PERSPECTIVES ON PATENTABLE SUBJECT MATTER

Perspectives on Patentable Subject Matter brings together leading scholars to offer diverse perspectives on one of the most pressing issues in patent law: the basic question about which types of subject matter are even eligible for patent protection, setting aside the widely known requirement that a claimed invention avoids the prior art and is adequately disclosed. Some leading commentators and policy-making bodies and individuals envision patentable subject matter to include anything under the sun made by humans, whereas other thought leaders envision a range of restrictions for particular fields of endeavor, from business methods and computer software to matters involving life, such as DNA and methods for screening or treating disease. Employing approaches that are both theoretically rigorous and grounded in the real world, this book is well suited for practicing lawyers, managers, lawmakers, and analysts, as well as academics conducting research or teaching a range of courses in law, business, and public policy schools and in economics and political science departments, at either the undergraduate or graduate level.

Michael Abramowicz is a professor at the George Washington University Law School in Washington, DC, who specializes in law and economics, spanning areas including intellectual property, civil procedure, corporate law, administrative law, and insurance law. His research has been published in the *California Law Review, Columbia Law Review, Cornell Law Review, Harvard Law Review, Michigan Law Review, New York University Law Review, Stanford Law Review, University of Chicago Law Review, Virginia Law Review,* and *Yale Law Journal*. He is the author of the 2008 book *Predictocracy: Market Mechanisms for Public and Private Decision Making*.

James E. Daily is the postdoctoral research associate for and administrative director of the Hoover Project on Commercializing Innovation. As an attorney licensed in Missouri and a patent agent registered with the U.S. Patent and Trademark Office, his research interests include open source models of innovation, the role of open source in the marketplace, and the interactions between open source and intellectual property. He is also the creator and co-author of the blog "Law and the Multiverse" and the co-author of the 2012 book *The Law of Superheroes*.

F. Scott Kieff is on leave from his post as Fred C. Stevenson Research Professor at the George Washington University Law School in Washington, DC, having been nominated by President Barack H. Obama, and confirmed by the Senate, to serve as a commissioner of the U.S. International Trade Commission. Before taking up his government post, he was also the Ray and Louise Knowles Senior Fellow at Stanford University's Hoover Institution, where he directed the Hoover Project on Commercializing Innovation. He has also regularly served as a testifying and consulting expert, mediator, and arbitrator for law firms, businesses, government agencies, and courts and on a range of government panels relating to the business and technology sectors. He worked on this book while in his academic positions, before being sworn in and taking his government post.

Perspectives on Patentable Subject Matter

Edited by

MICHAEL ABRAMOWICZ

George Washington University Law School

JAMES E. DAILY

Washington University in St. Louis School of Law

F. SCOTT KIEFF

George Washington University Law School

CAMBRIDGE
UNIVERSITY PRESS

CAMBRIDGE
UNIVERSITY PRESS

32 Avenue of the Americas, New York, NY 10013-2473, USA

Cambridge University Press is part of the University of Cambridge.

It furthers the University's mission by disseminating knowledge in the pursuit of education, learning, and research at the highest international levels of excellence.

www.cambridge.org
Information on this title: www.cambridge.org/9781107070912

First published 2015

Printed in Great Britain by Clays Ltd, St Ives plc

A catalog record for this publication is available from the British Library.

Library of Congress Cataloging in Publication Data
Perspectives on patentable subject matter / edited by Michael Abramowicz, James E. Daily, F. Scott Kieff.
pages cm
ISBN 978-1-107-07091-2 (hardback)
1. Patent laws and legislation. I. Abramowicz, Michael, editor. II. Daily, James, editor. III. Kieff, F. Scott, editor.
K1505.P45 2014
346.04'86–dc23 2014020981

ISBN 978-1-107-07091-2 Hardback

Contents

Contributors

Michael Abramowicz Professor, George Washington University Law School

John R. Allison Mary John and Ralph Spence Centennial Professor of Business Administration, University of Texas at Austin

Kevin Emerson Collins Professor of Law, Washington University in St. Louis

Christopher A. Cotropia Professor of Law and Austin Owen Research Fellow, University of Richmond

James E. Daily Research Technologist, Washington University in St. Louis School of Law, Center for Empirical Research in the Law

John F. Duffy Samuel H. McCoy II Professor of Law and Armistead M. Dobie Professor of Law, University of Virginia

Bronwyn H. Hall Professor of Economics, Emerita, University of California, Berkeley

Christopher M. Holman Professor of Law, University of Missouri–Kansas City

F. Scott Kieff Professor, George Washington University Law School, and Ray and Louise Knowles Senior Fellow at Stanford University Hoover Institution on War, Revolution, and Peace*

* Kieff took a leave of absence from George Washington University Law School and resigned from Stanford University Hoover Institution to take up his post as a commissioner at the U.S. International Trade Commission (USITC). He worked on this book before taking up his government post. The views expressed in this book are those of the authors of the various chapters and do not necessarily reflect those of the co-editors. Nor are the views expressed in this book properly attributable to the USITC.

Josh Lerner Jacob H. Schiff Professor of Investment Banking, Harvard University

Gerard N. Magliocca Samuel R. Rosen Professor of Law, Indiana University

Michael J. Meurer Abraham and Lillian Benton Scholar and Professor of Law, Boston University

Kristen Osenga Professor of Law, University of Richmond

Arti K. Rai Elvin R. Latty Professor of Law, Duke University

Bhaven N. Sampat Associate Professor at the Mailman School of Public Health, Columbia University

Pamela Samuelson Richard M. Sherman Distinguished Professor of Law, University of California at Berkeley

Jason Schultz Associate Professor of Clinical Law, New York University

Ted R. Sichelman Professor of Law, University of San Diego

Acknowledgments

This book consists of articles written by the participants in the Patents & Entrepreneurship in Business & Information Technologies conference held at the George Washington University Law School (GW Law) on June 12 and 13, 2009. The conference was sponsored and hosted by the GW Law Intellectual Property Center, with support from the Ewing Marion Kauffman Foundation and the Microsoft Corporation. We would like to thank John Berger, our Cambridge University Press editor, for his efforts and patience. We are particularly grateful to the individuals whose work makes up this book.

This book is part of broader work conducted under the auspices of the Project on Commercializing Innovation at Stanford University's Hoover Institution, which studies the law, economics, and politics of the whole range of legal and business relationships that can be used to bring ideas to market. We would like to thank the Hoover Institution – particularly Richard Sousa, its senior associate director – for the support of the Project on Commercializing Innovation. More about the Project is available on the Web at www.innovation.hoover.org.

Finally, we must note again that F. Scott Kieff worked on this book while serving as Fred C. Stevenson Research Professor, George Washington University Law School, and Ray & Louise Knowles Senior Fellow, Stanford University Hoover Institution on War, Revolution, and Peace, before taking up his government post as a commissioner at the U.S. International Trade Commission (USITC). He took a leave of absence from the George Washington University Law School and resigned from Stanford University Hoover Institution before becoming a commissioner. The views expressed in this book are those of the chapter authors and do not necessarily reflect those of the other chapter authors or co-editors. Nor are the views expressed in this book properly attributable to the USITC.

Michael Abramowicz, James E. Daily, and F. Scott Kieff

Introduction

*Michael Abramowicz, James E. Daily, and F. Scott Kieff**

This book consists of articles written by participants in the Patents & Entrepreneurship in Business & Information Technologies conference held at the George Washington University Law School on June 12 and 13, 2009. The conference focused on whether the patent system is helpful or harmful to entrepreneurs in the fields of business and information technologies. In recent years, the use of business methods and information technologies has grown exponentially in our society, and the application of patent rights in these fields has been the subject of much debate. Although patents have been historically viewed as an important legal mechanism for fostering entrepreneurial activity in well-developed fields such as mechanical, chemical, and pharmaceutical innovation, it has been more controversial whether this conventional wisdom applies in these emerging areas. Some argue that patent protection could inhibit advances in areas such as software and financial engineering, whereas others insist that protection is as critical in these areas as it was for the emerging technologies of the past. The interface between the patent system and these areas of entrepreneurship highlights critical questions, such as whether the difficulties in these fields reveal more general problems with the existing patent system and whether the patent system can be, or should be, modified so that it better accommodates the practical needs of entrepreneurs in these and other fields.

Although many areas of the law are in flux, and any area tightly intertwined with fast-moving fields of technology might be expected by at least some to evolve rapidly,

* Kieff worked on this book while serving as Fred C. Stevenson Research Professor, George Washington University Law School, and as Ray & Louise Knowles Senior Fellow, Stanford University Hoover Institution on War, Revolution, and Peace, before taking up his government post as a commissioner at the U.S. International Trade Commission (USITC). He took a leave of absence from George Washington University Law School and resigned from Stanford University Hoover Institution to take up his government post. The views expressed in this chapter are those of the chapter authors and do not necessarily reflect those of the other chapter authors. Nor are the views expressed in this book properly attributable to the USITC.

the field of patentable subject matter has been especially volatile over the past few decades and is showing no signs of settling down quickly. Each season's hottest case seems to enjoy little more than the proverbial fifteen minutes of fame before it is overshadowed by the next. Practitioners and commentators who focus on this area of the law well recognize that the field of patentable subject matter is strewn with countless examples of the one final, hottest, newest High Court case that will settle these questions once and for all – until the next many such cases come along to leave the field just as muddy as before.

No book devoted to such a rapidly changing legal environment could accurately claim for long that it was fully up to date. Fortunately, such constant updating is not necessary for a book such as this one, which is devoted to a general audience, because the same core issues and key tensions in the field of patentable subject matter have tended to play out repeatedly over the years. Thus, the field can be well explored by using almost any reasonably broad collection of cases as a reference point. In contrast, the central cost of waiting to update each thought to address more recent cases, especially in depth, would yield undue delay with no substantive benefit to the reader, somewhat like waiting for Beckett's Godot. Instead, we carefully selected prominent authors who have prepared particularly insightful chapters at particular points in time over the past few years that provide analysis and insight that are for practical purposes timeless when applied to the presently foreseeable legal landscape in this area.

An initial question concerning the patentability of business methods and software inventions is whether the patent system should include categorical bars on such inventions and, if not, whether they should be treated differently at all from other inventions. The recent Supreme Court decision *Bilski* v. *Kappos* considered patentable subject matter in the realm of business method patents. The Court issued its opinion in the summer of 2010, holding that the claimed system to hedge energy prices using weather projections was an abstract idea, ineligible for patent protection. Consistent with the Court's rejection, Pamela Samuelson and Jason Schultz argue in Chapter 1, *"Clues" for Determining Whether Business and Service Innovations Are Unpatentable Abstract Ideas*, for the rejection of an overbroad interpretation of patentable subject matter such as that advocated by the petitioner in *Bilski*. They begin by arguing that the history and structure of the statute limit the appropriate construction of patentable processes to those that are technological. Then, they suggest that allowing patents on nontechnological methods is unnecessary and likely to be harmful to innovation in those industries. Finally, they contend that removing the long-standing technological limit on patentable processes would undermine the institutional competence of the U.S. Patent and Trademark Office (PTO) and the federal courts to protect innovation.

In contrast, in Chapter 2, *Still Aiming at the Wrong Target: A Case for Business Method and Software Patents from a Business Perspective*, Kristen Osenga argues that the current debate on patentability for business methods as a category is misplaced.

She begins by discussing the rise and recent fall of business method patents and surveys the scholarly literature discussing business method and software patents. She then argues that the patentability inquiry is tied to examination and that the focus should be on improving the PTO's examining techniques and ensuring that patent applications are being held to the appropriate level of scrutiny for written description, enablement, novelty, and nonobviousness. She suggests that if the negative effects on competition and innovation can be addressed through this more thorough examination, then business method and software patents are not categorically bad and should be permitted.

The question of patentability for these fields may require an entirely different framework. Kevin Emerson Collins in Chapter 3, *Semiotics 101: Taking the Printed Matter Doctrine Seriously*, suggests a reconsideration of the printed matter doctrine and argues that semiotics can serve as a framework within existing doctrine for determining the acceptability of patentability of computer programs. He suggests a new approach to patentable subject matter, different from the contemporary patentable subject matter framework, based on a revised version of the printed matter doctrine. Collins notes the conventional view that a printed diagram is not a patentable invention, and he argues that there is an aspect of the printed matter doctrine that is worth identifying and saving in the modern age. He then considers semiotics – the interpretation of signs – and notes that if an inventor has discovered a new way of understanding the world (interpretant), the inventor cannot claim a meaningful invention (sign-vehicle). Collins combines the two theories and uses insights from a semiotic reformulation of the printed matter doctrine to offer suggestions about how computer software should be considered under § 101.

Most academics and practitioners who have significant experience with questions about patentable subject matter recognize that the reasoning courts and commentators tend to demonstrate when thinking about patentable subject matter as a question facing one particular field of technology (such as computers and business methods) often will be the same basic reasoning that they would use when thinking about a different field of technology (such as biology or medicine), and vice versa. In Chapter 4, *Patent Eligibility as a Policy Lever to Regulate the Patenting of Personalized Medicine*, Christopher M. Holman elucidates many of the links in the bodies of case law devoted to these different areas of technology. He then explores several practical implications of these insights for the field of biomedicine in general and personalized medicine in particular. Holman concludes by exploring a set of implications of these developments in the law of patentable subject matter for the types of business models that are likely to evolve and thrive in this important area of technology, including some important interactions with the public patient population.

Assuming that some form of protection for software, business methods, and biomedical inventions remains available, as seems likely, the question that then emerges is what the appropriate standard of protection should be. In Chapter 5, *The Inducement Standard of Patentability*, Michael Abramowicz and John F. Duffy propose a renewed focus on the "inducement standard" when determining whether an invention is sufficiently nonobvious to justify patentability. The inducement standard was first articulated in the seminal patent law case *Graham* v. *John Deere*. It states that the purpose of the nonobviousness test is to identify and protect only inventions whose creation is attributable to the patent system. The academic consensus following *Graham* holds the inducement standard to be a useful theoretical construct, but one without practical implications. Abramowicz and Duffy argue that in fact the inducement standard, properly understood, should guide the PTO and the courts in implementing the nonobviousness standard. The theoretical and practical framework they defend can help show why software and business method patents often should receive more skeptical treatment than, for example, pharmaceutical inventions.

The business and entrepreneurial communities are important stakeholders in the patent system, and relying on these communities for guidance may be an alternative standard to that employed by the current patent system. In Chapter 6, *Patenting the Curve Ball: Business Methods and Industry Norms*, Gerard N. Magliocca proposes that patent subject matter eligibility should be interpreted to exclude a process unless the applicant can show that a norm of permitting protection exists within the relevant business community. He suggests three benefits that an industry customs test would have over the current patent system. First, fewer business method patents would be issued under this modified standard. This would stem some of the problems with the poor notice and costly litigation associated with these patents. Second, the use of norms resolves the need to define a scope of patentability across business method categories, an approach that had created substantial confusion. Third, the current view of process patents empowers those who seek to defect from a community ethic. His analysis steers a different course in the debate regarding whether business methods should be patented and suggests that they should be patentable subject matter when the relevant community believes it to be appropriate. He also suggests that the PTO and the courts would do better by following the norm of the industry, rather than setting new standards with respect to business process patents.

Empirical studies highlight the complex relationship between innovation of business and financial methods and the current patent system. In Chapter 7, *Business and Financial Method Patents, Innovation, and Policy*, Bronwyn H. Hall explores the relationship between the patent system and innovation through an economist's perspective, surveying theoretical and empirical approaches as well as the impact on patent quality. Her examination of theoretical works reveal that whether patents are a socially useful way to encourage innovation turns on the characteristics of the innovation process and the complexity of the products patented. She identifies two main conclusions from her survey of empirical works. First, introducing or strengthening a patent system (e.g., lengthening the patent term or broadening subject matter coverage) usually results in an increase in patenting, but it is unclear that an increase in innovative activity will result at all times and in all places. Hence, she offers support to those who argue that a unitary patent system is far from optimal for supporting innovation. Second, the patent system has a tendency to affect the organization of industry by allowing trade in knowledge and facilitating the vertical disintegration of knowledge-based industries and the entry of new firms that possess only intangible assets. Hall notes that this tendency is particularly apparent with respect to business method and internet patents. She draws a tentative conclusion that business and financial patents fall under a category of innovations where it is less obvious that the benefits of the patent system outweigh the costs.

Litigation of financial patents is crucial to delineating the boundaries of these patents. The definition of patent rights has implications for how these rights eventually affect innovation. In Chapter 8, *The Litigation of Financial Innovations*, Josh Lerner conducts an empirical study of litigation stemming from patents related to financial products and services. Lerner finds that the financial patents being litigated are disproportionately those issued to individuals; litigated patents appear to be more important than other financial patents (i.e., they have more claims and disproportionately cite and are cited by other patents); and larger entities are disproportionately targeted in litigation. He discusses how his findings are consistent with the economic theory that high-stakes disputes should lead more frequently to litigation. However, he notes that other factors also contribute to how financial patents are litigated. Overall, he concludes that there are certain patterns in financial patent litigation, but how these suits may affect innovation remains to be determined.

Another issue in the area of patent and entrepreneurship is the behavior of innovators and how patents may affect the behavior of these individuals and entities. In Chapter 9, *Patent Search and Cumulative Innovation*, Michael J. Meurer focuses his examination of the patent system on cumulative innovation, the process of one innovator building on the efforts of earlier innovators. Economists widely recognize that cumulative innovation poses a serious challenge to those who try to design an optimal patent system. When one innovation builds on another, the patent system can be used to divide profits between two distinct innovators. In the area of information and communications technologies, Meurer recognizes that this model does not work well. Instead, he proposes a modified model of cumulative innovation to account for factors that cause patents to differ from property.

The behaviors of patent holders examined through case studies of particular entities also underscore the complex relationship between patents and entrepreneurship. Although much attention has been directed to the problem of nonpracticing entities or patent trolls, practicing entities also engage in behavior that exploits the defects in the patent system. In Chapter 10, *The Vonage Trilogy: A Case Study in "Patent Bullying,"* Ted Sichelman presents an in-depth case study of infringement suits alongside empirical research that assesses the prevalence of large-firm versus small-firm suits. For the in-depth case study, Sichelman presents "patent bully" suits filed by large established companies that threaten or institute costly patent infringement actions of dubious merit against smaller companies to suppress competition or garner licensing fees. In particular, he identifies suits initiated by incumbent telecommunications carriers (Sprint, Verizon, and AT&T) against Vonage, an early-stage company providing consumer telephone services over the internet. In considering the merits of each suit in turn and the defense raised by Vonage, he points out several weaknesses in Vonage's defense and recognizes that, as a startup, Vonage has limited budgets that may reduce attorney effectiveness. As a result, Sichelman concludes that the patent bullies were able to hinder Vonage's technologies from competing, despite the weak merits of their suits, through leveraging the current patent system. Sichelman further determines that empirical studies confirm this pattern of patent bullying. He concludes by examining potential solutions to this issue, such as compulsory licensing and one-way fee shifting.

Another example where the behavior of patent holders under the current system may affect entrepreneurship is with universities that hold software patents. In Chapter 11, *University Software Ownership and Litigation: A First Examination*, Arti K. Rai, John R. Allison, and Bhaven N. Sampat systematically examine the ownership and litigation of university software patents. Their empirical research reveals that the number of software patents that a university owns is highly dependent on a tendency to seek patents in other areas. Their data also suggest that universities with higher patent propensities in other fields also tend to patent more software. Because the authors recognize that software is likely to follow a different commercialization path than invention in other fields, they argue that patenting and exclusive licensing of software may yield a higher proportion of situations where the exclusive licensee uses a patent to hold up an entity that has successfully commercialized without the need for an exclusive license. In conclusion, they indicate that university software patents have largely been used to extract rents in holdup litigation, rather than to foster commercialization.

Although broader scale patent reform has been often raised as a solution to resolve the uncertainties in protecting business and information technology, the problems with the current system may not be sufficiently severe to justify extreme changes. In Chapter 12, *The Individual Inventor Motif in the Age of the Patent Troll*, Christopher A. Cotropia starts with the individual inventor motif and explores whether there has been an attitude change in light of the existence of "patent trolls" in recent years. Cotropia lays out the premises that the individual inventor has been revered as an American icon and that the patent system seeks to assist and protect the individual inventor. Although Cotropia recognizes that there is no statutory basis for this premise, there is historical, legislative, judicial, and administrative evidence to support the motif. He offers as support congressional statements and testimony in discussions of the recent proposed patent reform legislation, the PTO's response to recently proposed sets of patent rules, and recent Supreme Court patent decisions. Cotropia then turns to the concern of patent holdup in the current system and describes the impact that patent trolls have on the individual inventor motif. He concludes that the motif has essentially remained unchanged; however, there is a disconnect between the rhetoric of the individual inventor motif and the substantive impact of legal changes on the same inventors.

Finally, in Chapter 13, *Anything Under the Sun Made by Humans: Patent Law Doctrines as Endogenous Institutions for Commercializing Innovation*, James E. Daily and F. Scott Kieff take a New Institutional Social Sciences approach in arguing that a broad, easily satisfied patentable subject matter requirement is socially beneficial. For Daily and Kieff, narrower, more subjective notions of patentable subject matter place greater discretion in the hands of administrative agencies and the courts, both of which are subject to political influence, whether directly – as part of a political branch of government – or indirectly, such as through the filing of briefs by the Solicitor General's Office. They conclude that the end result is likely to be weaker patents, less certainty, and less innovation.

The ongoing controversy surrounding the modern patent system and its relationship with entrepreneurship in business and information technology is multifaceted. The chapters in this volume provide diverse perspectives on the various debates surrounding patents in business and information technologies.

1

"Clues" for Determining Whether Business and Service Innovations Are Unpatentable Abstract Ideas

*Pamela Samuelson and Jason Schultz**

I. INTRODUCTION

In June 2010, the U.S. Supreme Court ruled in *Bilski* v. *Kappos* that Bernard Bilski's method for hedging risks of price fluctuations for commodities was an abstract idea that was ineligible for patent protection.[1] Four of the Justices would have gone further to hold that business methods were unpatentable subject matter; that is, not the kind of "process" for which patent protection was available.[2] Although the Court as a whole was not persuaded that business methods should be deemed categorically ineligible for patent protection,[3] in part because the term "business method" is difficult to define with precision,[4] Justice Kennedy, writing the opinion of the Court for himself and three other Justices, recognized that "some business method patents raise special problems in terms of vagueness and suspect validity."[5] After *Bilski*, these methods are likely to be deemed too abstract to be patentable.

* Pamela Samuelson is the Richard M. Sherman Distinguished Professor of Law, Berkeley Law School. Jason Schultz is an Assistant Clinical Professor of Law, Berkeley Law School. This chapter is a derivative work of a brief amicus curiae that the authors submitted on behalf of the Ewing Marion Kaufmann Foundation, the Electronic Frontier Foundation, and several entrepreneurs in support of the U.S. Patent and Trademark Office's rejection of Bernard Bilski's patent application for failure to claim patentable subject matter. *See* Brief of Entrepreneurial & Consumer Advocates as Amici Curiae Supporting Respondent, *Bilski* v. *Kappos*, 130 S. Ct. 3218 (2010) (No. 08–964). A version of this article was originally published in the *Lewis and Clark Law Review*. *See* Pamela Samuelson & Jason Schultz, *"Clues" for Determining Whether Business and Service Innovations Are Unpatentable Abstract Ideas*, 15 LEWIS & CLARK L. REV. 109 (2011). We wish to thank Eric Talley for his help with the arguments concerning innovation, competition, and financial arbitrage.

1 Bilski v. Kappos, 130 S. Ct. 3218, 3231 (2010).

2 *Id.* at 3231–32 (Stevens, J., concurring) (Justice Stevens was joined by Justices Ginsburg, Breyer, and Sotomayor).

3 *Id.* at 3228 (majority opinion).

4 *Id.* (indicating that it was unclear "how far a prohibition on business method patents would reach, and whether it would exclude technologies for conducting a business more efficiently").

5 *Id.* at 3229. Justice Scalia did not join the subpart of Justice Kennedy's opinion in which this sentence appears. *Id.* at 3223.

Justice Kennedy went on to say that it was important to set a high bar for patentability of these kinds of inventions, because otherwise "patent examiners and courts could be flooded with claims that would put a chill on creative endeavor and dynamic change."[6] To avoid this chilling effect on business innovation, a limiting principle was needed so that the U.S. Patent and Trademark Office (PTO) and the courts could determine which kinds of methods affecting business operations should be eligible (or not) for patent protection. Justice Kennedy pointed to the Court's prior rulings on the unpatentability of abstract ideas as likely to provide useful guidance for achieving this purpose.[7] Drawing on these precedents, the Court of Appeals for the Federal Circuit might, he thought, be able to "defin[e] a narrower category or class of patent applications that claim to instruct how business should be conducted, and then rule that the category is unpatentable because, for instance, it represents an attempt to patent abstract ideas," adding that "this conclusion might well be in accord with controlling precedent."[8]

Although Justice Kennedy's opinion does not spell out with precision how to distinguish between unpatentable abstract ideas and patentable processes, it does offer some "clues" for drawing such distinctions that deserve attention going forward.[9] Part II of this chapter discusses the clues we think are most likely to be useful to the PTO and the courts in developing a jurisprudence about abstractness as a disqualification from patent protection. Part III explains why, in light of these clues and in line with sound patent policy, business and service method innovations, although not categorically unpatentable, should still generally be excluded from patent protection as abstract ideas. Part IV provides further support for this approach by suggesting that taking the clues of unpatentability seriously may facilitate administrative and judicial efficiency in reviewing patent claims when assessing whether they satisfy patent subject matter rules.

II. *BILSKI* DIRECTS US TO SEARCH FOR "CLUES" ABOUT ABSTRACTNESS

In this part, we mine the *Bilski* decision, the precedents on which it relies, as well as the Constitution, the Patent Act, and patent-related policies for clues that may aid in determining whether a claim is too abstract to qualify for patent protection or is instead sufficiently concrete to be eligible for patenting, assuming other criteria for patentability are satisfied. Although the rather amorphous clue-based approach to

6 *Id.* at 3229. Justice Stevens' concurring opinion also emphasized that business method patenting could have chilling effects on innovation in that field. *Id.* at 3254–55 (Stevens, J., concurring).

7 *Id.* at 3229 (majority opinion).

8 *Id.*

9 The Court in *Bilski* drew the "clue" metaphor from the Court's decision in Gottschalk v. Benson, 409 U.S. 63, 70 (1972) and endorsed its use for assessing patentable subject matter in the future. *Bilski*, 130 S. Ct. at 3226–27.

patent subject matter determinations may be frustrating for those looking for concise bright-line rules to patentability, it can be useful, especially when properly framed.

A. *Clues Derived from* Bilski *and Other Supreme Court Precedents*

Much like Sherlock Holmes or Harry Bosch, a patent examiner or a court searching for "clues" to patentability must both collect the clues and sift through them for a discernible pattern that leads to a sound conclusion. Often, it is easiest to begin with the most obvious clues and then move to those more nuanced or subtle. One clue readily discernible from the Court's *Bilski* decision is that the term "abstract idea" as a disqualification from patent protection is not limited to very high-level abstractions (e.g., the idea of cutting bread with a knife). For example, Bilski's first claim contained some relatively "concrete" elements, such as a commodity provider, a commodity, a price, and a market participant.[10] And yet, the Court was unanimous in regarding it as too abstract to qualify for a patent.[11]

A second clue comes from the Court's unanimous reaffirmation in *Bilski* that its decades-earlier ruling in *Gottschalk* v. *Benson* is still good law.[12] Benson had once hoped to obtain a patent on a multistep method of transforming binary coded decimals (BCDs) to pure binary form.[13] Under the patent subject matter standards used by the Federal Circuit for more than a decade prior to its ruling in *In re Bilski*,[14] Benson would have been eligible for a patent because his method was capable of yielding "a useful, concrete, and tangible result."[15] Yet, the Supreme Court in *Bilski* could not have been clearer in expressing its view that the Benson method was too abstract to qualify for patent protection. The Court reiterated in *Bilski*, as it had in *Benson*, that no one can patent an idea.[16] The practical effect of a patent on Benson's method would, however, have been the grant of a patent on an idea that would "wholly pre-empt [use of] the mathematical formula" or algorithm at issue.[17]

10 *Id.* at 3223–24 (quoting claim 1 of the Bilski patent).

11 *Id.* at 3230–31. See also Interim Guidance for Determining Subject Matter Eligibility for Process Claims in View of *Bilski v. Kappos*, 75 Fed. Reg. 43922, 43924 (U.S. Pat. & Trademark Office July 27, 2010) [hereinafter Interim Guidance] ("Moreover, the fact that the steps of a claim might occur in the 'real world' does not necessarily save it from a section 101 rejection. Thus, the *Bilski* claims were said to be drawn to an 'abstract idea' despite the fact that they included steps drawn to initiating transactions. The 'abstractness' is in the sense that there are no limitations as to the mechanism for entering into the transactions.").

12 Gottschalk v. Benson, 409 U.S. 63 (1972), *cited with approval in Bilski*, 130 S. Ct. at 3230, *and id.* at 3253 (Stevens, J., concurring).

13 *Benson*, 409 U.S. at 65.

14 *In re Bilski*, 545 F.3d 943 (Fed. Cir. 2008) (en banc). In *In re Bilski*, the Federal Circuit abjured the useful, concrete, and tangible result test in favor of the "machine-or-transformation" test. *Id.* at 959–60. *See also infra* notes 33–38 and accompanying text.

15 *See, e.g.*, State St. Bank & Trust Co. v. Signature Fin. Grp., Inc., 149 F.3d 1368, 1373 (Fed. Cir. 1998) (quoting *In re* Alappat, 33 F.3d 1526, 1544 (Fed. Cir. 1994)).

16 *Bilski*, 130 S. Ct. at 3230 (quoting *Benson*, 409 U.S. at 67).

17 *Benson*, 409 U.S. at 72, *quoted in Bilski*, 130 S. Ct. at 3230.

A second clue of unpatentability is, then, that mathematical formulas and algorithms as such, however novel or nonobvious they might be, are viewed by the Supreme Court as unpatentable abstractions.[18] In fact, when analyzing the Bilski patent, Justice Kennedy wrote, "The concept of hedging, described in claim 1 and reduced to a mathematical formula in claim 4, is an unpatentable abstract idea, just like the algorithms at issue in *Benson* and *Flook*."[19] Therefore, claims that are capable of being reduced to mathematical formulas or algorithms, even if they are not written as such, can be held as abstract ideas based on this clue.

A third clue to abstractness as a disqualifier from patent protection is evident in Justice Breyer's concurring opinion in *Bilski*, which emphasizes several points on which the Justices were unanimous, including the unpatentability of mental processes.[20] Mathematical formulas are one subset of a much larger set of processes that can be carried out in a person's mind or with only the aid of pencil and paper. Many business methods are also susceptible to being carried out in a business person's head (e.g., assessing the risk of lending money to clients with certain types of backgrounds); these methods should also be regarded as too abstract to qualify for patenting.[21] Some methods whose patentability some Justices questioned during oral argument in the *Bilski* case were also mental process innovations.[22]

A fourth clue of unpatentability on abstractness grounds, also derived from *Benson* as well as from *Bilski*, is the wide range of applications in which a claimed method could be practiced.[23] In *Benson*, the process claimed was "so abstract and sweeping as to cover both known and unknown uses of the BCD to pure binary conversion. The end use may (1) vary from the operation of a train to verification of drivers' licenses to researching the law books for precedents and (2) be performed through any existing machinery or future-devised machinery or without any apparatus."[24] The process's

18 During oral argument, Justice Kennedy was quite skeptical of the idea that patents could be granted for important innovations in the insurance industry, such as actuarial tables. *See* Transcript of Oral Argument at 10–11, *Bilski*, 130 S. Ct. 3218 (2010) (No. 08–964) [hereinafter Transcript of *Bilski* Oral Argument].

19 *Bilski*, 130 S. Ct. at 3231.

20 *Id.* at 3257–58 (Breyer, J., concurring) (quoting *Benson*, 409 U.S. at 67); *see also id.* at 3226 (majority opinion) ("Concerns about attempts to call any form of human activity a 'process' can be met by making sure the claim meets the requirements of § 101."); Interim Guidance, *supra* note 11, at 43925 ("The nature of the article transformed, *i.e.*, whether it is an object or substance, weighing toward eligibility, compared to a concept such as a contractual obligation or mental judgment, which would weigh against eligibility."), 43926 (listing "[m]ental activity" as an example of the patent-ineligible category of "general concepts").

21 *See, e.g.*, Brief for Kevin Emerson Collins as Amicus Curiae in Support of Neither Party, *In re Bilski*, 545 F.3d 943 (Fed. Cir. 2008) (No. 2007–1130) (en banc), *available at* http://www.patentlyo.com/patent/bilski.collins.pdf.

22 *See, e.g.*, Transcript of *Bilski* Oral Argument, *supra* note 18, at 5–7 (methods of resisting a corporate takeover, of choosing a jury, and of avoiding taxes).

23 *See* Interim Guidance, *supra* note 11, at 43925 ("Application of a law of nature having broad applicability across many fields of endeavor weighs against eligibility. . . . ").

24 *Benson*, 409 U.S. at 68.

breadth affected the Court's view of it as too abstract to qualify for patenting. In *Bilski*, Justice Kennedy wrote, "Allowing petitioners to patent risk hedging would pre-empt use of this approach in all fields, and would effectively grant a monopoly over an abstract idea."[25] Again, the wide-ranging impact of the claim was a clue to being too abstract.

A fifth clue of unpatentability on abstractness grounds would exist with processes that involve representing or transforming data from one form to another. Recall that the method at issue in *Benson* transformed the representation of data from BCD to pure binary form. It did not matter to the Court that this transformation could take place through the use of a programmed digital computer: the method was simply unpatentable.[26] Along similar lines, several Justices expressed skepticism about the patentability of data representation and communication during oral argument in the *Bilski* case.[27]

A sixth clue of unpatentability on abstractness grounds can be found in *Parker v. Flook*,[28] which the Court in *Bilski* also reaffirmed as a sound precedent.[29] In *Flook*, the claim was for an improved method of calculating alarm limits for a catalytic conversion process.[30] Although the claim contained a step that was to be performed after the calculations had yielded a solution, the Court characterized this step as insignificant "post-solution activity" that could not render the claimed method patentable subject matter.[31] *Flook* also made clear that mere field-of-use limitations would not overcome the abstractness objection to the patenting of a mathematical process.[32] The Court in *Bilski* endorsed *Flook* as another source of guidance for the unpatentability of abstract methods.[33]

Although we have thus far emphasized the clues that tip against patentability, the Court recognized that some clues will point to the existence of sufficient concreteness to support patentability. The most important of the clues identified in *Bilski* lies in the "machine-or-transformation" (MoT) test.[34] The Federal Circuit articulated

25 *Bilski*, 130 S. Ct. at 3231.

26 One of the claims in *Benson* was for the method carried out through the use of a general-purpose computer. Yet, the Court regarded this method to be equally unpatentable as the claim that did not specify the use of an apparatus. *Benson*, 409 U.S. at 65, 68–72. During oral argument in *Bilski*, several Justices were openly skeptical of the idea that merely computerizing an abstract process would render it patentable. *See, e.g.*, Transcript of *Bilski* Oral Argument, *supra* note 18, at 30–36.

27 Transcript of *Bilski* Oral Argument, *supra* note 18, at 9 (questioning the patentability of a method of teaching antitrust), 16 (questioning the patentability of a method of horse training), 22 (questioning the patentability of alphabets).

28 437 U.S. 584 (1978).

29 *Bilski*, 130 S. Ct. at 3230–31.

30 *Flook*, 437 U.S. at 585.

31 *Id.* at 590, *construed in* Diamond v. Diehr, 450 U.S. 175, 191 (1981) ("insignificant postsolution activity will not transform an unpatentable principle into a patentable process").

32 *Diehr*, 450 U.S. at 191–92 (discussing *Flook*).

33 *Bilski*, 130 S. Ct. at 3226.

34 *See id.* at 3224–28.

this test in its *Bilski* decision, saying that a claimed process is eligible for patent protection if "(1) it is tied to a particular machine or apparatus, or (2) it transforms a particular article into a different state or thing."[35] Although the Supreme Court rejected the Federal Circuit's endorsement of MoT as the "sole test" of patentability, it recognized it as "an important and useful clue" in patent subject matter determinations.[36] *Diamond* v. *Diehr* is an example of a method that was concrete enough to be patentable because the programmed computer's calculations in that case were elements of a process for transforming rubber from one physical state to another.[37] This method was also tied to a specific machine.[38]

B. *The Constitution's Emphasis on Promoting Progress Provides Another Clue to Determining Abstractness*

In addition to the clues one can find in the Supreme Court's jurisprudence, one can also look to other sources of authority for guidance on determining what constitutes an abstract idea. Although nothing in the text of the Constitution provides a direct explanation as to why "abstractions" are unpatentable, the patent clause and its context provide at least one "clue" for how courts should assess abstractness. As all who study patent law know, the Constitution speaks directly of the purpose of patent law: to promote the progress of the useful arts.[39] The relationship between this purpose, § 101, and the abstract idea limitation was reinforced throughout all three *Bilski* opinions, as well as the Court's prior § 101 case law.[40]

Thus, the principal constitutional clue to patentability is the progress of the useful arts.[41] To promote such progress, inventions need to be concrete, not abstract; they must also be specific, not general. Progress must be capable of being measured: it must have direct benefits that can be defined. Abstract ideas, in contrast, lack specific benefits that are measurable. Abstract ideas are also, as the Supreme Court

35 *In re Bilski*, 545 F.3d 943, 954 (Fed. Cir. 2008) (en banc).

36 *Bilski*, 130 S. Ct. at 3226.

37 *Diehr*, 450 U.S. at 184.

38 *Id.* at 177–78 (describing a process by which a specific digital computer sends a signal to a specific rubber-pressing machine to open at a specific time). We agree with the PTO's Interim Guidance notice that indicates that the more a process is tied to a specific machine, rather than just a general-purpose computer, the more likely it is to recite patentable subject matter. Interim Guidance, *supra* note 11, at 43925.

39 *See* U.S. CONST. art. I, § 8, cl. 8 (the purpose of patents is to "promote the Progress of . . . useful Arts."); KSR Int'l Co. v. Teleflex Inc., 550 U.S. 398, 427 (2007) ("[T]he results of ordinary innovation are not the subject of exclusive rights under the patent laws. Were it otherwise patents might stifle, rather than promote, the progress of useful arts.").

40 *Bilski*, 130 S. Ct. at 3226–31. *See also id.* at 3238–47 (Stevens, J., concurring); *id.* at 3258–59 (Breyer, J., concurring); *Bonito Boats, Inc.* v. *Thunder Craft Boats, Inc.*, 489 U.S. 141, 150–51 (1989); *Diehr*, 450 U.S. at 192 (processes are patentable when the claim "is performing a function which the patent laws were designed to protect"); *Graham* v. *John Deere Co. of Kan. City*, 383 U.S. 1, 9–11 (1966).

41 *See Bilski*, 130 S. Ct. at 3253 (Stevens, J., concurring) ("The Court has kept this 'constitutional standard' in mind when deciding what is patentable subject matter under § 101.").

has repeatedly recognized, "part of the storehouse of knowledge of all men . . . [which must be] free to all men and reserved exclusively to none,"[42] as well as "the basic tools of scientific and technological work" whose patent-free status contributes to the very progress that the Constitution aims to bring about.[43]

The constitutional focus on progress of the useful arts is consistent with the holding in *Bilski*. There, the Court found the claim at issue to be abstract in part because it covered a "basic concept" and a "fundamental economic practice long prevalent in our system of commerce and taught in any introductory finance class."[44] It also held that Bilski's claim was unpatentable because it could be "reduced to a mathematical formula."[45] In other words, stating the basic concept or fundamental economic practice did not promote any particular progress; rather, particular implementations of an idea are the methods that promote progress in a constitutional sense and thus a clue to concreteness.[46]

C. *The Patent Act's Emphasis on Machines, Manufactures, and Compositions of Matter Also Provides Clues to Distinguishing Abstract Ideas from Concrete Processes*

The history and structure of the Patent Act also provide clues as to what is and is not an abstract process. As the Supreme Court has noted, Congress did not authorize patenting of "any [process] under the sun."[47] In §101, Congress expressly limited patenting to four types of inventions – processes, machines, manufactures, and compositions of matter – leaving other forms of innovation in the public domain where freedom to innovate is prevalent.[48]

Although the word "abstract" does not appear in the Patent Act, the Court in *Bilski* connects the concept of abstractness as a limit on patent subject matter with the statutorily eligible category of "processes." Thus, the meaning of "abstract" in relation

42 *Funk Bros. Seed Co.* v. *Kalo Inoculant Co.*, 333 U.S. 127, 130 (1948), quoted in *Bilski*, 130 S. Ct. at 3225.

43 *Benson*, 409 U.S. at 67.

44 *Bilski*, 130 S. Ct. at 3231 (quoting *In re Bilski*, 545 F.3d 943, 1013 (Fed. Cir. 2008) (en banc) (Rader, J., dissenting)).

45 *Id.*

46 *See id.* at 3230 ("*Diehr* explained that while an abstract idea, law of nature, or mathematical formula could not be patented, 'an application of a law of nature or mathematical formula to a known structure or process may well be deserving of patent protection.'" (quoting *Diamond v. Diehr*, 450 U.S. 175, 187 (1981)). *See also id.* at 3258 (Breyer, J., concurring) (noting that abstract ideas are not patentable because allowing individuals to patent these fundamental principles would "'wholly pre-empt' the public's access to the 'basic tools of scientific and technological work[,]'" thus inhibiting the overall progress of the useful arts (quoting *Benson*, 409 U.S. at 67, 72)); *Diehr*, 450 U.S. at 184 (noting that machines must be "particular" machines under an MoT analysis).

47 *Bilski*, 130 S. Ct. at 3248 (Stevens, J., concurring).

48 35 U.S.C. § 101 (2006). *See Diehr*, 450 U.S. at 185 (noting that, although each individual term of the four is to be construed broadly, "every discovery is not embraced within the statutory terms" (emphasis added)); *Parker v. Flook*, 437 U.S. 584, 588–89 (1978).

to § 101 is a question of statutory interpretation because, in essence, the *Bilski* Court interpreted the word "process" to mean "nonabstract processes." Under the doctrine of *noscitur a sociis*, courts may look to surrounding terms to inform the meaning of any individual term in a statute.[49] In § 101 the word "process" is side by side with machine, manufacture, and composition of matter and cannot be understood in isolation from its statutory companions.[50] Thus, these three words – machines, manufactures, and compositions of matter – are themselves clues as to concreteness, and association with them would weigh against abstractness.[51] When combined with the constitutional clue of promoting progress, improvement or advancement of machines, manufactures, and compositions of matter provides an even stronger clue that a process is concrete and not abstract.[52]

The clues of "promoting progress" and the other categories of invention in § 101 are also consistent with the history of the Patent Act.[53] When Congress last amended § 101 in 1952, it did so at the height of the industrial age, an age where science and engineering focused on machines, manufacturing, and the creation of compositions of matter. These were the technologies that were patentable at the time, along with the processes of creating them.[54]

Not surprisingly, the prevailing understanding at that time was also that processes that lacked specific application to machines, manufacturing, or compositions of matter – such as processes for doing business, practicing law, arbitrating disputes,

49 *See United States* v. *Williams*, 128 S. Ct. 1830, 1839 (2008) ("a word is given more precise content by the neighboring words with which it is associated" (citing *Jarecki* v. *G.D. Searle & Co.*, 367 U.S. 303, 307 (1961)); *Babbitt* v. *Sweet Home Chapter of Cmtys. for a Great Or.*, 515 U.S. 687, 687 (1995) (noting that "a word is known by the company it keeps").

50 *See* 35 U.S.C. § 101. *See also* 35 U.S.C. § 100(b) (2006) (defining process as including "a new use of a known process, machine, manufacture, composition of matter, or material"). It is worth noting that the Court in Bilski did not use *noscitur a sociis* primarily because it found the word "process" defined in the Act under § 100(b). However, because we are looking to define "abstract," which does not appear in the statute, we do not anticipate any conflict in the courts over application of this canon. *See Bilski*, 130 S. Ct. at 3226 ("ambiguous [terms in statutes] may be given more precise content by the neighboring words with which it is associated" (quoting *United States v. Stevens*, 130 S. Ct. 1577, 1588 (2010)).

51 The MoT test is clearly one instance of this, as "machine" appears in § 101. 35 U.S.C. § 101.

52 *See* Interim Guidance, *supra* note 11, at 43925 ("Integral use of a machine or apparatus to achieve performance of the method weighs toward eligibility, as compared to where the machine or apparatus is merely an object on which the method operates, which weighs against eligibility."). *See also id.* (noting that the use of a machine or apparatus that contributes only "nominally or insignificantly to the execution of the claimed method" would weigh against patent eligibility).

53 As the Supreme Court has held, "a page of history is worth a volume of logic." Eldred v. Ashcroft, 537 U.S. 186, 200 (2003) (quoting *N.Y. Trust Co.* v. *Eisner*, 256 U.S. 345, 349 (1921)).

54 Utilizing the other inventive categories of § 101 as clues to patentability also comports with the historical origin of "process," which the Court has held is synonymous with "art." *Diamond* v. *Diehr*, 450 U.S. 175, 182–84 (1981). As others have pointed out, "[t]he term 'useful arts,' as used in the Constitution . . . is best represented in modern language by the word 'technology.'" Karl B. Lutz, *Patents and Science: A Clarification of the Patent Clause of the U.S. Constitution*, 18 Geo. Wash. L. Rev. 50, 54 (1949).

raising money for charity, or writing novels – were unpatentable.[55] When Congress amended § 101 in 1952, it merely ratified this prevailing understanding.[56] As Judge Giles Rich, one of the principal drafters of the 1952 Act, explained soon after the act was passed,

> Of course, not every kind of an invention can be patented. Invaluable though it may be to individuals, the public, and national defense, the invention of a more effective organization of the materials in, and the techniques of teaching a course in physics, chemistry, or Russian is not a patentable invention because it is outside of the enumerated categories of "process, machine, manufacture, or composition of matter, or any new and useful improvement thereof." Also outside that group is one of the greatest inventions of our times, the diaper service.[57]

What all of Judge Rich's examples (the diaper service, a more effective organizational approach, and improved techniques for teaching courses) share in common is that they are abstract in nature. Even if they may use concrete manufactures, compositions of matter, or machines (a washing machine and detergent in the case of a diaper service, telephones in implementing an improved method of organization, and a blackboard and chalk in teaching), the processes themselves are not patentable because their association with these concrete components does not involve a specific concrete application of the process to improve or advance a particular machine, manufacture, or composition of matter.[58]

This is also consistent with the function of the patent laws historically, which was to protect not only new machines, manufactures, and compositions of matter but also the "working or making of any manner of new manufactures within this realm."[59] One example of such workings and makings is James Watt's famous 1769 patent on a "[m]ethod of diminishing the consumption of fuel in [steam]-engines."[60] These kinds of processes – the working and making of machines and manufactures – advanced these technological subject matters, thereby advancing

55 *See Bilski*, 130 S. Ct. at 3239–46 (Stevens, J., concurring); *In re Bilski*, 545 F.3d 943, 1001–02 (Fed. Cir. 2008) (en banc) (Mayer, J., dissenting) (collecting cases that rejected patenting of nontechnological methods).

56 *See* Nationwide Mut. Ins. Co. v. Darden, 503 U.S. 318, 322 (1992) (holding that where no contrary indication is present, courts presume Congress intended to ratify, rather than overturn, the prevailing legal understanding at the time).

57 Giles S. Rich, *Principles of Patentability*, 28 Geo. Wash. L. Rev. 393, 393–94 (1960) (quoting 35 U.S.C. § 101).

58 This same approach can be used to explain why several of the Justices at the Bilski oral argument expressed skepticism toward patents on such methods as speed dating and an improved method of teaching antitrust law, even though these methods would inevitably involve concrete objects such as electronic timers, laptops, visual projectors, and microphones. *See* Transcript of *Bilski* Oral Argument, *supra* note 18, at 7–9.

59 *In re Bilski*, 545 F.3d at 968 (Dyk, J., concurring) (emphasis omitted) (quoting Statute of Monopolies, 1623, 21 Jac. 1, c. 3 (Eng.)).

60 *Id.* at 970 (alterations in original) (emphasis and citation omitted).

the useful arts.[61] Thus, each time the Supreme Court has historically spoken to the patentability of processes, it has reinforced that valid ones should advance the development, understanding, or application of a machine, manufacture, or composition of matter.[62]

III. THE ABSTRACTNESS "CLUES" AND SOUND PATENT POLICY SUGGEST THAT BUSINESS AND SERVICE PROCESSES ARE STILL OFTEN UNPATENTABLE

The clues discussed in Part II are important considerations when courts or the PTO considers the patentability of all types of processes. However, they are particularly important when considering the patentability of business and service processes – not only because these types of processes have not been historically recognized as patentable[63] but also because heightened scrutiny of patents in these industries comports with sound patent policy. Although the Court in *Bilski* rejected a categorical prohibition on such processes being patentable, all nine Justices recognized the dangers of allowing patents in these areas.[64] Thus, it is particularly important for the PTO and the Court to use these clues to scrutinize patent applications on such processes.

In particular, strict application of these clues for ferreting out abstract ideas from patentable business and service processes protects the public interest for four reasons. First, there are generally sufficient incentives for innovation already in these industries and thus less patent protection is necessary; second, the research and development (R&D) costs that typically justify patent protection are lower for business and service processes; third, business and service innovation is far more diffuse and collaborative than innovation in other industries; and fourth, overextending patent protection to business and service industries would disrupt settled

61 *See* Tilghman v. Proctor, 102 U.S. 707, 722 (1880) (manufacturing processes are within the meaning of the term "art"); Cochrane v. Deener, 94 U.S. 780, 788 (1876) (finding patentable processes to be "a mode of treatment of certain materials to produce a given result"); Corning v. Burden, 56 U.S. (15 How.) 252, 267–68 (1853) (noting patentable processes must produce a certain effect or manufacture by means of "chemical action, by the operation or application of some element or power of nature, or of one substance to another"). See also Bilski v. Kappos, 130 S. Ct. 3218, 3240 (2010) (Stevens, J., concurring) (noting the emphasis in the English Statute of Monopolies on allowing process patents for the "mode, method, or way of manufacturing" (citation omitted)).

62 *See* Jacobs v. Baker, 74 U.S. (7 Wall.) 295, 297 (1868) ("But if the subject-matter be neither a machine nor a manufacture, nor a composition of matter, then . . . it must be an art, for there can be no valid patent except it be for a thing made, or for the art or *process of making* a thing.") (quoting George Ticknor Curtis, A Treatise on the Law of Patents for Useful Inventions in the United States of America 91 (2nd ed. 1854))); *Corning*, 56 U.S. at 267 (a patentable art includes "methods, or operations . . . called processes" such as the "arts of tanning, dyeing, making water-proof cloth, vulcanizing India rubber, [and] smelting ores").

63 *See Bilski*, 130 S. Ct. at 3237–47 (Stevens, J., concurring).

64 *Id.* at 3230 (majority opinion).

expectations and impose substantial additional costs on investors and innovators. We next discuss each of these reasons in more detail and map them to several of the earlier clues.

A. *Patent Protection Is Generally Unnecessary to Promote Innovation in Business and Service Processes*

"[F]rom the outset, federal patent law has been about the difficult business 'of drawing a line between the things which are worth to the public the embarrassment of an exclusive patent, and those which are not.'"[65] Patents on business and service methods often fall in the latter category. Prior to the Federal Circuit's ill-conceived *State Street Bank*[66] decision, business and service innovations thrived in the United States without patent protection.[67]

Service industries may use more technology today, such as programmed computers, than they did in the past, but patents are rarely sought or needed to encourage innovation for new business models or services.[68] In a recent survey of more than 1300 high-technology entrepreneurs, close to three-fourths of software and e-commerce startups (which are among the most technologically driven participants in modern business and service industries) reported that they do not own patents and have not applied for them, compared with less than a quarter of similarly situated biotechnology and medical device companies.[69] Software and e-commerce companies report also seeking patent protection almost five times less frequently than computer hardware startups.[70] Thus, even in technology-driven business and service industries, patent protection is largely disfavored as a source of incentives for innovation; for nontechnological businesses and services, it would provide even less. Instead, business and service-oriented industries rely on a wide variety of other

65 *See* Bonito Boats, Inc. v. Thunder Craft Boats, Inc., 489 U.S. 141, 148 (1989) (quoting 13 THOMAS JEFFERSON, THE WRITINGS OF THOMAS JEFFERSON 335 (Andrew A. Lipscomb ed., Thomas Jefferson Mem'l Ass'n 1903)).

66 State Street Bank & Trust Co. v. Signature Fin. Group, Inc., 149 F.3d 1368 (Fed Cir. 1998).

67 *See* Leo J. Raskind, *The* State Street Bank *Decision: The Bad Business of Unlimited Patent Protection for Methods of Doing Business*, 10 FORDHAM INTELL. PROP. MEDIA & ENT. L.J. 61, 93 (1999) (citing the rapid growth of fast-food restaurants, self-service gasoline stations, quick oil change facilities, ATMs, and alternative long-distance telephone services as examples of business innovations that occurred without patent incentives).

68 Abstractness of many software innovations for which patents may be sought has contributed to difficulties in patents performing the important function of defining the metes and bounds of patent claims. *See, e.g.*, JAMES BESSEN & MICHAEL J. MEURER, PATENT FAILURE: HOW JUDGES, BUREAUCRATS, AND LAWYERS PUT INNOVATORS AT RISK 187–214 (2008).

69 Stuart J. H. Graham et al., *High Technology Entrepreneurs and the Patent System: Results of the 2008 Berkeley Patent Survey*, 24 BERKELEY TECH. L.J. 1255, 1255, 1277 (2009).

70 *Id.* at 1277, 1283 (reporting that patents offer "relatively mixed to weak incentives to engage in innovation" in these areas). *See also id.* at 1286 (reporting that patents provide between "slight" and "no incentive at all" for internal process innovations), 1290–92 (reporting "patenting" as the least important incentive for innovation and maintaining competitive advantages).

incentives that promote innovation. These include first-mover advantages, complementary assets, trade secrets, and customer loyalty.[71]

First-mover advantages are particularly prevalent in business and service innovation because they provide competitive advantages that cannot be copied, such as consumer brand loyalty and heightened switching costs.[72] For example, in frequent flyer programs, the first airline to convince a customer to invest often remains the primary program for that customer – despite robust competition from other airlines – because of the customer's substantial investment in the program and the high switching costs associated with starting over.[73] Such programs also face little danger of the kind of copying and free-riding that patents are meant to prevent. One airline can copy the general rules and structure of another's program, but the true value and competitive advantage lie in customers' investment and loyalty to their account and achieving the benefits it offers.[74] At the same time, competition keeps the pressure on airlines to continue innovating and responding to consumer demand, so that the switching costs do not become worthwhile to the customer. Patent incentives, in contrast, would not encourage such competition – if customer-friendly programs such as frequent flying were patentable, then the first airline would gain the spoils, and other airlines would be prevented from innovating and competing.[75]

Patent monopolies are equally unnecessary for many service-driven internet companies such as Google, Twitter, YouTube, and Facebook. These companies have few, if any, patents and almost never enforce them.[76] Yet they command

[71] *Id.* at 1290–92 (noting that first-mover advantages, complementary assets, and trade secrecy are the most important strategies for securing competitive advantages among software and e-commerce startups), 1292 (noting, in summary, that software and internet startups strongly prefer first-mover advantages to patents when seeking incentives to innovate). *See also* Bilski v. Kappos, 130 S. Ct. 3218, 3254 (2010) (Stevens, J., concurring).

[72] *See* Stefania Fusco, *Is the Use of Patents Promoting the Creation of New Types of Securities?*, 25 Santa Clara Computer & High Tech. L.J. 243, 256 (2009) (citing Peter Tufano, *Financial Innovation and First-Mover Advantages*, 25 J. Fin. Econ. 213, 214–15, 234–35 (1989)). *See also* Adam B. Jaffe & Josh Lerner, Innovation And Its Discontents: How Our Broken Patent System Is Endangering Innovation and Progress, and What to Do About It 47 (2004) (discussing brand loyalty and consumer learning curves as strong first-mover advantages over competitors); Wesley M. Cohen, Richard R. Nelson, & John P. Walsh, *Protecting Their Intellectual Assets: Appropriability Conditions and Why U.S. Manufacturing Firms Patent (or Not)* 28 (Nat'l Bureau of Econ. Research, Working Paper No. 7552, 2000), *available at* http://www.nber.org/papers/w7552.pdf; Helios Herrera & Enrique Schroth, *Profitable Innovation Without Patent Protection: The Case of Derivatives* 6 (Centro de Investigación Económica, Working Paper No. 03–02, 2003), available at http://ftp.itam.mx/pub/academico/inves/herrera/03–02.pdf.

[73] Fredrik Carlsson & Åsa Löfgren, *Airline Choice, Switching Costs and Frequent Flyer Programmes*, 38 Applied Econ. 1469, 1469–70 (2006).

[74] *Id.* at 1474.

[75] *See also* Fred Smith & Brian Dumaine, *How I Delivered the Goods*, Fortune Small Bus., Oct. 1, 2002, at 28, *available at* http://money.cnn.com/magazines/fsb/fsb_archive/2002/10/01/330568/index.htm (describing Federal Express's first-mover advantages).

[76] *See generally* Graham et al., *supra* note 69.

significant market shares through their first-mover statuses, innovation-driven cultures, technological and data lock-ins, and emphasis on customer service and loyalty.[77]

In addition to first-mover advantages, business and service industries can use complementary assets to secure their market positions and recoup their investment. Lawyers who provide high-quality corporate services to clients may also attract those clients when additional matters such as litigation arise. A good doctor will attract the family and friends of patients. A good plumber will attract repeat business for additional household problems. These business advantages – and the innovation and quality required to maintain them – are based on loyalty and reputation, not patent incentives.[78]

Other nonpatent incentives for innovation in the business and service industries include ongoing professional development and expertise (e.g., the more one performs and improves one's service, the higher quality performance one offers) and customization (e.g., solving a particular client's problem often provides information on the client and the problem that competitors may lack).[79]

Rather than the repetition of identical items, which is characteristic of manufacturing and quite vulnerable to copying, it is the individualized qualities of the service marketplace that provide competitive advantage.[80] Put another way, the provision of services cannot be duplicated in the same way that a product or device can be copied; thus, the classic free-riding problem in patent-intensive industries is avoided.[81]

77 *See* Sara Kehaulani Goo, *Building a 'Googley' Workforce*, WASH. POST, Oct. 21, 2006, *available at* http://www.washingtonpost.com/wp-dyn/content/article/2006/10/20/AR2006102001461.html. *See also* JONATHAN ZITTRAIN, THE FUTURE OF THE INTERNET – AND HOW TO STOP IT 102–03 (2008) (discussing platform lock-in).

78 *See generally* Pamela Samuelson, *What Effects Do Legal Rules Have on Service Innovation?*, *in* HANDBOOK OF SERVICE SCIENCE 603 (Paul P. Maglio, Cheryl A. Kieliszewski, & James Spohrer eds., 2010), *available at* http://ssrn.com/abstract=1421946; *Hearing on Issues Relating to the Patenting of Tax Advice Before the Subcomm. on Select Revenue Measures of the H. Comm. on Ways & Means*, 109th Cong. 77 (2006) (statement of Ellen Aprill, Associate Dean of Academic Programs, Professor of Law, and John E. Anderson Chair of Tax Law, Loyola Law School, Los Angeles, California) (noting that existing economic incentives for tax planning already provide ample inducement for the development, promotion, and implementation of new strategies). *See also generally* Eric Goldman, *Online Word of Mouth and Its Implications for Trademark Law*, *in* TRADEMARK LAW AND THEORY: A HANDBOOK OF CONTEMPORARY RESEARCH 404, 410 (Graeme B. Dinwoodie & Mark D. Janis eds., 2008).

79 *See* MICHAEL POLANYI, THE TACIT DIMENSION 72–89 (1966) (discussing the highly detailed, often context-specific knowledge actually required to do a complex job well); Robert P. Merges, *The Uninvited Guest: Patents on Wall Street* 10–11 (UC Berkeley Pub. Law & Legal Theory Research Paper Series, Research Paper No. 126, 2003), *available at* http://ssrn.com/abstract=410900 (citing Tufano, *supra* note 72, at 235) (reporting a bankers' view that innovation is the best way to advertise expertise).

80 *See* Frances X. Frei, *Breaking the Trade-Off Between Efficiency and Service*, HARV. BUS. REV., Nov. 2006, at 93, 93–101; Conrad Lashley, *Towards an Understanding of Employee Empowerment in Hospitality Services*, 7 INT'L J. CONTEMP. HOSPITALITY MGMT. 27, 27–32 (1995).

81 *See* Merges, *supra* note 79, at 10–11 (citing Robin Cowan, Paul A. David & Dominique Foray, *The Explicit Economics of Knowledge Codification and Tacitness*, 9 INDUS. & CORP. CHANGE 211, 211–53

The characteristics and practices in business and service professions we have identified here provide policy reasons for heeding the abstractness clues that will frequently be evident in applications seeking patents for business and service innovations – indicating that patent protection is unnecessary in many, if not most, cases to provide incentive for innovation in these fields. These practices link directly to the constitutional and statutory clues noted earlier because patents on such processes would generally not promote additional progress in these areas, and certainly not the progress of particular machines, manufactures, or compositions of matter.

B. *By Their Nature, Business and Service Innovators Have Not Needed Patent Incentives Because They Have Had Less Intensive R&D Costs than Technological Innovators*

Patents should only be granted to those inventions "which would not be disclosed or devised but for the inducement of a patent."[82] The high R&D costs of technology innovation, coupled with the low costs of copying, are a major reason why patent incentives help promote innovation in technology-intensive industries.[83]

Business and service innovations, however, do not typically require the substantial up-front investments – for example, engineering teams, R&D labs, expensive equipment, and/or clinical trials – that undergird the perceived need for patent protection in manufacturing industries.[84] Without high up-front costs to recoup, there is simply less need to protect business and service innovations with patents. Lower R&D costs also allow innovators to recoup their investments more quickly without the need for twenty years of patent protection, thus making competitive advantages such as first-mover adequate for cost recovery.

In light of these lower R&D costs, the constitutional and statutory clues we have noted strongly suggest that, where there is no economic need for patent protection to promote specific innovations – especially innovations related to machines, manufactures, or compositions of matter – the PTO and the courts should heavily scrutinize process patent applications in order to ferret out abstract ideas from receiving protection. Specifically, where R&D costs are low, the legal and administrative gatekeepers for patenting should take particular care to consider the *Flook* clues of insignificant post-solution activity and mere field-of-use limitations to ensure

(2000)) (noting that customized knowledge is difficult to codify and even harder to transfer from one person to another).

82 Graham v. John Deere Co. of Kan. City, 383 U.S. 1, 11 (1966).

83 *See* Bessen & Meurer, *supra* note 68, at 216.

84 *See* Bilski v. Kappos, 130 S. Ct. 3218, 3254 (2010) (Stevens, J., concurring) (noting that business innovation generally does not require the same enormous costs in terms of time, research, and development as more traditional technological innovation); Andrew A. Schwartz, *The Patent Office Meets the Poison Pill: Why Legal Methods Cannot Be Patented*, 20 Harv. J.L. & Tech. 333, 369 (2007) (noting that "[t]here is no need to buy or build expensive machinery or run tests on prototypes" in service professions as in the practice of law).

against the unnecessary protection of abstract ideas. Where patent applicants have not invested significant R&D in the tangible elements of their claims (such as the use of a telephone as part of a business process), the *Flook* clues are more likely to apply.

C. *Business and Service Innovations Are Often More Diffuse and Collaborative and Thus Fall Outside of the Classic Patent "Reward" Paradigm*

Classic patent economics presumes that the costs of innovation will be efficiently internalized within single firms or individuals and that innovators will need exclusive rights to encourage investment and recoup those costs.[85] In most technological industries such as pharmaceutical, electronics, and manufacturing firms, single entities bear the full R&D costs of initial development, refinement, production, maintenance, and ongoing innovation. These R&D costs are typically passed on to consumers as part of the price of specific products, but consumers have typically played a very minimal and indirect role in the actual practice of research and development.

In service and business industries, however, such economics do not map easily or appropriately because innovation is often derived from collaboration with customers.[86] For example, professional service innovations are often discovered and developed on-site with clients at their place of business or as a result of a client's own innovative approaches to the problem the provider is helping solve. Even when the subject matter is technological, consumers frequently innovate new processes and then voluntarily transfer that knowledge back to the producers of the technology without patenting it and at no charge.[87]

Thus, patents for business and service innovation may often fail to allocate rewards appropriately and may potentially bar some user-innovators from practicing the very methods they underwrote or to which they contributed. The constitutional and statutory clues discussed earlier help ensure that users and customers can continue to innovate in general areas of process improvement without fear that a single actor

[85] Bessen & Meurer, supra note 68, at 216.

[86] Mary Jo Bittner, Stephen W. Brown & Matthew L. Meuter, *Technology Infusion in Service Encounters*, 28 J. Acad. Marketing Sci. 138, 138–49 (2000).

[87] *See* Jeroen P.J. de Jong & Eric von Hippel, *Measuring User Innovation in Dutch High Tech SMEs: Frequency, Nature and Transfer to Producers* 3–4 (MIT Sloan Sch. of Mgmt., Working Paper No. 4724–09, 2009), *available at* http://ssrn.com /abstract=1352496; Fred Gault & Eric von Hippel, *The Prevalence of User Innovation and Free Innovation Transfers: Implications for Statistical Indicators and Innovation Policy* 2, 4, 19 (MIT Sloan Sch. of Mgmt., Working Paper No. 4722–09, 2009), *available at* http://ssrn.com/abstract=1337232. See also Eric Von Hippel, The Sources of Innovation 25–26 (1988); Yochai Benkler, *Coase's Penguin, or, Linux and the Nature of the Firm*, 112 Yale L.J. 369, 372 (2002).

will gain patent protection for the basic concepts or wide-ranging applications of processes in these areas.[88]

D. *Extensive Patent Protection on Business and Services Would Disrupt Settled Expectations and Impose Substantial Additional Costs on Innovators and Investors*

Setting aside the lack of necessity and inapplicability, extensive patenting of business and service processes would also actively hurt innovation and disrupt settled expectations.[89] As the Supreme Court observed, "[t]he balance between the interest in motivating innovation and enlightenment by rewarding invention with patent protection on the one hand, and the interest in avoiding monopolies that unnecessarily stifle competition on the other, has been a feature of the federal patent laws since their inception."[90]

Business and service industries attract a high proportion of individual entrepreneurs, small businesses, and other so-called startups.[91] These entrepreneurs already face disproportional regulatory costs that inhibit their advancement in the marketplace vis-à-vis larger firms.[92] Imposing a new layer of significant additional costs for patent searches, legal counsel, litigation defense, and license negotiation would further drain their resources, potentially deterring investment and entry.[93] Moreover, if the PTO grants broad business and service process patents, small startup businesses would face an entirely new regime of business regulation – essentially requiring them to request private permits to operate from their competitors that have patents, independent of whatever technology the new business uses to compete. A prohibition on such broad patenting is strongly supported by the "clues" that processes with wide-ranging applications, that constitute basic concepts, or that

88 *See supra* notes 23–25 and accompanying text (wide-ranging application and basic concept clues).

89 *See* Festo Corp. v. Shoketsu Kinzoku Kogyo Kabushiki Co., 535 U.S. 722, 739 (2002) (noting that courts should be cautious not to disrupt settled expectations when deciding patent cases).

90 Pfaff v. Wells Elecs., Inc., 525 U.S. 55, 63 (1998).

91 *See* Small Bus. Admin., Office of Advocacy, The Small Business Economy: A Report to the President 20–21 (2009), *available at* http://www.sba.gov/advo /research/sb_econ2990.pdf (showing that 41.88% of new financial services are small businesses and 43.88% of new professional and business services are small businesses). See also Robert W. Fairlie, Kauffman Found., Kauffman Index of Entrepreneurial Activity 1996–2009 (2010), *available at* http://www.kauffman.org /uploaded-files/kiea_2010_report.pdf (noting that the entrepreneurial activity rate – the percentage of American non–business-owning adults who start a business each month – increased slightly in 2008 over 2007).

92 *See* W. Mark Crain, Small Bus. Admin., Office of Advocacy, The Impact of Regulatory Costs on Small Firms 5–6 (2005), *available at* http://www.sba.gov/sites/default/files/The_Impact_of%20_Regulatory_Costs_of_Small%20Firms.pdf.

93 *See* Bilski v. Kappos, 130 S. Ct. 3218, 3255–56 (2010) (Stevens, J., concurring) (noting the substantial costs that will likely be imposed on businesses by increased business method patenting).

contain fundamental economic principles are more likely to be abstract ideas and should not be patentable.[94]

The potential for follow-on innovation is another reason to heavily scrutinize business and service process patent applications. In an ideal marketplace, one firm often discovers an innovative aspect of the business and others quickly follow, experimenting with and modifying the original method or product to find other advances.[95] In technological industries, follow-on innovation is often impeded by a plethora of preexisting patents. In patent-intensive industries, firms often develop large patent portfolios in order to navigate these so-called patent thickets.[96] Although this practice often leads to market inefficiencies, many technology industries have adapted reasonably well to the existence of patent thickets in their fields because they must already invest in patents to offset the significant R&D costs they are incurring.[97]

In many business and service industries, however, this is not the case. These firms have traditionally not sought nor obtained patent protection. If some firms can easily acquire broad and potentially abstract patents on these methods, competing firms and new market entrants may have little choice but to develop defensive patent portfolios and blocking patents of their own to avoid the potentially catastrophic risk of injunctions on their primary business models.[98] Ironically, to acquire these patents, business and service firms would have to divert resources away from their R&D budgets to pay legal fees and PTO fees, thereby potentially reducing innovation in their fields.[99] All of this goes against the current settled expectations of innovators and investors in these fields.[100]

[94] *See supra* notes 23–25 and accompanying text. *See also Bilski*, 130 S. Ct. at 3229 (majority opinion) ("The Information Age empowers people with new capacities to perform statistical analyses and mathematical calculations with a speed and sophistication that enable the design of protocols for more efficient performance of a vast number of business tasks. If a high enough bar is not set when considering patent applications of this sort, patent examiners and courts could be flooded with claims that would put a chill on creative endeavor and dynamic change.").

[95] *See* Alan Greenspan, Chairman, Fed. Reserve Bank, Remarks at the 2003 Financial Markets Conference of the Federal Reserve Bank of Atlanta: Market Economies and Rule of Law (Apr. 4, 2003), *available at* http://www.federalreserve.gov /BoardDocs/speeches/2003/20030404/default.htm.

[96] Carl Shapiro, *Navigating the Patent Thicket: Cross Licenses, Patent Pools, and Standard-Setting*, 1 INNOVATION POL'Y & ECON. 119, 120–21 (2001).

[97] *See id.* at 120, 129–30.

[98] *See, e.g.*, NTP, Inc. v. Research in Motion, Ltd., No. 3:01CV767, 2003 U.S. Dist. LEXIS 26837, at *5 (E.D. Va. Aug. 5, 2003) (staying permanent injunction of RIM's Blackberry Wireless Email Service pending appeal due in part to a "demonstrated and increasing use" by the public); BESSEN & MEURER, *supra* note 68, at 176 (noting evidence of large incumbents using patent injunctions anticompetitively as a means of discouraging entry by small inventors). *See also generally* Colleen V. Chien, *Of Trolls, Davids, Goliaths, and Kings: Narratives and Evidence in the Litigation of High-Tech Patents*, 87 N.C. L. REV. 1571, 1582–83 (2009) (describing the need for defensive patenting in patent-intensive industries).

[99] *See* Graham et al., *supra* note 69, at 1311 (noting that many startups, even in technology sectors, do not file patents because of their high cost).

[100] *See* Bilski v. Kappos, 130 S. Ct. 3218, 3255 (2010) (Stevens, J., concurring) (noting that "[i]nnovation in business methods is often a sequential and complementary process in which imitation may be a 'spur to innovation' and patents may 'become an *impediment*.'") (quoting James Bessen & Eric

The potential perils of patent protection in the context of financial innovation are particularly ominous. A chief driver of financial innovation is the profit earned through perfect or near-perfect arbitrage. In other words, by repackaging and restructuring existing financial assets in new forms or combinations, arbitragers can take advantage of price discrepancies between two otherwise equivalent bundles of assets. Arbitrage is a fundamental activity in financial markets. Moreover, it is one that has been quite active since at least the Middle Ages, when Venetian bankers were able to exploit regional differences in gold and silver exchange rates to turn a considerable profit.[101] Because arbitrage activities offer short-term profits that are often close to being risk-free, such activities do not need the decades-long protection of patents to incentivize their innovation and use.

Moreover, the activities of quick-acting arbitrageurs are critical to efficiency and price discovery in financial markets. Virtually every accepted technique within financial engineering for valuing financial assets, from the capital asset pricing model to arbitrage pricing theory to the Black Scholes options pricing formula, depends critically on the existence of arbitrageurs who will identify and quickly dissipate arbitrage opportunities.[102]

By its very nature, patent protection allows a patentee to delay her activities of profit extraction, unafraid of competition by others. In an arbitrage context, this implies that a patentee arbitrageur may decide to "milk" her strategy for many months, years, or even decades, and her property right to exclude others from the same strategy will induce her arbitrage position to become relatively gradual. Thus, application of the constitutional and statutory clues to scrutinize financial patents would help ensure market efficiency, price discovery, and the viability of benchmark valuation models in finance. This also comports with the *Bilski* Court's finding that attempts to patent fundamental economic practices should generally be rejected as attempts to patent abstract ideas.[103]

IV. USING ABSTRACTNESS CLUES TO CLOSELY SCRUTINIZE PATENT APPLICATIONS ON BUSINESS AND SERVICE PROCESSES WILL IMPROVE ADMINISTRATIVE AND JUDICIAL EFFICIENCY

Applying the clues to patentability discussed earlier will also help the PTO and the courts use public resources more appropriately. Whether a claim qualifies as patentable subject matter under § 101 is a threshold inquiry[104] Any claim that fails

Maskin, *Sequential Innovation, Patents, and Imitation*, 40 RAND J. ECON. 611, 613 (2009) (emphasis in original)).

[101] *See* IVO WELCH, CORPORATE FINANCE: AN INTRODUCTION 248 (2009).

[102] *See, e.g.*, MARK GRINBLATT & SHERIDAN TITMAN, FINANCIAL MARKETS AND CORPORATE STRATEGY 230–31 (2d ed. 2002) (discussing the critical role of arbitrage in financial derivatives pricing).

[103] *Bilski*, 130 S. Ct. at 3231.

[104] *See id.* at 3225 ("The § 101 patent-eligibility inquiry is only a threshold test.").

to meet the requirements of § 101 must be rejected, even if the requirements of §§ 102, 103, and 112 are met.[105] Therefore, a robust set of § 101 clues for abstractness can help improve patent quality and the efficiency of decision makers who examine and decide patent subject matter eligibility.

A. *Use of Robust § 101 Clues Allows the PTO to Efficiently Reject Abstract Patent Applications*

A robust set of §101 clues to abstractness gives the PTO a meaningful, efficient, and predictable framework against which to test patent applications at the threshold of the examination process, before significant costs are incurred. Every year, the PTO struggles to review and grant patents on appropriate inventions. The longer the PTO takes to review applications, the less protection and the fewer incentives are returned to innovators.[106] Since *State Street*, there has been a dramatic increase in the number of business and service method patent applications, adding to this problem.[107] After *Bilski*, the PTO and the courts will need to rely even more heavily on the clues to patentability to prevent threats to freedom to innovate from abstract patent claims.

Issuing a § 101 rejection is among the easiest ways for the PTO to take final action on patent applications.[108] Unlike rejections under § 102 (lack of novelty) or § 103 (obviousness), § 101 determinations are made on the claim language alone and thus do not require extensive research into the state of the art or the details of other documents. This can save examiners significant research time and lead to faster rejections of abstract applications.

For example, consider the following method from an actual application for directing funds to a charity, in which the primary claim is as follows:

A method of directing funds to a charity, comprising:

> receiving a first signal from a donor computer, the first signal including instructions, a request or advice indicating a desire to direct one or more payments to a donor-selected charity, at least a portion of the payment to be transferred from a giving

[105] *See* 35 U.S.C. § 103 (2006); 35 U.S.C. § 112 (2006); Diamond v. Diehr, 450 U.S. 175, 188–91 (1981); Kewanee Oil Co. v. Bicron Corp., 416 U.S. 470, 483 (1974); 35 U.S.C. § 102 (2006).

[106] *See* Jaffe & Lerner, *supra* note 72, at 131, 185–86.

[107] Kevin M. Baird, *Business Method Patents: Chaos at the USPTO or Business as Usual?*, 2001 U. Ill. J.L. Tech. & Pol'y 347, 348 (2001) (noting backlog of business method applications at the PTO).

[108] *See In re Bilski*, 545 F.3d 943, 950 n.1 (Fed. Cir. 2008) (en banc) (noting that a PTO examiner may reject a claim solely on the basis of § 101 and independently of any other substantive requirement and suggesting that examiners first identify and reject claims on that basis). *See also* Interim Guidance, *supra* note 11, at 43923 (instructing examiners to reject claims under § 101 if there is a prima facie case of subject matter ineligibility and then consider rebuttal arguments and evidence if presented).

account, the giving account having been established to hold funds for charitable gift-giving.[109]

This is essentially an abstract process for charity fundraising. It embodies a "basic concept" much like the patent claim in *Bilski* and does not advance the development, understanding, or application of a machine, a manufacture, or a composition of matter. Instead, much like Judge Rich's example of a diaper service, it merely uses technology (a donor computer) as an insignificant part of its solution without promoting its progress. Using the abstractness clues, the PTO could easily and quickly reject this application and focus its resources on other applications of more merit.

B. *Use of Robust § 101 Clues Allows Courts to Efficiently Dismiss Frivolous Patent Litigation*

A set of robust § 101 clues would also empower courts to reject patent claims that were erroneously granted to improper subject matter. Much has been made of the avalanche of patent litigation in the federal court system, especially as it relates to so-called patent trolls – entities that acquire patents for rent-seeking but that do not actually produce products covered by the patent.[110] As Justice Kennedy recently observed, "An industry has developed in which firms use patents not as a basis for producing and selling goods but, instead, primarily for obtaining licensing fees."[111] These lawsuits are problematic because they are so costly.[112] Rarely does one win or lose such cases on summary judgment, and parties often have little choice but to settle to avoid the cost of litigating through trial and possible appeal.[113]

Utilizing the clues of § 101 will allow at least some defendants who are fighting patent trolls and other suspect litigants to bring relatively straightforward motions to dismiss and for summary judgment on § 101 issues.[114] This could have a substantial effect on reducing unwarranted and inappropriate patent litigation in the federal court system.[115]

[109] U.S. Patent Application No. 2006/0212390 (filed Mar. 15, 2006).

[110] *See, e.g.*, Chien, *supra* note 98, at 1577–82.

[111] eBay Inc. v. MercExchange, L.L.C., 547 U.S. 388, 396 (2006) (Kennedy, J., concurring).

[112] *See, e.g.*, Jaffe & Lerner, *supra* note 72, at 76.

[113] *See id.* at 14.

[114] *See* AT&T Corp. v. Excel Commc'ns, Inc., 172 F.3d 1352, 1355 (Fed. Cir. 1999) (noting, on appeal from a motion for summary judgment, that § 101 determinations are an issue of law).

[115] *Compare* John R. Allison & Mark A. Lemley, *Empirical Evidence on the Validity of Litigated Patents*, 26 AIPLA Q.J. 185, 187, 208 tbl. 1 (1998) (finding that from 1989 through 1996, even before *State Street*, expansive subject matter doctrines resulted in less than 1% of patents being invalidated by courts for improper subject matter), *with* CyberSource Corp. v. Retail Decisions, Inc., 620 F. Supp. 2d. 1068, 1081 (N.D. Cal. 2009) (ruling, after the *Bilski* en banc decision, that a business method patent was invalid subject matter on motion for summary judgment and observing that "[t]he closing bell may be

V. CONCLUSION

In his *Bilski* concurrence, Justice Stevens expressed a "real concern that patents on business methods would press on the limits of the 'standard expressed in the Constitution,' more likely stifling progress than 'promot[ing]' it."[116] Even though the majority of the Court held that business methods can qualify as patentable processes, we believe this concern remains. To address it, the PTO and the courts should fully embrace the constitutional, statutory, and judicial clues outlined earlier in light of the policy objectives we have described to help determine whether such methods are abstract ideas or concrete processes.

ringing for business method patents"), Fort Props., Inc. v. Am. Master Lease, LLC, 609 F. Supp. 2d 1052 (C.D. Cal. 2009) (holding a real estate business method patent invalid under *Bilski's* machine-or-transformation test), *and* Research Corp. Techs. v. Microsoft Corp., No. CV-01–658-TUC-RCJ, 2009 WL 2413623, at *9 (D. Ariz. July 28, 2009) (holding two patents invalid on motion for summary judgment under *Bilski's* machine-or-transformation test).

[116] Bilski v. Kappos, 130 S. Ct. 3218, 3253 (2010) (Stevens, J., concurring) (alteration in original) (quoting Graham v. John Deere Co. of Kan. City, 383 U.S. 1, 6 (1966) and U.S. CONST. art. I, § 8, cl. 8).

2

Still Aiming at the Wrong Target

A Case for Business Method and Software Patents from a Business Perspective†

*Kristen Osenga**

INTRODUCTION

Haste in every business brings failures. – Herodotus

Ten years ago, business method inventions went from being ineligible for patent protection to eligible, nearly overnight. In 2008, the tide shifted just as quickly in the other direction, calling into question which, if any, business method and software inventions can be patented. In the intervening years, there has been much angst surrounding patents on business methods and software. The evils of these patents have been hailed by everyone from judges[1] to academics[2] to mainstream

† Editors' Note: This chapter was written prior to the Supreme Court's decision in *Bilski* v. *Kappos*, which affirmed the Federal Circuit's decision in *In re Bilski* but modified its rationale. 561 U.S. 593, 130 S. Ct. 3218 (2010). Contrary to the Federal Circuit, the Court held that the machine-or-transformation test was not the sole test for determining the patent eligibility of a process. Rather, that test was only "a useful and important clue... for determining whether some claimed inventions are processes under § 101." *Bilski*, 130 S. Ct. at 3227. However, Osenga's argument is not based on the precise rationale of the Federal Circuit's decision. In fact, this chapter recognizes that the result of the Supreme Court's grant of certiorari in *Bilski* would likely lead to a reduction in the scope of patentable subject matter for business methods. So although this chapter should be read with an understanding of the later history of the *Bilski* case, its discussion of the broader arguments for and against business method and software patents remains instructive.

* Professor of Law, University of Richmond School of Law.

1 *See, e.g.*, Lab. Corp. of Am. Holdings v. Metabolite Labs., Inc. 548 U.S. 124, 138 (2006) (Breyer, J., dissenting) (noting that even if the claims in question were valid, it is important to debate whether the granting of business method patents "adequately reflects the 'careful balance' that the 'federal patent laws... embody'"); *In re Bilski*, 545 F.3d 943, 998 (Fed. Cir. 2008) (Mayer, J. dissenting) ("Business method patents do not promote the 'useful arts' because they are not directed to any technological or scientific innovation.").

2 *See, e.g.*, Malla Pollack, *The Multiple Unconstitutionality of Business Method Patents*, 28 Rutgers Computer & Tech. L.J. 61 (2002); Rochelle Cooper Dreyfuss, *Are Business Method Patents Bad for Business?*, 16 Santa Clara Computer & High Tech. L.J. 263 (2000).

media.[3] In fact, it is media coverage of this type of patent that may shape the layperson's perspective on intellectual property law generally.[4]

To be sure, there are abundant examples of problematic patents on business method and software inventions, such as the much maligned Amazon one-click patent.[5] But there are problems with patents on many other types of inventions, particularly those in burgeoning fields that had previously not been covered by patent protection.[6] In the case of business methods and software, these concerns have prompted some to suggest that patents should not be granted for these inventions.[7] Recently the Court of Appeals for the Federal Circuit seems to have embraced this suggestion and has made it much more difficult to obtain patent protection for business method and software inventions. And now, the Supreme Court is poised to consider the issue.

In an earlier article, *Ants, Elephant Guns, and Statutory Subject Matter*,[8] I argue that the opposition to business method and software patents is misplaced. Because of the firestorm surrounding these patents, the PTO and the courts are using proxy-type inquiries to cut off the patentability analysis of these inventions at the threshold step. I contend that it is inappropriate to use the statutory subject matter inquiry to avoid more difficult questions of patentability and policy. Instead the PTO should be examining and the courts should be reviewing these inventions on an individual basis and on their merits, just as we do with every other type of invention.

It is not just the PTO and the courts that are avoiding difficult inquiries by wielding the statutory subject matter sword. Scholarship from the legal and business fields has

3 *See, e.g.*, Peter J. Howe, 'Business Methods' Patents Raise the Stakes, Boston Globe (July 5, 2005) C1; Jonathan Krim, *Patenting Air or Protecting Property? Information Age Invents a New Problem*, Wash. Post (Dec. 11, 2003) E01.

4 Consider that there has even been coverage of business method patents in the *New York Times Magazine*. *See, e.g.*, James Gleick, *Patently Absurd*, N.Y. Times Mag. at 47 (Mar. 12, 2000) (describing the patent system as "in crisis" because of business method patents and further claiming that "[a] series of unplanned mutations have transformed patents into a positive threat to the digital economy.").

The *New York Times Magazine* is a supplement to the paper that typically includes longer feature stories, along with fashion and style photography. *See* Wikipedia. At the end of May 2009, its cover story was about Conan O'Brien taking over the *Tonight Show* seat. This is clearly not the business section of the paper.

5 The Amazon patent is U.S. Patent No. 5,960,411, *Method and system for placing a purchase order via a communications network*. For some of the back story about this patent's history, *see, e.g.*, Evan Ratliff, *Patent Upending*, Wired (June 2000) (*available at* http://www.wired.com/wired/archive/8.06/patents.html) (last visited Mar. 20, 2011).

6 *See, e.g.*, Raj Bawa, *Nanotechnology Patent Proliferation and the Crisis at the U.S. Patent Office*, 17 Albany L.J. Sci. & Tech. 699 (2007) (describing problems relating to the growing field of nanotechnology); Natasha N. Aljalian, *The Role of Patent Scope in Biopharmaceutical Patents*, 11 B.U. J. Sci. & Tech. L. 1, 61 (same for biopharmaceutical inventions). *See also* Katherine J. Strandburg et al., *Law and the Science of Networks: An Overview and an Application to the "Patent Explosion."* 21 Berkeley Tech. L.J. 1293, 1321–22 (2007) (noting that the "issuance of a burgeoning number of patents" has led to a perception that the entire patent system is "off balance").

7 *See* Pollack, *supra* note 2; Dreyfuss, *supra* note 2.

8 Kristen Osenga, *Ants, Elephant Guns, and Statutory Subject Matter*, 39 Arizona St. L.J. 1087 (2007).

called for an end to business method and software patents, basing their arguments on misplaced proxy-type reasoning.[9] In this chapter, I argue that, if we can dig into the literature and expose these proxy arguments about business method and software patenting, a solid case can be made that business method and software patents, done right, can be good for business.

In Part I, I briefly discuss the rise and recent fall of business method patents. Part II covers the scholarly literature discussing business method and software patents. In Part III, I explain the proxy argument that I have made elsewhere and show how it plays in the recent decisions surrounding the patent eligibility of business method and software inventions. I then explain why the analysis of business method and software patents in the literature uses the same proxy-type arguments to avoid more difficult questions of patentability and policy. Finally, I conclude by explaining how business method and software patents, if administered properly, are actually good for business.

I. THE RISE AND FALL OF BUSINESS METHOD PATENTING

Nothing is illegal if a hundred businessmen decide to do it. – Andrew Young

The rise of patent eligibility for business method and software inventions is a tale that been told many times over.[10] Although it is possible to find issued patents describing methods of doing business dating back to the late 1700s,[11] the story gets more interesting some two hundred years later. After a string of Supreme Court cases in the 1970s and 1980s that led to the eligibility of software for patenting,[12] the

9 Some of the scholarship covers exclusively business methods, whereas other works cover software. This chapter treats both simultaneously, because there is significant overlap between these two types of invention and they share similar characteristics. *See, e.g.*, remarks of Bob Hunt, *The Limits of Abstract Patents in an Intangible Economy*, Brookings Institution conference, transcript available at http://www.brookings.edu/~/media/Files/events/2009/0114_patents/0114_patents_transcript.pdf, Jan. 14, 2009, at p. 17 (Brookings Transcript) (last visited Mar. 20, 2011) (noting a study that found four out of five business method patents are also software patents); Bronwyn Hall, *Business Method Patents, Innovation, & Policy*, NBER Working Paper at 2 (2003), *available at* http://papers.ssrn.com/sol3/papers.cfm?abstract_id=463160 (last visited Mar 20, 2011). There are some scholars, however, who separate the two types of invention, encouraging patent protection of software but not business methods. *See, e.g.*, Dreyfuss, *supra* note 2, at 280 ("we are keeping the bath water (business method patents) when all we really need or want is the baby (patents on software)").

10 For just a few exemplary explications of the history of business method and software patents, see Thomas F. Cotter, A *Burkean Perspective on Patent Eligibility*, 22 BERKELEY TECH L.J. 855, 862–69 (2007); Osenga, *supra* note 8, at 1092–1103; John R. Thomas, *The Patenting of the Liberal Professions*, 40 B.C. L. REV. 1139, 1148–62 (1999).

11 *See* patent to Jacob Perkins, "Detecting Counterfeit Notes," granted 3/19/1799 (more detail destroyed by PTO fire of 1836); Patent to John Kneass, "A Mode of Preventing Counterfeiting," granted 4/28/1815. Business methods were first called into question for eligibility for patenting in 1908, *Hotel Security Checking Co. v. Lorraine Co.*, 160 F. 467 (2nd Cir. 1908).

12 *See* Gottschalk v. Benson, 409 U.S. 63 (1972); Parker v. Flook, 437 U.S. 584 (1978); Diamond v. Diehr, 450 U.S. 175 (1981).

Federal Circuit held in the late 1990s that there was no such thing as a business method exception to patentable subject matter, opening the patent eligibility door for these inventions as well.[13] In short order, this holding led to a flood of filings of patent applications directed toward business method inventions.[14] Applications covering these inventions increased from some 1300 filed in 1998 to nearly 8000 filed in 2001.[15]

As the number of patent applications covering business method inventions quickly skyrocketed, the objections to these patents also grew. Courts, industry, and mainstream media all lodged complaints against the patent eligibility of business methods and software inventions.[16] Interestingly, many of these complaints might be unfounded – they were based either on supposition, disdain, or, at best, a handful of anecdotes about unrepresentative business method patents, such as Amazon's one-click process.[17] The hostility of the various parties grew palpable as systemic criticisms abounded about the PTO's failure to adequately examine patent applications in general, and particularly applications for these types of invention.[18]

Perhaps in response to this loudening chorus calling for the end of patent protection for business method and software inventions, the PTO and the courts began to close the door. In 2007, the Federal Circuit issued two important opinions, *In re Nuijten*[19] and *In re Comiskey*,[20] that began to rein in the previously broad expanse of patent-eligible subject matter. In the *Nuitjen* case, the Federal Circuit concluded that, regardless of utility, claims directed to electrical signals did not fall within the four categories of patent-eligible subject matter: processes, machines, articles of manufacture, and compositions of matter.[21] In the *Comiskey* case, the court held that, even though a set of steps has practical application, it can still be an abstract idea or algorithm that is ineligible for patenting, particularly if it is only a set of mental steps.[22] These cases, and similar appeals working their way through the PTO, laid the foundation for the death knell that was to come – the Federal Circuit's *In re Bilski* case.

13 *See State Street Bank & Trust Co. v. Signature Financial Group, Inc.*, 149 F.3d 1368 (Fed. Cir. 1998); *AT&T Corp. v. Excel Comm'ns, Inc.*, 172 F.3d 1352 (Fed. Cir. 1999).

14 Starling David Hunter III, *Have Business Method Patents Gotten a Bum Rap? Some Empirical Evidence*, 6 J. Info Tech. Theory & Application 1, 1 (2004).

15 *See id.*

16 *See* notes 1–3, *supra;* Hunter, *supra* note 14, at 1–2.

17 *See* Hunter, *supra* note 14, at 2–3.

18 *See* Osenga, *supra* note 8, at 1114–15; Hunter, *supra* note 14, at 3 (highlighting "disdain" for business method patents, "distrust of motives" and the examination process at the PTO, and "dismay" at the consequences that may flow from these patents).

19 500 F.3d 1346 (Fed. Cir. 2007).

20 499 F.3d 1365 (Fed. Cir. 2007).

21 *Nuitjen*, 500 F.3d at 1354.

22 *Comiskey*, 499 F.3d at 1376–77.

In 1997, Bilski filed a patent application on a method of hedging risk to be practiced by a commodity provider.[23] When the commodity provider enters into a contract to sell to a consumer at one fixed rate, the provider makes a second hedging transaction at a second rate with a second consumer, thereby reducing the risk associated with market fluctuations.[24] The PTO rejected the claims under § 101 because the invention was "not implemented on a specific apparatus and merely manipulates [an] abstract idea and solves a purely mathematical problem without any limitation to a practical application."[25] Bilski appealed the examiner's rejection to the Board of Patent Appeals and Interferences (BPAI), which affirmed the rejection of the claims as nonstatutory subject matter.[26]

Bilski then appealed to the Federal Circuit, and oral argument was held before a three-judge panel in October 2007, shortly after the September 2007 decisions in *Comiskey* and *Nuitjen*. Before an opinion was issued, the Federal Circuit *sua sponte* ordered an en banc rehearing to consider the question of patent-eligible subject matter under § 101.[27] Oral argument was heard on May 8, 2008, and the opinion was issued on October 30, 2008. The court's opinion was expressly limited to determining what constitutes a patent-eligible "process" under 35 U.S.C. § 101.[28] After reviewing its own statutory subject matter jurisprudence, as well as precedent from the Supreme Court, the Federal Circuit implemented the "machine-or-transformation" (MoT) test for determining whether a method is a patent-eligible process.[29] On June 1, 2009, the Supreme Court granted Bilski's petition for writ of certiorari to review the Federal Circuit's decision.[30*] Based on comments made by sitting Supreme Court

23 *Ex parte Bilski*, No. 2002–2257, 2006 WL 5738364 (BPAI Sept. 26, 2006), *aff'd on other grounds, In re Bilski*, 545 F.3d 943 (Fed. Cir. 2008).

24 Claim 1 is an exemplary claim and recites:

> A method for managing the consumption risk costs of a commodity sold by a commodity provider at a fixed price comprising the steps of:
>
> (a) Initiating a series of transactions between said commodity provider and consumers of said commodity wherein said consumers purchase said commodity at a fixed rate based upon historical averages, said fixed rate corresponding to a risk position of said consumer;
> (b) Identifying market participants for said commodity having a counter-risk position to said consumers; and
> (c) Initiating a series of transactions between said commodity provider and said market participants at a second fixed rate such that said series of market participant transactions balances the risk position of said series of consumer transactions.

25 *Ex parte* Bilski, No. 2002–2257, slip op. at 3.

26 *See id.*

27 *In re Bilski*, 264 Fed. Appx. 896 (Fed. Cir. 2008).

28 *In re Bilski*, 545 F.3d at 951.

29 *Id.* at 954. In doing so, the court overturned its earlier "useful, concrete, and tangible result" test for statutory subject matter. *Id.* at 956.

30 *See Bilski v. Doll*, No. 08–964, 556 U.S. 1268 (June 1, 2009) (order granting petition for writ of certiorari).

* Editors' Note: This article was written prior to the Supreme Court's decision in *Bilski* v. *Kappos*, which affirmed the Federal Circuit's decision in *In re Bilski* but modified its rationale. 561 U.S. 593, 130

Justices in other cases,[31] it is not clear that the patent eligibility for business method and software inventions is going to be as expansive as it was before.

Although the reaction to *Bilski* from intellectual property practitioners is mixed (but largely negative),[32] the reaction from business and industry has been fairly positive.[33] The happiness of members of the business and entrepreneurial community with *Bilski* likely flows from their concerns about business method and software patents. These concerns are discussed in the next section.

II. THE BUSINESS OF BUSINESS METHOD PATENTING

Stop going for the easy buck and start producing something with your life. Create, instead of living off the buying and selling of others. – Martin Sheen (as character Carl Fox) in Wall Street

As noted earlier, it is not just the PTO and the courts that are calling for the cessation or, at least, the restriction of patent eligibility for business method and software patents. Scholars writing about the business of business method and software patents have also called for changes in patent protection of these inventions, some going so far as to state that these patents "play a central role in the failure of the patent system as a whole."[34] There are, of course, some who claim the evidence does not bear this out and that there have been patents on these inventions for years without causing a catastrophe in the patent system.[35] Yet, the criticisms persist and must be addressed. The bulk of the complaints coming from the literature can be summed up in three main, and quite interrelated, categories: abstractness and breadth, low quality, and negative effects on innovation and competition.[36]

S. Ct. 3218 (2010). Contrary to the Federal Circuit, the Court held that the MoT test was not the sole test for determining the patent eligibility of a process. Rather, that test was only "a useful and important clue . . . for determining whether some claimed inventions are processes under § 101." *Bilski*, 130 S. Ct. at 3227.

31 *See* note 1, *supra*. One of the Justices who questioned business method patents, Justice Souter, retired from the bench in 2009. It is unknown whether his replacement will share a similar viewpoint. [Editors' Note: His replacement, Justice Sotomayor, joined Justice Stevens's concurrence in *In re Bilski*, which would have held that all business methods are patent-ineligible for failing to describe a process under § 101. *Bilski*, 130 S. Ct. at 3232.]

32 *See, e.g.*, Gary Odom, *Milking Bilski*, The Patent Prospector Blog, *available* at http://www.patenthawk.com/blog/2008/11/milking_bilski.html (Nov. 1, 2008) (last visited Mar. 21, 2011) (providing a summary of commentary on the then just-issued *Bilski* opinion, as well as allowing an open comment thread that demonstrates both positive and negative viewpoints).

33 *See, e.g.*, remarks of David Kappos, Brookings Transcript at 80–1 ("I view the Bilski decision as being a good piece of work on the part of the Federal Circuit and an important step in the right direction . . . ")

34 James Bessen & Michael J. Meurer, Patent Failure 214 (2008).

35 *See* Hunter, *supra* note 14, at 1–2.

36 *Cf. id.* at 14, at 4 (dividing the complaints about business method patents into three categories – process issues (examination problems), patents qua patents (quality), and proliferation (stifling

A. *Abstract Technology and Broad Claims*

One of the primary complaints about business method and software patents is that they cover abstract technologies and claim broad territory. Their abstractness and breadth then allow the patentee to adversely affect innovation by encompassing entire industries and competition through opportunistic litigation.[37]

There is a distinction between abstractness and breadth, although patent claims can certainly be both abstract and broad. The abstract nature of business method and software patents is attributed to the fact that they often claim results, rather than the method to achieve the results.[38] Breadth, in contrast, refers simply to an expansive scope of protection. Both abstractness and breadth arise where patent claims are not limited to a distinct embodiment, where vague language is used (either inadvertently or strategically), or wherever the boundaries of the invented technology are unclear.[39] Abstractness and breadth work together to permit patent claims that cover technologies that may not even be known to the inventor.[40]

There are a few reasons why abstractness and breadth are troublesome. First, inventors are being rewarded for something they did not invent and may not even know about.[41] This goes against the reward theory for patents, which justifies the patent monopoly as being necessary to encourage inventors to invent and innovate.[42] Second, the abstract nature makes it difficult for competitors to determine the boundaries of the patentee's exclusive rights.[43] The notice provided by the patent is low, the costs of determining boundaries are high, and the costs are not linear.[44] Finally, and this overlaps with another set of criticisms discussed later, the breadth and abstractness of these patent claims dominate potential downstream uses.[45]

innovation and competition). *See also* Rob Tiller (vice president and assistant general counsel for IP of Red Hat), *Brookings Conference on Software and Business Method Patents Highlights Need for Reform*, *available at* http://press.redhat.com/2009/01/19/brookings-conference-on-software-and-business-methods-highlights-need-for-reform (last visited 5/19/09) (claiming the dysfunctionality of the patent system for business methods is a result of unmanageable litigation risks, unpredictable and fuzzy boundaries, and difficulty in identifying prior art).

37 *See, e.g.*, Bessen & Meurer, *supra* note 34, at 199–200; Robert P. Merges, *As Many as Six Impossible Patents Before Breakfast*, 14 Berkeley Tech. L. J. 577, 590 (1999).

38 *See* remarks of David Kappos, Brookings Transcript, *supra* note 33, at 79. *See also id.* at 85 ("[T]he patenting of abstractions, especially business methods, has drive a real ends justifies the means kind of philosophy in the patent system, whereby we're approaching patents in a way that's covering the results, right, not how the results are achieved, and that I think is very, very dangerous.").

39 *See* Bessen & Meurer, *supra* note 34, at 200.

40 *See id.* at 199.

41 *See id.* at 200.

42 *See, e.g.*, Julie E. Cohen & Mark A. Lemley, *Patent Scope and Innovation in the Software Industry*, 89 Calif. L. Rev. 1, 5 n. 5 (2001).

43 *See* Bessen & Meurer, *supra* note 34 at 200.

44 *See* remarks of Peter Menell, Brookings Transcript, *supra* note 9, at 14–15.

45 *See* remarks of Rochelle Dreyfuss, Brookings Transcript at 89–90; *see also* remarks of Josh Sarnoff, Brookings Transcript at 117.

B. *Quality Issues*

Another common complaint about business method and software patents is that an inordinate number are "bad" or of low quality. Although there are a few different definitions of what constitutes a "bad" patent, it is safe to say that any patent that protects an invention that was well known before the application is filed is not good.[46] These patents impose numerous and substantial costs on the system,[47] including rewarding the patentee for something she did not invent, taking the invention out of the public domain, and causing notice problems because competitors believe the invention to be freely available.

Although the problem of patent quality is not limited to business method and software patents, the crisis seems to be exacerbated in this area for several reasons. The most common and pervasive argument is that the prior-art field for these business method and software inventions is not fully developed because they have only been eligible for patenting for the last decade; before that, these types of inventions were kept secret. Even when these inventions were disclosed, it was not in traditional publications that are easily searchable by the PTO.[48] As one scholar has noted, "knowledge about business methods resides mainly in the practices and policies of the firms that use them, [and] even common methods may not be documented in the sorts of materials that examiners can efficiently consult."[49] Another contention is that these patents are difficult to examine properly because of abstract technology and breadth, described earlier. Because the patent (or application) covers a wide swath of territory, including possibly unknown territory, it is nearly impossible for the PTO to ensure that the process is novel and nonobvious. Another contention is that it is particularly difficult to apply the standards of patentability to business method and software inventions because these requirements are not absolute – novelty is not a black-or-white standard.[50]

Patent quality has been the subject of empirical study. For example, Starling Hunter reviewed a sample of business method patents for the amount of prior-art citation. He argues that because these patents cite as much, if not more, prior

[46] *See* Dreyfuss, *supra* note 2, at 268. *See also* Bronwyn Hall, *supra* note 9, at 13 (noting that high-quality patents are those that protect "an invention that is truly 'new,' rather than an invention that is already in widespread use but not yet patented").

[47] *See* Jay P. Kesan & Andres A. Gallo, *Why "Bad" Patents Survive in the Market and How Should We Change? – The Private and Social Costs of Patents*, 55 Emory L.J. 61 (2006). One of these costs is also opportunistic litigation, which is discussed in more detail later.

[48] *See* Dreyfuss, *supra* note 2, at 269.

[49] *See id.*

[50] *See id.* at 268 (noting that the level of "newness" required for patentability depends on the field of invention); *see also* Justin Hughes, *The Philosophy of Intellectual Property*, 77 Georgetown L.J. 287, 294 (1988) ("The novelty, however, does not have to be absolute. What is important is that at the time of propertization the idea is thought to be generally unknown. The res cannot be common currency in the intellectual life of society at the time of the propertization.").

art during prosecution than patents in other technology areas, there is no reason to believe that business method patents are of any lesser quality than patents generally.[51] However, others argue that the amount of prior art cited is an incomplete definition of quality and that these patents still prove to be troublesome.[52]

C. *Adverse to Innovation and Competition*

The problems of abstractness, breadth, and low patent quality all give rise to concerns about adverse effects on innovation and competition, which is why the literature comes down on the side that business method and software inventions should not be eligible for patenting.

1. Effects on Innovation

The literature contends that business method and software patents decrease innovation. The standard story is that patents are a necessary evil, trading a monopoly for the incentive to innovate and disclose.[53] Generally, patent systems are important if there are high front-end costs or expenses to develop a new technology and low back-end costs, making it easy and inexpensive to duplicate the technology.[54] Patent systems create problems where the technology is cumulative or sequential, because it is difficult to get rights to build on the preceding technology.[55]

In the case of business method and software patents, the argument is made that the benefits are simply insufficient and the costs are too high. As Adam Jaffe has stated in testimony before Congress, "the patent system – intended to foster and protect innovation – is generating waste and uncertainty that hinder and threaten the innovative process," particularly in fields such as business methods and software where products are complex and progress is incremental and cumulative.[56] There are three main arguments presented for why patents on business method and software inventions adversely affect innovation: These patents are unnecessary, they tie up downstream innovation, and they affect research and development (R&D) spending.

First, some argue that patents are not necessary to encourage innovation on business method and software inventions. Generally, patent protection is thought to encourage disclosure and prevent free-riding, thereby incentivizing further innovation in an area.[57] However, "[n]owhere in the substantial literature on innovation is

[51] *See* Hunter, *supra* note 14. *See also* John R. Allison & Emerson H. Tiller, *The Business Method Patent Myth*, 18 Berkeley Tech. L.J. 987 (2003).

[52] *See* Bessen & Meurer, *supra* note 34.

[53] *See* Hall, *supra* note 9, at 24.

[54] *See id.* at 16.

[55] *See id.*

[56] *See* Iain M. Cockburn & Megan MacGarvie, *Patents, Thickets, and the Financing of Early Stage Firms: Evidence from the Software Industry*, NBER Working Paper 2007, p. 2 (quoting Jaffe).

[57] *See* Dreyfuss, *supra* note 2, at 274–75.

there a statement that the United States economy suffers from a lack of innovation in methods of doing business [even before patents were available for these inventions]. Compared with the business practices of comparable economies we seem to be innovators. . . ."[58] Thus, there is no justification on the upside for business method and software patents.

Second, the argument is that business method and software patents have at least one significant downside. Because of their abstractness and breadth, these patents "may effectively appropriate all possible solutions to a particular problem. This direct restraint upon the ability of competitors to develop alternatives to the patented invention thwarts a principal aspiration of the patent system – fostering new alternatives."[59] This argument extends beyond all possible solutions to a problem, because downstream products are also affected by patent protection.[60] This argument is common, even in fields outside of business method and software;[61] however, combined with the lack of justification on the front end, the literature argues this cost is too high.

Finally, some literature argues that the increase in patent protection for business method and software inventions results in a decrease in R&D spending, which signals a decrease in innovation.[62] Other literature counters this argument by stating that R&D spending is not a good proxy for innovation, in part because this spending is affected by many other factors.[63]

2. Effects on Competition

Patents on business methods and software are also said to have negative effects on competition. One argument is that these patents may have adverse effects on the market entry and exit of competitors in these fields. Another argument is that these patents are frequently wielded in opportunistic lawsuits that drive competitors out of business or protect business from normal competition.

With respect to entry and exit, "[e]conomic analysis says first that competition may suffer when we grant a monopoly right to the inventor of a business method but it will

58 *See* Leo J. Raskind, *The State Street Bank Decision: The Bad Business of Unlimited Patent Protection for Methods of Doing Business*, 10 Fordham Intell. Prop., Media & Ent. L.J. 61, 92 (1999).

59 *See* David J. Kappos, John R. Thomas & Randall J. Bluestone, *A Technological Contribution Requirement for Patentable Subject Matter: Supreme Court Precedent and Policy*, 6 Nw. J. Tech. & Intell. Prop. 152, 169 (2008).

60 *See* Dreyfuss, *supra* note 2, at 265 (noting that advancements in technology are not enough – a "killer application" of the technology is required to inspire people to adopt the new developments).

61 *See, e.g.*, Michael A. Heller & Rebecca S. Eisenberg, *Can Patents Deter Innovation? The Anticommons in Biomedical Research*, 260 Science 698 (1998) (claiming that the proliferation of intellectual property rights in the biomedical sciences decreases innovation and research in the field).

62 *See* James Bessen & Eric Maskin, *Sequential Innovation, Patents, and Imitation*, 40 RAND J. Econ. 611 (2009); James Bessen & Robert M. Hunt, *An Empirical Look at Software Patents*, 16 J. Econ. & Mgmt. Strategy 157 (2007).

63 *See* Iain M. Cockburn & Megan J. MacGarvie, *Entry, Exit and Patenting in the Software Industry*, NBER Working Paper 2006, p. 2. Some of these factors are competitive interaction, knowledge spillovers, nature of technology opportunities, and appropriability conditions.

benefit if this right facilitates entry into the industry by new and innovative firms."[64] Patents can facilitate entry by signaling quality of the entrants or giving entrants access to profits from licensing, but it can also impede entry because patents and patent thickets may create a significant barrier to entrants.[65] In fact, in the software field, firms are less likely to enter product markets where there are more patents.[66] This may cause a decrease in competition, although patents may strengthen the position of players already in a market.[67] Beyond entry and exit, business method and software patents adversely affect competition because, as Rochelle Dreyfuss notes, "Winning and losing is supposed to depend on execution, not on exclusive rights to the moves that need to be executed."[68]

Business method and software patents also affect competition through the potential for opportunistic litigation. Litigation is problematic in any technology area, because there are reasons beyond patent validity and infringement for a defendant to settle a lawsuit. First, because patent claim construction is difficult and technology may be complex,[69] the defendant may not be confident that the court will reach a correct decision.[70] Second, until discovery is taken, it may be nearly impossible to distinguish between a strong lawsuit and a weak one.[71] Finally, even a weak lawsuit will cost money to defend, and it might be cheaper to simply settle.[72]

These problems are alleged to be exacerbated in the case of business method and software patents because of abstractness and breadth, described earlier. Some argue that, even though many in the software industry are against patenting, a major share of patent lawsuits involve software patents; these scholars claim that abstractness and breadth lead to patents being acquired by nonsoftware and business method firms, which are happy to engage in litigation and patent enforcement efforts and which create patent thickets outside the software industry.[73] Abstractness and breadth also lead to notice problems, as described earlier, which allow for opportunistic litigation.[74]

64 *See* Hall, *supra* note 14, at 3.

65 *See* Cockburn & MacGarvie, *supra* note 63 at 3, 13–15.

66 *See id.* at 33.

67 *See id.* at 33–34.

68 *See* Dreyfuss, *supra* note 2, at 276.

69 Business methods, however, are generally considered to be relatively simplistic, not complex.

70 James Bessen & Michael J. Meurer, *Lessons for Patent Policy from Empirical Research on Patent Litigation*, 9 Lewis & Clark L. Rev. 1, 16 (2005).

71 *See id.*

72 *See id. See also* Kesan & Gallo, *supra* note 47, at 69 n. 36 ("Although [bad patents] are prone to attacks on their validity, bad patents may nevertheless deter meritorious challenges: '[S]mall companies may not be willing to invest resources in such a challenge, especially with the presumption of validity that attends PTO decisions. Rather, it may make sense for these companies to accept a license fee from the patentee, thereby leaving the inappropriate patent unchallenged.'")

73 *See* Bessen & Meurer, *supra* note 34 at 214.

74 *See id.* at 213 ("In sum, patents on software are *not* just like other patents. . . . We attribute these problems [prone to litigation and boundary disputes] to the abstract nature of software technology; too many software patents claim all technologies with similar form or all means of achieving a result, when the actual invention is much more limited and often trivial.")

III. THE PROXY OF THE BUSINESS METHOD PATENTING INQUIRY

When two men in business always agree, one of them is unnecessary. – William Wrigley, Jr.

As I argue in *Ants, Elephant Guns, and Statutory Subject Matter*, the PTO and the courts are using subject matter rejections as proxies for other, more difficult questions of patentability and policy.[75] Subject matter rejections are particularly attractive because they are not based on prior art and are a "threshold inquiry," allowing the application to be disposed of at an early stage.[76] And yet, inquiries into novelty and nonobviousness have been hopelessly entwined into the § 101 analysis, leading to a confusion of both.[77] In that earlier piece, I analyzed how each of the then-current and former tests for patent eligibility extended beyond the appropriate scope of the § 101 statutory subject matter inquiry. Many of the same arguments can be applied to the current standard set forth in *Bilski*, as well as to the reasons set forth in the scholarly literature for eliminating patent eligibility for business method and software patents.

As noted earlier, the current standard for patent eligibility of a process is the MoT test. The Supreme Court has granted Bilski's petition for writ of certiorari, and the case will be part of the Court's 2009 Term. However, as noted earlier, it is unclear that the Court will expand the Federal Circuit's standard for patent eligibility, and it may even constrict it. In any case, the test imposed by *Bilski* suffers from the same defect as the tests that were previously in use – the questions being asked are not directed toward determining statutory subject matter, but are rather proxies for more difficult questions of patentability and policy.

The machine prong of *Bilski* asks whether the process "is tied to a particular machine or apparatus."[78] The machine used to satisfy this prong must impose meaningful limits and may not be merely "insignificant extra-solution activity."[79] Most currently pending business method applications and issued patents do not include a recitation of a machine. Many software patents and applications recite simply a "general purpose computer," which may become a problem given the Federal Circuit's comment that "[w]e leave to future cases the elaboration of the precise contours of machine implementation, as well as the answers to particular questions, such as whether or when recitation of a computer suffices to tie a process

75 *See* Osenga, *supra* note 8, at 1115–17.

76 *See id.* at 1116 ("This type of rejection is not based on prior art, and because patentable subject matter is a threshold issue, it allows the application to be disposed of at an early stage."); *In re* Comiskey, 499 F.3d 1365, 1373 n. 7 (Fed. Cir. 2007) ("The § 101 issue is an antecedent question to the [other requirements for patentability].").

77 *Id.*

78 *Bilski*, 545 F.3d at 954.

79 *Id.* at 961–2.

claim to a particular machine."[80] The "machine" inquiry, however, is really a proxy for the actual question at issue: How does the method work? This question is more properly posed under § 112: Did the applicant fully describe and enable her invention? If the applicant does not explain how a process is to be implemented, either by machine or otherwise, she fails to satisfy the written description and/or enablement requirements, and the patent should not be granted or should be invalidated for that reason, not for lack of statutory subject matter.

The transformation prong of *Bilski* asks whether the process "transforms a particular article into a different state or thing."[81] The transformation "must be central to the purpose of the claimed process,"[82] and the articles undergoing transformation must be physical objects or representative of physical objects.[83] But again, the "transformation" question is a proxy for the real question: Is it useful? That is a question better asked under § 101 utility. Although § 101 utility and § 101 patent eligibility both reside in the same statutory section, the inquiries are distinct; that is, something can be "useful but not subject matter (gravity), . . . subject matter but not useful (purified chemical compositions from plants and animals with no known uses), or [neither useful nor subject matter] (e-c2 and naturally occurring chemical compositions with no known uses.)"[84] Further, these two issues are subject to review by the Federal Circuit under different standards.[85]

Just as the PTO and courts are using the statutory subject matter inquiry as a proxy to avoid more difficult questions of patentability and policy, the arguments raised in the scholarly literature in support of eliminating business method and software patents are largely not about statutory subject matter at all. Claiming that business method and software inventions should not be eligible for patenting misplaces the focus or aims at the wrong target.

The arguments about abstractness and breadth are very similar to the concerns that the PTO and the courts have been addressing using, most recently, the MoT test. If the patent claims are sufficiently enabled and describe the invention in the inventor's possession, both of which are required by § 112, then the concerns about overbreadth and abstractness will be minimized. Specifically, the concerns that the patent will cover things that the inventor never contemplated or that the patent will cover all possible solutions relate less to situations where the inventor is held to the

80 *Id.* at 962.
81 *Id.* at 954.
82 *Id.* at 962.
83 *Id.* at 963.
84 Robert A. Kreiss, *Patent Protection for Computer Programs and Mathematical Algorithms: The Constitutional Limitations on Patentable Subject Matter*, 29 N.M. L. Rev. 31, 75 (1999).
85 *See* Kevin Casey et al., *Standards of Appellate Review in the Federal Circuit: Substance and Semantics*, 11 Fed Cir. B.J. 279, 361 (2002) (noting that subject matter is a question of law reviewed de novo, but utility is a question of fact reviewed for clear error).

obligation to fully describe his invention (and the courts are then faithful in only giving him exclusive rights to the extent his patent describes).

The arguments about patent quality are inextricably linked to other requirements of patentability, which is precisely why lumping this problem into a discussion of patent eligibility is so wrong. Whether or not the PTO can adequately examine these types of inventions should have nothing to do with the existence of patent protection on business methods and software. Of course, there is a problem with patent quality, a problem that extends beyond business methods and software. In fact, many people claim that the invention claimed in the *Bilski* application is painfully obvious. But the answer to this problem is not to deny patent protection to a whole area of innovation; rather the solution must be to improve examination standards and deny patents for particular applications that are not novel, obvious, or fail to be adequately described or enabled.

Similarly, the complaints that business method and software patents negatively affect innovation and competition contain some proxy-type arguments. For example, the concern that these patents will affect downstream innovation is related to the abstractness and breadth issues, which boil down to a difficult inquiry under § 112. The concern about opportunistic litigation is made much more palpable when the patent in question is weak, which is related to abstractness, breadth, and patent quality. All of these issues are better addressed under the other patentability requirements, namely §§ 102, 103, and 112.

IV. THE POSITIVES OF BUSINESS METHOD PATENTING

Innovation is the specific instrument of entrepreneurship . . . the act that endows resources with a new capacity to create wealth." – Peter Drucker

So what is good about business method and software patents? If we deal with the troublesome issues described in the literature, maybe there is no real problem. In fact, what may be causing the problems going forward are actually the solutions that have erroneously been put into place. Consider a scenario where the fields of business method and software patents are allowed to mature. The body of prior art becomes rich, and the examining corps gains expertise. Patents are only granted for inventions that are fully enabled and described and that are novel and nonobvious, just like in every other field. Then patents on business method and software inventions become less suspect and higher quality, and all is right with the world.[86]

Instead, the patent eligibility tests set up by the PTO and the courts, beginning in 2006 and culminating with the *Bilski* opinion, will have the opposite effect.

[86] This is not merely a pipe dream. *See* Martin Campbell-Kelly (cited in Bessen & Meurer, *supra* note 34, at 188) ("History shows us that software patents are not so different from other patents in the information technology industries, and that the patent system is capable of adjusting to the particularities of individual industries.").

Because these inventions are no longer eligible for patenting, prior art will again become scarce, and the only expertise the examiners will get is in making quick rejections for lack of statutory subject matter. Instead of moving forward toward a system of higher quality business method and software patents, we are taking two steps backward.

But let us go back to the first scenario. Business method and software patents have improved in quality. The issues of abstractness, breadth, and quality are no longer serious concerns, at least no more so than in any technology area. Are patents on these inventions still bad for business? I think the answer is no.

Looking at the remaining complaints about business method and software patents, the primary concerns seem to be that these patents are not needed for innovation and that they affect R&D spending and market entry and exit. The main thrust of the argument that patents are not needed for innovation in this sector hinges around the idea that there was no shortage of innovation in this area even without protection. The reality, though, is that many business method and software inventions (not to mention many other types) are created out of need – the so-called user innovation.[87] The idea of user innovation is borne out by looking at who obtains patents on business method and software inventions. Only one in ten patents is obtained by a financial services firm or payment system company, the typical business method businesses.[88] More than one third of business method patents are granted to information and communication technology firms.[89] Other business method and software patents are scattered throughout various industries, many stemming from a problem that necessitated a solution that ended up being innovative. The idea that people invent to solve a problem they have is not unique to business methods and software, and yet we do not question the grant of patents in those other areas.[90] The argument that patents are not needed to encourage innovation in the business method and software fields, in the absence of other issues such as quality, abstractness, and breadth, seems to have less import about whether or not there should be business method and software patents.

Finally, the only remaining complaints about the negative effects of business method and software inventions are their potential to decrease R&D spending and adversely affect market exit and entry. And yet, the empirical literature, as discussed earlier, does not bear out these concerns. It may skew how we look at these events, but there is no clear indicator that patents cause a lack of competition and innovation, and in fact, they may even promote these things.

[87] *See, e.g.*, Katherine J. Strandburg, *Users as Innovators: Implications for Patent Doctrine*, 79 U. Colo. L. Rev. 467 (2008).

[88] *See* remarks of Bob Hunt, Brookings Transcript, *supra* note 9, at 16. This number has been rising, however. *See id.*

[89] *See id.*

[90] *See id.* at 468.

So if business method and software patents can be properly examined by the PTO for requirements of patentability – including § 102 novelty, § 103 nonobviousness, and § 112 written description and enablement – and if the negative effects on competition and innovation can be addressed through this more thorough examination, then business method and software patents are really not all that bad.

In fact, an argument can be made that these patents, if done right, are good for business. Although business methods and software can be produced with minimal front-end cost, more so for business methods than software, both types of invention are amenable to free-riding, because they are easily and inexpensively duplicable. Further, business method and software patents encourage disclosure of inventions that heretofore had been kept as trade secrets, a tradeoff for the grant of the monopoly.

CONCLUSION

The current state of patent eligibility for business method and software inventions is in disarray, but much of the discussion is focused in the wrong place. The tests implemented by the PTO and the courts, as well as examined in the literature, are aimed at the wrong target. The real problem is not substantive, determining whether these types of invention should be eligible for patent protection. Instead the quandary is much more procedural: Can the PTO adequately examine patent applications covering business method and software inventions? Procedural difficulties should not drive the law, particularly where the law being implemented shuts out the reality of business and industry today.

Rather than continuing the dialog about whether business methods and software are statutory subject matter, we should take aim at the PTO's examining techniques and ensure that patent applications are being held to the appropriate level of scrutiny for written description, enablement, novelty, and nonobviousness. Because the bulk of the concerns about these patents arise from other patentability questions, this change would go a long way toward determining if business method and software patents are truly different from those in any other burgeoning field. Until this is fixed, there is no way we are going to hit the right target.

3

Semiotics 101

Taking the Printed Matter Doctrine Seriously

*Kevin Emerson Collins**

INTRODUCTION

The contemporary printed matter doctrine restricts the products of human ingenuity that can be patented under § 101 of the Patent Act.[1] Roughly stated, it dictates that "information recorded in [a] substrate or medium" is not eligible for patent protection – regardless of how nonobvious and useful it is – if the advance over the prior art resides in the "content of the information."[2] For example, the printed matter doctrine prevents an inventor from claiming a diagram or text explaining how to perform a technological procedure, even though a technical diagram is an artifact of human ingenuity that satisfies the major statutory requirements for patent protection. Among its attributes, it can be both useful – it helps a technologist perform the procedure more quickly, reliably, and precisely – and nonobvious – a person having ordinary skill in the art may not have been motivated to make the diagram before the inventor's discovery. However, the printed matter doctrine prevents a patent claiming this type of diagram from issuing. Similarly, the printed matter doctrine prevents an inventor from claiming an old machine with new labels, regardless of the

* Professor of Law, Washington University in St. Louis School of Law. I thank Michael Abramowicz, Barton Beebe, Dan Burk, Deven Desai, John Duffy, Justin Hughes, Mark Lemley, John Mikhail, Efthimios Parasidis, Peggy Radin, Michael Risch, Joshua Sarnoff, Pam Samuelson, Ted Sichelman, and Kathy Strandburg for comments on drafts of this chapter at various stages. In addition, I thank the attendees of conferences AND workshops at the Washington University School of Law, the George Washington University Law School, the Michigan State University College of Law, the Thomas Jefferson School of Law, and the University of Cincinnati College of Law. Finally, I thank the participants in the Patentable Subject Matter Roundtable at the University of California Berkeley School of Law, at which the nascent ideas that led to this chapter were aired. A version of this chapter was originally published in the *Indiana Law Journal*. *See* Kevin Emerson Collins, *Semiotics 101: Taking the Printed Matter Doctrine Seriously*, 85 IND. L.J. 1379 (2010).

[1] The Federal Circuit grounds the printed matter doctrine alternately in 35 U.S.C. §§ 101 & 103, but there is no principled basis for the statutory distinction. *See infra* Part I.B.

[2] 1. DONALD S. CHISUM, CHISUM ON PATENTS § 1.02[4], at 1–25 to 1–26 (2009).

nonobviousness of what the labels mean and the utility of the relabeled machine to society. The advance over the prior art is understood to reside not in the mechanics of the machine, but rather in the content of the information conveyed by the labels.

The Court of Appeals for the Federal Circuit has repeatedly stated that "'[a] printed matter rejection' . . . stands on questionable legal and logical footing."[3] The infirmities of the printed matter doctrine are notorious and numerous. For example, it is arguably more exception than rule, because many types of information with newly invented content are patentable.[4] It also employs a "point of novelty" or "patentable weight" approach that runs against the most recent pronouncements on the doctrine of patent eligibility by the Supreme Court and the Federal Circuit.[5] The Patent and Trademark Office (PTO) dresses up legal fictions as factual truths to enforce it, especially in the context of software-on-disk claims.[6] Additionally, it has no recognized statutory grounding, because § 101 of the Patent Act simply states, in relevant part, that inventors may patent a "process, machine, manufacture, or composition of matter."[7]

Furthermore, the printed matter doctrine plays a marginal role, at best, in the common explanations of how the patent regime works, likely in large part because nobody can explain how the printed matter doctrine works. It receives only passing mention in most patent law casebooks used to teach the next generation of patent lawyers.[8] The Federal Circuit and the PTO frequently label their printed matter opinions as "unpublished" and "nonprecedential," respectively, so that the opinions cannot be cited as precedent.[9] Perhaps most strikingly, the Federal Circuit simply ignored the printed matter doctrine when it took the bold step of announcing en banc a new "machine-or-transformation test" (MoT) for patentable subject matter in *In re Bilski*.[10] It proclaimed the MoT to be the "sole" test for patent eligibility without considering the continued validity of the printed matter

3 *In re* Lowry, 32 F.3d 1579, 1583 (Fed. Cir. 1994) (quoting *In re* Gulack, 703 F.2d 1381, 1385 n.8 (Fed. Cir. 1983)).

4 *See infra* Parts I.A.1 & 3.

5 *See infra* Part I.A.4.

6 *See infra* notes 89–93 and accompanying text.

7 35 U.S.C. § 101 (2006). *See infra* Part I.B.

8 One popular casebook dismisses the printed matter doctrine with a single note, stating that "like the mental steps doctrine, the printed matter rule also appears to have declined in importance." Robert Patrick Merges & John Fitzgerald Duffy, Patent Law and Policy: Cases and Materials 141 (4th ed. 2007). Another casebook fails to even mention the printed matter doctrine. *See* F. Scott Kieff, Pauline Newman, Herbert F. Schwartz & Henry E. Smith, Principles of Patent Law: Cases and Materials (4th ed. 2008).

9 *See, e.g.*, *In re* Smith, 70 F.3d 1290 (Fed. Cir. 1995) (unpublished table decision); *Ex parte* Shanahan, No. 2004–2334, 2005 WL 191069 (B.P.A.I. Jan. 1, 2005). Parties may cite unpublished opinions issued after January 1, 2007, as precedent. Fed. R. App. P. 32.1. In the Federal Circuit, however, judges may refer to unpublished opinions in new opinions only to note the persuasiveness of the reasoning, not as "binding precedent." Fed. Cir. R. 32.1(d).

10 545 F.3d 943 (Fed. Cir. 2008) (en banc), *cert. granted sub nom.* Bilski v. Doll, 129 S. Ct. 2735 (2009). The Supreme Court has accepted certiorari to review the Federal Circuit's decision in *Bilski*, so the

doctrine.[11] Over the last half-century, courts abandoned many restrictions on patent eligibility that were not understood to have explicit moorings in § 101 and were often difficult to administer.[12] However, the implicit consensus best practice with respect to the printed matter doctrine appears to be not to eliminate the doctrine outright, but simply to tidy up appearances by sweeping it under the rug whenever possible and hiding its conceptual poverty.

Breaking from the implicit consensus, this chapter argues that the PTO, the courts, and commentators should take the printed matter doctrine seriously. Taking a cue from the doctrine's staying power, they should recognize that it does important work in restricting the set of artifacts of human ingenuity that can be patented. They should embrace it as a central feature of a well-tempered patent regime. The difficulty with this approach, of course, is the open recognition of an unruly doctrine that "stands on questionable legal and logical footing."[13] This chapter, therefore, initially confronts and then resolves this difficulty. It reveals the hidden conceptual coherence and statutory grounding of the printed matter doctrine, providing it with a sound legal and logical footing and demonstrating how to take it seriously.

The key move in this reconceptualization is to recognize that the printed matter doctrine is not really about "information" and its "content" at all.[14] Rather, it is based on *semiotic* principles. Semiotic analysis is most commonly associated with expression and culture, and it may therefore seem at first glance to be more relevant to other forms of intellectual property such as trademarks and copyrights.[15] However, this chapter takes the original approach of viewing technological inventions through a semiotic lens and demonstrates that patent scholars and practitioners, too, have

validity of the machine-or-transformation test remains unsettled as of the publication of this chapter. Bilski v. Doll, 129 S. Ct. 2735 (2009).

[11] *Bilski*, 545 F.3d at 955–56 ("[T]he machine-or-tranformation test, properly applied, is the governing test for determining patent eligibility of a process under § 101."). Furthermore, the claim "as a whole" approach to patent eligibility mandated in *Bilski* overtly conflicts with the "point of novelty" or "patentable weight" approach that structures the printed matter doctrine. *See infra* notes 94–98, 108–27 and accompanying text.

Editors' Note: This chapter was written prior to the Supreme Court's decision in *Bilski v. Kappos*, which affirmed the Federal Circuit's decision in *In re Bilski* but modified its rationale. 561 U.S. 593, 130 S. Ct. 3218 (2010). Contrary to the Federal Circuit, the Court held that the machine-or-transformation test was not the sole test for determining the patent eligibility of a process. Rather, that test was only "a useful and important clue . . . for determining whether some claimed inventions are processes under § 101." *Bilski*, 130 S. Ct. at 3227.

[12] *See infra* note 146.

[13] *In re* Lowry, 32 F.3d 1579, 1583 (Fed. Cir. 1994) (quoting *In re* Gulack, 703 F.2d 1381, 1385 n.8 (Fed. Cir. 1983)) (internal quotation marks omitted).

[14] *See supra* note 2 and accompanying text.

[15] The foremost example of scholarship on semiotics and intellectual property is Barton Beebe, *The Semiotic Analysis of Trademark Law*, 51 U.C.L.A. L. Rev. 621 (2004). Other intellectual property scholars address semiotic issues in substance, if not in name, in copyright scholarship. *See, e.g.*, Justin Hughes, *"Recoding" Intellectual Property and Overlooked Audience Interests*, 77 Tex. L. Rev. 923, 952–63 (1999) (discussing whether copyright should grant an author the right to influence and stabilize the meaning of her work to the public).

much to learn from semiotics.[16] Semiotics is the study of the *sign*, and a sign exists whenever something stands for something else to somebody.[17] Texts and diagrams are archetypal examples of signs, but signs are not limited to such conventional writings. The invention of new signs contributes in many ways to the "Progress of [the] useful Arts" that the patent regime is by constitutional design intended to promote.[18] A close examination of the nature of the property interests in newly invented signs that the patent regime sanctions should therefore be an intuitively promising undertaking for anyone interested in understanding the reach of patent protection.

One of the most fundamental insights of semiotic analysis is that semiotic meanings are not intrinsic in worldly things.[19] They are not literally "content" in the sense of being contained within the molecules that comprise a printed diagram. Rather, semiotic meanings result from active processes of interpretation that occur in people's minds.[20] Printed diagrams, wind vanes, and medical symptoms are all meaningful in a semiotic sense because they are components of signs: They are objects or events that mean something other than their intrinsic structure to interpreting minds. The semiotic meanings of scribbles on paper and spots on human skin are not predetermined by their formal or functional properties. They are meaningful to us because our interpreting minds have the capacity to understand that worldly things represent other things (worldly or not) and because we have learned social conventions that fix what they represent. This chapter argues that the printed matter doctrine turns this descriptive observation about the mind-centric nature of semiotic meaning into an instrumental rule for limiting the reach of patent-eligible inventions. Couched in a semiotic framework, the printed matter doctrine can be reconceptualized as the *sign doctrine*. It dictates that an invention is ineligible for patent protection if the invention is a newly invented sign and the advance over the prior art resides only in the mind of an interpreter.[21] Standing alone, newly invented

[16] Patent scholarship has employed the philosophy of language – a discipline that can be thought of as a specialized branch of semiotics – to shed light on how the language in a patent claim describes things and actions. *See, e.g.*, Kevin Emerson Collins, *The Reach of Literal Claim Scope into After-Arising Technology: On Thing Construction and the Meaning of Meaning*, 41 CONN. L. REV. 493, 536–53 (2008); Craig Allen Nard, *A Theory of Claim Interpretation*, 14 HARV. J.L. & TECH. 1 (2000); Kristen Osenga, *Linguistics and Patent Claim Construction*, 38 RUTGERS L.J. 61 (2006); Margaret Jane Radin, *The Linguistic Turn in Patent Law* (2005) (draft on file with author). To date, however, no patent scholarship has employed semiotics to examine the nature of the newly invented things and actions that can be described by a valid patent claim.

[17] *See infra* note 167.

[18] U.S. CONST. art. I, § 8, cl. 8.

[19] *See infra* text accompanying notes 175–77.

[20] *See infra* text accompanying note 175. The mind-centric definition of semiotics employed in this chapter follows the approach of noted semiotics scholar Umberto Eco, but it is not the only possible definition of the proper semiotic field. *See infra* Part II.C.

[21] This chapter refers to the reconceptualized doctrine alternatively as the sign doctrine and the printed matter doctrine couched in a semiotic framework.

semiotic meanings are not eligible for patent protection. Similarly, attaching new semiotic meanings to old worldly things does not make the worldly things patentable. Whereas the information-centric formulation of the printed matter doctrine purports to curtail the patenting of artifacts and events that exist in the extra-mental world of extension, its semiotic reformulation reveals that its actual function is to restrict the reach of patent protection into the human mind.

In the core printed matter cases – that is, the cases in which the inventions are identified as information recorded on substrate, and the relevance of the contemporary printed matter doctrine is already self-evident – the sign doctrine and its semiotic framework do not significantly disrupt the status quo of patent eligibility.[22] In other words, the problem with the contemporary printed matter doctrine is not that the PTO and the courts have frequently reached incorrect outcomes in core cases. Rather, the problem is the gap between what courts are saying and what they are doing. Courts lack the conceptual tools to describe how and why they are reaching their outcomes. The contemporary printed matter doctrine is plagued by doctrinal exceptions and legal fictions because the PTO and the courts are attempting to achieve semiotically motivated ends without employing semiotic concepts to draw the needed distinctions. The semiotic framework that structures the sign doctrine is therefore a conceptual apparatus that enables courts to both explain what they are doing when they employ the printed matter doctrine and justify why they are doing it. The semiotic framework dispels the conceptual incoherence of the printed matter doctrine by shifting the doctrine's conceptual focus from information and its content to signs and the mental representations that they entail.

In addition to providing conceptual clarity, the reconceptualization of the printed matter doctrine in a semiotic framework has another important role to play in the core printed matter cases: It reveals the doctrine's otherwise absent statutory grounding. The key move here is to recognize the importance of interpreting the text of § 101 in light of the structure of the Patent Act in general and its disclosure provisions in particular. The printed matter doctrine plays a critical, although not commonly recognized, role in shaping the deep structure of the patent regime: It protects the disclosure side of the "duality of claiming and disclosing" from privatizing incursions by claims.[23] In enacting the Patent Act, Congress did not simply create privately held rights to exclude. It did not unilaterally bestow benefits on inventors who generate technological progress. Rather, it structured the patent regime as a "bargain" in which inventors and the public exchange valuable rights.[24] The public, via the

[22] *But see infra* text accompanying notes 249–55 (discussing some historical printed matter cases that the semiotic framework cannot explain).

[23] Graeme B. Dinwoodie & Rochelle Cooper Dreyfuss, *Patenting Science: Protecting the Domain of Accessible Knowledge*, *in* The Future of the Public Domain: Identifying the Commons in Information Law 191, 193 n.4 (Lucie Guibault & P. Bernt Hugenholtz eds., 2006).

[24] Pfaff v. Wells Elecs., Inc., 525 U.S. 55, 63 (1998); Bonito Boats, Inc. v. Thunder Craft Boats, Inc., 489 U.S. 141, 150–51 (1989).

federal government, grants an inventor limited rights to exclude others from making, using, or selling the claimed embodiments of an invention, and as the "quid pro quo of the right to exclude," the inventor discloses newly discovered information that she otherwise could have kept secret.[25] Importantly, the disclosure obligations are not merely obligations to publicize information in the weak sense of making information known to the public: They require a patent applicant to publicize information in a strong sense – to give the public a use privilege in the invention *qua* knowledge, free of the strings of property. Disclosures are "additions to the general store of knowledge" or public domain that must be free for all to use from the moment of their publication so as to "stimulate ideas and the eventual development of further significant advances in the art."[26] But for the printed matter doctrine, however, the disclosure side of the duality of claiming and disclosing would collapse. Couched in a semiotic framework, the printed matter doctrine prevents the worldly artifacts that represent knowledge to human minds from being patentable inventions when the advance over the prior art solely lies in the "stuff" that is represented in the mind. If patent disclosures are to generate a public domain of knowledge, this is precisely the type of advance that should be free for all to use, and it therefore should not be the type of invention that is eligible for patent protection. A semiotically oriented printed matter doctrine allows courts to see through an inventor's attempts to pass off an advance in knowledge that must be disclosed and publicized as a patentable "process, machine, manufacture, or composition of matter."[27]

To repeat, the semiotic framework allows the printed matter doctrine to be taken seriously because it conceptually clarifies and statutorily legitimizes the core printed matter cases. However, this is only half of the story. If taken seriously, a semiotic framework for the printed matter doctrine would also have prescriptive bite outside of the core printed matter cases. The historical printed matter doctrine has focused on artifacts that superficially resemble information recorded on a substrate, but semiotics as a discipline provides no reason to restrict the application of the sign doctrine to such artifacts. Semiotics posits that signs pervade our environment.[28] By shifting the focus of the printed matter doctrine away from information to signs, a semiotic framework for the printed matter doctrine brings into question the patent eligibility of some inventions that escaped scrutiny under the traditional printed matter doctrine.

To illustrate the impact of the shift from the conventional printed matter doctrine to the sign doctrine – that is, a shift in conceptual focus away from information and its content to signs and their mental representations – this chapter addresses the patent eligibility of one specific type of software invention: the *computer model*. As defined

[25] Kewanee Oil Co. v. Bicron Corp., 416 U.S. 470, 484 (1974).

[26] *Id.* at 481.

[27] 35 U.S.C. § 101 (2006).

[28] *See infra* note 191.

in this chapter, computer models are signs: They exist when programmed computers are understood by their human users to represent (i.e. model) real-world systems.[29] For a simple example of a computer model, assume that a researcher discovers that the concentrations of two chemicals are inversely correlated in human blood: A high level of chemical A indicates that a patient has a low level of chemical B, and vice versa.[30] The researcher could seek a claim to a programmed computer: "a computer device for diagnosing a chemical B deficiency that correlates a high level of chemical A with a low level of chemical B."[31] This claim describes a computer model: The claimed programmed computer is useful because it is understood by its human users to model a real-world system, and it is nonobvious because the way in which the real-world system functions was unexpected at the time of the invention. Under the contemporary doctrine of patent eligibility as articulated by the Federal Circuit in either *State Street Bank & Trust Co.* v. *Signature Financial Group*[32] or *In re Bilski*,[33] this newly invented computer model would likely be viewed as a relatively uncontroversial, patent-eligible claim.[34] However, semiotic analysis suggests a hard second look. The tangible artifact described by the claim is not the computer model in its entirety, but rather a *programmed computer* – a computer executing a mathematical function with semantically meaningless variables.[35] More specifically, allowing for a degree of simplification, it is a computer programmed to execute the formula $y = 1/x$. Such a programmed computer was presumptively old in the art at the time the researchers made their discovery about the inverse correlation between chemicals A and B in human blood. The computer model invention at issue is therefore simply a shift in what the programmed computer represents to its human user. The meanings of the variables y and x are not formal or functional properties of the programmed computer in and of itself. All that needs to occur for the old programmed computer to function as a new sign and to model the newly discovered real-world system of chemicals in human blood is for a human computer user to change her mind about the meaning of the programmed computer. The computer user need only posit that x represents chemical A and that y represents chemical B to use the newly invented computer model. This computer model is therefore a close semiotic cousin of a printed technical diagram with new text; even

[29] *See infra* Part IV.B.

[30] This simplistic example is a variation of the facts presented in *Lab. Corp. of Am. Holdings* v. *Metabolite Labs., Inc.*, 548 *U.S.* 124 (2006) (Breyer, J., dissenting from the dismissal of the writ of certiorari as improvidently granted).

[31] *See infra* notes 294, 325–29 and accompanying text (addressing this variant).

[32] 149 F.3d 1368, 1373 (Fed. Cir. 1998) (articulating the "useful, concrete, and tangible result" test for patent eligibility).

[33] 545 F.3d 943, 961–63 (Fed. Cir. 2008) (en banc), *cert. granted sub nom. Bilski v. Doll*, 129 S. Ct. 2735 (2009) (articulating the "machine-or-transformation" test for patent eligibility).

[34] *See infra* Part IV.C.

[35] This chapter employs the term "programmed computer" as a semiotic term of art to differentiate it from a computer model. *See infra* notes 294–95 and accompanying text.

more so, it is like an old machine with new textual labels. Under the sign doctrine, it is a product of human ingenuity that should not be eligible for patent protection because, first, it is a sign and, second, the only advance over the prior art resides in the mind of a human interpreter.

This chapter proceeds in four principal parts. Part I reviews the contemporary printed matter doctrine, highlighting its internal conceptual incoherence, its awkward fit with other patent law doctrines, and its lack of a statutory grounding. Parts II and III make the arguments that allow the printed matter doctrine to be taken seriously. Part II offers a course in "Semiotics 101": a semiotics primer strategically targeted on the principles that prove to be relevant to the § 101 doctrine of patent eligibility. Part III illustrates the virtues of reconceptualizing the printed matter doctrine as the sign doctrine in the core printed matter cases. The semiotic framework offers a conceptually coherent explanation for the rough contours of the outcomes that the PTO and the courts are already reaching in these cases. It also points the way to a textual grounding for the printed matter doctrine in the Patent Act. Part IV examines an unexpected consequence of taking the printed matter doctrine seriously. It turns from the core printed matter cases to technologies that function as signs but are not intuitively understood to be information recorded on a substrate. More specifically, Part IV employs semiotic analysis to suggest that the patentability of certain types of programmed computers under § 101 may need to be reconsidered. In particular, it argues that the routine patentability of computer models under the contemporary doctrine of patent eligibility and the categorical unpatentability of old mechanical devices with new labels under the printed matter doctrine cannot be reconciled as a matter of semiotic logic.

I. THE INFORMATION-CENTRIC PRINTED MATTER DOCTRINE

This part summarizes the contemporary printed matter doctrine. Part I.A focuses on conceptual infirmities, demonstrating that the doctrine is, at its best, more exception than rule and, at its worst, an accumulation of unacknowledged, yet plainly evident, legal fictions. Part I.B turns to statutory mysteries, illustrating that the courts have not identified how the printed matter doctrine is anchored in the Patent Act. Part I.C notes the lack of any calls for eliminating the printed matter doctrine despite its conceptual infirmities and statutory mysteries. It argues that its widespread acceptance strongly suggests that the printed matter doctrine performs a much-needed function in that it excludes certain useful and nonobvious products of human ingenuity from the patent regime.

A. *Doctrinal Infirmities*

As its name suggests, the printed matter doctrine had its historical origins in the technology of printing characters and images on paper. The Court of Customs and

Patent Appeals (CCPA) stated in *In re Russell* that the printed matter doctrine meant that "[t]he mere arrangement of printed matter on a sheet or sheets of paper, in book form or otherwise, [did] not constitute" an invention that was eligible for patent protection.[36] Today, books, ledgers, and technical diagrams remain paradigmatic examples of the products of human ingenuity that are patent ineligible because of the printed matter doctrine. However, as technology progressed through the twentieth century, courts recognized that the printed matter doctrine should not be tied to a specific technology. A recording of a book on a magnetic tape is no different in principle from a stack of printed papers in between hard covers, so the existence of printing per se could not remain the lynchpin of the doctrine.[37] Courts therefore generalized the printed matter doctrine into a technology-neutral rule that states that claims to "information recorded in any substrate or medium" cannot be patented when it is the "content" of the information that differentiates the claimed subject matter from the prior art.[38]

Regardless of how simple this rule about recorded information and its content may seem, it is anything but clear in its application. Part I.A.1 illustrates that the printed matter doctrine does not govern the patentability of many inventions that are readily understood to be information with content, and Part I.A.2 considers the Federal Circuit's unsuccessful attempt to resolve this problem by restricting the printed matter doctrine to recorded information that is not processed by machines. These first two subparts employ DNA molecules and software recorded on tangible media as paradigmatic examples of inventions that present conceptual difficulties for the contemporary printed matter doctrine. Part I.A.3 addresses the long-standing

36 *In re* Russell, 48 F.2d 668, 669 (C.C.P.A. 1931); *accord In re* Sterling, 70 F.2d 910, 912 (C.C.P.A. 1934); *see also In re* Reeves, 62 F.2d 199, 200 (C.C.P.A. 1932). The CCPA heard appeals from the PTO before the creation of the Federal Circuit in 1982.

37 *See, e.g., Ex parte* Carver, 227 U.S.P.Q. (BNA) 465, 467 (B.P.A.I. 1985) (bringing the printed matter doctrine to bear on cassette tapes and finding them to be patent-eligible subject matter).

38 1 Chisum, *supra* note 2, § 1.02[4]. The value of the history of the printed matter doctrine in understanding the doctrine's contemporary state is easy to overstate. The courts' track record is not perfect; there are exceptional cases in which the printed matter doctrine probably should have invalidated a claim but did not. *See, e.g.*, Rand, McNally & Co. v. Exchange Scrip-Book Co., 187 F. 984 (7th Cir. 1911) (holding a railroad scrip-book with coupons expressed in monetary value rather than in miles to be a patentable invention). Furthermore, even ignoring errant data points, there is no coherent narrative arc to describe the doctrine's historical evolution. *See* Morton C. Jacobs, Note, *The Patentability of Printed Matter: Critique and Proposal*, 18 Geo. Wash. L. Rev. 475 (1950) (teasing several themes out of the historical printed matter cases). For example, the printed matter doctrine originated as a corollary of the exclusion of business methods from patent eligibility, *id.* at 476, but the business methods exclusion is today defunct, at least as an express subject-matter-specific exception. *Bilski*, 545 F.3d at 960. Similarly, the printed matter doctrine and the mental steps doctrine were once recognized as two sides of the same coin. *See, e.g., Ex Parte* Jenny, 1961 WL 7968 (B.P.A.I. June 30, 1960) (employing principles established in the mental steps doctrine to craft the printed matter doctrine). Although the courts continue to apply the printed matter doctrine, they abandoned the mental steps doctrine during their struggle with the patent eligibility of computer software and programmed computers. *In re* Musgrave, 431 F.2d 882, 890 (C.C.P.A. 1970).

functional-relation exception to the printed matter doctrine. Part I.A.4 examines the patentable-weight approach to patent eligibility that structures the printed matter doctrine.

1. Some Recorded Information Is Patentable

One conceptual wrinkle in the contemporary printed matter doctrine is that it only applies to a small subset of the tangible artifacts that are intuitively understood to be recorded information with new content.[39] Many artifacts that are readily identified as information with new content remain eligible for patent protection under the printed matter doctrine. If the printed matter doctrine means what its rhetoric actually says about barring the patenting of information based on its content, then it is difficult to understand why the printed matter doctrine does not produce a much larger exclusion from patent eligibility.

For example, consider claims to isolated and purified DNA molecules that reflect the sequence of nucleotides in genes expressed in living cells. The patentability of isolated and purified DNA is uncontroversial, at least under the printed matter doctrine.[40] Yet, DNA is commonly described as nothing more than genetic

39 To avoid unnecessary confusion, one definition of information should be identified at the outset and recognized as irrelevant to the type of information that is at issue in the printed matter doctrine. Claude Shannon is widely credited with developing "information theory" – a mathematical theory for "measuring the amount of information that a particular code or channel [can] transmit." J. Mingers, *The Nature of Information and Its Relationship to Meaning, in* PHILOSOPHICAL ASPECTS OF INFORMATION SYSTEMS 74 (R.L. Winder, S.K. Probert & I.A. Beeson eds., 1997); *see generally* FRED I. DRETSKE, KNOWLEDGE AND THE FLOW OF INFORMATION 3–39 (1981) (offering a readable overview of Shannon's information theory). Shannon's information theory addresses information in a purely quantitative fashion. It has nothing to do with the "content" of information in the sense of its meaning. As Shannon himself stated, "[f]requently the messages have *meaning*; that is they refer to or are correlated according to some system with certain physical or conceptual entities. These semantic aspects of communication are irrelevant to the engineering problem" addressed by information theory. CLAUDE E. SHANNON & WARREN WEAVER, THE MATHEMATICAL THEORY OF COMMUNICATION 31 (1949) (emphasis in original). In terms of Shannon information, both the rolling of an eight-sided die to determine who jumps out of a plane first and the running of a race between eight evenly matched horses are informationally equivalent events. *See* DONALD M. MACKAY, INFORMATION, MECHANISM AND MEANING 56–57 (1969) ("Communication engineers [working with Shannon information] have not developed a concept of information at all. They have developed a theory dealing explicitly with only one particular feature or aspect of messages . . . their unexpectedness or surprise value."). Shannon's theory should be called the "mathematical theory of communication" in order to avoid confusion with a theory about information in which semantic content is relevant, as it is in the printed matter doctrine. Luciano Floridi, *Information, in* THE BLACKWELL GUIDE TO THE PHILOSOPHY OF COMPUTING AND INFORMATION 352–53 (L. Floridi ed., 2003).

40 The fact that printed matter challenges have not been brought against gene patents does not mean that the patent eligibility of isolated and purified molecules of DNA under § 101 is uncontroversial. *See, e.g.*, Ass'n for Molecular Pathology v. U.S. Patent & Trademark Office, 669 F. Supp. 2d 365, 397–98 (S.D.N.Y. 2009) (arguing that DNA claims are not eligible for patent protection because they are natural phenomena). Additionally, the permissive nature of the standard for assessing the nonobviousness of gene patents established by the Federal Circuit has been questioned, Arti K. Rai, *Intellectual Property Rights in Biotechnology: Addressing New Technology*, 34 WAKE FOREST L. REV. 827, 836

information – a "code" or "blueprint" for the proteins and RNA molecules that constitute living organisms.[41] DNA is information embedded in a substrate of nucleotides strung together to form a molecule, rather than in the form of printing on paper.[42] Furthermore, it is the informational content of a DNA molecule that differentiates it from the prior art of other DNA molecules. The linear sequence of nucleotides in an expressed gene encodes the structure of the proteins and RNA molecules that the cellular machinery involved in the processes of transcription (the copying of DNA into mRNA) and translation (the production of proteins from mRNA templates) will produce.[43] Different DNA sequences deterministically yield different proteins, making DNA molecules instances of information with different content. The difference between a newly isolated and purified strand of DNA and prior-art DNA molecules resides in the content of the DNA-as-information; that is, in the protein-building instructions that the DNA molecule provides to the cellular machinery.[44]

The artifacts described by software-on-disk claims are another, and perhaps even more intuitive, example of recorded information with new content that is patentable under the contemporary printed matter doctrine.[45] By the early 1990s, both method claims describing the steps performed by computers executing software and apparatus claims describing computers programmed with software were frequently held

(1999) (arguing that the status of DNA as both "a chemical compound" and "more fundamentally" as "a carrier of information" should influence the courts' decisions about the nonobviousness of DNA), and the statutory utility requirement invalidates some patents claiming gene fragments, *In re* Fisher, 421 F.3d 1365, 1378 (Fed. Cir. 2005).

41 *See* Stephen M. Downes, *Biological Information, in* THE PHILOSOPHY OF SCIENCE: AN ENCYCLOPEDIA 64, 64 (Sahotra Sakar & Jessica Pfeiffer eds., 2005) (reviewing the origins of the concept of genetic information).

42 Rebecca S. Eisenberg, *Molecules vs. Information: Should Patents Protect Both?*, 8 B.U. J. SCI. & TECH. L. 190, 196 (2002) (discussing the dual status of DNA as information and molecule).

43 *See generally In re* O'Farrell, 853 F.2d 894, 895–99 (Fed. Cir. 1988) (offering a basic primer on transcription and translation).

44 In the chemical and biochemical fields, DNA is the low-hanging fruit of the argument that the restrictions on patentability imposed by the printed matter doctrine do not apply to all instances of recorded information with content. However, it is arguably a conceptual error to frame DNA as unique in raising the question of whether molecules are information with content. There is an interesting debate over what could be called DNA exceptionalism: Is DNA different from other molecules in that it is a "code" or "blueprint" for the cell, or is it simply one information bearer among the many information-bearing molecules implicated in a cell's metabolic pathways? *See* Downes, *supra* note 41, at 64. The critique of DNA exceptionalism demonstrates that the DNA-is-information argument can be generalized into an everything-is-information argument, making the rhetorical focus of the printed matter doctrine on information and its content even more problematic. *Cf.* Dan L. Burk, *The Problem of Process in Biotechnology*, 43 HOUS. L. REV. 561, 582–88 (2006) (discussing the difficulty of using the concept of information to limit the scope of what can be patented).

45 For an argument that analogizes the patentability of software-on-disk inventions and isolated and purified DNA molecules, see D.C. Toedt, *Software as "Machine DNA": Arguments for Patenting Useful Computer Disks Per Se*, 77 J. PAT. & TRADEMARK OFF. SOC'Y 275, 276 (1995) ("Program- and data-storage devices encoding computer programs and data seem to be closely analogous to DNA sequences, which are routinely patented.").

to be eligible for patent protection.[46] However, courts found that the manufacture and sale of copies of computer software embedded on disks did not directly infringe either method or apparatus claims, so patent applicants sought the additional protection offered by software-on-disk claims.[47] When confronted with the issue in its opinion in *In re Beauregard*, the PTO initially resisted issuing software-on-disk claims under the printed matter doctrine.[48] Under the information-centric rhetoric of the printed matter doctrine, this conclusion seems reasonable. Computer software is self-evidently information recorded on a medium. (If software recorded on a disk is not recorded information, what is?) Furthermore, the difference between the software-on-disk claims and the prior art resides in the content of the recorded information. Before the Federal Circuit reviewed the PTO's decision in *Beauregard*, however, the PTO gave way on this point, announcing that it would treat "computer programs embodied in a tangible medium, such as floppy diskettes" as patentable subject matter under § 101.[49] The Federal Circuit has not ruled on this interpretation of the printed matter doctrine.

2. Only Machine-Processed Information Is Patentable?

In *In re Lowry*, the Federal Circuit attempted to explain why the printed matter doctrine does not apply in general to all recorded information or in particular to computer-readable "information stored in a memory."[50] It interpreted the printed matter cases as factually limited to "'novel arrangements of printed lines or characters, useful and intelligible only to the human mind.'"[51] Inversely, it interpreted the printed matter doctrine to have "no factual relevance where 'the invention as defined by the claims *requires* that the information be processed not by the mind but by a machine.'"[52] In gross, the Federal Circuit set up a dichotomy of

46 *See, e.g.*, Arrhythmia Research Tech., Inc. v. Corazonix Corp., 958 F.2d 1053, 1060 (Fed. Cir. 1992) (holding that method and apparatus claims directed to the analysis of EKG signals described statutory subject matter under § 101).

47 *See* Vincent Chiappetta, *Patentability of Computer Software Instruction as an "Article of Manufacture": Software as Such as the Right Stuff*, 17 J. Marshall J. Computer & Info. L. 89, 110–11 (1998) (discussing the advantages of software-on-disk claims for patentees).

48 *See* 53 F.3d 1583, 1583 (Fed. Cir. 1995); Chiappetta, *supra* note 47, at 120.

49 *Beauregard*, 53 F.3d at 1584. *But see infra* text accompanying notes 55–58 & 89–93 (discussing limitations that the PTO has placed on the patentability of *Beauregard* claims).

50 32 F.3d 1579, 1583 (Fed. Cir. 1994).

51 *Id.* (quoting *In re* Bernhart, 417 F.2d 1395, 1399 (C.C.P.A. 1969)); *see also In re* Jones, 373 F.2d 1007, 1013 (C.C.P.A. 1967) ("Certainly, there is no 'printing' in this case in the form of words or other symbols intended to convey intelligence to a reader.... The user of the disc is not supposed to contemplate it as he would a mathematical table, weighing scale chart, or the like in order to derive some information.").

52 *Lowry*, 32 F.3d at 1579. *But cf. infra* note 254 (noting that, in a semiotic framework, the language in *Lowry* limiting the printed matter doctrine to indicia intelligible to the human mind was not necessary to the holding).

machine-processed and human-intelligible information, and it limited the restrictive effect of the printed matter doctrine to the latter.

At first glance, this machine-versus-mind structure for the printed matter doctrine seems to resolve the puzzle of the patentability of both software-on-disk and isolated-and-purified DNA claims.[53] A human being cannot look at either a computer disk or a DNA molecule with naked eyes and "read" it. Both are embodiments of information that must be processed by machines to unlock its content. Information recorded on a computer disk must trigger a response in a general-purpose computer through a deterministic process. DNA functions as an information-bearing molecule in a cell because it triggers a response in an organic machine through the processes of transcription and translation.[54] However, on closer inspection, the notion that the printed matter doctrine simply does not apply to any information that must be processed by a machine – whether mechanical (e.g., punch cards in a weaving loom), electronic (e.g., software on a disk), or organic (e.g., DNA) – does not describe the ends that are being reached through the application of the printed matter doctrine. In seeking to explain the puzzle of why some information is patentable, it creates two new puzzles that are just as troubling: the *first-then* and *both-and* puzzles.

First, in comparison to the exception from patent eligibility that the printed matter doctrine is presumed to generate, the notion that the printed matter doctrine does not apply to any information that must be processed by a machine is fatally underinclusive. Many artifacts at the heart of what cannot be patented under the contemporary printed matter doctrine involve information that must be processed by a machine before being intelligible to humans. For example, a book recorded on a magnetic tape is information that must be initially processed by a machine, because humans cannot read magnetic tapes.[55] Taken literally, a printed matter doctrine that accepts as patentable all information that must be processed by a machine would uphold a claim to an audio book on a cassette tape conveying useful and nonobvious technological information to a listener. Similarly, *Beauregard* claims may describe either computer programs that are viewed as giving the computer new functionality (".exe" files, for short) or digitized versions of human-readable printed matter, such as books or instruction manuals (".txt" files for short).[56] The ".txt" files are not meaningfully different from audio tapes. They are information that must be initially processed by a machine, which in this instance is a computer programmed with software such as a word processor or a music player, so they are not

53 *See supra* Part I.A.1.

54 *See supra* text accompanying notes 41–44.

55 *See supra* note 37 and accompanying text (noting that the printed matter doctrine applies to cassette tapes).

56 The concept of a ".txt" file is not intended to be limited to files that display text. As used here, a recording of a song as an MP3 to be played on a portable music player is also a ".txt" file.

"'novel arrangements of printed lines or characters, useful and intelligible only to the human mind.'"[57] Nonetheless, they are not eligible for patent protection. In sum, the Federal Circuit has in effect proposed a dichotomy between information that must be processed by machines, to which the printed matter doctrine is inapplicable, and information that can only be understood by the human mind, to which the printed matter doctrine applies. This approach misses the mark because the printed matter doctrine should apply to some information that is first processed by a machine and that then becomes intelligible to humans. The relevant distinction is a distinction between two types of functionality that the information triggers in a machine, and this is not a distinction that can be captured by querying whether the information must be processed by a machine.[58]

Second, the two categories of information that the Federal Circuit identifies in *Lowry* exclude the most interesting and the most problematic type of information. *Lowry* suggests how courts applying the printed matter doctrine should address both information that must be processed by a machine (ignore it) and information that is only intelligible to the human mind (scrutinize it to see if it is the content of the information that is the advance over the prior art).[59] However, many examples of recorded information that are today routinely held to be patentable suffer from a both-and problem: They can be both processed by machines and intelligible to human minds at the same time. Computer software ".exe" files are examples *par excellence* of the both-and problem. Computer software on a disk can both be processed by a machine to generate a particular type of functionality, and when displayed on a screen or printed out on paper as source code, it is intelligible to computer programmers as a kind of language.[60] DNA, too, is both-and information. The information in a DNA molecule can be processed by the cellular machinery that gives rise to transcription and translation, *and* when fed through a sequencer, it is intelligible to a human mind.[61] Even a punch card can both cause a programmable weaving loom to execute a particular design and be intelligible to a knowledgeable industrial weaver who has learned how to read punch cards. A simple dichotomy of information that is either processed by machines or intelligible to the human mind ignores the both-and problem with which the printed matter doctrine must grapple.

57 *Lowry*, 32 F.3d at 1583 (quoting *In re* Bernhart, 417 F.2d 1395, 1399 (C.C.P.A. 1969)).

58 *See infra* text accompanying notes 89–93 (describing the doctrine that the PTO has developed to distinguish ".txt" files from ".exe" files).

59 *See supra* text accompanying notes 50–52.

60 *See* Dan L. Burk, *Patenting Speech*, 79 TEX. L. REV. 99, 101–05 (2000) (considering the implications for patent law of treating software as speech by programmers to other programmers); Chiappetta, *supra* note 47, at 141–43 (discussing an "implementation" and "language" dichotomy in software). Technically, software suffers from a combination of the first-then and both-and problems, because the software recorded on a disk is not intelligible to a computer programmer as code until after it has been processed by a machine.

61 DNA molecules, too, suffer from a combination of the first-then and both-and problems.

3. The Functional-Relation Exception

Another wrinkle in the printed matter doctrine is an exception to the doctrine's rule of exclusion that has a pedigree almost as long and well established as the default rule itself. The exception is today referred to as the functional-relation exception: A claim encompassing printed matter may be patentable if the information is "functionally related" to the substrate.[62] This exception applies even if the content of the printed matter must be considered to demonstrate that the printed matter is an advance over the prior art.

Courts initially developed the exception through a series of cases in which claims to human-readable printed matter shared a factual theme: The printed matter was designed to be physically torn apart or punched in new ways.[63] In these ticket-tearing cases, the invention clearly lay at least in part in "[t]he mere arrangement of printed matter on a sheet or sheets of paper" and thus fell under the default rule of exclusion of the printed matter doctrine.[64] However, when the improvements that differentiated the claimed inventions from the prior art resided in a combination of the structural qualities of the substrate and the physical location of the printing on the substrate in relation to those structural qualities, the courts upheld claims to printed matter per se.

For example, in *Cincinnati Traction Co.* v. *Pope*,[65] the Sixth Circuit addressed a claim to a book of streetcar transfer tickets with three physical sections separated by perforations.[66] Each ticket had a stub attached to the book, a coupon in the middle, and a transfer ticket at the loose end.[67] The tickets allowed the company to restrict the use of transfers issued in the morning to the morning hours and prevent the use of morning transfers in the evening.[68] The conductor could issue morning transfer tickets without the coupons and afternoon transfer tickets with the coupons, and the company would only accept transfer tickets in the evenings with the coupons attached.[69] Furthermore, the tickets allowed railroad companies

62 *In re* Gulack, 703 F.2d 1381, 1386 (Fed. Cir. 1983); *see also In re* Miller, 418 F.2d 1392, 1396 (C.C.P.A. 1969).

63 *See, e.g.*, Cincinnati Traction Co. v. Pope, 210 F. 443 (6th Cir. 1913) (transfer tickets); Flood v. Coe, 31 F. Supp. 348 (D.D.C. 1940) (price tags on garments); Mitchell v. Int'l Tailoring Co., 170 F. 91 (C.C.S.D.N.Y. 1909) (device for advertising goods); Benjamin Menu Card Co. v. Rand, McNally & Co., 210 F. 285 (C.C.N.D. Ill. 1894) (combined menu and meal check); *cf.* Boggs v. Robertson, 13 U.S.P.Q. (BNA) 214 (D.C. 1931) ("[W]here the paper or physical body upon which the matter is printed is designed to be used with the printed matter, as by tearing apart or punching, it becomes . . . an actual physical article of manufacture within the terms of [the Patent Act].").

64 *In re* Russell, 48 F.2d 668, 669 (C.C.P.A. 1931).

65 210 F. 443.

66 *Id.* at 444–45.

67 *Id.*

68 *Id.* at 445.

69 *Id.*

to monitor their conductors more closely.[70] Because the coupons from morning transfers would still be attached to the stubs remaining in conductors' ticket books, the company could ensure that conductors did not conspire with the passengers and issue afternoon transfers in the morning.[71] The Sixth Circuit upheld the claim under the printed matter doctrine, stating that the claimed invention "clearly involves physical structure" and that "[t]he presence of conventional indications and legends [on the structure] does not rob the structure of patentability."[72]

Flood v. *Coe*[73] provides another example of a ticket-tearing case. The claimed invention was a ticket for tagging garments in retail stores.[74] Prior-art tickets were divided horizontally into two sections, each of which contained printing descriptive of both the garment to which the ticket was attached and the price of the garment.[75] At sale, one section remained attached to the garment and one section was torn off and retained by the retailer.[76] The claimed invention improved on the prior-art tickets in three ways: It made the division between the two sections vertical, it placed the price at the very bottom of both vertical sections, and it left a space in the middle band of the ticket, above the price and below the description of the garment.[77] The benefit of the new ticket was that the prices could be torn off the bottom and new prices could be written in each of the columns in the blank space (now at the bottom of the ticket), without removing the ticket from the garment and without interfering with the descriptions. The District Court for the District of Columbia upheld the claim as a patentable invention, stating that the arrangement of printed matter on a substrate is patentable when "[t]here is a definite and decided relationship between the physical structure [of the substrate] and the printed matter" or "there is a cooperative relationship between the printed indicia and the structural features" of the substrate.[78]

In more recent cases, what was originally described as a *structural*-relation exception to the printed matter doctrine in the ticket-tearing cases has morphed into a *functional*-relation exception. The facts and holdings in these more recent functional-relation cases are impossible to describe with a single overarching narrative. The functional-relation exception has become malleable to the point of not having any identifiable form at all. Today, it is a doctrine that places few hard constraints on legal decision makers and instead gives them access to rhetoric that allows them to reach the outcomes in printed matter cases that they believe are correct.

70 *Id.* at 444.
71 *Id.* at 444–45.
72 *Id.* at 446–47.
73 31 F. Supp. 348 (D.D.C. 1940).
74 *Id.* at 348–49.
75 *Id.*
76 *Id.*
77 *Id.* at 349.
78 *Id.*

The shift in rhetoric from a structural- to a functional-relation exception occurred in *In re Miller*.[79] In *Miller*, the CCPA addressed a claim to measuring cups and spoons in which the advance over the prior art resided in the mislabeling of the measuring receptacles to facilitate the making of fractionated recipes.[80] For example, in a set of spoons collectively labeled the "one half recipe" set, the one-half teaspoon measure was labeled as the "1 teaspoon" measure, meaning that a chef would automatically half the recipe if she were to use the measures with labels corresponding to the amounts listed in the recipe.[81] While acknowledging that there was no new structural relationship between the substrate (the spoons) and the printed labels, the CCPA upheld the claims because it found "a new and unobvious functional relationship" between the spoons and the labels.[82] What the CCPA seemed to have been focused on is the nonobvious relationship between the utility of the substrate (the spoon's utility in measuring ingredients) and the content of the human-readable printed matter (the meaning of the factually incorrect labels). In *Miller*, the key to the functional relationship appears to have been the fact that the content of the human-readable printed matter was a property of the substrate. Furthermore, the relationship was nonobvious because the property was a fictitious one, namely a size other than the actual size of the spoon.

In *In re Gulack*,[83] the Federal Circuit upheld a claim under the functional-relation exception to the printed matter doctrine that the CCPA had minted in *Miller*.[84] The claim described an entertainment or education device consisting of a band or ring with a series of numbers printed thereon.[85] The numerical series had a cyclical nature: Each successive number was related to the previous one by a specified mathematical relationship, and the "last" number in the series had this same relationship to the "first," meaning that there were in fact no last or first numbers in the series.[86] Mathematically speaking, the numbers formed an endless loop.[87] The Federal Circuit held the printed matter to be functionally related to the substrate because "the digits exploit[ed] the endless nature of the band."[88] In *Gulack*, the key to the functional relationship appears to have been the isomorphism of the nature of the mathematical relationships among the numbers and the physical, spatial arrangement of the printed indicia on the band. Under this reasoning, simply printing the numbers in a circle on a piece of paper would

79 418 F.2d 1392 (C.C.P.A. 1969).
80 *Id.* at 1393–95.
81 *Id.* at 1394–95.
82 *Id.* at 1396.
83 703 F.2d 1381 (Fed. Cir. 1983).
84 *Id.*
85 *Id.* at 1382–84.
86 *Id.*
87 *Id.* at 1386–87.
88 *Id.* at 1387.

seem to be patentable subject matter because the functional relationship between the mathematical sequence of numbers and the printed indicia is preserved.

More recently, the PTO has seized on the functional-relation exception to the printed matter doctrine as a means of justifying differential treatment for *Beauregard* claims describing ".txt" and ".exe" files.[89] The PTO has declared that there are two types of descriptive material that can be put onto computer disks: functional and nonfunctional.[90] As the names suggest, functional descriptive material is described as "structurally and functionally interrelated to the medium" on which it is recorded, whereas nonfunctional descriptive material is described as lacking a functional relationship to its medium.[91] The PTO posits that ".exe" computer programs, such as e-book readers, are functional descriptive material and that ".txt" files, like e-books themselves, are nonfunctional descriptive material.[92] The dichotomy of functional and nonfunctional descriptive material allows the PTO to achieve the intuitively desired end result of making ".exe" files patent eligible and ".txt" files patent ineligible. The only problem with the functional–nonfunctional dichotomy is that it does not exist: There is no difference as a matter of fact between the data-disk relationship that exists when the data is a ".txt" e-book and when the data is an ".exe" e-book reader.[93] However important the distinction between an e-book file and an e-book reader is to patent law as a normative matter – and however "correct" the end result of the PTO's distinction between patentable, functional descriptive material and unpatentable, nonfunctional descriptive material may seem – the PTO's interpretation of the functional-relation exception to printed matter doctrine in *Beauregard* claims is conceptually bankrupt and has no grounding in factual reality.

4. The Patentable-Weight Approach

A patentable-weight approach to patent eligibility is implicit in the default rule of the printed matter doctrine under which "information recorded in any substrate or medium" cannot be patented when it is the "content" of the information that differentiates the claimed subject matter from the prior art.[94] The printed matter doctrine does not categorically bar the patenting of any artifact that comprises information recorded on a substrate or medium. Rather, it only bars the patenting of information when the difference between the claimed subject matter and the prior

89 *See supra* notes 56–58 and accompanying text.

90 Examination Guidelines for Computer-Related Inventions, 61 Fed. Reg. 7478, 7481 (Feb. 28, 1996) [hereinafter Examination Guidelines].

91 *Id.*

92 *Id.*

93 *See* John R. Thomas, *Of Text, Technique, and the Tangible: Drafting Patent Claims Around Patent Rules*, 17 J. MARSHALL J. COMPUTER & INFO. L. 219, 260 (1998) (asserting that the distinction is "simply a misstatement of fact").

94 1 CHISUM, *supra* note 2, § 1.02[4].

art lies in the content of the information.[95] Couched in the rhetoric commonly used by courts, the printed matter doctrine means that the content of the information cannot be given "patentable weight" in the assessment of the claim's novelty or nonobviousness (unless, of course, the information is functionally related to the substrate).[96] If the claim describes an improvement over the prior art without any consideration of the content of the printed matter – that is, without giving the printed matter any weight – then the subject matter described by the claim can be patented. However, if the content of the information is the only locus of the invention – that is, the content of the information must be given patentable weight in order to demonstrate that the claim describes a novel and nonobvious improvement over the prior art – then the claim is not eligible for patent protection under § 101.[97] In other contexts, such as the now dormant or defunct "mental steps" doctrine, this same approach to patent eligibility is referred to as a "point of novelty" approach: If the content of the information is the point of novelty (or nonobviousness) that demonstrates that the entire claim is a novel and nonobvious advance over the prior art, then the claim does not describe a patentable invention.[98]

The patentable-weight approach to patent eligibility is today commonly viewed as conceptually problematic for two distinct reasons. First, it leads to the counterintuitive conclusion that the status of an artifact or method as patentable subject matter is contingent on the content of the prior art. Second, it runs against the grain of the claim-as-a-whole approach that both the Supreme Court and the Federal Circuit today accept as the dominant approach to doctrine of patent eligibility.

The status of an object or method as patentable subject matter is usually presumed to be capable of being determined in a binary, yes-or-no fashion simply by examining the object or method itself. Whether an object or process either is, or is not, a "process, machine, manufacture, or composition of matter" that is eligible for patent protection under § 101[99] is a status inherent in the object or method, and the historical context in which an invention occurs is presumed to be irrelevant to the identification of patent eligibility.[100] In other words, patent eligibility under § 101 is presumed to be an "intrinsic" property of the claimed artifacts, not a "relational" property of the claimed artifacts that is contingent on the historical context in which an invention

95 In colloquial terms, the printed matter doctrine bars the patenting of information when the invention resides in the content of the information.

96 The CCPA seems to have first used this rhetoric in *In re* Miller, 418 F.2d 1392, 1395–96 (C.C.P.A. 1969).

97 Because it mixes together concepts of patent eligibility, novelty, and nonobviousness, the printed matter doctrine is sometimes applied under the auspices of §§ 102 and 103 rather than § 101. *See infra* notes 136–41 and accompanying text.

98 *In re* Musgrave, 431 F.2d 882, 889 (C.C.P.A. 1970) (describing the "point-of-novelty" approach to patent eligibility under the mental steps doctrine in the course of abandoning the mental steps doctrine).

99 35 U.S.C. § 101 (2006).

100 Diamond v. Diehr, 450 U.S. 175, 189–91 (1981); *In re* Bergy, 596 F.2d 952, 959–64 (C.C.P.A. 1979).

occurs.[101] Statutorily, the same point can be made by noting that both the novelty of an invention under § 102 and its nonobviousness under § 103 are presumed to be irrelevant to the invention's eligibility for patent protection under § 101.[102]

The patentable-weight approach to patent eligibility challenges these presumptions. The way in which it undermines these presumptions is easiest to see when the printed matter doctrine is brought to bear on a claim describing a mechanical device, such as a scale for weighing objects, with textual labels. A mechanical scale is a clear example of an object that falls within the category of a "machine" in § 101.[103] Under a patentable-weight approach to patent eligibility, the scale is eligible for patent protection if the claim is limited in scope to scales with a nonobvious mechanism for translating the weight of the object into the position of a pointer. However, if the advance over the prior art in a later claim resides in a new set of indicia placed next to the pointer of the same scale, then the scale is no longer patent eligible at this later point in time under the printed matter doctrine with its patentable-weight approach.[104] The advance over the prior art resides in the content of the printed matter. Because of the awkward nature of the resulting statutory conclusion – an assertion that the same scale that earlier had been a § 101 "machine" is no longer a § 101 "machine" at a later point in time – courts have become wary of a patentable-weight approach to § 101 doctrine.

Although the counterintuitive consequences of the patentable-weight approach are most apparent in the context of machines with labels, they are also present even when claims describe printed matter per se. For example, consider a piece of paper with writing on it that conveys a specific idea.[105] If the fibrous structure of the paper or the chemical composition of the ink is novel and nonobvious in relation to the prior art, then the artifact is eligible for patent protection as a "manufacture" under § 101.[106] The inventor would want to claim either the paper or the ink generically. However, she could also file a dependent claim to the paper or ink in a form that

[101] The "intrinsic" properties of a thing are properties that are "entirely about that thing," whereas the "relational" or "extrinsic" properties of a thing are properties that "may depend, wholly or partly, on something else" other than the thing at issue. David Lewis, *Extrinsic Properties*, 44 Phil. Stud. 197, 197 (1983). Patent eligibility is a relational property of the claimed subject matter under a patentable-weight approach to § 101 because patentability turns on the historical context in which a thing is situated.

[102] *Diehr*, 450 U.S. at 189–91; *Bergy*, 596 F.2d at 959–64.

[103] 35 U.S.C. § 101 (2006).

[104] The later claim is a scale-plus-labels claim, whereas the earlier claim was simply a scale claim. However, even the scale-plus-labels claim would be a patentable "machine" under § 101 if it were to be filed as a dependent claim on the earlier date on which the mechanical operation of the scale was nonobvious. At this earlier time, the scale-plus-labels claim would depend from the independent scale claim, and allowing the scale-plus-labels claim to issue would not deprive the public of any rights that it would otherwise possess.

[105] *See, e.g.*, *infra* text accompanying notes 154–55 (discussing a hypothetical claim to a diagram based on its content).

[106] 35 U.S.C. § 101 (2006).

conveys the specific idea (a diagram claim), and the public would not be any worse off if such a dependent claim were to issue. Regardless of the scope of the claim, the artifact is eligible for patent protection. However, if neither the fibrous structure of the paper nor the chemical composition of the ink is novel and nonobvious in relation to the prior art, then the diagram claim is not eligible for patent protection under the printed matter doctrine. Thus the identical artifact is a patent-eligible "manufacture" under § 101 if one set of prior art is presumed, but it is not patent eligible if another set of prior art is presumed. Just as with the machine-plus-label claim, the self-same artifact can be patentable subject matter when the prior art is relatively impoverished and can be unpatentable subject matter when the prior art is more developed. Because of the patentable-weight approach, the printed matter doctrine always makes patent eligibility a "relational" rather than "intrinsic" property of the claimed artifacts.[107]

Not only does the patentable-weight approach to patent eligibility counterintuitively make the status of an artifact as patentable subject matter contingent on the historical context in which an invention occurs, it also runs against the grain of the claim-as-a-whole approach to patent eligibility that predominates in most judicial applications of § 101 doctrine. Despite the lack of any direct support in the text of the Patent Act, the Supreme Court has stated repeatedly that "laws of nature, natural phenomena, and abstract ideas" are not eligible for patent protection under § 101.[108] To implement this prohibition, the Court has distinguished two types of claims implicating newly discovered "laws of nature."[109] Claims to "laws of nature" in the abstract are not patent eligible under § 101, but claims describing applications of "laws of nature" in new products and processes are patent eligible.[110] The claim-as-a-whole approach to patent eligibility is one tool that the Court has developed to distinguish abstract claims from applied ones.

For example, in *Diamond* v. *Diehr* the Court addressed "whether a process for curing synthetic rubber which includes in several of its steps the use of a mathematical formula and a programmed digital computer is patentable subject matter under 35 U.S.C. § 101."[111] The Court had already identified a mathematical formula

[107] *See supra* note 101. There is one type of claim that is per se unpatentable under the printed matter doctrine: a claim that only recites limitations describing the content of printed matter. Here, the patent applicant is by definition alleging that it is the content of the printed matter that differentiates the claimed invention from the prior art. However, the notion that a particular type of claim is per se unpatentable is different from the notion that the artifacts described by the claim are per se unpatentable.

[108] Diamond v. Diehr, 450 U.S. 175, 185 (1981); *see also* Diamond v. Chakrabarty, 447 U.S. 303, 309 (1980) (stating that "laws of nature, physical phenomena, and abstract ideas" are not patent eligible).

[109] The distinction between the categories remains unclear, so "laws of nature" is employed here as a shorthand for all of the categories.

[110] *Diehr*, 450 U.S. at 188, 191–92.

[111] *Id.* at 177.

as a "law of nature,"[112] so the question presented was whether the claim to the computer-assisted process of curing rubber that employed a mathematical formula to calculate the optimal cure time described a "law of nature" in the abstract.[113] The Court emphatically stated that the proper focus was on the nature of the claim "as a whole."[114] The claim at issue described a process of curing rubber "beginning with the loading of a mold with raw, uncured rubber and ending with the eventual opening of the press at the conclusion of the cure."[115] The curing of rubber is a traditionally patentable process, so the Court held that the claim as a whole was a patentable application of whatever "laws of nature" were implicated in the method's computer-executed steps.[116]

In *Diehr*, the Court not only used a claim-as-a-whole approach to patent eligibility but it also expressly dismissed the idea of using a patentable-weight or point-of-novelty approach.[117] The Court stated that it is impermissible to query whether the point of novelty of a claimed invention resides in a newly discovered "law of nature" and to invalidate the claim as unpatentable subject matter if it does.[118] It stated that "[i]n determining the eligibility of [a] claimed process for patent protection under § 101, . . . claims must be considered as a whole. It is inappropriate to dissect the claims into old and new elements and then to ignore the presence of the old elements in the analysis."[119]

To reinforce the need for the claim-as-a-whole approach on a pragmatic level, the Court highlighted the potential for a point-of-novelty approach, if "carried to its extreme," to undermine the patentability of the chemical and biochemical inventions that lie at the heart of traditionally patentable subject matters.[120] Because the chemical arts at a deep level are based on nothing but the "natural principles" of the periodic table of elements, the patentability of many inventions in the chemical arts would be threatened by a point-of-novelty approach carried to its extreme.[121] If the therapeutic property of a drug is a "natural principle" of a drug, then new-use claims for the drug arguably would not recite patentable subject matter under a point-of-novelty approach to patent eligibility for "natural principles."[122]

112 *Id.* at 186.
113 *See id.* at 191–92.
114 *See id.* at 192.
115 *Id.* at 184.
116 *Id.*
117 *Id.* at 188–89, 192.
118 *Id.* at 188.
119 *Id.* at 188. *But see* Parker v. Flook, 437 U.S. 584 (1978) (relying on reasoning that strongly resembles the methodology prohibited in *Diehr* to invalidate a patent claim under § 101).
120 *Diehr*, 450 U.S. at 189 n.12.
121 *See* Funk Bros. Seed Co. v. Kalo Inoculant Co., 333 U.S. 127, 135 (1948) (Frankfurter, J., concurring); Dan L. Burk, *Biotechnology and Patent Law: Fitting Innovation to the Procrustean Bed*, 17 Rutgers Computer & Tech. L.J. 1, 26–33 (1991).
122 Brief for 22 Law and Business Professors as Amici Curiae Supporting Appellants, at 17–18, *In re Bilski*, 545 F.3d 943 (Fed. Cir. 2008) (en banc) (No. 2007–1130) 2008 WL 1842281.

The claim-as-a-whole approach to patent eligibility articulated in *Diehr* has had a strong impact on the Federal Circuit. In its en banc decision in *In re Bilski*,[123] the Federal Circuit announced a new machine-or-transformation (MoT) test for patent eligibility that focuses on the tangibility of the claimed invention considered as a whole.[124] Roughly captured, the MoT test states that claims are eligible for patent protection only if they are tied to a particular machine or if they change an article into a different state or thing.[125] *Bilski* reaffirms that the printed matter doctrine is the black sheep of the doctrine of patent eligibility. It positions the MoT test as the "sole" test for patent eligibility under § 101, placing the continued vitality of the printed matter doctrine in limbo.[126] It states categorically that the claim-as-a-whole approach articulated in *Diehr* must govern all inquiries into patent eligibility, raising questions about the viability of the patentable-weight approach without which the printed matter doctrine would be unrecognizable.[127] Whether the printed matter doctrine has survived *Bilski* would seem to be an open question. If it has survived, it has done so largely because it has been swept under the rug and conveniently overlooked.

B. *Statutory Mysteries*

The Patent Act does not expressly mention either the printed matter doctrine or a restriction on the patentability of information. In part for this reason, the Federal Circuit has repeatedly noted that "[a] 'printed matter rejection' . . . stands on questionable legal and logical footing."[128]

The portion of § 101 that is understood to give rise to the doctrine of patent eligibility states that inventors may patent a "process, machine, manufacture or

[123] *In re Bilski*, 545 F.3d 943 (Fed. Cir. 2008) (en banc), *cert. granted sub nom.* Bilski v. Doll, 129 S. Ct. 2735 (2009).

[124] *Id.* at 954.

[125] *Id.* at 961–63.

[126] *Id.* at 955–56. The Federal Circuit framed its analysis in *Bilski* as a case that was about construing the word "process" in § 101. *Id.* at 949. It is therefore plausible to argue that *Bilski* does not apply to object claims describing a "machine, manufacture, or composition of matter" that are most commonly at issue in the core printed matter cases. 35 U.S.C. § 101 (2006). However, this formalistic argument is tenuous. The Supreme Court has generalized from the status of object claims under § 101 to develop rules for method claims. *See* Gottschalk v. Benson, 409 U.S. 63, 67–68 (1972). Furthermore, the printed matter doctrine applies to method claims that implicate the reading and comprehension of text by a human interpreter. King Pharms., Inc. v. Eon Labs, Inc., 593 F. Supp. 2d 501, 513–14 (E.D.N.Y. 2009).

[127] *Bilski*, 545 F.3d at 958. Despite its categorical statement, however, the Federal Circuit left open the possibility of a point-of-novelty approach coming in through the back door by noting that the machine or transformation implicated in the claim "must impose meaningful limits on the claim's scope" and "must not merely be insignificant extra-solution activity." *Id.* at 961–62.

[128] *In re* Lowry, 32 F.3d 1579, 1583 (Fed. Cir. 1994) (quoting *In re* Gulack, 703 F.2d 1381, 1385 n.5 (Fed. Cir. 1983)) (internal quotation marks omitted). The Federal Circuit in *Lowry* and *Gulack* was discussing the status of the printed matter doctrine as an artifact of § 103, but the same questions pertain to the status of the printed matter doctrine as an artifact of § 101.

composition of matter."[129] There are two interpretive techniques conventionally employed to wring congressional intent from this text, and neither supports the printed matter doctrine. First, the plain meaning of the words that mark the four categories can be dispositive. For example, the Federal Circuit has held that a claim to a "signal" not embedded in a tangible storage medium is not eligible for patent protection because the statutory category "manufacture" encompasses only tangible artifacts.[130] This statutory, plain-meaning strategy cannot support the printed matter doctrine. Not only are books articles of manufacture but the printed matter doctrine also governs the patent eligibility of information embedded on substrates such as mechanical scales (machines), toys (manufactures), or sheets of plastic (compositions of matter), all of which are clearly within the plain meanings of the statutory categories.[131] Second, the doctrine of patent eligibility has been indirectly grounded in § 101 through the Supreme Court's statement that "laws of nature, natural phenomena, and abstract ideas" are "[e]xcluded from such patent protection."[132] These three judicially crafted exclusions from patent eligibility do not support the printed matter doctrine either. The "laws of nature" and "natural phenomena" exclusions prevent patents from encompassing things that are simply discovered in nature and dusted off by humans, but not invented by humans.[133] The "content" of the information at issue in printed matter cases is about more than the discovery of natural things. It is typically about human-made inventions, such as the molecular structure of a chemical that does not exist in nature or a method of using the human-made chemical. The naturalist bias in the exclusions of "laws of nature" and "natural phenomena" from patent eligibility means that these exclusions cannot support the printed matter doctrine. The prohibition on claims to "abstract ideas" does have an intuitive resonance with the printed matter doctrine, and it comes the closest to a source of support for the doctrine.[134] However, the printed matter

[129] 35 U.S.C. § 101 (2006).

[130] *In re* Nuijten, 500 F.3d 1346 (Fed. Cir. 2007).

[131] *But see* 1 Chisum, *supra* note 2, § 1.02[4] ("Under traditional doctrine, 'printed matter' by itself did not constitute a 'manufacture.'"). In the context of the infringement provision in § 271(g), the Federal Circuit has interpreted the word "manufacture" as a verb to exclude "the production of information." Bayer AG v. Housey Pharms., Inc., 340 F.3d 1367, 1371–72 (Fed. Cir. 2003). In the context of the infringement provision in § 271(f), the Supreme Court has interpreted the word "component" to exclude software "in the abstract" because it is equivalent to the "design information presented in a blueprint." Microsoft Corp. v. AT&T Corp., 550 U.S. 437, 449–52 (2007). However, the Court also held that software recorded on a tangible medium was a "component." *Id.*

[132] Diamond v. Diehr, 450 U.S. 175, 185 (1981).

[133] *See* Parker v. Flook, 437 U.S. 584, 593 & n.15 (1978) (stating that these exclusions from patent eligibility address discoveries that simply reveal relationships that have always existed in nature). For the purposes of the argument made here, the author brackets his skepticism about the solidity of the invention/discovery dichotomy.

[134] The exclusion of abstract ideas from patent eligibility is complicated by an ambiguity in the notion of an abstract idea. In a first set of "abstract idea" cases, the prohibition on patenting abstract ideas bars the patenting of a claim that is too broad because its scope is defined only by an abstract idea. For example, in *O'Reilly* v. *Morse*, Morse's famous claim eight impermissibly sought to privatize all "use

doctrine turns its back on the claim-as-a-whole approach to patent eligibility that the Court has stated must be used to identify impermissible claims to "abstract ideas" (as well as both "laws of nature" and "natural phenomena").[135] The problem addressed by the printed matter doctrine is that the point of novelty of an invention is an abstract idea, not that the claim as a whole describes an abstract idea.

In addition to the lack of statutory support for the printed matter doctrine in the language that establishes the four categories in § 101 – or, perhaps precisely because of it – the printed matter doctrine has an unstable statutory locus. The doctrine has long had an ambiguous status as an artifact of both the novelty analysis of § 102 and the patent-eligibility analysis of § 101.[136] Today, the practice seems to be that claims describing books or computer disks that intuitively describe information recorded on a substrate per se are analyzed under § 101,[137] whereas claims describing printed matter on or in combination with conventionally patentable machines and manufactures are analyzed under either the novelty provisions in § 102 or the nonobviousness provisions in § 103.[138] The reason for this statutory schizophrenia is likely the counterintuitive result of bringing a patentable-weight approach to patent

of... electro-magnetism, however developed for marking or printing intelligible characters, signs, or letters, at any distances." 56 U.S. (15 How.) 62, 129 (1853). Every individual embodiment within Morse's claim eight is arguably tied to a tangible, nonabstract machine (overlooking ESP), but the claim attempts to impermissibly privatize an abstract idea because the outer bounds of the claim are established with reference to an abstract idea. Here, the problem is that the language used to delineate the claim relies on an abstract idea. In contrast, in a second set of cases, the abstract-ideas exclusion seems to bar the patenting of immaterial processes such as human thought. *In re* Comiskey, 554 F.3d 967, 979 (Fed. Cir. 2009) ("However, mental processes – or processes of human thinking – standing alone are not patentable even if they have practical application."). Here, the claim language may be drawn very narrowly – it may describe one very specific mental process in great detail – but the "stuff" described by the claim, namely a mental process, is simply too abstract in some way to be patented. Thus, there is an ambiguity in the notion of an abstract idea: Is the impermissible abstractness located in the describing language or in the things and actions that the language describes? This ambiguity between describing language and the "stuff" described by language has parallels in many other patent law concepts. *See, e.g.*, Collins, *supra* note 16, at 502–03 (noting that the notion of the "scope" of a claim in patent law can invoke either the meaning of the describing language – meaning-scope – or the size of the set of things that the language describes – thing-scope). The abstract-ideas exclusion has greater resonance with the printed matter doctrine when abstractness is taken as a property of the stuff described rather than a property of the describing language.

135 *See supra* notes 108–22 and accompanying text (contrasting the patentable-weight approach of the printed matter doctrine to the claim-as-a-whole approach); *cf.* Comiskey, 554 F.3d at 979 (holding that "a claim that involves both a mental process [that is, an abstract idea] and one of the other categories of statutory subject matter (i.e., a machine, manufacture, or composition) may be patentable under § 101").

136 *See, e.g.*, *In re* Sterling, 70 F.2d 910 (C.C.P.A. 1934) (finding that the same claims to printed matter were neither novel nor patentable subject matter).

137 *See, e.g.*, Examination Guidelines, *supra* note 90, at 7481.

138 *See, e.g.*, *In re* Ngai, 367 F.3d 1336 (Fed. Cir. 2004) (applying the printed matter doctrine as a part of a § 102 novelty analysis to a claim to a kit of chemicals in combination with written instructions); *In re* Gulack, 703 F.2d 1381 (Fed. Cir. 1983) (applying the printed matter doctrine as part of a § 103 nonobviousness analysis to a claim to a circular band with printed indicia). Judge Linn of the Federal Circuit has even suggested that the printed matter doctrine should be applied as part of the

eligibility to bear on machines and manufactures: It is awkward to recognize that a device is a patent-eligible "machine" when its mechanics are nonobvious but that the same device with labels is no longer a "machine" if the content of the labels is the only difference from the prior art.[139]

However, splitting the printed matter doctrine between § 101 and § 102 and 103 raises more questions than it resolves. The same counterintuitive result still exists when the patentable-weight approach to patent eligibility is brought to bear on the claims that are today analyzed under § 101 because they are intuitively viewed as describing recorded information per se. A disk with specific information recorded thereon is a statutory "manufacture" when the structure of the disk is a patentable improvement over the prior art, but it is no longer a "manufacture" when it is the content of the information that differentiates the disk from the prior art.[140] It makes no sense to shift only part of the printed matter doctrine to § 103. Furthermore, the text of § 103 – unlike the text of § 101 – expressly states that the nonobviousness analysis must be conducted by looking at "the subject matter as a whole."[141] Selectively ignoring certain limitations that differentiate a claimed invention from the prior art would therefore seem to be yet more problematic on a statutory level under § 103 than it would be under § 101. No other doctrine is administered as a hybrid of § 101 and of § § 102 and 103, so the split reinforces the impression that the printed matter doctrine is the ugly duckling of contemporary patent law.

C. *Normative Desirability*

Given the doctrinal and statutory shortcomings of the printed matter doctrine, it is unsurprising that the Federal Circuit believes that "[a] 'printed matter rejection'... stands on questionable legal and logical footing."[142] For similar reasons, commentators have questioned the doctrine's future viability.[143] What is surprising, however, is that there have been so few calls for the outright elimination of the printed matter doctrine from inventors who seek broader patent protection.[144] There

utility doctrine of § 101. *In re* Nuijten, 500 F.3d 1346, 1365–67 (Fed. Cir. 2007) (Linn, J., concurring in part and dissenting in part).

139 *See supra* notes 103–07 and accompanying text.

140 *See supra* notes 105–07 and accompanying text.

141 35 U.S.C. § 103(a) (2006).

142 *In re* Lowry, 32 F.3d 1579, 1583 (Fed. Cir. 1994) (quoting *In re* Gulack, 703 F.2d 1381, 1385 n.5 (Fed. Cir. 1983)) (internal quotation marks omitted).

143 *See, e.g.*, 1 CHISUM, *supra* note 2, § 1.02[4], at 1–26 ("A question of interest is whether and to what extent the traditional exception for printed matter will survive in view of court decisions that are critical of non-statutory exceptions to the four categories of patentable subject matter."); Dan L. Burk & Mark A. Lemley, *Policy Levers in Patent Law*, 89 VA. L. REV. 1575, 1672 (2003) ("The Federal Circuit eliminated the long-standing rule against patenting business methods in 1998, and the related 'printed matter' doctrine is on uncertain footing as well." (footnote omitted)).

144 One reason for this silence may be the relatively low economic stakes of printed matter cases involving board games and the like. *See* R. Carl Moy, *Statutory Subject Matter and Hybrid Claiming*, 17

have been vocal critics – both judicial and nonjudicial – of many other historical and contemporary limits on patent-eligible subject matter.[145] In contrast, there are no lobbyists before Congress, litigants in courtrooms, or judges at the bench arguing that the printed matter doctrine should simply be taken off the books right now.[146] The frailty of the printed matter doctrine should, in theory, make it an easy target for any inventor and patentee who wants to internalize a larger share of the welfare benefits that her invention offers to society. Yet, there is no gathering wave of sentiment against the contemporary printed matter doctrine. There is no angry mob outside of the PTO demanding that technical diagrams or e-book files be eligible for patent protection when the content of the information conveyed is useful, novel, and nonobvious.

There is a lesson to be learned from this relatively uncontroversial persistence of the core of the printed matter doctrine, despite its conceptual and statutory shortcomings. Although far from an analytical proof, the simple persistence of the printed matter doctrine strongly suggests that the doctrine restricts patentable subject matter in a manner that reflects widely shared understandings of what patent protection should be and that it rests on normative justifications that should not be lightly dismissed.[147] The fact that the Federal Circuit has marginalized the printed matter doctrine, but has not outright eliminated it, should be taken as a clue that the effect of the doctrine has significant normative value, even if that value has not yet been articulated with precision.[148] In sum, the contemporary printed matter

J. Marshall J. Computer & Info. L. 277, 279 (1998). Another reason may be that the patent ineligibility of core printed matter claims is so intuitive and self-evidently correct that inventors realize that such claims will never issue.

145 *See, e.g.*, *In re* Musgrave, 431 F.2d 882 (C.C.P.A. 1970) (criticizing and abandoning the mental steps doctrine); Donald S. Chisum, *The Patentability of Algorithms*, 47 U. Pitt. L. Rev. 959 (1986) (criticizing the exclusion of algorithms in the abstract from patent eligibility). Many amicus briefs were filed in the Supreme Court in *In re Bilski* by representatives of the software, biotech, and accounting industries suggesting that the Federal Circuit's "machine-or-transformation" test interpreted patent eligibility too narrowly. *See, e.g.*, Brief of Amicus Curiae Novartis Corp. Supporting Petitioners, Bilski v. Doll, No. 08–964 (U.S. filed Aug. 6, 2009) (arguing against restrictions on patent eligibility in biotechnology).

146 *But see* Andrew F. Knight, *A Potentially New IP: Storyline Patents*, 86 J. Pat. & Trademark Off. Soc'y 859, 863–64 (2004) (arguing that storyline patents are eligible for patent protection because the printed matter doctrine "rests on shaky legal authority and, in any event, has been whittled away to an archaic common law has-been").

147 *Cf.* Thomas F. Cotter, *A Burkean Perspective on Patent Eligibility*, 22 Berkeley Tech. L.J. 855, 858 (2007) (arguing that "some of the traditional limitations on patentable subject matter . . . may yet have much to recommend them").

148 A normative justification of what the PTO and the courts are doing when they apply the printed matter doctrine is beyond the scope of this chapter. However, the justification tracks the justification of why the knowledge conveyed by a patent disclosure must remain free for all to use *qua* knowledge, even during the term of a patent. *See infra* Part III.C (arguing that the printed matter doctrine is an implicit negative corollary of the patentee's statutory disclosure obligations).

The outcomes reached by courts in the printed matter cases can also be justified indirectly by framing the printed matter doctrine as a channeling doctrine that allocates responsibilities among doctrine displays an odd amalgam of conceptual incoherence and normative acceptance, of statutory aloofness and self-evident correctness.

To the extent that the printed matter doctrine is under any kind of attack today, the most common argument is not designed to expand patent-eligible subject matter by removing the restrictions on patent eligibility that are traditionally attributed to the printed matter doctrine. Rather, the argument is that the printed matter doctrine is the appendix of the patent regime: It is a superfluous doctrinal organ that no longer plays any role in restricting the scope of patent protection because all of the artifacts that it excludes from the patent regime would be excluded by the other, well-established validity doctrines – such as novelty,[149] nonobviousness,[150] and utility[151] – if only they were given the chance to do their jobs.[152] Whatever its merits when brought to bear on some of the other strands of the § 101 doctrine of patent eligibility, however, this appendix argument is unconvincing with respect to the printed matter doctrine. The printed matter doctrine has substantive bite. It restricts the set of novel, nonobvious, and useful artifacts of human ingenuity that are eligible for patent protection. Most importantly for the arguments presented in this chapter, it restricts the reach of patent protection into technical texts and diagrams in a manner that the other validity doctrines do not.[153]

different intellectual property regimes. *Cf.* Dastar Corp. v. Twentieth Century Fox Film Corp., 539 U.S. 23, 34 (2003) (limiting the application of the Lanham Act to avoid creating a "species of mutant copyright law"). The "essence" of copyright, "[w]hat has distinguished copyright from other forms of intellectual property, [and] what has been at its base but not at the base of others," is arguably "that the *content* of a copyrighted work has always had some nonfunctional aesthetic, informational, or entertaining qualities which are communicated to a human audience." Pamela Samuelson, *CONTU Revisited: The Case Against Copyright Protection for Computer Programs in Machine-Readable Form*, 1984 DUKE L.J. 663, 749 (1984) (emphasis in original). *But see id.* at 753 (noting that copyrights in machine-readable computer software run counter to this rule). Perhaps copyright law, including its idea/expression dichotomy, should have the sole authority to determine the public/private balance with respect to what lies at its core, namely to the "informational . . . qualities" of the "content" that a work "communicate[s] to a human audience." *Id.* at 749. For copyright law to be the final arbiter of that public/private balance, the printed matter doctrine must keep patent protection out of the mix. *Cf.* Dennis Karjala, *Distinguishing Patent and Copyright Subject Matter*, 35 CONN. L. REV. 429, 448–49 (2003) (arguing that the definition of a "useful article" in copyright law should be employed to limit the subject matter of both copyright and patent).

149 35 U.S.C. § 102 (2006).

150 *Id.* § 103.

151 *Id.* § 101.

152 For an example of this appendix argument directed at the doctrine of patent eligibility in its entirety, see Michael Risch, *Everything Is Patentable*, 75 TENN. L. REV. 591, 606–09 (2008) (articulating a "rigorous patentability" standard for patent eligibility); *see also* Burk & Lemley, *supra* note 143, at 1642–44 & n.235 (arguing that the role played by the historical § 101 case *O'Reilly* v. *Morse* is today performed by the disclosure doctrines); F. Scott Kieff, *The Case for Registering Patents and the Law and Economics of Present Patent-Obtaining Rules*, 45 B.C. L. REV. 55, 108 (2003); Kristen Osenga, *Ants, Elephant Guns, and Statutory Subject Matter*, 39 ARIZ. ST. L.J. 1087, 1088 (2007) (addressing computer software in particular).

153 With respect to patent claims describing paintings, songs, and fictional novels, the appendix argument has a greater intuitive resonance. *Cf.* Risch, *supra* note 152, at 633–35 (addressing the patentability of

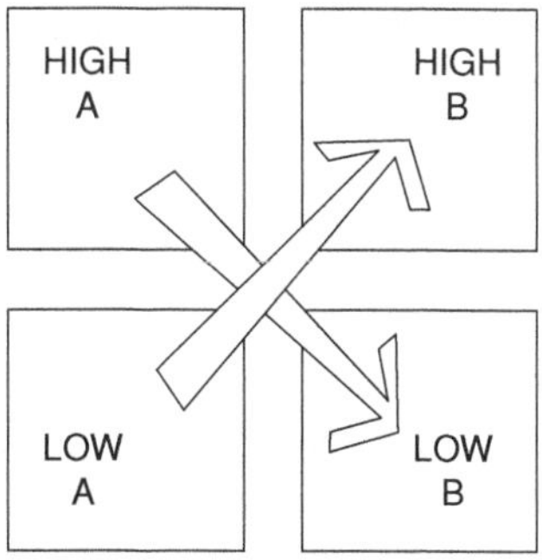

FIGURE 3.1. A hypothetical disease diagnosis chart.

For a simple example, consider a hypothetical claim to a printed diagram that enables a doctor to diagnose a disease.[154] A researcher discovers that the concentrations of two chemicals are inversely correlated in human blood: A high level of chemical A indicates that a patient has a low level of chemical B, and vice versa. This discovery paves the way for a new method of testing for a deficiency of chemical B: detecting a chemical B deficiency by correlating a high level of chemical A with a low level of B. Assume that the researcher seeks to claim something like "a device for determining the existence *vel non* of a chemical B deficiency consisting of a diagram" that encompasses the diagram illustrated in Figure 3.1. This claim describes a core example of an artifact that is not a patent-eligible invention under the printed matter doctrine: The artifact is printed matter per se, and the invention resides in the "content" of the printed matter.[155]

Absent the printed matter doctrine, however, it is difficult to identify with certainty any doctrine that would invalidate the claim to the technical diagram.[156] The claimed

"Books, Art, and Music"). It is true that the artistic creations that are the archetypes of copyrightable subject matter lack the type of technical utility possessed by the archetypes of patentable subject matter such as drugs and methods of manufacturing or using drugs. *Cf.* Karjala, *supra* note 148, at 448–49. However, in the mechanical arts, human amusement, entertainment, or aesthetic satisfaction is frequently accepted as a statutory utility. *Cf. In re* Dembiczak, 175 F.3d 994, 1002–03 (Fed. Cir. 1999) (upholding the nonobviousness of a claim to a trash bag with a jack-o'-lantern depicted thereon); *infra* note 163 (noting the inability of the utility doctrine to query whether the advance over the prior art is statutorily useful). It is therefore unclear why the amusement provided by a painting to its viewer would not be a statutory utility too.

154 In this hypothetical, the discovery is derived from *Lab. Corp. of Am. Holdings* v. *Metabolite Labs., Inc.*, 548 U.S. 124, 125–26 (2006) (Breyer, J., dissenting from the dismissal of the writ of certiorari as improvidently granted); *cf. supra* text accompanying notes 30–35 (discussing the same discovery). However, there was no claim to a printed diagram at issue in *Laboratory Corp.*

155 *See supra* note 39 and accompanying text (defining the printed matter doctrine).

156 The exercise of guessing what a court without recourse to the printed matter doctrine would do if faced with a diagram claim should be taken with a grain of salt. Because there is a widespread consensus that printed diagrams should not be eligible for patent protection, *see supra* text accompanying notes 145–46, courts would in all likelihood contort some doctrine – any doctrine, if necessary – to deny patent protection to printed diagrams. The point made in the following text is only that there is nothing in

diagrams are novel based purely on their intrinsic structural properties, because nobody had any motivation to make the claimed combination of text, boxes, and arrows before the researcher arrived at her discovery.[157] Furthermore, the claimed diagrams are nonobvious if their content is nonobvious. They produce an unexpected result: They convey unexpected information to a reader.[158] Finally, the invention also has utility of the kind required by the patent statutes.[159] Utility cases such as *Brenner* v. *Manson*[160] and *In re Fischer*[161] forbid patent applicants from patenting a new chemical before there is a believable guess about a practical and specific use for the chemical.[162] The diagram suffers from no such uncertainty: It is useful because it can help a doctor diagnose a specified disease in a particular patient in a more reliable manner than relying on memory alone would produce.[163]

In sum, the printed matter doctrine is not superfluous. If the artifacts that it excludes from patent protection are to remain beyond the reach of the patent regime, legislative or judicial actors must actively craft a patent doctrine to exclude them. No matter how counterintuitive the notion of a patent regime in which printed diagrams are patentable might be, there is nothing "natural" or inevitable about the

the internal logic of the validity doctrines that precludes the patenting of a printed diagram. A printed diagram should present an easy case of something that cannot be patented, but – absent the printed matter doctrine in some form – the case is an awkward one.

157 Novelty would be practically assured if the full names of the chemicals were to be printed on the diagram.

158 *See In re* O'Farrell, 853 F.2d 894, 903–04 (1988) (noting the importance of unexpected results in the nonobviousness analysis).

159 Richard Gruner has argued that artifacts that are not patentable under the printed matter doctrine lack statutory utility: "[W]here new content is recorded in printed matter, no patentable invention is created because the . . . utility of the newly created printed matter rest[s] in features other than the structure or functional attributes of the entity created." Richard S. Gruner, *Intangible Inventions: Patentable Subject Matter for an Information Age*, 35 Loy. L.A. L. Rev. 225, 404 (2001); *cf. In re* Nuijten, 500 F.3d 1346, 1365–67 (Fed. Cir. 2007) (Linn, J., concurring in part and dissenting in part) (suggesting that the printed matter doctrine should be a part of the utility doctrine). This argument misses the mark. The utility of a printed diagram does reside in part in its structural and functional features: The structure of a printed diagram allows an interpreter to find it meaningful, and the function of a printed diagram is to convey information to an interpreter. Furthermore, the utility of many useful artifacts rests in part in features other than their intrinsic properties. For example, the utility of a DNA molecule rests in large part in the structural and functional features of the cellular machinery of transcription and translation. *See supra* note 43 and accompanying text.

160 383 U.S. 519 (1966).

161 421 F.3d 1365 (Fed. Cir. 2005).

162 *Brenner*, 383 U.S. at 533–36; *Fischer*, 421 F.3d at 1369–78.

163 The utility doctrine also cannot fill the role played by the printed matter doctrine because there is no precedent in the utility doctrine for the patentable-weight analysis that lies at the heart of the printed matter doctrine. *See supra* notes 94–98 and accompanying text. A kit of chemicals plus a sheet of written instructions clearly has statutory utility because the chemicals are useful. However, due to the patentable-weight analysis of the printed matter doctrine, the combination is not patentable if the difference between the prior art and the claimed invention resides in the "content" of the information conveyed by the printed matter. *In re* Ngai, 367 F.3d 1336, 1339 (Fed. Cir. 2004) (invalidating a claim to a kit of chemicals plus instructions on how to use them under the printed matter doctrine when the advance over the prior art resided in the instructions).

effects of the printed matter doctrine.[164] The effects of the printed matter doctrine are so familiar and intuitive that it may be tempting to take the doctrine for granted. However, the knowledge that constitutes the public domain of patent disclosure will be free only if courts take the active step of enforcing the printed matter doctrine.[165]

II. SEMIOTICS 101

This part offers an introductory course in "Semiotics 101."[166] Part II.A explores the triadic model of the sign, commonly associated with Charles Sanders Peirce. Part II.B presents Peirce's threefold taxonomy of signs. Part II.C emphasizes a common restriction on the proper domain of semiotic analysis that places the human mind at the center of semiotic inquiry.

A. *Peirce's Triadic Sign*

Semiotics is the study of signs, and signs are entities that involve something standing for something else to somebody.[167] To conceptualize the operation of a sign, Peirce and his followers posit a triadic model of the sign.[168] They argue that every sign

[164] *But cf.* R. Polk Wagner, *Information Wants to Be Free: Intellectual Property and the Mythologies of Control*, 103 COLUM. L. REV. 995, 1005–09 (2003) (arguing that the knowledge spillovers of intellectual property protection are inevitable).

[165] *See infra* Part III.C (arguing that printed matter doctrine is an implicit negative corollary of a patentee's disclosure obligations).

[166] Semiotics is a sprawling discipline with many competing conceptual frameworks. This part does not attempt a comprehensive introduction to semiotics. *See, e.g.*, WINFRIED NÖTH, HANDBOOK OF SEMIOTICS (1990). Nor does it attempt a neutral or objective introduction comprised of the most commonly discussed or widely shared principles in the discipline. *See, e.g.*, DANIEL CHANDLER, SEMIOTICS: THE BASICS (2002). It does not purport to exhaust the utility of semiotics as a tool to understand legal processes. *See, e.g.*, Susan W. Tiefenbrun, *Legal Semiotics*, 5 CARDOZO ARTS & ENT. L.J. 89, 96 (1986) (proposing a definition of "legal semiotics"). This part only presents "Semiotics 101" in a very narrow sense with the pun fully intended: It is a strategically chosen introduction to the basic principles of semiotics (a 101-level course) that the author believes to be the most fruitful background to lead to an explanation of how a semiotic framework can structure the printed matter doctrine (a § 101 doctrine).

[167] CHANDLER, *supra* note 166, at 13 ("Anything can be a sign as long as someone interprets it as 'signifying' something – referring to or *standing for* something other than itself."); UMBERTO ECO, A THEORY OF SEMIOTICS 17 (1976) ("[A] sign [is] *everything* that, on the grounds of a previously established social convention, can be taken as *something standing for something else*."); CHARLES W. MORRIS, FOUNDATIONS OF THE THEORY OF SIGNS 3 (1938) ("[A] sign refers to something for someone."); CHARLES SANDERS PEIRCE, COLLECTED PAPERS § 2.228 ("A sign . . . is something which stands to somebody for something in some respect or capacity.").

[168] *Cf. infra* note 177 (presenting the competing dyadic model of the sign). Working in the late 1800s and into the early 1900s, Peirce originated discussion of the triadic model in modern semiotics, but triadic models of the sign can be traced back to antiquity. *See* W.C. Watt, *Semiotics*, § 1, *in* 8 ROUTLEDGE ENCYCLOPEDIA OF PHILOSOPHY 676 (Edward Craig ed., 1998). Scholars who have adopted a triadic model of the sign have built on Peirce's work in divergent ways, so there is considerable disagreement on the substantive "details of the triadic analysis even among those who accept that all

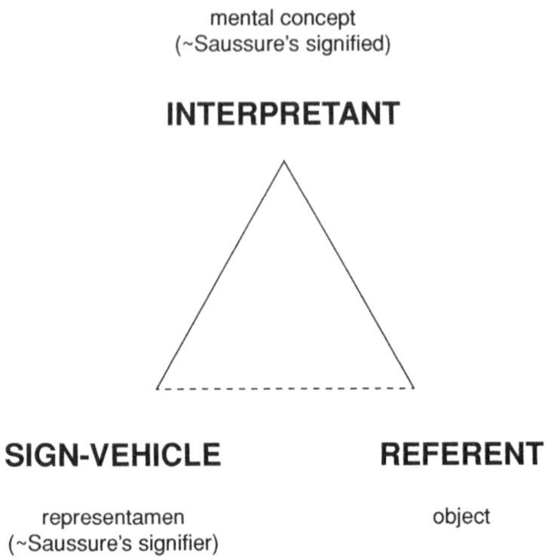

FIGURE 3.2. The Peircean sign.

involves three distinct components: a *sign-vehicle*, an *interpretant*, and a *referent*.[169] The Peircean sign is commonly depicted as a triangle, as in Figure 3.2.[170]

The *sign-vehicle* is the perceptible form of the sign; it is the physical artifact that an interpreter perceives.[171] The particular combination of curves that make up the letter "S" and the formal properties of the dots, dashes, and blank spaces that make up a message transmitted in Morse code are both sign-vehicles, as are the undulating sound waves that convey the sound of the word "dog." The *interpretant* is roughly the concept that the sign-vehicle invokes in the mind of a person for whom the sign

three components . . . must be taken into account." 1 JOHN LYONS, SEMANTICS 99 (1977). This chapter culls details from Peirce and his interpreters, sacrificing historical accuracy and fine distinctions for brevity and readability when the lost nuances are not relevant to the semiotic framework for patent eligibility.

169 Peirce's preferred nomenclature was the *representamen*, the *interpretant*, and the *object*. *See* PEIRCE, *supra* note 167, § 2.228. The terms used in the text of this chapter are derived from NÖTH, *supra* note 166, at 89, and they are chosen for their relatively intuitive qualities. (Quotes directly from Peirce's writings in the footnotes, however, use the Peircean terminology.) Departure from Peirce's terminology is par for the course. *See* LYONS, *supra* note 168, at 95 (discussing variations in the terminology used to discuss the triadic model of the sign).

170 *See, e.g.*, C.K. OGDEN & I.A. RICHARDS, THE MEANING OF MEANING 11 (10th ed. 1949); CHANDLER, *supra* note 166, at 30.

171 The sign-vehicle corresponds to the *signifier* in Saussure's dyadic model of the sign. *See infra* note 177. Peirce emphasized that sign-vehicles are both immaterial types and material tokens of those types. *Cf.* PEIRCE, *supra* note 167, § 2.246 (discussing replicas, sinsigns, and legisigns). Because only tokens of signs can be made, used, or sold by people, and can lead to the infringement of patent claims, this chapter treats the sign-vehicle as a material entity. In other words, it discusses semiotics in the context of what Saussure referred to as *parole* (an instance of speech) rather than *langue* (the system of speech). FERDINAND DE SAUSSURE, COURSE IN GENERAL LINGUISTICS 13 (Charles Bally & Albert Sechehaye eds., Roy Harris trans., Duckworth 1983) (1916).

is meaningful.[172] The *referent* of a sign is the thing in the world that is described, indicated, or referred to by a sign.[173] Both interpretants and referents are within the ambit of the general term *semiotic meaning* as employed in this chapter.[174] For precision, a sign-vehicle is described as *signifying* its interpretant and *referring to* its referent.

Peirce's sign "involves a rejection of the equation of 'content' and meaning; the meaning of a [sign-vehicle] is not contained within it, but arises in its interpretation" by an interpreter in the form of an interpretant.[175] In other words, the sign-vehicle is not the sign, despite the commonplace nature of the language in which the material sign-vehicle is employed as a synecdoche for an entire sign. Stop-signs-as-artifacts – the physical, red, octagonal things located at intersections – are not signs in and of themselves. They are sign-vehicles and therefore only components of signs. The sign is the combination of the perceived thing (the sign-vehicle), the mental concept that the sign triggers in the mind of an interpreter (the interpretant), and the things or events in the world to which the sign refers (the referents).[176] The sign-vehicle is a

[172] Peirce, *supra* note 167, § 3.72 ("cognition produced in the mind"); *see also* Lyons, *supra* note 168, at 102 (defining the interpretant as "the mental effect produced by the sign" or "the concept associated with the sign in the triangle of signification"). The interpretant corresponds to the *signified* in Saussure's dyadic model of the sign. *See infra* note 177. The notion that a sign involves a self-contained concept is a misleading simplification of Peirce's interpretant. Peirce considered the interpretant to be a sign unto itself that can only be understood in terms of further interpretants and thus further signs, leading to a process of "unlimited semiosis." Chandler, *supra* note 166, at 31–33; *cf.* Saussure, *supra* note 171, at 110–20 (implying that signifieds are structural entities defined only by their *value* – that is, by their relations to other signifieds).

[173] *See infra* note 176 (discussing the nature of the referent).

[174] Peirce's model demonstrates that signs are wound up with two very different types of meaning. *Sense* is an ideational or mentalistic phenomenon and is lodged in the interpretant, whereas *reference* deals with the worldly things implicated in referents. For a detailed presentation of the distinction between sense and reference, as well as an argument about its relevance in the context of claim construction, see Collins, *supra* note 16, at 536–53.

[175] Chandler, *supra* note 166, at 32.

[176] The presence of the referent in Peirce's model of the sign does not always tie a sign directly to a material thing, an individual thing, or even a thing that exists in the actual world. *See* Chandler, *supra* note 166, at 33 (noting that "Peirce's [referent] is not confined to physical things and [that] it can include abstract concepts and fictional entities"); Ogden & Richards, *supra* note 170, at 9 n.1 (noting that the referent should not be "restricted to material substances"). A sign may indicate a particular thing in the world as its referent – that is, the word "Fido" may refer to my dog. Alternatively, a sign may pick out a class of referents in the world – that is, the word "dog" may refer not to my dog but to the species in general. Peirce, *supra* note 167, § 2.232 ("The Objects [of a sign] may each be a single known existing thing . . . or a collection of such things. . . ."). The referent may be perceptible in the actual world, but, alternatively, it may be simply imaginable, because it may be a class without any actual individuals contained within it. Morris, *supra* note 167, at 5 ("No contradiction arises in saying that every sign has [a referent] but not every sign refers to an actual existent. . . . [A referent] is not a thing, but a kind of object or a class of objects – and a class may have many members, or one member, or no members. . . . This distinction makes explicable the fact that one may reach into the icebox for an apple that is not there. . . ."); Peirce, *supra* note 167, § 2.232 ("The Objects [of a sign] may each be a . . . thing believed formerly to have existed or expected to exist. . . ."). Even attributes or qualities of things – such as the property *blackness* – can be the referents of a sign, as can events –

particularly useful term for the perceived component of the sign precisely because it wears on its sleeve a warning against the misleading synecdoche.[177]

B. *Peirce's Taxonomy of Signs*

Peirce was enamored with taxonomies of the sign, and the most famous of his taxonomies is his simple tripartite schema of *symbols*, *icons*, and *indices*.[178] Importantly, there is no one-to-one correspondence between sign-vehicles, interpretants, and referents on the one hand and symbols, icons, and indices on the other. Peirce's taxonomy classifies relationships between the sign's components.[179]

1. Symbols

Morse code, traffic lights, and most words, both written and spoken, are meaningful because they function as symbols. A sign is a symbol when the relationship between

such as "a *killing*." *Id.* § 1.551 (property); *id.* § 2.230 (event); *id.* § 2.232 ("a known quality or relation or fact"). Thus, Peirce technically referred to signs as standing not for objects themselves, but as standing for referents in some respects and identified those respects as the *ground* of the representamen. *Id.* § 2.228 ("The sign stands for something, its *object*. It stands for that object, not in all respects, but in reference to a sort of idea, which I have sometimes called the *ground* of the representamen." (emphasis in original)).

[177] Despite the wide-ranging nature of the referent, *see supra* note 176 and accompanying text, the presence of the referent in the triadic model of the sign ties the sign to the world in a way that would not be possible in its absence. In contrast, an alternative dyadic model of the sign popularized by Saussure "brackets the referent." Chandler, *supra* note 166, at 16. *See generally* Saussure, *supra* note 171 (postulating a dyadic model of the sign). For Saussure, the sign is the combination of a *signifier* (the analog of the sign-vehicle) and a *signified* (the analog of the interpretant), and the meaning of a signified is determined not by reference to worldly things but only in relation to other mental signifieds. Chandler, *supra* note 166, at 18–22. Saussure's model is conspicuous in its absolute neglect of the things for which signs stand, dealing with the signified exclusively as "a concept in the mind – not a thing but a notion of a thing." *Id.* at 16; *see also* Ogden & Richards, *supra* note 170, at 6 (criticizing Saussure for "neglecting entirely the things for which signs stand"). Thus, whereas both Saussurian and Peircean models of the sign accommodate meaning-as-sense, only the Peircean model accommodates meaning-as-reference. Chandler, *supra* note 166, at 33–34; *cf. supra* note 174 (discussing the distinction between sense and reference).

This chapter adopts the triadic model of the sign for three reasons. First, new signs often come into being when researchers discover new facts or formulate new hypotheses about the nature of the actual world, and it is thus useful to be able to talk about the things in the world to which a sign refers when discussing signs as inventions. Second, the referent is a useful descriptive tool for portraying what the Federal Circuit has done in *Bilski*: Data are meaningful because they are sign-vehicles, and *Bilski* makes the tangibility of the sign's referent dispositive of patentability. *See infra* notes 317–20 and accompanying text. Third, computer models are meaningful because they are either icons or indices. *See infra* notes 297–303 and accompanying text. It is difficult to discuss these types of signs using a dyadic model of the sign because they implicate the referent by definition. *See infra* notes 186–92 and accompanying text.

[178] *See, e.g.*, Peirce, *supra* note 167, §§ 2.304, 5.484. The tripartite schema is Peirce's simplest taxonomy, but not his only one. *See* Nöth, *supra* note 166, at 44 (noting that Peirce postulated 59,049 classes of signs); *id.* at 45 (discussing a ten-category classification).

[179] Terence Hawkes, Structuralism and Semiotics 129 (1977).

the sign-vehicle and the referent is ontologically arbitrary.[180] "[T]here is nothing 'treeish' about the word 'tree.'"[181] The word "tree" signifies the concept TREE in the mind of an interpreter and refers to the pulpy, leafy things swaying outside of my window only because of an arbitrary convention known to the interpreter. It is an historical accident that the English word "tree" signifies the concept TREE. The concept TREE could just as well be conveyed by the sign-vehicle "soup" or "urgh" in English, and it is conveyed by other signifiers in other languages, such as "arbre" in French.[182] A symbol is therefore a sign "whose special significance or fitness to represent just what it does represent lies in nothing but the very fact of there being a habit, disposition, or other effective general rule that it will be so interpreted."[183]

2. Icons

Icons involve sign-vehicles that are perceived by an interpreter to have qualities that resemble or imitate their referents.[184] The resemblance is often in visual perception (a stick figure standing for a person or a scale model representing a building) or sound (onomatopoetic spoken words). The resemblance can also exist in terms of the mapping of internal structural or functional relations among parts, making a diagram an icon.[185] Thus, for Peirce, icons include "every diagram, even although there be no sensuous resemblance between it and its [referent], but only an analogy between the relations of the parts of each."[186] Peirce frequently noted the utility of diagrams as aids in the reasoning process.[187]

3. Indices

The index is the least familiar of Peirce's three types of signs. As used in this chapter, the index is a sign in which the sign-vehicle is directly connected in some nomic

[180] LYONS, *supra* note 168, at 101 (discussing Saussure's dyadic model of the sign that accommodates only Peircean symbols).

[181] CHANDLER, *supra* note 166, at 22.

[182] LYONS, *supra* note 168, at 100–01.

[183] PEIRCE, *supra* note 167, § 2.299; *see also id.* §§ 2.292, 2.299, 4.447 & 4.531.

[184] *Id.* § 2.299 ("[A] quality that [an icon's representamen] has *qua* thing renders it fit to be a representamen [of an icon]."); *id.* ("A sign may be *iconic*, that is, may represent its object mainly by similarity."). Iconicity is a scalar variable, because all icons have some conventional attributes not based on resemblance. CHANDLER, *supra* note 166, at 40–41.

[185] PEIRCE, *supra* note 167, § 4.447 ("A geometrical diagram is a good example of an icon.").

[186] *Id.* § 2.279; *id.* § 2.282 ("Many diagrams resemble their objects not at all in looks; it is only in respect to the relations of their parts that their likeness consists.").

[187] *Id.* § 4.531 ("Icons are especially requisite for reasoning. A Diagram is mainly an Icon, and an Icon of intelligible relations."); *id.* § 4.447 ("A geometrical diagram is a good example of an icon. . . . [I]t is of the utmost value for enabling its interpreter to study what would be the character of such an object in the case any such did exist.").

way to the referent, such as through a natural law or an engineered coupling that generates spatial co-occurrence, temporal sequence, or cause and effect.[188] The shadow on a properly constructed sundial functions as an index because it indicates the time of day: The position of the shadow on the slab (the sign-vehicle) refers to the time of day (the referent) and signifies the concept TIME OF DAY (the interpretant) in the mind of a person who is looking at the sundial.[189] When the relevant nomic connection is known to an interpreter, smoke can function as an index of fire, thunder as an index of lightning, a medical symptom as an index of a disease, the position of a wind vane as an index of the direction in which the wind is blowing, and the level of mercury in a thermometer as an index of the temperature at that location.[190]

C. *The Lower Threshold of Semiotic Inquiry: Causation Versus Signification*

There is no universally agreed-on limit to the proper domain of semiotic inquiry. How many of the meaningful phenomena in the world are meaningful because they function as signs, and how many are meaningful for other reasons? On what Umberto Eco has called the "upper threshold" on the complexity of the phenomena within the "semiotic field," there is rarely any limit at all: Semioticians routinely treat all human endeavors, whether cultural or other, as their sandbox and examine how signs construct the social reality with which we engage.[191] However, there is more disagreement on what Eco calls the "lower threshold."[192] Following Eco, this

[188] Elizabeth W. Bruss, *Peirce and Jakobson on the Nature of the Sign*, *in* THE SIGN: SEMIOTICS AROUND THE WORLD 81, 88 (Richard W. Bailey, Ladislave Matejka & Peter Steiner eds., 1978). Bruss describes indexicality as "a relationship rather than a quality. Hence the signifier need have no particular properties of its own, only a demonstrable connection to something else. The most important of these connections are spatial co-occurrence, temporal sequence, and cause and effect." *Id.* Peirce distinguished between "genuine" and "degenerate" indices. PEIRCE, *supra* note 167, § 5.74. The hygrometer is a genuine index. Through "[i]ts connection with the weather" it "actually conveys information." *Id.* "[O]n the other hand any mere land-mark by which a particular thing may be recognized because it is as a matter of fact associated with that thing, a proper name without signification, a pointing finger, is a degenerate index." *Id.* This chapter addresses only genuine indices.

[189] *Id.* § 2.285; *cf. id.* § 2.286 (noting that a barometer is an index of the likelihood of rain and that a weathercock is an index of the direction of the wind).

[190] CHANDLER, *supra* note 166, at 33 (offering these examples among others).

[191] ECO, *supra* note 167, at 21. Signs are widely recognized as constructing reality and mediating human experience, but the precise role that signs play in constructing reality is hotly debated. A strong stance is that signs construct reality per se because "there is no external reality beyond sign systems," whereas a more tempered stance suggests that signs construct the reality that we experience and that "studying semiotics can assist us to become more aware of the mediating role of signs and of the roles played by ourselves and others in constructing social realities." CHANDLER, *supra* note 166, at 10–11. Given that patent law and discussions of technological progress traffic in concepts such as the "laws of nature" that are discovered and put to work by inventors, the semiotic analysis of patent law presented here takes the conservative approach and adopts the moderate stance.

[192] ECO, *supra* note 167, at 19–21.

chapter erects a relatively high hurdle that must be surmounted to demonstrate the existence of a sign and the presence of a semiotic meaning.[193]

To understand what is at stake in Eco's delineation of the lower threshold of semiotic inquiry, consider two things that can be described as "meaningful" in a colloquial manner. The first is the stop sign discussed earlier – a clear example of a sign that is meaningful to the mind of a human interpreter.[194] The second is chemical X, a chemical that a bacterium secretes when it is unable to find food and that slows down certain metabolic functions of other bacteria that encounter it. (The evolutionary benefit of the secretion of chemical X is that bacteria conserve energy in a nutrient-poor environment.) In a colloquial sense, it is not jarring to say that chemical X is "meaningful" because of the behavior that the bacterium exhibits when it encounters chemical X. Chemical X can be described as conveying a message that is interpreted by the bacterium to "mean" something along the lines of "time to slow down certain metabolic functions." Although both a stop sign and a molecule of chemical X can be described as meaningful, the nature of the meaning that a stop sign has to a driver and the nature of the "meaning" that chemical X has to the bacteria are radically different. Chemical X is "meaningful" to the bacterium only because it triggers a metabolic reaction in the bacterium. The laws of physics on a molecular scale fully explain the nature of the "meaning" that chemical X has to the bacterium as an interpreter. The three-dimensional shape of chemical X and the biochemical properties of the bacterium's receptors and other metabolic pathways fully determine the "meaning" of chemical X – that is, the bacterium's behavior that constitutes the reaction to the presence of chemical X. In contrast, the behavior that the driver displays in response to the stop sign does not exhaust the meaning of the stop sign to the driver. In fact, the driver may comprehend the meaning of a stop sign and yet may display no extroverted behavior at all. The stop sign has meaning to the driver because of the mental state that it triggers in the driver's mind, not because of any action that it causes the driver to take.

Some definitions of the proper domain of semiotics encompass chemical X and describe the meaning that chemical X has to the bacterium as a semiotic phenomenon.[195] Eco, however, defines semiotics more restrictively. He takes the

[193] The embrace of the Peircean triadic sign, rather than the Saussurian dyadic sign, means that this chapter already exceeds one common boundary for semiotic inquiry on the lower threshold. *Cf. supra* note 177 (discussing Saussure's dyadic sign). Saussure focused on the study of "the sign . . . as a communicative device taking place between two human beings intentionally aiming to communicate or to express something." Eco, *supra* note 167, at 15. In contrast, Peirce's definition of the sign "does not demand, as part of a sign's definition, the qualities of being intentionally emitted and artificially produced." *Id.* at 15. As a consequence, Peircean semiotics readily accommodates the study of both natural phenomena and human behavior not intentionally emitted by its sender as signs, whereas Saussurian semiotics does not. *See id.* at 14–17.

[194] *See supra* notes 175–76 and accompanying text. The technical diagram discussed earlier is also a good example. *See supra* text accompanying note 154.

[195] The field of *endosemiotics*, or signaling between microbiota, defines the semiotic field in this more inclusive manner. Watt, *supra* note 168, at 677 (describing a chemical as conveying the semiotic

distinction between what a stop sign means to a driver and what chemical X "means" to a bacterium to be the distinction that defines the lower threshold of semiotics. Chemical X is not a sign simply because it causally triggers a behavior in the interpreter. In Eco's terminology, things that are "meaningful" insofar as they cause specified behaviors are *stimuli* or *signals*, not sign-vehicles.[196] Defined in the negative, a sign-vehicle is an entity that acquires meaning through a mechanism other than through deterministic cause and effect. It is "a physical phenomenon which provokes reactions in mechanisms and organisms, *without being the cause of these reactions*."[197] The physical reactions provoked in interpreters by signs – to the extent that there are any extroverted reactions at all by the interpreters – are mediated by minds and mental states. In a positive manner, Eco defines semiotics to involve only the study of things that stand for other things by *social convention*.[198] The key concept is that, simply through a social agreement, the semiotic meaning of the stop sign can change. In contrast, the effect of chemical X on the organism cannot change without a change in the chemical composition of the organism. The behavioral response is hardwired into the bacterium. Eco's paradigm examples of interpretants are mental phenomena.[199] Semiotic meaning is a phenomenon that occurs largely, if not solely, when there is a mind in the picture. Minds can employ social conventions to allow one thing to stand for or represent another thing, but it is difficult to comprehend how something that does not qualify as a mind would achieve this end.[200]

meaning that "there is a dearth of food hereabouts" to a bacterium). *See generally* THOMAS A. SEBEOK, THE SIGN AND ITS MASTERS (1979) (developing a theory of endosemiotics).

[196] ECO, *supra* note 167, at 16, 19.

[197] *See* Roscislaw Pazukhin, *The Concept of the Signal, in* 16 LINGUA POSNANIENSIS 25, 41 (1972) (defining the term "signal" but employing the same concept that this chapter calls a sign) (emphasis added); *see also* NÖTH, *supra* note 166, at 112.

[198] *See* ECO, *supra* note 167, at 16, 19 (asserting that "everything can be understood as a sign if and only if there exists a convention which allows it to stand for something else" and that "behavioral responses [that] are not elicited by convention . . . *cannot* be regarded as signs" (emphasis in original)).

[199] *Id.* (treating "the human addressee [as] the methodological . . . guarantee of the existence of signification").

[200] The mind-centric school of semiotics has a long history. Augustine defined a sign as "a thing which, over and above the impression it makes on the senses, causes something else to come into the mind as a consequence of itself." Watt, *supra* note 168, § 1, at 676. Although Eco does not make this connection, the presence of a mind can be identified through the concept of *intentionality* that is a staple in the intellectual diet of philosophers of the mind. Intentionality is the property of "aboutness" that many mental states possess and that signs are understood to possess in a manner that is derivative of those mental states. *See* Daniel C. Dennett & John C. Haugeland, *Intentionality, in* OXFORD COMPANION TO THE MIND 383–86 (1987); JOHN HAUGELAND, HAVING THOUGHT: ESSAYS IN THE METAPHYSICS OF MIND 127–70 (1998). However, an analytical definition of a mind is not critical for the day-to-day operation of a patent regime that adopts a semiotic framework. There is an intuitive difference between minds on the one hand and the mechanical and biological things on the other that will prove dispositive in the vast majority of patent cases. A small set of cases involving claims to zoosemiotics (the study of animals' use of signs), reflexive reactions by humans, and artificial intelligences yet to be defined will prove to be the exceptions to this rule.

Importantly, the world is not neatly divided into the mutually exclusive categories of artifacts that function as sign-vehicles on the one hand and artifacts that function as stimuli and signals on the other. In the most interesting cases of overlap, an article can come to signify to an interpreting mind the very behavior that it already causes an interpreter to perform. Things that are already signals and stimuli can become sign-vehicles as well, and they can support semiotic meanings once a social convention and a mind come into play. Chemical X can be a stimulus that *causally triggers* a reaction in a bacteria and a sign-vehicle that both *signifies* the concept of that behavior in the mind of a microbiologist and *refers to* the worldly behavior itself.

The status of an artifact as both a stimulus and a sign-vehicle can often be traced to the fact that the type of sign at issue is an index, rather than an icon or a symbol. In an index, the sign-vehicle is nomically linked to the referent.[201] Chemical X is the sign-vehicle of an index because its presence in a culture of bacteria is linked to slower metabolic processes in the bacteria as cause is nomically linked to effect. However, it is critical to keep the status of chemical X as a stimulus and the status of chemical X as an index distinct. Causation and signification cannot be collapsed into a single process. Chemical X must function as a stimulus to give rise to indexical meaning,[202] but it may function as a stimulus without giving rise to indexical meaning. Indexical meaning arises only when humans come to understand the cause-and-effect relationship between chemical X and the bacteria's behavior and establish a social convention based on it.[203] Chemical X has been a stimulus that causes a bacterium to slow down its metabolism ever since natural selection chose bacteria that responded to chemical X in this fashion. However, chemical X has only functioned as a sign-vehicle and referred to the slowing down of the bacteria's metabolic functions since the date on which a biologist discovered the causal relationship and communicated it to others. Only at this point is "this relationship . . . made conventional" and the "*semiotic convention* . . . established."[204] Thus, according to Eco, "[t]here is a sign every time a human group decides to use and to recognize something as the vehicle of something else," even if that something caused the something else to actually occur before the human group established its convention.[205] Chemical X takes on a semiotic meaning as an index only when, to a human observer, chemical X (sign-vehicle) refers to the agent causing slowing down

[201] *See infra* Part II.B.3.

[202] Or, at least, it must be correlated to the slowing down of the bacteria's metabolism in some way, even if the nomic link is not a direct relationship of cause and effect. *See supra* text accompanying note 188 (noting that nomic, correlative covariation can also lay the foundation for an index).

[203] *Cf.* Peirce, *supra* note 167, § 2.299 ("The [sign-vehicle of the] index is physically connected with its object; they make an organic pair, but the interpreting mind has nothing to do with this connection, *except remarking it, after it is established.*" (emphasis added) (footnote omitted)).

[204] Eco, *supra* note 167, at 17 (emphasis in original). To differentiate the conventional relationships that are semiotic from the nonconventional relationships that are not, Eco coins a distinction between *codes* and *s-codes*. *Id.* at 36–38 (emphasis added).

[205] *Id.* at 17.

of the bacteria (referent) and signifies the mental concept BACTERIAL METABOLISM IS SLOWING DOWN (interpretant).

The importance of maintaining a distinction between the indexical meaning of a thing functioning as a sign-vehicle and the nonsemiotic "meaning" of the same thing functioning as a stimulus can also be seen in the ability of the two types of meaning to change independently. As described by a scholar who has adopted a broader definition of the semiotic field,

> [w]hat Eco describes is . . . the shift from natural semiosis to its cultural interpretation, which is a shift between two levels of semiosis. While events of natural semiosis remain unaffected by cultural conventions, their interpretation changes with time and culture. Even that mode of interpretation which comes closest to reality of the facts of natural semiosis, namely, scientific explanation, is still affected by culture, as the changes in the world models of physics show. In archaic times, for example, lightning was once understood as the gesture of a supernatural being. Modern meteorology explains it as an electrical phenomenon.[206]

The semiotic meaning of chemical X may change over time, even if the physiological effect that it causally triggers in a bacterium remains unchanged. For example, assume that future scientists discover that the slowing down of the metabolic processes of the bacteria leads to a spike in the concentration of chemical Y, the nutrient on which bacteria feed and that is going uneaten. If high concentrations of chemical Y are dangerous for human health, then the high concentration of chemical X that previously signified BACTERIAL METABOLISM IS SLOWING DOWN now signifies LOCATION UNFIT FOR HUMAN HABITATION as well. Although the underlying "natural phenomena" and "laws of nature" that are wound up in the cause-and-effect relationships remain unchanged, the social conventions that layer semiotic meanings on top of them are human-made constructs that can shift and evolve with some degree of independence.

III. RECONCEPTUALIZING THE CORE PRINTED MATTER CASES

Limiting its scope to the core printed matter cases – that is, the cases in which the inventions are intuitively identified as information recorded on a substrate and the potential relevance of the contemporary printed matter doctrine is already clear – this part demonstrates that the printed matter doctrine is in its effect, if not its rhetoric, already sensitive to semiotic principles. Part III.A articulates the sign doctrine by reinterpreting the printed matter doctrine in semiotic terms, and it emphasizes that the job that the printed matter doctrine is tasked to perform is to limit the incursion of patent protection into the representational processes of the human mind. Part III.B illustrates that the sign doctrine and its semiotic framework resolve many of the

[206] NÖTH, *supra* note 166, at 213–14.

incoherencies of the contemporary, information-centric printed matter doctrine. Part III.C argues that semiotic reasoning points the way to a firm grounding for the printed matter doctrine in the Patent Act. Part III.D demonstrates that the patentable-weight approach to patent eligibility should be understood as a feature, not a bug, of the printed matter doctrine when it is reinterpreted as the sign doctrine and understood to achieve semiotically motivated ends.

A. *The Sign Doctrine: From Information and Content to Signs and Interpretants*

The idea that the core printed matter cases involve signs is not a stretch. Printed matter, such as a diagram for diagnosing a chemical B deficiency discussed earlier,[207] is clearly meaningful, and the components of Peirce's triadic sign can be readily identified.[208] The physical printed matter itself – the formal patterns of markings on the page perceived by a reader – is the sign-vehicle. The referent is the state of affairs in the world for which the sign-vehicle stands: the actual concentrations of chemicals A and B in a patient's blood. The interpretant is the set of mental concepts that form in the mind of the reader/interpreter of the diagram: It is the mental understanding of what the world is and how it functions that the reader may gain from exposure to the printed matter. All three of these components together make up the sign: The sign is the combination of the sign-vehicle, the interpretant, and the referent. Critically, and despite the misleading shorthand in which everyday language describes the printed matter itself as a sign (for instance, a stop sign), the printed matter as an artifact viewed in isolation is the sign-vehicle, not the sign in its entirety.[209] The sign-vehicle has "content" only in a loose sense of the word. The sign-vehicle does not contain its semiotic meaning within its physical structure. Instead it has a semiotic meaning because it directly signifies a mental interpretant in the mind of an interpreter and indirectly, via the interpretant, refers to a referent that exists in the world.[210]

What precisely has the researcher who seeks protection for the diagram contributed to technological progress? Each component of the sign must be considered independently, at least at first. Concerning the referent, the researcher has made what the Supreme Court identified as a "discovery" rather than a patentable invention.[211] The inventor has discovered a new property of human blood in the actual world, namely that the concentrations of chemicals A and B are inversely related. This correlation presumably existed in human blood before the researchers undertook

[207] *See supra* text accompanying notes 154.
[208] *See supra* notes 170–71 and accompanying text (presenting Peirce's triadic sign).
[209] *See supra* notes 175–77 and accompanying text (discussing the misleading synecdoche).
[210] *See supra* notes 175–77 and accompanying text (noting that the meaning of a sign is not contained within the sign-vehicle).
[211] Parker v. Flook, 437 U.S. 584, 593 & n.15 (1978).

their research. All that the researchers have done is to recognize the existence of the referent in the world and "reveal[ed] a relationship that has always existed."[212] However, the researchers have a much stronger argument to having invented, not simply discovered, the interpretant. Prior to the researchers' work, no human mental state existed in which the inverse correlation between chemicals A and B was the object of thought. The mental interpretant of the correlation between chemicals A and B that forms in the mind of the human interpreter of the diagram may be novel, nonobvious, and useful.[213] Finally, concerning the sign-vehicle, the researchers may have done either of two different things, depending on the content of the prior art. They may have piggybacked on existing social conventions and manufactured a new sign-vehicle to signify to an interpreter the concept corresponding to the newly discovered referent. Alternatively, they may have repurposed an existing sign-vehicle, enabling an interpreter to associate a newly invented interpretant – and, indirectly, a newly discovered referent – with the existing sign-vehicle. Any single claim may encompass sign-vehicles of both types. In either case, however, the nonobviousness of the sign turns entirely on the nonobviousness of the interpretant. The sign-vehicle is either a preexisting entity or an entity that is nonobvious to make only because the interpretant that it signifies is nonobvious.

The basic effect of reinterpreting the printed matter doctrine in a semiotic framework is to shift courts' focus away from information and its content and toward signs and their interpretants during the analysis of the types of products of human ingenuity that can and cannot be patented. When the printed matter doctrine is reconceptualized in a semiotic framework and recast as the sign doctrine, the core printed matter cases can be seen to follow a simple rule: A *claim that describes a sign is not eligible for patent protection if the sole locus of the nonobvious improvement over the prior art resides in a mental state*. Semiotically framed, what courts are already doing under the banner of the printed matter doctrine – but not what they are saying they are doing – is invalidating claims that describe a sign in which the only nonobvious advance over the prior art resides in the processes that occur in the minds of interpreters.[214] It is the interpretant of a sign, not the content of information more broadly, that cannot be given patentable weight.

[212] *Id.* at 593 n.15. Many signs have human-made entities, rather than natural phenomena, as their referents. For example, in the rhetoric of *Parker* v. *Flook*, a diagram depicting the structure of a human-made chemical depicts the results of an invention, not simply the results of a discovery. Under a semiotic framework, the status of the referent as an invented or discovered entity is irrelevant.

[213] Whether the interpretant is novel and nonobvious hinges on the nature of the discovery at issue. If the researchers were the first to recognize that the correlation might exist, then the interpretant would be novel and possibly nonobvious. However, if the researchers' work simply provided empirical verification for the correlation that had long been hypothesized, then the interpretant might not be novel.

[214] *But see infra* notes 248–55 and accompanying text (discussing how a semiotic framework would, if rigorously applied, expand patent eligibility in core printed matter cases).

B. *Curing Doctrinal Infirmities*

A semiotic perspective on the evolution of the printed matter doctrine suggests that courts erred in their choice of the doctrine's technology-neutral formulation.[215] The doctrine was originally aimed at printing on paper, but this technology-specific focus proved to be unsustainable. Courts took printed matter to be an archetype of information with content when they should have taken printed matter to be an archetype of a sign with an interpretant. Once couched in terms of information, the printed matter doctrine was destined to be conceptually incoherent. The printed matter doctrine lost its coherence because neither the PTO nor the courts had access to the semiotic concepts that are required to describe the semiotically motivated distinctions they intuitively realized that they needed to make in the core printed matter cases. To exclude the types of inventions that did not comport with widely shared notions of what should be patented, the PTO and the courts allowed the effect of the printed matter doctrine to veer off sharply from its information-centric rhetoric. What they did diverged from what they said. Reinterpreting the printed matter doctrine as the sign doctrine and embracing a semiotic framework is in large part a valuable exercise because it brings to light the otherwise difficult-to-perceive conceptual coherence in the outcomes that the courts and the PTO are already reaching in many of the core printed matter cases.[216]

1. Interpretants Entail Human Intelligibility

The thesis that the printed matter doctrine is already a doctrine that is in its effects – but not in its rhetoric – based on semiotic principles explains why the Federal Circuit gravitated toward a definition of information and its content that focuses on human intelligibility.[217] Interpretants entail intelligibility in a human mind.[218] A semiotic reformulation of the printed matter doctrine as the sign doctrine embraces the notion that the printed matter doctrine deals with the worldly things that the human mind finds to be meaningful.[219]

Under the sign doctrine, patents that describe sign-vehicles and that grant inventors rights to exclude the public from using signs are commonplace. The sign-vehicles of signs are often the "machine[s], manufacture[s], and composition[s] of

[215] *See supra* notes 36–38 and accompanying text (presenting the evolution of the printed matter doctrine to its contemporary technology-neutral formulation).

[216] *But see infra* notes 248–55 and accompanying text (discussing how a semiotic framework would, if rigorously applied, expand patent eligibility in core printed matter cases).

[217] *See supra* Part I.A.2.

[218] *See supra* notes 172, 199–200 and accompanying text.

[219] The semiotic framework explains the historical kinship of the printed matter doctrine and the now defunct or dormant mental steps doctrine that expressly addressed the patentability of human mental processes. *See, e.g., Ex Parte* Jenny, 130 U.S.P.Q. 318 (Pat. Off. Bd. App. 1960) (employing principles established in the mental steps doctrine to refine the printed matter doctrine).

matter" that lie at the core of patentable subject matters.[220] The steam engine is the sign-vehicle of a sign that has the industrial revolution as its referent (and the mental understanding of the industrial revolution as its interpretant), yet a patent on the steam engine does not run afoul of the sign doctrine. Television sets routinely display signs that are intelligible to those who are watching, yet they remain patentable inventions under a semiotically oriented printed matter doctrine. Mercury thermometers are useful because the level of mercury in the thermometer serves as the sign-vehicle of an index that has the temperature of the air as its referent, yet thermometers can be patented when they contain improvements in their physical engineering.[221] Ink on paper is a patentable invention when the chemical formula of the ink is useful, novel, and nonobvious.[222] The sign doctrine bars the patenting of a sign only when the sole locus of nonobvious advance over the prior art resides in the sign's interpretant. The steam engine, television set, and thermometer all function as sign-vehicles, but they contain novel and nonobvious improvements in the physical engineering of the sign-vehicle proper.

The key to distinguishing permissible claims to signs from impermissible ones is not to inquire whether the patent claim describes a sign-vehicle but rather to determine whether what is novel and nonobvious is the semiotic meaning that a human interpreter should understand when she perceives a sign-vehicle.[223] The semiotic framework for patent eligibility, therefore, focuses the exclusion from patentable subject matter not generally on meaningful things but specifically on improvements in human understanding itself.

2. Of Signals and Stimuli

The semiotic framework explains why many artifacts that are nothing more than information recorded on a substrate remain patentable under the printed matter doctrine, even when it is the content of the information that is the advance over the prior art.[224] Many artifacts are tangible embodiments of information because they are signals or stimuli, and signals and stimuli pass below the lower threshold of the semiotic field.[225] A signal or stimulus carrying informational content passes below the lower threshold of the semiotic field because its "meaning" or "content" is the behavior that it causes in a biological, mechanical, or electronic interpreter. Its structure can be nonobvious because it has the unexpected property of causing this behavior, and no interpretant or social convention needs to be considered.

[220] 35 U.S.C. § 101 (2006); *cf.* Burk, *supra* note 60, at 113 (discussing the expressive qualities of technology).

[221] *See infra* Part IV.A (discussing the patentability of mechanical measuring devices).

[222] *Cf. supra* text accompanying notes 105–07.

[223] *See supra* text accompanying note 214.

[224] *See supra* Part I.A.1.

[225] *See supra* Part II.C.

All chemicals and biological molecules are stimuli and signals that carry information because they physically cause chemical and biological interpreters to adopt particular states of affairs. In particular, the DNA of an expressed gene is a stimulus: It is the bearer of information in a nonsemiotic sense because a cell is a biological interpreter that responds in a deterministic manner to the presence of the DNA.[226] Thus, "genetic 'codes' are below [Eco's] semiotic threshold, since they are not based on social conventions."[227] Long before the discovery of the genetic code and the advent of molecular biology, DNA molecules bore information without a human interpretant or a sign anywhere in the picture.

Similarly, to the extent that software-on-disk claims are eligible for patent protection under *Beauregard*, it is because the information recorded on the disk serves as a signal that deterministically causes a computer to adopt a particular state of affairs.[228] The binary ones and zeros recorded on an old-fashioned computer punch card or a newfangled USB drive are signals or stimuli: The mechanical or electronic devices into which they are fed are interpreters that, when functioning properly, produce responses through deterministic processes. No interpretants are required for software recorded on a disk to "mean" something in the nonsemiotic sense to a computer as an interpreter.[229]

Furthermore, the semiotic framework explains the both-and problem that the contemporary printed matter doctrine is unable to address in a coherent manner.[230] The both-and puzzle arises when an artifact is both a signal/stimulus that causes a behavior in a mechanistic or organic interpreter and a sign-vehicle that signifies an interpretant in the mind of a human interpreter. More specifically, it arises when the sign at issue is an index, and the referent of the index is the very behavior that the artifact-as-stimuli causes in the machine or organism.[231] DNA is an example of the both-and problem: It is a stimulus that causes a cell-as-interpreter to produce a protein, and it is a sign-vehicle of an index that signifies the same protein to a molecular biologist who understands the genetic code (through the mediation of a sequencer). Cells and molecular biologists "read" DNA through entirely different mechanisms. Software recorded on a disk is an example of the both-and problem for the same reason. The software is a signal that causes a computer-as-interpreter to perform a particular behavior, and it is a sign-vehicle of an index that signifies the

[226] *See supra* notes 41–44 and accompanying text (discussing DNA as a form of information).

[227] NÖTH, *supra* note 166, at 213.

[228] *See supra* notes 45–49, 56–58, 89–93 and accompanying text (discussing *Beauregard* claims).

[229] As Pamela Samuelson stated:

> There is one very simple but important difference between a book which contains a set of instructions about how to do a particular task and a computer program in machine-readable form which contains a similar, if considerably more elaborate, set of instructions on the same subject: The former informs a human being about how the task might be done; the latter does the task.

Samuelson, *supra* note 148, at 727.

[230] *See supra* notes 59–61 (discussing the both-and puzzle).

[231] *See supra* note 201 and accompanying text.

same behavior to a computer scientist who understands the programming language (through the mediation of a decompiler).

In a semiotic framework, both-and artifacts are usually eligible for patent protection. The important question to determine patentability in a semiotic framework is whether the nonobvious advance over the prior art resides solely in a mental act of human understanding; that is, an interpretant in the mind of a human interpreter.[232] Insofar as they function as sign-vehicles, newly invented both-and artifacts will commonly signify novel and nonobvious interpretants, but these interpretants will rarely be the only locus of the advance over the prior art. The physical structure of the both-and artifact will often be nonobvious because of the reaction that it causes in the organic or mechanical interpreter. DNA is an advance over the prior art because of its function as a stimulus: Its structure causes a cell to produce a protein. To understand the irrelevance of the interpretant, consider a hypothetical in which human understanding is taken out of the picture. Even if humans did not understand the genetic code, an isolated and purified gene would be patentable because it could be used to provoke a cell to produce a protein. Similarly, software on a disk is an advance over the prior art because its structure causes a computer to exhibit a particular behavior. Even if computer programmers forgot how to read and understand a programming language, the computer software recorded on a disk would remain patentable because it would still cause the machine to exhibit a specific behavior. The status of both-and artifacts as stimuli means that their patent eligibility can be proven even if nonobvious interpretants associated with them when they function as sign-vehicles for human readers are not given patentable weight.[233]

[232] *See supra* Parts III.A and III.B.1.

[233] Depending on the trajectory of the future evolution of technology, there may need to be an exception to the patent eligibility of both-and artifacts. The printed matter doctrine may need to incorporate a safety valve that restricts the reach of patent protection that is similar to the merger doctrine in copyright. *See* Morrissey v. Procter & Gamble Co., 379 F.2d 675 (1st Cir. 1967) (holding that original expression may be copied without violating a copyright if the expression is but one of a few ways of expressing an idea). For example, assume that the art of computer programming – and the art of compilers in particular – evolves to the point at which the functions performed by a software program can be described by a computer programmer in plain English and automatically translated into executable object code. In this world, it would be very difficult to use the English language recorded on a computer disk to convey concepts about the computer program without infringing a *Beauregard* claim to the computer program. Any English description of the program that serves as a sign-vehicle that represents the computer's behavior to a human mind would also be a signal or stimuli that causes the computer to perform the behavior. In this future world, sign-vehicles and signals will have merged. If both-and artifacts are patent eligible, the categorical sanctioning of the patentability of both-and artifacts would in effect be the categorical allowance of patents on nearly all of the sign-vehicles that can convey knowledge about the program. If carried over into patent law, the merger doctrine would hold both-and artifacts to be patent ineligible when a signal must remain beyond the reach of patent protection to ensure that representations of knowledge about an invention reside in the public domain.

3. Signals That Cause Machines to Generate Sign-Vehicles

The semiotic framework also provides the conceptual tools required to explain the first-then puzzle – the fact that some artifacts, such as analog tapes or computer disks encoded with books, must be processed by machines but yet intuitively should not be eligible for patent protection.[234] The same conceptual tools explain the currently inexplicable distinction that the PTO has drawn in *Beauregard* claims between descriptive material that is functionally related to its substrate (an ".exe" file) and descriptive material that is not functionally related to its substrate (a ".txt" file).[235]

In a semiotic framework, a signal embedded on a computer-readable medium is not guaranteed to be patentable simply because it physically causes the computer to exhibit a specific behavior. Both functional descriptive material and nonfunctional descriptive material are signals that cause a behavior in a general-purpose computer. In a semiotic framework, the important question addresses the nature of the behavior that the signals provoke in the computer. Sometimes, the behavior that a signal causes the computer to perform is the production of a sign-vehicle. For terminological clarity, the sign-vehicle produced by the computer-as-interpreter can be called the *secondary sign-vehicle* and the sign in which it participates can be called the *secondary sign*. When a signal causes the production of a secondary sign, there is quite obviously another sign wound up with the claimed invention to which the PTO must pay attention in the patent-eligibility analysis. If the sole advance over the prior art resides in the interpretant signified by the secondary sign-vehicle that a signal causes a machine to produce, the signal is no more eligible for patent protection than a direct claim to the sign-vehicle would be. A claim to a printed book (sign-vehicle) that is nonobvious in relation to the prior art only because of its semiotic meaning is no different from a claim to a computer disk that causes a machine programmed with prior-art software to display the same book (secondary sign-vehicle). The patentable-weight analysis of the printed matter doctrine must apply to any interpretant, regardless of whether the interpretant is associated with a sign-vehicle or with the behavior that the claimed subject matter triggers in a machine or organism.

4. Limiting the Exclusion: Newly Engineered Sign-Vehicles

The semiotic framework also enables a reevaluation of the structural- and functional-relation exceptions to the printed matter doctrine in their pre-*Beauregard* applications.[236] Construed in semiotic terms, the printed matter doctrine states that

[234] *See supra* notes 55–58 and accompanying text.

[235] *See supra* notes 89–93 and accompanying text.

[236] The arguments in Part III.B.3 address the functional-relation exception in the context of *Beauregard* claims.

a claim to a sign-vehicle is not eligible for patent protection if the sole locus of the improvement over the prior art resides in the interpretant that it signifies to an interpreter.[237] The negative corollary of this limited rule is that there are many situations in which newly engineered sign-vehicles are eligible for patent protection.

For example, as already discussed, the negative corollary leads to the conclusion that newly engineered sign-vehicles are patent eligible when they have been engineered to possess nonsemiotic properties in addition to their semiotic properties. Sometimes, the nonsemiotic properties are structural properties of the sign-vehicle itself. A sheet of paper with a specific diagram printed on it is a sign-vehicle that is eligible for patent protection if the chemical composition of the ink in which the diagram is printed is a nonobvious invention.[238] Sometimes, the nonsemiotic properties are the structural properties of the sign-vehicle that deterministically cause reactions in other systems. Newly engineered signals and stimuli are usually patent eligible for this reason despite the fact that they are frequently sign-vehicles as well.[239] In either case, the advance over the prior art resides in a property other than the ability of the sign-vehicle to signify interpretants and, indirectly, refer to referents.

The structural- and functional-relation cases, which are traditionally viewed as exceptions to the printed matter doctrine, populate another category of newly engineered sign-vehicles that are eligible for patent protection under the negative corollary. Sign-vehicles have historically been patentable under the printed matter doctrine when they have been engineered so as to improve the efficiency of the process of signification without an accompanying improvement in what is signified.[240] More specifically, the efficiency gains can occur either on the production side, in which case speakers can generate sign-vehicles more rapidly or with less effort, or on the reception side, in which case speakers can more readily understand the interpretants associated with the sign-vehicles.

The inventions in the structural-relation, ticket-tearing cases are examples of newly engineered sign-vehicles that are eligible for patent protection because of production-side efficiencies.[241] The inventors achieved nonobvious advances in the structural features of the sign-vehicles that made them labor-saving devices for sign producers. In *Cincinnati Traction Co.* v. *Pope*,[242] the inventor of the tripartite ticket did not argue that the referent or the interpretant was newly discovered or invented, respectively. Street railways were using time-limited transfer tickets before the

[237] *See infra* Part III.A.

[238] *See supra* text accompanying note 222.

[239] *See supra* Part III.B.2.

[240] The notion that the two different signifiers can be associated with the identical signified is semiotically naive. *Cf.* Chandler, *supra* note 166, at 17 (noting that, for Saussure, the signified and signifier were as inseparable as two sides of a page). However, it is a useful simplification for understanding the sign doctrine.

[241] *See supra* text accompanying notes 63–78.

[242] 210 F. 443 (6th Cir. 1913).

invention of the tripartite ticket at issue.[243] The tripartite ticket was a newly engineered sign-vehicle that allowed streetcar conductors to generate a time-limited transfer ticket more quickly and to increase the verifiability of the tickets that had been issued. Similarly, in *Flood* v. *Coe*, the tickets for tagging garments in retail stores signified the identical interpretants to customers that prior art garment tickets had signified, but the new spatial arrangement of the printed matter on the substrate reduced the workload of the workers in the retail stores who had to reprice the ticketed merchandise.[244]

In re Gulack, and its functional-relation exception from the printed matter doctrine, is an example of a claim to printed matter that was patentable because the sign-vehicle was newly engineered to promote reception-side efficiencies in the semiotic process.[245] The "nonobvious" circular configuration for the digits representing the mathematical sequence presumptively made the endless nature of the sequence more readily understandable to the reader.[246] The claimed invention does not convey a newly invented interpretant, because the mathematical sequence (referent) is not put forth as newly discovered, and thus the human act of understanding of that sequence (interpretant) is not alleged to be newly invented. Rather, the sign-vehicle has been newly engineered to make it more iconic: In comparison to the prior art, the claimed invention increases the perceived resemblance between the sign-vehicle and the referent.[247] The increase in the perceived resemblance presumptively makes it easier for the interpreter to formulate the proper interpretant that accurately reflects the nature of the referent.

The semiotic reformulation of the structural- and functional-relation exceptions to the printed matter doctrine explains courts' outcomes in most of the pre-*Beauregard* cases in which the exceptions have been invoked to justify the patentability of printed matter: Newly engineered sign-vehicles are patentable insofar as they entail production efficiencies or reception efficiencies.[248] However, if taken seriously, it also reveals one area in which the semiotic framework would have prescriptive bite

243 *Id.* at 444.

244 31 F. Supp. 348, 348–49 (D.D.C. 1940).

245 703 F.2d 1381 (Fed. Cir. 1983).

246 Whether the circular configuration was nonobvious raises a question of fact that is beyond the scope of the inquiry here.

247 *See supra* Part II.B.2.

248 *In re Miller* is arguably the exception – a case that held an invention to be patentable under the functional-relation exception to the printed matter doctrine but that should not be patentable under the semiotic framework. 418 F.2d 1392 (C.C.P.A. 1969). *Miller* did not involve a newly engineered sign-vehicle. The inventor simply placed new labels on old measuring spoons that instructed the user how to use the spoons in a particular fashion, something along the lines of "if you are making a half-recipe, use this spoon if the recipe calls for a cup of an ingredient." *See id.* at 1394. If *Miller* qualifies as patent eligible under the printed matter doctrine, then it is difficult to understand why machine-plus-labels are not eligible for patent protection. *See infra* Part IV.A (explaining why old machines with new labels are not eligible for patent protection). Pragmatically, however, *Miller* may be cabined as an exceptional case because it involved factually incorrect labels.

in the core printed matter cases. More specifically, it suggests one way in which the adoption of the sign doctrine and its semiotic framework might *expand* the set of artifacts of human ingenuity that are eligible for patent protection. Historically, the printed matter doctrine started out as a categorical rule that simply excluded all printed matter from patent eligibility,[249] and some vestiges of this rule remain in the contemporary printed matter doctrine. These vestiges make the exclusion from patent eligibility attributable to the contemporary printed matter doctrine an overinclusive proxy for the exclusion that can be justified on purely semiotic grounds.

For example, concerning production efficiencies, it is semiotically irrelevant whether a claim describes printed matter that is easier to use because it can be physically folded, punched, or torn in a new manner or, alternatively, because the printed matter is simply structured differently in the sense of ink being at different locations on a page. Imagine a bound book of tickets in which a number must be written by the ticket seller on the stub of each ticket. If prior-art ticket books had the space for writing the number near the binding of the stubs, a book of tickets with the space near the free end of the stub where the tickets have been removed might be patentable because the numbers would be easier to record.[250] Similarly, documents written in a new form of shorthand would be eligible for patent protection under a semiotic framework because the shorthand results in production efficiencies without affecting what the writing signifies.[251] In linguistic terms, matter printed in newly invented systems of *syntax* should be eligible for patent protection under a sign doctrine that rigorously follows semiotic reasoning, but printed matter should not be patent eligible because it has a newly invented *semantic* meaning.[252]

Concerning reception efficiencies, there are also printed matter inventions that are not eligible for patent protection under the traditional printed matter doctrine that should be eligible for patent protection under purely semiotic reasoning. Perhaps the most important of these inventions historically are documents embodying new methods of arranging and indexing printed matter. The spatial arrangement of printed matter on a sheet can clearly make it easier for an interpreter to understand the printed matter, as can a well-designed index for a book. In several cases that lie at the heart of the printed matter canon, claims to an index arranged in a particular fashion have been held not to be patentable subject matter.[253] When interpreted as

[249] *See supra* text accompanying note 37.

[250] The nonobviousness of the physical engineering of the sign-vehicle under section 103 in this simple example is highly questionable.

[251] Although the printed matter doctrine was not considered, production efficiencies also explain why the Supreme Court held Morse code itself to be a patentable invention as a "system of signs." *See O'Reilly v. Morse*, 56 U.S. 62, 86, 112 (1853).

[252] Syntax is "the structure of phrases and sentences and the constraints on well-formedness of sentences," and semantics is "the meaning of words and sentences." VICTORIA A. FROMKIN, LINGUISTICS: AN INTRODUCTION TO LINGUISTIC THEORY 7 (2000).

[253] *See* Jacobs, *supra* note 38, at 480–81 (discussing printed matter cases involving "a new method of arranging or indexing information").

part of a semiotic framework, however, the printed matter doctrine should sanction the patentability of an index arranged in a nonobvious manner. The index does not alter the ideas represented by a book; it does not affect the nature of what the book signifies. It simply provides an understanding efficiency.[254] For the same reasons, drawings rendered in new systems of perspective or diagrams employing new graphic conventions – that is, new systems of syntax – provide understanding efficiencies that should make them eligible for patent protection under the sign doctrine when its exclusion is narrowly tailored to its semiotic principles.[255]

C. *Solving Statutory Mysteries: A Structural Interpretation of § 101*

A semiotic perspective on the printed matter doctrine also reveals how the doctrine is grounded in the Patent Act.[256] When viewed semiotically, the printed matter doctrine is grounded in a *structural* interpretation of § 101 – an interpretation that examines the meaning of § 101 within the context of the Patent Act as a whole and its disclosure provisions in particular.[257]

One of the deepest structural principles of the Patent Act is its "duality of claiming and disclosing."[258] Congress did not unilaterally bestow benefits on inventors who generate technological progress. Rather, it structured the patent regime as a "bargain" in which inventors and the public exchange valuable

[254] The reconsideration of the historical printed matter cases involving indexes also sheds new light on the Federal Circuit's holding in *In re* Lowry, 32 F.3d 1579 (Fed. Cir. 1994). In *Lowry*, the Federal Circuit upheld a claim to a computer-readable data structure under the printed matter doctrine. *Id.* at 1582–84. *Lowry* is often taken to stand for the fact that the printed matter doctrine does not apply to computer technology in the same way that it applies to traditional print media. *Id.* at 1583 (chastising the PTO for "erroneously extend[ing] a printed matter rejection . . . to a new field. . . . "). However, from a semiotic perspective, the *Lowry* holding does not require a computer-specific exception to the general rule. The computer-readable data structure is an organization of data akin to an index. Under the semiotic framework, new, more efficient electronic organizations of computer-readable data should be patentable because new, more efficient spatial organizations of human-readable data should be patentable too.

[255] *Cf. supra* note 252 and accompanying text (arguing that documents printed in newly invented systems of syntax can be patented without running afoul of a narrowly construed sign doctrine). Despite the fact that improvements in semiotic efficiency do not run afoul of the sign doctrine when it is narrowly tailored to its semiotic principles, there are good reasons not to upset the status quo and recognize them as patent eligible. A bright-line rule that excludes all claims to newly invented printed matter per se simplifies the analysis, because the distinction between inventions in syntax and semantics may not always be self-evident. The overinclusiveness of its exclusion may be justified by invoking the traditional benefit-of-administrability justifications of rules rather than standards. *See* FREDERICK SCHAUER, PLAYING BY THE RULES: A PHILOSOPHICAL EXAMINATION OF RULE-BASED DECISION-MAKING IN LAW AND IN LIFE (1991).

[256] *Cf. supra* Part I.B (discussing the doctrine's nonstatutory nature).

[257] *See* Kevin Emerson Collins, *Claims to Information qua Information and a Structural Theory of Section 101*, 4 I/S: A J. OF L. AND POL'Y FOR THE INFO. SOC'Y 11, 22–26 (2008), *reprinted in* PATENT CLAIMS: JUDICIAL INTERPRETATION AND ANALYSIS (2009) (discussing a structural interpretation of § 101).

[258] Dinwoodie & Dreyfuss, *supra* note 23, at 193 n.4 (2006).

rights.[259] The public, via the state, grants an inventor limited rights to exclude others from making, using, or selling the claimed embodiments of an invention, and, as the "quid pro quo of the right to exclude," the inventor discloses newly discovered knowledge that she otherwise could have kept secret.[260] The disclosure requirements of § 112 of the Patent Act impose an affirmative obligation on the patent applicant.[261] Disclosure runs against the inventor's self-interest; it is a "price" that "is *exacted from*" the patentee in return for patent protection.[262] Importantly, the disclosure is not merely an obligation to publicize knowledge in the weak sense of making it known to the public. Rather, disclosures are "additions to the general store of knowledge" that must be free for all to use so as to "stimulate ideas and the eventual development of further significant advances in the art."[263] From the moment of publication, the public is free to use the knowledge that it gains from the disclosure, even in ways that are detrimental to the patentee.[264] Thus, the disclosure obligation requires a patent applicant to publicize knowledge in a strong sense – to give the public a use privilege in the invention *qua* knowledge, free of the strings of property.

The existence of the duality of claiming and disclosing as part of the deep structure of the Patent Act is widely accepted, but its implications have not been fully explored. The duality, and its granting of public privileges of access in particular, cannot be taken for granted. There is no self-enforcing line that separates the resources that can be privatized by a claim and those that must be publicized by the disclosure. Knowledge does not have any inherent "architectural" property that makes it immune from the propertizing effect of patent claims.[265] In a form that is useful to humans, knowledge is not an ethereal, immaterial entity: It is a phenomenon rooted in both the electrochemical states of our brains and the worldly things that

[259] Pfaff v. Wells Elecs., Inc., 525 U.S. 55, 63 (1998); Bonito Boats, Inc. v. Thunder Craft Boats, Inc., 489 U.S. 141, 150–51 (1989).

[260] Kewanee Oil Co. v. Bicron Corp., 416 U.S. 470, 484 (1974).

[261] 35 U.S.C. § 112 ¶ 1 (2006).

[262] Eldred v. Ashcroft, 537 U.S. 186, 216 (2003) (emphasis in original).

[263] *Kewanee Oil*, 416 U.S. at 481.

[264] 1 Chisum, *supra* note 2, § 7.01 ("[O]n issuance . . . the patent immediately increases the storehouse of public information available for further research and innovation."); Timothy R. Holbrook, *Possession in Patent Law*, 59 S.M.U. L. Rev. 123, 133 ("[T]he disclosure in the patent is . . . designed. . . to enrich the state of the art contemporaneously with the invention."). Patent law encourages competitors to use the disclosure to "design around existing patents." Intel Corp. v. VIA Techs., Inc., 319 F.3d 1357, 1367 (Fed. Cir. 2003); *see also* Vitronics Corp. v. Conceptronic, Inc., 90 F.3d 1576, 1583 (Fed. Cir. 1996). Competitors can design around a patent only if they have free use of the newly invented knowledge conveyed by the patent disclosure. In addition to this preexpiration role, the disclosure also plays a postexpiration role in that it ensures that the public possesses the right to make the claimed invention after expiration. Grant v. Raymond, 31 U.S. (6 Pet.) 218, 247 (1832).

[265] Lawrence Lessig, Code and Other Laws of Cyberspace 24–29 (1999) (arguing that there is nothing inherent in the architecture of cyberspace that prevents its regulation). *But see* Wagner, *supra* note 164, at 1005–09 (arguing that "perfect control" may be justified in intellectual property because information inevitably escapes the property owner's control and generates externalities).

our minds understand to be meaningful.[266] Because of the worldly, material basis of knowledge, the disclosure side of the duality of claiming and disclosing is in jeopardy of being curtailed or eliminated unless doctrinal restrictions on the patent eligibility of worldly things and mental processes are built into patent law. Unless patentable subject matter is restricted, patentees can dress up the worldly resources that comprise inventive knowledge itself as patentable inventions. Unless patentable subject matter is restricted, patentees can describe in a claim, and thus purport to privatize, the resources that the patentee should be obligated to publicize. Disclosures create a public domain of knowledge only if there are doctrinally enforced limits on the nature of the claims to which inventors are entitled.

A structural interpretation of § 101 allows courts and examiners to enforce those limits and ensure that patent applicants fulfill their disclosure obligations. Structural statutory interpretation requires courts to look to "the structure and purpose of the Act" as a whole when construing statutory language.[267] The duality of claiming and disclosing is a deep, structural principle of patent protection, and § 101 must be construed so as to preserve it.[268] When § 101 is viewed in the context of the Patent Act as a whole and the disclosure obligations of § 112 in particular, it is clear that there is one category of claims that Congress did not sanction as patent eligible: claims that interfere with the public's free use of "the general store of knowledge" created by patent disclosures.[269]

The sign doctrine is nothing more than a prohibition on patent eligibility that is required to prevent patent applicants from shirking their disclosure obligations. Signs – or, more precisely, signs with newly invented interpretants – are real-world resources that must be free for all to use to ensure that the knowledge disclosed in a patent specification remains free for all to use *qua* knowledge. Reconceptualized in semiotic terms, the printed matter doctrine prevents the issuance of a patent when all that the inventor has achieved is an advance in human understanding.[270] This result is mandated by the disclosure side of the duality of claiming and disclosing that structures the Patent Act as a whole.

The fact that the printed matter doctrine is implicit in the structure of the Patent Act as a whole also lowers the stakes of the Federal Circuit's difficult-to-explain

[266] *Cf.* Karl R. Popper, Objective Knowledge: An Evolutionary Approach 73–74 (1979) (discussing subjective and objective knowledge).

[267] N.Y. State Conference of Blue Cross & Blue Shield Plans v. Travelers Ins. Co., 514 U.S. 645, 655 (1995); *see also* William N. Eskridge, Jr., Dynamic Statutory Interpretation 118–19 (1994) (discussing Justice Scalia's structural approach to statutory interpretation). The Supreme Court has used a yet more inclusive variant of this canon of structural statutory construction to interpret the Lanham Act in light of other intellectual property laws. *See* Dastar Corp. v. Twentieth Century Fox Film Corp., 539 U.S. 23, 37 (2003) ("[R]eading the phrase 'origin of goods' . . . in light of the copyright and patent laws. . . . "). Reading § 101 in light of the Patent Act is a far less ambitious structural move.

[268] *See supra* text accompanying notes 258–66.

[269] Kewanee Oil Co. v. Bicron Corp., 416 U.S. 470, 481 (1974).

[270] *See supra* text accompanying note 223.

application of the doctrine under the dual statutory provisions in §§ 101 and 103.[271] The structure of the Patent Act as a whole mandates the existence of the printed matter doctrine, but it does not mandate that courts must construe any section in particular to embody the printed matter doctrine. It is reasonable to think of the printed matter doctrine as an artifact of the § 101 doctrine of patent eligibility because there is a particular type of invention – a newly invented interpretant – that cannot be patented, regardless of how novel, useful, and nonobvious it is. This is the route that this chapter has taken, but this choice is more a matter of convenience than necessity. It is also entirely possible to construe §§ 102 and 103 in light of the structure of the Patent Act as a whole so as to make the sign doctrine an artifact of the novelty and nonobviousness analyses: In assessing whether a claimed invention embodies an advance over the prior art, courts could ignore any advance that resides solely in newly invented interpretants. When the sign doctrine is grounded in a structural theory of statutory interpretation, its statutory locus is broader than any single statutory provision.

D. *Embracing the Patentable-Weight Approach in a Limited Realm*

A semiotic framework demonstrates that the patentable-weight approach to patent eligibility is practical and coherent when it is employed as part of the sign doctrine. The patentable-weight approach should be recognized as a feature, not a bug, of the sign doctrine for two reasons.

First, on a conceptual level, the semiotic framework explains why it is appropriate for the patentability of an artifact to hinge on the content of the prior art and thus on the historical context in which an invention was made.[272] There is no reason to expect patent eligibility to be an intrinsic property of an artifact in a semiotic framework. Semiotic meanings are not intrinsic properties of artifacts, nor are they contained within artifacts; sign-vehicles do not have "content" in the sense of meanings contained within them.[273] Printed matter is meaningful only because of the mental process of interpretation in the mind of an interpreter. Signs, not sign-vehicles, are the entities within which meanings reside. If a single component of a sign is artificially cabined off from the sign's other components – for instance, if the sign-vehicle is examined in isolation – it should be unsurprising that its eligibility for patent protection depends on something other than that single component's intrinsic properties.

To understand the value of a patentable-weight approach to the doctrine of patent eligibility in the context of semiotically meaningful things, consider the absurd

[271] *See supra* text accompanying notes 136–41 and accompanying text.
[272] *See supra* notes 99–107 and accompanying text.
[273] *See supra* text accompanying note 175.

results of taking a claim-as-a-whole approach to patent eligibility seriously. In other words, consider a hypothetical *sign-as-a-whole* approach to patent eligibility. Under a sign-as-a-whole approach, courts would have to take note of all of the components of a sign – the sign-vehicle, the interpretant, and the referent – every time an inventor claimed a sign. If any of those individual components described patentable subject matter, then the claim as a whole would describe patentable subject matter. Because every sign has a perceptible sign-vehicle that is an extra-mental thing, every sign would be eligible for patent protection under the sign-as-a-whole approach.[274] Despite their insistence on a claim-as-a-whole approach to patent eligibility, courts have understandably never shown interest in a sign-as-a-whole approach. Such an approach would not reach normatively acceptable ends. Only a patentable-weight approach can effectively prevent the privatization of advances in human understanding.

Second, the use of a patentable-weight approach to structure the sign doctrine does not run afoul of the Supreme Court's insistence in *Diehr* that a claim-as-a-whole approach should guide the § 101 prohibition on the patenting of "laws of nature."[275] Statutorily, the two strands of § 101 doctrine derive from entirely distinct modes of statutory interpretation. The interpretation of § 101 in *Diehr* emphasized that §§ 102 and 103 are distinct from § 101 and that the word "new" in § 101 should not be construed as a reference to the novelty doctrine.[276] In contrast, the interpretation of § 101 that supports the printed matter doctrine is informed by the structure of the Patent Act as a whole and the disclosure obligations placed on patent applicants.[277] There is no reason to expect the doctrinal rules that derive from distinct modes of interpreting § 101 to adopt the same approach to patent eligibility. The Court's disapproval of the point-of-novelty approach when applied to "laws of nature" expressed in *Diehr* need not pertain to the printed matter doctrine.[278] Pragmatically, the recognition of two statutorily distinct strands of the doctrine of patent eligibility allays the concerns about the mischief that a point-of-novelty approach "taken to its extreme" would cause when preventing the patenting of "laws of nature."[279] The point-of-novelty approach need only apply to inventions implicating semiotic meanings. It need not govern the patent eligibility of inventions implicating "laws of nature." The claim-as-a-whole approach can continue to determine how patent eligibility is brought to bear on "laws of nature."

274 *But see In re* Nuijten, 500 F.3d 1346 (Fed. Cir. 2007) (holding that perceptible but intangible "signals" are not patentable subject matter).

275 *See supra* notes 108–27 and accompanying text.

276 Diamond v. Diehr, 450 U.S. 175, 189–91 (1981).

277 *See supra* Part III.C.

278 *See supra* notes 108–27 and accompanying text (discussing this disapproval).

279 *See supra* notes 120–22 and accompanying text (discussing this potential for mischief).

IV. QUESTIONING THE PATENTABILITY OF COMPUTER MODELS

When the printed matter doctrine is brought to bear on claims that are conventionally viewed as describing information recorded on a substrate – that is, when the doctrine is employed in the core printed matter cases – the value added by the semiotic framework comes in large part from a more coherent explanation of what courts and the PTO are already doing when they apply the printed matter doctrine.[280] With respect to other technologies, however, the semiotic framework has the potential to play a prescriptive role that restricts the set of patent-eligible claims. Semiotic analysis posits that signs pervade our environment.[281] If the printed matter doctrine is about signs and not recorded information, courts should be on the lookout for claims that run afoul of the printed matter doctrine whenever there are semiotically meaningful things at issue, even if those things do not intuitively resemble recorded information.

This part considers the impact of the sign doctrine on one technology that is not conventionally understood to be information recorded on a substrate: the computer model.[282] Part IV.A sets the stage by revealing the semiotic logic that has driven the courts' application of the printed matter doctrine to mechanical measuring devices: New mechanical measuring devices are eligible for patent protection, but old mechanical measuring devices with new labels are not. Part IV.B defines a computer model as a programmed computer in which computer users understand variables to stand for real-world systems, and it illustrates that computer models are signs. Part IV.C reviews the Federal Circuit's treatment of computer models as routinely patentable technologies. Part IV.D demonstrates the semiotic error that infects the Federal Circuit's assessment of the patentability of computer models. By eliding the sign-vehicle and the sign, the Federal Circuit has inappropriately reified semiotic meanings into worldly things. As a matter of semiotic logic, the limits that courts impose on the patentability of mechanical measuring devices under the printed matter doctrine cannot be reconciled with the courts' permissive attitude toward the patentability of computer models.

[280] *But see supra* notes 248–55 and accompanying text (discussing the prescriptive bite of the semiotic framework in core printed matter cases).

[281] *See supra* note 191 and accompanying text.

[282] This part does not consider the narrow issue of the patentability of software-on-disk claims that have long been understood to present a challenge for the printed matter doctrine. *See supra* text accompanying notes 89–93, 234–35 (discussing the distinction between functional descriptive material and nonfunctional descriptive material in *Beauregard* claims). Nor does it seek to undermine the patent eligibility of computer software broadly writ. *Cf.* Brief of the Software Freedom Law Center as Amicus Curaie in Support of Respondent, Bilski v. Kappos, No. 08–964 (U.S. filed Oct. 1, 2009) (arguing that software "standing alone" is patent ineligible). Many software inventions remain patentable under the sign doctrine. *See infra* note 327 and accompanying text (differentiating patent-ineligible advances in representation from patent-eligible advances in software engineering).

A. *Mechanical Measuring Devices and Indexical Meaning*

Courts applying the printed matter doctrine recognize the distinction between a new machine and a new set of labels placed on an old machine. For example, in *In re Lockert*,[283] a patent applicant sought to claim a prior-art scale with new printed indicia or labels that instructed the user to think differently about the meaning of the result generated by the scale.[284] For the purpose of simplicity, assume that the scale was a standard weighing device with a pointer on a fulcrum that pointed to a value on a continuous spectrum. The court rejected the claim because the invention resided in "the mere arrangement of printed matter": The claimed invention would be a patentable improvement over the prior art only if the content of the new labels was considered.[285] The actual claim described labels that indicated the amount of postage that was required to mail a package under the newly adopted postal shipping fees,[286] but the claim could have described any labels and the result would have been the same. The claim could, for example, have described labels indicating how far an object would be thrown when placed on a specific catapult. Even if the formula for determining this distance was nonobvious – and thus the information generated by the scale was nonobvious – the claim to the prior-art scale with new indicia would not be eligible for patent protection under the printed matter doctrine because the content of the labels could not be given patentable weight.

Semiotically speaking, a scale is no different from a weather vane, sundial, or mercury thermometer, all of which are canonical examples of indices.[287] Furthermore, in *Lockert*, the only "thing" that the inventor invented was a new interpretant or social convention understood in the mind of the user of the scale. In the old scale without the new labels, the position of the pointer on the spectrum (sign-vehicle) is nomically correlated to the weight of the object placed on the scale (referent), and it signifies the concept WEIGHT OF THE OBJECT in the mind of the human interpreter of the scale who understands the social convention built on top of the nomic correlation (interpretant).[288] With its new labels, the pointer can function as the sign-vehicle in a new sign. The position of the pointer on the spectrum (sign-vehicle) is now nomically correlated to the cost of mailing the object placed on the scale (referent)

[283] 65 F.2d 159 (C.C.P.A. 1933).

[284] *Id.*

[285] *Id.* at 161.

[286] *Id.* at 159.

[287] *See supra* Part III.B.3 (discussing Peircean indices).

[288] The scale gives rise to an index wherein the nomic connection is that the sign-vehicle is caused by the referent. This differentiates the scale from stimuli and signals that can function as indices because the nomic connection is that the sign-vehicle causes the referent. *See supra* note 201 and accompanying text.

in the mind of the human interpreter (interpretant). With yet different labels, the position of the pointer on the spectrum (sign-vehicle) could be nomically correlated to the distance that a particular catapult will throw the object (referent) in the mind of the human interpreter (interpretant). For the scale to mean new things, the only thing that has to change is the social convention that the interpreter uses to associate the sign-vehicle with an interpretant and thus, indirectly, to link the sign-vehicle to a referent. The pointer on the scale has no single "natural" or intrinsic meaning. The meaning of the scale is not "content" in the sense that it is contained within the scale as an object. What the position of the pointer means to a human interpreter is a semiotic meaning because it resides in the mind of an interpreter and arises from prevailing social conventions.

The semiotic framework not only explains why an old scale with new labels is not eligible for patent protection but it also accommodates the fact that scales with newly invented mechanical devices are "machines" that are eligible for patent protection under § 101, despite the fact that the scales are useful because they give rise to indexical meanings.[289] Sign-vehicles are eligible for patent protection when they have newly engineered nonsemiotic properties.[290] If a patent applicant limits the scope of her claim to a scale with a nonobvious mechanical mechanism for linking the weight of the object placed on the scale to the position of a pointer on a scale, there is an advance over the prior art that resides in the solution to a classic problem of mechanical engineering. The improvement over the prior art lies in the ingenuity of the engineering of the device that gives rise to indexical meaning; that is, the engineering that couples one real-world system (the weight of the object on the scale) to another real-world system (the position of the pointer) in a nomic fashion. The improvement does not reside solely in the interpretant that the sign-vehicle signifies.

In sum, the critical distinction that needs to be drawn to bring the sign doctrine to bear on mechanical measuring devices is the distinction between (a) new semiotic meanings for existing machines and (b) machines with new mechanical engineering that nomically couples distinct systems. In the context of mechanical devices, the distinction is intuitive because it corresponds roughly to the distinction between (a) new labels on old machines and (b) new machines.[291] Because this semiotic distinction is readily grasped, courts have successfully implemented it. They have extended the semiotic framework for the printed matter doctrine from static books and diagrams to dynamic mechanical machines that give rise to indices. As explored later, however, courts have failed to grasp this basic semiotic distinction in the context of computer-software inventions.

[289] *See* 35 U.S.C. § 101 (2006).

[290] *See supra* text accompanying notes 238–39.

[291] *But see infra* note 332 (discussing the borderline cases of novel machines that are nonobvious only because of their semiotic meanings).

B. *Computer Models Are Signs*

Mechanical devices are not the only types of § 101 machines that can function as the sign-vehicles of signs. Programmed computers, too, can be meaningful because they are wound up with signs. Specifically, programmed computers can be the sign-vehicles of signs when the behavior of the software program being executed on the computer mimics the behavior of a real-world system.[292] In this situation, a programmed computer functions as a component of a *computer model*.

For a simple example of a computer model, consider the invention of a programmed computer that diagnoses a patient based on an inverse relationship between two chemicals in human blood.[293] Researchers discover that in the real world – that is, in the molecules that actually comprise human blood – a high level of chemical A is correlated with a low level of chemical B, and vice versa. The programmed computer takes as an input a variable that represents the concentration of chemical A (either high or low) and produces as an output a variable that represents the concentration of chemical B (either low or high, respectively). The programmed computer functions as a model in the everyday way in which the word "model" is commonly used: It is built so that its behavior resembles the behavior of a real-world system. Computer models may range from the highly complex (for instance, a computer model for predicting weather) to the extremely simple (for instance, a computer for diagnosing chemical B deficiencies), but the basic concept remains unchanged.

To see that computer models are signs, it is important to draw a distinction between two different entities. First, there is a *programmed computer*: a computer executing a program that manipulates meaningless or semantically empty variables according to certain mathematical rules. Allowing for some simplification, the programmed computer in the device for diagnosing chemical B deficiencies is a computer programmed with software that manipulates variables according to the mathematical rule $y = 1/x$. Second, there is the computer model in which the behavior of the computer means something to the user of the programmed computer. The variable x means chemical A and the variable y means chemical B; thus the programmed computer models the relationship between chemicals A and B in human blood – only because of interpretants in the minds of computer users. The programmed computer and the computer model must be kept distinct to avoid the misleading synecdoche in which sign-vehicles are elided with signs.[294] The programmed computer is only one component of the computer model. The variables' meanings are not properties that are intrinsic to the computer that is programmed to execute the

[292] The notion that the key feature of software is the behavior that it provokes in a computer is explored at length in Pamela Samuelson, Randall Davis, Mitchell D. Kapor & J.H. Reichman, *A Manifesto Concerning the Legal Protection of Computer Programs*, 94 COLUM. L. REV. 2308 (1994).

[293] The discovery that gives rise to this invention is the same discovery discussed earlier in the text accompanying notes 154–55, but the claimed invention is different.

[294] *See supra* text accompanying notes 175–77.

rule $y = 1/x$. The computer itself cannot support an interpretant, and it is indifferent to the nature of the data's referents.[295]

To the computer, the data are not semiotically meaningful sign-vehicles but rather nonsemiotic signals: They cause the computer to adopt a predetermined internal state of affairs through a physical, causal mechanism.[296] The identical computer program (sign-vehicle) can have a perceived resemblance to, and can therefore be used to model or stand for, a vast array of different real-world systems (referents). The same programmed computer can mean different things to different users or even to the same user at different times, if the users associate different interpretants with the programmed computer. All that needs to change for the semiotic meaning of a computer model to change is for the computer user to think about the programmed computer in a different way, associate a new mental interpretant with the computer, and understand that the computer refers to a different real-world system. A programmed computer that executes the formula $y = 1/x$ can model the relationship between chemicals A and B in human blood or the relationship between the quantity of a young law professor's scholarship and her likelihood of being denied tenure. The meaning of a computer model is semiotic in nature and is thus in the eyes – or, more accurately, the mind – of the beholder.

More specifically, a computer model can be either of two different types of Peircean signs. It can be an icon or an index, depending on whether the data are input into the system through a deterministic process. Initially, assume that the programmed computer is a freestanding calculator in which a user inputs data on a keyboard and a display shows the result. The Peircean icon maps perfectly onto the computer model.[297] The programmed computer is the sign-vehicle. In the earlier example, this is the electronic device that manipulates data using the formula $y = 1/x$. The real-world system being modeled is the referent, the amounts of the chemicals A and B in a patient's blood. The interpretation given to the programmed computer by the computer user is the mental interpretant. The computer model is an icon because the computer user perceives a resemblance between the behavior of the real-world system (referent) and the behavior of the programmed computer (sign-vehicle).[298] The resemblance is in the nature of a diagram – a subspecies of an icon – because there is "an analogy between the relations of the parts of each."[299]

[295] *Cf. supra* note 200 (arguing that interpretants require intentional mental states and that only minds can possess intentional mental states). The fact that all programmed computers are elaborate Turing machines highlights the semiotically meaningless nature of the data to the computer. *See* J. David Bolter, Turing's Man: Western Culture in the Computer Age 43–47 (1984) (explaining Turing machines).

[296] *See supra* text accompanying note 196 (defining a signal).

[297] *See supra* Part II.B.2.

[298] *See supra* note 184 and accompanying text.

[299] Peirce, *supra* note 167, § 2.279.

Under only slightly modified conditions, computer models can give rise to Peircean indices rather than Peircean icons.[300] If the computerized device that executes the formula $y = 1/x$ obtains its input data automatically from a chemical analyzer that measures the amount of chemical A in a sample of human blood, then the combination of the chemical analyzer and the programmed computer (the "chemical-detector machine") gives rise to an index. The chemical-detector machine is semiotically analogous to a sundial and a scale.[301] The scale engineers a nomic correlation between properties of the object being weighed and the position of the pointer on the spectrum. Similarly, the chemical-detector machine engineers a nomic correlation between the concentration of chemical A in the blood sample and the value of the computer's output variable. The output variable of the chemical-detector machine is the sign-vehicle of a sign that can have the concentration of chemical B as its referent because the user of the chemical-detector machine understands the social convention that links the sign-vehicle to the referent. The sign-vehicle of an index is meaningful in a semiotic sense only because of a contingent social convention and the interpretant that forms in the mind of an interpreter.[302] As with the scale, the chemical-detector machine can have many different meanings. For example, if further research reveals that a chemical B deficiency is correlated with an increased risk of a heart attack, then the meaning of the machine may change without any change in the intrinsic workings of the machine itself.[303] For the chemical-detector machine to transform from a machine for detecting chemical B deficiencies into a machine for determining the risk of a heart attack, all that needs to change is the interpretant in the mind of the machine's user.

C. *The Routine Patentability of Computer Models Under the Contemporary Doctrine of Patent Eligibility*

The Federal Circuit views newly invented computer models as routinely patentable inventions. They are all eligible for patent protection under the "useful, concrete and tangible result" test of *State Street Bank & Trust Co.* v. *Signature Financial Group*,[304] and, if their referents are tangible entities, they remain eligible for patent protection under the more restrictive MoT test of *In re Bilski*.[305]

[300] *See supra* Part II.B.3.

[301] *See supra* notes 189, 287.

[302] *See supra* notes 201–06 and accompanying text (demonstrating the reliance of indexical meaning on social convention).

[303] *Cf.* Kevin Emerson Collins, *Constructive Nonvolition in Patent Law and the Problem of Insufficient Thought Control*, 2007 Wis. L. Rev. 759, 818–24 (using this shift in meaning to demonstrate the difficulty of administering a claim based on a social convention).

[304] 149 F.3d 1368, 1373 (Fed. Cir. 1998).

[305] 545 F.3d 943, 961–63 (Fed. Cir. 2008) (en banc). The Supreme Court has accepted certiorari to review the Federal Circuit's *Bilski* decision, so the validity of the MoT test remains unsettled as of the publication of this chapter. *See* Bilski v. Doll, 129 S. Ct. 2735 (2009). [Editors' Note: This chapter was

In its infamous "useful, concrete and tangible result" test of *State Street Bank*, the Federal Circuit looked to the meaning of the data manipulated as the key determinant of the patent eligibility of programmed computers.[306] *State Street Bank* involved a claim to a Hub and Spoke® data-processing system for administering mutual funds in which "mutual funds (Spokes) pool their assets in an investment portfolio (Hub) organized as a partnership."[307] As one of its functions, "the system also allow[ed] for the allocation among the Spokes of the Hub's daily income, expenses, and net realized and unrealized gain or loss."[308] In an oft-quoted passage, the Federal Circuit held that the claimed system of programmed computers was patentable subject matter because the data manipulated by the program had specified meanings that were useful to the computer users:

> Today, we hold that the transformation of data, representing discrete dollar amounts, by a machine through a series of mathematical calculations into a final share price, constitutes a practical application of a mathematical algorithm, formula, or calculation, because it produces "a useful, concrete and tangible result" – a final share price momentarily fixed for recording and reporting purposes and even accepted and relied upon by regulatory authorities and in subsequent trades.[309]

The programmed computer may manipulate and produce "numbers," but the program is patentable subject matter so long as the scope of the claim is limited to numbers that mean something "such as price, profit, percentage, cost, or loss."[310] Inversely, if a claim implicating a mathematical algorithm is not limited to the manipulation of meaningful data, and thus does not produce data that have a specified meaning, then the claim recites a mathematical idea in the abstract and is not

written prior to the Supreme Court's decision in *Bilski v. Kappos*, which affirmed the Federal Circuit's decision in *In re Bilski* but modified its rationale. 561 U.S. 593, 130 S. Ct. 3218 (2010). Contrary to the Federal Circuit, the Court held that the MoT test was not the sole test for determining the patent eligibility of a process. Rather, that test was only "a useful and important clue . . . for determining whether some claimed inventions are processes under § 101." *Bilski*, 130 S. Ct. at 3227.]

306 *State St. Bank*, 149 F.3d at 1373–75. The turn to meaning as the determinant of the patent eligibility of a programmed computer originated in the Federal Circuit's earlier case *Arrhythmia Research Tech., Inc.* v. *Corazonix Corp.*, 958 F.2d 1053 (Fed. Cir. 1992).

307 *State St. Bank*, 149 F.3d at 1370.

308 *Id.* at 1371.

309 *Id.* at 1373.

310 *Id.* at 1375; *see also id.* at 1374 ("[T]he mere fact that a claimed invention involves inputting numbers, calculating numbers, outputting numbers, and storing numbers, in and of itself, would not render it nonstatutory subject matter, unless, of course, its operation does not produce a 'useful, concrete and tangible result.'"). Similarly, discussing *Arrhythmia Research*, the Federal Circuit noted in *State Street Bank* that "the transformation of electrocardiograph signals from a patient's heartbeat by a machine through a series of mathematical calculations constituted a practical application of an abstract idea (a mathematical algorithm, formula, or calculation), because it corresponded to a useful, concrete or tangible thing – the condition of a patient's heart." *Id.* at 1373. *Accord* AT&T Corp. v. Excel Commc'ns, Inc., 172 F.3d 1352, 1358 (Fed. Cir. 1999) (holding a software claim to be patent eligible because the "PIC indicator represent[ed] information about the call recipient's PIC").

patent eligible.[311] Because the variables manipulated by computer models have specified meanings that are useful to computer users, computer models are categorically patent-eligible subject matter under *State Street Bank*.

The "useful, concrete and tangible result" test was an "anything goes" test for patent eligibility,[312] and *Bilski* represents the Federal Circuit's attempt to rein in patentable subject matter. *Bilski* identifies physicality or tangibility as the hallmark of historically patentable subject matter, and it deems some products of human ingenuity to be insufficiently tethered to this historical core to merit patent protection.[313] To instrumentalize this tangibility approach, *Bilski* articulates the MoT test for patent eligibility: A method claim is patent eligible only if "(1) it is tied to a particular machine or apparatus, or (2) it transforms a particular article into a different state or thing."[314] The claim at issue in *Bilski* described a method of entering into contracts in order to hedge "consumption risk."[315] Applying the MoT test, the Federal Circuit upheld the PTO's rejection of Bilski's claim. The claimed method neither required a particular machine – the method could in theory be performed with only spoken words and a handshake – nor transformed an article into a different state or thing. It transformed only legal rights, and the Federal Circuit held that legal rights are an abstract construct, not a physical article whose transformation could give rise to a patentable invention.[316]

Bilski did not involve a claim to a programmed computer, but the Federal Circuit nonetheless addressed at length the application of the transformation prong of the MoT test to programmed computers.[317] Method claims reciting the operations

311 *Id.* at 1373 n.4 ("By keeping in mind that the mathematical algorithm is unpatentable only to the extent that it represents an abstract idea, this confusion [about the section 101 mathematical algorithm exception] may be ameliorated."). The Federal Circuit's motivation for adopting meaning as the key indicia of the patent eligibility of programmed computers was to implement the Supreme Court's holding in *Gottschalk* v. *Benson*, 409 U.S. 63, 70–71 (1972) (holding that claims to mathematical formulas in the abstract are not eligible for patent protection).

312 Cotter, *supra* note 147, at 895.

313 *In re Bilski*, 545 F.3d 943, 961–63 (Fed. Cir. 2008) (en banc), *cert granted sub nom.*, Bilski v. Doll, 129 S. Ct. 2735 (2009).

314 *Id.* at 954 (Fed. Cir. 2008). The concerns about abstraction and intangibility that give rise to the MoT test usually play out in method claims rather than product claims. *But see In re* Nuijten, 500 F.3d 1346 (Fed. Cir. 2007) (holding that signals are not patent-eligible "articles" under § 101). For this reason, the MoT test rarely applies to artifact claims. Claims to programmed computers are an exception to this rule because apparatus and method claims to software inventions are interchangeable. *See infra* note 324.

315 *Bilski*, 545 F.3d at 949. Allowing for some simplification, the claim described a method in which a commodity provider enters into two contracts with two distinct parties: she contracts with a consumer of the commodity who has a given risk position and a third party who has a counter-risk position to that consumer. *Id.* at 964. This simplified description is misleading to the extent that the novelty and nonobviousness of the claim are at issue, but it communicates the basic facts needed to understand the Federal Circuit's holding on patent eligibility.

316 *Id.* at 964.

317 *Id.* at 962–63. The court in *Bilski* chose not to address the application of the machine prong to programmed computers. *Id.* at 962.

performed by a software program executed on a general-purpose computer present a particularly interesting problem under the transformation test articulated in *Bilski*. A programmed computer manipulates electronic signals. Are electronic signals sufficiently tangible to qualify as "articles" whose transformation can give rise to a patentable invention under § 101, or are they abstractions like legal rights? To answer this question, the court distinguishes data that are "representative of physical objects and substances" from data that are not (and that are thus representative of either abstractions or nothing at all).[318] The former data "constitute 'articles' such that their transformation is sufficient to impart patent-eligibility under § 101," but the latter data do not.[319] Under the MoT test of *Bilski*, computer models are patent-eligible inventions, provided that they model tangible real-world systems.[320] In semiotic terms, what the Federal Circuit did in *Bilski* was to focus on the tangibility of the referents of a computer model to assess the tangibility of the claimed invention. It shifted the focus from the physicality of the electrons in a computer processor to the physicality of the things that the electrons represent when the electrons are construed as semiotically meaningful data. The Federal Circuit drew a distinction not between two types of signals-as-artifacts, but rather between two types of data-as-signs.

The Federal Circuit already relied on the semiotic meaning of data as the key indicia of the patent eligibility of a programmed computer in *State Street Bank*.[321] *Bilski* and its overt reliance on the physicality of what the data represent bring this reliance to the surface. The rhetoric of the MoT test announced by the Federal Circuit in its *Bilski* opinion practically begs for a semiotic analysis of the patent eligibility of computer-software inventions.

D. *The Federal Circuit's Semiotic Error*

The Federal Circuit has committed a fundamental semiotic error in its analysis of the patent eligibility of newly invented computer models. It has collapsed the sign into the sign-vehicle and thereby reified semiotic meanings into intrinsic properties

[318] *Id.* at 963, 964.

[319] *Id.* at 962.

[320] In a blog post several days after the *Bilski* decision, the author offered a semiotic description of the MoT test using the terminology from the better known Saussurian model of the sign: "In the language of semiotics, the tangibility analysis has shifted from a concern about the tangibility of the signifier – the physical configuration of matter that forms a symbol – to a concern about the tangibility of the signified – the informational content of or the thing represented by the symbol." Posting of Kevin Emerson Collins to Patently-O, http://www.patentlyo.com/patent/2008/11/professor-colli.html (Nov. 1, 2008, 2:58 P.M.); *cf. supra* note 177 (presenting Saussure's dyadic model of the sign). Technically, however, Saussurian terminology is not up to the task of describing the *Bilski* decision. The MoT test turns on the tangibility of the referent, and Saussure employed a dyadic model of the sign that "brackets" the referent. *See supra* note 177. The Saussurian signified resembles the Peircean interpretant. *See supra* note 172. So, there is no such thing as a tangible signified (except insofar as a materialist sees a token of a signified in the synaptic firings of the brain).

[321] *See supra* text accompanying notes 306–11.

of worldly things.[322] It has treated an existing programmed computer that has a newly invented meaning to its user as a newly invented, extra-mental artifact.

The Federal Circuit has long recognized that a computer programmed with a new software program is a new machine for the purposes of both the novelty and nonobviousness analysis.[323] If any computer software is to be patentable, this is a necessary doctrinal stance. The underlying ontological presumption is that new software causes small-scale physical changes within the machine – different gates are open at different times, so electrons are moving around in different patterns – that in turn cause the programmed computer to demonstrate new behaviors.[324] The semiotic framework for the printed matter doctrine does not challenge this presumption. Computers with new programs must continue to be recognized as new machines. What is required, however, is a shift to a semiotic perspective on what constitutes a new computer program and thus a new machine.

Consider again the computer model of the inverse relationship between the concentrations of chemicals A and B in human blood.[325] The computer program in this example is software that executes the formula $y = 1/x$, and the programmed computer is an apparatus that manipulates data using the formula $y = 1/x$. The first computer programmer to make software that executes the formula $y = 1/x$ has clearly generated a new machine that may or may not be nonobvious, depending on the state of the art in computer programming at the time of the invention. In other words, advances in software engineering are patent eligible under the sign doctrine.[326] However, although a computer programmed with new software is a new machine,

[322] *See supra* notes 175–77 and accompanying text.

[323] *E.g.*, *In re* Bernhart, 417 F.2d 1395, 1400 (C.C.P.A. 1969) ("[I]f a machine is programmed in a certain new and unobvious way, it is physically different from the machine without that program; its memory elements are differently arranged.").

[324] Apparatus claims describing programmed computers and method claims describing the execution of software programs on computers are today presumed to rise and fall together. *See, e.g.*, Arrhythmia Research Tech., Inc. v. Corazonix Corp., 958 F.2d 1053 (Fed. Cir. 1992). Historically, however, method claims were viewed less favorably and arbitrary, formalistic distinctions pervaded the standards governing the patentability of software. *See In re* Prater, 415 F.2d 1393 (C.C.P.A. 1969) (rejecting method claims and upholding apparatus claims); Julie E. Cohen & Mark A. Lemley, *Patent Scope and Innovation in the Software Industry*, 89 CAL. L. REV. 1, 9–10 (2001) (discussing the now-defunct doctrine of "magic words").

[325] *See supra* text accompanying note 294.

[326] Programmed computers can be nonobvious, patentable machines for precisely the same reasons that mechanical measuring devices can be nonobvious, patentable machines. The software engineering required to make a computer execute the formula $y = 1/x$ may be a nonobvious advance, in the same way that the mechanical engineering required to make a pointer on a scale move in response to the weight of an object may be a nonobvious advance. *See supra* text accompanying notes 289–90. More generally, a newly invented computer model is eligible for patent protection under the sign doctrine if an advance over the prior art in software engineering is required to construct the claimed programmed computer. If the computer model is claimed generically, an advance in software engineering that makes the programmed computer capable of behaving in a manner that is analogous to the newly discovered real-world system (referent) is required for a patent-eligible invention. If the computer model is claimed in a manner that limits the scope of the claim to the use of a particular type of

a new computer model does not necessarily involve a new programmed computer. Even if the programmed computer that executes the formula $y = 1/x$ is old in the art, the researchers who discover the inverse correlation between chemicals A and B in human blood can lay claim to the invention of a new computer model. They have discovered new referents, and they can instruct users of the programmed computer to understand that the variables x and y signify newly invented interpretants. This discovery/invention is not a patent-eligible invention under the sign doctrine because the only advance over the prior art resides in the mind of a computer user. In sum, under the sign doctrine, it is important to differentiate patent-eligible advances in software engineering from patent-ineligible inventions in what software represents in the minds of its users.

Given the contemporary state of computer technology, only a trivial effort is required to create a programmed computer that executes the formula $y = 1/x$. In fact, it is almost inconceivable that such a device does not already exist in the prior art. Under the sign doctrine, a contemporary claim to a computer model along the lines of "an electronic device for measuring the concentration of chemical B in human blood" should therefore not be eligible for patent protection.[327] The meaning of the computer model is not intrinsic in the programmed computer; the only advance over the prior art lies in the minds of computer users. The old programmed computer has a new meaning and is able to function as a component of a new model only because of the interpretant that exists in the mind of the computer user and the social convention understood by the user that links the sign-vehicle to the interpretant and referent. However, under *State Street Bank* or *Bilski*, the newly invented computer model would be a patentable invention because the data have specific meanings or they refer to tangible substances, respectively.[328] In the context of computer models, the Federal Circuit has yet to learn the lesson that the "content" of a sign is not truly contained within a sign-vehicle.[329]

Whether the claimed computer model functions as an index or an icon is irrelevant to the patent-eligibility analysis. In the indexical computer model, there is a nomic connection between the output of the chemical-detector machine (sign-vehicle) and the real-world system (referent), but the semiotic meaning of the output is lodged in a social convention and a mental interpretant that forms in the mind of the user

programmed computer, however, only the particular type of programmed computer that is claimed needs to embody an advance over the prior art to achieve patent eligibility.

327 An inventor could, however, still patent an improved programmed computer that executed the formula $y = 1/x$ more rapidly or with fewer resources. *See supra* note 327. Therefore, an inventor can claim a computer model of the concentrations of chemicals A and B in human blood if the claim is limited to the use of the improved programmed computer, just like an inventor can claim a scale as an indexical sign if the claim is limited to a scale with an improved mechanism for creating the nomic connection between the weight of the object and the pointer. *See supra* notes 289–90 and accompanying text.

328 *See supra* Part IV.C.

329 *See supra* text accompanying note 175.

of the chemical-detector machine.[330] As a matter of semiotic logic, the fact that old mechanical measuring devices with new labels are unpatentable subject matter cannot be reconciled with the fact that indexical computer models are routinely patentable inventions.[331] Presuming that the combination of the chemical analyzer and the programmed computer that executes the formula $y = 1/x$ is old in the art, all that the inventor has done is put new labels on an old machine, indicating that x means chemical A and y means chemical B.[332]

The argument for the patentability of the iconic computer model is even weaker. In the iconic computer model, there is no link at all between the programmed computer (sign-vehicle) and the real-world system (referent), except a combination of convention understood by the interpreter and a resemblance perceived by the interpreter.[333] For a mechanical analog of the iconic computer model, consider the "spinner-machine" depicted in Figure 3.3 made by adding labels to a spinner from a board game for children.

This spinner-machine is a mechanical device that performs a basic mathematical or logical function: It establishes an inverse correlation between two variables. To use the machine, the operator places the tail of the arrow in the box corresponding to the known value of variable A, and the device produces a result indicating the corresponding value of variable B. If variable A is low, then the device determines that variable B is high. Inversely, if variable A is high, then the device determines that variable B is low.

The spinner-machine is a model of a real-world system in the exact same way that the iconic programmed computer that inversely correlates two variables can function as a model of a real-world system. The two machines are semiotically indistinguishable. The spinner-machine and the programmed computer (the sign-vehicles) both stand for the real-world system of chemical concentrations discovered by the researcher (the referents) because of the mental concepts in the minds of

330 *See supra* notes 300–03 and accompanying text.

331 *See supra* Part IV.A (discussing the nonpatentability of old machines with new labels).

332 A more difficult problem arises when the chemical analyzer and the programmed computer are both old in the art, but the combination of the two is new. In this situation, the invention is novel, but its nonobviousness raises an interesting question. The motivation to combine the chemical analyzer and programmed computer follows directly from the fact that the combination (the chemical-detector machine) can give rise to an index in which the concentration of chemical B in a patient's blood is the referent. When should a nonobvious interpretant render a novel machine nonobvious? This same question complicates the status of newly invented mechanical measuring devices under the sign doctrine. For example, consider the inventor who has discovered the "law of nature" that determines how far a given catapult will throw a stone of a particular weight. *See supra* text accompanying note 286. Now assume as well that prior-art scales were not very good at measuring the weight of catapult stones, perhaps because the basket in which the thing to be weighed was put could not readily accommodate large stones. If the inventor puts new labels on a new scale that can weigh large stones, is the invention patentable under the sign doctrine?

333 *See supra* notes 297–99 and accompanying text.

FIGURE 3.3. A "spinner-machine."

the people who use the devices (the interpretants). Viewed as a question of semiotic logic, there is no good semiotic reason why one should be a patentable invention but the other should not. A patent regime in which the spinner-machine is eligible for patent protection is difficult to imagine, however, so the routine patentability of iconic computer models should be treated as suspect at best.

CONCLUSION

The printed matter doctrine is not about information and its content, as the rhetoric of its contemporary judicial formulation suggests. Rather, it is about signs and their interpretants. The printed matter doctrine should therefore be reinterpreted in semiotic terms as the sign doctrine. The sign doctrine requires that claims to meaningful artifacts be held ineligible for patent protection if the nonobvious advance over the prior art resides solely in a representation (interpretant) in the mind of an interpreter.

Judicial recognition of a semiotic framework for the printed matter doctrine would have two principal effects. First, the semiotic framework allows the printed matter doctrine to be taken seriously. It provides a conceptually coherent and statutorily justified explanation for the muddled and nonstatutory reasoning that courts and the PTO currently employ in core printed matter cases. Second, the semiotic framework suggests that the Federal Circuit should reconsider the routine patentability of newly invented computer models. When addressing computer models, the Federal Circuit today elides the sign-vehicle with the sign and therefore commits a classic semiotic error: It inappropriately reifies a newly invented semiotic meaning into a new intrinsic property of a tangible, extra-mental artifact. As a result, it sanctions a patent on a meaningful thing even when the only invention at issue resides in the mind of the person who understands the thing's newly invented semiotic meaning. Claims to newly invented computer models literally describe a programmed computer (a sign-vehicle), yet the only inventive aspect of the claimed technology may be a new mental state in the mind of a computer user (an interpretant).

4

Patent Eligibility as a Policy Lever to Regulate the Patenting of Personalized Medicine

*Christopher M. Holman**

INTRODUCTION

This chapter considers the implications of a recently reinvigorated patent eligibility doctrine for innovation in personalized medicine. Part I begins with a brief overview of personalized medicine, followed in Part II by a discussion of the critical role that molecular diagnostic method claims will likely play in providing effective patent protection for inventions relating to personalized medicine. Part III reviews recent developments in patent law that have breathed new life into the previously moribund doctrine of patent eligibility, most notably the Supreme Court's 2010 *Bilski* v. *Kappos* (*Bilski II*)[1] decision and the Federal Circuit's decision in *Prometheus* v. *Mayo* (*Prometheus III*)[2] applying *Bilski II* to claims reciting a method for practicing personalized medicine. In that part, I argue that, by declining to set forth any clear criteria for assessing compliance with the doctrine, the Supreme Court has in effect sanctioned the use of patent eligibility as a "wildcard" to invalidate patent claims deemed "unworthy" of patent protection. Part IV discusses how the lower courts, particularly the Federal Circuit, and the U.S. Patent and Trademark Office (PTO) might leverage the discretion inherent in the *Bilski II* fundamental test for patent eligibility as a policy lever to regulate the scope of patent claim coverage available for inventions relating to molecular diagnostics and personalized medicine, in a manner that achieves perceived policy objectives of the patent system. For example, in *Prometheus III* the panel interpreted vaguely delineated parameters in the test for patent eligibility in a manner supporting the availability of reasonably extensive method claim coverage for personalized medicine inventions; however, it drew a line at claims that would be infringed by a doctor merely recognizing the clinical significance of a diagnostic test results or communicating that information to a

* Professor of Law, University of Missouri-Kansas City School of Law.

[1] Bilski v. Kappos, 561 U.S. 593, 130 S.Ct. 3218 (2010).

[2] Prometheus Laboratories v. Mayo Collaborative, 628 F.3d 1327 (2010).

patient. Part V offers some concluding thoughts on the implications of these developments for the availability of adequate patent protection for personalized medicine innovations.

I. THE ASCENT OF PERSONALIZED MEDICINE

The term "personalized medicine" has been coined to describe a relatively recent movement to incorporate molecular diagnostic testing (particularly, but not exclusively genetic testing) into the practice of clinical medicine. In personalized medicine, a molecular diagnostic test is used to identify a medically significant biomarker, such as a genetic mutation or an elevated level of a metabolite, the presence of which correlates with the suitability of a particular therapeutic treatment for the particular patient tested.[3] The goal of personalized medicine is to provide, in an efficient and cost-effective manner, "the right treatment, for the right patient, at the right time."[4] Personalized medicine has been getting a lot of buzz lately, spurred by advances in genomics research, including the completion of the Human Genome Project, and more recently by dramatic advances in DNA sequencing technology that many believe will soon bring down the cost of determining an individual's entire genomic sequence to less than $1000.[5]

It is widely anticipated that personalized medicine will play an increasingly important role in pharmaceutical development in particular and in health care in general. For example, FDA Commissioner Margaret Hamburg has stated that personalized medicine "is likely to be one of the most important themes for healthcare of the future."[6] She recently co-authored an article appearing in the *New England Journal of Medicine* with Francis Collins, the head of the National Institutes of Health (NIH), espousing the enormous potential benefits of personalized medicine and their shared vision of the scientific and regulatory structure needed to support its growth.[7] In 2007, then-Senator Barack Obama sponsored the Genomics and Personalized Medicine Act of 2007, which would have provided the framework for the establishment of a Personalized Medicine Interagency Working Group.[8] The Department of Health and Human Services has instituted a Personalized Healthcare

3 PERSONALIZED MEDICINE COALITION, THE CASE FOR PERSONALIZED MEDICINE 1 (2006).

4 Michael Rugnetta & Whitney Kramer, *Paving the Way for Personalized Medicine*, SCIENCE PROGRESS 3 (September 2009).

5 KEVIN DAVIES, THE $1000 GENOME (2010).

6 Margaret Hamburg, Commissioner, Food & Drug Administration, *Bringing Home the Genome: The FDA's Role in Realizing Personalized Medicine*, Address at Personalized Medicine Coalition Luncheon (February 25, 2010), *available at* http://www.personalizedmedicinecoalition.org/sites/default/files/files/Hamburg%20Transcript.pdf.

7 Margaret A. Hamburg & Francis S. Collins, *The Path to Personalized Medicine* 363 NEW ENG. J. MED. 301 (2010).

8 Genomics and Personalized Medicine Act, S.976, 110th Cong. (2007). *See also* Genomics and Personalized Medicine Act, H.R. 6498, 110th Cong. (2008).

Initiative to facilitate the translation of advances in genetic research into improved individual clinical care.[9]

Personalized medicine has the potential to provide numerous benefits to individual patients and to society at large by providing more effective and less costly therapeutic treatment. For example, it has been shown that prescribed drugs are in many instances ineffective for a large number of the patients taking them, and in some cases only 30% of the patients receiving a drug actually experience any benefit.[10] Individual patients can have entirely different responses to the same drug, often based on genetic variations or other biomarkers amenable to detection by diagnostic testing. A drug that could save one patient's life might be extremely toxic to another. Similarly, a drug dosage that is optimal for some patients might be too high for others, leading to serious adverse side effects, and be subtherapeutic for other patients with a genetic predisposition to metabolize and thereby neutralize the drug quickly. Molecular diagnostic testing to prescreen for patients who will truly benefit from the drug, and to determine the optimal dosing regimen, could dramatically improve the status quo, benefiting patients while substantially reducing the huge amounts currently expended by payers (such as the U.S. government) on ineffective treatment.

Tailoring the drug to the individual patient could also reduce adverse reactions and increase patient compliance. Furthermore, the principles of personalized medicine can reduce the time and cost of moving drugs through clinical trials and even facilitate the approval of drugs that might otherwise fail to achieve FDA approval or be withdrawn from the market for lack of an acceptable safety/efficacy profile with respect to the population at large.

The approval of Herceptin (trastuzumab) for the treatment of women with HER2-positive breast cancer has been pointed to as a poster child for personalized medicine. Herceptin, an antibody-based biological drug developed by Genentech, failed in its initial attempt to achieve FDA regulatory approval, based on Phase III trials that in 1997 showed the drug to be ineffective in the overall population tested.[11] However, subsequent evaluation of the trial results revealed that the drug was effective for the approximately 30% of patients whose breast cancer is characterized by overexpression of a cell surface protein called human epidermal growth factor receptor 2 (HER2).[12] In 1998, FDA approved Herceptin for treatment of breast cancer patients identified by genetic diagnostic testing to be HER2-positive. The diagnostic test also received FDA approval, and the ability of the test to accurately target the subset of patients who would benefit from the drug convinced most third-party payers, including Medicare, to provide reimbursement for both the drug and the genetic testing.[13]

[9] Health and Human Services, *Personalized Health Care*, *available at* http://www.hhs.gov/myhealthcare/.

[10] Personalized Medicine Coalition, *supra* note 3, at 3.

[11] *Id.* at 6.

[12] *Id.*

[13] *Id.* at 8.

In short, pairing of Herceptin with HER2 genetic diagnostic testing transformed a failed drug candidate into a highly effective therapeutic, illustrating the life-saving potential of personalized medicine.

II. DIAGNOSTIC METHOD CLAIMS WILL PLAY A CRITICAL ROLE IN THE PATENTING OF PERSONALIZED MEDICINE

The pharmaceutical industry relies heavily on patent protection to provide the necessary incentive for investment in the costly and risky endeavor of modern drug research and development. In fact, many would argue that no other technological sector is so dependent on strong and effective patent protection. Traditionally, patenting in the pharmaceutical sector has focused primarily on chemical compounds (i.e., drug active ingredients, drug formulations, processes for producing these compounds and formulations, and methods for using them in the treatment of specific diseases).[14]

By far, composition-of-matter patents claiming a drug's active ingredient (COM patents) have proven the most effective in this regard.[15] COM patents are the gold standard, generally providing innovators with broad and effective patent coverage, because they broadly cover any unauthorized production, use, or sale of any product comprising the active ingredient, even in new formulations or for new indications. Generic competitors rarely succeed in challenging COM patents, so normally generic competition does not begin until after expiration of these patents.[16]

Non-COM patents, in contrast, such as those claiming methods of treatment, processes of manufacture, or specific formulations, are as a rule substantially less effective in excluding generic competition. Although there are many examples of non-COM patents being effectively used by drug innovators, often to extend market exclusivity beyond the expiration of a COM patent, overall they have proven much more susceptible to challenge by generic competitors.[17] In most cases non-COM patents play an ancillary, supporting role to the more foundational protection provided by COM patents. Pharmaceutical companies will in many cases decide against developing a potentially promising drug candidate if it appears that COM patent protection will not be available for the active ingredient.

Given the critical importance of COM patent protection in conventional pharmaceutical development, the question arises as to whether innovators in personalized medicine will be able to obtain adequate patent protection to justify investment in this increasingly important sector of pharmaceutical innovation. Advances in personalized medicine will generally arise out of the discovery that some biomarker observable by molecular diagnostic testing, such as a genetic variation or mutation,

[14] Bernstein Global Wealth Management, *Paragraph IV Litigation: A Guide for the Perplexed* at 6 (October 2007) (hereafter the "Bernstein Report").

[15] *Id.* at 6.

[16] *Id.*

[17] *Id.*

is in some way predictive of a preferred therapeutic treatment regimen.[18] In some cases, the innovator might be able to rely on a traditional approach to pharmaceutical patenting and still achieve a sufficient period of market exclusivity to reap an adequate return on its investment.

For example, consider a pharmaceutical company that, in the course of seeking approval to market a new drug, discovers that, although the drug is safe and highly effective for some patients, it is inappropriate for patients carrying a specific genetic variation, either for lack of efficacy or because of safety concerns specifically correlated with a genetic variation. If the company has a COM patent on the new drug's active ingredient, it can capitalize on its personalized medicine discovery by using the information to ensure that clinical trials exclude patients who should not be receiving the drug, thus expediting and facilitating FDA approval of a drug for the subpopulation that can benefit from it.[19] A patent claiming the personalized medicine invention more specifically is not required for the innovator to reap a benefit from the invention.

But what happens when COM patent protection is not available for an inventor who discovers a therapeutically relevant correlation between a molecular biomarker and the optimal use of a drug, either because the drug is at or near the end of its patent term by the time the correlation is discovered or because the correlation was discovered by someone other than the owner of the COM patent? Under such circumstances, the inventor's ability to obtain an adequate return on investment will likely hinge on the availability of effective patent protection directed toward the diagnostic method used for detecting the biomarker in a patient.[20] The remainder of this chapter focuses on the role that patent eligibility might play in regulating the availability and scope of molecular diagnostic method claims and how it could affect the ability of innovators in personalized medicine to obtain adequate patent protection for their discoveries.

III. RECENT DEVELOPMENTS IN THE DOCTRINE OF PATENT ELIGIBILITY IMPLICATING THE PATENTABILITY OF DIAGNOSTIC METHODS

A. *The LabCorp Appeal Breathes New Life into the Patent Eligibility Doctrine*

Prior to 1980, it remained unclear the extent to which innovations relating to new but increasingly important technologies such as computer programming and biotechnology would be treated as patent-eligible subject matter under § 101 of the U.S.

[18] Personalized Medicine Coalition, *supra* note 3, at 1.

[19] *See, e.g.*, the Herceptin example provided in Part I.

[20] Genentech, the biotechnology company that markets Herceptin, is listed as the assignee of a number of patents claiming the HER2-positive diagnostic test as a diagnostic method. *See, e.g.*, U.S. Patent No. 8,076,066 (filed Mar. 23, 2007).

patent statute.[21] During the 1970s the Supreme Court twice struck down, as patent ineligible, claims directed toward the use of mathematical algorithms in computer programs – thereby establishing a gatekeeping role for this largely judge-made doctrine in policing against the expansion of patent law to encompass innovations that might satisfy statutory requirements of patentability, such as utility and nonobviousness, but nonetheless are deemed by the court unsuited for the right of exclusivity conferred by a patent.[22]

However, in 1980 and 1981 the Supreme Court decided two cases, one in the context of biotechnology and the other involving a computer program, which substantially expanded the recognized scope of patent-eligible subject matter, reflecting a more expansive vision of the role of patents in incentivizing advancement in these increasingly critical technologies. These decisions, *Diamond* v. *Chakrabarty*[23] and *Diamond* v. *Diehr*,[24] articulated a definition of patent-eligible subject matter that encompasses essentially any human-made product or process, with the only explicit caveat being a prohibition against patenting certain so-called fundamental principles. Examples of fundamental principles specifically identified in Supreme Court decisions from this era include principles of nature, natural phenomena, physical phenomena, abstract ideas, and mental steps. For the sake of simplicity, in this chapter I often boil these down to what I consider to be two primary categories of fundamental principles: natural phenomena and abstract ideas.[25]

Chakrabarty and *Diehr* roughly coincided with the creation of the Court of Appeals of the Federal Circuit, and from its inception in 1982 through 2005 the generally pro-patent Federal Circuit took this relatively permissive approach to patent eligibility and ran with it, progressively expanding the recognized scope of patent-eligible subject matter. One of the most significant decisions in this regard was *State Street Bank & Trust Co.* v. *Signature Financial Group*,[26] in which the court disabused the patent community of a previously widely held assumption that methods of doing business lie outside the realm of patentable subject matter. The U.S. Patent and Trademark Office (PTO), dutifully following the court's lead, expanded its view of patent-eligible subject matter and began issuing patents claiming subject matter bearing less and less semblance to what has traditionally been viewed as "technology."[27]

But this expansion led to a backlash, particularly from stakeholders outside the patent system's core constituencies of inventors and patent attorneys, who charged

21 Christopher M. Holman, *Bilski: Assessing the Impact of a Newly Integrated Patent Eligibility Doctrine on the Pharmaceutical Industry and the Future of Personalized Medicine*, 10 CURR. TOPICS MED. CHEM. 1937, 1939 (2010).

22 Gottschalk v. Benson, 409 U.S. 63 (1972) and Parker v. Flook, 437 U.S. 584 (1978).

23 Diamond v. Chakrabarty, 447 U.S. 303 (1980).

24 Diamond v. Diehr, 450 U.S. 175 (1981).

25 To my mind, principles of nature, natural phenomena, and physical phenomena are all essentially synonymous, and the patenting of purely mental steps constitutes a form of patenting an abstract idea.

26 State Street Bank & Trust Co. v. Signature Financial Group, 149 F.3d 1368 (Fed. Cir. 1998).

27 Holman, *supra* note 21, at 1939.

that the expansion of recognized patent-eligible subject matter was inconsistent with the purpose of the patent system, often tending to impede rather than incentivize innovation, and they called on the courts or Congress to rein in the trend. Patents on molecular diagnostic methods, especially those relating to genetic diagnostic testing (often characterized as "gene patents") came under particularly strident attack, based in large part on a perception that these patents could impede the development of new diagnostic tests and block patient access to already existing tests.[28]

The criticism took on increasing force as it found voice in a number of studies and reports commissioned to investigate the potential negative consequences of patents on innovation in biology and medicine, some with a particular emphasis on the availability of genetic diagnostic testing services.[29] Patents owned by Myriad Genetics that claim methods of testing for genetic variations in the BRCA genes (associated with breast and ovarian cancer) have been a most notable lightning rod for controversy and are currently the subject of a highly publicized judicial challenge, *The Association for Molecular Pathology* v. *US Patent and Trademark Office* – a sweeping assault on DNA patents and other patents based on genetic discoveries that has been orchestrated by the ACLU and Public Patent Foundation and is currently on appeal to the Federal Circuit.[30]

Nonetheless, in spite of the criticism, prior to 2005 the doctrine of patent eligibility remained largely moribund.[31] Although no one disputed the black-letter law that abstract ideas and natural phenomena are patent ineligible, the Supreme Court had provided scant guidance as to just what exactly that meant in practice, and it had come to be generally assumed that a small quantum of human intervention was sufficient to transform a fundamental discovery into a patent-eligible invention. As a practical matter, patent eligibility was simply not an issue for the vast majority of innovations, including the increasing number of important inventions relating to fundamental biological discoveries. So long as a patent claim was limited to some nominally useful application of a biological natural phenomenon and met the other statutory requirements such as novelty, nonobviousness, and adequate description, it

[28] Christopher M. Holman, *The Impact of Human Gene Patents on Innovation and Access: A Survey of Human Gene Patent Litigation*, 76 U.M.K.C. L. Rev. 295 (2007) (see citations provided herein). *Stifling or Stimulating – The Role of Gene Patents in Research and Genetic Testing Before the Subcomm. on Courts, the Internet and Intellectual Property*, 110th Cong. (2007) (statement of Dr. Marc Grodman, CEO, Bio-Reference Laboratories, Inc.).

[29] Comm. on Intellectual Property Rights in Genomic & Protein Research & Innovation, Nat'l Research Council, Reaping The Benefits of Genomic and Proteomic Research: Intellectual Property Rights, Innovation, and Public Health (2006); Revised Draft Report on Gene Patents and Licensing Practices and Their Impact on Patient Access to Genetic Tests (the SACGHS Report), *available at* http://oba.od.nih.gov/oba/SACGHS/SACGHS%20Patents%20Report%20Approved%202-5-20010.pdf.

[30] The Association for Molecular Pathology v. US Patent and Trademark Office, 702 F.Supp.2d 181 (S.D.N.Y. 2010).

[31] Mark A. Lemley et al., *Life After Bilski*, 63 Stan. L. Rev. 1315 (2011), *available at* http://ssrn.com/abstract=1725009.

was generally assumed to be patentable. For many years, this assumption was never seriously contested in the courts.

However, in 2005 the Supreme Court breathed new life into the doctrine of patent eligibility when it granted certiorari in *LabCorp* v. *Metabolite*.[32] Significantly, in view of the focus of this chapter, the patent claim that drew the Supreme Court's attention in *LabCorp* was directed toward a molecular diagnostic method. In fact, the claimed method might reasonably be characterized as an example of personalized medicine, at least under a relatively broad definition of that term, because it provides a method of using molecular diagnostic testing to identify individual patients who would benefit from a specific course of therapeutic treatment.

More specifically, the patent claim at issue in *LabCorp* arose out of the discovery by university researchers that an elevated level of total homocysteine (a naturally occurring metabolite) in a patient's body correlates with vitamin B deficiency. In the context of personalized medicine, elevated total homocysteine can function as a biomarker for diagnosing a medically relevant physiological state. The challenged patent claim broadly recites a method of diagnosing for vitamin B deficiency that entails performing a diagnostic test to determine the level of total homocysteine in a patient's blood and then correlating an observation of elevated total homocysteine with a deficiency of vitamin B. In practice, a doctor would use the claimed method to identify an individual patient likely to benefit from a personalized course of therapeutic treatment: use of a vitamin B supplement.

In the district court and before the Federal Circuit, the alleged infringer argued that the patent claim was invalid for failure to satisfy various requirements of patentability, including lack of novelty and obviousness.[33] The issue of patent eligibility does not appear to have been raised, not surprising in view of the doctrine's generally dormant status at that time. However, on petition for certiorari the defendant raised the issue of patent eligibility, and the Supreme Court granted the petition for the express purpose of deciding that issue – in particular, the question to be considered was whether the claim was invalid for violating Supreme Court precedent barring the patent eligibility of "laws of nature, natural phenomena, and abstract ideas."

The prohibition against patenting these fundamental principles was, of course, well established, at least as an abstract principle, but the case law provided little guidance as to exactly what it meant for a claim to patent a fundamental principle, particularly in the context of a diagnostic method claim originating out of the discovery of a naturally occurring biological correlation. The decision to grant certiorari signaled that at least some of the Justices were concerned that the recognized scope of patent-eligible subject matter had expanded too much in the years since

[32] Laboratory Corp. of America Holdings v. Metabolite Laboratories, Inc. 548 U.S. 124, 125 (2006) (Breyer, J., dissenting from dismissal of writ of certiorari).

[33] Metabolite Laboratories, Inc. v. Laboratory Corp. of America Holdings, 370 F.3d 1354 (Fed. Cir. 2004).

Chakrabarty and *Diehr* were decided, perhaps warranting another intervention by the Court to recalibrate the doctrine.

Ultimately, the Supreme Court dismissed *LabCorp* without deciding on the merits of the case, presumably because the patent eligibility of the claim was never addressed in the lower courts and as such the record was not sufficiently developed to permit comprehensive consideration of the issue. The Department of Justice (DOJ), in an amicus brief filed with the Court on behalf of the U.S. government, recommended against granting the petition for certiorari for this reason, but speculated that the claim might very well be patent ineligible if its scope were found to encompass every "substantial practical application" of a law of nature.[34] However, the DOJ went on to point out that the lower courts had not provided a sufficiently rigorous analysis of the scope of the claim to make such a determination.

Nonetheless, three Justices joined in an opinion authored by Justice Breyer dissenting from the majority's decision not to decide the case, arguing that the Court should have decided the case in a manner that would have held the method claim to be patent ineligible.[35] In their view, the correlation between total homocysteine level and vitamin B deficiency is a natural phenomenon, and the challenged patent claim was invalid because, in Justice Breyer's words, the claim "embodies" the natural phenomenon. The *LabCorp* dissent voices many of the concerns raised by critics of the patent system, arguing that too much patent protection can impede rather than promote progress in science and technology and attributing an important role to patent eligibility as a gatekeeper to guard against such overprotection.

Significantly, under Justice Breyer's approach to patent eligibility, the explicit recitation of a tangible, physically transformative step is not necessarily sufficient to render a method claim patent eligible. The claim at issue in the case specifically recites a positive step of assaying a patient's blood for total homocysteine level, a procedure that requires the physical processing of a blood sample and the use of sophisticated laboratory equipment. Prior to the *LabCorp* dissent, most patent practitioners would have probably assumed that the involvement of such a clearly technological and tangible set of process steps was sufficient to render the claim patent eligible. However, in his analysis Justice Breyer essentially dissected the claim into two parts: the assay step, which he assumed (I think correctly) was not independently patentable due to prior art, and the correlation step, which marked the point of novelty and invention. In reaching his ultimate conclusion of patent ineligibility, he focused entirely on the correlation (which he characterized as a natural phenomenon), essentially treating the initial assaying step as irrelevant to the inquiry.

34 Metabolite Laboratories, Inc. v. Laboratory Corp. of America Holdings, Brief for the United States as Amicus Curiae, 2005 WL 3533248 (2005).

35 Laboratory Corp. of America Holdings, 548 U.S. at 125 (Breyer, J., dissenting).

Justice Breyer then went further, postulating that even if the claim were amended to explicitly recite a step of acting on the information gathered using the method (i.e., by treating the patient for the identified vitamin deficiency), the claim would still be patent ineligible for embodying a natural phenomenon. In adopting this approach to analyzing for patent eligibility, Justice Breyer completely disregards what most patent practitioners at the time would have considered a fundamental principle of patent law (i.e., that all claim limitations must be taken into account when considering the scope and validity of a patent claim).

Although the *LabCorp* dissent is not binding legal precedent, as a practical matter it reinvigorated the doctrine, planting the seed for future patent-eligibility–based challenges, particularly with respect to claims relating to biology and molecular diagnostics. In its aftermath, the issue of patent eligibility was raised in three cases involving method claims directed toward inventions arising out of the discovery of a biological phenomenon applied in a clinical context.

The earliest of these cases, *Classen* v. *Biogen* (*Classen I*),[36] involved patent claims reciting methods for modifying an immunization schedule to reduce the incidence or severity of immune-mediated disorders. The methods generally comprise immunizing a group of patients according to one vaccination schedule and comparing the incidence or severity of immune-mediated disorders with that of a control group of patients immunized pursuant to a different schedule. No doubt emboldened by Justice Breyer's *LabCorp* dissent, the alleged infringer challenged the patent eligibility of the claims, and the district court judge obliged by holding that the relationship between vaccination schedule and autoimmune disorders is "without question" a natural phenomenon and that the challenged claims were invalid for embodying the phenomenon.

The next eligibility-based patent challenge, arising in *Ariad* v. *Eli Lilly*,[37] was not so successful. The patents at issue arose out of the inventors' discovery of the NF-kB transcription regulation pathway, and they broadly claimed essentially any method for inhibiting NF-kB activity in a cell. Ariad sued Eli Lilly for patent infringement, claiming that the mechanism of action of some of its drugs involved inhibition of NF-kB activity. However, the district court judge in this case rejected the patent eligibility challenge, finding that Lilly had failed to prove by clear and convincing evidence that the alleged natural phenomenon existed in living cells in a way encompassed by the challenged patent claims (based in large part on some critical evidentiary rulings that went against Lilly). Ultimately, the issue of patent eligibility was rendered moot when the en banc Federal Circuit invalidated the claims for failure to satisfy the written description requirement.[38] The district court's patent eligibility analysis seems highly suspect, and *Ariad* v. *Eli Lilly* probably has little if any significance for future cases involving questions of patent eligibility.

36 Classen Immunotherapies, Inc. v. Biogen Idec, 2006 WL 6161856 (D. Md. 2006).
37 Ariad Pharmaceuticals v. Eli Lilly, 2007 WL 2011279 (D. Mass. 2007).
38 Ariad Pharmaceuticals v. Eli Lilly, 598 F.3d 1336 (Fed. Cir. 2010).

The third patent-eligibility–based challenge, *Prometheus* v. *Mayo* (*Prometheus I*),[39] is the most relevant to the focus of this chapter because it involves claims directed toward an invention that is clearly an example of personalized medicine. The patents at issue arose out of the discovery that, by monitoring the level of certain thiopurine drug metabolites (i.e., drug breakdown products created as the drug is metabolized) in a patient's body, it is possible to adjust drug dosage to optimize safety and efficacy for that particular patient. The thiopurine drugs in question are used to treat individuals with immune-mediated gastrointestinal disorders such as Crohn's disease, but their use is often accompanied by serious adverse side effects, including hepatotoxicity. Because different patients metabolize the drug differently, it had been difficult for doctors to ascertain the proper dosage, and some doctors had reportedly been hesitant to prescribe the drugs at all for fear of toxic side effects. The challenged patent claims in Prometheus I recite methods of treating individuals suffering from autoimmune disease comprising the steps of administering the drug to the patient, performing a diagnostic test to determine the level of certain drug metabolites in the patient's body, and recognizing that if the metabolite level exceeds a specified upper threshold the dosage should be decreased, while if the metabolite level is less than a lower threshold the dosage should be adjusted upward.

The district court judge in *Prometheus I* found the challenged claims "clearly analogous" to the claim at issue in *LabCorp* and, although acknowledging that Breyer's dissent is not binding precedent, found its substance to be "persuasive." Thus inspired by Breyer's reasoning, the judge held the challenged claims patent ineligible on two alternate grounds: (1) The claims are directed toward patent-ineligible "mental steps" (i.e., a doctor being warned by the metabolite levels that an adjustment in dosage may be required), and (2) the claims wholly preempt all practical uses of a "natural phenomenon" (i.e., the correlation between the level of drug metabolite and therapeutic efficacy and toxicity).

The patent owner in *Prometheus I* argued that its claims were patent eligible because they explicitly recited the physically transformative steps of administering a drug to a patient and determining the level of drug metabolite in the patient's body. However, apparently taking Justice Breyer's cue, the district court blithely disregarded these steps in its analysis, dismissing them as "merely data-gathering steps." With the "administering" and "determining" steps of the claimed method effectively ignored in the analysis, the sole remaining claim limitation was the mental step of recognizing the correlation between the drug metabolite level and the optimal dosage, which the district court characterized as a natural phenomenon.

The patent owner further argued that, because the drug metabolites only exist in the human body as a result of human intervention (i.e., by administration of the thiopurine drugs), the correlation cannot properly be considered a *natural* phenomenon. However, the judge rejected this argument, holding that because

39 Prometheus v. Mayo, 2008 WL 878910 (S.D. Cal. 2008).

thiopurine drugs "are converted naturally by enzymes within the patient's body to form an agent that is therapeutically active,... the correlation results from a natural body process" and is thus an unpatentable "work of nature." The judge then proceeded to conclude that the claims were patent ineligible for "wholly preempting" this supposedly natural phenomenon.

In an effort to rebut the allegation that the claims wholly preempt all uses of the correlation, the patent owner identified at least six potential uses of the correlation that it argued were outside the scope of the claims. However, the judge dismissed all of these uses as insubstantial, concluding that the "subject matter recited in the claims has 'no substantial practical application' outside the context of the claims."

Classen I and *Prometheus I* were both appealed to the Federal Circuit. However, before the parties submitted their briefs, the en banc Federal Circuit created a new (but ultimately short-lived) "definitive" and universal test for patent eligibility applicable to all method claims, as discussed in the next section.

B. Bilski I *and the Short-Lived Reign of the Machine-or-Transformation Test*

In 2008, with appeals pending in *Classen I* and *Prometheus I*, the Federal Circuit took up the issue of patent eligibility en banc in *In re Bilski* (*Bilski I*). The claims at issue were directed toward methods of hedging risk in energy investments, but the holding of the case was broad and expressly applicable to all method claims. In *Bilski I*, the majority proposed that under binding Supreme Court precedent the fundamental test for patent eligibility is whether the claim recites fundamental principle and, if so, whether it would preempt substantially all uses of that fundamental principle.[40] Observe that this is essentially the same test for patent eligibility proposed by the DOJ in its LabCorp amicus brief, and it ascribes to patent eligibility an explicit role in policing claim scope.

However, the *Bilski I* majority went on to point out that, in practice, applying this fundamental test is "hardly straightforward." The court noted that many of the process claims that arise out of twenty-first-century technological innovation bear little resemblance to the process claims specifically addressed in the patent eligibility cases decided by the Supreme Court, and as a consequence the controlling precedent provides little practical assistance to guide the inquiry outside the specific facts of those cases.[41] The solution adopted by the court was to institute a more predictable, objective, and administrable test for patent eligibility that would effectively function as a proxy for the more fundamental inquiry of whether the claim substantially preempt all uses of a fundamental principle.

To this end, the *Bilski I* court articulated what has come to be known as the "machine-or-transformation test" (MoT) and elevated it to a preeminent position

[40] *In re Bilski*, 545 F. 3d 943, 954 (Fed. Cir. 2008).
[41] *Id.*

as the sole and definitive test for patent eligibility of all method claims, applicable across the entire spectrum of technologies and innovation. The majority argued (unconvincingly in my view) that this approach was grounded in applicable Supreme Court precedent, which it characterized as having implicitly "enunciated [that MoT is the] definitive test to determine whether a process claim is tailored narrowly enough to encompass only a particular application of a fundamental principle rather than to preempt the principle itself."[42] As defined by the Federal Circuit, the machine-or-transformation test is a two-part inquiry, pursuant to which "an advocate may show that a process claim [is patent eligible] either by showing that his claim is tied to a particular machine, or by showing that his claim transforms an article."[43]

Bilski I emphasizes, however, that the mere involvement of a machine or transformation in a claimed method is not necessarily sufficient to render the claim patent eligible. In a manner hearkening back to the approach adapted by Justice Breyer in *LabCorp*, *Bilski I* held that involvement of a machine or transformation in a claimed process can be disregarded in assessing the patent eligibility of a method claim if the step involving a machine or transformation represents nothing more than mere "insignificant extra-solution activity." The court expressed particular skepticism with respect to the significance of data-gathering steps, noting that "at least in most cases, gathering data would not constitute a transformation of any article, and adding a data-gathering step to an algorithm is insufficient to convert the algorithm into a patent-eligible process."

Bilski I raised some serious concerns for the biotechnology sector, particularly companies and other institutions engaged in the development of genetic tests and personalized medicine. In a strongly worded dissent to *Bilski I*, Judge Rader (now chief judge of the Federal Circuit) voiced his fear that the MoT test threatened to preclude effective patent protection for life-saving diagnostic innovations, thereby undermining and discouraging future research.[44] In his words, the MoT test "inadvertently advises investors that they should divert their unprotectable investments away from the discovery of scientific relationships within the body [which could be used] to diagnose breast cancer or Lou Gehrig's disease or Parkinson's or whatever."

Some of the angst arose out of uncertainty as to how specific a method claim would need to be with respect to the involvement of a "particular" machine or transformation to satisfy the MoT test. For example, would the inclusion of a step requiring the use of a general-purpose computer in a claimed method be sufficient to satisfy the test? Diagnostic methods typically rely on the analysis of data, and data gathering in the context of molecular diagnostics generally implies the use of some machine and/or the transformation of some substance (e.g., a chemical transformation). Would this be sufficient to render the claim patent eligible, or

42 *Id.*
43 *Id.* at 961.
44 *Id.* at 1014 (Rader, J., dissenting).

would a court simply disregard these sorts of data-gathering steps in the analysis by characterizing them as mere "insignificant extra-solution activity." *Bilski I* seemed fairly explicit in its statement that, in general, a data-gathering step would not be sufficient to confer patent eligibility on a method claim involving recognition of a fundamental principle – regardless of whether the data gathering involves the use of a machine or transformation – if the gathering of data is inherent in carrying out the method.

The Federal Circuit's first opportunity post-*Bilski I* to apply the MoT test in the context of biotechnology was the appeal of *Classen* (*Classen II*),[45] and the outcome was not encouraging. In a terse, unpublished (and thus thankfully nonprecedential) opinion, the panel affirmed the lower court's decision finding the claims at issue patent ineligible. In its opinion, the Federal Circuit did not comment on the district court's rationale for invalidating the patents (which was arrived at prior to *Bilski I* and thus not based on the MoT test), but simply stated that the claims were patent ineligible for failure to satisfy the MoT test because the claimed processes are neither "tied to a particular machine or apparatus" nor do they "transform [] a particular article into a different state or thing."

On its face, the logic behind *Classen II* appears suspect. The invalidated claims explicitly recite a step of immunizing patients with a vaccine, which if successful substantially transforms the immunized individual by enhancing her immunity to the targeted disease. Although the panel provides no explanation of the rationale used in deciding to disregard the immunization step in its MoT test analysis, it presumably must have concluded that the immunization step is mere "data-gathering," inherent to the practical implementation of the fundamental principle implicated by the claim, and thus not central to the claim – in the words of *Bilski I*, mere "insubstantial extra-solution activity." The alternative explanation – that the panel concluded that immunization of a patient is not transformative – would imply that pharmaceutical method of treatment claims are patent ineligible, but it seems highly implausible that the Federal Circuit would knowingly define transformation in a manner that would implicitly render this important class of pharmaceutical patents invalid.

The biotechnology community was not exactly sure what to make of the cryptic pronouncement of *Classen II*, but its constituents clearly perceived that the yet to be decided appeal of the *Prometheus I* decision could have important ramifications for the industry. Representatives of these constituencies submitted numerous amicus briefs to the Federal Circuit, voicing their concern that if affirmed *Prometheus I* could adversely affect the patenting of important innovations in diagnostics, personalized medicine, and even conventional pharmaceuticals.[46] Under the district court's

[45] Classen Immunotherapies, Inc. v. Biogen Idec et al., 2008 WL 5273107 (Fed. Cir. 2008).

[46] *See, e.g.*, amicus briefs submitted to the Federal Circuit in *Prometheus* on behalf of BayBio et al., Genetic Alliance, and the Biotechnology Industry Organization.

ruling, the patent eligibility of molecular diagnostic and personalized medicine methods in particular seemed highly suspect.[47]

Perhaps even more troubling, the logic espoused by the district court, if applied literally to other method claims, would appear to preclude the patenting of pharmaceuticals in general. After all, if the interaction of a drug with the human body is a natural phenomenon (the conclusion of the district court), a patent claiming the drug (or a method of treatment using the drug) would seem to be patent ineligible for wholly preempting all substantial practical applications of the phenomenon. Fortunately, apparently cognizant of these concerns, the Federal Circuit decided the appeal (*Prometheus II*) in a manner clearly intended to preserve the patenting of diagnostics and pharmaceuticals.[48]

Although the district court's decision in *Prometheus I* was based primarily on its conclusion that the claims substantially preempt all practical uses of a natural phenomenon, on appeal the intervening controlling precedent of *Bilski I* dictated that the panel decide the case within the rubric of the MoT test. Applying the test in a very different context from which it arose, the panel reversed the district court and held that all of the challenged patent claims clearly satisfy the transformation prong of the MoT test.

The critical difference between the patent eligibility analysis as conducted by the district court and Federal Circuit, which dictated the disparate outcomes, lies primarily in the significance attributed by the respective courts to the "administering" and "determining" steps in the claims. In contrast to the district court's dismissal of these steps as mere "data-gathering," the Federal Circuit characterized each as "central to the purpose of the claim" (i.e., the treatment of the patient) and thus relevant to the question of patent eligibility. Note that the weight afforded by this panel of the Federal Circuit to the drug administration step appears inconsistent with the approach taken by a different panel in *Classen II*, which as noted earlier disregarded an explicit step of administering a vaccine to a patient in its MoT analysis, even though administering a vaccine seems just as central to the claims at issue in that case.

I think the most likely explanation for the facial inconsistency between *Classen II* and *Prometheus II* is that the Federal Circuit considered Dr. Classen's claims "unworthy" of patent protection and employed the doctrine of patent eligibility as a useful expedient to invalidate the claims, rather than sending the case back to the district court to reach the same conclusion under more conventional grounds, such as obviousness or lack of enablement. However, under *Bilski I* the panel was compelled to decide the case under the MoT test and was probably unsure how to rationalize its decision to invalidate the claims for lack of patent eligibility in a

47 See *infra*, this section.

48 Prometheus Labs, Inc. v. Mayo Collaborative Services, 581 F.3d 1336 (Fed. Cir. 2009), *cert. granted, vacated, and remanded*, 130 S.Ct 3543 (2010).

manner that would not inadvertently implicate the patentability of a host of other biology-based inventions deemed more worthy of protection, such as methods of pharmaceutical treatment and personalized medicine. To this end, they issued a terse, nonprecedential opinion that arrives at the desired outcome with respect to the Classen claims, but provides no explicit explanation of its MoT analysis, thereby minimizing the relevance of the decision beyond the facts of the case. In my opinion, the panel should have simply issued a Rule 36 affirmance without any explanation, because, in spite of its brevity, the *Classen II* opinion generated unnecessary uncertainty as to how the MoT test would be applied to biotechnology inventions in future cases.

Returning to *Prometheus II*, with respect to the "administering" step the panel held that the administration of a drug to a patient results in a transformation of the human body, as well as physical changes to the drug as the body metabolizes it. The court found that the "asserted claims are in effect claims to methods of treatment, which are always transformative when a defined group of drugs is administered to the body to ameliorate the effects of an undesired condition." The *Prometheus II* panel appears to have been fully cognizant that the test for patent eligibility, if applied too stringently, could threaten the validity of drug method of treatment claims. Such an outcome would be bad public policy, given the important role these claims play in incentivizing investment in pharmaceutical innovation, and the panel addressed this potential concern by clarifying that any method claim reciting administration of a drug to a patient is patent eligible under the MoT test.

With regard to the "determining" step, the court held that determining the amount of drug metabolite in a patient's body likewise necessarily involves a transformation, because the determination cannot be made by "mere inspection," but instead requires some form of physical manipulation to isolate molecules from a patient's sample and determine their concentration. Under this holding, it would seem that any form of molecular diagnostic testing, such as genetic testing, should be considered patent eligible, because they all require some transformative clinical and laboratory manipulations to detect the molecule of interest. In adopting this approach, the panel presumably sought to ensure that any molecular diagnostic method that involves actual isolation, detection, and/or measurement of a biological molecule, such as genetic diagnostic testing that requires analysis of DNA molecules (as opposed to the mere analysis of genetic sequence information), would remain patent eligible.

The Federal Circuit did agree with the district court judge that the final "wherein" clause of the Classen claims, which the district court construed as requiring that a doctor be warned that an adjustment of dosage might be required, constitutes a mere mental step and is thus patent ineligible per se. However, the panel stressed that inclusion of a mental step in a claim does not negate the transformative nature of prior steps – in this case the administering and determining steps – and thus does not detract from the patent eligibility of the claimed method as a whole. The outcome-determinative difference between *Prometheus I* and *Prometheus II* was that the lower court disregarded the administering and determining steps as mere data gathering, whereas the Federal Circuit included them in its analysis of the claim. Significantly, however, under the Federal Circuit approach a claim that only recites recognition of a physiologically significant biomarker or correlation, without explicitly reciting steps that actively transform physical matter, would apparently be patent ineligible.

Shortly after *Prometheus II*, a district court invoked the MoT test to invalidate genetic diagnostic method claims in *Association for Molecular Pathology* v. *US Patent and Trademark Office*, the challenge to gene patents mentioned earlier.[49] These claims are directed toward methods for identifying mutations in a patient's BRCA gene sequence that correlate with an increased risk of developing breast or ovarian cancer. The claimed methods generally involve a step of either "analyzing" or "comparing" the BRCA nucleotide sequence of a patient with a wild-type BRCA nucleotide sequence to check for the presence of a deleterious mutation.

One interesting aspect of *Association for Molecular Pathology* lies in a significant dispute as to the scope of the challenged diagnostic method claims. The district court judge adopted the broad construction of the claims proffered by the plaintiffs, under which the term "nucleotide sequence" refers to genetic sequence information, and pursuant to which the claims were assumed to encompass the purely mental process of "comparing" or "analyzing" genetic sequence information. The patent owner, Myriad Genetics, in contrast, argued unsuccessfully for a narrower interpretation, pursuant to which "nucleotide sequence" refers to actual polynucleotides (i.e., DNA or RNA molecules) and the step of "comparing" or "analyzing" these molecules necessarily entails physically isolating polynucleotides from a patient's tissue sample and then processing and analyzing the molecules.[50] The distinction is highly relevant under *Bilski I*, because the physical manipulation of samples using sophisticated laboratory equipment entails physical transformations and machines that would not be required for the mere mental comparison of genetic sequence information.

On a motion for summary judgment, the district court judge ruled Myriad's diagnostic method claims patent ineligible for failing to adequately recite the use of a machine or transformation.[51] Given the claim construction adopted by the court, this aspect of the decision seems reasonable and in keeping with dicta in *Prometheus II* stating that a claimed process involving only mental steps fails the MoT test per se. Interestingly, however, the judge goes even further and opines that

> [e]ven if the challenged claims were to include the transformations associated with isolating and sequencing human DNA, these transformations would constitute no

49 The case also involves claims to isolated DNA molecules, but they are not the focus of this chapter.

50 Molecular biologists routinely to refer to DNA molecules as "sequences," but this terminology might have been unfamiliar to the judge.

51 In fact, all of the challenged product and process claims were held patent ineligible in the ruling.

> more than "data-gathering step[s]" that are not central to the purpose of the claimed process.... Consequently, even if the method claims-in-suit were construed to include the physical transformations associated with isolating and sequencing DNA, they would still fail the "machine or transformation" test under Section 101 for subject matter patentability.

This gratuitous speculation regarding the patent eligibility of hypothetical claims explicitly reciting the isolation and sequencing of DNA molecules seems clearly inconsistent with *Prometheus II*, which was controlling precedent at the time *Association for Molecular Pathology* was decided. Recall that in *Prometheus II*, the Federal Circuit held that a step of determining the amount of drug metabolite in a patient's body is transformative, because the determination inherently involves obtaining a sample from a patient and using analytical laboratory processes and equipment to determine the amount of drug metabolite present. It then proceeded to hold that this transformation was sufficient to render the claim patent eligible under the MoT test, because the transformative step is aimed at the central purpose of the claim and thus cannot be simply disregarded in the analysis as mere "insubstantial extra-solution activity." To my mind, the "transformations associated with isolating and sequencing human DNA" are just as central to the purpose of Myriad's diagnostic method claims as the transformations inherent to determining the level of drug metabolite are to Prometheus's claims.

C. Bilski II *Reinstates a More Flexible Approach to Assessing Patent Eligibility*

The preeminence of the MoT test was to prove short-lived. *Bilski* I was appealed to the Supreme Court, which granted certiorari and in June 2010 issued its decision under the name *Bilski* v. *Kappos* (*Bilski II*).[52] *Bilski II* held that Federal Circuit had erred in characterizing the MoT test as the definitive and sole test for analyzing the patent eligibility of method claims, and it emphatically reiterated that the test for patent eligibility remains the same as it was in 1980 (i.e., fundamental principles cannot be patented).

To my mind, perhaps the most notable aspect of *Bilski II* is the plurality's decision to provide virtually no additional guidance with respect to how the lower courts are to apply the test for patent eligibility in future cases, beyond simply pointing to the statutory definition of "process" and referring to earlier Supreme Court precedent as "guideposts." The Court makes a couple of unambiguous statements regarding what the test for patent eligibility is *not* – the MoT test is not the sole test for patent eligibility, and there is no absolute bar to the patent eligibility of business methods – but has virtually nothing to say about what the test for patent eligibility

[52] Bilski v. Kappos, 130 S.Ct. 3218 (2010).

is.[53] The *Bilski II* plurality emphasizes that the case was decided narrowly and provides only the most minimal explanation as to how it arrived at its conclusion that the claims at issue are all patent ineligible.

What little explanation *Bilski II* provides does not hold up particularly well under scrutiny. The Court begins by asserting that the claims "explain the basic concept of hedging," which is clearly not the case. Some of the independent claims do appear quite broad, but they are limited to a specific type of risk hedging in the commodity market and in no way "explain" the concept of hedging. The Court then states that the claims would "pre-empt [the concept of risk hedging] in all fields." But the claims are clearly not that broad, and if they were they would be invalid on their face under § 102 for lack of novelty, obviating any need for invoking the patent eligibility doctrine. As the decision specifically points out, risk hedging "is a fundamental economic practice long prevalent in our system of commerce and taught in any introductory finance class." The Court never addresses the fact that the claims would necessarily be invalid under §§ 102 and 103 if they were actually as broad as the Court characterizes them.

The Court then turns to the remaining claims at issue in the case, dependent claims that by definition are narrower in scope than the claims on which they depend. The Court characterized these claims as "broad examples of how hedging can be used in commodities and energy markets." While implicitly acknowledging that these claims would not preempt all uses of risk hedging, it nonetheless justified its decision by pointing out that under earlier Supreme Court precedent "limiting an abstract idea to one field of use or adding token post-solution components" does not render a claim patent eligible, and it held the dependent claims patent ineligible because they do not add enough to the "underlying abstract principle."

Significantly, while rejecting the notion that the MoT test is the exclusive test for patent eligibility of method claims, *Bilski II* acknowledges that it can be highly probative of patent eligibility and suggests that in most cases patent-eligible claims will involve a machine or transformation. In a sense *Bilski II* amounts to a do-over, resetting the standard for patent eligibility to its vaguely defined pre-*Bilski* state, but refraining from introducing any additional restrictions or clarifications that might limit the Federal Circuit's discretion in future cases.

In my view, the conflicting interpretations of patent eligibility set forth in *Bilski I* and *Bilski II* reflect a conflict between the Federal Circuit's aspiration for relatively bright-line tests for patent eligibility and the Supreme Court's insistence on the use of more flexible, ambiguously defined standards. In establishing the MoT test as the sole and definitive test for patent eligibility of method claims, the Federal Circuit attempted to provide the lower courts and PTO with a relatively objective

[53] Donald Chisum has made the similar observation. *See* Donald S. Chisum, *Patenting Intangible Methods: Revisiting* Benson (1972) *After* Bilski (2010) (October 27, 2010), *available at* http://ssrn.com/abstract=1698724.

and administrable test for patent eligibility that could be applied in a predictable and technology-neutral manner.

In this respect, *Bilski II* is reminiscent of other recent Supreme Court decisions striking down relatively bright-line, easier to administer rules created by the Federal Circuit in favor of more vague, subjective, and malleable standards. For example, in *Festo* the Supreme Court struck down a bright-line rule created by the Federal Circuit imposing an absolute bar on a finding of infringement under the doctrine of equivalents with respect to claim elements that have been narrowed by amendment, in favor of a rebuttable presumption that equivalents had been surrendered.[54] Similarly, in *KSR* the Supreme Court struck down the so-called teaching-suggestion-motivation test as the definitive test for obviousness in favor of a less rigid, more fluid standard.[55] In each case, the Supreme Court imposed its apparently strong preference for loosely defined standards that can be applied in a more discretionary manner on a case-by-case basis.

In a dissent to the Federal Circuit's recent en banc decision in *Ariad* v. *Eli Lilly*, Judge Rader observed that the majority had essentially sanctioned the use of the Lilly written description requirement as a doctrinal "wildcard" to invalidate patent claims that a court deems "unworthy" of protection.[56] By this, I believe he meant that as a result of the court's failure to articulate any objective or principled criteria for evaluating compliance with the Lilly written description requirement, the doctrine provides courts with a doctrinal shortcut to invalidate disfavored patent claims without conducting the more "neutral, empirical, and predictable" analysis required by more objective and well-established patentability doctrines such as enablement.[57]

In my opinion, not only is Judge Rader correct in his assessment of the Lilly written description requirement but the same can also be said with respect to patent eligibility under the current standard. *Bilski II* clearly affirms that the doctrine remains viable and is available as a threshold requirement to screen for "unworthy" patent claims, such as the risk hedging claims at issue in the case. But by declining to provide any clear guidance as to how the analysis is to be performed, the Court has imbued the lower courts and PTO with a great deal of discretion when applying the standard in future cases. In essence, patent eligibility can function as an easy out for a court or patent examiner faced with a patent claim that seems inappropriate, but for which there might be no clear route for invalidation using other more established doctrines of patentability such as obviousness or lack of enablement. I think *Classen I* and *Classen II* represent examples of a district court and the Federal Circuit, respectively, deploying patent eligibility in this manner.

[54] Festo Corp. v. Shoketsu, 535 U.S. 722 (2002).
[55] KSR International Co. v. Teleflex Inc., 550 U.S. 398 (2007).
[56] Ariad Pharmaceuticals, 598 F.3d at 1366.
[57] *Id.*

As the Federal Circuit correctly noted in *Bilski I*, the fundamental test of whether a claim "patents a fundamental principle" is difficult to apply in practice. Although *Bilski II* rejects the notion that the MoT test is the sole test for patent eligibility, it does acknowledge that it is often highly informative of the ultimate question of whether the claim patents a fundamental principle, and it sanctions its continued use as a tool for assessing patent eligibility. Significantly, the Supreme Court did not offer up any alternative analytical approach to aid in assessing the patent eligibility of method claims. Lower courts, seeking some sort of objective criterion for patent eligibility, will likely continue to rely heavily on the MoT test, particularly with respect to biotechnology inventions, which are difficult to analogize to the algorithms and methods of risk hedging that have been the subject of the relevant Supreme Court precedent. So far, this appears to be the case – Lemley et al. recently noted the continuing heavy reliance on the MoT test in the district courts and PTO Board of Patent Appeals and Interferences (BPAI).[58]

An objective test for patent eligibility amenable to administration in a predictable manner across a diverse spectrum of technologies is particularly important in the context of PTO examination. To the extent possible, the PTO aspires to provide clear and objective standards of patentability to its large corps of patent examiners, most of whom are not lawyers and have only rudimentary training in legal analysis. Prior to *LabCorp*, patent eligibility was rarely the basis for patent examiner rejections of claims, probably due at least in part to the vague and subjective nature of the fundamental test. Not surprisingly, the MoT test continues to figure prominently in PTO examination guidelines issued in response to *Bilski II*.[59]

As a practical matter, I think that claims found to be in compliance with the MoT test will enjoy a de facto rebuttable presumption of patent eligibility at the PTO. Conversely, method claims that lack what the PTO deems to be sufficient involvement of a machine or transformation will face a de facto rebuttable presumption of patent ineligibility. Under *Bilski II*, of course, an applicant must be afforded an opportunity to rebut this presumption by arguing that, regardless of the lack of involvement of a machine or transformation, the claim does not patent a fundamental principle. In most cases, however, I think this will be a difficult argument on which to prevail.

Immediately after deciding *Bilski II*, the Supreme Court granted certiorari in *Classen II* and *Prometheus II*, vacated both decisions, and remanded to the Federal Circuit to reconsider in a manner consistent with *Bilski II*. As I finalize this chapter, *Classen* and *Association for Molecular Pathology* are both still pending before the Federal Circuit. The decision on remand in *Prometheus* (*Prometheus III*) came out just as I was completing the chapter and is discussed in the following section.

58 Lemley et al., *supra* note 31, at 4.

59 Interim Guidance for Determining Subject Matter Eligibility for Process Claims in View of *Bilski v. Kappos*, 75 Fed. Reg. 43922 (2010).

D. Prometheus III *Applies* Bilski II *to Personalized Medicine*

On remand, a different panel of Federal Circuit judges came to essentially the same conclusion in *Prometheus* v. *Mayo* (*Prometheus III*) as the original panel had, reversing the district court and finding the claims patent eligible.[60] *Prometheus III* states that "in light of [*Bilski II*] patent eligibility in this case turns on whether Prometheus's asserted claims are drawn to a natural phenomenon, the patenting of which would entirely preempt its use as in *Benson* or *Flook*, or whether the claims are drawn only to a particular application of that phenomenon as in *Diehr*."[61] In essence, *Prometheus III* seems to interpret *Bilski II* as establishing preemption as a prerequisite for patent ineligibility, which, depending on how strictly "preemption" is defined, could substantially cabin the doctrine of patent eligibility (which I suspect is the panel's intent).

In fact, as explained earlier, it is clear that under *Bilski II* preemption is not a prerequisite for a finding of patent ineligibility, and limiting a fundamental principle to a particular application does not necessarily ensure patent eligibility. *Bilski II* does state that a claim limited to a particular application of a fundamental principle "may well be deserving of patent protection," but then proceeds to find relatively narrow claims patent eligible even though they do not preempt the abstract idea of risk hedging. In any event, the *Prometheus III* panel quickly concluded that the claims are not preemptive, but rather are drawn to particular applications of a natural phenomenon, which under the panel's interpretation of *Bilski II* equates with patent eligibility.

The preemption analysis in *Prometheus III* is terse and provides little explanation as to how the panel arrived at its conclusion that the claims are not preemptive. Recall that in *Prometheus I* the district court judge based his decision on a determination that the claims preempt all substantial practical applications of the correlation between the drug metabolite and the optimal dosage. *Prometheus III* never addresses this point and provides no hint as to what, if any, practical uses of the correlations might fall outside the scope of the claims. Instead, the only explanation provided is a statement that, rather than preempting the correlations, the claimed methods use them in "the treatment of a specific disease by administering specific drugs and measuring specific metabolites." One might speculate that under this approach a broader claim, perhaps one not limited to a specific disease or one encompassing less specifically defined drugs or drug metabolites, might be considered patent ineligible. My sense, however, is that the panel intended to foster an expansive interpretation of what it means to be patent eligible, and to that end it chose not to articulate any more concrete definition of patent ineligibility than the vague standard set forth in *Bilski II*.

60 Prometheus Laboratories v. Mayo Collaborative, 628 F.3d 1327 (2010).

61 *Id.* at 12–13.

Significantly, after succinctly explaining that the claims satisfy the preemption test, *Prometheus III* embarks on an extended analysis of the claims for compliance with the MoT test. The Court emphasizes that, although *Bilski II* had rejected the notion that the MoT test is the definitive test for patent eligibility of all method claims, it had characterized it as a "useful and important clue, an investigative tool" for determining patent eligibility. The MoT analysis in *Prometheus III* is substantially the same as that provided in *Prometheus II* and arrives at the same conclusion (i.e., that the "administering" and "determining" steps in the claims were both central to the purpose of the claim and independently sufficiently transformative to satisfy the transformation prong of the MoT test). *Prometheus III* appears to base its ultimate conclusion of patent eligibility primarily on MoT analysis, consistent with my prediction that the MoT test will continue to play a central role in patent eligibility analysis.

IV. AMBIGUITY IN *BILSKI II* FACILITATES ITS DISCRETIONARY IMPLEMENTATION AS A POLICY LEVER

Not surprisingly, opinions vary regarding the appropriate role of patents in the advancement of personalized medicine. Some argue that the availability of adequate patent protection for the clinical application of newly discovered biomarkers and medically significant correlations will be necessary to incentivize the substantial investment required to make personalized medicine a reality.[62] Others counter that patents broadly covering the use of these discoveries are unjustified and threaten to impede rather than promote progress in clinical medicine.[63] Given the importance of personalized medicine to the future of health care, it is important that the patent system balance these concerns by providing the appropriate incentives to facilitate development of personalized medicine, while at the same time avoiding overprotection that could stymie it.

The vaguely defined parameters of the test for patent eligibility under *Bilski II* provide the lower courts and PTO ample discretion to selectively deploy the doctrine as a policy lever to further perceived public policy objectives of the patent system. For example, *Bilski II* and the Supreme Court precedent on which it rests impose virtually no constraints with respect to how a court decides what does or does not

[62] Michael Schuster and Pauline Farmer-Koppenol, *Post-Bilski: Patent Strategy for Personalized Medicine* (2010), *available at* http://patentlawcenter.pli.edu/2010/08/23/post-bilski-patent-strategy-for-personalized-medicine; *The Association for Molecular Pathology v. U.S. Patent and Trademark Office*, Brief of Amici Curiae Christopher M. Holman and Robert Cook-Deegan in Support of Neither Party, 2010 WL 4853323 (2010).

[63] *The Association for Molecular Pathology* v. *U.S. Patent and Trademark Office*, Brief of Amici Curiae American Medical Association et al. in Support of Plaintiffs, 2012 WL 2885872; Daniel Ravicher, *Gene Patent Decision Emancipates Personalized Medicine*, Huffington Post (2010), *available at* http://www.huffingtonpost.com/daniel-b-ravicher/gene-patent-decision-eman_b_521324.html.

constitute a "fundamental principle" or what it means to "patent" or "claim" a fundamental principle. Of particular significance to the scope of patent protection available for molecular diagnostics and personalized medicine, the Supreme Court has left a virtually clean slate on which to define what it means for a method claim to impermissibly "claim" a biological natural phenomenon. Furthermore, because the MoT test will likely continue to play a key role in assessing patent eligibility, various vaguely defined elements of this test might also be adjusted as policy levers. In this part, I discuss the range of alternate interpretations the courts could apply to these elements and how the choice of interpretation might dictate the range of patent protection available for diagnostic methods and personalized medicine.

A. *What Constitutes a Biological "Fundamental Principle"?*

Bilski II is adamant that "fundamental principles" are patent ineligible, but the Supreme Court has never provided anything resembling a concrete definition of the term. All of the relevant Supreme Court decisions addressing the patent eligibility of process claims have involved one category of fundamental principle, the abstract idea. But as frankly acknowledged by Justice Stevens in *Bilski II*, the Supreme Court has "never provided a satisfying account of what constitutes an unpatentable abstract idea."[64]

With respect to the other category of fundamental principle – natural phenomena – the Court has provided even less guidance. *Chakrabarty* implicitly held that human-made living organisms are not natural phenomena, but the only examples of natural phenomena that have been identified by the Supreme Court are nonbiological (e.g., gravity and other fundamental laws of physics).

As a threshold matter, it seems self-evident that a claim cannot properly be characterized as claiming a natural phenomenon unless the allegedly claimed phenomenon is in fact "natural." For example, Justice Breyer in his *LabCorp* dissent identified the correlation between the level of total homocysteine in the human body and the existence of a vitamin B deficiency as a natural phenomenon. In *Association for Molecular Pathology*, the district court judge characterized the correlation between certain naturally occurring variations in the BRCA sequence with a predisposition to cancer as a natural phenomenon. It seems reasonable to categorize these correlations as natural phenomena, seeing as both involve a physiological relationship that exists naturally in the human body, prior to and independent of any human intervention.

In contrast, the characterization of the correlation between drug metabolite levels and optimal dosage in *Prometheus* strikes me as questionable. Unlike the naturally occurring metabolite in *LabCorp* or the naturally occurring genetic mutations in *Association for Molecular Pathology*, the drug metabolites in *Prometheus* do not exist

64 Bilski, 130 S.Ct. at 3236 (Stevens, J., concurring).

naturally. They are the metabolic breakdown products of a non-naturally occurring drug that has been introduced in the body. Absent human intervention – particularly the development and chemical synthesis of the drug and administration of the drug to human patient – the drug metabolite does not exist. Human intervention was a necessary prerequisite to the presence of the drug metabolite in the body, and hence to the correlation implicated by the claims.

The judge in *Prometheus I* based his conclusion that the correlation is a natural phenomenon on the fact that the interaction of a drug metabolite with the human body is governed by fundamental principles of chemistry and biology. The flaw in this logic is that that most inventions are based on interactions between human innovation and natural phenomena. Any drug interacts with the human body through the same natural processes as the drug metabolites in *Prometheus*, so under the judge's broad interpretation of the term any use of an entirely synthetic human-made drug to treat a disease is a natural phenomenon. In fact, under this approach virtually any invention would seem to constitute a natural phenomenon. For example, an airplane wing interacts with air according to fundamental principles of physics, so under the district court's logic airplane flight is a natural phenomenon.

On the initial appeal of *Prometheus* to the Federal Circuit, I filed an amicus brief arguing that the district court had erred in characterizing a correlation involving a synthetic, non-naturally occurring drug breakdown product as a natural phenomenon.[65] The correlation does not and cannot occur naturally, because it only arises as a result of the administration of a synthetic drug to a patient. I pointed out that under the rationale used by the district court it would be difficult if not impossible to effectively patent newly discovered drugs. Applying the court's logic more generally, the interaction of any drug with the human body would apparently qualify as a natural phenomenon, from which it would flow that any claim encompassing substantially all practical uses of that phenomenon would be preemptive and hence patent ineligible. But this would imply that a composition-of-matter patent directed toward the drug would be patent ineligible, because it covers any use of the drug. A method-of-treatment claim using the drug would also apparently be patent ineligible if it covered the method of treatment that rendered the drug useful, because the claim would substantially cover the known practical uses of the phenomenon.

The courts could potentially use their discretion in defining what it means to be a biological natural phenomenon as a policy lever to distinguish between disfavored "pure" molecular diagnostic method claims (i.e., diagnostic methods not tied to any particular therapy or medicine) versus methods of personalized medicine deemed more worthy of patent protection. For example, the phenomena implicated by the claims at issue in *LabCorp* and *Association for Molecular Pathology* truly do occur naturally. By characterizing these phenomena as natural, a court would be able to

65 *Prometheus Laboratories Inc.* v. *Mayo Clinic*, Brief of Amici Curiae Interested Patent Law Professors in Support of Neither Party, 2009 WL 462602.

invoke patent eligibility as a doctrine to invalidate overly broad claims tending to encompass all practical applications of the phenomena.

In contrast, the purported natural phenomenon in *Prometheus* only arises as a consequence of active human intervention and thus could more plausibly be characterized as a non-natural phenomenon, obviating the applicability of the patent eligibility doctrine. This distinction would give courts a doctrinal policy lever for discriminating between disfavored diagnostic testing method claims, which broadly encompass testing for the presence of a naturally occurring biomarker, and more favored personalized medicine claims, such as those at issue in *Prometheus*, that are directly tied to the administration of a human-made drug. For example, the discovery of a correlation between a genetic mutation and the suitability of a drug for a particular patient might be more amenable to broad patent protection than the discovery of a correlation between a genetic mutation and a more "natural" phenotype, such as a propensity for developing cancer.

However, *Prometheus III* chose not to adopt this approach, passively going along with the questionable logic of *Prometheus* I and accepting its conclusion that the correlation between drug metabolite level and optimal drug dosage is a "natural phenomenon." *Prometheus III* never even acknowledges the argument that a correlation arising out of the interaction of a non-naturally occurring, human-made drug metabolite with the human body is not "natural." Of course, in this particular case the distinction between natural and unnatural phenomena was rendered moot by the court's ultimate conclusion that the claims are patent eligible on other grounds. By accepting the fiction that the correlation is a natural phenomenon, the court was able to reach the issue of what it means to "claim" a natural phenomenon.

Perhaps the panel felt it was better to address that important question sooner rather than later, in order to establish judicial precedent addressing this critical question. In any event, it used the opportunity to reassure the biotechnology community that the Federal Circuit was not inclined to interpret the prohibition against claiming biological natural phenomena in a manner that would dramatically restrict the scope of patent protection available for methods of treatment and methods of molecular diagnostic testing. In a future case, perhaps the Federal Circuit will explicitly take up the question of where to draw the line between natural and unnatural biological phenomena.

B. *What Does It Mean to "Claim" a Fundamental Principle?*

Another key question left largely unanswered by *Bilski II* is what the Court means when it says that a claim is patent ineligible if it "patents" or "claims" a fundamental principle. The vague and undefined language provides another highly variable parameter in the test for patent eligibility that courts might exploit as a policy lever.

Clearly, in this context the Court is not using the terms "patent" or "claim" in their ordinary sense. In normal patent parlance, a patent claim only "claims" subject matter falling within the scope of the claim (i.e., methods that if practiced would infringe the claim), but under *Bilski II* a claim need not literally "claim" a fundamental principle to be patent ineligible. This is illustrated most plainly by the fact that some of the dependent claims deemed patent ineligible in *Bilski II* were limited to fairly specific applications of the abstract idea of risk hedging in energy or commodity markets, and hence they fell far short of literally "claiming" the abstract idea of hedging risk.

In fact, it is difficult to imagine how one could literally "claim" the medically significant correlations that have been identified as natural phenomena in recent patent eligibility cases. The Patent Act explicitly specifies that only products and processes can be patented, which clearly rules out a claim literally reciting, for example, the correlation between genetic variations in the BRCA genes and an individual's likelihood of developing cancer, which is neither.[66]

On the other hand, the prohibition against claiming a fundamental principle cannot be interpreted so broadly as to preclude patent protection for any method that involves some new and useful application of a fundamental principle. The claimed inventions held patent eligible in *Diehr* and *Chakrabarty*, for example, both relied heavily on fundamental principles. Indeed, few if any inventions do not involve some natural phenomenon or abstract idea. As pointed out by the DOJ in its *LabCorp* amicus brief, "it is now commonplace that an application of a law of nature or mathematical formula to a new structure or process may well be deserving of patent protection."[67]

Although *Bilski II* never explicitly articulates what it means to "claim" a fundamental principle, it appears to adopt the approach taken by Justice Breyer in his *LabCorp* dissent, pursuant to which a claim is patent ineligible if it "embodies" a fundamental principle. Of course, this approach – equating "to claim" or "to patent" with "to embody" – begs the question of what it means for a claim to embody a fundamental principle. Apparently it is not necessary for a claim to substantially preempt all practical applications of a fundamental principle (i.e., the standard advanced by the DOJ in its *Prometheus* amicus brief) for the claim to impermissibly "embody" the fundamental principle, because at least some of the claims, particularly the relatively narrow dependent claims, found patent ineligible in *Bilski II* clearly do not preempt all practical applications of risk hedging. As explained by the Court, patent ineligibility "cannot be circumvented by limiting a claim to a particular technological environment or adding insignificant post-solution activity" (130 S.Ct. 3218, 3231). The Court declined, however, to elaborate as to the specific circumstances

66 *In re Nuijten*, 515 F.3d 1361 (Fed. Cir. 2008) (patent protection is only available for the four specific categories enumerated in 35 U.S.C. § 101: machines, articles of manufacture, composition of matter (all of which are "products"), and processes).

67 *LabCorp* v. *Metabolite*, Brief for the United States as Amicus Curiae, 2005 WL 3533248 at 19–20 (citing *Diehr*, 450 US at 187).

under which limiting a claim to a particular technological environment would be insufficient or what would render an activity "insignificant."

In effect, the amorphous "embodiment" standard allows courts to use patent eligibility as a wildcard to invalidate claims deemed overly broad or otherwise unworthy of patent protection, without requiring any formal claim construction or the identification of specific subject matter covered by the claim that renders it patent ineligible. The invalidation of the dependent claims in *Bilski II* demonstrates that under this standard even relatively narrow claims can be susceptible to invalidation, based on little more than a conclusory statement that the claim embodies a natural phenomenon.

I suspect that the *Bilski II* plurality saw the claims at issue as illustrative of the sort of claims that should not be considered patent eligible; however, it could not agree on how to articulate exactly what it is about the claims that it found objectionable without risking creating an unduly restrictive test for patent eligibility that would have the unintended consequence of threatening the patent eligibility of future patent claims perhaps more deserving of protection. By keeping the inquiry open-ended, the Supreme Court allowed lower courts the flexibility to invoke patent ineligibility against other claims unsuited for patent protection. Somewhat akin to pornography, it might be difficult to articulate a prospective definition of what it means to claim a fundamental principle, but the Court knows a patent-ineligible claim when it sees one.

The downside of an amorphous "embodiment" test, of course, is that it provides little objective guidance that might facilitate attempts by the lower courts and the PTO to apply the test in a predictable and consistent manner or that would assist patent practitioners in their attempts to draft patent claims that provide adequate scope of protection for their clients without crossing the line into patent ineligibility. In an attempt to provide a more objective and administrable standard for what it means to claim a fundamental principle, it has often been proposed that courts should apply a "preemption" test, pursuant to which a claim is patent ineligible if it effectively preempts all substantial practical applications of a fundamental principle.

The preemption test owes its origin to language appearing in the Supreme Court's 1972 *Gottschalk* v. *Benson* decision to the effect that a claim that "wholly preempts" all "substantial practical applications" of a fundamental principle is the practical equivalent of a patent on the fundamental principle itself, and hence patent ineligible.[68] Prior to *Bilski II*, the DOJ implied that it viewed preemption as the test for patent eligibility, stating in its *LabCorp* amicus brief that under earlier Supreme Court precedent "no one can patent a process that comprises every substantial practical application of a law of nature, because such a patent in practical effect would be a patent on the law of nature itself."[69] The district court in *Prometheus I*

[68] Gottschalk v. Benson, 409 U.S. 63, 71–72 (1972).

[69] *LabCorp v. Metabolite*, Brief for the United States as Amicus Curiae, 2005 WL 3533248 at 20 (internal quotes omitted).

also explicitly used the preemption test. Subsequent to *Bilski II*, the Federal Circuit has indicated that preemption remains a critical consideration in assessing patent eligibility, but has interpreted it more liberally than the DOJ or *Prometheus I* – in a manner suggesting that in most cases a claim limited to practical applications of a fundamental principle will satisfy the test, regardless of whether or not the claim leaves any substantial practical applications of the fundamental principle unclaimed.

Note that the "preemption" test implicates claim scope more explicitly than the "embodiment" test. The DOJ *LabCorp* brief postulates, for example, that a claim directed toward the practical application of natural phenomenon is generally patent eligible, so long as the claim does not preempt substantially *all* of the practical applications of the phenomenon. Under this approach patent eligibility effectively functions as a tool for policing claim scope, a role that has traditionally been the province of the enablement requirement, although increasingly the written description requirement is being invoked for this purpose.

Although Justice Breyer's *LabCorp* dissent promotes the use of an embodiment test for patent eligibility and does not engage in any formal consideration of claim interpretation or claim scope, it does conjecture that the breadth of the claim at issue was such that it would cover any practical use of a natural phenomenon, implying that he views consideration of preemption as at least relevant to the question of patent eligibility. Similarly, *Bilski II* adopts an embodiment standard, but acknowledges a role for consideration of claim scope and preemption, pointing out that some of the broader claims at issue in the case "pre-empt use of [risk hedging] in all fields, and would effectively grant a monopoly over an abstract idea."[70]

The advantage of the preemption test over the more flexible but amorphous embodiment test is that it provides a relatively objective and administrable standard. It is also more consistent with other doctrines of patentability, because it explicitly considers the scope of the properly construed claim, as opposed to some vaguely defined assessment of what the claim "embodies." Not surprisingly, given the premium that the PTO places on predictability and bright-line guidance, the PTO promoted the use of the preemption test in proposed examination guidelines published shortly after the Supreme Court granted certiorari in *LabCorp*.[71] The PTO's more recent patent eligibility guidelines, based on *Bilski II*, continue to find preemption an extremely important factor in the analysis for patent eligibility, although in keeping with *Bilski II* preemption is not absolutely required for a finding of patent ineligibility.[72]

Although the preemption test might be less ambiguous than the embodiment test, it is nonetheless amenable to substantial judicial discretion in its application. This is

70 *Bilski*, 130 S.Ct. at 3231.

71 PTO, Interim Guidelines for Examination of Patent Applications for Patent Subject Matter Eligibility (Interim Subject Matter Eligibility Guidelines), 1300 Off. Gaz. Pat. Office 142, 146 (Nov. 22, 2005).

72 Interim Guidance for Determining Subject Matter Eligibility for Process Claims in View of *Bilski v. Kappos*, 75 Fed. Reg. 43922 (2010).

exemplified by the decisions in *Prometheus I* and *Prometheus III*, wherein the district court judge and Federal Circuit, respectively, applied their own interpretations of the preemption test to arrive at diametrically opposite conclusions. Even though the patent owner identified at least six practical applications of the alleged natural phenomenon that it argued were not covered by the claim, the district court was able to dismiss this argument by simply finding that none of these applications were sufficiently "substantial." When the Federal Circuit decided the case, the panel justified an opposite outcome by concluding that because the claims recite specific applications of the phenomenon they do not wholly preempt the phenomenon. Significantly, the Federal Circuit did not feel compelled under *Bilski II* to provide any meaningful explanation of how it arrived at his conclusion and, in particular, what substantial applications of the natural phenomenon might fall outside the scope of the claims.

The manner in which the preemption test was applied in *Prometheus III* seems in conflict with the approach set forth by Justice Breyer in his *LabCorp* dissent. The claim at issue in *LabCorp* is entirely analogous to the *Prometheus* claims; it includes a step of measuring specific metabolites, which the panel in *Prometheus III* specifically identified as a step rendering the claims patent eligible. *Prometheus III* acknowledged the tension, but declined to attribute any significance to it, pointing out that as a dissent Justice Breyer's opinion is not controlling law and then declining to discuss *LabCorp* any further.

Courts might apply a patent eligibility test based on "preemption" of a biological natural phenomenon as a policy lever to police against patent claims perceived to be unduly expansive in scope. For example, a claim broadly encompassing any possible means of diagnosing a genetic mutation could be treated as patent ineligible, whereas a more limited claim restricted to some specific means for identifying mutation would be patent eligible. Much of the criticisms that have been raised against genetic diagnostic testing method claims, including some of Myriad's claims that have been challenged in *Association for Molecular Pathology*, have centered on the contention that the claims are effectively impossible to design around, because they arguably would cover any methodology for testing for BRCA mutations. Preemption analysis could address these concerns.

Alternatively, the preemption test could be applied in a manner that supports patent eligibility for even very broad diagnostic method claims. For example, a claim broadly reciting a method for diagnosing a physiological state of clinical significance, such as the level of total homocysteine (*LabCorp*) or the presence of a genetic variation (*Association for Molecular Pathology*), does not cover the physiological state as it exists in nature. A genetic sequence functions and exerts its physiological influence in the body, as dictated by the laws of chemistry and biology, and none of this is covered by a patent claim limited to the human-directed endeavor of diagnostic testing. *Bilski II* would not appear to preclude a court from holding that, even though the genetic variation and its correlation with a propensity toward cancer are a fundamental principle, claims broadly reciting a diagnostic test for the variation are patent eligible because they do not implicate the correlation as it exists and manifests itself in nature. This would appear to be consistent with the approach taken by the *Prometheus III* panel, which held that claims broadly directed to the practical application of a natural phenomenon were sufficiently limited in scope to satisfy the preemption test, even though the district court had found that the claim covered all substantial practical applications of the phenomenon.

Under the preemption standard, the patent eligibility of a method claim would seem at times to hinge on the state of technology at the time the claim is analyzed. This could occur in cases where a claim that initially preempts all practical applications of a fundamental principle later becomes susceptible to circumvention by an after-arising technology and is thus no longer preemptive. For example, consider a patent claim that broadly covers methods of identifying a genetic mutation. If at the time the patent is filed the only practical means for detecting the mutation requires DNA analysis, the claim could in a practical sense preempt access to the genetic information. But genetic mutations manifest themselves in the protein encoded by the gene, so at least in principle the same information could be derived by analyzing the protein directly, by a process falling outside the scope of the claim. Would the claim, originally patent ineligible because it preempted all practical means for accessing the natural phenomenon of a patient's genetic sequence, be rendered patent eligible by the development of an after-arising technology that makes it practical to exploit the phenomenon in a manner not encompassed by the claim? On the one hand, the claim no longer preempts a natural phenomenon, so a determination of patent ineligibility is no longer justified by the claim's preemptive effect. On the other, it seems problematic to me that under this logic the eligibility of an invention for patent protection can depend critically on independent technological innovations by third parties.

In any event, this discussion illustrates how, by exploiting the ambiguity as to what it means to patent or claim a fundamental principle, a court might modulate the effect of patent eligibility on the patenting of personalized medicine. Employing the preemption test, the doctrine could be used as a policy lever to prevent overly broad patent coverage of a biological natural phenomenon, such as a genetic variation or other medically significant biomarker. Of course, there are other doctrines of patentability more commonly invoked to police claim scope, most notably the enablement and written description requirements, which I would argue are the more appropriate and objective doctrinal tools to deal with overly broad patent claims.

C. *What Role Will the MoT Test Play in Assessing the Patent Eligibility of Diagnostic Method Claims?*

As noted earlier, although *Bilski II* clarified that the MoT test is not the sole, definitive test for patent eligibility, the decision did acknowledge the test's usefulness as an investigational tool, and it allows courts essentially unfettered authority to continue using the test on a case-by-case basis. Early indications are that courts will continue to rely heavily, if not exclusively, on the MoT test in assessing patent eligibility. For example, in *Prometheus III* the Federal Circuit's analysis focused almost entirely on the MoT test. Lemley et al. recently observed that district courts and the PTO's BPAI continue to rely heavily on the MoT test.[73]

The MoT test can be invoked flexibly by a court to achieve a desired policy outcome. On the one hand, a court can choose to completely ignore it in assessing patent eligibility. This is precisely what the Federal Circuit did recently in *Research Corporation Technologies* v. *Microsoft Corp*., wherein it based its finding of patent eligibility solely on the "functional and palpable" applicability of the invention in the field of computer technology, with no mention of the MoT test.[74] Alternatively, the court can rely entirely on the MoT test, which is close to what the Federal Circuit did in *Prometheus III*. In both of these cases, I suspect that the panel's ultimate conclusion of patent eligibility was driven by its perception that these were real, technological inventions worthy of patent protection. In *Prometheus III*, the panel was able to articulate a strong rationale for concluding that the claims included transformative method steps, and thus it found it advantageous to rely heavily on the MoT test in explaining its conclusion. In *Research Corporation Technologies*, in contrast, the involvement of a particular machine or physical transformation is perhaps less apparent, so the panel chose to deemphasize the MoT test, as *Bilski II* allows it to do.

Not only can courts deploy the MoT test as a policy lever by selectively emphasizing or deemphasizing its relevance to the analysis of the particular claims under consideration but also a court choosing to base its decision on this test can exercise a great deal of discretion in interpreting its requirements. The Supreme Court never disputed the Federal Circuit's formulation or application of the MoT test in *Bilski I*, only its characterization of the MoT test as the sole and definitive test for patent eligibility. The MoT test itself, as set forth in *Bilski I*, includes a number of vaguely defined parameters, amenable to discretionary manipulation by courts as policy levers.

In *Bilski I*, for example, the Federal Circuit emphasized that to satisfy the MoT test a claimed method must involve the use of a particular machine. But just how explicit does the claim need to be with respect to the use of a machine, and to what degree of "particularity" must the machine be identified? In the immediate aftermath of *Bilski I*, for example, commentators queried whether the involvement of a general-purpose computer would be sufficiently "particular" to satisfy the test. A court faced with an unworthy patent claim could selectively calibrate the stringency with which it enforces the requirement of particularity to justify finding the claim invalid for failure to recite the use of a particular machine, while retaining the

73 Lemley et al., *supra* note 31.

74 Research Corporation Technologies v. Microsoft Corp., 627 F.3d 859 (Fed. Cir. 2010).

discretion to impose a more lenient definition particularly in cases wherein it is perceived that the claim is more legitimate.

A stringent interpretation of this aspect of the MoT test, requiring the literal recitation of a specifically identified machine for a claim to be patent eligible, would substantially limit the scope of a typical diagnostic or personalized medicine method claim. This interpretation of the MoT test would find favor with critics of these patents, who object to broad claims that purport to encompass any and all means of testing for a biomarker but are more receptive to diagnostic method patents limited to specific testing methodologies and equipment.

Alternatively, a court could apply the MoT test more permissively, such that any method that inherently involves the use of a machine could be found in compliance, regardless of whether the claim is implicitly or explicitly restricted to use of a particular machine. This was the approach advocated by the patent owners in *Prometheus II* and *Association for Molecular Pathology*. In *Prometheus*, the patent owner argued that "the patents inextricably rely on numerous machines to process the bodily sample, determine the metabolite levels, and thereby calibrate the proper dose." Similarly, in *Association for Molecular Pathology*, the patent owner argued that the use of laboratory equipment is inherent in analyzing and comparing DNA molecules. These arguments were rendered moot in *Prometheus III* when the Federal Circuit decided in favor of the patent owner on other grounds (i.e., compliance with the transformation prong of the MoT test). The district court rejected the argument in *Association for Molecular Pathology*, but perhaps the Federal Circuit will revisit the issue when it decides that case on appeal.

Another variable for calibrating the impact of the MoT test is the manner in which a court defines what it means for a method step to be "transformative." *Prometheus III* suggests that the Federal Circuit is inclined to enforce this indicium of patent eligibility permissively in the context of biotechnology and personalized medicine. As discussed earlier, in that decision the panel held that administering a drug to a patient and determining the level of drug metabolite in a patient's body are both inherently transformative and both independently sufficient to confer patent eligibility on a method claim. This bodes well for the patent eligibility of personalized medicine claims that positively recite a step of administering treatment to the patient or physically analyzing a biological sample.

Even if a method claim explicitly recites a step involving a machine or transformation, *Bilski I* and *Bilski II* explicitly sanction disregarding this step in the patent eligibility inquiry if the court concludes that the step is mere "extra-solution activity" or mere "data-gathering."[75] The district court took this route in *Prometheus I*, as did the Federal Circuit (at least implicitly) in *Classen II*. This represents yet another discretionary aspect of the test for patent eligibility, allowing a court or the PTO to

75 Bilski, 130 S.Ct. at 3231 ("limiting an abstract idea to one field of use or adding token post-solution components [does] not make the concept patentable").

conveniently disregard explicit claim limitations reciting tangible, physical process steps requiring the use of machines and/or physical transformations in its patent eligibility analysis.

The disparate outcomes in *Prometheus II* and *Prometheus III* illustrate the effect of a court's selective disregard of transformative method steps in the MoT analysis by characterizing them as mere "extra-solution activity." All of the claims at issue in these cases included a step of determining the level of drug metabolite in a patient's body, which inherently involves transformative activities, such as the isolation and processing of a biological sample. In *Prometheus I* the court justified its decision to completely ignore this step in its analysis by simply characterizing it as insubstantial extra-solution activity. In contrast, the Federal Circuit looked at the same step and found it to be "central to the purpose of the claims," and thus relevant to (and ultimately determinative of) the question of patent eligibility.

Further illustrating the discretionary nature of the test, when another panel of the Federal Circuit decided *Classen II*, it implicitly treated the step of administering vaccine to patients as mere extra-solution activity; it was thus able to disregard the step and conclude that the claim was invalid for failure to include any machine or transformation. Similarly, in *Association for Molecular Pathology* the district court advocated an approach that would dismiss data acquisition steps as mere extra-solution activity and would have found claims including steps requiring the isolation and analysis of DNA patent ineligible under the MoT test. In short, the amorphous nature of the test offers courts great discretion to consider or ignore a method step in its patent eligibility analysis, in order to arrive at the legal conclusion that the court believes will further the policy objectives of the patent system.

V. CONCLUDING THOUGHTS

In *Bilski II* the Supreme Court appears to have made a conscious decision to establish a test for patent eligibility that maintains broad discretion for lower courts to interpret the requirement on a case-by-case basis in a manner that furthers the policy objectives of the patent system. The Federal Circuit will play a key role in fleshing out the contours of the doctrine as it is applied to specific technologies, particularly involving biology and other subject matter far removed from the risk hedging methods at issue in *Bilski II* and the computer programs considered in earlier Supreme Court precedent on which *Bilski II* depends. Recent decisions such as *Research Corporation Technologies* and *Prometheus III* indicate that at least some judges on the Federal Circuit do not interpret *Bilski II* as a mandate to dramatically contract the scope of patent-eligible subject matter, at least so long as a claimed invention appears to relate to subject matter that would fall under a relatively broad definition of "technology," particularly in the computer sciences and biotechnology.

The courts will likely exploit the ambiguity in *Bilski II* to deploy patent eligibility as a policy lever to regulate the extent to which genetic diagnostic testing and personalized medicine innovations are afforded patent protection. For example, patents on pure genetic diagnostic tests, such as Myriad's broad method claims to diagnosing for genetic variation in the BRCA genes, are highly unpopular in many quarters. In contrast, patent claims directed toward methods of genetic diagnostic testing for use in conjunction with a particular class of drugs, the prototypical example of personalized medicine, would likely meet with much less objection. Patent eligibility might be selectively enforced as a policy lever in a manner that would acknowledge the significance of this distinction, at least implicitly.

For example, in *Prometheus III* the Federal Circuit emphasizes that the personalized medicine claims at issue are patent eligible because they relate to a specific class of drugs. This approach could serve as the basis for a principled distinction between patent-eligible personalized medicine claims and patent-ineligible pure genetic diagnostic testing claims, such as Myriad's claims, which are not tethered to any specific drug or medical intervention.

An alternative approach to distinguishing between pure diagnostic and personalized medicine claims would be to focus the inquiry on whether or not the claim implicates a truly natural phenomenon. For example, the claims at issue in *LabCorp* and *Association for Molecular Pathology* both relate to naturally occurring physiological correlations that exist absent any human intervention, whereas the *Prometheus* claims involves what I would argue is a non-natural phenomenon. Similarly, a court might conclude that, because Herceptin is a human-made, non-naturally occurring drug, the correlation between a patient's HER2-positive status and whether that patient will benefit from treatment with Herceptin is not a natural phenomenon, and thus claims broadly directed toward practical application of the correlation do not implicate the patent eligibility doctrine.[76]

Patent eligibility might also be invoked as a policy lever to regulate both the manner in which personalized medicine innovations are claimed and the scope of claim coverage. Under *Prometheus III*, a claimed method relating to personalized medicine or molecular diagnostic testing would appear to be patent eligible so long as it recites a positive step of treating a patient and/or performing some sort of clinical or laboratory-based test for the presence of a biomarker. In contrast, a claim drafted so broadly as to encompass the mere mental recognition of the existence of the biomarker correlated with a medically relevant physiological state will be found patent ineligible. The former claim entails tangible and physical technology, the traditional stuff of patents, whereas the latter encompasses intangible conceptual analysis that many people believe should not be patented. I think the line drawn by *Prometheus III* is reasonable and will likely be the general approach adopted by the courts and the PTO when analyzing the patent eligibility of claims relating to personalized medicine and diagnostic testing.

76 Personalized Medicine Coalition, *supra* note 3, at 6.

One can readily imagine claims falling somewhere in between these two extremes, and it is unclear where the courts and PTO would come down with respect to such claims. For example, would a claim reciting a computer-implemented method for analyzing DNA sequence information be found patent eligible? I think *Bilski II* allows courts ample discretion to decide the question either way, and I think a Federal Circuit panel faced with the question would decide the manner based on the perceived public policy implications of the decision. The recent Federal Circuit decision in *Research Corporation Technologies* – holding that an invention that presents "functional and palpable applications in the field of computer technology" and that addresses "a need in the art" was patent eligible – suggests that a method claim directed toward the analysis of genetic information could be patent eligible if limited to computer-implemented modes of practicing the invention (and as such presenting no danger of infringement by a doctor merely thinking about the correlation).

One concern raised by all this is that requiring inventors to specifically recite method steps of performing laboratory diagnostic tests and/or administering drugs to patients could, as a practical matter, render the patent claims difficult to enforce. Under the doctrine of divided infringement, to prove infringement the patent owner is generally required to prove that a single party performed all of the steps recited in the claim.[77] It would be difficult to hold a diagnostic testing company liable for direct infringement for a method claim that recites a step of treating a patient. In some cases a patient or doctor might be found directly infringing such a claim, but in practice doctors and patients are not realistic targets for lawsuits.

A diagnostic testing company or perhaps a generic drug company selling the drug might potentially be found liable under a theory of indirect infringement, based on a showing that it induced or contributed to the patient's direct infringement, but this might also be difficult to establish.[78] For example, if there are substantial non-infringing reasons for performing the diagnostic test, and the testing company does not promote use of the test in an infringing manner, the diagnostic testing company would probably not be found liable for indirect infringement. Likewise, if the method relates to the use of a drug that can also be used without first performing the genetic test, and a generic drug company does not promote use of the test in conjunction with the drug, the patent owner would be unable to demonstrate indirect infringement of the patent by the generic drug company. In effect, although the patent accurately claims an important invention, from a practical point of view it might be commercially worthless to the patent owner.

In contrast, a personalized medicine method claim reciting performance of a diagnostic test and administration of a drug could be particularly valuable for a branded drug company if the FDA-mandated label for the drug indicates that the

77 Muniauction Inc. v. Thomson Corp., 532 F.3d 1318 (Fed. Cir. 2008).

78 35 U.S.C. § 271 (b) and (c).

diagnostic test should be performed before administering the drug. For example, imagine a drug company that discovers a diagnostic test to identify a population of patients for whom a drug is not appropriate. If that information is provided on the drug's label, FDA might very well require a generic drug company to include the same warning on a generic version of the drug. A generic drug company could potentially be held liable for inducing infringement of the patent, based on inclusion of the warning on the label for the generic version of the drug.

This scenario illustrates one potential way in which a personalized medicine method claim of moderate scope could be commercially valuable. Of course, the policy implications of this use of the patent are mixed. On the one hand, some might object to a branded drug company obtaining a de facto extension in patent exclusivity in this manner – such extensions are sometimes referred to pejoratively as "evergreening." On the other hand, the patent could be seen as providing an important incentive for investment in the research necessary to discover and validate potentially life-saving tests to optimize drug safety and efficacy.

As is usually the case with patents, the patenting of innovations in personalized medicine will create a tension between the desire for lower costs for existing products versus the need for adequate incentives for future innovation. Moving forward, *Bilski II* gives the Federal Circuit the discretion to develop the patent eligibility doctrine in a manner that seeks to balance these competing concerns.

5

The Inducement Standard of Patentability

*Michael Abramowicz and John F. Duffy**

"The inherent problem was to develop some means of weeding out those inventions which would not be disclosed or devised but for the inducement of a patent."[1]

– A unanimous Supreme Court in *Graham* v. *John Deere*

INTRODUCTION

The opening quotation is one of the most memorable and insightful lines from arguably the most important patent law case of the twentieth century, the Supreme Court's 1966 decision in *Graham* v. *John Deere*.[2] *Graham*'s preeminent place in the patent canon is well justified, because it is the Supreme Court's seminal opinion on a patent law doctrine – the "nonobviousness" requirement – that is typically introduced as "the most important of the basic patent requirements,"[3] "central to determining patentability,"[4] "the key to defining what is a patentable invention,"[5] or simply "the ultimate condition of patentability."[6] The basic rule of nonobviousness

* Michael Abramowicz is a Professor of Law at the George Washington University Law School. John F. Duffy is the Samuel H. McCoy II and Armistead M. Dobie Professor of Law at the University of Virginia School of Law.

[1] Graham v. John Deere Co., 383 U.S. 1, 11 (1966).

[2] *Id.*

[3] Robert P. Merges & John F. Duffy, Patent Law and Policy 611 (4th ed. 2007).

[4] Michael J. Meurer & Katherine J. Strandburg, *Patent Carrots and Sticks: A Model of Nonobviousness*, 12 Lewis & Clark L. Rev. 547, 548 (2008).

[5] Alan L. Durham, *Patent Symmetry*, 87 B.U. L. Rev. 969, 970 (2007) ("Obviousness is the key to defining what is a patentable invention.").

[6] This phrase comes from the title of Nonobviousness – The Ultimate Condition of Patentability (John F. Witherspoon ed., 1980), a prominent collection of articles celebrating the twenty-fifth anniversary of the codification of the obviousness doctrine in 35 U.S.C. § 103 (2000 & Supp. IV 2004). Other authors have since used the same phrase to describe the doctrine. *See, e.g.*, Daralyn J. Durie & Mark A. Lemley, *A Realistic Approach to the Obviousness of Inventions*, 50 Wm. & Mary L. Rev. 989, 990 (2008).

is easy enough to recite: Under 35 U.S.C. § 103, a patent may not be granted on an invention that "would have been obvious at the time the invention was made to a person having ordinary skill in the art."[7] But the apparent simplicity of the requirement belies the complexities and difficulties that have historically bedeviled the doctrine.[8] The inducement standard, as articulated in *Graham*, appears to be vitally important to understanding the statutory nonobviousness requirement, because it offers a simple explanation for why society should deny patents on some innovations: If the innovation would be created and disclosed even without patent protection, denying a patent on the innovation costs society nothing (because the innovation would be developed anyway) and saves society from needlessly suffering the well-known negative consequences of patents, including the restriction on output caused by a patentee's exclusive rights and the administrative and litigation costs associated with running a patent system.

Yet despite its apparent promise as the theoretical basis for the most important patentability doctrine, *Graham*'s inducement standard has achieved only a modicum of influence.[9] Though frequently cited, the inducement standard is often relegated to a passing mention or to a footnote in introducing the patentability standard.[10] Some articles have devoted more extended attention to the inducement standard, but these too have generally highlighted the difficulties in using the standard to

7 35 U.S.C. § 103(a).

8 *See, e.g.*, Durham, *supra* note 3, at 971 ("Obviousness is a difficult issue to resolve. It requires one to imagine how a claimed invention might have looked to a different person . . . at a different time . . . and without resorting to hindsight based on knowledge of the claimed invention. . . . "); Eisenberg, *supra* note 3, at 886–87 (stating that "the implementation of [the nonobvious] standard poses certain administrative challenges"); Gregory Mandel, *The Non-Obvious Problem: How the Indeterminate Nonobvious Standard Produces Excessive Patent Grants*, 42 U.C. Davis L. Rev. 57, 59 (2008) (explaining that the indeterminacy of the nonobvious standard results in too many patent grants even though "[t]he nonobvious standard is not simply too low, but both too high and too low. It is indeterminate."); Joshua McGuire, *Nonobviousness: Limitations on Evidentiary Support*, 18 Berkeley Tech. L.J. 175 (2003) ("To obtain a patent, one must have patentable subject matter that is useful, novel, nonobvious, and adequately described; however, the standard for a nonobvious invention is often difficult to apply.").

9 Some commentators, meanwhile, have criticized *Graham* for failing to articulate a clear test. T. J. Chiang, for example, notes, "The opinion gave all the appearance of expecting a solution to appear out of thin air once the formula was followed. The lack of an articulable rule meant that determinations of obviousness took the appearance – and arguably the reality – of resting on judicial whim. . . . " Tun-Jen Chiang, *A Cost-Benefit Approach to Patent Obviousness*, 82 St. John's L. Rev. 39, 49 (2008).

10 For example, Professor Rebecca Eisenberg begins the analysis in a recent article by noting, "*In theory*, [the nonobviousness] standard prevents the issuance of patents on inventions that, although new, are so close to the prior art that they are likely to be forthcoming even without the incentive of a patent." Rebecca S. Eisenberg, *Pharma's Nonobvious Problem*, 12 Lewis & Clark L. Rev. 375, 381 (2008) (emphasis added). The footnote to that sentence quotes *Graham*'s articulation of the inducement standard, *id.* at 381 n.13, but inducement theory is never again mentioned in the remainder of the article. Similarly, Professor Mandel quotes the *Graham*'s inducement standard in a footnote. *See* Mandel, *supra* note 8, at 85 n.121 (2008). Yet Mandel describes the sentence from *Graham* as "dicta" and concludes that the *Graham* Court did not hold "that this is what the statutory nonobviousness standard actually measures." *Id.*

decide cases or to shape legal doctrine.[11] For example, Ed Kitch's classic verdict on *Graham*'s inducement standard emphasized that the nonobviousness requirement, as articulated by the courts, provides only an "awkward" tool "to sort out those innovations that would not be developed absent a patent system," with the "focus" of the legal doctrine always being on other issues.[12] Kitch's view has become the consensus. Thus, in a widely cited and influential 2003 report, the Federal Trade Commission summarized the testimony of numerous legal and economics scholars as demonstrating that, even though the inducement standard represents "the right way to assess whether to grant a patent" from a "theoretical perspective," the standard is not "administrable," so "the more manageable standards of the patent statute have evolved to serve as the means by which to measure when to grant a patent."[13]

In some ways, we agree with these prior assessments of the inducement standard. There is a certain awkwardness in the relationship between the inducement standard and the nonobviousness requirement, at least as that requirement has previously been articulated by the courts. Moreover, the Supreme Court in *Graham* did not provide a rigorous foundation for deriving the inducement standard from the statutory language. The absence of such a legal foundation may explain why the courts and the Patent and Trademark Office (PTO) have typically avoided looking to the inducement standard for guidance in interpreting and applying the statutory nonobviousness requirement. The one exception, an insightful but ultimately flawed panel opinion by Judge Posner, relied on the inducement standard to invalidate a patent, but nevertheless failed to identify any administrable test or metrics for applying the inducement standard to the specific facts of that case or other cases.[14] Posner's panel opinion was reversed en banc,[15] and that history has perhaps cemented the notions that the inducement standard conflicts with the statutory obviousness standard, is anti-patent, or is simply too difficult to apply in actual cases. This chapter aspires to show those notions to be wrong and to revitalize the inducement standard as the touchstone for understanding and refining the obviousness doctrine. The result

11 Glynn Lunney considers the inducement standard in his treatment of obviousness doctrine, but in his view, the lack of "empirical evidence [for] determining the point at which a patent becomes necessary to induce desirable invention" is a stumbling block to using the inducement standard more extensively in crafting patentability doctrine. Glynn S. Lunney, Jr., *E-Obviousness*, 7 Mich. Telecomm. Tech. L. Rev. 363, 416 (2000). Similarly, Samuel Oddi has provided a treatment of inducement theory. *See* A. Samuel Oddi, *Un-Unified Economic Theories of Patents – The Not-Quite-Holy Grail*, 71 Notre Dame L. Rev. 267, 277–81 (1996). But he views the theory as merely one of several competing theories of the patent system, *see id.* at 268, and he does not attempt to refine obviousness doctrine to conform to an inducement standard.

12 Edmund W. Kitch, Graham v. John Deere Co., *New Standards for Patents*, 1966 Sup. Ct. Rev. 293, 301.

13 Federal Trade Comm'n, To Promote Innovation: The Proper Balance of Competition and Patent Law and Policy ch. 1, at 11 (2003).

14 *See infra* notes 108–130 and accompanying text.

15 See Roberts v. Sears, Roebuck & Co., 697 F.2d 796 (7th Cir. 1983), *opinion vacated as noted in* Roberts v. Sears, Roebuck & Co., 723 F.2d 1324, 1329 (7th Cir. 1983) (en banc).

should be more coherent, defensible, and predictable decision making than is possible either under the current doctrine or under Judge Posner's treatment, which missed important implications of the inducement standard.

There are two motivations for undertaking this project. First, the time is right. In its 2007 decision *KSR International* v. *Teleflex, Inc.*,[16] the Supreme Court overturned a quarter-century-old test for nonobviousness that the nation's expert appellate court for patent law, the Court of Appeals for the Federal Circuit, had meticulously constructed. The *KSR* decision has precipitated a vibrant debate among scholars seeking to help the courts rebuild a pragmatic obviousness doctrine that yields predictable answers and is more theoretically sound than the Federal Circuit doctrine rejected in *KSR*.[17] That reconstruction project can have little hope of enduring success without reexamining and reevaluating the ultimate goal of the nonobviousness requirement.

A second and more important motivation is the promise of the inducement standard in providing significant insights into some of the most difficult theoretical and practical problems in the field. Economic analysis of patent law frequently begins with the assertion that patents present a social tradeoff: providing incentives for innovation at the expense of accepting the deadweight loss associated with monopoly-like exclusive rights.[18] Even beyond the law and economics literature,

[16] 550 U.S. 398 (2007). The Court rejected the Federal Circuit's test as excessively rigid and formalistic. *Id.* at 419. The Supreme Court explained that "familiar items may have obvious uses beyond their primary purposes, and in many cases a person of ordinary skill will be able to fit the teachings of multiple patents together like pieces of a puzzle," precluding bright-line tests. *Id.* at 420.

[17] *See, e.g.*, Durie & Lemley, *supra* note 5, at 998 (arguing for a more realistic inquiry into obviousness and noting that "[i]n *KSR*, the Supreme Court ostensibly made the obviousness inquiry more 'flexible' and 'pragmatic'"); Eisenberg, *supra* note 10 (analyzing the effect of *KSR* on the application of the nonobvious standard to pharmaceutical patents); Jeanne C. Fromer, *The Layers of Obviousness in Patent Law*, 22 Harv. J.L. & Tech. 75, 76 (2008) (discussing the proper object of the nonobviousness inquiry and stating that "[d]espite this overarching purpose [of encouraging innovation] highlighted in *KSR*, neither courts nor scholars have analyzed or settled on the obviousness inquiry's object, that is, the thing which must be nonobvious"); Michael J. Meurer & Katherine J. Strandburg, *Business Law Forum: Nonobviousness – The Shape of Things to Come: Patent Carrots and Sticks: A Model of Nonobviousness*, 12 Lewis & Clark L. Rev. 547, 548 (2008) (measuring the effect of the nonobvious standard on the "choice of research projects" and stating that "[t]he KSR decision clears the way for new thinking about the obviousness issue, which, despite its importance, is surprisingly undertheorized"); Joseph Scott Miller, *Remixing Obviousness*, 16 Tex. Intell. Prop. L.J. 237, 240 (2008) (discussing the impact of *KSR* on the concept of the person having ordinary skill in the art and advancing a "framework for determining whether a combination claim is nonobvious"); Joshua D. Sarnoff, Bilcare, KSR, *Presumptions of Validity, Preliminary Relief, and Obviousness in Patent Law*, 25 Cardozo Arts & Ent. L.J. 995, 1036 (2008) ("Whatever the legal or factual status of the obviousness inquiry, *KSR* has enormous importance as it has clearly raised the bar for determining when inventions are non-obvious and thus patentable.").

[18] *See, e.g.*, Richard Gilbert & Carl Shapiro, *Optimal Patent Length and Breadth*, 21 RAND J. Econ. 106, 106 (1990) (referring to "the conventional analysis of optimal patent length, based on the tradeoff between the incentives for innovation and the extent of static monopoly deadweight loss"); William D. Nordhaus, Invention, Growth, and Welfare: A Theoretical Treatment of Technological Change 76 (1969) (creating a model for calculating the optimal patent term by balancing increased incentives for innovation against greater deadweight loss).

legal scholars often frame intellectual property law generally and patent law in particular as presenting a conflict between the public and private domains – a choice between openness and exclusivity.[19] If, however, the law follows *Graham*'s inducement standard, such tradeoffs and conflicts do not necessarily exist.

Under a rigorously enforced inducement standard, patents would cover only those innovations that otherwise would not be created or disclosed – in other words, patents would cover only innovations that, without the patent system, *would not have been in the public domain anyway*. The patent system would then have only positive effects on the public domain: Patents would cover only inventions that would otherwise not be in the public domain, and when the patents expire, the inventions would enter into and enrich the public domain. Similarly, the apparent deadweight losses created by patent rights would be an illusion because, if patent rights had not been available, the invention would not have been available from competing firms but instead would have been either unavailable or covered by trade secrecy. As we show in this chapter, the optimal implementation of the inducement standard may not achieve such a Panglossian resolution because, at least in some circumstances, patents should be allowed even if they merely induce *earlier* innovation. Thus, the analysis suggested by the inducement standard helps identify more clearly the precise the economic tradeoff at issue: Patents produce earlier innovation, but at the cost of higher prices and associated deadweight loss in a later period (when the invention would have existed even without the inducement of the patent). This point highlights another deep theoretical strength of the inducement standard, because it holds out the hope of grounding patentability decisions law in a more rigorous economic framework and thereby bringing patent law closer to the vast body of modern regulatory law, which commonly uses economic analysis in making specific decisions about the scope and extent of regulation.

19 See, e.g., James Boyle, *The Second Enclosure Movement and the Construction of the Public Domain*, 66 L. & CONTEMP. PROBS. 33, 38 (2003) (describing the "limits to intellectual property rights" as the "antierosion walls around the public domain" and more generally arguing that expansions of intellectual property rights erode the public domain); Niva Elkin-Koren, *What Contracts Cannot Do: The Limits of Private Ordering in Facilitating a Creative Commons*, 74 FORDHAM L. REV. 365 (2005) (noting the effect of the expansion of IP rights on the contraction of the public domain); Christine D. Galbraith, *A Panoptic Approach to Information Policy: Utilizing a More Balanced Theory of Property in Order to Ensure the Existence of a Prodigious Public Domain*, 15 J. INTELL. PROP. L. 1, 4 (2007) (advocating for a more accessible public domain, because "[u]nfortunately, the public domain appears to be diminishing as the recent trend in formulating information policy is to utilize an organizing concept of private property ownership"); Pamela Samuelson, *Enriching Discourse on Public Domains*, 55 DUKE L.J. 783, 791 (2006) (acknowledging the tension between intellectual property rights and protecting the public domain and quoting *International New Service* v. *Associated Press*, 248 U.S. 215, 250 (1918) (Brandeis, J., dissenting) ("The general rule of law is, that the noblest of human productions – knowledge, truths ascertained, conceptions, and ideas – become, after voluntary communication to others, free as the air to common use.")); John R. Therien, *Exorcising the Specter of a "Pay-Per-Use" Society: Toward Preserving Fair Use and the Public Domain in the Digital Age*, 16 BERKELEY TECH. L.J. 979, 1035 (2001) (arguing that "the judiciary must protect the public domain and fair use, whether impinged upon by technology-derived statutory rights or the technology itself").

The chapter's rehabilitation of the inducement standard begins, in Part I, with an investigation of doctrinal difficulties associated with *Graham*'s inducement standard. As Professor Kitch noted more than forty years ago, the nonobviousness requirement seems at first to be an awkward way to implement an inducement standard. We agree that perhaps one natural interpretation of the statutory text points toward a *cognitive* definition of nonobviousness that focuses on whether individuals have epistemic awareness of technological solutions to problems. In embracing the inducement standard as the ultimate theory underlying nonobviousness, the *Graham* Court embraced an *economic* definition of nonobviousness and implicitly rejected a cognitive approach in interpreting the statute. The Court, however, failed to provide a sufficient legal justification for that interpretation, and that failure has almost certainly made courts and lawyers wary of placing too much reliance on the theoretical standard. Yet establishing a legal justification for the inducement standard is not so difficult. The statute itself sets the obviousness standard by reference to a highly fictional concept, the "person having ordinary skill in the art." Defining that fictional person's abilities by reference to economic incentives rather than technological cognition is no more radical than the now familiar use of economics to define the behavior of the fictional reasonable person in tort law.[20]

The awkwardness of the inducement standard is, however, only partially remedied by the development of a more rigorous legal basis justifying the use of the standard in patentability determinations. Part II introduces ambiguities, puzzles, and other difficulties associated with the inducement standard. Because the inducement standard has not been taken seriously in the past, these ambiguities and difficulties have not been resolved. Our analysis leads to three necessary clarifications of *Graham*'s inducement standard.

First, *Graham*'s articulation of the inducement standard may be fairly criticized for treating a fundamentally dynamic issue – invention – as if it were static, with no time frame specified or implicit. *Graham*'s inducement standard asks which inventions would be devised and disclosed even without the inducement of a patent, but it is silent on the crucial question: devised and disclosed *by when*? Even with no patent system, it is hard to imagine that many inventions would remain undevised and undisclosed *forever*. Thus, if the *Graham* inducement standard were interpreted as trying to identify "those inventions which would not [*ever*] be disclosed or devised but for the inducement of a patent,"[21] then almost nothing would be patentable. Yet, if the inducement standard were interpreted as trying to identify "those inventions which would not [*immediately*] be disclosed or devised but for the inducement of a patent,"[22] almost everything would be patentable because patent law presumably provides at least marginal incentives for inventing earlier. Both extremes must be

[20] *See* United States v. Carroll Towing Co., 159 F.2d 169 (2d. Cir. 1947) (L. Hand, J.).

[21] *Graham*, 383 U.S. at 11.

[22] *Id.*

wrong. We show that *Graham*'s inducement standard is best interpreted as requiring patents to cover only those inventions that, but for the inducement of a patent, would not have been disclosed or devised for a substantial period of time. Our reformulation produces a dynamic inducement standard that is consistent with the growing body of literature that views the patent system as attempting not so much to *increase* but to *accelerate* invention.

A second insight relies on an important feature of the patent system: competition. The modern patent system does not grant monopolies to industry participants that the sovereign happens to favor. Rather, patents are awarded competitively, and the competition to obtain patents has important implications for the practical enforcement of the patentability standard. Our dynamic adjustment to the inducement standard introduces the concept of a "substantial period of time," which naturally leads to the question of just *how* substantial a time period is necessary. Yet the competitive structure of the patent system makes the answer to that question less important than it first seems. The strong incentives of the patent system, coupled with the competition to obtain patents, should accelerate the time of innovation by a very long period, often by longer than the patent term itself, except in certain specific circumstances – the circumstances that make a patent-motivated innovator insignificantly better (i.e., insignificantly earlier) than an innovator not motivated by the patent system. Those circumstances can serve as proxies for the inducement standard so that, by looking for such circumstances, government officials and judges can identify inventions not induced by the patent system without invoking any complex models of technological acceleration. These circumstances include a rapid decline in the cost of innovation – for example because of the development of a technology that is an input into the new technology – and a positive demand shock shortly before invention, especially where multiple firms respond to the shock by developing the technology and even more so if some of those firms do not appear to be patent motivated.

A third and final clarification to *Graham*'s inducement standard resolves the ambiguity in the concept of "invention." Once it is recognized that the inducement standard must be interpreted dynamically – so that the inquiry is whether the inducement of the patent accelerated the arrival of the invention – then a crucial question becomes what precisely must be accelerated: the conception of an invention or its practical, commercial implementation. Our conclusion is that *Graham*'s standard should be interpreted as requiring the inducement of an earlier arrival of the commercialized invention, not merely the "invention" in theory or on paper in a patent disclosure. A contrary approach would induce what we call "speculative patents" – patents that describe possible future applications of embryonic technologies. Such speculative patents, if they were to be allowed, might have a high option value – they will be valuable if technological development takes a particular course. But if the patents do little or nothing to advance the actual arrival of new technology in practical terms, then they have little or no social value.

This third clarification to the inducement standard provides insight into what has so far been a muddled debate about the meaning and desirability of so-called patent trolls. The term "patent troll" has been generally if somewhat loosely defined in the literature as a "nonpracticing entity," an entity that has never commercialized or "practiced" its patented technology.[23] Such nonpracticing entities have generated enormous controversy in recent years, and as the label "troll" suggests, some patent practitioners have a visceral sense that, at least in some circumstances, such nonpracticing entities stand in the way of true innovators. But under orthodox patent doctrine and theory, it should not matter whether an entity practices a patent, because the quid pro quo of the patent is said to encompass merely the disclosure in the patent document. Our approach to the *Graham* inducement standard shows why it can matter whether an entity is practicing its invention: Although a nonpracticing patentee might accelerate the actual practice of an invention, it is difficult to believe that has happened if other parties have independently invented and commercialized the technology without even planning to seek patent protection. Such circumstances would seem to be powerful evidence that the inducement of the patent was unnecessary to generate the invention, and thus that the patent may be invalid under the inducement standard.

Whereas Parts I and II are devoted to resolving the previously perceived legal and theoretical awkwardness of the inducement standard, Part III focuses on the other major criticism of the standard – that it is unadministrable. Many doctrines of patent law can be subjected to the simplistic objection that they lack mathematical precision, and prior approaches to the nonobviousness standard have been especially vulnerable to such attacks. A reinterpreted inducement standard need not demonstrate perfection: It can be an administrative success if it is a bit better than current doctrine as a helpful theoretical and pragmatic guide for applying the obviousness doctrine. We believe the inducement standard easily satisfies that test. As a theoretical matter, it provides a sound basis for interpreting "the person having ordinary skill in the art" not only as a person possessing technological knowledge but also as someone who is responsive to both economic incentives and economic limitations. Those economic incentives and limitations help not only answer the previously intractable question of just *how* obvious something must be to be obvious under the statute but also unify patent law with bodies of regulatory law as a diverse as common law torts, antitrust law, and modern federal administrative law. Beyond its theoretical successes, the inducement standard can also be a practical success.

[23] Former Assistant General Counsel of Intel Peter Detkin claims to have created this term in 2001 while describing companies that do not create patents, but rather buy them, and then demand unusually high license fees by threatening costly litigation in the alternative. *See* Peter N. Detkin, *Leveling the Patent Playing Field*, 6 J. Marshall Rev. Intell. Prop. L. 636, 636 (2007). The broadest definition describes a patent troll as an entity that extracts profits by offering a target entity an option of purchasing a license or facing litigation. Thomas S. Kim & Michael D. Stein, *Patent Value: Increased Interest Extends Beyond "Trolls,"* Legal Intelligencer, July 25, 2005.

For example, it provides concrete guidance for how the nonobviousness standard should apply in fields such as software, where the costs of achieving any particular innovation may decrease over time[24] and mechanisms other than patents (such as copyright protection) likely provide very significant inducements for innovation. The inducement standard suggests that patent examiners and judges should be especially vigilant in enforcing the nonobvious requirement in such fields because, even without the inducement of patents, many innovations would have been produced perhaps at only slightly later times.

Any disagreement about the specifics of our interpretation of the inducement standard should not obscure the overarching project. *Graham*'s inducement standard provides an intuitively simple and powerful framework to justify granting patents for some innovations and denying patents for others. If *Graham*'s articulation of the inducement standard is not flawless, it is nonetheless sufficiently meritorious and prominent to be worth saving. Our reinterpretation of the inducement standard merely ties it to three fundamental features of the patent system: It is dynamic, pragmatic, and competitive. The first two of those features are evident in the constitutional goal of the patent system – to "promote the Progress of... useful Arts."[25] "Progress" reminds us that invention is dynamic and that producing invention earlier in time is a central objective of the system. The constitutional reference to the "useful Arts" makes clear that the specific form of progress we should care about lies in the practical realm. Finally, although patents reduce short-term competition to lower prices, they foster a long-term competition among innovators to find and develop tomorrow's technology.

I. REHABILITATING THE INDUCEMENT STANDARD: A DOCTRINAL FOUNDATION

It may seem exceptionally odd to begin with a doctrinal justification of a standard *already supported by Supreme Court precedent*. Yet any candid assessment must acknowledge that, despite its endorsement by the Supreme Court in 1966, the inducement standard has not shaped subsequent doctrinal development of the patentability standard. A reason for this startling absence of influence is that

[24] One input for generating software innovation is almost certainly computing power, because experiments in software likely need to be repeatedly tested on fast computers. The cost of computing power has been dramatically falling ever since the "Moore's Law" prediction decades ago, where Moore noted that the number of transistors that can be placed on an integrated circuit had doubled every year from 1958 to 1965 and predicted that the trend would continue "for at least 10 years." Gordon E. Moore, *Cramming More Components onto Integrated Circuits*, Electronics Mag. 4–5 (1965). His prediction has proved so far to be accurate, so much so that that the law is now used in the semiconductor industry to guide long-term planning and set targets for research and development. *See* Cornelius Disco & Barend van der Muelen, Getting New Technologies Together 206–07 (1998).

[25] U.S. Const. art I, § 8, cl. 8.

neither in *Graham* nor in subsequent cases has the Supreme Court attempted either to reconcile the inducement standard with the statutory text or to provide a general theoretical or doctrinal foundation for the inducement standard. Thus, the inducement standard has been viewed as a theoretical tangent in the *Graham* opinion or perhaps even as an unhelpful distraction from the statutory inquiry.

The statutory text must be the starting point for any attempt to supply the inducement standard with a doctrinal foundation. As discussed in Part I.A, that text might seem at first glance to point toward a cognitive test of obviousness. Yet a cognitive approach to the statutory nonobviousness requirement raises numerous questions while offering little or no guidance for answering those questions. Part I.B then compares the inducement standard and the statutory text in more detail and finds that the most important features of the inducement standard are easily harmonized with the statutory text and structure. Part I.C examines the inducement standard in light of general regulatory theory and practice. Doctrine outside patent law illustrates the justification for using an economic approach to interpret legal provisions. The inducement standard can serve as the guide for an economic approach to the obviousness test. Finally, Part I.D further analyzes what the inducement standard requires, arguing that it is an objective test, exploring the rare case in which non-patent incentives to invent are considerable, and emphasizing that an invention can be patent induced if in the absence of patent incentives someone could have been expected to invent and keep the invention a trade secret.

A. *The Difficulties with a Cognitive Approach*

Section 103(a) of the Patent Act provides the statutory foundation for the obviousness doctrine:

> A patent may not be obtained . . . if the differences between the subject matter sought to be patented and the prior art are such that the subject matter as a whole would have been obvious at the time the invention was made to a person having ordinary skill in the art to which said subject matter pertains. Patentability shall not be negatived by the manner in which the invention was made.

The word "obvious" is consistent with a cognitive approach, because one of its standard definition is "easily discovered, seen or understood,"[26] and the last of these words focuses on the mental process of understanding or cognition.[27] Perhaps because the word "obvious" names the statutory doctrine, courts and commentators

[26] Webster's New World Dictionary 937 (3d ed. 1994). The word derives from the Latin prefix *ob-* (meaning "in the way of" or "on") and the Latin word *via* ("street"). The word "ob-via" could be accurately translated as "lying in the street."

[27] The words "easily discovered," meanwhile, are consistent with an economic approach. *See infra* text accompanying note 72.

have tended to assume, implicitly or explicitly,[28] that the doctrine focuses on the degree of cognitive difficulty in conceiving the invention.

A purely cognitive approach to applying the statutory standard runs into immediate difficulty when the standard is read in its entirety, because obviousness is tested by reference to what would have been obvious not to any actual person, but to "a person having ordinary skill in the art"[29] – abbreviated typically, if inelegantly, as "Phosita." As discussed later, the courts have constructed this person with attributes acknowledged to be highly fictional, and those fictional attributes make it difficult or impossible to gain any real intuition as to the cognitive processes of the mythical Phosita. That stumbling block is only the beginning of the problems for a cognitive approach.

1. The Imaginary Person of Extraordinary Knowledge and Ordinary Creativity

The courts have rejected the proposition that the construct of a "person having ordinary skill in the art" should be defined by reference to the actual or average abilities of real individuals. In *Kimberly-Clark Corp.* v. *Johnson & Johnson*[30] – a decision the Federal Circuit rendered only two years after its creation – Judge Rich emphasized that this person was a "hypothetical person" and "an imaginary being," and he forthrightly acknowledged that "the courts have always applied a standard based on an imaginary worker of their own devising."[31] The Federal Circuit has since held that whatever an actual expert "did or did not *personally* realize at the time based on his actual knowledge is irrelevant" to applying the statutory nonobviousness standard because the "relevant inquiry" is always directed toward "what a hypothetical ordinarily skilled artisan would have gleaned from [the prior art]."[32] Furthermore, the court has repeatedly recognized that this "legal construct" of the "hypothetical person"[33] – this "ghost"[34] – "is akin to the 'reasonable person' used as a reference in negligence determinations."[35]

28 *See, e.g., In re* Kahn, 441 F.3d 977, 988 (Fed. Cir. 2006) (focusing on "the understandings and knowledge of persons having ordinary skill in the art"); Colleen M. Seifert, *Now Why Didn't I Think of That? The Cognitive Processes That Create the Obvious*, 12 Lewis & Clark L. Rev. 489 (2008) (offering a psychological critique of the courts' approaches to nonobviousness, but on the assumption that nonobviousness is an epistemic phenomenon); Dorothy Whelan, Note, *A Critique of the Use of Secondary Considerations in Applying the Section 103 Nonobviousness Test for Patentability*, 28 B.C. L. Rev. 357 (1987) (suggesting that the purpose of secondary considerations "is to ascertain the state of mind of a hypothetical worker having ordinary skill").

29 35 U.S.C. § 103(a) (2000 & Supp. IV 2004).

30 745 F.2d 1437 (Fed. Cir. 1984).

31 *Id.* at 1454.

32 Amazon.com, Inc. v. Barnesandnoble.com, Inc., 239 F.3d 1343, 1364 (Fed. Cir. 2001) (emphasis in original).

33 *In re* Rouffet, 149 F.3d 1350, 1357 (Fed. Cir. 1998).

34 Panduit Corp. v. Dennison Mfg. Co., 810 F.2d 1561, 1566 (Fed. Cir. 1987).

35 *Rouffet*, 149 F.3d at 1357; *see also Panduit*, 810 F.2d at 1566 (noting that, in applying the obviousness test, "the decisionmaker confronts a ghost, i.e., 'a person having ordinary skill in the art,' not unlike the 'reasonable man' and other ghosts in the law").

The reference to the "reasonable person" of tort law is an important signal. At least one school of thought during the last century – one might even say the dominant school – has viewed the "reasonable" person as different from the "average" person.[36] The reasonable person in tort is instead "an ideal creature" whose behavior is controlled "not [by] what is, but [by] what ought to be."[37] Lon Fuller and William Perdue long ago recognized that reasonable person tests have "an element of circularity" and are "subject to manipulation by the simple device of defining the characteristics of the hypothetical man."[38] This circularity can be eliminated only with an appropriate normative foundation, such as economics.[39]

Without such a framework, the concept of a "person having ordinary skill" is similarly question begging. The cognitive approach does not provide a normative foundation, let alone a clear doctrinal test, for determining what constitutes the level of "ordinary skill." It would be circular to define "ordinary skill" by reference to inventors, because the statute defines invention by reference to ordinary skill.[40] The Federal Circuit has held, "Inventors, as a class, according to the concepts underlying the Constitution and the statutes that have created the patent system, possess something – call it what you will – which sets them apart from the workers of *ordinary* skill."[41] This follows as a matter of definition, but if we cannot get a handle or even a name for this "something," the law will inevitably reflect a series of ad hoc ungrounded policy judgments.

In the absence of a compelling normative framework, the courts have defined the person of *ordinary* skill to be a rather *extraordinary* creature, an idiot savant with extraordinary knowledge and virtually no creativity. The mind of this hypothetical person comes equipped with a complete and thorough knowledge of all legally pertinent prior art, far more knowledge than could be possessed by any average or actual researcher.[42] Thus, the hypothetical person, as constructed by the courts, is

36 Francis A. Bohlen, *Mixed Questions of Law and Fact*, 72 U. PA. L. REV. 111, 114 (1924) ("The 'reasonable man' is not the average man.").

37 *Id.*; *see also* PAGE KEETON ET AL, PROSSER AND KEETON ON TORTS 173–74 (5th ed. 1984) (emphasizing that the reasonable person is described by the courts as a "community ideal of reasonable behavior" and not as any actual person who might very well do unreasonable things from time to time).

38 Lon Fuller & William R. Perdue, Jr., *The Reliance Interest in Contract Damages*: 1, 46 YALE L.J. 52, 85 (1936). For recognition of similar circularity problems in other areas, see Orin S. Kerr, *Four Models of Fourth Amendment Protection*, 60 STAN. L. REV. 503, 511 (2007), which identifies circularity in the Fourth Amendment's "reasonable" expectation of privacy, and James Weinstein, *The Federal Common Law Origins of Judicial Jurisdiction: Implications for Modern Doctrine*, 90 VA. L. REV. 169 (2004), spotting circularity in test of *World-Wide Volkswagen Corp.* v. *Woodson*, 444 U.S. 286, 297 (1980), which makes a court's jurisdiction turn on whether defendants could "reasonably anticipate being haled into court there."

39 That foundation in turn allows for critique of the test announced. *See, e.g.*, Allan M. Feldman & Jeonghyun Kim, *The Hand Rule and* United States v. Carroll Towing Co. *Reconsidered*, 7 AM. L. & ECON. REV. 523 (2005) (identifying inefficiencies in Hand's formulation).

40 35 U.S.C. § 103 (referring to "a person having ordinary skill in the art").

41 *Standard Oil*, 774 F.2d at 454.

42 *See, e.g.*, MERGES & DUFFY, *supra* note 3, at 729 (recognizing that, in degree of knowledge, the person having ordinary skill is a "superperson" in the art).

deemed to know about pieces of prior art that would have been not only extremely difficult to find – for example, a single copy of a doctoral dissertation in a library of a foreign country,[43] an entry in a commercial catalog circulated overseas,[44] or a few uses of an unpublished process somewhere inside the country[45] – but even *impossible* to find (e.g., patent specifications still being held in secret by the PTO,[46] publications not yet written,[47] and inventions still held in secret by other inventors).[48] Meanwhile, the Federal Circuit at one time described the person of ordinary skill as someone "who thinks along the line of conventional wisdom in the art and is not one who undertakes to innovate."[49]

Constructing the person of ordinary skill in this way may have seemed the most straightforward path to making the cognitive test administrable. A court could perhaps imagine the logical processes of a well-read robot and hold innovations obvious only where the prior art "connect[ed] the dots . . . very, very clearly."[50] That case law, however, does not survive the Supreme Court's decision in *KSR* v. *Teleflex*, which stated that "[a] person of ordinary skill is also a person of ordinary creativity, not an automaton."[51] Whatever administrability benefit the courts derived from their textually implausible construction of "ordinary" is thus lost today. The cognitive approach provides no guide for determining what constitutes "ordinary creativity." Even if creativity could be measured by something like IQ, the cognitive approach provides no basis for determining, even at a conceptual level, what would be an appropriate cutoff.

It might seem that the cognitive approach might be salvageable if the courts did use real people as a reference point.[52] But doing so would introduce new potential for arbitrariness. Skill exists on a continuum, ranging from the student just learning a subject to the world's foremost expert. Ordinary skill is somewhere in the middle. We cannot define ordinary skill as the level of those who are awarded patents, because this too would be circular. Perhaps we might then define the level as that needed to earn a livelihood in a field *without* earning patents. This is close to the solution that

43 *In re* Hall, 781 F.2d 897, 198 (Fed. Cir. 1986).

44 35 U.S.C. § 102(a).

45 *Id.*

46 Hazeltine Research, Inc. v. Brenner, 382 U.S. 252, 254 (U.S. 1965) (holding that § 102(e) patent applications are a source of prior art for purposes of §103).

47 *In re* Foster, 438 F.2d 1011 (C.C.P.A 1971) (holding that § 102(b) material may be used as part of an obviousness analysis); TorPharm Inc. v. Ranbaxy Pharms., Inc., 336 F.3d 1322 (Fed. Cir. 2003) (same).

48 *In re* Bass, 474 F.2d 1276 (C.C.P.A 1973).

49 Std. Oil Co. v. Am. Cyanamid Co., 774 F.2d 448, 454 (Fed. Cir. 1985).

50 Fed. Trade Comm'n, *supra* note 13, ch. 4 at 11 (recounting the 2002 testimony of Steven Kunin, Deputy Commissioner for Patent Examination Policy, U.S. Patent and Trademark Office and describing his perception of the Federal Circuit's case law on obviousness).

51 550 U.S. 398, 421 (2007).

52 Courts do sometimes use real people to help define the level of ordinary skill, but often in passing. *See infra* note 228 and accompanying text. Perhaps this is because of the courts' emphasis that the construct is hypothetical or perhaps because the cognitive approach offers no good way of answering the question.

we will reach under the inducement standard,[53] but the cognitive approach does not provide an explanation for why this is the level that should matter. Moreover, the level of ordinariness would then be higher for fields where there happen to be a group of people who need knowledge of the field to perform their work, even if those individuals are performing a type of work that does not involve innovation. But why should this happenstance of job specialization matter? The people who ought to matter, we argue, are those who would be *inventing without patents*. This observation flows not from a cognitive approach, but from the inducement standard.

2. The Degree of Obviousness and the Commingling of Economic Factors

In addition to the theoretical difficulties in defining the person having ordinary skill, courts applying the statutory obviousness standard must also confront the ultimate question of *how* obvious must something be to be viewed as "obvious," and therefore unpatentable, as a matter of law. Even if the courts were to follow a cognitive approach to obviousness, they would still confront this "how obvious" question, and the cognitive approach provides no guidance except for the insight that, cognitively, problems can present a full spectrum of difficulty – from the extremely obvious to the extremely hard.[54] The cognitive approach is especially ill equipped to resolve the "how obvious" question in part because cognition is an epistemic phenomenon that takes place at a particular moment in time, whereas invention occurs across time. Once the hypothetical person of ordinary skill becomes the focus of the obviousness inquiry, the natural question would be how much effort it would take this person to arrive at the solution, but a cognitive approach, rigorously followed, instead seems to ask about the chance that the person of ordinary skill would see the solution at the outset.

It should not be surprising then that the doctrine of nonobviousness in fact does not adhere to a rigorous cognitive definition of nonobviousness. The category of what is "obvious" as a matter of patent law clearly extends to more than just situations where the person of ordinary skill could consider the problem in an instant and immediately intuit the solution. In *KSR*, the Supreme Court made clear that the obviousness standard can be met in some situations where several *potential* solutions to a problem are "obvious to try."[55] The Court wrote:

> When there is a design need or market pressure to solve a problem and there are a finite number of identified, predictable solutions, a person of ordinary skill has good reason to pursue the known options within his or her technical grasp. If this

[53] *See infra* Part I.B.2.

[54] The case law rarely recognizes even this, instead dichotomizing "'ordinary innovation' or 'ordinary creativity' on one hand and 'real innovation' on the other," despite psychological evidence that "creativity is believed to vary along a continuum." Mandel, *supra* note 8, at 120–21.

[55] 550 U.S. at 421.

> leads to the anticipated success, it is likely the product not of innovation but of ordinary skill and common sense.[56]

Thus, a solution can be deemed legally obvious even though the person having ordinary skill would have had to "pursue" "a finite number" of potential solutions until an "anticipated success" is realized.

The "obvious to try" doctrine presents judges following a purely cognitive approach with a set of unappealing choices. Consider, for example, two potential research projects, both of which are obvious to try. Each research project requires researchers to explore a fairly large number of potential alternatives to find a solution. The testing of each alternative is routine, demanding nothing more than time and competent labor. In each case, the researcher can be fairly confident that a solution will be found, but prior to undertaking experiments, the exact solution cannot be predicted. Finally, assume that, for one research project, the testing of all possible solutions can be concluded at low cost within a few hours, whereas for the other, testing will take years and hundreds of millions of dollars.

The inducement standard provides a clear intuition about whether the fruits of each research project should be patentable: The patent probably should be granted for the years-long project, but not for the hours-long project. Yet if judges follow a purely cognitive approach, without peeking at the utterly different economics of the two scenarios, they will find the two scenarios difficult or impossible to distinguish. The judges might feel compelled to find neither patentable, following literally the Supreme Court's reference to "a finite number of identified, predictable solutions." Or the judges, attracted to the cognitive approach, might be tempted to hold the results of both research projects to be patentable, for in both, the end solution cannot be recognized at the outset.

This problem is not hypothetical. In *In re Deuel*,[57] the Federal Circuit considered whether it was obvious to isolate the DNA sequence coding for a particular human protein where (1) the protein had previously been discovered and (2) techniques were available by which a researcher could isolate the DNA sequence coding for any protein once the protein was known. The PTO adopted an appropriate methodological approach, looking to the practicalities – that is, the economics – of the problem. The agency concluded the DNA sequence was obvious because the agency found that, once a protein's amino acid sequence is known (indeed, even if it is only partially known), well-known screening techniques could find the corresponding DNA sequence for the protein by "effectively sampl[ing] all the DNA of the mammalian cell" in a process that would take "at worst, only a few weeks."[58]

[56] *Id.*

[57] In re Deuel, 51 F.3d 1552 (Fed. Cir. 1995).

[58] *Ex parte* Deuel, 33 U.S.P.Q.2D (BNA) 1445, 1452 (PTO Bd. Appeal & Interferences 1994) (quoting James D. Watson et al., *Recombinant DNA – A Short Course* (1983), then a standard reference in the field). We would not automatically assume that any process that would be expected to take only a

Although holding the isolated DNA sequence obvious made good policy sense, the Federal Circuit nonetheless reversed the agency. The court's decision serves as a paradigm of the pure cognitive approach. The court reasoned that knowledge of the amino acid sequence of a protein does not necessarily render obvious the corresponding DNA sequence because there were "an enormous number of DNA sequences" that could potentially code for the protein.[59] In its prior decision *In re Bell,*[60] which was repeatedly cited in *Deuel,*[61] the Federal Circuit had determined that "more than 10^{36} different nucleotide sequences" could encode the particular protein at issue there.[62] Numbers like 10^{36} – one undecillion, or *trillion, trillion, trillions* – are certainly enormous. No one could guess the DNA sequence until the screen procedures were complete. To the PTO, the cognitive difficulty posed by that multitude of possibilities did not matter as long as known screening procedures could be used to isolate the correct DNA sequence without any difficulty or any undue experimentation.[63] To the Federal Circuit, however, "the existence of a general method of isolating ... DNA molecules is essentially irrelevant to the question whether the specific molecules themselves would have been obvious."[64] This logic suggests that the court would have reached the same outcome even if the screening could be completed in a matter of minutes on inexpensive equipment.

Deuel makes perfect sense from a cognitive perspective, but it was terrible policy and a poor interpretation of the statutory patentability standard. The decision was widely criticized by academics and, toward the end of its life, began to draw criticism even within the Federal Circuit.[65] Soon after the Supreme Court decided *KSR* v. *Teleflex,*[66] the PTO took the opportunity to assert that the analysis in *Deuel* had to be disavowed in light of the new Supreme Court teachings.[67] In *In re Kubin,*[68] the pragmatic position of the agency finally prevailed. The Federal Circuit overruled *Deuel* and specifically embraced the argument that, in determining the obviousness

few weeks could not be patented. The question is whether inventors could be expected to take the time in the absence of patent protection, and this might depend in turn on the potential benefits from completing the invention. *See infra* Part III.B.1.

59 51 F.3d. at 1558.

60 *In re Bell*, 991 F.2d 781 (Fed. Cir. 1993).

61 *See, e.g., Deuel*, 51 F.3d at 1559, 1560.

62 *Bell*, 991 F.2d at 784.

63 In *Bell*, the PTO had reasoned that standard techniques could be "easily" applied to isolate the DNA coding for a particular known protein. 991 F.2d at 785 (quoting the reasoning of the PTO Board). The Federal Circuit rejected that reasoning, *see id.*, so in *Deuel* the agency tried to use synonyms for "easily."

64 51 F.3d at 1559.

65 *See, e.g., In re* Fisher, 421 F.3d 1365, 1378 (Fed. Cir. 2005) (Rader, J., dissenting) (arguing that *Deuel* should be overruled).

66 550 U.S. 398 (2007).

67 *Ex parte* Kubin, 2007 Pat. App. LEXIS 13, at *11 (PTO Bd. Pat. App. & Interferences 2007) (reasoning that *KSR* "cast doubt on the viability of *Deuel*").

68 561 F.3d 1351 (Fed. Cir. 2009).

of DNA sequences coding for a particular protein, the courts must take into account "the ease and predictability" of techniques for isolating those DNA sequences.[69]

"Ease" is, of course, a relative term, and that is its strength. The term invites judgment about the economic factors that make the process of developing something new more or less difficult. Finding the right DNA sequence out of a trillion, trillion, trillion possibilities should be considered easy if standard, low-cost techniques can resolve the problem in a short time, and there would be ample incentive to undertake the effort even without patents. Finding the right answer among a mere ten or twenty possibilities may be considered difficult if testing each possibility requires enormous expense, time, and effort. As in *Deuel*, the purely cognitive approach to obviousness has no place for considering those factors. *Deuel*'s demise shows that the courts have not been able to maintain a purely cognitive approach. Mixing economic considerations into the analysis – or, better still, making economic factors the centerpiece of analysis rather than merely relevant factors – is desirable not only because it generates better patent policy but also because it represents the better interpretation of the statute, and it reconciles patent law with other areas of regulatory theory. To those matters, we now turn.

B. *The Inducement Standard and the Statutory Text*

The intellectual weaknesses of a cognitive approach and the courts' decisions that stray from this approach in service of the patent system's policy goals do not themselves establish a legal justification for embracing an economic interpretation of the statutory nonobviousness requirement. The statutory text, it might be argued, still does not point toward an economic approach to defining patentability such as the inducement standard, and thus the courts should muddle along with a cognitive approach, despite its glaring flaws, with arbitrary exceptions made where necessary. Yet careful analysis of the statute proves that the inducement standard provides a stronger framework for interpreting the statutory text than the cognitive approach.

Our analysis focuses on a straightforward interpretation of three critical words in § 103: "A patent may not be obtained . . . if the differences between the subject matter sought to be patented and the prior art are such that the subject matter as a whole would have been *obvious* at the time the invention was made to a *person* having *ordinary* skill in the art to which said subject matter pertains."[70] We interpret "obvious" to mean its dictionary definition of "easily discovered," "ordinary" to mean "nonpatent induced," and "person" to mean "human or entity." We freely admit that there are alternative possible interpretations of each of these words standing alone, but each of these interpretations is readily defensible under ordinary principles

[69] *Id.* at 1360; *see also id.* at 1358 (holding that *KSR* discredited the holding of *Deuel*).
[70] 35 U.S.C. § 103 (emphasis added).

of statutory interpretation. In addition, reading these three words in this way makes them cohere with one another, with *Graham*, and, as we show later,[71] with regulatory law more generally. One could reject some aspect of this interpretation and still allow some role for the inducement standard, but the combination of all three of these points shows that *Graham* is not an extra-textual gloss on or theory of the statute, but a reasonable reading of it.

1. "Obvious" and Ease of Discovery

The word "obvious" can mean not only "easily understood" but also "easily discovered."[72] As the *Deuel* example shows, a standard based on the *ease of discovery* is not difficult to reconcile with an economic test, because it recognizes both that something may be obvious even if it takes some searching and that the concept of obviousness is, like the concept of "easily," a matter of degree and context. Even under a dictionary definition of the term "obvious," courts need to evaluate how difficult a discovery must be before it can no longer be considered easy. There are three plausible approaches. First, the courts could try to articulate an absolute standard – a degree of anticipated time, difficulty, and expense beyond which a discovery will be considered not obvious. Although that approach is linguistically plausible, it is also indeterminate. The statute provides no guides for the courts to decide the level at which to fix this absolute standard. Perhaps the courts could do so – holding, for example, that an anticipated expense of $1,000,000 will be the threshold for nonobviousness – but this would be arbitrary.[73]

The second approach is the inducement standard: Innovations should be considered "easily discovered" if they would otherwise be devised and disclosed without the strong incentives of the patent system. This approach provides a guide for setting the level. It is sensitive to the context, and it recognizes that the word "obvious" in the statute encompasses achievements generated by ordinary economic forces where these achievements are "easily discovered." A third approach is to determine ease in reference to the person of ordinary skill. This approach does not so much solve the problem of defining a standard as it does merely push the problem down the line. However, the approach becomes congruent with the second approach if the inducement standard is used to define the skills possessed by the person of ordinary skill.

71 *See infra* Part I.C.

72 *See supra* text accompanying note 26.

73 Of course, the courts do sometimes announce holdings that include bright-line numeric thresholds. *See, e.g.*, Maryland v. Shatzer, 130 S. Ct. 1213 (2010) (announcing a bright-line test assessing whether a break in custody of more than fourteen days occurred). Doing so in this context would be undesirable because the appropriate threshold likely varies considerably from one context to another. Where the benefits of an invention are relatively small, an amount considerably less than $1,000,000 should perhaps be sufficient for patenting. *See infra* text following note 244.

2. "Ordinary" Skill

Graham's inducement standard does provide a way to interpret the level of "ordinary skill." It should be interpreted to be the level that would exist *without the inducement of patents*. That insight provides courts with a coherent and theoretically rigorous way to define the capabilities of the hypothetical person of ordinary skill while avoiding the difficulties we found with either endowing the person with omniscient knowledge and minimal creativity or with seeking to identify the relevant level of ordinary skill on the basis of a cognitive approach to nonobviousness.[74] Defining the level of ordinary skill does not do all the work of the inducement standard; we still need to consider the motivations of people with this level of skill in the absence of patents to determine what would have happened absent patent protection. But it moves us much closer to an administrable doctrine with a normatively defensible foundation.

The inducement standard thus offers an escape from the otherwise unanchored and potentially circular "reasonable person" test of the Patent Act, in much the same way that economic analysis provided content to the reasonable person test of tort law. The standard establishes a baseline that is independent of the patent system because it looks to the economic forces that would exist without patents. The person of "ordinary" skill is the person who would be in the industry even if the patent system did not exist, and an innovation should be considered "obvious" or "easily" discoverable if nonpatent incentives would be sufficient. The practical importance of this resolution can be understood by considering a field – for example, pharmaceutical research – in which the vast majority of the actual practitioners in the field are expected to be very creative. Research pharmaceutical firms presumably hire only those researchers whom the firms believe to be creative enough to secure patents. Patent law ought not look to the level of skill of these researchers and arbitrarily label them all ordinary. Rather, it should compare these researchers' work with the relatively little that would be produced in the absence of patent incentives.

3. The "Person" Who Possesses the Skill

Further conceptual improvement can be made by understanding that a "person" can be conceived of not merely as an individual but also as a corporation or some other entity. An entity, of course, naturally includes different people offering different types of contributions, and in most cases it makes more economic sense to ask about the economic incentives that an entity would face absent patent inducement than to ask about the economic incentives of hypothetical individuals. With this clarification, the inducement standard asks not only what some *individual* blessed with economic common sense and a lab in the garage would do in a world without patent incentives but also what entities would do. Inventions are often developed by teams of inventors,

74 *See supra* Part I.A.1.

and thus it makes economic sense for the inducement standard to apply at more than the individual level. If, for example, no individual would pursue a project, but a group of individuals certainly would, even without patent incentives, then we should characterize the invention as patent induced. This step furthers the project of making the person of ordinary skill less hypothetical; this element is still hypothetical in the sense that it is "ordinary" and thus operating without patent incentives, but no longer do we need to imagine a person with extraordinary capabilities. We need only consider what an entity would easily discover, using typical research protocols, given a particular incentive structure.

It might appear that this change would require rewriting the statute, but the very first section of the U.S. Code, the Dictionary Act, provides that "[i]n determining the meaning of any Act of Congress, unless the context indicates otherwise . . . the words 'person' and 'whoever' include corporations, companies, associations, firms, partnerships, societies, and joint stock companies, as well as individuals."[75] We know of no prior suggestions that the Dictionary Act should be applied to the patent statute, but this is likely a consequence, rather than a cause, of the conception of the person of ordinary skill in cognitive rather than economic terms. And we recognize that the courts have not always followed the Dictionary Act.[76] But even skeptics about the Act[77] seem troubled only where it conflicts with *other* principles of interpretation. That an entity is a legal "person" is a commonplace,[78] and it may be a particularly appropriate fiction once the obviousness doctrine is conceived in economic terms. Nothing in the context of § 103 suggests that "person" should exclude entities. There may well be statutes – say, a typical murder statute – in which the Dictionary Act would clearly not apply to the word "person." But, as we have seen, there is already a long-standing tradition in patent law of treating the "person of ordinary skill" as a hypothetical rather than a real person, and the Dictionary Act provides a means of honoring the sense behind this tradition that a real person cannot be intended without doing violence to the statutory text.

C. *Reconciling the Patentability Standard with General Regulatory Theory*

Embracing an economic approach such as the inducement standard, while rejecting a purely cognitive approach to obviousness, provides one final important benefit: It

75 1 U.S.C. § 1 (2004).

76 *See* Nicholas Quinn Rosenkranz, *Federal Rules of Statutory* Interpretation, 115 Harv. L. Rev. 2085, 2121–24 (2002) (discussing judicial interpretation of the Act).

77 *See, e.g.*, 1 Laurence H. Tribe, American Constitutional Law § 2–3, at 125–26 n.1 (3d ed. 2000), *cited and discussed in* Rosenkranz, *supra* note 76, at 2117.

78 *See generally* Susanna Kim Ripken, *Corporations Are People Too: A Multi-Dimensional Approach to the Corporate Personhood Puzzle*, 15 Fordham J. Corp. & Fin. L. 97 (2009) (examining the history and exploring the underpinnings of the law's treating corporations as people).

generates theoretical consistency between patent law and a much broader range of federal regulatory law in which economic approaches are ubiquitous.

A starting place is the federal common law of torts, where negligence has long been defined as conduct falling below the standard of care that would be followed by a reasonable person.[79] Tort law is an especially good field for comparison to patent law in this context because tort law's "reasonable person" has frequently been cited as a hypothetical construct that is analogous to the statutory "person having ordinary skill in the art" used in defining nonobviousness. One could imagine a cognitive approach to defining the care that would be employed by a reasonable person (e.g., an approach that asked how much care actual, average, or perhaps even hypothetical individuals would think of taking in particular circumstances). Yet for more than a half-century, that has not been the approach taken by the federal courts. The set of decisions made by actual individuals – in other words, the *customary* level of care – is not the ultimate touchstone of negligence. Rather, the courts have overtly tied the standard of reasonable care to an economic calculus, mostly famously outlined in Learned Hand's opinion in *United States* v. *Carroll Towing*.[80]

The obviousness doctrine of patent law could be distinguished from the negligence standard of federal tort law on the grounds that patent law is a statutory field, not an area of common law. In a common law field, judges have inherent lawmaking powers, whereas in statutory fields, judges are supposed to follow the policy dictates of statutory law as encoded by the legislature. Judicial importation of economic analysis into a common law field is thus less troubling than a similar step would be in a statutory field. Yet although the distinction between statutory and common law fields is significant in many contexts, it is not so here for two reasons.

First, the nonobviousness requirement evolved first as a common law doctrine developed by the courts themselves.[81] Congress's codification of the requirement in 1952 is widely understood to be a legislative validation of the general thrust of the doctrine as it had been evolving in the courts.[82] Indeed, the Supreme Court in *Graham* expressly held that the statutory nonobviousness requirement "was intended to codify judicial precedents."[83] Where Congress endorses the general thrust of judicially created common law through codification, the resulting statute might

79 *See, e.g.*, Davidson Steamship Co. v. United States, 205 U.S. 187, 193 (1907) ("There is an obligation on all persons to take the care which, in the ordinary circumstances of the case, a reasonable and prudent man would take, and the omission of that care constitutes negligence.").

80 United States v. Carroll Towing, 159 F.2d 169, 173 (2d Cir. 1947). *See generally* Chiang, *supra* note 9, at 43–46 (recounting the development of the common law of obviousness before codification); John F. Duffy, *Inventing Invention: A Case Study of Legal Innovation*, 86 TEX. L. REV. 1 (2007) (providing a history of the development of the obviousness doctrine).

81 A critical turning point in doctrinal development was the Supreme Court's decision in *Hotchkiss* v. *Greenwood*, 52 U.S. 248 (1850).

82 *See* Giles S. Rich, *The Vague Concept of "Invention" as Replaced by Section 103 of the 1952 Patent Act*, *in* NONOBVIOUSNESS – THE ULTIMATE CONDITION OF PATENTABILITY, *supra* note 6, at 400, 409.

83 *Graham*, 383 U.S. at 3.

well be interpreted as maintaining a significant role for further judicial development and refinement of the law. The obvious analogy comes from the other branch of federal monopoly law, antitrust. The Supreme Court has expressly interpreted the Sherman Act as "drawing on common law tradition"[84] and has repeatedly held that, in interpreting that statute, the courts maintain a greater degree of policy-making power than they do with respect to other statutory enactments.[85]

Second, even in the statutory area, the federal courts have not balked at importing economic analysis into vaguely worded regulatory statutes. Again, the antitrust laws are one obvious example. Section 1 of the Sherman Act prohibits "*[e]very* contract, combination in the form of trust or otherwise, or conspiracy, in restraint of trade,"[86] and yet the Supreme Court soon imposed on the statute a reasonable gloss that was defined in economic terms.[87] Like the Sherman Act, the Patent Act concerns the permissible (indeed, desirable) extent of monopolies in our economic system, and like the Sherman Act, the Patent Act is based on economic goals.[88] Furthermore, in interpreting the Copyright Act, the Supreme Court has also imported economic analysis in determining, for example, the extent of "fair use" that may be made of copyrighted works.[89] More generally, modern regulatory statutes are typically interpreted to include economic analysis. Although in many regulatory areas the executive branch supplies that interpretive gloss,[90] the source of the interpretive gloss merely

[84] National Soc. of Professional Engineers v. United States, 435 U.S. 679, 688 (1978); *see also* Leegin Creative Leather Prod., Inc. v. PSKS, Inc., 551 U.S. 877 (2007) ("From the beginning the Court has treated the Sherman Act as a common-law statute.").

[85] *See, e.g., Leegin*, 551 U.S. at 899 (noting that "[j]ust as the common law adapts to modern understanding and greater experience, so too does the Sherman Act's prohibition on 'restraint[s] of trade' evolve to meet the dynamics of present economic conditions").

[86] 15 U.S.C. § 1 (2004) (emphasis added).

[87] *See* Standard Oil Co. v. United States, 221 U. S. 1, 60, 62 (1911) (announcing that a "standard of reason" or "rule of reason" was to be applied in enforcing the Sherman Act); *id.* at 55, 58 (recognizing that the conceptions of unreasonable restraints on trade depend on "economic conceptions"). The *Standard Oil* Court's imposition of an economic reasonableness test onto the Sherman Act was controversial. In dissent, Justice Harlan accused the Court majority of "judicial legislation" because it had decided "to insert the word 'unreasonable' in the act." *Id.* at 90 (Harlan, J., concurring in part and dissenting in part).

[88] *See, e.g.*, Mazer v. Stein, 347 U.S. 201, 219 (1954) (noting that the constitutional "clause empowering Congress to grant patents and copyrights" is based on an "economic philosophy . . . that encouragement of individual effort by personal gain is the best way to advance public welfare through the talents of authors and inventors in 'Science and useful Arts'").

[89] *See, e.g.*, Harper & Row, Publrs. v. Nation Enters., 471 U.S. 539, 559 & 566 n.9 (1985) (relying on economic theory in interpreting the permissible scope of fair use). Although the statutory language of the current fair use statute, 17 U.S.C. § 107 (2004), includes at least one factor that points toward economic analysis (factor 4, "the effect of the use upon the potential market for or value of the copyrighted work," § 17(4)), the statute itself is a codification of a judicial gloss imposed on the Copyright Act prior to any legislative recognition of fair use. *See* Campbell v. Acuff-Rose Music, 510 U.S. 569, 577 (1994) (recognizing the statutory provision as a restatement of judicially created doctrine).

[90] *See, e.g.*, Executive Order No. 12866 § 1(b)(6) (1993) (requiring that, to the extent permitted by law, Executive Branch agencies should engage in cost-benefit analysis and should regulate only if the

reflects Congress's decision to allocate substantive lawmaking powers to administrative agencies in the modern regulatory state. Where Congress has not granted administrative agencies substantive lawmaking powers (as in the patent field), the courts need not eschew economic analysis. Rather, courts may properly recognize that, in numerous areas – ranging from pure common law (tort law), to areas of mixed statutory and common law (like antitrust), to modern statutory-administrative areas (like environment law[91]) – economic analysis is a broadly accepted interpretive gloss.

Viewed in this larger context, *Graham*'s inducement standard, with its economic gloss on the statutory nonobviousness standard, is not anomalous. Rather, the anomaly is the paucity of economic analysis in lower court applications of the nonobviousness standard. An electronic search of all Federal Circuit decisions since 1982 found fewer than two dozen cases in which economic factors are even mentioned as part of the nonobviousness analysis.[92] Moreover, in the majority of those cases, the courts were *distinguishing* economic from technological factors and were holding that the economic factors were not relevant in determining nonobviousness. At most, the survey was able to identify only six cases in a quarter-century that had overtly applied economic analysis in deciding patent obviousness issues, and none of those cases had been decided in the last decade. That vacuum of economic analysis need not exist. Incorporating basic economic wisdom into patentability decisions would help harmonize patent law with the overarching thrust of regulatory law in many other fields. *Graham*'s inducement standard points the way toward that end.

benefits of regulation exceed the costs); *see also* Entergy Corp. v. Riverkeeper, Inc., 129 S. Ct. 1498 (2009) (sustaining the EPA's decision to require economic cost-benefit analysis in administering a statute that did not clearly forbid such analysis).

91 Barton H. Thompson, Jr., *What Good Is Economics?*, 37 U.C. Davis L. Rev. 175, 176 (2003) ("One cannot study environmental law today without encountering economic analyses. Economics is everywhere – in legislative hearings and debates, regulatory documents, judicial opinions, legal casebooks, and academic articles.").

92 With the Lexis file of all Federal Circuit decisions, the following search was executed on February 14, 2010: "patent and econom! w/200 (obviou! or nonobviou!) and (overview(patent or patent!) or core-terms (patent or patent!))." (The restrictions "(overview(patent or patent!) or core-terms (patent or patent!))" were designed to exclude any nonpatent cases.) The search yielded sixty-eight cases. Those cases were independently coded by two coders into three categories: (1) false positives (i.e., cases that did not involve any use of economic principles in obviousness analysis); (2) cases in which the courts distinguished economic factors from technological factors and held that economic factors were not relevant to obviousness analysis; and (3) cases in which courts were using economic factors as proxies or considerations for either obviousness or nonobviousness. Of the sixty-eight cases, fifty-two cases were coded by at least one coder as false positives, and in fifty of those cases, both coders agreed on the classification (intercoder agreement = .96). Sixteen of the cases were coded by at least one coder as falling within category (2), with agreement on coding in twelve of those cases (intercoder agreement = .75). Only six cases were classified by at least one coder as falling into category (3), and in only two cases did the coders agree on the classification (intercoder agreement = .33). None of the cases classified in category (3) by either coder was decided in the last decade.

D. *Implications of the Inducement Standard*

Our preceding textual analysis justifies the use of an economic rather than cognitive approach to the nonobviousness standard. This still leaves several questions about what the inducement standard would require, and we address three important questions here.

1. Objectivity

One question is whether the courts should ask whether the particular inventor would have invented without patent incentives or whether any inventor would have done so. Because *Graham*'s articulation of the inducement standard employs the passive voice (referring to the inventions that "would not be disclosed or devised"), the inducement standard could be read as subjective: Would *this inventor* have devised and disclosed without the patent inducement? But the more natural reading of the passage, and the reading more justifiable on policy grounds,[93] is an objective one. The passive voice employed in the sentence highlights the invention, not the inventor. The *Graham* Court appeared to favor the latter approach, an objective patentability standard,[94] and an objective patentability standard is almost certainly compelled by the second sentence of § 103, which forbids reliance on the inventor's actual inventive process as a ground for rejecting a patent.[95] Properly construed,

93 A subjective inducement standard might be easier to administer because the PTO and the courts could look merely to historical facts about how a particular inventor derived the invention. Moreover, where an innovation is discovered merely by chance, without actually being motivated by the promise of a patent, it is unclear why society is better off rewarding the discovery with a patent. *But see* Sean B. Seymore, *Serendipity*, 88 N.C. L. Rev. 185 (2009) (defending patentability of serendipitous inventions, while arguing that conception occurs after the initial accident).

Yet a subjective standard would have significant drawbacks. Courts and patent examiners would have to determine the mental state of individual inventors – a difficult task compounded by the inventor's superior technical knowledge. Legally knowledgeable inventors could often feign additional efforts if they believed that their actual efforts in making the discovery might demonstrate that the invention was too subjectively obvious. Indeed, even in the case of a chance discovery, the patent applicant could delay seeking a patent while pretending to do additional experiments that are in fact unnecessary. An objective standard does not exclude the possibility that how hard the inventor worked may be indirectly relevant, as evidence of how hard a problem was expected to be. *See infra* Part III.B.2.

Finally, the choice in favor of an objective standard aligns patentability decisions with other areas of law that are designed to regulate economic behavior. Tort law, for example, applies an objective standard of reasonableness and generally affords the clumsy or inattentive no adjustment. Susan Randall, *Corrective Justice and the Torts Process*, 27 Ind. L. Rev 1, 19 (1993) ("[I]ndividuals who cannot conform to the standard of the reasonable person, as an unfortunate consequence of subnormal intellectual capacity or some other shortcoming, may be held liable for conduct which represents their best efforts."). So too, the rule of reason in antitrust law is based on an objective analysis of the economic behavior. *See* United States v. Brown Univ., 5 F.3d 658, 671 (3d Cir. 1993).

94 Graham v. John Deere Co., 383 U.S. 1, 15 n.7 (1966).

95 35 U.S.C. § 103(a) (2000) ("Patentability shall not be negatived by the manner in which the invention was made.").

the inducement standard looks objectively to determine whether any person would likely have devised and disclosed the invention without a patent inducement.

2. Trade Secrecy and Disclosure

Under the Court's articulation of the inducement standard, an invention is patentable if it would not be devised *or disclosed* but for the inducement of a patent. For inventions that would not be created at all without the promise of a patent, it is easy to understand the social benefits of granting the patent. For inventions that would be created but held as trade secrets in the absence of the patent system, the social calculus is more complex. The position taken under the *Graham* standard – which permits patents on such inventions – might be open to question as a matter of policy, but that position does make *Graham*'s inducement standard easier to reconcile with the statutory text.

Consider, for example, an alternative inducement standard that allowed patenting only if the invention would not have been *devised* but for the inducement of the patent system. If that standard were followed, patents would have to be denied for inventions that were difficult to discover but that would have been made without the inducement of the patent system *because they could be held as trade secrets*. The problem for this hypothetical alternative inducement standard is that, in certain circumstances, the incentives associated with trade secrecy protection are strong.[96] Indeed, trade secrecy protection can theoretically provide even more powerful incentives than patents because trade secrecy rights are potentially infinite in duration. Because of those incentives, some innovations induced by trade secrecy may have been difficult to discover, and thus courts are likely to view them to be not obvious, at some basic, commonsense interpretation of the statutory language.[97]

The actual inducement standard endorsed by the *Graham* Court does not, however, suffer from this problem. *Graham*'s inducement standard requires innovations to be viewed as unpatentable only if they would be created *and shared* without any patent inducement. Such innovations are likely to be relatively easy – meaning inexpensive – to create because such an inventor must find a means of recouping the investment made in an innovation that anyone can freely copy. Thus, the position on trade secrecy taken by the *Graham* inducement standard narrows any potential

96 *See, e.g.*, David S. Levine, *Secrecy and Unaccountability: Trade Secrets in Our Public Infrastructure*, 59 FLA. L. REV. 135, 157 (2007) ("Because a trade secret lasts, at least in theory, as long as a trade secret holder maintains its secrecy, the possibility that the information will never enter the public domain is very real.").

97 The alternative inducement standard would also seemingly require decision makers to investigate the extent to which inventions could be kept secret, with patents denied to inventions that were capable of being held in secret. In a sense, the alternative inducement standard would make secrecy the preferred policy, with patenting allowed only if the incentives associated with trade secrecy are inadequate. That approach would seem to be contrary to long-standing patent precedent and to present another hurdle for reconciling the statutory text with the alternative inducement standard.

gap between the inducement standard and the statutory text: If an innovation is sufficiently difficult that no one would engage in the creative activity absent the possibility of either trade secret or patent protection, then the invention should not be viewed as easily discovered or "obvious." The end result is also sensible: Where an invention is sufficiently difficult that the incentives of either trade secrecy or the patent system are needed to induce its creation, the law will permit protection of the invention under either regime.

A more challenging policy critique of the *Graham* standard would suggest that it might sometimes make it too easy to patent. Consider technological information that is easily developed and known by multiple firms in an industry, but each firm would protect the information as trade secret because there is no benefit from public disclosure. Protection of such secrets is consistent with the "exchange-for-secrets" theory, a venerable (if historically controversial) rationale for patents.[98] But this theory is a better justification for permitting patents to cover information that would otherwise be held in secret by a single firm. Allowing patents on widely held secrets imposes more social costs (because it halts preexisting competitive use of the information) and fewer benefits (because placing information in the public domain is likely to provide little social benefit where most or all of the parties who could make use of the information previously had access to it). But this problem in any event is not severe. Typically, easily developed information is likely to spill out of trade secrecy and enter the public domain long before a twenty-year patent would place the technology in the public domain. So it would only be a small group of inventions, for which there is some reason to believe that no such spillover would occur, for which the inducement standard would give excessive protection.

3. Nonpatent Inducements for Innovation

Graham's inducement might, in contrast, also be viewed as establishing too stringent of an obviousness standard where the nonpatent inducements for innovation are especially powerful. Consider, for example, a situation where the government, a foundation, or a wealthy philanthropist offers a prize (or a subsidy or grant) for creating and disclosing a particular type of advance – for example, a better treatment for a particular disease.[99] Assume that the prize is sufficiently large that it spurs teams of top researchers to seek the innovation. After years of hard work, one team succeeds, claims the prize, and *seeks a patent*. Such an innovation would seem difficult or impossible to label "obvious" in any linguistic sense. Yet an argument might be made that the patent should be denied under the inducement standard because the

[98] David G. Luettgen, *Functional Usefulness vs. Communicative Usefulness: Thin Copyright Protection for the Nonliteral Elements of Computer Programs*, 4 Tex. Intell. Prop. L.J. 233, 261–62 (1996) (explaining the rationale of this theory and its tension with justifications for patent law).

[99] *See, e.g.*, Keionline.org, *Prize for the Development of New Treatments for Chagas Disease*, http://www.keionline.org/misc-docs/b_b_igwg/prop2_chagas_prize.pdf (last visited June 9, 2010) (proposing a prize for new treatments of a particular disease).

powerful incentives created by the prize would have led to the innovation being devised and disclosed even without the possibility of a patent.

Much turns, however, on the conditions under which the prize or subsidy was granted. Federal research subsidies are now typically granted under the rule, codified in legislation, that grant recipients *will* be able to seek patents on the fruits of their federally funded research.[100] The possibility of a patent likely will affect the amount and intensity of the grantee's research and thus can be viewed as a proximate cause of the innovation. The inducement standard would then not be a significant barrier to patenting. Indeed, because the inducement of a possible patent existed prior to any offer for a prize, the hypothetical suggests that the invention was so difficult to achieve that it could not be devised or disclosed but for the inducement of a patent *plus other incentives*. Even if it could be shown in a particular case that a particular federally funded invention would have been invented at about the same time *without* the patent incentive, there is a strong argument for reading the Bayh-Dole Act, in conjunction with the patent statute, to allow patentability if the combination of the patent incentive and federal funding sufficiently accelerated the invention.

If the government, foundation, or philanthropist wants to preclude patenting, then the award of the grant or prize could be conditioned on the grantee or winner dedicating the patent rights to the public domain.[101] (Such a contractual condition is clearly wise if the grantor or prize funder wants to preclude patenting.) This arrangement, however, poses no special problem for the inducement standard. The conditioned grant or prize looks largely identical to standard employment contracts in for-profit firms, which award workers with money (in the form of a salary and other benefits) in exchange for, inter alia, an assignment of patent rights in any inventions created at work.[102] Because the patentability standard is objective, it cannot matter whether the individual actually seeking the patent intends to assign the rights (in exchange for a salary) to a firm for commercial exploitation or to assign the rights (in exchange for a grant or prize) to the public domain.

Nonetheless, although grants and prizes do not usually present a situation where the inducement standard produces results divergent from an intuitive sense of "obviousness," we do not discount the possibility that the inducement standard could produce such results in some circumstances. Sometimes even nonpatent incentives

[100] *See* 35 U.S.C. § 202(a) (allowing nonprofit and small business entities to retain title to any "subject invention," which is defined to encompass any invention created "in the performance of work under a [federal] funding agreement," id., § 201(e)).

[101] Alternatively, the prize sponsor could allow patenting but require that any resulting product be sold at a low price. *See, e.g.*, Aidan Hollis & Thomas Pogge, Incentives for Global Health, Health Impact Fund: Making New Medicines Accessible for All 3 (2008) (describing rules of the Health Impact Fund that would require specified prices for prize recipients).

[102] The Netflix Prize similarly required that the winner provide Netflix a royalty-free license. *See* Netflix, http://www.netflixprize.com/rules (last visited May 17, 2011).

such as tenure hopes might have clearly been sufficient for some inventions, and indeed the existence of such incentives highlights that patent protection often is not necessary to induce invention after a supply shock made invention much easier or a demand shock made invention much more useful.[103] The inducement standard is most congruent with an intuitive sense of "obviousness" where the nonpatent inducements are relatively weak in comparison to the patent inducement. If the nonpatent inducements are powerful, then those inducements may spur the creation of relatively difficult inventions. At least for the general run of cases, the PTO and courts should focus on and apply the inducement standard because it is supported by Supreme Court precedent, it provides a compelling economic justification for granting patents in some circumstances and denying them in others, and it gives specific intuitions for how to administer the obviousness doctrine, as we show in Part III.

II. REFINING THE INDUCEMENT STANDARD

Graham's inducement standard lends itself to economic analysis because it focuses on the incentives for creativity provided by a patent's exclusive rights. The question whether the invention would not have been "disclosed or devised but for the inducement of a patent" demands an inquiry into (1) the economic incentives or inducements that would exist without the patent and (2) the expected economic costs of generating the invention. Where there would be sufficient inducements to cover the costs of generating invention even absent patent protection, a patent would entail costs and no benefit. Yet although the inducement standard provides that basic economic intuition, the standard needs to be refined or clarified in at least three important respects. Not surprising, these three refinements concern points that are fundamental to patent policy: time, competition, and the meaning of "invention."

A. *Time*

Time is one of the most important features in the patent system. Patents are relatively short property rights, and parties often engage in intense competition known as patent racing to be the first in time to obtain a patent.[104] (Whether "first in time" is defined by reference to the date of invention or the date of application filing

[103] *See infra* Part II.B.

[104] *See generally* Jean Tirole, The Theory of Industrial Organization 400 (1988) (discussing potential costs and benefits of patent races); Christopher A. Cotropia, *The Folly of Early Filing in Patent Law*, 61 Hastings L.J. 65, 85–86 (2009) (assessing the efficiency of racing); Glenn C. Loury, *Market Structure and Innovation*, 93 Q.J. Econ. 395 (1979) (offering a model of the dynamics of patent races); Suzanne Scotchmer, *Incentives to Innovate*, in The New Palgrave Dictionary of Economics and the Law 273, 275 (Peter Newman ed., 1998) (summarizing competing conclusions of the literature).

matters not for these purposes.[105]) More generally, the patent system is frequently modeled as a system designed to produce not so much more innovation but earlier innovation.[106]

Yet despite the importance of time to the patent system, *Graham* articulates an atemporal inducement standard. Plainly, the standard has to be modified to take in account time, and the basic insights here are straightforward. If the prospect of a patent induces invention to occur twenty years or more earlier than it otherwise would have occurred, then the issuance of the patent is unambiguously desirable (assuming, of course, that the invention is socially valuable[107]). With the inducement of the patent, society has the technology at an earlier time (albeit under exclusive rights). After the expiration of the patent (which we will assume to last for twenty years), the technology enters the public domain at a time equal to or earlier than it otherwise would have if there had been no patent inducement. At the other extreme, a patent is almost certainly undesirable where it induces invention to be devised and disclosed only a day or two earlier than would otherwise have occurred without the patent inducement. In that case, society would have obtained the technology free of exclusive rights very soon even without the patent inducement. Society is then burdened with having the technology exist under exclusive rights for a long period of time, and society gains the technology at an insubstantially different time. Between those two extremes, there can be reasonable debate about the precise amount of temporal acceleration needed to justify a patent.

For our immediate purposes, we may leave that temporal period vaguely defined by requiring the inducement of a patent to accelerate invention by a substantial period of time, where substantiality is some period of years. Extreme patent skeptics might put that period close to twenty years. Patent enthusiasts could reasonably argue that, if the inducement of a patent advances the arrival of technology by only a few years, society is better off having the earlier arrival of the technology, even though the deadweight losses associated with the patent will continue for many more years. In principle, "substantial" should be defined as the amount of time where the social benefits of the invention's existing for that time period are equal to the social costs of patent protection for the patent term minus that period. As we soon see, a precise numeric definition of that period of time is less necessary than it may first seem.

An excellent case to illustrate this temporal refinement of the inducement standard is the brilliant – yet, in our view, ultimately wrong – opinion by Judge Posner

[105] *See generally* Toshiki Takenaka, *Rethinking the United States First-to-Invent Principle from a Comparative Law Perspective*, 39 Hous. L. Rev. 621 (2002) (critiquing the United States' approach and arguing for specific changes).

[106] *See, e.g.*, John F. Duffy, *Rethinking the Prospect Theory of Patents*, 71 U. Chi. L. Rev. 439, 444 (2004) (noting that one advantage of earlier invention is that inventions fall into the public domain sooner).

[107] The patent system generally does not consider the social desirability of an invention. *See* Juicy Whip, Inc v. Orange Bang, Inc, 185 F.3d 1364, 1367–68 (Fed. Cir. 1999).

in the panel opinion from *Roberts* v. *Sears, Roebuck & Co.*[108] Posner's panel opinion is the only reported court of appeals case that has ever attempted to apply *Graham*'s inducement standard. Posner recognized that the standard needed temporal adjustment. He reasoned, "The framers of the Constitution and the Patent Code would not have wanted patents to be granted where the invention would have been made anyway, *and about as soon*, without any hope of patent protection."[109] Where the invention would be made "about as soon" without a patent inducement, Posner understood that the patent "would confer no benefits that might offset the cost of monopoly."[110] He identified the obviousness doctrine as the correct doctrinal vehicle to deny patents in such circumstance, and for good measure, he cited *Graham* and Kitch's article on obviousness – the leading judicial and academic authorities to endorse the inducement standard.[111] So far, Posner's reasoning mirrors our own approach.

Then Posner turned to applying the inducement standard. The invention before the court was famous.[112] It was a "quick-release" socket wrench – a wrench that allowed the user to push a button to release the socket attached to the wrench.[113] Socket wrenches were very old in the art. Also very old were the ideas that the socket head could be attached to the wrench by a spring-loaded ball bearing and that the wrench could encompass some releasing mechanism.[114] Peter Roberts, the inventor, set out to fix what he saw as a problem with the existing designs: Releasing the socket from the wrench was "difficult . . . particularly when the sockets are small and the user's hands are greasy."[115] Roberts' novel quick-release mechanism provided a button, typically on the top of the wrench (see Figure 5.1), that would quickly and easily release the ball bearing "so that it longer holds the socket, which then can be easily withdrawn from the [wrench] or in fact can actually fan off . . . due to gravity."[116] The release button was positioned so that it could be easily pushed by the same hand used to hold the wrench.

Posner acknowledged that Roberts had made a "genuine" contribution in designing "a device in which [the preexisting] ideas worked smoothly to enable sockets

[108] 697 F.2d 796 (7th Cir. 1983), *opinion vacated as noted in* Roberts v. Sears, Roebuck & Co., 723 F.2d 1324, 1329 (7th Cir. 1983) (en banc).

[109] 697 F.2d at 797 (emphasis added).

[110] *Id.*

[111] *See* Kitch, *supra* note 12 and accompanying text.

[112] For mainstream media coverage of the David-vs.-Goliath case that grew out of the invention, see *Wrenching Sears*, TIME (Oct. 23, 1978), *available at* http://www.time.com/time/magazine/article/0,9171,946093,00.html; *Sears Loses Patent Suit; Clerk Wins $5 Million in Sears Case*, N.Y. TIMES, Apr. 3, 1982.

[113] U.S. Patent No. 3,208,218 (filed April 24, 1964; issued Sept. 28, 1965) (entitled "Quick Release for Socket Wrenches").

[114] *See* U.S. Patent No. 1,660,989 at pp. 1–2 (Feb. 28, 1928) (disclosing both the use of a ball bearing to secure the socket head and a mechanism, albeit an awkward one, for releasing the socket).

[115] U.S. Patent No. 3,208,218, *supra* note 113, at col. 1, ll. 15–16.

[116] *Id.*

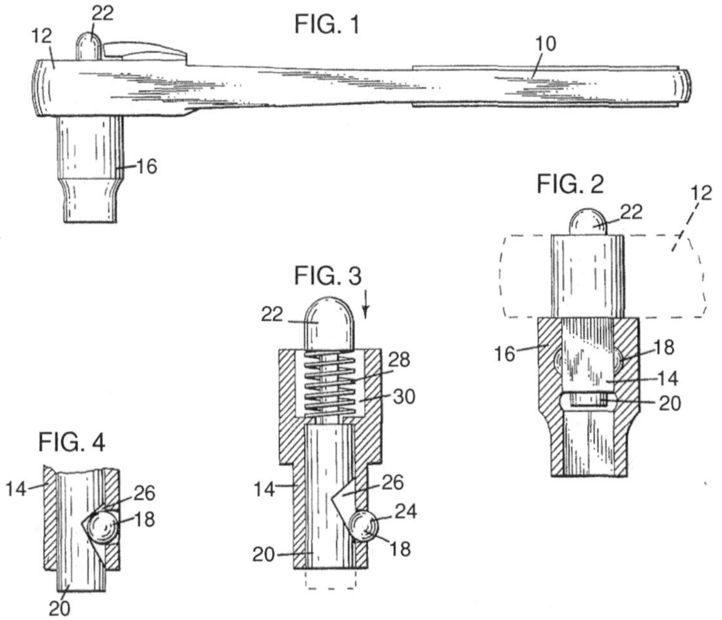

FIGURE 5.1. Roberts' quick-release socket wrench: The ball bearing (24) is used to lock the socket head in place, as was typical in preexisting socket wrenches. In Roberts' wrench, pushing the button (22) allows the ball bearing to move into the notch (26) and thereby to release the socket head.

to be changed easily with one hand." But that contribution "was entitled to patent protection only if it was the kind of contribution unlikely to be induced except by the promise of a monopoly, and we do not think it was that kind of invention, because we think it would have been made anyway, and soon."[117] Once again, Posner appropriately adjusts the inducement standard to account for time: The invention should be viewed as obvious only if it would have been made "soon" without the inducement of a patent.

But how did Judge Posner know that Roberts' invention would have been made "soon"? The invention was "simplicity itself" and "its essential elements were well known when it was invented."[118] Posner noted that "Gonzalez and Carpenter separately had patented socket wrenches that had the essential elements of the Roberts patent; true, the emphasis was on the locking rather than the release function, but these are reciprocals."[119] Thus, in Posner's view, all that needed to be done was for a person skilled in the art to recognize that a "reciprocal" of existing elements was

[117] 697 F.2d at 797.
[118] *Id.*
[119] *Id.* at 797–98.

needed, and this should happen quickly because "[e]veryone knew there was a market for a quick-release wrench; everyone knew the elements of such a wrench.... It was just a question of coming up with a workable embodiment of these ideas, a task for which no special training, expensive equipment, or prolonged testing and refining were necessary."[120]

Yet there is one glaring oddity about Posner's reasoning: Although he correctly modifies the inducement standard to account for time, he otherwise does not mention time at all in the opinion. All the prior-art patents are cited by the inventor's name only, without referencing either the patent issuance number or date.[121] When dates are added to the prior patents, we discover that the Carpenter patent – the patent that Posner heralds as having all the essential elements needed to make Roberts' invention – was issued in 1928, three and a half *decades* before the time of Roberts' invention.[122] In expressing confidence that, even without the inducement of a patent, the elements of the 1928 Carpenter patent could be modified "soon" to produce a quick-release wrench, Judge Posner offered nothing more than *ipse dixit* contradicted by history: No one in the art had been able to make the necessary changes for an extremely long time, and the one person who was able to do it – Roberts – seems to have been induced by a possibility of a patent.[123] Although other pieces of prior art cited in Posner's opinion were closer in time to Roberts' invention, the opinion did not maintain that any of those pieces of art contained additional elements or ideas that were not already in the 1928 Carpenter patent.[124]

The en banc Seventh Circuit held that Posner's panel opinion was wrong to rule Roberts' wrench invalid as a matter of law.[125] Overturning the panel's flawed reasoning was amply justified, but the en banc court also went out of its way to disavow Posner's modified inducement standard.[126] The en banc court's rejection

[120] *Id.* at 798.

[121] *See, e.g., id.* at 797–98 (referring to the "Roberts patent" and comparing it to "DePew," "Gonzalez," "Carpenter," and "Wilson").

[122] See U.S. Patent No. 1,660,989 (Feb. 28, 1928).

[123] In 1963, Roberts spent about six months designing his improved wrench and developing a prototype. *See Roberts*, 697 F.2d at 797. He submitted his prototype to Sears in May 1964, one month after the filing of his patent application. *Roberts*, 573 F.2d at 978. The sequence of events strongly suggests that Roberts spent time creating the invention in the hope of obtain a patent and then marketing the patent to Sears.

[124] In reverse chronological order, the other pieces of prior art considered by Posner were (1) the Gonzales patent, U.S. Pat. No. 3,172,675 (filed Feb 19, 1963; issued March 9, 1965), which like Carpenter provided a mechanism for holding and locking in sockets; (2) the De Pew patent, U.S. Pat. No. 3,069,191 (filed April 13, 1961; issued Dec. 18, 1962), which did not discuss wrenches at all but was instead a device for holding loads being lifted by "winch or other power means"; and (3) the Wendling patent, U.S. Pat. No. 2,987,334 (filed June 22, 1959; issued June 6, 1961), which was a tool holder with an "interlock mechanism which positively prevents accidental disengagement thereof." None of these pieces of prior art even attempted to address the problem of building a "quick-release" mechanism.

[125] The en banc court remanded the case for a new trial because the district court submitted the case to the jury in a procedurally flawed manner. *See* 723 F.2d at 1343.

[126] *Id.* at 1329 n.5.

of his analysis led Judge Posner to write a dissenting opinion that, in addition to repeating his earlier analysis, also chastised the majority for refusing to apply economic analysis to the problem. "[L]awyers and judges," Posner wrote, may seem to find "the language of economics repulsive. Yet the policies that have given shape to the patent statute are quintessentially economic, and the language of economics is therefore the natural language in which to articulate the test of obviousness."[127] Once again, we agree entirely with Posner's general approach, and we also agree that the en banc majority did not "succeed very well in articulating an alternative test."[128] But Judge Posner's poor application of the economic test, resulting in the invalidation of a patent on an invention that intuitively seems extraordinarily clever, may have alienated the en banc court and, in the process, given the inducement approach a bad name. In our view, the en banc court should have rejected only Posner's application of the inducement standard, not the inducement standard itself or an economically based test. Given the failure of the literature and case law to point out the relevance of the timing of prior art,[129] however, the en banc court's approach was at least understandable. It reflected a common, though mistaken, intuition that the inducement standard cannot be applied in a principled or consistent way.[130]

B. *Competition*

Patent rights are distributed through a competition to be first in time, and that competition has implications for the inducement standard. Competition is most likely to speed invention when both the costs of innovation and the value of patent rights are relatively stable. Where this is so, competition to obtain the patent should advance the time of innovation by long periods, provided that the patent confers significantly greater market protection than can be obtained otherwise. To demonstrate this point, we here construct a model of invention that relies on a few straightforward assumptions about invention and competition. Though simple, the model illustrates the circumstances under which the time when innovations will be created and disclosed will depend little on whether there is a patent system. Our model will support several conclusions: (1) Where the cost of innovation is falling rapidly, patents ordinarily should not issue, because inventors would likely have strong incentives to invent within a short period of time; (2) Where the cost of innovation is constant or falling slowly, patents are more likely to be justified because the patent incentive will generally lead to invention long before it would have occurred with nonpatent first-mover advantages; (3) Where nonpatent incentives to invent are much greater, patent inducement is less likely and thus patents are less likely to be justified; (4) Where

[127] *Id.* at 1347.
[128] *Id.*
[129] *See* John F. Duffy, *A Timing Approach to Patentability*, 12 LEWIS & CLARK L. REV. 343, 357–61 (2008) (identifying other cases that failed to take proper account of the timing of inventions).
[130] *See supra* notes 12–13 and accompanying text; *infra* Part III.

market demand unexpectedly increases greatly shortly before invention, patents are less likely to be justified; and (5) Where an invention will not be useful for some time, perhaps because supporting technologies are not yet sufficiently advanced, patents probably will not be justified because earlier innovation is not socially beneficial. The most difficult cases are those in which the patent incentive accelerates invention for a substantial period that is nonetheless substantially shorter than the patent term.

Four assumptions are necessary to create the model. First, the process of innovation has a cost, which may decrease with time. The assumption that innovation has *some* cost should not be difficult to defend. If innovations were costless, then the patent system would be difficult to justify because innovation would simply happen, like manna descending from the heavens.[131] The decreasing costs of invention also accord with basic notions of progress: Past advances in technology provide necessary predicates, insights, and tools that make subsequent advances easier.

Second, innovations have some positive value that may increase with time. This potential growth in the value of an innovation can be justified by the increasing size of markets and the gradual accumulation of wealth. Alternatively, an innovation could increase in value because complementary technologies or markets arise. For example, a method of speeding checkout procedures for online transactions might become considerably more valuable after cheaper bandwidth leads to an explosion in the number of internet users.

Third, part of an innovation's social value can be captured by the innovator through either (i) patents or (ii) nonpatent, non–trade-secret mechanisms, such as first-mover advantages, copyrights, or trademarks. (We exclude trade secrecy from the alternative mechanisms for capturing part of an invention's value because, as previously explained, *Graham*'s inducement standard looks to whether the innovation would be devised *and* disclosed without patent incentives.[132]) We also assume that a patent allows an innovator to capture a larger fraction of an innovation's value than would the nonpatent, non–trade-secret mechanisms alone. Obviously, if patents and nonpatent incentives are similar in size, innovation will not be retarded by denying patent protection.

Fourth and most importantly, we assume that competition for innovations – either patent racing or competition to be the first in the market – will allow innovation to occur when the portion of the innovation's value that can be privately appropriated just equals and begins to exceed the cost of developing the innovation.[133] This is a

[131] *See* Yoram Barzel, *Optimal Timing of Innovations*, 50 Rev. Econ. & Stat. 348 (1968) (noting that all economic models of the patent system assume that innovation is a positive function of the resources devoted to research).

[132] *See supra* Part I.B.3.

[133] A more elaborate assumption would recognize that success might occur only with some probability. In that case, an attempt at innovation will occur only when the expected costs are equal to the expected benefits, discounting for the possibility of failure. *See* Duffy, *supra* note 106, at 480–82 (offering a

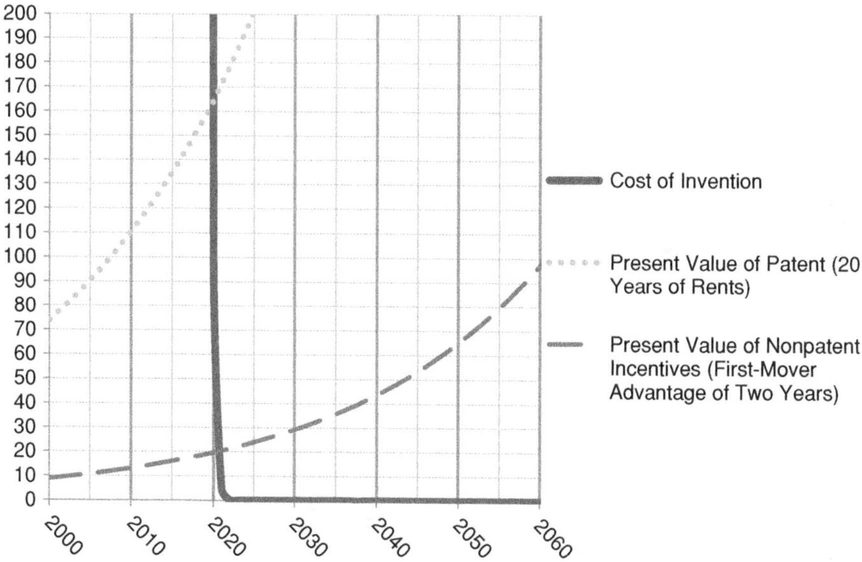

FIGURE 5.2. Innovation cost shock: The costs of innovation are falling at 95% per year. Patent protection would induce innovation a few months prior to the time of innovation without patent protection.

standard assumption in industrial organization models[134] and follows from the more general assumption that firms maximize wealth. Competition is therefore essential to determining the timing of innovation.

Figure 5.2 justifies our conclusion that patents ordinarily should not issue when the costs of the innovation are declining dramatically. The costs are assumed to decline at a rate of 95% per year near a particular point in time (represented arbitrarily as the year 2020). The solid, nearly vertical line near the year 2020 is the cost of the invention. The dotted and dashed lines gradually increasing from left to right are, respectively, the private value of a patent on the innovation (which is assumed to be twenty years of rents on the innovation) and the private value of the innovation without patent or trade secrecy protection (which is assumed to be equivalent to two years worth of rents on the innovation from first-mover advantages). The situation portrayed is a stark case where the issuance of a patent should not be viewed as

model in which attempts to invent have only probabilistic success); *see also* Mark T. L. Sargent, *Economics Upside-Down: Low-Price Guarantees as Mechanisms for Facilitating Tacit Collusion*, 141 U. PA. L. REV. 2055, 2076 n.102 (1993) (noting that "the assumption of zero economic profits for the industry does not imply that each firm is earning zero economic profits").

134 *See, e.g.*, Susan Rose-Ackerman, *Unfair Competition and Corporate Income Taxation*, 34 STAN. L. REV. 1017, 1025 n.28 (1982) ("In equilibrium in a competitive industry marginal firms earn zero 'economic' profits and positive accounting profits. Their accounting profits include both a return to the equity capital invested in the firm, reflecting the opportunity cost of that capital, and the value of the entrepreneurs' time.").

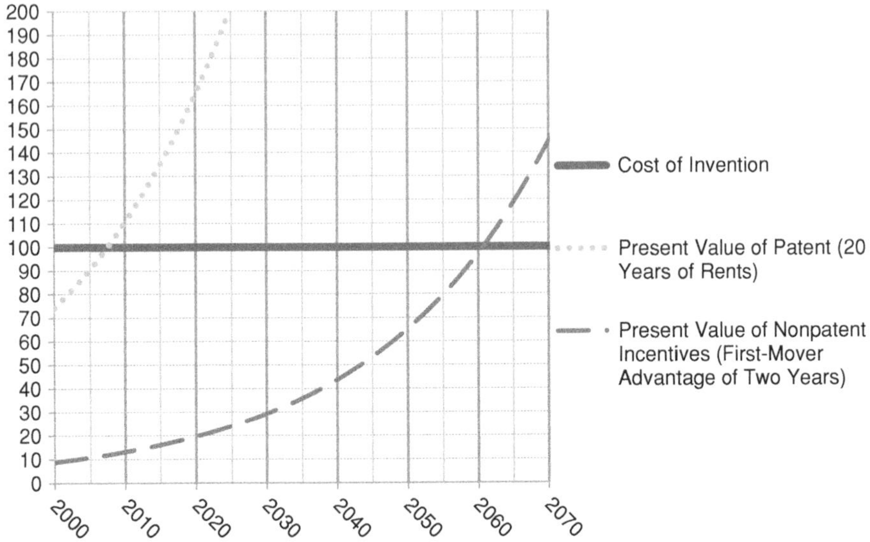

FIGURE 5.3. Constant cost of innovation: The cost of innovation is constant. Patent protection would induce innovation fifty years prior to the time of innovation without patent protection.

meeting *Graham*'s inducement standard. Without the inducement of a patent, the innovation would be devised and disclosed just a few months into the year 2020 (where the dashed line intersects the cost line). With the inducement of a patent, the innovation would be devised and disclosed just shortly before 2020 (where the dotted line intersects the cost line). If such an innovation were protected by a patent, society would bear the costs of twenty years of patent protection for almost no gain. Worse still from the standpoint of social welfare, the promise of patent protection may induce an intense race to be first so that many times the social resources are expended to obtain the innovation just a few months earlier. These conclusions are also relatively insensitive to changes in other assumptions.[135]

By contrast, Figures 5.3, 5.4, and 5.5 show cases where the cost of innovation is not falling dramatically in time, but all other parameters are the same as in Figure 5.2. These figures thus help explain why patents should generally issue in these cases. Patent protection can induce earlier innovation by a period of a half-century, where the cost of innovation is constant (in Figure 5.3); by just a little more than twenty years, where the cost of innovation is falling 6% per year (in Figure 5.4); or by about eight years, where the cost of innovation is falling by 20% per year (in Figure 5.5). The grant of the patent is unambiguously beneficial in Figures 5.3 and 5.4

[135] In Figure 5.2 the discount rate (interest rate) is assumed to be 6% and the market growth rate is assumed to be 4%. A patent would induce innovation only a few months earlier if the discount and growth rates fall anywhere within a range of 0–20%.

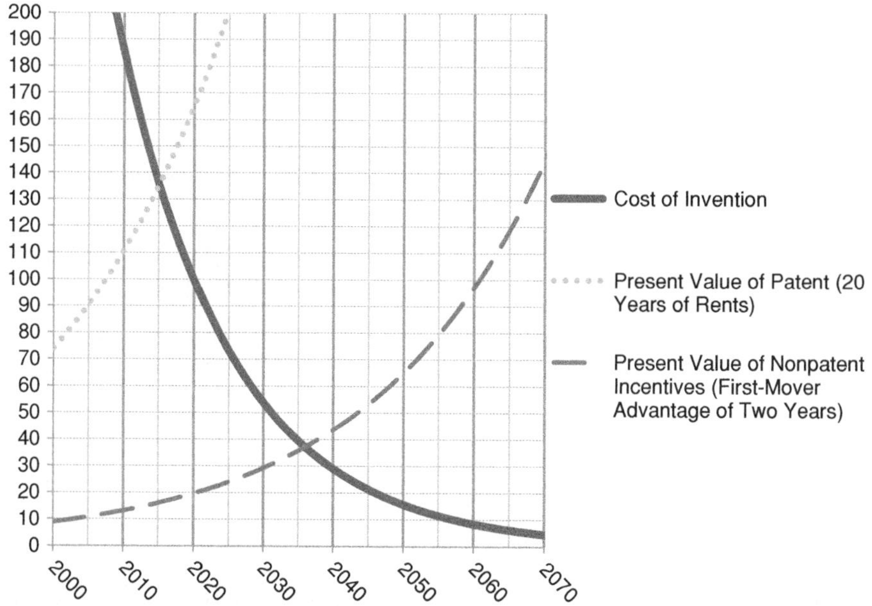

FIGURE 5.4. Slowly declining innovation costs: The cost of innovation is falling slowly (6% per year). Patent protection would induce innovation twenty years prior to the time of innovation without patent protection.

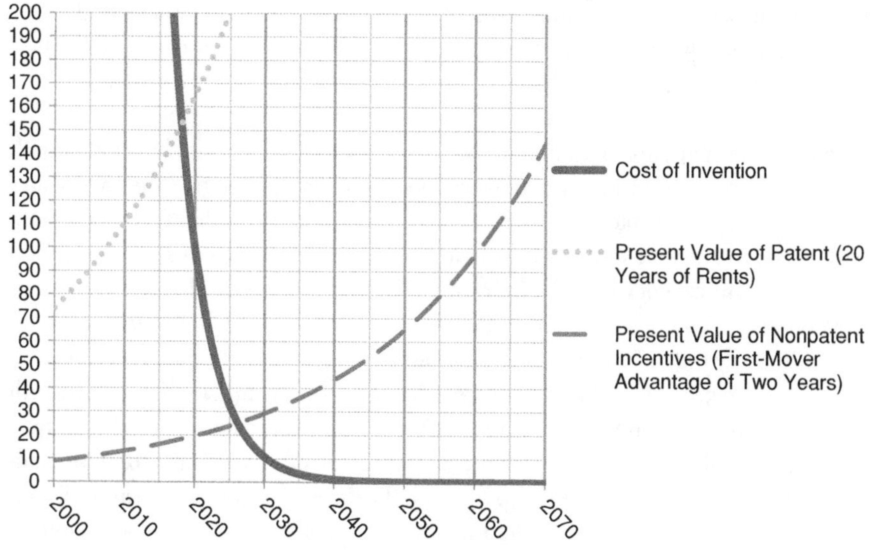

FIGURE 5.5. Moderately fast decline in innovation costs: The cost of innovation is falling moderately fast (20% per year). Patent protection would induce innovation several years prior to the time of innovation without patent protection.

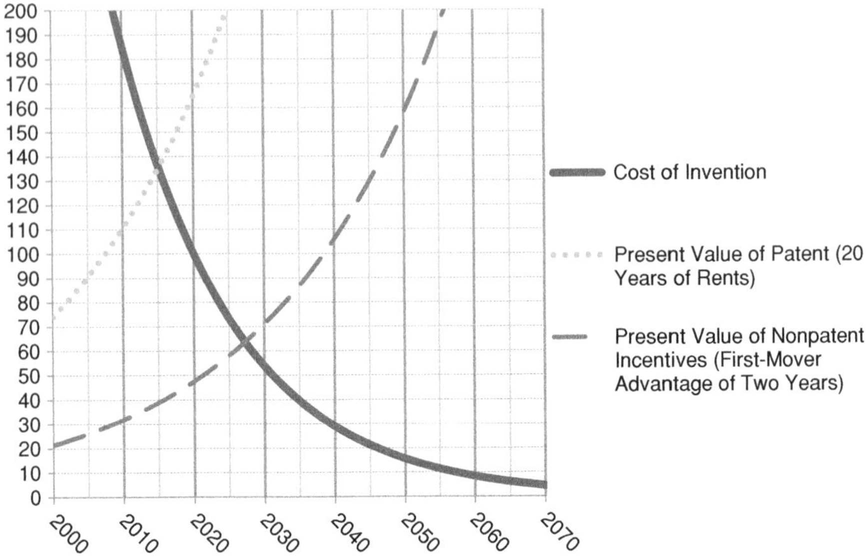

FIGURE 5.6. Slowly declining innovation costs with nonpatent incentives equal to five years of rents: The cost of innovation is falling slowly (6% per year), and nonpatent incentives equal five years worth of rents. Patent protection would induce innovation twelve years prior to the time of innovation without patent protection.

because the patent advances the arrival of the technology by a period longer than, or about equal to, the patent life. Thus, the grant of the patent induces the invention sooner and either enriches or at least does not diminish the public domain. The situation shown in Figure 5.5 is a more difficult case as a matter of public policy. The innovation arrives substantially earlier with patent protection, but the patent's exclusive rights extend into a period when society could have had the innovation without any patent protection. Even though there is some tradeoff in this region, eight years might well still seem to satisfy the refined inducement standard, which permits patents except where the innovation would be devised and disclosed soon in the absence of patent protection. Figures 5.2–5.5 illustrate that innovations should typically satisfy the inducement unless the cost of innovation is falling very quickly.

Figures 5.2–5.5 assumed that nonpatent incentives were equal to two years worth of rents on the innovation. Such nonpatent incentives could come from first-mover advantages, trademarks, copyright protection, or some other mechanism. If the nonpatent incentives are greater, the gap between the time of invention with and without patent incentives narrows, and patent protection is less successful in inducing innovation substantially earlier than would otherwise be. Conversely, if the nonpatent incentives are smaller (e.g., where technology is easily copied and any first-mover advantage is slight), then the temporal gap widens. The former point is illustrated in Figure 5.6, which assumes that nonpatent incentives are equal to five years worth

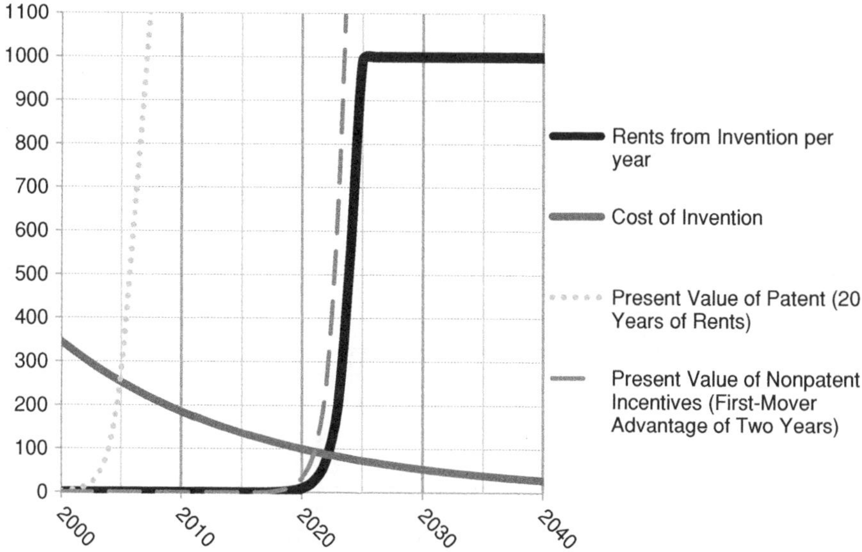

FIGURE 5.7. Market shock scenario: The market for innovation experiences exponential growth from 2020–25, while the cost of innovation is falling slowly (6% per year). Patent rights induce innovation long before the innovation is useful in the market.

of rents on the innovation and otherwise reflects the same assumptions as Figure 5.4. Patents now induce innovation approximately twelve years instead of twenty years earlier. This not only highlights the importance of courts' considering nonpatent incentives in implementing the inducement standard[136] but also shows that patents can substantially accelerate invention even where nonpatent incentives at early invention are considerable.

Another circumstance to be investigated is where the market for an innovation expands dramatically, as shown in Figure 5.7. The amount of rents associated with the innovation is the heavy line rising dramatically after 2020; the other parameters are assumed to be changing at moderate levels, with the cost of invention declining at 6% and the discount rate holding at 6% through the period. At first glance, this scenario appears to satisfy the inducement standard, or at least the inducement standard as modified to take into account time, because the patent incentive causes the innovation to be devised and disclosed by patenting more than a decade earlier than would be otherwise. Yet looks are deceiving here. Although the innovation is *patented* at an early time, the use of the innovation – the actual practical benefit of the innovation – does not occur until much later. In this numeric example, although patenting occurs approximately at 2005, the innovation is not capable of any significant use until 2021–22 (perhaps because some crucial piece of complementary

[136] *See supra* Part I.B.4.

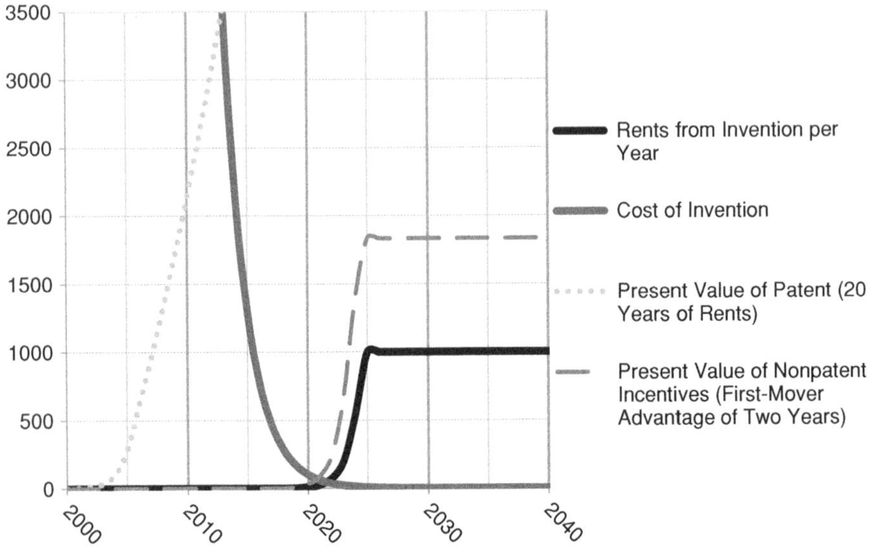

FIGURE 5.8. Scenario involving a market shock and rapidly falling innovation costs: The market for innovation experiences exponential growth from 2020–25, while the cost of innovation is falling rapidly (40% per year). Patent rights induce innovation long before the innovation is useful in the market, and the patent remains in force many years after the innovation would have been created and disclosed without the patent inducement.

technology is not yet available). As the innovation becomes capable of use – as the market for the innovation grows – nonpatent incentives would induce creation and disclosure. In the example, this occurs in 2021.

The scenario depicted in Figure 5.7 may, moreover, be overly optimistic in favor of patents: Although allowing a patent will have little social benefit (because the patent merely induces innovation at a time when it is not yet useful), granting the patent might seem to have little social cost (because the patent will expire relatively soon after the time when the innovation begins to be used in the market). A more realistic account, however, would recognize that someone patenting inventions years before they may be useful faces great uncertainty about which patents ultimately will be useful.[137] Many early patents will cover inventions that turn out to be worth little or nothing because of market or technological developments in the interim. Thus, the cost of developing a patent on an invention that will be useful years in the future should be adjusted to take into account the costs of patenting other inventions that turn out to be useless. These costs will be greater the further in advance of possible commercialization that patenting occurs. Figure 5.8 models this relationship by

[137] *See generally* Christopher A. Cotropia, *Describing Patents as Real Options*, 34 J. Corp. L. 1127 (2009) (exploring the implications of recognizing the option value of patents).

assuming that the cost of innovation declines by 40% per year, as awareness of what inventions will be useful increases.

With these assumptions, patent protection will induce the innovation at a time closer to when the need arises, though still substantially before the innovation would be created absent patent protection. In the example, patenting will induce the innovation in 2012, and then the patent will last until 2032. The patent will thus extend several years after the technology has matured, the innovation is widely used, and the rents associated with the patent are high. The social benefit of the earlier innovation is minimal, and the competition to obtain the patent succeeds only in pushing back the time of innovation to a point when producing the invention is unnecessarily expensive because of the uncertainty about whether it will be useful.

In sum, the competition to innovate should mean that, if the rewards associated with twenty years of patent exclusivity are much greater than nonpatent rewards, then patents will generally be successful in inducing innovation at a much earlier time. That general conclusion is subject to one important exception and one important caveat. The exception occurs where the costs of inventing are falling rapidly. In that circumstance, patent protection may not advance the time of innovation much. This exception produces the important insight that was missing from Judge Posner's analysis in *Roberts*. Patents are most likely to fail the inducement standard where the innovation has *recently become obvious* (i.e., where the costs of innovating have recently and dramatically declined). Perhaps Judge Posner's intuition was that mechanical patents are generally obvious, but in fact the relative lack of recent advances in mechanical design tends to point to nonobviousness.

The final caveat is that even when the patent does succeed in inducing much earlier innovation, the early innovation may be socially worthless if the innovation will not be marketed for some time. This caveat leads us to our third refinement of *Graham*'s inducement standard – that the inducement standard must focus not merely on whether the patent induces earlier creation of new information but also on whether the patent can be expected to induce earlier innovation in practical terms. We now turn to that point.

C. *Invention*

The *Graham* standard seeks to identify "those inventions" that are patent induced. But what is meant by "invention"? The Supreme Court has sometimes stated that "[t]he disclosure required by the Patent Act is 'the quid pro quo for the right to exclude.'"[138] That formulation might suggest that the mere paper disclosure in a patent application should be viewed as an "invention" for purposes of applying the inducement standard: If the promise of a patent yields a filed patent application years

[138] J.E.M. Ag Supply, Inc. v. Pioneer Hi-Bred International, Inc., 534 U.S. 124, 142 (2001) (quoting Kewanee Oil Co. v. Bicron Corp., 416 U.S. 470, 484 (1974)).

before the invention would have been created without any patent inducement, then perhaps the inducement standard should be viewed as satisfied.

Yet although some Supreme Court pronouncements focus on *disclosure* of information as the public good generated by the patent system, other statements from the Court emphasize the *practical benefits* obtained by the public. Thus, for example, the Court in *Brenner* v. *Manson* maintained that the "basic quid pro quo contemplated by the Constitution and the Congress for granting a patent monopoly is the *benefit derived by the public* from an invention with substantial utility."[139] *Brenner* v. *Manson* is widely understood as holding that a substantial utility is a necessary element of "invention" under the Patent Act. Under that formulation, the inducement standard should look to whether the possibility of a patent has induced not mere disclosure, but useful public benefits. Such public benefits arise only if the invention leads not merely to earlier disclosure but also to earlier practical application. Acceleration of the disclosure of an invention ordinarily serves no social goal if the mere paper disclosure does not accelerate the actual arrival of an invention in the marketplace. The patent system should thus distinguish purely speculative patent applications from applications that are prophetic in the sense that they herald the arrival of important new technologies, but do so by meaningfully accelerating the arrival of those technologies.

1. Speculative Patents

This theoretical point is best illustrated by example. Consider U.S. Patent 7,346,850, a "System and method for iconic software environment management."[140] This patented software innovation generates a "graphical thumbnail" image of what a document would look like if it were to be opened in a particular program.[141] The innovation is useful because it gives users a quick "preview" of the document's appearance without the bother of launching the program. The innovation does, however, demand additional computing resources – such as memory and CPU cycles – to provide the preview, and the preview will not be helpful unless it is done quickly. In 1998, when the patent application was first filed, this innovation may have been impractical given the speed and memory capacity of most computers of the time. Later, as computers improved, the feature became more practical, and the feature unsurprisingly has since been introduced.[142]

Let us assume that, but for the inducement of a patent, this preview innovation would not have been devised and disclosed until 2003 or so – a half-decade after the 1998 filing date of the application, which is the patentee's nominal "invention" date.

139 *See, e.g.*, Brenner v. Manson, 383 U.S. 519 (1966) (emphasis added).

140 U.S. Patent No. 7,346,850 (issued Mar. 18, 2008; originally filed June 12, 1998).

141 *Id.* (abstract).

142 *See, e.g.*, Microsoft, *The Taskbar (Overview)*, http://windows.microsoft.com/en-us/windows-vista/The-taskbar-overview (last visited June 9, 2010) (describing the preview feature in Microsoft Windows 7).

Should the innovation be considered nonobvious? Not necessarily. If the practical implementation of the innovation has been advanced little by the inducement of the patent, then the social tradeoff is similar to what we graphically represented in Figures 5.5 and 5.6 in Part II.B. The disclosure of the invention occurs very early in time, but the actual arrival of the invention in practical terms changes little. Such patents might be called *speculative patents*, which disclose not so much nonobvious information helpful in realizing an invention but rather mere prognostications about future needs and capabilities.

A more difficult case involves the controversial patent at issue in the Blackberry litigation. The "electronic mail system with RF communications to mobile processors" claimed in one patent[143] may or may not have been easy to imagine in 1994, but any difficulty was probably due at least in part to the fact that the hardware infrastructure existing at the time did not yet make such a system plausible. What makes the case more difficult is that the patent arguably discloses genuine, if small, technological contributions.[144] Certainly, the inducement standard ought not discriminate against a patent merely because the inventor is so remarkable as to produce an invention years ahead of when it would otherwise be produced, provided that – and this is the crucial point – the earlier production of the information provides a substantial benefit to society through accelerating the arrival of the invention in practical terms.[145] Yet if the technological contributions are sufficiently small in comparison to the total effort needed to generate a commercial product, then granting a patent may not accelerate the arrival of the invention and might even delay it.

An alternative solution to the problem of speculative patents is for the law to impose a much more robust demonstration of practical utility as a prerequisite for obtaining a patent. For example, Michael Risch argues in a recent article that patents should not be granted unless the applicant demonstrates that, at the time of patent application filing, "a) there is a market for the invention, and that b) the invention can be manufactured at a cost sufficient to fulfill market demand."[146] Risch makes clear that, under his proposal, many ideas would remain unpatentable until they were commercially realized. Although such a heightened utility requirement has its attractions, it also has significant drawbacks. In particular, the heightened utility requirement would likely bar patents on pioneering research that has no immediate commercial application but that will substantially accelerate the time of ultimate commercialization. Current utility doctrine allows for patents on such inventions,

[143] U.S. Patent No. 5,438,611 (filed May 23, 1994).

[144] One contribution in the patent is that storage in the RF receiver memory permits the reception of the information without the RF receiver being connected to the destination processor, thus eliminating the requirement that the destination processor be turned on and carried with the user of the destination processor. *Id.* at col. 18 l. 42–46.

[145] Such an inventor already pays a price in a reduced patent term. *See* Duffy, *supra* note 106, at 444.

[146] Michael Risch, *Reinventing Usefulness*, 2010 B.Y.U. L.J. 1195, 1240–1241 (2011).

provided that they can produce some "credible," "specific," and "substantial" – but not necessarily commercial – utility.[147] The nonobviousness requirement then provides the more flexible means by which patents may be denied to paper inventions that seem to embrace more speculation than technical achievement.

In sum, because society should gain some benefit if it is to tolerate the costs associated with granting a patent, the inducement standard focuses on the practical or commercialized invention, not merely a paper description of the invention. Three caveats are critical. First, the inducement standard does not insist that the *patentee* commercialize the invention or even that the patentee find someone who will commercialize the invention. Some commentators have proposed "innovation patents,"[148] which would insist that one commercialize an invention before receiving a patent on it, and some countries employ "working requirements"[149] under which patentees must engage at least in some minimal commercialization activity. These, however, can have perverse consequences, because patentees may inefficiently engage in commercialization simply to meet the legal requirement. In addition, it may be difficult to determine what constitutes sufficient activity.[150] Under the economic approach, the patentee is rewarded for the technological accomplishment and is not required to commercialize it. The patentee might well commercialize the patent and use this as *evidence* of acceleration, but commercialization is not required, and such evidence in any event is not dispositive, because the patentee might have commercialized the invention even without a patent.[151] Meanwhile, commercialization by others who did not have the patent may be evidence *against* acceleration, because that suggests that commercialization might have occurred even without the patentee's development; however, such evidence could count in the opposite direction where the commercializers appear to have copied the invention or lost a patent race.

Second, the courts need not even be confident that the invention in fact will be commercialized. All that matters is that, if this turns out to be an invention to be commercialized within the lifetime of the patent, the invention will likely have substantially accelerated commercialization. If commercialization never occurs, then the patent will be worthless and is not worth worrying about.[152] What the inducement

[147] *In re* Cortright, 165 F.3d 1353, 1356 (Fed. Cir. 1999), *In re* Fisher, 421 F.3d at 1369–74.

[148] *See* William Kingston, *Innovation Patents and Warrants, in* PATENTS IN PERSPECTIVE 68, 70 (Jeremy Phillips ed., 1985). William Kingston, *The "Thesis" Chapters, in* DIRECT PROTECTION OF INNOVATION 1–87 (William Kingston ed., 1987). For a discussion, see Ted Sichelman, *Commercializing Patents,* 62 STAN. L. REV. 341, 398–400 (2010).

[149] For a history, see Janice M. Mueller, *The Tiger Awakens: The Tumultuous Transformation of India's Patent System and the Rise of Indian Pharmaceutical Innovation,* 68 U. PITT. L. REV. 491, 593–97 (2007). The United States has long eschewed working requirements. *See* Cont'l Paper Bag Co. v. E. Paper Bag Co., 210 U.S. 405, 429 (1908).

[150] *See* Sichelman, *supra* note 148, at 397 (assessing incentives provided by working requirements).

[151] *See infra* Part III.B.2.b.

[152] There may still be some social costs to such patents, although the high cost of applying for a patent means that there would be little incentive to apply for patents on inventions almost certain not to be

standard seeks to block is the granting of a patent when a technological contribution represents only a tiny portion of the total effort that would be required for commercialization and the patent incentive did not accelerate such commercialization. The inducement standard thus considers the expected cost of generating the technology in comparison to the total cost of the project.

Third, the inducement standard should not be seen as inherently blocking granting of patents where a single commercialized product reflects many patents. The combination of many patents into a single product creates serious challenges for patent law and theory, and some commentators have worried that "patent thickets" may create an "anticommons" that will retard rather than advance innovation.[153] Perhaps there are some areas of technology in which products encompass many patents, and one can conclude that commercialization generally would occur at more or less the same pace even absent patent inducement. If so, the inducement theory would suggest that many such patents are invalid. But there may be other areas where many technologies are combined and where in fact the patent incentive is critical to development of all these technologies collectively. The inducement standard should apply to the group of patents as a whole, and patents should be granted. Holdouts and other familiar problems of patent law may ensue,[154] but our goal in this chapter is not to overcome them.

What is particularly worrisome from our perspective is the case in which a patent contributes nothing other than prophecy or perhaps something that is relatively trivial – the time and cost involved in developing it would not be expected to delay commercialization – but nonetheless is critical. This is especially likely when a patent reads like an idea – maybe it would be great to allow a user to view a miniature version of a document by mousing over an icon or to allow e-mail by wireless phone – and simply describes some of the steps that any competent practitioner would quickly realize one would need to do to make the project work. The patent literature sometimes notes that the possibility that one might invent around a patent decreases a patentee's ability to hold out for large undeserved sums,[155] but speculative patents can cover such fundamental (if simple) aspects of a technology that they will be

commercialized within the patent term. *See* Jonathan S. Masur, *Process as Purpose: Costly Screens, Value Asymmetries, and Examination at the Patent Office*, 2 J. LEGAL ANALYSIS (2010) (manuscript at 4) (noting that patents of "*low* private value and *low* (or negative) social value [may] increase the search costs and risk imposed on commercial firms").

[153] *See* Michael A. Heller & Rebecca S. Eisenberg, *Can Patents Deter Innovation? The Anticommons in Biomedical Research*, 280 SCI. 698 (1998) (discussing the anticommons problem in the patent context). *But see* Richard Epstein & Bruce N. Kuhlik, *Navigating the Anticommons for Pharmaceutical Patents: Steady the Course on Hatch-Waxman*, Univ. of Chi. Law Sch. John M. Olin Law & Econ. Working Paper No. 209 (2d Ser.) (2004) (available at http://ssrn.com/abstract_id=536322) (arguing that patent thickets are not a serious problem).

[154] Possible remedies include antitrust law, *see* Thomas F. Cotter, *Patent Holdup, Patent Remedies, and Antitrust Responses*, 34 J. CORP. L. 1151 (2009), and private ordering, *see* F. Scott Kieff, *Engineering a Deal: Toward a Private Ordering Solution to the Anticommons Problem*, 48 B.C. L. REV. 111 (2007).

[155] *But see* Ian Ayres, *Tradable Patent Rights*, 60 STAN. L. REV. 863, 874–75 (2007) (noting that inventing around often may be impractical).

difficult to invent around. These patents are worrisome because they may in fact retard commercialization, because the patentee may credibly insist on a substantial portion of the rents from a new technology. Moreover, they may be a waste from a transactions costs perspective. The possibility of such valuable patents encourages prospective patentees to imagine technological capabilities that might exist in the future and describe how they might be used, whether or not such prophecy has beneficial economic consequences.

2. Kitch's Prospect Theory

We are, of course, not the first patent theorists to focus on the significance of commercialization to the patent standard. Most famously, Edmund Kitch in 1977 advanced a prospect theory of the patent system, arguing that the granting of a patent may be useful because the grant of the patent itself may promote commercialization.[156] A patent on a nascent technology, Kitch argues, can "increase[] the efficiency with which investment in innovation can be managed,"[157] can give the patentee "an incentive to make investments to maximize the value of the patent without fear that the fruits of the investment will produce unpatentable information appropriable by competitors,"[158] and can facilitate contracting.[159] More recently, F. Scott Kieff has amplified Kitch's analysis by focusing on how granting a patent on new technology may tend to promote commercialization of that technology.[160] For both Kitch and Kieff, then, patents can accelerate commercialization.

It might seem that an inference based on the importance of commercialization is that patenting should wait until *after* commercialization, so that there are incentives to take this step. Yet in fact, the literature on the prospect theory suggests the opposite, for two distinct reasons. First, an inventor who holds a patent may be more likely to commercialize than an inventor who hopes to have a chance of receiving a patent after commercialization.[161] Second, when an inventor holds a patent before commercialization, there is likely to be less duplication in commercialization efforts.[162] The ex post effects of this may be equivocal; sometimes duplication in commercialization is what we call "competition."[163] But, the ex ante effect of early patenting is that the invention is likely to be made earlier, when inventors

[156] Edmund W. Kitch, *The Nature and Function of the Patent System*, 20 J.L. & ECON. 265 (1977).

[157] *Id.* at 276.

[158] *Id.*

[159] *Id.* at 277–78.

[160] F. Scott Kieff, *Property Rights and Property Rules for Commercializing Inventions*, 85 MINN. L. REV. 697 (2001).

[161] *Id.* at 710.

[162] *See* Duffy, *supra* note 106, at 444 (discussing "the prospect features of the patent system – particularly the preference for the grant of patent rights early, before most of the resources have been committed to developing the technology and before much wasteful duplication can occur").

[163] *See* Robert P. Merges & Richard R. Nelson, *On the Complex Economics of Patent Scope*, 90 COLUM. L. REV. 839, 872 (1990).

anticipate that if patents are awarded relatively early, the amount that they might lose in a patent race is limited.[164] If the race is not simply to create an invention, but to create and then commercialize the invention, the race will not be as attractive to enter, because the expected costs of entry are higher. This argument suggests that the prospect approach of granting patents on nascent technologies may be useful not solely for its ex post effects but also for its ex ante effects.

The ex ante effect of accelerating invention, however, is not a social benefit if it does not also translate into acceleration of commercialization. A promise of a prospect patent surely leads to speculative patents being issued earlier than they otherwise would, but to no useful end. Our analysis thus suggests a distinction between a speculative patent and a prophetic prospect patent that reflects a significant technological advance. Granting a patent prospect on an invention may be appropriate when commercialization efforts will follow thereafter, because then the promise of the patent accelerates invention and the resulting commercialization. Even if commercialization will not follow immediately, a prospect patent will be appropriate if, by some time after commercialization would be expected to occur, the invention would not have been created in the absence of the patent system. The inducement standard thus separates cases in which the ex ante prospect theory rationale supports patenting from those in which it does not.

The more traditional ex post rationale for prospect theory, however, could be advanced against our approach and in favor of speculative patents. On this theory, even if a speculative patent reflects no or minimal technological advance, granting of a property right may accelerate commercialization. We should, the theory goes, grant speculative patents, because it is useful to grant property rights to *someone*, as a way of spurring additional discovery. The most straightforward approach is then to grant the property rights over a technological area to the first person who recognizes the future existence of that area. Moreover, a benefit of granting rights in this way is that potential patentees will compete to recognize future technological areas first. As a result, the patent will be awarded to the party who agrees to take the patent right for the shortest possible patent term.[165]

We acknowledge potential benefits to such an approach, but believe that its costs exceed the benefits.[166] Once such a patent exists, the patent holder will have greater incentive to work on solving relevant technological and market problems, because the initial patent increases the share of producer surplus that the patent holder can

[164] Duffy, *supra* note 106, at 469–75.

[165] There is a disadvantage to this as well, however, even granting the proposition that patents will accelerate commercialization ex post. The usable portion of the patent term may end up being so small that there is little incentive to commercialize. *See* Michael Abramowicz, *The Danger of Underdeveloped Patent Prospects*, 92 CORNELL L. REV. 1065 (2007) (providing an overview of this problem).

[166] *See* Michael Abramowicz, *The Uneasy Case for Patent Races over Auctions*, 60 STAN. L. REV. 803 (2007).

expect to receive.[167] But the incentive of other parties to work on the technological problems may be reduced, if they believe that they will have to pay a tax to the first patent holder. This latter consideration may help explain the findings of those who have cast empirical doubt on the proposition that consolidating property rights tends to accelerate invention.[168] Although we cannot purport to conclusively resolve the problem, we suspect that granting property rights on a technological area to someone who has done nothing to accelerate development will likely reduce rather than increase overall investment in the technology.[169]

This suggests that one should not grant a patent unless the inventor has solved a relatively significant percentage of the technological problems that need to be solved before commercialization can occur or unless others have already done so and the inventor has contributed one of the missing pieces. In these cases, the invention itself will generally (though not always) accelerate commercialization, and the ex post effects of granting a patent seem likely to accelerate invention as well. Once an inventor has worked out a large portion of a puzzle and possesses at least a blocking right against anyone else who might complete another piece of the puzzle,[170] this inventor will have strong incentives (considerably stronger than anyone else's) to complete the puzzle and commercialize it. By contrast, a speculative patent holder's best strategy may be to sit around, hope that others will do the hard work of invention and commercialization, and then sue for infringement. This is, of course, the story of a "patent troll," a nonpracticing entity that has contributed little technology but hopes to use patenting as a source of profit.[171] The inducement standard could thwart this strategy, while still preserving the ability of those who have made genuine technological contributions to be nonpracticing entities who license their technology to others.

3. Merges' Model of Nonobviousness

Perhaps the most significant obstacle in the existing legal literature to our interpretation of the *Graham* inducement standard lies in a classic article on the economics of the nonobviousness standard, written by Robert Merges.[172] The article is an obstacle because Merges explicitly addresses the question that the literature has otherwise largely ignored – whether the degree to which an invention increases the probability

[167] Duffy, *supra* note 106, at 483–91.

[168] *See* Merges & Nelson, *supra* note 163, at 896.

[169] *See* Abramowicz, *supra* note 166, at 845–47 (explaining how an auction design might stimulate additional research spending).

[170] For discussions of blocking patents, see Ariad Pharm., Inc. v. Eli Lilly & Co., 598 F.3d 1336, 1364–66 (Fed. Cir. 2010); and Robert Merges, *Intellectual Property Rights and Bargaining Breakdown: The Case of Blocking Patents*, 62 Tenn. L. Rev. 75 (1994).

[171] *See supra* note 23 and accompanying text.

[172] *See* Robert P. Merges, *Uncertainty and the Standard of Patentability*, 7 High Tech. L.J. 1 (1992).

of *commercial* success is relevant to the obviousness test – and because Merges concludes that it is not relevant. We nonetheless argue that Merges' broad argument in fact supports our position and then refute the specific argument that Merges makes against considering commercial success in the obviousness inquiry.

Merges' model shows that patent protection may augment the incentives of an individual inventor to undertake technological experiments and then to bring these experiments to market. For Merges, the nonobviousness requirement rewards inventions that reduce uncertainty about the probability of success.[173] If initially a research path seems to have only a small probability of producing a successful technical result, but after some set of costly experiments, a successful result is achieved, then the invention resulting from the research path is likely to count as nonobvious, because the probability of success is now considerably higher. Merges recognizes that firms often will innovate without patent protection – for example because of first-mover advantages – but patent protection can increase incentives to take on low-probability or high-cost projects.

Merges' approach is not a restatement of the inducement standard of patentability. Indeed, although he identifies the *Graham* approach as "[t]he conventional ideal standard of patentability,"[174] he identifies an objection that would be powerful without our view of *Graham* as promoting inventions that accelerate technology – arguing that "very few patents would be granted today under this standard, since so few industries consider patents essential."[175] Nonetheless, Merges' approach is conceptually largely consistent with the *Graham* approach under our interpretation. His preferred standard "rewards one who successfully invents when the uncertainty facing her prior to the invention makes it more likely than not that the invention won't succeed,"[176] and he would measure uncertainty "from the perspective of the average skilled inventor in the field."[177] When a research path appears unlikely to produce a successful invention, incentives to undertake that research path may be inefficiently low in the absence of patents. If the probability is sufficiently low, first-mover advantages may be inadequate and inventors will not undertake such research. Thus, the inventions that are induced by patent law will generally be those that ex ante appear to be low probability. Merges also recognizes that cost may be important.[178] Although he would not make cost central to the patentability

[173] *Id.* at 29–32.

[174] *Id.* at 19.

[175] *Id.* Even in some industries that do not consider patents essential, patents may accelerate invention and commercialization.

[176] *Id.*at 19. Merges' model, however, does not establish the 50% success probability level as always the relevant threshold for judging nonobviousness.

[177] *Id.* at 20.

[178] Merges cites the case of "a fairly certain experiment, leading to a product likely to succeed in the market, but involving very high experimentation costs and/or costs of commercial failure." *Id.* at 32.

standard, he argues that the patentability threshold should be lower "for very high-cost research."[179] Our interpretation of the *Graham* test recognizes a central role for both uncertainty and cost, because in the absence of patent protection, either a low probability of success or high costs of experimentation would generally significantly delay commercialization.

Although we believe that the inducement standard, properly conceived, provides a better integrated explanation of and justification for the nonobviousness standard than separate focuses on probability and cost, Merges' model provides support for our approach. We agree that, when an experiment has a high probability of succeeding and is relatively inexpensive, patent law is not needed to induce the resulting invention. Our chief improvement on Merges' model is the focus on whether invention accelerates the date of acceleration, which makes the static model dynamic and embraces concerns about both probability and cost. Merges' model nonetheless provides indirect support for this variation on the inducement standard. One justification for patentability, Merges notes, is that patents may increase the incentive to engage not only in technological experimentation but also in development and commercialization of the results of experiments. It should be a small step from this recognition to our argument that the nonobviousness standard should be designed to exclude from patentability inventions that would not significantly accelerate commercialization.

"The model," Merges writes, "shows that patents may have a greater impact on incentives to *develop* than incentives to invent. Once a promising result is in hand, the heightened payoff from a patent more directly affects the expected value of developing the product."[180] Merges' model thus shows that factoring commercial uncertainty into the obviousness inquiry improves efficiency, moving the patent system closer to a hypothetically ideal system from the perspective of the *Graham* inducement standard. The patent system should be willing to count as nonobvious an invention when the invention and its development sufficiently lower uncertainty about the ultimate success of a research path, including consideration of commercial uncertainty. For Merges, in sum, "the key factor is the level of uncertainty facing the inventor just prior to the crucial experiment leading up to the patent."[181]

Perhaps surprisingly, then, Merges does not conclude that the probability of commercial success should affect the definition of nonobviousness. Merges asks, "Why focus on uncertainty at the initial experimental stage, when uncertainty at the second, or commercialization stage, can also drive expected returns below the break-even point, hence discouraging perhaps useful research?" Merges offers "two primary reasons,"[182] developed in just two brief paragraphs, that reduction in commercial uncertainty should not be relevant to a nonobviousness assessment.

179 *Id.* at 4; *see also id.* at 43–55.

180 *Id.* at 33.

181 *Id.*

182 *Id.* at 34.

The first argument is that there is "intrinsic social value of producing information in the face of highly uncertain technical challenges."[183] In contrast, he claims that "information about what the market desires would seem to produce relatively few positive externalities."[184] This is irrelevant to the issue of whether nonobviousness should be judged by the extent to which an invention reduces commercial uncertainty. When technological experimentation reduces uncertainty, it will also have the effect of reducing commercial uncertainty. Thus, analysis of the degree to which an invention reduces commercial uncertainty is a measure of the technological achievement. Even if, contrary to our later argument, there is no social value in encouraging information about the marketplace, it may still be useful to measure technical achievement in commercial terms. Just as cost-benefit analysis seeks to use dollars as a common metric for aggregating a wide range of considerations, so too is reduction of commercial uncertainty a useful measure of technological achievement.

Nominally in supporting his first argument, but in fact making an entirely separate argument, Merges states that "assess[ing] commercial or market uncertainty . . . would seem to be even more difficult than assessing technical uncertainty, as in the current patent system."[185] As is revisited later, assessing commercial uncertainty (and in particular the degree to which an innovation has reduced such uncertainty) presents a timing challenge, because patents are generally awarded before commercialization. If patent examiners can assess in hindsight whether scientists would have believed that a particular approach would be successful, however, why should they not be able to assess in hindsight whether businesspeople would have thought that an approach would be successful? And just as a firm might be able to produce internal evidence that its scientists doubted that a particular approach would work (for example, because they initially tried some other approach), so too might a firm be able to produce evidence that potential funding sources were skeptical that the business could succeed. Indeed, there is a good reason that commercial success is sometimes called objective evidence of nonobviousness; sometimes (though not all the time) it may be assessed more objectively than purely technological information by a court.[186]

Finally, Merges argues that a promising experiment produces valuable information "*even if it never leads to a viable commercial product*."[187] One interpretation of this argument is that the degree to which an invention is expected to accelerate commercialization is a poor measure of technological achievement and thus of the degree to which an invention should be thought of as nonobvious. We agree that

183 *Id.*

184 *Id.* For an argument that free-rider problems may also prevent optimal production of "information about what the market desires," see Michael Abramowicz & John F. Duffy, *Intellectual Property for Market Experimentation*, 83 N.Y.U L. Rev. 337, 346–51 (2008).

185 Merges, *supra* note 172, at 34.

186 *See infra* Part III.B.2.

187 Merges, *supra* note 172, at 34 (emphasis in original).

many technically remarkable inventions never will in fact lead to viable commercial products, because some other requirement for successful commercialization, such as consumer demand, will never materialize. Properly conceived, the inducement standard demands measuring not absolute value, but relative value in comparison to the experimentation needed for complementary technologies.[188] We suspect that our approach would deny patentability to significant advances only when those advances are so abstract that it seems almost impossible that they could accelerate technology. Such advances might be unpatentable subject matter anyway.[189]

III. ADMINISTERING THE INDUCEMENT STANDARD

Still confronting us is the task of moving from the *Graham* inducement standard to a functional doctrinal definition. This task reflects at least two challenges. The first challenge is that, even if the inducement standard is the appropriate theoretical basis for distinguishing obvious from nonobvious inventions, decision makers might have trouble applying the test directly. It might even seem to invite dangerous inconsistency to ask decision makers to imagine a hypothetical world without patent incentives, in part because different people might have different opinions about the effect of patent protection on innovation. Even so, the *Graham* inducement standard can generate a structured approach that provides common law guidance on nonobviousness to decision makers. Moreover, the structured approach should be largely familiar. As the statute demands, we would begin by asking decision makers to consider what would be obvious to a person having ordinary skill in the art, having been instructed that an entity could count as a person, and the question would be whether this person would find it economically obvious to attempt a research path absent patent incentives.

The second challenge results from our argument that the extent to which a patent accelerates commercialization bears on the degree of nonobviousness. Commercialization, we have argued, ought not be required in advance of patenting, because such an extension of patent races would tend to postpone invention,[190] but depending on the circumstances, it might serve as evidence either in favor of or against inducement.[191] It might appear, however, that even if evidence from market experiments is theoretically relevant, patent law simply cannot take that information into account, because market experimentation generally occurs after a patent is granted.

[188] *See infra* text following note 244.

[189] *See* Bilski v. Kappos, 130 S. Ct. 3218, 3229–31 (2010) (reaffirming that abstract ideas are unpatentable under 35 U.S.C. § 101).

[190] *See supra* notes 148–50 and accompanying text.

[191] It will militate in favor of inducement where the patentee promptly commercializes and no one else does, and against inducement where one or more other parties commercialize but the patentee does not.

But we believe that common law rules can give extra credit in the validity determination to a patentee who has engaged in commercialization that would have been unlikely to have occurred in the absence of receipt of a patent, and can penalize a patentee when others who were not seeking patent protection commercialize the invention without patent inducement. The key is that courts often will be differently situated from examiners and may be able to take into account evidence not available when granting patents. Indeed, the courts, beginning with the Supreme Court in *Graham* itself,[192] have developed a series of secondary considerations of nonobviousness.[193] The secondary considerations as understood by courts today make more sense in light of the inducement theory, and an appreciation of the role of commercialization can further clarify and improve how the courts apply the secondary considerations.

Thus, in addition to asking decision makers to consider the obviousness question from the perspective of the person having ordinary skill in the art, courts ideally should offer further guidance on the secondary considerations. Our analysis would continue to place considerable emphasis on many of the traditional secondary considerations of nonobviousness, such as a long-felt need for an invention and the failure of others. An additional consideration of nonobviousness that we would add to the inquiry is the cost of the experimentation leading to the invention. This is not dispositive, because the relevant factor is what the invention would have been *expected* to cost, but it is helpful. Meanwhile, we would recast the most historically important of the secondary considerations, commercial success, so that the relevant question would be *unexpected* commercial success, which tends to show that a risky project would not have been undertaken without patent incentives. Finally, we would add several considerations of obviousness, guided by our analysis of the competitive dynamics of the patent system.[194] For example, the fact that there was a positive demand shock shortly before the invention would tend toward obviousness, as would a rapidly declining cost of invention. In total, this would provide considerable guidance to decision makers beyond what they receive now, without changing the overall structure of the obviousness inquiry.

The approach that we suggest, although representing a shift in emphasis to which the courts would need to acclimate, would be more administrable than the current system. First, it avoids the inevitable confusion that results from doctrinal incoherence. As we have shown, courts currently nominally apply a cognitive approach

[192] Graham v. John Deere Co., 383 U.S. 1, 17–18 (1966).

[193] The courts' weight on them is sufficiently great that the label "secondary" can be misleading. *See* Kevin Rhodes, Comment, *The Federal Circuit's Patent Nonobviousness Standards: Theoretical Perspectives on Recent Doctrinal Changes*, 85 NW. U. L. REV. 1051, 1070–72 (1991). These considerations may be even more important under recent case law. *See* Amanda Wieker, *Secondary Considerations Should Be Given Increased Weight in Obviousness Inquiries Under 35 U.S.C. § 103 in the Post-*KSR v. Teleflex *World*, 17 FED. CIR. B.J. 665 (2008).

[194] *See supra* Part II.B.

to nonobviousness but then smuggle economic considerations into the analysis.[195] Second, the different parts of our test, the Phosita analysis and the secondary considerations, are more cohesive. Today, it sometimes seems that the two parts of the nonobviousness inquiry are almost unrelated,[196] but we emphasize that each part is a tool for addressing the fundamental question of patent inducement. Third, our test provides more guidance than existing tests, because it highlights fundamental policy choices. Current decision makers receive essentially no guidance on *how* nonobvious an invention must be, but our insistence that they consider whether technology is substantially accelerated provides structure to the inquiry. We do not say definitively what counts as "substantial," but the duration of the patent term is a natural point of comparison, and we invite decision makers to compare the dynamic benefit of any estimated number of years of acceleration with the static costs of the patent term. Fourth, our approach better takes advantage of the natural comparative advantages of patent examiners and courts, and we identify factors on which the courts should be less deferential because relevant information would not have been available to examiners.

A. *Methodological Questions*

1. Heuristics vs. Direct Application

Past commentators have embraced the inducement standard as a theoretical account of the purpose of the obviousness doctrine, but have assumed that the standard would not be administrable.[197] This observation makes sense on the assumption that decision makers would simply be told to apply the inducement standard in an open-ended fashion. The Supreme Court, in propounding the inducement standard, was not insisting that decision makers apply it directly in an unstructured way, but rather in a way recognizing that the inducement standard was a useful description of what common law courts had been trying to achieve in developing the obviousness doctrine. Our call is for this evolutionary process to continue. Appellate judges developing frameworks for the obviousness test should see the inducement standard as a lodestar, as should PTO officials who are developing guidelines for examiners. District judges or patent examiners could, and ideally should, consider the inducement standard directly. Having a deeper theoretical understanding of the nonobviousness inquiry should tend to improve decision making. Our goal, though, is to refine the existing administrative framework of the nonobviousness inquiry to nudge decision makers toward taking into account relevant concerns, even if they reflect little on first principles in day-to-day patent administration. Our approach emphasizes heuristics

195 *See supra* Part I.A.2.

196 *See, e.g.*, Endress + Hauser, Inc. v. Hawk Measurement Sys. Pty., 892 F. Supp. 1107, 1116 (S.D. Ind. 1995) (separating the two parts of the analysis into two unintegrated, separately numbered sections).

197 *See supra* notes 13–14 and accompanying text.

such as the person having skill in the art and secondary considerations of nonobviousness that should work tolerably well even when decision makers are unaware of the justifications for them.

There are several reasons to prefer this approach over one that seeks to use the inducement standard as an unfiltered doctrinal test. First, we recognize the need for caution in attempts to solve the nonobviousness problem merely by conjuring up a perfect verbal explanation of what it means to be nonobvious. Switching from a cognitive approach to a more pragmatic one may help ground the inquiry, but any definition must ultimately be interpreted by a patent examiner or a judicial decision maker. The extent to which subtle distinctions in a definition actually affect legal decision makers is an empirical question.[198] It is not clear how much of a difference instructing the decision maker to apply the inducement standard would make. Decision makers might well make serious errors, and even the best definitions may be somewhat prone to cognitive errors such as hindsight bias.[199] Providing heuristics can lead to more consistent decision making, even if the heuristics are an imperfect approximation of the underlying theoretical concept.

Second, for some inventions, it may be impractical for decision makers to try to identify the market conditions at the time of an invention in a way that would be helpful in applying our definition. In principle, the relevant inducement standard question is how long it would take for the *market* to have produced a particular invention absent patent incentives, but a decision maker may have little information about the market beyond the inventor. And yet another layer of complexity would result from trying to determine how firms might have acted differently in the absence of patent law. As a result, it is useful to have a test that allows the decision makers at least initially to focus on the inventor, while also taking into account objective proxies for market conditions. We do not rule out the possibility that, sometimes in high-end patent litigation, it might be appropriate to have testimony from expert economists that bears directly on the inducement question. In the ordinary case and at least initially, however, decision makers must be able to focus on a relatively small number of easily digested pieces of information.

Third, asking decision makers to apply the inducement standard directly would be a revolution, and it is hard to see how such a revolution would take place. Even if the Supreme Court embraced the standard, it seems unlikely that the Court could

[198] For a recent argument that administrative law doctrines have almost no effect on the outcomes of cases, see Richard Pierce, *What Do the Studies of Judicial Review of Agency Actions Mean?* (2010) (unpublished manuscript, on file with author).

[199] *See* Gregory N. Mandel, *Patently Non-Obvious: Empirical Demonstration that the Hindsight Bias Renders Patent Decisions Irrational*, 67 Ohio St. L.J. 1391 (2006) (discussing the problem of hindsight bias in the patent context). The inducement standard presents a problem of hindsight, because once the technology is developed, decision makers might imagine that one would not need the patent system to develop it. It might seem to add to this the challenge of foresight, because the decision makers must anticipate whether the invention would accelerate commercialization, at least in cases in which commercialization has not already occurred.

properly insist that decision makers consider the standard directly. If a jury must make a validity determination,[200] for example, it would be awkward for the Supreme Court to invalidate jury instructions that included the text of § 103. What the Court can do by embracing the inducement standard is persuade lower courts that, if they do not give adequate attention to the inducement standard, there is a risk that they will reach incorrect results that superior courts will reverse. Our goal is to show how some modest clarifications of principles that decision makers already apply can steer them in the right direction. The changes we recommend still might not seem modest to someone who is steeped in current practices, but we believe that these changes will be less tumultuous than the current path of maintaining nonobviousness as an essentially cognitive inquiry but injecting into the analysis considerations that are undoubtedly economic in nature.

2. Courts vs. Agencies

A significant debate in patent law concerns the relative importance of the PTO and of the courts in deciding questions of patent validity. On one side, Mark Lemley has argued that a patent office should be rationally ignorant. Recognizing that it has a relatively small amount of time in which to decide whether to issue a patent, the office might grant some patents despite some uncertainty about whether invalidating prior art might be found, leaving the courts a role to play in invalidating the patent.[201] F. Scott Kieff has gone further, arguing that the patent system should be replaced with a registration system.[202] With appropriate fee-shifting rules,[203] Kieff maintains that the courts should be trusted with validity and infringement litigation. On the other side are those who insist that it is critical for investors to know whether a patent is valid before they back either the patent-protected product or one that might be accused of infringement.[204] This implies that the courts should almost always defer to PTO decisions. Existing law is somewhere between these extremes.

[200] Although patent validity, in general, and obviousness, in particular, are issues of law, *see Graham*, 383 U.S. at 17, current Federal Circuit case law allows juries to render verdicts on obviousness questions, *see, e.g.*, Richardson v. Suzuki Motor Co., 868 F.2d 1226, 1234 (Fed. Cir. 1989) (claiming that "[i]t is established that the jury may decide the questions of anticipation and obviousness"). The Federal Circuit case law on this point conflicts with the decisions of other circuits rendered before the creation of the Federal Circuit. *See, e.g.*, Sarkisian v. Winn-Proof Corp., 688 F.2d 647, 651 (9th Cir. 1982) (en banc) (holding that, because obviousness is a question of law, jury verdicts on the issue must be considered advisory only, and that "[t]he court must, in all cases, determine obviousness as a question of law independent of the jury's conclusion").

[201] *See* Mark A. Lemley, *Rational Ignorance at the Patent Office*, 95 Nw. U. L. Rev. 1495 (2001).

[202] *See* F. Scott Kieff, *The Case for Registering Patents and the Law and Economics of Present Patent-Obtaining Rules*, 45 B.C. L. Rev. 55 (2003).

[203] *Id.* at 119 & n.278.

[204] The Supreme Court, however, has sometimes adopted relatively vague and uncertain rules despite this concern. *See* Festo Corp. v. Shoketsu Kinzoku Kogyou Kabushiki Co., 535 U.S. 722, 732 (2002) ("Each time the Court has considered the doctrine [of equivalents], it has acknowledged this uncertainty as

The courts grant a strong presumption of patent validity, even where the PTO never considered allegedly invalidating prior art,[205] but it is still not uncommon for a court to find a patent invalid.[206] That courts sometimes disagree with the PTO's nonobviousness determinations,[207] and that the Federal Circuit often disagrees with the determinations of lower federal courts, reinforces that the existing obviousness test allows for a great deal of disagreement.

Whether or not the economic approach increases or decreases the predictability of the obviousness test, it might appear likely to increase the divide between the PTO and the courts. We have argued that commercialization activity, both by the patentee and by other parties, may be relevant to the inducement standard. Patent applications are generally filed before commercialization, however, and the PTO then must make a decision whether to award a patent before commercialization evidence fully develops. The courts, meanwhile, should generally be in a better position to analyze commercialization, both because adjudication will generally take place years after a patent is issued[208] and because judges may have more time to consider this evidence than harried examiners generally do. Application of the inducement standard, one might worry, will create two laws of nonobviousness, one in the administrative agency and one in the courts.

This need not, however, be cause for concern. There are good reasons for the PTO and the courts to share the task of determining patent validity, and the conventional wisdom at least is that it makes sense to have an early determination of nonobviousness by the agency and a later, more thorough review by the courts. This

the price of ensuring the appropriate incentives for innovation, and it has affirmed the doctrine over dissents that urged a more certain rule.").

[205] z4 Techs., Inc. v. Microsoft Corp., 507 F.3d 1340, 1354–55 (Fed. Cir. 2007) (holding, consistent with a long line of Federal Circuit precedents, that clear and convincing evidence is needed to invalidate a patent even where the PTO failed to consider the relevant art). We believe that such doctrine conflicts with basic principles of administrative law. Courts generally presume the actions of administrative agencies to be valid. *See, e.g.*, Hynes v. Grimes Packing Co., 337 U.S. 86, 101 (1949) ("An administrative order is presumptively valid."); Citizens to Preserve Overton Park v. Volpe, 401 U.S. 402, 415 (1971) ("Certainly, the Secretary's decision is entitled to a presumption of regularity."). But that presumed validity yields entirely "if the agency has . . . entirely failed to consider an important aspect of the problem. . . . " Motor Vehicle Mfrs. Ass'n v. State Farm Mut. Auto. Ins. Co., 463 U.S. 29, 43 (1983).

[206] *See* Kimberly A. Moore, *Judges, Juries, and Patent Cases: An Empirical Peek Inside the Black Box*, 99 MICH. L. REV. 365, 380, 390 tbl.4 (2000) (reporting patents held invalid in 33% of 1151 validity determinations in U.S. patent trials from 1983 to 1999). It may be dangerous to extrapolate too much from this statistic, because the cases that are tried may be a unrepresentative sample of all disputes. *See* Peter Siegelman & Joel Waldfogel, *Toward a Taxonomy of Disputes: New Evidence Through the Prism of the Priest/Klein Model*, 28 J. LEGAL STUD. 101 (1999) (offering empirical support for the proposition that plaintiff win rates will be a function of structural parameters, such as the parties' uncertainty, given the existence of settlement before trial).

[207] *See, e.g.*, Perfect Web Tech., Inc. v. InfoUSA, Inc., 587 F.3d 1324 (Fed. Cir. 2009).

[208] *See, e.g.*, Samson Vermont, *Litigation Risk Analysis: The Economics of Patent Litigation, Part IV: More Patent Facts and Stats*, 2 PAT. STRATEGY & MGMT. (Oct. 2001) (stating that for the average litigated patent, final judgment is not rendered until 12.3 years after the patent application was filed).

conventional wisdom makes even more sense once the obviousness test is viewed in economic rather than purely cognitive terms. If, after all, the only question is whether a hypothetical person at a hypothetical time would understand that a particular technological solution exists for some problem, then it might seem strange to delay decision making, aggravating concerns about hindsight bias.[209] If all the prior art is presented to an examiner, the additional time that courts have to consider evidence might seem to have little relevance. When obviousness is conceived in purely cognitive terms, the question is whether one who knows the prior art will easily conceptualize the invention, and it might seem that a quick reaction to that question best allows the decision maker to simulate the mindset of the inventor.[210] However, if the inducement standard suggests that an economic approach is more appropriate than a cognitive one, and if the economic approach requires more analysis, we should be willing to accept a greater discrepancy in roles for the agency and the court.

We doubt, however, that explicit adoption of an economic approach would increase the discrepancy significantly. The courts, after all, have already incorporated economic considerations into the process of evaluating patent validity. One vehicle through which they do this are the secondary considerations of nonobviousness, and in particular the consideration that has often been labeled the most important of these in litigation – commercial success.[211] Although PTO procedure allows examiners to take into account commercial success,[212] because of timing problems, patent applications do not generally report evidence of market success. A discrepancy thus already exists, and as long as the heuristics that we recommend hew reasonably closely to the existing secondary considerations, agency and judicial decisions should be no more discrepant than previously. Indeed, the adoption of a cohesive obviousness test may present an opportunity to make agency and judicial decisions less discrepant, even if timing issues prevent the agency from taking some of the secondary considerations into account. Adoption of the economic approach allows all of the secondary considerations to be conceived in terms of the inducement standard, and as long as the agency can take into account some of the secondary considerations, the agency and the courts may be more likely to agree. Agency–court disagreement may be greater when the agency conceives of nonobviousness in cognitive terms while the courts alone add in to the mix a number of primarily economic factors.

[209] *See supra* note 199 and accompanying text.

[210] *Cf.* Malcolm Gladwell, Blink (2005) (arguing that instantaneous decisions are sometimes better than reasoned ones). *But see* Richard Posner, *Blinkered*, New Republic, Jan 24, 2005, *available at* http://www.tnr.com/article/blinkered (offering a critique of Gladwell's argument).

[211] *See infra* Part III.B.2.b.

[212] *See, e.g.*, Manual of Patent Examining Procedure § 716.03 (8th ed. 2001, rev. July 2008), *available at* http://www.uspto.gov/web/offices/pac/mpep/mpep.htm.

B. A Structured Economic Inquiry

The existing framework for applying the obviousness doctrine can, with minor extensions and adjustments, accommodate the inducement standard's insights. An economic approach retains the statute's focus on the person having ordinary skill in the art, but considers not simply what this person would think about technology, but also the economic incentives that this person faces. Part III.B.1 elaborates on this inquiry, and Part III.B.2 explains how the secondary considerations of nonobviousness can reinforce the economic approach.

1. Phosita

Ideally, the Phosita test[213] should reflect a central insight of the inducement standard: that whether an invention is obvious depends on how costly an experiment would be and the probability that the experiment would be successful. The obviousness test should generally protect inventions that are expensive to generate, either because an experiment that might produce the invention is itself expensive or because it is unlikely to lead to the invention. Fortunately, the Phosita heuristic can accommodate these insights as long as the test no longer isolates the Phosita's state of mind regarding technology from economic considerations. The required addition to the test would be that an invention should be considered obvious when a Phosita would have considered it obvious that it would be worth trying the experiment in question, even if it would be impossible to obtain a patent on the results or to keep them trade secret.[214] This approach is consistent with the "easily discovered" definition of obvious and simply turns the Phosita into a person (or an entity[215]) with economic common sense as well as technological knowledge.

This approach embraces the inducement standard by insisting that the decision maker consider what the Phosita would have done absent patent incentives or the protection of trade secrecy. As such, we are vulnerable to some of the concerns that we had about simply instructing decision makers to apply the inducement standard, though we think that these concerns are not as severe. This instruction would keep the court's focus on the person having ordinary skill in the art, while ideally noting that an entity can be a "person." An expert might well testify about what such a person thought about economic feasibility, for example by noting the investments in machines and personnel that would have been necessary to accomplish an experiment. But we would not need a phalanx of market experts

[213] *See supra* Part I.A.1.

[214] Note that the question is *not* whether the Phosita would have tried the experiment personally. It might be that any individual Phosita would conclude that the experiment is *so* obvious that some other Phosita would likely do it. The question is whether it would be worth the effort of some Phosita, even if imperfect information leaves some slim possibility that no one will actually do the experiment on the assumption that others are doing it.

[215] *See supra* Part I.B.3.

expounding on market structure and projections. If this principle were clarified in common law, it could easily be absorbed into practice without worrying about how decision makers would interpret an entirely new framework.

The law can nudge decision makers to consider inducement by turning the Phosita into someone with ordinary sensitivity to the economic realities of innovation without patents. This approach avoids turning Phosita into an economic superman or superwoman, one who understands all economic models or has perfect economic foresight. The Phosita instead becomes closer to the reasonable person of tort law. In practice, tort decision makers do not ordinarily perform detailed cost-benefit analyses to realize the Hand formula,[216] and there is similarly no reason to worry that giving Phosita some economic common sense will open the floodgates so that sophisticated economic models will be needed to make everyday patent decisions. We would not necessarily prohibit such modeling; perhaps there could be the rare case in which such modeling might be helpful. But the experience of tort law at least suggests that just because a hypothetical reasonable person takes into account economic considerations does not mean that the legal regime must be interpreted in a way that provides full employment for economists.

Our Phosita is of course a hypothetical entity, as an objective standard necessarily requires. But we do not think it is any more hypothetical than the Phosita of present patent law, and indeed we suspect that our changes might allow emergence of a Phosita that is somewhat less hypothetical than the present one. The present Phosita, we have noted, is assumed to have a perfect knowledge of all prior art, but ordinary creativity in assembling disparate pieces of this art.[217] Our move away from a cognitive test suggests less emphasis on what the Phosita *knows* and more emphasis on what the Phosita can *discover* and on how much such discovery would cost. An implication is that more emphasis should be placed on a well-known piece of prior art than on one that is in a journal obscure even to experts in the relevant fields, and more on a piece of prior art that can be easily found with Internet searches than one that, rather than use common words in a field, invents its own lexicon[218] in such a way as to hide the invention from all but the most determined searcher. All prior art would, of course, remain relevant to the novelty inquiry,[219] but the inquiry into obviousness would more closely track the experience of real scientists who attempt to discern the prior art.[220] This refinement on the Phosita test is independent of our primary suggestions, because one could conceive of an omniscient Phosita who

[216] *See* Stephen G. Gilles, *The Invisible Hand Formula*, 80 VA. L. REV. 1015, 1020 (1994) (noting that it is puzzling that jury instructions do not generally reference the Hand Formula directly).

[217] *See supra* Part I.A.1.

[218] *See* CCS Fitness, Inc. v. Brunswick Corp., 288 F.3d 1359, 1366 (Fed. Cir. 2002) (noting that patentees can define terms as they choose).

[219] 35 U.S.C. § 102 (2000) (setting forth the novelty requirement).

[220] In many industries, such scientists themselves may appear hypothetical, because lawyers commonly advise scientists not to consider issued patents for fear that they might expose themselves to willful infringement liability. *See* Mark A. Lemley, *Ending Patent Law's Willfulness Game*, 18 BERKELEY

also takes into account economic concerns, but the possibility helps show that our approach need not make the Phosita test more hypothetical and less administrable, and indeed it could have the reverse effect.

A counterargument is that the Phosita test is settled doctrine, and any major change in the conception of the Phosita will be unsettling. We agree, but it does not appear that patent doctrine can continue merrily along in any event given developments in the Supreme Court. In particular, the courts must flesh out the *KSR* decision's recognition that an invention could be obvious because it is obvious to try.[221] The Federal Circuit has already moved in this direction, sensibly recognizing the relevance of factors such as the cost of experimentation.[222] But the result of these case law developments is doctrinal disjointedness that will remain as long as the courts combine a cognitive definition of nonobviousness with ad hoc doctrines importing economic considerations.

Consider the following example: Even in the absence of a patent system, there would be AIDS researchers, both working for philanthropic causes and for companies that might hope to achieve some commercial benefit by being the first to introduce such a vaccine (for example, because of the benefits of trademark protection).[223] If it became obvious to such researchers, for example because of some scientific discovery, that it would be worth trying to perform a set of research steps, even without a patent incentive, then any resulting vaccine should count as obvious. But if it would not obviously be worthwhile for these scientists to devote their scarce research funds to a research path that would have led to the invention, then the resulting invention should count as nonobvious. The Phosita concept thus implicitly takes into account expected cost and expected probability of success. An inventor who develops a theory to try a research path that others would not have considered should be able to obtain a patent, whether this is because the research path would have been seen as too expensive or too unlikely to produce a positive outcome, or simply because the research path was so clever that individuals without a patent incentive would not likely have conceived of it. A proper understanding of the "obvious to try" concept flows naturally from our approach.

A virtue of this approach is that it implicitly takes into account the issue of the cost of the time of the person having ordinary skill in the art. One problem with the Phosita approach as generally conceived is that, even once we take into account the potential cost of executing the experiment, it might seem that the cost of the

Tech L.J. 1085, 1100–02 (explaining how willful infringement doctrine interferes with patent law's disclosure function).

221 *See* KSR Int'l v. Teleflex, Inc., 550 U.S. 398 (2007); *supra* note 51 and accompanying text.

222 *See In re* Kubin, 561 F.3d 1351 (Fed. Cir. 2009); *supra* notes 68–69 and accompanying text.

223 The standard, of course, is objective, so philanthropic inventors should be as eligible for patents as anyone else. Even inventors who seek to promote the public domain sometimes may seek patents. *See, e.g.*, Grant Gross, *Red Hat: Our Software Patents Are Defensive, and We'll Share*, May 29, 2002, http://www.linux.com/archive/articles/23154 (explaining Red Hat's decision to seek software patents).

Phosita is not directly relevant. The test asks whether the invention would have been obvious to someone with ordinary skill in the art, not what the person charges or how many hours (or how many such people) would be required to achieve. Case law sometimes sets a somewhat arbitrary level for the education level or experience of the Phosita,[224] without considering whether someone at that threshold would have sufficient incentives to innovate in the absence of patent protection. Worse, ordinary skill is likely to be set higher in fields where artisans are more expensive,[225] thus ratcheting up the patentability standard for fields that are inherently difficult to practice, even where no one would be practicing absent patent incentives. Our approach does not do this. Whether an experiment is worth the time of a Phosita depends implicitly on the alternative uses of a Phosita's time. If, without the patent or trade secret incentive for a particular invention, a Phosita would have thought it better to work on other matters, that is enough for patentability.

Our approach to the Phosita test also conveys the appropriate baseline, a world in which the inventor makes decisions to invent but for reasons other than patent and trade secrecy. The inducement standard asks whether there would have existed alternative incentives (such as first-mover advantages and copyright law) for the invention. But we do not expect decision makers to read the business literature on first-mover advantages[226] or to acquaint themselves with more modern versions of Stephen Breyer's back-of-the-envelope calculations about copyright incentives.[227] We suspect, for example, that decision makers would be more wary of a software invention if presented with testimony indicating that either the patentee or its rivals were intent on producing the product embodying some process in any event and that patenting was a secondary consideration and, in contrast, that decision makers could be made to understand that pharmaceutical research is so expensive and so easily copied that incentives to conduct it are ordinarily quite limited.

We do not mean to imply that the construct of a hypothetical person with economic common sense is perfect. There may be situations in which it could lead the decision maker astray, though it should be possible for common law decision making and instructions to decision makers to limit this danger. Take, for example,

[224] *See, e.g.*, Bose Corp. v. JBL, Inc., 112 F. Supp. 2d 138, 155 (D. Mass. 2000) (specifying that the Phosita "would have worked as a loudspeaker designer for two to three years").

[225] *See* Joseph P. Meara, Ph.D., *Just Who Is the Person Having Ordinary Skill in the Art? Patent Law's Mysterious Personage*, 77 Wash. L. Rev. 267, 280–81 (2002) (noting that the education level required will be higher for "those involved in drug discovery" than those involved "in the art of fly wraps for the legs of horses").

[226] *See, e.g.*, Roger A. Kerin et al., *First-Mover Advantage: A Synthesis, Conceptual Framework, and Research Propositions*, 56 J. Marketing 33, 34–39 (1992) (providing overview of the literature); Marvin B. Lieberman & David B. Montgomery, *First-Mover Advantages*, 9 Strategic Mgmt. J. (Special Issue) 41, 42–47 (1988) (same).

[227] *See* Stephen Breyer, *The Uneasy Case for Copyright: A Study of Copyright in Books, Photocopies, and Computer Programs*, 84 Harv. L. Rev. 281, 294–95 (1970) (estimating costs for a first publisher and a copier).

the situation in which only the top experts in a field would recognize the wisdom of a particular approach, but they would do so even absent any inducement of patents. If, for example, some development in topology would have led a number of Nobel Prize winning physicists to conceive of a particular invention even without patent protection, then those prize winners ought to set the level of ordinary skill. This situation will not happen often, but it emphasizes that in theory, the level of skill in the art may depend on the importance of the problem to be solved. This is particularly the case for inventions that are the result of intellectual contemplation. On extraordinarily important problems, highly trained scientists are likely to offer at least some analysis even without patent protection. If many such scientists surely would have made a particular intellectual contribution, then the only relevant question should be whether it would be obvious to try any necessary follow-up experimentation in the absence of the patent system. The Phosita construct does not clearly convey this question. It is easy to imagine refinements to the approach that could remedy this lack of clarity, however.

One refinement would be a clarification that an "art" must be delineated by the type of person who ordinarily would make the specific type of contribution represented by the invention. Currently, in litigation, the level of ordinary skill in the art receives relatively little attention, with the parties often simply stipulating that the relevant skill level is that of a Ph.D. scientist in the relevant field.[228] This stipulation is somewhat indeterminate, however. Where do we divide the line between Ph.D.'s who are ordinary and those who are inventors? Moreover, it produces strange policy results. If the possibility of patents leads to an increase in the education that students in a given field receive, then patent law responds by making it harder to win patents, thus pushing the trend in the opposite direction. And it suggests that work that can only be done by above-average Ph.D.'s should always receive patent protection, regardless of whether they would have done the same work absent patent protection. Defining an "art" not as a reference to the field of inquiry but as a type of contribution within this field would address this concern.

For example, if a software patent involves a complex pattern for organizing interactions among different code modules, the relevant art may be software architecture rather than software programming. This approach demands that the decision maker hone in on just what the innovation is to determine who the applicable person is. Sometimes, a particular patent may combine the contributions of people in different roles, and at least one indispensable contribution must be of the sort that would not have been made by the ordinary contributor of that type in the absence of patent

[228] *See, e.g.*, Herbert F. Schwartz, *Panel I:* KSR v. Teleflex: *The Nonobviousness Requirement of Patentability*, 17 FORDHAM INTELL. PROP. MEDIA & ENT. L.J. 875 (2007) (stating that sometimes "people just punt on it and they stipulate that the person of ordinary skill in the art has a Ph.D. in nuclear engineering, and then people go on to something else"). There are cases, however, in which the issue is litigated. *See* Meara, *supra* note 225 (providing an overview of doctrine and critiquing the tests as not well connected to the concerns of obviousness doctrine).

incentives. For example, a pharmaceutical invention may be the result of both a decision to test some set of isomers and of the actual testing. The invention might be patent induced because the decision to test those isomers was nonobvious. That would depend on whether the people who design experiments would likely have recognized the benefits of the research plan absent patent inducement. Or, it might be patent induced because the results of the testing were nonobvious. This inquiry would focus on the probability of success given the original design and the cost of experimentation. In other words, we must consider each research step individually, rather than simply considering from the outset what the result of experimentation is likely to be.

The Phosita construct still faces one significant challenge, and it is central to our conceptualization of the nonobviousness standard. In the absence of the patent incentive, a Phosita might think it not obviously worthwhile to conduct an experiment because it would make sense to wait before conducting the experiment. Perhaps it is unclear whether there would be a market for such an invention or whether some cheaper approach to experimentation might be developed. The wording that we have adopted so far might suggest that an invention resulting from an experiment in such circumstances would count as nonobvious, but the inducement standard counsels the reverse result.[229] We can, however, add a clarification. The decision maker should analyze the claimed invention by asking whether it would make sense for the Phosita to undertake the research process in the absence of a patent incentive once any complementary technologies needed for commercialization already existed.[230] If the patent incentive would still be needed to induce the claimed invention, then the claimed invention is nonobvious. This approach ensures that the inventor receives no bonus or penalty for invention before more important complementary technologies exist.

Suppose, for example, that a patent application claims a machine that can determine in what order clothes removed from a dryer should be folded, taking into account factors such as the susceptibility of the fabric to wrinkles and the location of each item of clothing in the pile. In theory, such a machine could be used today to advise people doing laundry about what order to fold their clothes, but there would be almost no market for it, because people already perform this task well. It is possible, though, that in a few years, robots will be able to fold laundry.[231]

[229] *See supra* Part II.C.

[230] This approach would make little sense with a cognitive definition of nonobviousness, because the creation of an invention may lead to the creation of other inventions that, had they been invented first, would make the first invention cognitively obvious. But it does make sense when the question is whether it would be economically obvious to undertake the work to conduct the experiments that might lead to successful attainment of the first invention, where the benefit of the first invention depends entirely on the second.

[231] *See* YouTube, http://www.youtube.com/watch?v=gy5g33SoGzo (last visited May 23, 2011) (demonstrating a primitive prototype).

The decision maker then should ask, *if* a robot to fold laundry existed, would it be obvious for a Phosita even without patent incentives to develop the folding-order-determination invention. The answer may depend on the sophistication of the invention. Given the technology to fold laundry robotically, a Phosita undoubtedly would need some mechanism for determining in what order to fold it. The invention should thus receive a patent covering only claims that represent an inventive accomplishment beyond what the Phosita would do without a patent incentive. Our approach thus refuses the speculative patent – for example, to the patent applicant who has not done much more than recognize that once robots can fold clothes, they will need to know to be extra careful with linen – while recognizing the possibility that genuine technological accomplishments often occur in advance of commercial application.

2. Secondary Considerations

Although the construct of the Phosita is mentioned in § 103 itself and is thus well established in the law, the broader case law on nonobviousness is today in an uncertain state. The Federal Circuit formerly followed the so-called teaching-motivation-suggestion test, finding that one of these was required to make an invention nonobvious.[232] In *KSR* v. *Teleflex*,[233] the Supreme Court rejected the teaching-suggestion-motivation test, seemingly adopting a more flexible test of nonobviousness. *KSR* creates an interpretive vacuum. Perhaps in future cases, the Supreme Court or the Federal Circuit could seize on the inducement standard of *Graham* to clarify case law. In addition to potentially leading to the changes in the conception of Phosita that we suggested earlier, the Court also could focus on refining the analysis of the secondary considerations of nonobviousness.

A. CONSIDERATIONS OF NONOBVIOUSNESS. The origin of the secondary considerations, *Graham* itself,[234] makes this an attractive doctrinal path for further development of the nonobviousness standard. Moreover, the Federal Circuit has placed considerable emphasis on the secondary considerations, and so an increased focus on or clarification of these considerations need not be a great divergence from the

[232] *See, e.g.*, C.R. Bard, Inc. v. M3 Sys., Inc., 157 F.3d 1340, 1352 (Fed. Cir. 1998) (discussing the test). The inducement standard will lead to the same results as the old test in many cases. Where there is a teaching, motivation, or suggestion indicating that a particular approach is likely to produce success, then often there will be enough incentive for someone to follow through on this teaching, suggestion, or motivation, even without patent protection. But the inducement standard shows that this will lead to both false negatives and false positives. Sometimes, even without a teaching, motivation, or suggestion in the prior art, and even without a patent incentive, an invention might have been developed early enough to allow commercialization on close to the same timetable. On the other hand, a teaching, motivation, or suggestion might be so uncertain or expensive to pursue with further research that such research would not have occurred without a patent incentive.

[233] 550 U.S. 398 (2007).

[234] Graham v. John Deere Co., 383 U.S. 1, 17–18 (1966).

status quo. The foremost of these factors, under Federal Circuit law,[235] is whether the invention has produced commercial success.[236] Another factor, which one commentator describes as "the most prevalent form of nonobviousness relied on by patent applicants during patent examination,"[237] is whether the experiment producing the invention has produced "unexpected results."[238] Other factors include whether others have tried but failed to create the invention or solve the same problem,[239] whether there was a long-felt need for the invention,[240] whether competitors have agreed to license the invention,[241] whether others skilled in the art have approved of the invention,[242] and whether infringers have copied the invention.[243] Some of these factors, such as the failure of others and long-felt need, could be easily considered by examiners as well as by courts, whereas others, such as licensing and copying, may be ascertainable only in litigation. Commentators have proposed additional secondary considerations, such as whether the invention has provided the inventor market power.[244]

The inducement standard approach supports these secondary considerations in general, while also suggesting caveats. Inventions, we have seen, will generally be patent induced where the experiments leading to them are *expected* to be *low probability* and/or *high cost* relative to the rents to be earned from invention. The decision maker considering the Phosita can directly consider issues of probability and expected cost by focusing on the difference between the claimed subject matter and the prior art. The secondary considerations can assist the decision maker by identifying objective signs of low-probability and high-cost experimentation. The secondary considerations should reflect an understanding of the economics of patent races so that the decision maker need not necessarily directly understand the details of such

[235] Reed Marcy has noted:

> Beginning in 1982, the Federal Circuit started to elevate the once-secondary consideration of commercial success to the level of a primary factor equal to or greater than the other three factual prongs of the *Graham* test. . . . Subsequent decisions by the Federal Circuit have borne out the theory that commercial success has been raised to the level of a primary, or even the prime, factor.

Reed W.L. Marcy, *Patent Law's Nonobviousness Requirement: The Effect of Inconsistent Standards Regarding Commercial Success on the Individual Inventor*, 19 Hastings Comm./Ent. L.J. 199, 207 (1996).

[236] *See, e.g.*, *In re* Sernaker, 702 F.2d 989, 996 (Fed. Cir. 1983) (discussing the relevance of commercial success).

[237] Harris A. Pitlick, *Some Thoughts About Unexpected Results Jurisprudence*, 86 J. Pat. & Trademark Off. Soc'y 169, 169 (2004).

[238] *See, e.g.*, Takeda v. Alphapharm, 492 F.3d 1350, 1354 (Fed. Cir. 2007).

[239] *See, e.g.*, Knoll Pharm. Co., Inc. v. Teva Pharm. USA, Inc., 367 F.3d 1381, 1385 (Fed. Cir. 2004).

[240] *See, e.g.*, Uniroyal, Inc. v. Rudkin-Wiley Corp., 837 F.2d 1044, 1054 (Fed. Cir. 1988) (finding evidence of a long-felt need).

[241] *See, e.g.*, WMS Gaming, Inc. v. Int'l Game Tech., 184 F.3d 1339, 1360 (Fed. Cir. 1999).

[242] *See, e.g.*, In re Piasecki, 745 F.2d 1468, 1473 (Fed. Cir. 1984).

[243] *See, e.g.*, Ecolochem, Inc. v. S. Cal. Edison Co., 227 F.3d 1361, 1380 (Fed. Cir. 2000).

[244] *See* Andrew Blair-Stanek, *Increased Market Power as a New Secondary Consideration in Patent Law*, 58 Am. U. L. Rev. 707 (2009).

a model. Ideally, the decision maker should be informed that the secondary considerations help identify cases in which inventions are the result of low-probability, high-cost experimentation, so that the decision maker can appreciate the relevance of the secondary considerations.

The secondary considerations do largely focus the decision maker on this inquiry. The focus on unexpected results, for example, is consistent with the point that low-probability experimentation should generally be rewarded, although it does not take cost directly into account. The fact that others have tried and failed supports the notion that success was uncertain, although it does not indicate whether success would have remained uncertain between the time of invention and commercialization. The consideration of long-felt need for the invention, however, helps compensate for this deficiency, because if such a need long existed, there is a good chance that the invention would be ready for commercialization. The approval of others points to the expected difficulty of the task; others having ordinary skill in the art would likely not admire efforts that they themselves might well have taken and soon, even absent patent incentives. Licensing and copying sometimes may be an indication that independent invention would be difficult, but because the decisions of others reflect their view of patent law, we must ensure that we do not place so much weight on this consideration as to make the obviousness doctrine circular.

Ideally, a decision maker animated by the inducement standard would not simply assign some weight to each of the secondary considerations. Rather, the various secondary considerations are useful clues in helping the decision maker apply elements of the inducement standard. The considerations should be seen not so much secondary as evidentiary, and they should be understood as interdependent. For example, even if the inventor has not had any commercial success, evidence that others have copied the invention and in turn had commercial success might help the inventor establish that other factors necessary to commercialization were present and yet competitors could not figure out how to proceed on their own. Evidence of commercialization by others would point in the opposite direction if it seemed that the others had developed the invention independently, another secondary consideration.

A textual counterargument to this interpretation of the secondary considerations might argue that any proxy for the cost of experimentation should be irrelevant. The last sentence of § 103 states, "*Patentability shall not be negatived* by the manner in which the invention was made."[245] Some commentators see this sentence as indicating that the courts must consider only the end product of invention, not the process by which the invention was produced.[246] As others have noted,[247] however,

[245] 35 U.S.C. § 103 (2000 & Supp. IV 2004) (emphasis added).

[246] *See, e.g.*, Varu Chilakamarri, *Structural Nonobviousness: How Inventiveness Is Lost in the Discovery*, 10 VA. J.L. & TECH. 7, 12 (2005).

[247] *See, e.g.*, George M. Sirilla & Hon. Giles S. Rich, *35 U.S.C. . . . 103: From* Hotchkiss *to Hand to Rich, The Obvious Patent Law Hall-of-Famers*, 32 MARSHALL L. REV. 437, 511–12 (1999) (recounting Judge Rich's recollection as the principal drafter of the Patent Act).

and as the official legislative history prominently confirms,[248] the sentence was a reaction to case law indicating that patentability must reflect a "flash of genius,"[249] and it makes clear that inventions resulting from detailed experimentation are also entitled to patentability. The inducement standard, meanwhile, would not prevent patentability of inventions reflecting a flash of genius, as long as the expected cost of invention was high. Section 103 does not state that evidence of the manner of invention cannot be considered; its passive wording indicates that the manner of invention may be relevant, but cannot alone be sufficient to determine patentability. The fact that the inducement standard is objective[250] helps make sense of this puzzle. It does not matter how the inventor arrived at the invention, but the expected difficulty of producing the invention is central to the obviousness doctrine.

This analysis at least counters the argument that a factor such as long-felt need should not be relevant because long-felt need is a proxy for the cost of experimentation and the statute deems the cost of experimentation irrelevant. Properly understood, long-felt need *is* a proxy for the expected cost of experimentation. This understanding also suggests that the actual cost of experimentation should join the pantheon of secondary considerations. Quite possibly, the last sentence of § 103 explains why courts have not adopted cost as a secondary consideration. Once the inducement standard places the secondary considerations into economic context and clarifies the importance of experimentation's expected cost, it should be possible to consider the actual cost of experimentation as a proxy for expected cost. There is some danger that because of hindsight bias decision makers might place too much weight on this consideration and refuse patentability for experiments that turned out to be low cost or grant patentability because of unnecessary high costs. But a very high actual cost of experimentation should at least be allowed as evidence, although not necessarily dispositive, of nonobviousness.

B. CONSIDERATION OF COMMERCIAL SUCCESS. But what of the purportedly most important consideration, commercial success? Before he developed the prospect theory of the patent system,[251] Edmund Kitch was skeptical about the use of commercial success evidence.[252] One basis for his skepticism is that only patents on commercially successful products will be litigated.[253] Later, Kitch defended the

[248] "The second sentence states that patentability as to this requirement is not to be negatived by the manner in which the invention was made, that is, it is immaterial whether it resulted from long toil and experimentation or from a flash of genius." 35 U.S.C.A. § 103 (2004) at 1952 Notes, *cited in* Graham v. John Deere, 383 U.S. 1, 16 n.8 (1966).

[249] Hamilton Standard Propeller Co. v. Fay-Egan Mfg. Co., 101 F.2d 614, 617 (6th Cir. 1939) ("The patentee did not display any flash of genius, inspiration or imagination.").

[250] *See supra* Part I.B.2.

[251] Kitch, *supra* note 156.

[252] Kitch, *supra* note 12, at 332–34.

[253] "Since it is unlikely that patents that are not commercially successful will be brought to litigation, [considering commercial success] amounts to a suggestion that borderline cases be decided in favor of patentees." *Id.* at 333.

commercial success criterion based on the development of his prospect theory, noting that "[t]he fact that a product or process within the terms of the patent claim is commercially successful tells the court that the patent serves as the foundation for a series of now valuable contract rights."[254] This argument, however, cannot easily justify the use of commercial success to determine nonobviousness, because obvious inventions, if sufficiently valuable, can also serve as a foundation for contract rights.

In his earlier work, Kitch offers a persuasive argument that commercial success will not necessarily be a strong indication of nonobviousness, arguing that the chain of inferences from commercial success back to nonobviousness is long and weak:

> First, that the commercial success is due to the innovation. Second, that . . . potential commercial success was perceived before its development. Third, the potential commercial success having been perceived, it is likely that efforts were made [by a number of firms] to develop the improvement. Fourth, the efforts having been made by men of skill in the art, they failed because the patentee was the first to reduce his development to practice.[255]

Moreover, Kitch showed that commercial success may point in the opposite direction. If a product would be commercially successful, there may be less need for a patent to induce its creation.[256] "At the very least," he argues, "these two arguments should cancel each other and leave commercial success with no role to play in a non-obviousness inquiry."[257]

The reason that commercial success seems to produce equivocal results is that we are interested in the ratio of the private benefit provided by a successful experiment in the absence of the patent system to the cost of experimentation.[258] Actual commercial success provides some evidence that the expected degree of commercial success was high. That has two alternative implications. First, the nonpatent private benefit of successful experimentation may have been relatively high, tending toward obviousness. Second, there must either have been a great deal of experimentation (the inferential link that Kitch considers) or a low probability of success, tending either way toward nonobviousness. And so, our approach provides support for Kitch's observation that the effects may crudely cancel out.

Commercial success thus seems intimately related to nonobviousness, but the relationship between them is not as simple as the current emphasis on commercial success in patent litigation would suggest. To unravel the puzzle of how to interpret commercial success evidence, we must consider not just the perspective of an individual inventor or firm but also market dynamics. Under stable conditions, the total combined economic effort of all firms racing for a particular invention will be equal to the present discounted value of the patent right. Each firm must consider

[254] Kitch, *supra* note 156, at 283.
[255] *Kitch, supra* note 12, at 332.
[256] *Id.* at 333–34.
[257] *Id.* at 334.
[258] *See supra* text following note 244.

not only whether experimentation will be successful but also what its probability is of winning the patent. Thus, where technology and markets develop roughly as expected, firms will earn *on average* zero economic profit.[259] Where racing firms collectively earn large positive profits, something unexpected has occurred, and to determine the implications of that commercial success, we must figure out the nature of the deviation from stable economic conditions.

To make commercial success relevant in the secondary considerations analysis, we must thus define clearly what type of success is relevant. What is relevant is the level of commercial success, taking into account the investments of both the inventor and all other racing firms, *relative* to expectations, once sufficient information existed to justify (at least to the inventor) technological research and commercialization conditional on research success. Unexpectedly high commercial success defined in this way implies patent inducement and nonobviousness, whereas unexpected low commercial success implies the opposite. These implications, however, are relatively weak. Even where commercial success is high relative to expectations, for example, it might be that the expected level of commercial success was still large enough that development would have occurred even without a patent incentive.

The evidence of unexpected commercial success that may thus be most relevant is evidence about the difficulty of obtaining funding for a research project. Suppose that a particular approach to research, which would be ready for commercialization if successful, was a marginal prospect for investors, so at the time of the initial investment, it was a close call as to whether any firm interested in pursuing this approach would be funded. The research eventually results, however, in a commercialized product for which a patent would be valuable. There is then a strong likelihood that if the patent incentive had not existed, the research and development would not have occurred. At times, relatively objective evidence of this, such as rejections from venture capitalists or memoranda indicating considerable skepticism within an organization about a particular approach, may be available, and such evidence could even be made available to patent examiners. Strong evidence of interest among potential funders may be more equivocal, because it may be difficult to determine whether adequate interest would have existed absent the patent incentive.

C. CONSIDERATIONS OF OBVIOUSNESS. Unexpected commercial success, like the other secondary considerations that the courts have considered, thus may provide evidence of nonobviousness. Perhaps the absence of the secondary considerations provides some indirect evidence of obviousness, but it is also possible to devise secondary considerations that provide direct evidence of obviousness, consistent with the model we developed in Part II. These considerations become apparent by asking why an invention would not have been invented earlier if it was obvious. There are at least two possibilities. First, the cost of invention may have fallen rapidly. For

[259] *See supra* note 134 and accompanying text.

example, if an invention depends on a research tool that did not exist until shortly before the research leading to the invention was conducted, the invention could not have been invented earlier. Similarly, an improvement patent cannot be invented before the patent that it is improving. Second, the benefits of invention may have risen rapidly. For example, the 9/11 terrorist attacks increased demand for security-related products, so the fact that a patent serving this demand was not invented earlier does not show nonobviousness. Such a recently felt need is the reverse of the long-felt need that can be a secondary consideration of nonobviousness. Another example can be found in *Honeywell International* v. *United States*.[260] The disputed patent claim element in that case involved filtering part of the red-color band for night vision goggles, and the patent issued just as the government was deciding that filtering this color band would be useful for night vision goggles to be used by pilots flying fixed-wing aircraft.

The occurrence of an exogenous shock that decreases the cost of an invention or increases the benefit of an invention should count as a secondary consideration of obviousness. As with other secondary considerations, it cannot by itself resolve the issue. It is certainly possible, for example, that an improvement patent following closely after the original patent would not have been invented for a long time after the original absent patent incentives, and it should then count as nonobvious. But including such an exogenous shock as a secondary consideration will serve as a reminder to the decision maker that there is a possible reason for the failure of earlier invention. At least, it will avoid the danger that a decision maker will make the mistake of concluding that an invention is nonobvious because of the newness of the context. And it will remind patent examiners especially to be more vigilant about allowing patents that follow major shocks. Such a secondary consideration might well have thinned the avalanche of patent applications that followed the development of the Internet.

The near-simultaneous independent invention of the invention by a party that was not itself motivated by patents should also count as a strong secondary consideration of obviousness. Independent invention itself is equivocal, because it could simply indicate the existence of a patent race.[261] But where one party does not seek a patent and it appears that this failure to seek a patent is not simply a strategic gambit to deny the other party a patent, that strongly suggests that a patent incentive was not needed to motivate the invention. For example, if an independent software programmer at a company that had a policy of never seeking patents developed a process at about the same time as a software company that sought to patent the process, it should be difficult for the latter to obtain a patent even if it was the first to invent. An

260 *See* Honeywell Int'l v. United States, 609 F.3d 1292 (Fed. Cir. 2010), *petition for cert. filed*, Oct. 8, 2010 (No. 10–491).

261 Our analysis thus differs slightly from that of T. J. Chiang, who persuasively explains the relevance of independent invention but seems to place somewhat more weight on this consideration than we would. *See* Chiang, *supra* note 9, at 94–100.

important caveat is that if the independent inventor planned to keep the invention trade secret, that should not preclude patenting, because the *Graham* test seeks to identify inventions that would not be "devised or disclosed" absent the patent system.

It may also be relevant, but is far from dispositive, that there is a vibrant group of inventors working in the general area of the invention without seeking patents. Sometimes, the presence of such a group might suggest that, even absent the patent incentive, someone else would have developed the invention soon. For example, if an international open science consortium plans to sequence genomes from a number of species, the fact that a patent-induced inventor is able to sequence a genome first might not be enough to entitle that inventor to a patent. In contrast, because there are so many plausible targets of investigation in the pharmaceutical field, the existence of some number of open source researchers is probably largely irrelevant, unless there is reason to believe they are near a resolution of any particular problem. The vast majority of such research is likely to be patent induced, even if there are some who eschew patents and many for whom patents are a significant incentive along with other incentives, such as the desire to obtain government grants.

IV. CONCLUSION

The inducement standard of patentability might be seen in at least three ways. The first is as a theoretical benchmark for evaluating nonobviousness determinations, but one so far removed from doctrine and practice as to be useless as a guide to the patent agency and the courts. We have argued for a second view – that the inducement standard should directly influence the courts' continued common law development of the obviousness doctrine and that it may provide useful guidance in determining the patentability of individual inventions. Once nonobviousness is framed in economic rather than cognitive terms, the inducement standard becomes comprehensible and administrable within the existing doctrinal framework. So far, we have ignored a third approach – the application of the inducement standard on a macro level rather than a micro level to foreclose patenting to entire classes of inventions that, on average, seem unlikely to be patent induced.[262]

At oral argument in a recent case on whether the entire class of business methods should be excluded from patentable subject matter, Justice Breyer suggested such an approach. "I don't know whether across the board or in this area or that area patent protection will do no harm or more harm than good," Breyer stated.[263] Patent law, Breyer noted, induces inventors "to produce more" and "to disclose,"[264] but it

[262] For an article arguing that patentable subject matter doctrine should be designed to exclude protection for "self-realizing" inventions (i.e. those that would be developed even absent a patent incentive), see Alan Devlin & Neel Sukhatme, *Self-Realizing Inventions and the Utilitarian Foundation of Patent Law*, 51 Wm. & Mary L. Rev. 897 (2009).

[263] *See* Transcript of Oral Argument at 21, Bilski v Kappos, No. 08–964 (2009).

[264] *Id.*

has two costs. The inventors will "charge a higher price, so people use the product less,"[265] and the property rights will create transactions costs.[266] Breyer suggested that the outcome of the case should turn on whether business methods as a class need the inducement of patents to generate innovation, and that view was directly expressed in the opinion that Justice Breyer joined in the case.[267] But if the inducement standard can be properly applied, these two minuses can be explicitly balanced against the benefits associated with the acceleration of invention. And if one insists on acceleration at least the length of the patent term, the minuses disappear altogether. There will be errors, of course, in applying any approach, but the inducement standard can work sufficiently well that the courts need not use the much blunter instrument of patentable subject matter. A majority of the Supreme Court disagreed with Justice Breyer's macro-level embrace of the inducement standard, refusing to impose a categorical ban on business method patents.[268] Whatever the correctness of this decision, it makes it all the more important for the Supreme Court and lower courts to make micro-level assessments of nonobviousness if they are to accomplish the *Graham* Court's goal of granting patents only to "those inventions which would not be disclosed or devised but for the inducement of a patent."[269]

The inducement standard would likely invalidate a relatively high percentage of patents in precisely those areas where patentable subject matter has become most controversial: business methods, software, and financial instruments.[270] A characteristic that these areas share is that many (though not all) innovations can be generated at low cost and that there tend to be other incentives to innovate even in the absence of patents. Inventors in these areas do not wear lab coats, and innovation seems likely to require less experimentation of a more traditional scientific kind (which is frequently very expensive) and more intellectual experimentation (which may not be very expensive). The inducement standard easily accommodates such intellectual experimentation, asking whether it would make sense to engage in the research process that produced a particular business method, software, or financial invention in the absence of a patent system. But in abandoning a cognitive approach, the inducement standard avoids the risk that a decision maker will conclude that because a complex and creative thought process was needed to arrive at the ultimate invention,

[265] *Id.*

[266] "[T]he act of getting permissions and having to get permission can really slow things down and destroy advance." *Id.*

[267] Bilski v. Kappos, 130 S. Ct. 3218, 3225–27, 3253–55 (2010) (Stevens, J., concurring in the judgment) (arguing that most business innovations will occur even without patent protection because "[i]nnovators often capture advantages from new business methods notwithstanding the risk of others copying their innovation").

[268] *Id.* at 3225–27 (majority opinion).

[269] Graham v. John Deere Co., 383 U.S. 1, 11 (1966).

[270] For an article in favor of allowing patentability in general in these areas, see Michael Risch, *Everything Is Patentable*, 75 Tenn. L. Rev 591 (2008).

the invention is by definition nonobvious.[271] Moreover, it may be particularly easy to craft a speculative patent in these fields – for example, by anticipating a type of business or software tool that will be useful in the future – and the inducement standard shows why these patents are invalid. By identifying the relevant baseline, which in the case of software includes the protections of copyright law, the inducement standard insists that inventions that would be routinely created anyway not receive protection. But it does so in a much more nuanced way than a categorical ban, and it can improve decision making in less controversial areas of patenting as well.

[271] The inducement standard could also be used to identify ideas that are so abstract that they should not be patentable. A useful illustration is the Supreme Court's notoriously difficult-to-harmonize cases on mathematical algorithms. In *Gottschalk* v. *Benson*, 409 U.S. 63 (1972), the Supreme Court rejected patentability of a claim on a numerical algorithm on patentable subject matter grounds, but in *Diamond* v. *Diehr*, 450 U.S. 175 (1981), the Court held that a machine or process executing a software algorithm could be patentable. The inducement standard asks whether the development algorithm can be expected to accelerate the commercialization of some process, and if so, the use of the algorithm in that process should qualify as nonobvious. This approach harmonizes the cases, though it is in tension with dicta in *Parker* v. *Flook*, 437 U.S. 584, 590 (1978), in which the Court argued that the Pythagorean Theorem would not have been patentable merely if the patent application explained how it could be applied to surveying techniques. At least, the use of the Pythagorean Theorem in such surveying should be patentable. A more concrete example of an abstract discovery that should have been patentable, had a patent been sought, was the discovery of human monoclonal antibodies. *See generally* Alberto Cambrosio & Peter Keating, *Between Fact and Technique: The Beginnings of Hybridoma Technology*, 25 J. HIST. BIO. 175 (1992) (providing an overview of the history). Although the original discoverers did not reduce their discovery to practice, they identified a clear path toward commercialization.

6

Patenting the Curve Ball

Business Methods and Industry Norms

*Gerard N. Magliocca**

"Inevitably, any policy to restrict abstract patents amounts to drawing a line between what is patentable and what is not, and, unfortunately, such lines are drawn in the shifting sands of words.... We thus do not know what it will take to appropriately restrict abstract patents in general or software patents in particular."[1]

Candy Cummings is not a household name, but he is credited with inventing a vital part of American civilization – the curve ball.[2] The ongoing controversy over whether and to what extent business methods should be patentable raises a fascinating question: Could a modern-day counterpart of Cummings who comes up with the next breakthrough pitch patent that invention?[3] Under the test set forth by

* Professor of Law, Indiana University – Indianapolis. Many thanks to Carlo Andreani, Dan Cole, Kevin Collins, and to my colleagues at the Roosevelt Study Center in Middelburg, The Netherlands, who hosted me while I worked on this chapter during my sabbatical. A version of this chapter was originally published in the *Brigham Young University Law Review*. *See* Gerard N. Magliocca, *Patenting the Curve Ball: Business Methods and Industry Norms*, 2009 B.Y.U. L. Rev. 875 (2009).

1 James Bessen & Michael J. Meurer, Patent Failure: How Judges, Bureaucrats, and Lawyers Put Innovators at Risk 244 (2008).

2 *See* Martin Quigley, The Crooked Pitch: An Account of the Curveball in American Baseball History (1984). As with many great leaps in technology, there is a dispute over who really invented the curve ball. *Cf.* United States v. American Bell Tel. Co., 128 U.S. 315, 354 (1888) (resolving a claim that Alexander Graham Bell was not the first inventor of the phone). Some give the nod to Fred Goldsmith, a contemporary of Cummings who pitched for the oddly named London Tecumsehs. *See id.* at 39. Nevertheless, the Veterans' Committee of the Baseball Hall of Fame inducted Cummings into Cooperstown based on its conclusion that he was the rightful claimant. *See id.* at 160. On this sort of matter, the Veterans' Committee is the final authority.

3 *See* State St. Bank & Trust Co. v. Signature Fin. Group, Inc., 149 F.3d 1368, 1373–77 (Fed. Cir. 1998) (holding that there is no "business method" exception for patents). The patentability of the curve ball is not an original hypothetical. *See, e.g.*, Rochelle Cooper Dreyfuss, *Are Business Method Patents Bad for Business?*, 16 Santa Clara Computer & High Tech L.J. 263, 276 (2000) ("What, for example, if Candy Cummings had patented the curve ball or Dick Fosbury his high jump 'flop?'"); Keith Maskus & Eina Vivian Wong, *Searching for Economic Balance in Business Method Patents*, 8 Wash. U. J. L. & Pol'y 289, 292–93 (2002) ("Suppose that a pitching coach on a minor-league baseball team

the en banc Federal Circuit in 2008, any process that "is tied to a particular machine or apparatus" or that "transforms a particular article into a different state or thing" is patentable so long as it is novel and nonobvious.[4] When it was first thrown, the curve ball was novel, was nonobvious in the sense that it revolutionized baseball (so much so that Cummings was inducted into the Hall of Fame for his idea), and could well be considered a process that transformed the ball into a different state.[5] Thus, if a pitch as groundbreaking as the curve ball were developed today, then its inventor probably (or at least plausibly) could obtain a patent.[6]

The problem with this conclusion is that most people would think it absurd to allow a player to patent a pitch, and it is unlikely that baseball leagues would let this happen.[7] Gamesmanship is a part of sports, but there is an ethic among athletes (save for the usual cheaters) that competition should occur on a level playing field based on individual ability.[8] Moreover, allowing one team or player to hold a monopoly on a key aspect of the sport would allow the patentee to dominate in a way that would hurt fan interest.[9] Put another way, there is a strong norm in the sports community that

developed an effective new pitch, the 'split-fingered curveball.' Perhaps the pitch itself would not be eligible for a patent, but the coach should be able to protect his instructional technique." (internal citation omitted)). Indeed, the issue was raised at oral argument in the Federal Circuit's recent en banc concerning process patents. *See* Christopher A. Harkins, *Throwing Judge Bryson's Curveball: A Pro Patent View of Process Claims as Patent-Eligible Subject Matter*, 7 J. Marshall Rev. Intell. Prop. L. 701, 723–24 (2008) (discussing these comments).

4 *In re Bilski*, 545 F.3d 943, 954 (Fed. Cir. 2008) (en banc), *petition for cert. filed sub nom.* Bilski v. Doll (U.S. Jan. 28, 2009) (No. 08–964); *see* 35 U.S.C. §§ 102–103 (2006) (laying out the novelty and nonobviousness requirements). There are some additional elements that must be met for patentability, most notably the enablement rule of 35 U.S.C. § 112, but nonobviousness and novelty are the most important (and most often contested) statutory factors.

5 *See supra* note 2. Gripping and throwing a rock or a bowling ball like a curve ball does not produce the same effect; thus the scope of any patentable "curve ball process" would be limited to a particular device. In this sense, one could say that a curve ball process is also tied to a particular apparatus (the ball) under that prong of the *Bilski* test.

6 *See* Harkins, *supra* note 3, at 734 (concluding that a curve ball could be patentable subject matter under 35 U.S.C. § 101). During the oral argument in *Bilski*, Judge Bryson stated that "[a] curveball is a baseball which has been, you could say, transformed into a baseball that has a great deal of spin on it and is being thrown at a pace which it didn't have at the time it was in the pitcher's hand." *Id.* at 724.

7 A sports league could address this problem by barring players from enforcing patents or by imposing a compulsory license for a nominal fee. *See* Carl A. Kukkonen, III, *Be a Good Sport and Refrain from Using My Patented Putt: Intellectual Property Protection for Sports Related Movements*, 80 J. Pat. & Trademark Off. Soc'y 808, 828 (1998) (making this point). If, however, the inventor was not a member of the league, then the only options would be to ban the pitch entirely or pay the fee demanded for its use as long as the license was open to all players.

8 *See* Dreyfuss, *supra* note 3, at 276 ("Sporting events are interesting because they pit humans against one another to determine whose abilities are superior. For that competition to be true, participants need to compete – literally – on a level playing field. Allowing one athlete to use a move that is denied to others would destroy the essence of the event.").

9 *See* Kukkonen, *supra* note 7, at 828 ("If Dick Fosbury had been granted a patent on his revolutionary style of high jumping, he could have dominated the sport for years."). Fans are not especially interested in seeing games that are fixed by gamblers, and it is doubtful that they would be any more enthusiastic about a contest where patent law gives one side a huge edge.

disseminating and using knowledge are more critical than supplying extra incentives for creativity. Thus, patent law is neither helpful nor necessary for that business.[10]

This chapter argues that patent subject matter eligibility should be interpreted to exclude a process unless an applicant can show that a norm exists within the relevant business community in support of patenting the class of innovations at issue.[11] The curve ball example encapsulates my view that the U.S. Patent and Trademark Office (PTO) and the courts would do better by being norm-followers rather than norm-entrepreneurs with respect to process patents.[12] Because the Federal Circuit's most recent effort to clarify the law governing these patents practically begged the Supreme Court to offer some fresh guidance, the time is ripe for a reconsideration of the entire subject.[13]

There are three benefits that come from replacing the current standard for process patentability, which ignores industry customs unless there is a statutory command to the contrary, with a test that relies on those norms.[14] First, fewer business method patents would be issued under this modified standard, which would be a positive reform because of the poor notice and costly litigation now associated with these process patents.[15] Second, using norms to define the scope of patentability can solve

[10] *See* John R. Thomas, *The Patenting of the Liberal Professions*, 40 B.C. L. Rev. 1139, 1176 (1999) (stating that "traditionally patent-free professions may resist the prospect of extensive appropriation of their techniques").

[11] *See* 35 U.S.C. § 101 (2006) (providing the definition of patentable subject matter). There is considerable evidence that courts take industry practices into account in tailoring the requirements of patent law, *see* Dan L. Burk & Mark A. Lemley, *Policy Levers in Patent Law*, 89 Va. L. Rev. 1575, 1577–79 (2003), but this chapter takes that thought one step further by arguing that patentability itself ought to be conditioned on business norms.

[12] This chapter builds on recent scholarship about how norms interact with intellectual property. *See, e.g.*, Thomas F. Cotter, *A Burkean Perspective on Patent Eligibility*, 22 Berkeley Tech. L.J. 855, 858 (2007) ("[A] Burkean-inspired approach to patent law – one that respects, though it does not worship, tradition and that generally prefers gradual to radical change – suggests that we consider again some traditional, but now dormant, restraints on patentable subject matter that may have embodied a degree of wisdom."); Jennifer E. Rothman, *The Questionable Use of Custom in Intellectual Property*, 93 Va. L. Rev. 1899, 1967–80 (2007) (evaluating when custom should and should not be used for IP).

[13] *See In re Bilski*, 545 F.3d 943, 956 (Fed. Cir. 2008) (en banc) ("[W]e agree that future developments in technology and the sciences may present difficult challenges to the machine-or-transformation test, just as the widespread use of computers and the advent of the Internet has begun to challenge it in the past decade. Thus, we recognize that the Supreme Court may ultimately decide to alter or perhaps even set aside this test to accommodate emerging technologies."), *petition for cert. filed sub nom.* Bilski v. Doll (U.S. Jan. 28, 2009) (No. 08–964).

[14] On the efforts of tax lawyers to get an exemption passed barring tax shelter patents, see Dan L. Burk & Brett H. McDonnell, *Patents, Tax Shelters, and the Firm*, 26 Va. Tax Rev. 981, 1002 (2007) ("[S]ince the interpretation of the patent statute by courts and by the Patent Office has led to the 'let it all in' approach to subject matter, there have been calls for Congress to intervene, at least with regard to tax shelter patents."). The Patent Reform Act of 2007, which was passed by the House of Representatives but died in the Senate, did contain a tax shelter exemption. *See* H.R. Res. 1908, 110th Cong. § 10 (2007).

[15] *See* Bessen & Meurer, *supra* note 1, at 150–55 (presenting empirical evidence that business method patents have much higher litigation rates than other patents); *see id.* at 187 (stating that these patents "often have unclear boundaries and give rise to opportunistic litigation").

the vexing problem that any attempt to craft a formal definition of a business method creates substantial confusion.[16] Third, the current view of process patents empowers those who seek to defect from a community ethic (e.g., the cheating athlete) and imposes an unjustified burden on many industries.[17]

Rather than reject or accept business method patents outright, therefore, this analysis steers a middle course that says they should be patentable subject matter when the relevant community believes that is appropriate. Naturally, this is bound to upset scholars who argue for a business method patent exclusion or those who believe that no restriction on these patents can be applied in a principled way.[18] Likewise, those who seek a clear answer to the question of whether software should be patentable may be disappointed, because that turns on a factual inquiry into the views of communities that are often divided on the issue.[19] Adopting a norm-sensitive approach toward business methods, however, would at least restrict patents' domain to those areas where it can do some good.

Part I explores the background law about business method patents and criticizes the Federal Circuit's view that groups who are not receptive to patents must seek relief from Congress. Part II lays out an alternative model that asks the PTO and the

[16] *See, e.g.*, John R. Allison & Starling D. Hunter, *On the Feasibility of Improving Patent Quality One Technology at a Time: The Case of Business Methods*, 21 Berkeley Tech. L. J. 729, 765 (2006) ("All attempts by courts and by Congress to arrive at a workable definition for business method patents have encountered intractable difficulties.").

[17] For example, a professional association might be forced to incur additional costs to protect its open innovation norm, *see supra* note 7, or might simply see its values undermined by a constant stream of defections. Of course, custom is not immune from public policy challenge. *See* The T.J. Hooper, 60 F.2d 737, 740 (2d Cir. 1932) (L. Hand, J.) (making a classic statement about the connection between custom and negligence). In the case of process patents, however, there is just no benefit that comes from imposing them on an unwilling group.

[18] *Compare* Jay Dratler, Jr., *Does Lord Darcy Yet Live? The Case Against Software and Business-Method Patents*, 43 Santa Clara L. Rev. 823, 833–36 (2003) (arguing that business method patents are contrary to the policies underlying Anglo-American patent law); Michael J. Meurer, *Business Method Patents and Patent Floods*, 8 Wash. U. J. L. & Pol'y 309, 310 (2002) (calling for the reversal of *State Street Bank* and the return of the business method exception); Leo J. Raskind, *The State Street Bank Decision: The Bad Business of Unlimited Patent Protection for Methods of Doing Business*, 10 Fordham Intell. Prop. Media & Ent. L. J. 61, 101 (1999) ("The broad sweep of the *State Street Bank* opinion remains a cause for concern."), *with* Burk & McDonnell, *supra* note 14, at 1001–02 (arguing that any limit on business method patents would be futile because it could be evaded through clever claim drafting); John R. Allison & Emerson H. Tiller, *The Business Method Patent Myth*, 18 Berkeley Tech. L. J. 987, 1021 (2003) ("[T]reating different technologies differently places too great a premium on *ex ante* definitions, such that the definitional scheme will be at least partially defeated because of the significant transaction costs associated with attorney efforts to opt into or out of a definition by carefully tailoring invention descriptions and patent claims.").

[19] *See* Bessen & Meurer, *supra* note 1, at 244 ("The empirical evidence makes us quite sure that *some* change is needed [for software patents]; however, we are uncertain what change is best."); Gerard N. Magliocca, *Blackberries and Barnyards: Patent Trolls and the Perils of Innovation*, 82 Notre Dame L. Rev. 1809, 1811–13 (2007) (comparing modern patent trolls to nineteenth-century patent sharks and suggesting the abolition of software and business method patents); *infra* text accompanying notes 97–102.

courts to conclude that an "ordinary person skilled in the art" would view the claim as falling within a class of patentable subject matter before granting an application for a process patent.

I. PATENTS WHETHER YOU LIKE THEM OR NOT

This part examines the statutory text and case law related to business method patents in light of the compelling arguments made by advocates for and against these patents.[20] Unfortunately, a careful review of the relevant sources yields almost no helpful guidance. As a result, the discussion turns to policy considerations and argues that the current statutory interpretation, which holds that most business processes are patentable unless Congress makes an exception, hurts innovation and provides the wrong incentives for many industries.[21] The en banc opinion of the Federal Circuit in *In re Bilski*[22] nibbled around the edges of this problem, but did not resolve the matter.[*]

A. *Wrestling with Indeterminacy*

The point of departure is the text of 35 U.S.C. § 101, which defines patentable subject matter and was last changed in 1952: "Whoever invents or discovers a new and useful process, machine, manufacture, or composition of matter or any new and useful improvement thereof may obtain a patent. . . ."[23] Because the statute states that "a new and useful process" and "any new and useful improvement" are patentable, the

[20] My analysis focuses on business methods because these are the process patents that receive the most scrutiny. The discussion in the text, however, does not define a business method, other than to say that it is a process rather than a machine, a manufacture, or a composition of matter. *See* 35 U.S.C. § 101 (laying out these categories of patentable subject matter). In part, this is because the term "business method" cannot really be defined with any precision. *See infra* text accompanying notes 52–57. Moreover, none of the cases or statutes about business method patentability defines the term. This may seem illogical – how can one assess if something is patentable without knowing what that something is? Patent law, unfortunately, is riddled with these sorts of inconsistencies.

[21] The policy discussion is premised on the principle that patents serve a utilitarian purpose and are supposed to promote innovation. *See* U.S. Const., art. I., § 8, cl. 8 (giving Congress the power "to promote the Progress of Science and useful arts, by securing for limited Times to Authors and Inventors the exclusive Right to their respective Writings and Discoveries").

[22] 545 F.3d 943 (Fed. Cir. 2008) (en banc), *petition for cert. filed sub nom.* Bilski v. Doll (U.S. Jan. 28, 2009) (No. 08–964).

[*] Editors' Note: This chapter was written prior to the Supreme Court's decision in *Bilski* v. *Kappos*, which affirmed the Federal Circuit's decision in *In re Bilski*, but modified its rationale. 561 U.S. ___, 130 S. Ct. 3218 (2010). Contrary to the Federal Circuit, the Court held that the machine-or-transformation test was not the sole test for determining the patent eligibility of a process. Rather, that test was only "a useful and important clue . . . for determining whether some claimed inventions are processes under § 101." *Bilski*, 130 S. Ct. at 3227.

[23] 35 U.S.C. § 101 (2006); *see* Diamond v. Diehr, 450 U.S. 175, 182 (1981) (stating that in 1952 Congress revised this section by replacing the word "art" with the word "process").

text does not appear to contemplate a categorical exception for so-called business methods.[24] This reading is buttressed by a statement in the legislative history of the 1952 Patent Act, which is frequently quoted by proponents of broad patentability – that § 101 was intended to "include anything under the sun that is made by man."[25]

Supporters of a business method exception have a robust response to these points, which is that when § 101 was last amended in 1952, and for decades thereafter, it was considered hornbook law that business methods were not patentable.[26] Even Judge Giles Rich, who wrote the crucial Federal Circuit opinion in *State Street Bank & Trust Co.* v. *Signature Financial Group, Inc.*[27] declaring that the business method exception never existed, relied on the exception in an earlier law review

[24] *See* Kevin Emerson Collins, *Claims to Interpretation Qua Information and a Structural Theory of Section* 101, 4 I/S: J. L. & POL'Y FOR INFO SOC'Y 11, 15 (2008) ("[A] plain-meaning textualist . . . might merely note that there is little to no statutory support for the exclusions as Section 101 merely states that 'any new or useful process, machine, manufacture, or composition of matter' is a patentable invention."); *see also Bilski*, 545 F.3d at 1012 (Rader, J., dissenting) ("The language of §101 conveys no implication that the Act extends patent protection to some subcategories of processes but not others. It does not mean 'some' or even 'most,' but all."). The courts do hold that "laws of nature, natural phenomena, and abstract ideas" are ineligible for patents, *id.* at *3, but those exclusions can be explained on the grounds that they are discovered, rather than invented, or are not useful within the meaning of the statute.

[25] Diamond v. Chakrabarty, 447 U.S. 303, 309 (1980) (quoting S. Rep. No. 1979, 82d Cong., 2d Sess., 5 (1952); H.R. Rep. No. 1923, 82d Cong., 2d Sess., 6 (1952); U.S. Code Cong. & Admin. News 1952, pp. 2394, 2399); *compare* State St. Bank & Trust Co. v. Signature Fin. Group, Inc., 149 F.3d 1368, 1373 (Fed. Cir. 1998) (citing this line for the proposition that "it is improper to read limitations into § 101 on the subject matter that may be patented where the legislative history indicates that Congress clearly did not intend such limitations"), *with* BESSEN & MEURER, *supra* note 1, at 27 ("[W]e are troubled by the expansionist view of the courts that 'everything under the sun made by man' should be patentable, including software, business methods, and even mental correlations. . . . We are quite sure that the patent system needs to recognize the limits of its grasp, even if we are not sure of the best way to implement those limits.").

Some of the opinions in *Bilski* challenged the broad interpretation of the legislative history in the 1952 Act. For instance, Judge Dyk contended that the phrase "made by man" referred only to manufactures. *See Bilski*, 545 F.3d at 976 (Dyk, J., concurring). Likewise, Judge Mayer pointed out that the "anything under the sun" language was qualified in the report from Congress. *See id.* at 1000 (Mayer, J., dissenting) (noting that the report also said an invention "is not necessarily patentable under § 101 unless the conditions of the title are fulfilled").

[26] *See In re* Patton, 127 F.2d 324, 327–28 (C.C.P.A. 1942) ("[I]t is sufficient to say that a system of transacting business, apart from the means of carrying it out, is not . . . patentable subject matter."); Hotel Sec. Checking Co. v. Lorraine Co., 160 F. 467, 469 (2d Cir. 1908) ("A system of transacting business disconnected from the means of carrying out the system is not . . . an art. Advice is not patentable."); Robert A. Kreiss, *Patent Protection for Computer Programs and Mathematical Algorithms: The Constitutional Limitations on Patentable Subject Matter*, 29 N.M. L. REV. 31, 85 (1999) (noting "the repeated comments made by courts, commentators, and the PTO over the years to the effect that business methods are not patentable subject matter"); Morton C. Jacobs, Note, *The Patentability of Printed Matter: Critique and Proposal*, 18 GEO. WASH. L. REV. 475, 476 (1950) (describing "the longstanding rule that abstractions, mental theories or business methods are not patentable subject matter" (footnote omitted)).

[27] 49 F.3d 1368 (Fed. Cir. 1998).

article.[28] This consensus began to unravel in 1980, when, in a decision involving genetically engineered bacteria, the Supreme Court quoted the "anything under the sun" language for the first time and set forth a strong presumption of patentability.[29] One year later, the Court relied on that presumption to hold that a process for curing synthetic rubber, in which software was the crucial component, was patentable – a decision that was the chief authority for the Federal Circuit cases during the 1990s that expanded patentable subject matter.[30] Nevertheless, a reasonable argument can be made that § 101 was enacted against the background assumption that business methods were not patentable and that the proper view of the statute was the one taken from the 1950s until the 1990s.[31]

[28] *See* Giles S. Rich, *Principles of Patentability*, 28 Geo. Wash. L. Rev. 393, 393–94 (1960) (stating that business methods were not patentable); *see also State Street Bank*, 149 F.3d at 1375 ("Since the 1952 Patent Act, business methods have been, and should have been, subject to the same legal requirements for patentability as applied to any other process or method."); Meurer, *supra* note 18, at 320 n.70 ("Although I think his treatment of the cases is reasonable, Judge Rich evades the longstanding PTO rule against patents on business methods and the consensus among commentators, including himself at an earlier date, that there was a business method exception.").

Although there are some pre-1952 patents that arguably did involve business methods, they do not establish that the exclusion of this category never existed. *Compare Bilski*, 545 F.3d at 974 (Dyk, J., concurring) (distinguishing these patents on various grounds), *with id.* at 989–90 (Newman, J., dissenting) (concluding from similar sources that business method patents were never excluded).

[29] *See Chakrabarty*, 447 U.S. at 309; Collins, *supra* note 24, at 15 (noting "the establishment of a default in favor of patentability in *Diamond v. Chakrabarty*").

[30] *See* Diamond v. Diehr, 450 U.S. 175, 184–85 (1981) (stating that "the fact that in several steps of the process a mathematical equation and a programmed digital computer are used" did not render the process unpatentable); *State Street Bank*, 149 F.3d at 1374 (reasoning that after *Diehr* "the mere fact that a claimed invention involves inputting numbers, calculating numbers, outputting numbers, and storing numbers, in and of itself, would not render it nonstatutory subject matter"); AT&T, 172 F.3d at 1356–57 (relying on an extended analysis of *Diehr* to validate a patent on a billing system for phone calls); Burk & McDonnell, *supra* note 14, at 984 ("[T]he acceptance of software within patentable subject matter undermined the prohibition on which the preclusion of business methods was also grounded.").

Diehr's effort to distinguish the Court's precedents rejecting software patents, especially *Parker* v. *Flook*, was unpersuasive and is widely criticized. *Compare Diehr*, 450 U.S. at 191–92 & n.14 (arguing that "insignificant postsolution activity will not transform an unpatentable principle into a patentable process" and that the software in *Flook* involved insignificant activity during a catalytic conversion process), *with id.* at 1065 (Stevens, J., dissenting) (arguing that *Flook* "made it clear that an improved method of calculation, even when employed as part of a physical process, is not patentable subject matter under § 101"); *id.* at 1071 ("[T]he postsolution activity described in the *Flook* application was no less significant than the automatic opening of the curing mold in this case."); *see also* Julie E. Cohen & Mark A. Lemley, *Patent Scope and Innovation in the Software Industry*, 89 Cal. L. Rev. 1, 9 (2001) ("*Diehr* seems difficult to distinguish from *Flook*."); Kevin Emerson Collins, *Propertizing Thought*, 60 S.M.U. L. Rev. 317, 349 (2007) ("*Flook* and *Diehr* are difficult to reconcile."). Indeed, the incoherence of the Supreme Court's cases on process patents helps explain why the Federal Circuit had such a hard time making sense of them in *Bilski*. *See infra* note 72.

[31] The Supreme Court has not addressed § 101 since *Diehr* and thus has expressed no view on the evolution of software and business method patents since then. *See* Collins, *supra* note 30, at 349–50 ("In large part because *Diehr* came after *Flook*, a default presumption of a method being applied rather than abstract has evolved over the last twenty-five years in the Federal Circuit. . . . ").

Not so fast, a supporter of business method patents would insist. Although there were numerous cases before and after the 1952 Act that said business methods were unpatentable, none of those decisions actually held that this was so.[32] In each case, the patent application was rejected on other grounds (e.g., obviousness or lack of novelty).[33] Accordingly, the statements about business method patentability were dicta and did not put a gloss on the sweeping language of § 101.[34] One response to this point, however, is that the absence of a holding on the issue is irrelevant because it "may simply reflect a widespread, unchallenged understanding that patentable subject matter did not extend so far."[35] An even more persuasive answer is that the patent bar clearly thought that the Federal Circuit changed the law in the 1990s, as reflected both by statements at the time and by the sharp increase in self-styled business method patent applications that followed the *State Street* decision.[36] That reaction is hard to reconcile with the view that the lack of holdings barring these patents was especially meaningful.[37]

Once again, some of the opinions in *Bilski* made this point about the proper construction of § 101. *See Bilski*, 545 F.3d at 974 (Dyk, J., concurring) (arguing that patents were not granted before 1952 "on methods of organizing human activity not involving manufactures, machines or the creation of compositions of matter"); *id.* at 999 (Mayer, J., dissenting) ("Because there is nothing in the language of the 1952 Act, or its legislative history, to indicate that Congress intended to modify the rule against patenting business methods, we must presume that no change in the rule was intended.").

32 *See State Street Bank*, 149 F.3d at 1375 ("The business method exception has never been invoked by this court, or the CCPA, to deem an invention unpatentable."); Michael L. Fuelling, *Manufacturing, Selling and Accounting: Patenting Business Methods*, 76 J. PAT. & TRADEMARK OFF. SOC'Y 471, 471–72 (1994) (noting that some commentators have been pointing this out since the 1930s).

33 *Compare* Hotel Sec. Checking Co. v. Lorraine Co., 160 F. 467, 469 (2d Cir. 1908) ("A system of transacting business disconnected from the means of carrying out the system is not, within the most liberal interpretation of the term, an art. Advice is not patentable."), *with id.* at 471 ("Admitting, arguendo, that a system such as Hicks describes is patentable, if absolutely novel, we are of the opinion that the improvements of Hicks over the system disclosed in the Smith patent are such as would occur to anyone conversant with the business."); *see also* Jacobs, *supra* note 26, at 475 & n.1 (stating that the case law "held that abstract ideas such as business methods and systems of knowledge were nonpatentable subject matter" but then adding that "[e]ach of these cases held that the printed arrangement itself lacked invention").

34 *See State Street Bank*, 149 F.3d at 1375 ("Application of this particular exception has always been preceded by a ruling based on some clearer concept of Title 35 or, more commonly, application of the abstract idea exception based on finding a mathematical formula.").

35 Cotter, *supra* note 12, at 877.

36 *See* Allison & Hunter, *supra* note 16, at 730–31 (stating that *State Street Bank* "was quickly followed by a dramatic increase in the number of applications for and grants of business method patents"); Meurer, *supra* note 18, at 313 ("The *State Street Bank* decision set off a flood of e-commerce patents."); Raskind, *supra* note 18, at 61 ("The Federal Circuit's recent endorsement of patent protection for methods of doing business marks so sweeping a departure from precedent as to invite a search for its justification."); *see also Bilski*, 545 F.3d at 1004 (Mayer, J., dissenting) (commenting that business method patent applications increased more than tenfold after *State Street* was decided).

37 For example, *State Street* noted that prior to 1996 the Manual of Patent Examining Procedures (used as guidance within the PTO) stated that "[t]hough seemingly within the category of process or method, a method of doing business can be rejected as not being within the statutory classes." *State Street Bank*, 149 F.3d at 1377 (quoting § 706.03 (a)); *see* Meurer, *supra* note 18, at 320 n.70 ("Defenders of

In sum, the legal authorities that apply to business method patents are inconclusive.[38] Both proponents and detractors of the current standard can marshal formidable arguments for their points of view. The discussion therefore turns to the policy implications of allowing patents on business processes.

B. A *Policy Stalemate*

Although the Federal Circuit's cases largely ignore the policy questions raised by expanding patentable subject matter, there is no shortage of opinions about that topic in the law reviews. Once again, both sides make a persuasive case about the value (or lack thereof) of business method patents and about the choice between excluding them from patentability and retaining the default rule that they are patentable. Although this may just mean that lawmakers face a tough decision on this issue, perhaps the problem is with the premise that an all-or nothing solution is the only option.

In the immediate aftermath of the liberalization of business method patentability, critics who were trying to gauge its impact offered several policy objections. First, they argued that allowing such patents would harm innovation by removing valuable ideas from the public domain; this claim was backed up by a parade of horribles (not unlike the curve ball example) asking whether industry would have benefited from the patenting of the assembly line, just-in-time inventory, or the hub-and-spoke airline system.[39] Second, they said that enlarging the universe of patentable processes would overwhelm the PTO in a "patent flood" and lead to the issuance of too many low-quality patents that produce nothing but nuisance litigation.[40] Third,

State Street admit this result, but blandly assert that *State Street* made practitioners aware of a class of inventions they previously overlooked.").

38 Following the decision in *State Street Bank*, Congress did enact a law that provided a limited defense to infringement actions involving a business method patent (without defining a business method). *See* First Inventor Defense Act of 1999, Pub. L. No. 106–113, 113 Stat. 1536 (codified at 35 U.S.C. § 273 (2006)) (providing an affirmative defense to patent infringement actions if the defendant had used a business method at least one year before the application was filed). It is wrong to say, however, that this should be treated as an endorsement of *State Street Bank*, especially because this provision remains untested in the courts. *See* Burk & McDonnell, *supra* note 14, at 1003 (stating that this provision was not "well-drafted or considered . . . is opaque and nearly incomprehensible, and . . . remain[s] obscure and largely unnoticed"); *see also* Allison & Hunter, *supra* note 16, at 766 (stating that that there were no reported cases on the First Inventor Defense Act as of 2006).

39 *See* Dreyfuss, *supra* note 3, at 264 ("Think how the airline industry might now be structured if the first company to offer frequent flyer miles had enjoyed the sole right to award them or how differently mergers and acquisitions would be financed . . . if the use of junk bonds had been protected by a patent."); Meurer, *supra* note 18, at 322 ("[B]asic business method innovations like the distribution system at Sears, the multi-divisional structure of the firm, and the Fed-Ex hub-and-spoke air delivery system are now likely to be patentable subject matter."); Raskind, *supra* note 18, at 64–65 ("Henry Ford's assembly line method of organizing production might also be characterized as a method of doing the business of automobile production.").

40 *See* Dreyfuss, *supra* note 3, at 267–68 ("The first problem is one that concerns many observers of the patent system. It is the frequency with which the Patent Office issues patents on shockingly mundane

they maintained that business method patents were unnecessary, because ordinary market competition and the first-mover advantage provided sufficient incentives for creativity in this area.[41]

The rebuttal to these initial criticisms has been equally forceful and convincing. Michael Abramowicz and John F. Duffy, for example, support the concept of business method patents with the rationale that firms need incentives for "market experimentation" when first-mover or branding advantages prove insufficient.[42] Other scholars argue that the novelty and nonobviousness requirements are more than able to screen out worthless patents, and they support that assertion with empirical research showing that business method patents are no lower in quality than other types of patents.[43] Finally, many people say that the definition of a business method is so fuzzy that any attempt to bar its patentability can be evaded with skillful claim

business inventions."); Robert P. Merges, *One Hundred Years of Solicitude: Intellectual Property Law, 1900–2000*, 88 CAL. L. REV. 2187, 2232 (2000) ("[T]he increased volume of patent applications stemming from this newly patentable subject matter has pushed the patent system into crisis."); Meurer, *supra* note 18, at 309–10 ("The decline of the business method exception to patentability will increase the frequency of patent floods.... Patent floods strain the resources of the U.S. Patent and Trademark Office (PTO) and adversely affect the quality of issued patents.").

41 *See* Dreyfuss, *supra* note 3, at 275 ("[N]either the free-rider nor the disclosure rationale justifies business method patents. Businesses are largely practiced in public. Accordingly, there is little need to especially encourage disclosure. Business methods are also hard to free ride on. They depend in strong ways on the social structure within the firms utilizing them – on compensation schemes, lines of reporting, supervising policies, and other business factors."); Raskind, *supra* note 18, at 92 ("Nowhere in the substantial literature on innovation is there a statement that the United States economy suffers from a lack of innovation in methods of doing business."); *see also* In re Bilski, 545 F.3d 943, 1005 (Fed Cir. 2008) (en banc) (Mayer, J., dissenting), *petition for cert. filed sub nom.* Bilski v. Doll (U.S. Jan. 28, 2009) (No. 08–964) ("Business innovations, by their very nature, provide a competitive advantage and thus generate their own incentives.").

42 *See* Michael Abramowicz & John F. Duffy, *Intellectual Property for Market Experimentation*, 83 N.Y.U. L. REV. 337, 340 (2008) ("[L]ate-entering competitors obtain two important second-mover advantages against early market experimenters. First, they do not have to bear the cost of investing in market development. Second, they can copy the first experimenter's market success and avoid repeating its failures."); *id.* at 344 (explaining that novel and nonobvious business method methods can involve "those cases where the market success is truly doubtful"). *But see* Dratler, *supra* note 18, at 845–47 (arguing that patent protection is appropriate only when there is a risk that the invention will fail to function at all, not when it will merely fail to succeed in the marketplace).

To be fair, Abramowicz and Duffy do not endorse all business method patents or all of the Federal Circuit's doctrines. *See* Abramowicz & Duffy, *supra*, at 398–99 ("Nor do we believe that business method patents and the watering down of the obviousness standard are necessarily positive developments. To the contrary, we believe these developments could lead to dramatically inefficient results unless other aspects of patent law are also modified.").

43 *See* John R. Allison & Emerson H. Tiller, *The Business Method Patent Myth*, 18 BERKELEY TECH. L. J. 987, 1004 (2003) ("Overall, our data demonstrate that Internet business method patents were no worse than patents in general during the late 1990s. Indeed, our empirical evidence suggests that they may have been better than average."); Collins, *supra* note 24, at 15 ("A more nuanced variant casts Section 101 as the vestigial appendix of patent doctrine.... [T]oday it is no longer necessary because any claim that is unpatentable under the patentable subject matter doctrine is also invalid under one of the now-refined invalidity doctrines."). *But see* BESSEN & MEURER, *supra* note 1, at 188 (criticizing Allison & Tiller's definition of patent quality). Allison and Tiller defined business method patents

drafting; thus, eliminating the exception was the correct choice because it reduced transaction costs for patents that would issue no matter what substantive test was used.[44]

Sifted through a decade of experience with business method patents, it is fair to say that two policy arguments – one pro and one con – retain their vitality and must be confronted. Contrary to the hopes of their boosters, business method patents do perform poorly as compared to other patents in the sense that they are litigated far more often.[45] A recent study by James Bessen and Michael J. Meurer establishes that software and business method patents account for nearly 40% of the total cost of patent litigation and that this proportion is increasing.[46] Furthermore, their data show that the patent system (outside of chemicals and drugs) is now providing a net disincentive for innovation – a result that is largely attributed to software and business method patents.[47] The novelty and nonobviousness gatekeepers, in other words, are preventing neither a patent flood nor the costly nuisance lawsuits that critics said would follow from the Federal Circuit's decisions.[48]

by relying on the PTO's classification of the applications, which is no more reliable than any other method but is better than nothing.

44 *See* Allison & Hunter, *supra* note 16, at 736 ("Carving out business method patent applications for harsher treatment would ultimately prove largely futile and possibly even counterproductive – futile because skilled patent attorneys can often draft applications so as to opt out of a predefined category, and counterproductive because of the increased transaction costs associated with tortuous drafting."); *see also* Cohen & Lemley, *supra* note 30, at 9 (describing "the doctrine of the magic words" that prevailed during the 1980s and early 1990s, under which "software was patentable subject matter, but only if the applicant recited the magic words and pretended that she was patenting something else").

45 *See* Bessen & Meurer, *supra* note 1, at 22 ("Critically, software patents *do* seem to exhibit some marked differences from other patents when it comes to litigation costs. Software patents are more than twice as likely to be litigated as other patents; patents on methods of doing business, which are largely software patents, are nearly *seven* times more likely to be litigated."). A similar pattern unfolded when the Patent Office expanded the subject matter covered by design patents in the late nineteenth century – an ill-fated experiment that led to another patent flood and a sharp increase in nuisance litigation. *See* Magliocca, *supra* note 19, at 1819–25 (describing this episode).

46 *See* Bessen & Meurer, *supra* note 1, at 22.; *see also id.* at 192–93 (presenting some data on this growing problem and stating that "software and business-method patents are different from most other patents, both in their litigation rates and frequency of claim-construction problems"). In this respect, Judge Newman's dissent in *Bilski* was very disappointing. Although her vigorous defense of process patents made many valid points, she also served up a rainbows-and-lollipops story that refused to acknowledge that these patents were presenting any problems. At one point, she did mention some of this criticism, but then quickly added that "this problem seems to be remedied." *See Bilski*, 545 F.3d at 997 (Newman, J., dissenting). That is nothing more than wishful thinking.

47 *See id.* at 144 ("By the late 1990s the risk of patent litigation for public firms outside of the chemical and pharmaceutical industries exceeded the profits derived from patents. This means that patents likely provided a net *dis*incentive for innovation for the firms who fund the lion's share of industrial R&D; this is, patents tax R&D."); *cf. Bilski*, 545 F.3d at 1004 (Mayer, J., dissenting) (providing a summary of absurd process patents granted by the PTO since *State Street Bank*).

48 Perhaps the Supreme Court's recent decision emphasizing the importance of a rigorous obviousness inquiry will help. *See* KSR Int'l Co. v. Teleflex, Inc., 127 S. Ct. 1727, 1741 (2007) (rejecting the Federal Circuit's lax "teaching, suggestion, or motivation" test for obviousness). That seems unlikely,

What makes business method patents so litigation prone is their abstract quality, which provides weak notice for firms and increases the probability of inadvertent infringement.[49] As Bessen and Meurer observe, "it is well-known among computer scientists that software technologies (algorithms, system structures) can be represented in many different ways, and . . . [t]his means that the technology claimed in a patent can be difficult to distinguish from alternatives. . . ."[50] The same holds true for most business methods, which often incorporate software or cover processes dealing with information management (e.g., financial instruments, negotiation tactics, styles of legal argument) that are subjective – an art rather than a science – and far less precise than a machine or a drug that can be described in concrete terms.[51] To the extent that firms simply do not know where the boundaries of these patents are, they are more likely to miss them in a due diligence search and infringe.[52]

Although all of this suggests that business method patents pose a threat to innovation, the very indefiniteness that makes these patents problematic also impedes every proposal for reform. There is still no definition of a business method in federal law, and the argument that none can be written that would make sense has merit.[53] One

however, because of the abstract nature of business methods and because it is not clear that *KSR* will change how the PTO operates. *Cf.* Meurer, *supra* note 18, at 334 n.132 (rejecting the view that tradeoffs involved in judging business method patents "should be implemented on a case-by-case basis via the nonobviousness standard of § 103. . . . I would respond by claiming that cost savings justify exclusion of business methods [under] § 101 because a *proper* nonobviousness analysis (based on the economic trade-off) would deny patents to most business method patent inventions"). Similarly, Judge Newman's argument in *Bilski* that § 112's requirement that claims must be made with particularity is an adequate gatekeeper is not borne out by the experience of the last decade. *See Bilski*, 545 F.3d at 996 (Newman, J., dissenting) (discussing the relevance of § 112).

49 *See* Bessen & Meurer, *supra* note 1, at 23 ("[S]oftware patents are much more likely than other patents to have their claim construction reviewed on appeal – an implicit indication that parties to lawsuits have fundamental uncertainty over the boundaries of these patents."); Magliocca, *supra* note 19, at 1821–22 (pointing out that the same kind of boundary confusion arose in the nineteenth century when the Patent Office allowed design patents to issue on common functional items such as farm tools).

50 Bessen & Meurer, *supra* note 1, at 23.

51 *See id.* at 198 (noting that courts have traditionally resisted patents on "principles of manufacture" for this reason and giving as an example Justice Story's rejection of a patent on "the art of cutting ice by means of any power, other than human power").

52 *See* Magliocca, *supra* note 19, at 1815 (explaining how this can lead to substantial sunk costs that an opportunistic litigant can exploit).

53 *See, e.g.*, Fuelling, *supra* note 32, at 480 (stating that "the decisional law never defines the term 'method of doing business'"). One bill introduced, but never passed, in the House of Representatives tried to define a business method as "(1) a method of – (A) administering, managing, or otherwise operating an enterprise or organization, including a technique used in doing or conducting business; or (B) processing financial data; (2) any technique used in athletics, instruction, or personal skills; and (3) any computer-assisted implementation of a method described in paragraph (1) or a technique described in paragraph (2)"). Business Method Patent Improvement Act of 2000, H.R. 5364, 106th Cong. (2000).

reason for this is that the definition is circular, because a business method is just a method used to conduct business.[54] Put another way, any process within an industry could be described as that industry's method of doing business. For example, some wonder if "a chemical refining process would be a business method for a firm in the business of refining petroleum products. Although probably not within the contemplation of most people who have given thought to business methods, why would the refining process not be included within such a definition?"[55] The answer, of course, is that chemical refining processes are not doing harm to the patent system and are supported by decades of prior art – neither of which can be said about business method and software patents.[56] Finding a formula that can capture that insight, however, is proving so elusive that even the most ardent critics of the Federal Circuit hesitate when it comes to the question of what should be done.[57]

One other facet of the process patent issue deserves some attention, and that is how the expansion of patentable subject matter affects the norms within particular business and professional groups. Some of the most exciting intellectual property research being done today focuses on how communities that are excluded from effective patent or copyright protection, such as chefs, magicians, and stand-up comedians, develop informal practices that govern ownership of and access to their creative material.[58] Although this could be viewed as just making the best of a bad situation, there is every reason to think that these customs (as in the curve ball example) actually encourage more sharing of knowledge and lower transaction costs

[54] *See* Allison & Hunter, *supra* note 16, at 767 (emphasizing this point). Dissenting in *Bilski*, Judge Mayer countered that a technological arts standard should be used to distinguish patentable subject matter from business methods. He said "a claimed process is technological to the extent it applies laws of nature to new ends," whereas "a process is non-technological where its inventive concept is the application of principles drawn not from the natural sciences but from disciplines such as business, law, sociology, or psychology." In re Bilski, 545 F.3d 943, 1009–10 (Fed. Cir. 2008) (en banc) (Mayer, J., dissenting), *petition for cert. filed sub nom.* Bilski v. Doll (U.S. Jan. 28, 2009) (No. 08–964). But software does not fit into this framework unless Judge Mayer is suggesting that software should not be patentable.

[55] Allison & Hunter, *supra* note 16, at 1019 n.104. This problem becomes even more complicated if software is included in the chemical process, which was the situation that the Court addressed in *Diehr*. *See supra* text accompanying note 30.

[56] *See* Bessen & Meurer, *supra* note 1, at 153 (stating that chemical patents are valuable in part because they are not frequently litigated); *id.* at 189 ("Chemical processes have always been patentable and have never been controversial in the United States.").

[57] *See supra* text accompanying note 1.

[58] *See* Emmanuelle Fauchart & Eric Von Hippel, *Norms-Based Intellectual Property Systems: The Case of French Chefs*, *available at* http://ssrn.com/abstract=881781 (last vistited Mar. 21, 2011); Jacob Loshin, *Secrets Revealed How Magicians Protect Intellectual Property Without Law*, *available at* http://ssrn.com/abstract=1005564 (last visited Mar. 21, 2011); Dotan Oliar & Christopher Sprigman, *There's No Free Laughs (anymore): The Emergence of Intellectual Property Norms and the Transformation of Stand-Up Comedy*, 94 Va. L. Rev. 1787 (2008); *see also* Kal Raustiala & Christopher Sprigman, *The Piracy Paradox: Innovation and Intellectual Property in Fashion Design*, 92 Va. L. Rev. 1687, 1769–75 (2006) (listing other examples such as fireworks, perfume, tattoos, and hairstyles).

in a way that makes the trade as a whole better off.[59] The chief threat to this sort of arrangement comes from defectors who can gain from violating these norms (e.g., copying without attribution) and hence must be reined in by some sort of informal sanctions lest the system collapse.[60]

Seen in this context, introducing patents into these communities only undermines their indigenous customs and gives more leverage to defectors.[61] It is not breaking news to say that law shapes norms, so when the doctrine holds that a business process can be owned outright and does not need to be shared, that change is bound to weaken any contrary cooperative practices.[62] For instance, when Congress enacted the Bayh-Dole Act to encourage the patenting of inventions in universities, observers noted that it actually eroded the prior ethos that professors would share their research freely with others.[63] The availability of patents also puts a potent weapon in the hands of any would-be defectors. Although they could still face reputational sanctions if they choose to apply for a patent rather than make their discoveries freely available, those disciplinary measures may not be enough if the patent is truly valuable. As a result, patents not only undermine sharing norms by making ownership more acceptable but they also limit the ability of professions to maintain their integrity against cheaters from inside and outside their ranks.[64]

Under the current "opt-out" posture taken by the Federal Circuit, if the American Medical Association wanted to prevent someone like Michael Debakey from patenting the heart bypass surgery procedure, its only hope would be to ask Congress

59 *See supra* text accompanying notes 7–9; Rothman, *supra* note 12, at 1924 ("[W]here parties either think that formal IP law has little or no role, or where legal enforcement is expressly disfavored by the community . . . the practices and norms that develop often reflect community members' preferred distribution of rights in intangible goods."); Thomas, *supra* note 10, at 1176 ("[T]he ability of a profession to serve the public good may also be affected by patenting, which could alter the willingness of professionals to disseminate and put into practice new learning.").

60 A familiar (perhaps all-too-familiar) example of this would be the way that federal appellate judges hire clerks. If everyone involved in that process sticks to a common understanding about a timeframe for receiving applications and conducting interviews, then the process as a whole works better. There will always be an incentive, however, for some judges to jump the gun. Whether shaming the renegades actually works is a question I shall not attempt to answer.

61 This assumes that the relevant profession is opposed to patents. If instead a group wants patent protection because it thinks that would lead to a better set of outcomes, then the analysis in the text does not apply.

62 The relatively high cost of obtaining a patent may protect a community from norm erosion by making it impractical for anyone to obtain one. Even if joke-telling were deemed a business method for a stand-up comic, it is hard to believe that any comic would bother spending the necessary time and money to get a patent.

63 *See, e.g.*, Arti Rai, *Regulating Scientific Research: Intellectual Property Rights and the Norms of Science*, 94 Nw. U. L. Rev. 77, 109 (1999) ("As might be predicted by law-and-norms theory . . . universities and individual researchers began to respond to the financial incentives of Bayh-Dole by rejecting communalism and increasing efforts to seek patents.").

64 A community could solve this problem by requiring its members to patent their work under something like the "Creative Commons" copyright for open-source software. *See* Rothman, *supra* note 12, at 1928. The shorter time horizon of a patent, however, might make this solution unworkable.

for a statutory exemption. With respect to surgical and medical patents, Congress did, in fact, grant such an exemption.[65] But for the vast majority of professional groups that reject patents, seeking a congressional exemption is no remedy at all because of the prohibitive costs of lobbying.[66] Besides, it is not at all clear that those who care about the patent system would want Congress involved in these issues. Dan Burk and Brett H. McDonnell point out that on "the rare occasion when legislative response has occurred, there is usually reason to wish that it hadn't. The previous history of remedial legislation regarding patentable subject matter is not encouraging."[67] What these professions really need is an "opt-in" system with a presumption against patentability unless they want to participate in the patent system. The problem, of course, is that business methods must be defined for that solution to work.

Accordingly, the policy debate over business method patents, like the discussion over the positive legal materials governing them, is indeterminate. On the one hand, there is considerable proof that the interpretation adopted by the Federal Circuit is a harmful tax on innovation. On the other hand, the definitional challenge makes it very tricky to replace the current test with one that will abolish the harmful patents without taking out the valuable ones.[68]

C. *The Federal Circuit's Opinion in* Bilski

In response to all of this criticism about business method patents, the Federal Circuit went en banc in 2008 and revisited its precedents.[69] Although the court reaffirmed

65 *See* Omnibus Consolidated Appropriations Act, 1997, Limitation on Patent Infringements Relating to a Medical Practitioner's Performance of a Medical Activity, Pub. L. No. 104–208, 110 Stat. 3009, § 616 (codified as amended at 35 U.S.C. § 287(c) (2006)) (barring infringement remedies and thereby effectively nullifying medical and surgical procedure patents); Thomas, *supra* note 10, at 1176 (stating that this action came after "condemnation of patents on methods of medical treatment by the American Medical Association House of Delegates"). *But cf.* Allison & Hunter, *supra* note 17, at 1020 ("Even if one believes that it was socially optimal to remove the threat of an infringement action so as to give physicians the freedom to use any procedure they choose, it is unlikely that a reasonable estimate of costs and benefits would lead to the same conclusion for business methods.").

66 *See* Thomas, *supra* note 10, at 1177 ("Whether business and other professionals will, like physicians, possess the wherewithal to persuade Congress to create particularized patent-free spheres of activity remains to be seen. Few occupations are as well-organized, imbued with a sense of profession and capable of employing the rhetoric of public service as the practice of medicine.").

67 Burk & McDonnell, *supra* note 14, at 1003.

68 *See* Dratler, *supra* note 18, at 879 ("The Federal Circuit's ultimate solution – virtually abandoning judgment and rejecting all categorical subject-matter limitations for computer programs entirely – can be understood primarily as a desperate search for certainty in an uncertain world.").

69 *See* In re Bilski, 545 F.3d 943, 1010 (Fed. Cir. 2008) (en banc) (Mayer, J., dissenting) ("We took this case en banc in a long-overdue effort to resolve primal questions on the metes and bounds of statutory subject matter. The patent system has run amok, and the USPTO, as well as the larger patent community, has actively sought guidance from this court in making sense of our § 101 jurisprudence."), *petition for cert. filed sub nom.* Bilski v. Doll (U.S. Jan. 28, 2009) (No. 08–964).

that business methods are patentable, its opinion in *Bilski* revised the test for assessing these process patents.[70] Ever since *State Street Bank* was issued in 1998, any process that yielded a "useful, concrete, tangible result" was deemed patentable under § 101.[71] But following an analysis of the most recent Supreme Court cases on the issue (all of which were more than twenty-five years old), *Bilski* held that this standard should be replaced by a machine-or-transformation test that asks whether a process "is tied to a particular machine or apparatus" or "transforms a particular article into a different state or thing."[72]

These new restrictions on patentable subject matter are a modest improvement over the previous standard. One of the most notable aspects of *Bilski* was its rejection of patents for purely mental calculations such as the commodity hedging strategy developed by the applicant in that case.[73] The Federal Circuit said that a "claimed process wherein all of the process steps may be performed entirely in the human mind is obviously not tied to any machine and does not transform any article into a different state or thing. As a result, it would not be patent-eligible under § 101."[74] Under that analysis, some business processes would clearly be excluded, such as a new style of argument in a courtroom or a better technique for haggling.[75]

70 *See id.* at 960 (reaffirming the conclusion in *State Street* that business methods as a class are patentable).

71 *See id.* at 959 (describing the standard associated with *State Street*).

72 *See id.* at 952–58 (discussing the case law and restating the operative test); *id.* at 959 ("[W]hile looking for 'a useful, concrete, and tangible result' may in many instances provide useful indications of whether a claim is drawn to a fundamental principle or a practical application of such a principle, that inquiry is insufficient to determine whether a claim is patent-eligible under § 101.").

Although I want to focus on the practical implications of *Bilski*, there are some things worth saying about the Federal Circuit's analysis. The chief flaw in the "machine-or-transformation" standard is that the Supreme Court once expressly disclaimed that this was the sole test for process patentability. *See* Gottschalk v. Benson, 409 U.S. 63, 71 (1972) ("It is argued that a process patent must either be tied to a particular machine or apparatus or must operate to change articles or materials to a 'different state or thing.' We do not hold that no process patent could ever qualify if it did not meet the requirements of our prior precedents."). The majority in *Bilski* concluded that the Court's omission of this qualification in a later decision meant that the "machine-or-transformation" test should be read as exclusive. *See Bilski*, 545 F.3d at 956 ("[T]his caveat was *not repeated* in *Diehr* when the Court refaffirmed the machine-or-transformation test."). This is a highly dubious (or, to be more polite, creative) interpretation of the cases. *See id.* at 982 (Newman, J., dissenting) ("It cannot be inferred that the Court silently imposed such a rule."). The problem for the Federal Circuit, however, is that the Supreme Court's cases on this question are a mess. *See supra* note 30. This helps explain why – right after *Bilski*'s attempt to reconcile these authorities – the en banc court suggested that review by the Justices was warranted. *See Bilski*, 545 F.3d at 956.

73 *See Bilski*, 545 F.3d at 949 (calling the claim "a method of hedging risk in the field of commodities trading"); *id.* at 963 ("Purported transformations or manipulations simply of public or private legal obligations or relationships, business risks, or other such abstractions cannot meet the test because they are not physical objects or substances, and they are not representative of physical objects or substances.").

74 *Id.* at 961 n.26.

75 *See In re* Ferguson, 558 F.3d 1359 (Fed. Cir. 2009) (applying *Bilski* to reject a patent application for a marketing strategy).

The application of the "machine-or-transformation" (MoT) test with respect to most process patents, however, is very unclear and may just end up providing more gainful employment for lawyers who excel at claim drafting.[76] First, the court declined to address the issue of "whether or when recitation of a computer suffices to tie a process claim to a particular machine."[77] This is a major omission because many business methods can be redrafted to include some connection with a computer (as software, for instance). Second, *Bilski* did not offer any helpful guidance on what was required to meet the transformation prong of the new test. As one dissenter said, "nearly every process claim can be rewritten to include a physical transformation."[78] Thus, the litigation of these instruments will probably not decrease because of the uncertainty surrounding the new standard articulated by *Bilski*.[79]

Here is the bottom line: The legal materials and the policy arguments do not resolve the question of whether business methods should be patentable if that question is whether they should always or never be patentable. My conclusion, however, is that this is the wrong approach. Instead, lawmakers should use a flexible standard that looks at the norms within particular communities, to the extent that is possible, and holds that processes can be patented only when their customs support patentability.

II. BRINGING CUSTOM INTO PATENT LAW

This part lays out an alternative interpretation of § 101 that would require the PTO and the courts to conclude that an "ordinary person skilled in the art" would consider a process patentable subject matter as a prerequisite for granting a claim. Through this standard, which is taken from the nonobviousness test in § 103, policy makers would be forced to defer to anti-patent norms within an industry, but would not have to define business methods to do so.[80] The analysis then explores how this approach might work in practice and looks at how it could affect software.

[76] *See id.* at 1008 (Mayer, J., dissenting) ("The majority's proposed 'machine-or-transformation test' for patentability will do little to stem the growth of patents on non-technological methods and ideas. Quite simply, in the context of business method patent applications, the majority's proposed standard can be too easily circumvented."); *id.* at 1015 (Rader, J., dissenting) (stating that "this opinion propagates unanswerable questions" and then listing several).

[77] *Id.* at 962.

[78] *Id.* at 1008 (Mayer, J., dissenting); *see id.* at 1010 (Mayer, J., dissenting) ("[A]lthough this court has struggled for years to set out what constitutes sufficient physical transformation to render a process patentable, we have yet to provide a consistent or satisfactory resolution of this issue.").

[79] *See id.* at 1010 (Mayer, J., dissenting) ("The majority . . . fails to enlighten three of the thorniest issues in the patentability thicket: (1) the continued viability of business method patents, (2) what constitutes sufficient physical transformation or machine-implementation to render a process patentable, and (3) the extent to which computer software and computer-implemented processes constitute statutory subject-matter.").

[80] *See* 35 U.S.C. § 103 (a) (2006).

A. *Expanding the Horizon of the Reasonable Person*

Let us begin with an observation about business methods, which is that, unlike other types of inventions, they generally evolve in the heat of market competition rather in a laboratory.[81] Opponents of business method patents use this point to say that there is no need for the extra incentives provided by intellectual property, but another way to think about this is that "[t]he interactive responses that shape business methods are largely shaped by customary practices."[82] In other words, the unique characteristics of each market niche play a major role in determining how firms organize themselves and relate to consumers. As many unsuccessful entrepreneurs learn the hard way, developing a better product or a more efficient way of doing things is not always enough. Market expectations, which can be set by players within an industry or by end users, often determine what is acceptable in a way that is hard for outsiders to understand.

Given the importance of market norms in framing business methods, a question that arises is who knows more about whether patents will lead to better processes: the people in that industry or lawmakers? When the tax bar loudly protested the suggestion that tax shelters could be patented, one recent article pooh-poohed these objections as "anxiety bordering on panic."[83] Now that may be true, but the confident assertion that patents are good for you even when you think they are not should at least give one pause.[84] In the case of software, most programmers adamantly opposed patents throughout the entire debate about whether § 101 should be extended over their work, and even now firms outside of the software business acquire most software patents.[85] Nevertheless, these concerns were waved off with equally confident and, as it turned out, false claims that software patents would not cause any significant problems.

What makes this issue especially interesting is that when it comes to determining whether a particular invention (or business method) is obvious, lawmakers do defer

[81] *See* Raskind, *supra* note 18, at 81 ("Courts should give weight to the fact that business methods are not derived from laboratory research and experimentation, but evolve in [and] are implemented in an environment of rivalry and emulation."); *see also* Meurer, *supra* note 18, at 315 (stating that business processes usually fall into two categories – administrative methods and customer service methods – that deal with how firms handle market constraints). Just to be clear, this is not a definition of business methods. It is only a trait that is helpful in framing the subsequent analysis.

[82] Raskind, *supra* note 18, at 81.

[83] Burk & McDonnell, *supra* note 14, at 982; *see also id.* ("[O]nce business methods are allowed as patentable subject matter, the presence of tax shelters among such methods is neither much of a doctrinal novelty nor much of a surprise.").

[84] Perhaps this is a closer question because legal academics might know a great deal about tax law. In my experience, however, tax lawyers are specialists whose work is incomprehensible to those in other legal disciplines.

[85] *See* Bessen & Meurer, *supra* note 1, at 189–90 (describing the opposition and stating that only 5% of software patents come from within the industry); *see id.* at 189 ("[S]uch broad opposition from *within* the affected industry and among the affected inventors seems to be unprecedented in U.S. patent history").

to industry expertise in the form of the "ordinary person skilled in the art" standard. Although the PTO or the courts must make an independent judgment on this legal question, it is inconceivable that either body would reject the uniform advice of scientists or engineers on the ground that they really do not know an obvious invention when they see one. In this instance, the law recognizes that the subtleties of technology are too complex for nonspecialists to grasp and that patentability cannot be determined by a rule. The same logic, in my view, applies to the nuances of how individual markets function and should frame how business method patents are handled.[86]

B. *The Operational Test*

Accordingly, my solution is simply to take the "ordinary person" standard and expand its reach to ask whether that same reasonable member of a technical or business community would think that the claim genre is patentable subject matter.[87] This view of § 101 would explicitly incorporate industry customs into the analysis and offers several advantages over the current approach.[88]

First, by imposing a higher burden on business method claim applicants, this test will reduce the number of these patents that are issued. It is hard to say how large that reduction will be or whether the new standard will target the most problematic patents (more on that in a moment).[89] But given the enormous litigation costs imposed by software and business method patents, anything that reduces their ranks without causing other problems would be welcome. At the same time, an "ordinary person" construction of § 101 would allow some business method patents to go through. In essence, the result would be a compromise between those who want to eliminate these patents and those who support the current liberal interpretation of § 101.

Second, using a somewhat vague and fact-intensive standard for this inquiry would go a long way toward solving the definitional issue that is tying the current debate

[86] *Cf.* Cotter, *supra* note 12, at 883 ("All of this reasoning leads me to conclude that, despite some potential drawbacks, the technological arts, mental steps, and physical transformation doctrines may have possessed some underappreciated virtues. Abandoning them entirely, in the interest of attaining a more rational, logical patent system, may well have been precipitate.").

[87] One obvious argument against this change is that § 103 contains language about an "ordinary person skilled in the art," whereas § 101 does not. There are at least two responses to this point. First, this kind of textual borrowing would fulfill the purpose of the legislation in a manner consistent with the goals and the structure of the statute. Second, the consensus that business methods were not patentable when the 1952 Act was passed can be read as implying that there is an equivalent ordinary person limit on § 101 because anti-patent norms did exist at the time in the relevant communities. *See supra* text accompanying notes 26–28.

[88] There might be a difference between the § 101 ordinary observer and the § 103 version, in the sense that the latter focuses on the technical aspects of an invention, whereas the former will be more interested in its commercial aspects. This distinction, however, does not diminish the value of the analogy.

[89] *See infra* text accompanying notes 97–102.

into knots. Instead of setting forth a categorical exclusion (or inclusion) that will almost certainly founder on the circularity of a business method, the definition will be supplied by industry participants on a case-by-case basis. Such a test should also alleviate concerns that long-established patent types (e.g., chemical processes) will be swept under any new restrictions. Where plentiful prior art exists, claimants will have no problem establishing, either with that evidence alone or with a few affidavits, that the custom of their trade supports patentability.

Third, the suggested expansion of the ordinary person test should not produce an intolerable level of uncertainty because the PTO, the courts, and applicants are already quite familiar with how this standard works. There is no question that a change from the "almost anything goes" rule now applied by the Federal Circuit will create some additional uncertainty, although one might say that the current approach just shifts the ambiguities from the application stage to the litigation stage.[90] Yet the types of evidence that would be considered and the way in which they are interpreted would be similar to an obviousness inquiry.[91] Prior art would naturally be relevant to the question of whether a particular industry thinks its discoveries are patentable.[92] So would expert testimony from people in the field or material from secondary sources such as trade journals. Thus, the suggested change would be modest from a methodological standpoint and should come within the competency of the officials charged with running the patent system.

Finally, adopting an ordinary person test for subject matter patentability would allow professions that do not want patents to be free from them unless they opt in. This will facilitate their autonomy (to the extent one thinks that is worth promoting) and let those with better information about market conditions make the call on whether patents are worthwhile.[93] In more organized trades, a professional association could take a position on patentability that would send a clear signal to all concerned about

90 Thus, Judge Newman was correct in her *Bilski* dissent when she said that "[u]ncertainty is the enemy of innovation." In re Bilski, 545 F.3d 943, 977 (Fed. Cir. 2008) (en banc) (Newman, J., dissenting), *petition for cert. filed sub nom.* Bilski v. Doll (U.S. Jan. 28, 2009) (No. 08–964). The issue is whether uncertainty at the application stage, which is what she was talking about, is more important than uncertainty at the litigation stage, which is what is occurring because of the proliferation of process patents.

91 One difference is that there may be no subject matter equivalent to the "secondary factors" that are used to identify obviousness. *See* Graham v. John Deere Inc., 383 U.S. 1, 17 (1966) (stating that "[s]uch secondary considerations as commercial success, long felt but unsolved needs, failure of others, etc" can be used to assess obviousness).

92 In cases where courts or examiners are confronted by some prior patents in the trade and must determine whether that amount is sufficient to justify the conclusion that a norm for patentability exists, the question of who is taking out these patents would be relevant. For example, if a major firm in the industry is the source of prior art, that would be more powerful evidence of a custom than if the patents were granted to outsiders or minor players that could be classified as defectors from a common understanding.

93 *See* Rothman, *supra* note 12, at 1908 ("Customary practices or norms that develop with the express purpose of formulating an aspirational set of practices should be given more weight than those that develop simply to avoid litigation or preserve relationships.").

the relevant practices.[94] Of course, this does suggest that the meaning of § 101 can change over time as a community reassesses the wisdom of patents. Because norms tend to be rather sticky, however, this probably does not inject an undue amount of doubt into the reliance interests served by patents.

The strongest counterargument to these points is that patent lawyers will find ways to draft their claims so that an invention does not fall within a prohibited category. Put another way, would the new standard just change the definitional problem from "What is a business method?" to "What business is this process in?" The answer is a qualified yes. Of course, lawyers will try to blur the boundaries and aid their clients – that is what attorneys do across all areas of doctrine. And although there will be some difficult cases there are good reasons to think that this definitional change will not pose a major problem.[95] The key point is that applicants would bear the burden of proof of showing what an ordinary person would conclude. As a result, redrafting the claim would not be enough: Applicants would also need to present evidence that their claim fell within the specified class and that an ordinary person skilled in the art would say that the item described was of a patentable type. This more rigorous examination should limit the typical legal shell games to a tolerable level.[96]

C. *The Application to Software*

The most important question that would arise if this proposal were adopted concerns what would happen to software patents. It is probably the case that professions or industries that have resisted business method patents thus far (law, medicine, sports, etc.) would find shelter under an ordinary observer standard. Although this would be a positive outcome, as a practical matter patents in those professions are not the ones causing most of the problems.[97] Software and the business methods that use software, not curve balls, are the source of the high litigation costs that are hurting innovation. My tentative conclusion is that the application of an ordinary person test would at least curb software patents and could lead to their abolition. No firm judgment can be made on this point, however, without further study.

94 *See* Thomas, *supra* note 10, at 16 ("[T]he tendency of professions to organize suggests that a vocal and established lobby will be on hand to debate the place of patenting within particular professional communities."). This proposal enhances the role of professional associations, because their declarations about patents would carry a lot of weight. However, if one thinks that these groups are controlled mainly by insiders who are not representative of the community as a whole, then that could be a problem.

95 It is worth noting that this sort of market inquiry is often undertaken in antitrust (to determine if a firm is monopolizing a market) and in trademark (to determine whether a mark has secondary meaning with a certain market niche).

96 Granted, this is a more powerful constraint in an adversarial context than in an ex parte application before the PTO.

97 *See* Bessen & Meurer, *supra* note 1, at 214 ("[S]oftware patents likely have a far greater influence on the performance of the patent system than do nonsoftware business processes.").

Identifying a norm within a community that includes Richard Stallman and Steve Ballmer is, to put it mildly, challenging.[98] There is some evidence of antipathy toward patents from software firms and programmers based on their past resistance and on the fact that most people within the industry do not patent their work.[99] Nevertheless, there are plenty of people in the business who take the opposite view (and not just at Microsoft).[100] Without a more detailed examination of attitudes and practices in that business, however, it is impossible to say whether a patentability norm exists or, if it does, what it covers. In other words, an ordinary person test could end software patents, but that framework does not necessarily lead to that result.

Another way to view the problem, however, is through the businesses that use (and write) their own software for specialized purposes. There are types of software (MS Word, Excel, TurboTax) that are designed for general use and would be properly classified as falling into the software market for purposes of a § 101 inquiry. Yet there are other programs that are designed for specific trades, such as banks, hotels, insurance, or lawyers. With respect to these business processes, one might wonder whether the norms of these particular trades should control. Drawing a distinction between general and specialized software makes sense because software is one of the few goods that can be developed for niche use by businesses outside the industry that uses them. By contrast, almost all tangible inventions such as machines are available for general use or are invented by R&D experts within a given trade. In either case, the patentability norms of the business that does the inventing would control because there is no other useful comparison. But for some business software, the spotlight could be placed either on firms that write programs or on end users who have in-house programmers doing the work and taking out the patents.

Shifting the focus from the software industry as a whole to the communities such as telecommunications, computers, and electronics that do most of the software patenting may seem unimportant, but in one respect it could be a big help. After all, that these businesses are taking out patents on software would suggest that they share a norm supporting patentability. Another possibility, however, is that these firms are against patents, but must get them for defensive purposes and cannot escape this suboptimal equilibrium without some help in solving their collective

98 *See generally* RICHARD M. STALLMAN, FREE SOFTWARE, FREE SOCIETY: SELECTED ESSAYS OF RICHARD M. STALLMAN (2002) (setting forth his influential ideas about open-source software and criticizing the proprietary model).

99 *See supra* text accompanying note 85. This is why, according to Bessen and Meurer, a proliferation of patents does not seem to pose a problem for software innovation itself. *See* BESSEN & MEURER, *supra* note 1, at 190 ("To date patents have had little negative effect within the software publishing industry because there are – despite the concerns of commentators – no substantial patent thickets within the industry."); *id.* ("[A]lmost all software patents are obtained by firms *outside* the software industry.").

100 My own conversations with people in the software business offer a cautionary note. Generally, they are quick to criticize patents, but then have a tendency to add qualifiers such as "unless it is obtained by a small firm." It may be that some coherent norm exists here, but its contours are far from clear.

action problem.[101] Using an ordinary person test for subject matter patentability offers a lifeline to these firms by giving significant weight to a policy statement by their professional associations about whether patents should be allowed. The same admonition would be meaningless under the current test because there is no effective means to discipline defectors. In essence, my proposal lowers the transaction costs involved in resolving this Prisoner's Dilemma by changing the necessary act from successfully lobbying Congress for a statutory exemption to obtaining an agreement in the industry on patent policy. Once again, it is difficult to say how much this change would reduce software patents, but it should at least make a dent in the problem.[102]

Accordingly, modifying the § 101 analysis with an "ordinary person" qualification comes as close as can be reasonably expected to addressing the current problems with business method patents. To a large extent, this is a compromise proposal that would allow some of these patents to issue while blocking others that are not supported by the relevant parties. Perhaps it is not a good solution, but it is probably better than any competing alternative.

CONCLUSION

The ongoing debate about business method patents may mark the peak of an intellectual property bubble. For decades, Congress and the courts steadily expanded the scope of patent, copyright, and trademark protection based on a belief that additional creative incentives always lead to more innovation. Now the costs of that approach, as they do with all manias, are coming due in the form of patent trolls and endless litigation.

As a result, what we need is a more pragmatic approach that pays heed to the expertise within a given industry before making the leap to patentability. Embracing long-established customs through an ordinary person test can accomplish this goal while avoiding the problems that are inherent in defining and evaluating business methods. Patent law can do many positive things, but producing better baseball is not one of them. Intellectual property must not be foisted on those who do not want or need it.

[101] *See* Gideon Parchomovsky & R. Polk Wagner, *Patent Portfolios*, 154 *U.* Pa. L. Rev. 1, 26–27 (2005) ("The defensive patenting theory holds that firms acquire patents to ward off possible lawsuits by using the patents as bargaining chips with potential plaintiffs.").

[102] Without further research, it is impossible to say how many industries that take out software patents do so for defensive reasons and would rather not.

7

Business and Financial Method Patents, Innovation, and Policy

*Bronwyn H. Hall**

INTRODUCTION

The explosion in business method patent applications and grants that occurred in 1999–2001 has abated somewhat, and the legal landscape has changed as a result of several court decisions. However, the many policy questions raised by the response of the financial, e-commerce, and software industries to the well-known *State Street Bank* decision on the patentability of business methods remain. Many scholars, both legal and economic, wrote on this topic shortly after the decision and the accompanying increase in patents in this technological area.[1] Although much of this literature provided a fairly thorough analysis of individual cases and what they signify, there was relatively little scholarship on the impact of business method patents based on a more broad-based or empirical approach. Notable exceptions are a series of studies of financial method patents by Lerner (2001, 2006a,b) and some studies of business method or financial patents by Allison and Tiller (2003), Hunt (2008), Wagner (2008), and Hall, Thoma, and Torrisi (2009).

This chapter examines the evolution of patenting in this area and reviews some of the literature on patents more broadly in an attempt to infer the implications of this literature for business method patents. The focus is on two issues: the role of

* University of California at Berkeley, University of Maastricht, and NBER. This is a substantially revised and expanded version of Hall (2003), a paper prepared for the Atlanta Federal Reserve Bank Conference on Business Method Patents, Sea Island, Georgia, April 3–5, 2003, and the EPIP Network Conference on New Challenges to the Patent System, Munich, Germany, April 24–25, 2003. Comments from participants in those conferences as well as from Robert Hunt and Josh Lerner are gratefully acknowledged. A version of this chapter was originally published in the *Scottish Journal of Political Economy*. *See* Bronwyn H. Hall, *Business and Financial Method Patents, Innovation, and Policy*, 56 SCOTTISH. J. POL. ECON. 443 (2009).

[1] See, for example, Bakels and Hugenholtz (2002), Bessen and Maskin (2006), Blind, Edler, and Nack (2001), Cockburn (2001), Cohen and Lemley (2001), Davis (2002a,b), Dreyfuss (2000), Hart, Holmes, and Reid (1999), Hunt (2001b), Kasdan (1999), and Lerner (2001).

TABLE 7.1. *Costs and benefits of the patent system*

Effects on	Benefits	Costs
Innovation	Creates an incentive for R&D; promotes the diffusion of ideas	Impedes the combination of new ideas and inventions; raises transaction costs
Competition	Facilitates entry of new small firms with limited assets; allows trading of inventive knowledge – markets for technology	Creates short-term monopolies, which may become long term in network industries

patents in encouraging innovation and the consequences of low patent quality for the performance of the system. I begin by briefly reviewing the facts about business method patents and then survey what economists know about the general relationship between patent systems and innovation in order to draw some implications for the likely impact of business method patents on innovation in industry. A discussion of the patent quality issue is followed by a summary of the policy recommendations made by those who have followed the evolution of legal standards as both software and business methods have become acceptable subject matter.

Most economists view the patent system as a necessary evil. With a patent grant we trade off short-term exclusive (monopoly) rights to the use of an invention in return for two things: (1) an incentive to create the innovation and (2) early publication of information about the innovation and its enablement. The argument is that, without the patent system, fewer innovations would be produced and those that were produced would be kept secret as much as possible to protect the returns from misappropriation. Mazzoleni and Nelson (1998) expand on this analysis and provide two further related arguments for the existence of a patent system: It serves as an inducement for the investments needed to develop and commercialize inventions, and it enables the "orderly exploration of the broad prospects" opened up by particularly novel inventions. In considering the economic impacts of the implicit subject matter extension implied by the increased use of patents to protect business methods, the tradeoff between these benefits and the welfare cost of the grant of a monopoly right is at least as important as it is in any other technological arena.

As our understanding of the uses and abuses of the patent system has grown, other benefits (to competition) and costs (to innovation) have emerged as important. Table 7.1 summarizes the basic dilemma: The patent system can generate both benefits and costs, for both innovation and competition. First, economic analysis says that *competition* may suffer when we grant a monopoly right to the inventor of a business method, but it will benefit if this right facilitates entry into the industry by new and innovative firms and allows the development of markets for technology. Second, *innovation* will benefit from the incentive created by a patent, but may suffer if patents discourage or raise the cost of combining and recombining of inventions to make new products and processes. Thus the relationship between patents, competition, and innovation is guaranteed to be a complex one and one that may vary over time and across industries.

I. BACKGROUND AND HISTORY

There is no precise definition of a business method patents, and in reading the literature it becomes clear that many scholars make little distinction between business method patents, internet patents, and software patents more broadly, at least when making policy recommendations. This is inevitable in the present day: Because many business method patents are in fact patents on the transfer of a known business method to a software and/or Web-based implementation, the distinction is hard to maintain. In addition, almost all patent offices draw some kind of line between a patentable business method and a method of doing something that does not have a "technical effect" (in the case of the European Patent Office; EPO) or is not "tied to a particular machine or apparatus" or does not transform one thing to another (the PTO after the *In re Bilski* decision). This line is inevitably fuzzy and has moved over time.*

For the purpose of examination, the PTO defines a business method patent fairly narrowly: as a patent classified in U.S. patent class 705, defined as "data processing: financial, business practice, management, or cost/price determination." Such patents are on methods used for a variety of purposes in business such as the following:[2]

- Financial – credit and loan processing, point-of-sale systems, billing, funds transfer, banking clearinghouses, tax processing, and investment planning
- Financial instruments and techniques – derivatives, valuation, index-linking
- Optimization – scheduling and resource allocation
- Marketing – advertising management, catalog systems, incentive programs, and coupon redemption
- Information acquisition, human resource management, accounting, and inventory monitoring
- E-commerce tools and infrastructure – user interface arrangements, auctions, electronic shopping carts, transactions, and affiliate programs
- Voting systems, games, gambling, and education and training

* Editors' Note: This article was written prior to the Supreme Court's decision in *Bilski v. Kappos*, which affirmed the Federal Circuit's decision in *In re Bilski* but modified its rationale. 561 U.S. ___, 130 S. Ct. 3218 (2010). Contrary to the Federal Circuit, the Court held that the machine-or-transformation test (MoT) was not the sole test for determining the patent eligibility of a process. Rather, that test was only "a useful and important clue . . . for determining whether some claimed inventions are processes under § 101." *Bilski*, 130 S. Ct. at 3227.

[2] See the USPTO White Paper (1999) for further description and categorization of these patents.

Examples of business method patents are the well-known one-click patents assigned to Amazon.com, the Dutch auction patent of Priceline.com, and, of course, the Signature Financial patent on a system of managing multiple mutual funds in a single account that was the subject of the *State Street* decision, which is described later.

A. *Brief Legal History*

Statutory subject matter for patenting is defined by § 101 of the U.S. code as any new and useful machine, article, process, or composition of matter.[3] Precedents set during the long legal history of patentability have interpreted this definition to exclude laws of nature, natural phenomena, and abstract ideas. It is the shades of difference in meaning between the definition of a "new and useful" item and an "abstract idea" that are the source of the debate surrounding business methods as a suitable subject matter for patentability and of the difficulty in clearly delineating that subject matter. Clearly it is possible to imagine an abstract idea that is new and useful, so the exclusion rests on the inclusiveness or exclusiveness of the words "machine, article, process, or composition of matter."

In 1998, the U.S. Court of Appeals of the Federal Circuit (CAFC) issued a decision that is widely viewed as having opened the door to widespread business method patenting, especially of financial methods, in the *State Street Bank and Trust* v. *Signature Financial Corporation* case.[4] The Signature patent at issue was a "pure" number-crunching software program application, which implemented a method of valuing mutual funds.[5] The Federal Circuit decision, authored by Judge Rich, stated clearly that section § 101 of the U.S. patent law is unambiguous – "any" means ALL, and it was improper to read limitations into § 101 not intended by Congress. Therefore, mathematical algorithms are nonstatutory only when "disembodied" and thus lacking a useful application. The court went on to make sure that the decision was precedent setting by stating that, with regard to the business method exception, "We take this opportunity to lay this ill-conceived exception to rest."

In a subsequent case, *AT&T* v. *Excel*, where the patent at issue contained a method claim about adding a data field to a record for use in a billing system, the Federal Circuit confirmed the *State Street* decision, saying that a physical transformation was

[3] 35 U.S.C § 101.

[4] State Street Bank and Trust Co., Inc. v. Signature Financial Group, Inc., 149 F.3d 1368 (Fed. Cir. 1998).

[5] The description of the patent in the court's decision was that it was "generally directed to a data processing system (the system) for implementing an investment structure which was developed for use in Signature's business as an administrator and accounting agent for mutual funds. In essence, the system, identified by the proprietary name Hub and Spoke, facilitates a structure whereby mutual funds (Spokes) pool their assets in an investment portfolio (Hub) organized as a partnership. This investment configuration provides the administrator of a mutual fund with the advantageous combination of economies of scale in administering investments coupled with the tax advantages of a partnership."

not required for a method claim to be statutory and that mathematical algorithms were patentable if "embodied" in an invention. That is, the *State Street* decision applies to methods as well as to machines.[6]

Two recent cases have changed the landscape in the business patent area, making it somewhat more difficult to obtain such a patent and also more difficult to enforce the patent, once obtained. In a high-profile case that ended in the Supreme Court, MercExchange sued e-Bay for infringement of a series of patents on computerized marketplaces.[7] The decision in this case is widely viewed as shifting the bargaining point between a nonworking patent holder and a potential infringer. In May 2006, the Court ruled that a four-factor test must be used to decide whether to issue a permanent injunction in a patent case.[8] Before an injunction is issued by the court, a patent owner must show (1) it has suffered irreparable injury, (2) monetary damages are inadequate compensation, (3) a remedy in equity is warranted, and (4) the public interest would not be disserved. Applying this test should make it more difficult for patent holders that do not offer a product embodying the invention in question to obtain injunctions against those who do.

The second important recent case is *In re Bilski*, which was decided by the Federal Circuit in October 2008.[9] This ruling addressed which technologies are eligible for patent protection, reinstating a test familiar from decisions in the 1970s and early 1980s and to some extent stepping back from the *State Street* test of patentability (that the invention need only have a "concrete, useful, and tangible result"). The new test for patentable software says that a process will be patentable if "(1) it is tied to a particular machine or apparatus, or (2) it transforms a particular article into a different state or thing."[10] The court expressed concern that a patent should not "pre-empt substantially all uses of a fundamental principle."[11] In addition to its implications for algorithmic patents, the decision is also viewed as ruling out medical methods as patentable subject matter.

Thus, the set of patents that could be classified as business method or financial method patents will change over time as the subject matter definitions used by the PTO change, either in response to court rulings or to other changes, including legislative. At the current time, there are two main patent classes containing these patents: 705 (data processing: financial, business practice, management, or cost/price determination) and 902 (electronic funds transfer). It is, of course, possible that patents we might view as business method patents are classified elsewhere in the patent system. For example, patent number 5,851,117, which describes a system for training janitors, is classified as 434, "education and demonstration," and patent number 6,015,947, which describes a method of teaching music, is classified as 84,

[6] AT&T Corp. v. Excel Communications, Inc., 172 F.3d 1352 (1999).

[7] eBay Inc. v. MercExchange L.L.C., 547 U.S. 388, 391–92 (2006)

[8] See http://www.supremecourtus.gov/opinions/05pdf/05–130.pdf.

[9] http://www.cafc.uscourts.gov/opinions/07–1130.pdf

[10] *In re Bilski*, 545 F.3d 943, 966 (Fed. Cir. 2008) (en banc).

[11] *Id.* at 953.

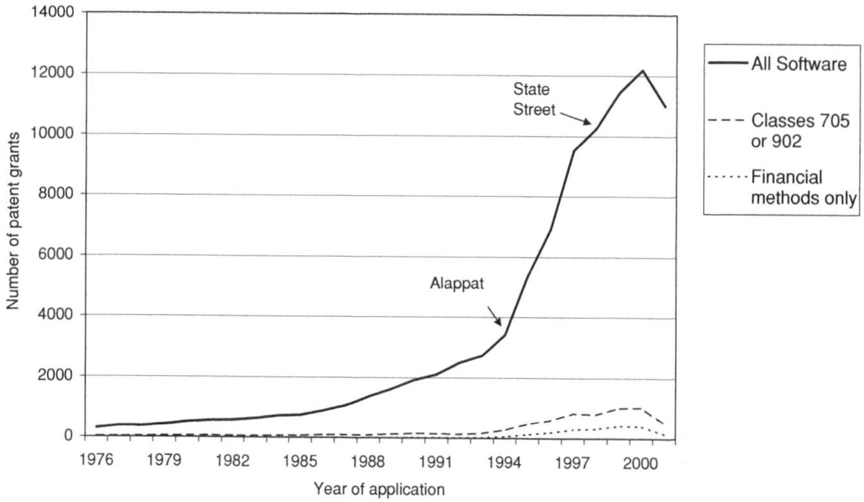

FIGURE 7.1. U.S. patent classes with software/business method patents applied for 1976–2006.

"music." In this chapter, I do not address patents in classes such as these, because the business method share of the class is quite small and it is not feasible to read each patent separately. The main patent classes that contain software and business method patents, broadly defined, are shown in Table 7.2. Among these classes, only 705 and 902 contain modern business method patents. About half of these patents are related to financial methods and payment services, and half to other business methods.[12]

Figures 7.1 (by year of application) and 7.2 (by year of grant) give an idea of the relative importance of software and business method patents according to various patent class definitions. Under a broad definition of software/business methods, the PTO is now granting about 10,000 to 12,000 patents per year, as opposed to fewer than a thousand per year before 1985.[13] Pure business method patents (those in class 705) are still a small share of the total, with about one thousand granted per year and with a notable decline in grants in 2001 and 2002, probably because the PTO instituted a second review for this class of patents.[14] Figure 7.3 shows the evolution

12 I define financial and payment service patents as the union of definitions due to Hall (2007) and Lerner (2006a): those 705 patents in subclasses 4, 14, 16–18, 21, 33, 35–45, 53–56, 64–79 plus any class 902 patents. See the appendix for a complete list of the subclasses. Although class 902 seems from its description to be a likely repository of many financial services patents, in fact there is only one patent with a primary classification in 902 granted by the end of 2006, which is when my data sample ends.

13 The definition used is the combined definition from Hall and MacGarvie (2006), which is based on previous work by Graham and Mowery (2003) and Bessen amd Hunt (2004).

14 In discussion of this chapter, Josh Lerner suggested that the decline may be partly due to strategizing on the part of firms to avoid having a potential business method patent classified into 705, so that it would not be scrutinized twice at the PTO. This seems likely, but there is no way to measure this effect using publicly available data.

TABLE 7.2. *Selected software and business method disputes*

Patent number	Patent class	Issue year	Description	Plaintiff	Defendant	Date filed	Court	Date of outcome	Outcome
					Infringement Suits				
4873662	711	1989	Hyperlink prototype patent	British Telecom	Prodigy (AOL, etc)	Dec 2000	New York	Sept 2002	Summary judgment; patent not valid; BT abandoned patent
5193056	705/36	1993	Data-processing system for hub-and-spoke financial services configuration	State Street	Signature Financial	1994	Mass.	1998	State Street Bank prevailed; business methods are patentable
5267314	713	1993	Public key encryption (SSL)	Leon Stambler	RSA Security, Verisign, etc	Feb 2001	Delaware		Trial began 2/26/03
5333184	379	1994	Call message recording for telephone systems (use of an algorithm to assign billing codes of IXCs in customer's records)	AT&T	Excel Communi-cations	1998		April 1999	CAFC reversed summary judgment, remanded to district court
5845265	705/37	1995	Computerized marketplace for goods	MercExchange	Return Buy	Sept 2001	VA, Eastern	Dec. 2002	ReturnBuy settled for nonexclusive license, details not disclosed
5774870	705/14	1998	Online incentive/award systems	Netcenter	Carlson Companies; others		CA, Northern		14 licensees with royalties of $6,000,000 per year collected by Netcenter
5794207	705/1	1998	(Dutch auction) method and apparatus for cryptographically assisted commercial network system designed to facilitate buyer-driven conditional purchase offers	Priceline/ Walker Digital	Microsoft/ Expedia	Oct 1999	Connecticut	Jan 2001	Settled with undisclosed royalty payments
5960411	705/26	1999	One-click internet shopping	Amazon.com	Barnes and Noble	Oct 1999	Washington	Mar 2002	Settled with royalties to Amazon.com
6009412	705/14	1999	online incentive/award systems	Netcentives/ Netcenter	Carlson Companies; others		CA Northern		14 licensees with royalties of $6,000,000 per year collected by Netcentives

5848265; 6085176; 6202051	705/37	2000	Use software search agents to comb multiple marketplaces; automated auctions	MercExchange	eBay	Sept 2001	VA Eastern	2006	Supreme Court overturned CAFC injunction; settled with undisclosed royalty payments in Feb. 2008
5897620	705/5	1999	(Dutch auction) method and apparatus for the sale of airline specified flight tickets	Priceline/ Walker Digital	Microsoft/ Expedia	Oct 1999	Conn.	Jan 2001	Settled with royalties not disclosed.
Selected re-examination requests									
5806063	707	1998	Y2K century windowing	McDonnell Douglas/Bruce Dickens		11999			Licensing letters 1999–2000; USPTO re-examined at inventor and PTO request, no outcome as of Feb. 2003
6368227	472	2002	swinging a swing sideways or in a circular motion instead of back and forth by pulling on the chains	Steve Olson		2003			USPTO-requested re-exam; no outcome noted.
Examples of licensing letters requesting royalties									
4698672	375	1986	JPEGlike compression standard	Compression Labs/Forgent		July 2002			Sony licensed the patent for $15M, other licenses have been asserted. The JPEG committee claims prior art invalidates the patent
5241671	707	1993	Multi-media search system with multiple paths (broad claims)	Compton's Encyclopedia/ Britannica				July 2003	Re-examined at PTO request Dec/93, certificate issued July 2002 (!), with narrowed claims
5933841, 6442574	715 (was 707)		Structured document browser	SB Communica-tions/ Ameritech	30 licensing letters	Feb 2003			prior art: Netscape 2.0 (1995); OWL International (1988) – first commercial hypertext system

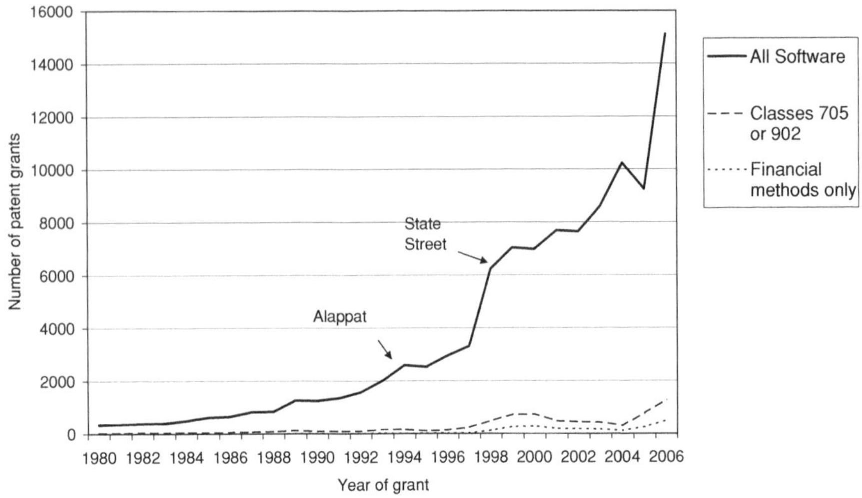

FIGURE 7.2. U.S. patent classes with software/business method patents granted 1976–2006.

of class 705 patents: Applications grow very slowly until the *In re Alappat* decision of 1994, which was widely viewed as opening the door to "pure" software patents in the United States.

Business method patents of some sort have existed for a long time, although not necessarily in large quantities. According to the U.S. PTO (1999), the earliest business method patents were for methods of printing money and detecting counterfeit

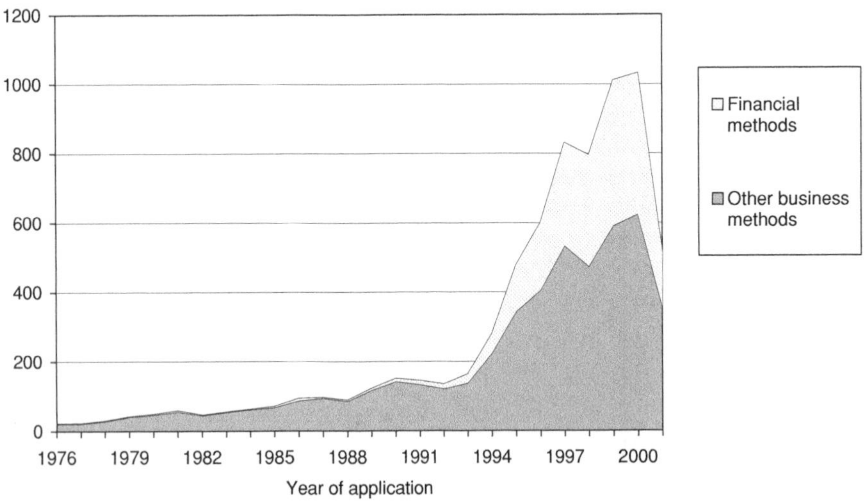

FIGURE 7.3. Business and financial method patents granted by 2006.

TABLE 7.3. *Patent classes with software or business method patents*

Class	Description
380	Cryptography
382	Image Analysis
395	Information Processing System Organization
700	Data Processing: Generic Control Systems or Specific Applications
701	Data Processing: Vehicles, Navigation, and Relative Location
702	Data Processing: Measuring, Calibrating, or Testing
703	Data Processing: Structural Design, Modeling, Simulation, and Emulation
704	Data Processing: Speech Signal Processing, Linguistics, Language Translation, and Audio Compression/Decompression
705	Data Processing: Financial, Business Practice, Management, or Cost/Price Determination
706	Data Processing: Artificial Intelligence
707	Data Processing: Database and File Management, Data Structures, or Document Processing
709	Electrical Computers and Digital Processing Systems: Multiple Computer or Process Coordinating
710	Electrical Computers and Digital Data Processing Systems: Input/Output
711	Electrical Computers and Digital Processing Systems: MemoryElectrical Computers and Digital Processing Systems: Processing
712	Architectures and Instruction Processing (e.g., Processors)
713	Electrical Computers and Digital Processing Systems: Support
715	Data Processing: Presentation Processing of Document
717	Data Processing: Software Development, Installation, or Management
902	Electronic Funds Transfer

bills.[15] A patent was issued in 1857 for the idea of including local advertising in a hotel register. Since the mid-1990s, the number of business method patents has increased substantially, largely due to the two previously mentioned court decisions and their aftermath, *In re Alappat* in 1994 and then *State Street* v. *Signature Financial* in 1998. Nevertheless, class 705 patents are still on the order of 0.5% of all patents applied for, whereas software patents are now about 6% of all patents, using the Hall-MacGarvie combined definition (2006). For comparison, Hall, Thoma, and Torrisi (2009) find that financial method patents were only about 0.2% of patent applications and 0.1% of patent grants at the EPO during the 1995–2002 period.

The success of the patent holder in the *State Street* and *ATT* v. *Excel* cases clearly emboldened others who held patents on internet-based methods of doing business. Table 7.3 lists some of these patents and the disputes in which they were involved:

[15] The first financial patent was granted on March 19, 1799, to Jacob Perkins of Massachusetts for an invention for "Detecting Counterfeit Notes." Patent number X2301 was granted to John Kneass on April 28, 1815, for a "A Mode of Preventing Counterfeiting." The hotel register patent is number 63,889. See USPTO (1999).

They include the well-known one-click patent of Amazon, the Priceline name-your-price auction, and the widely critiqued Y2K windowing patent.[16] The history of secure sockets layer (SSL) public key encryption technology is instructive: The original patent (4,405,829) was granted to MIT in 1983 on an application in 1976 that had been blocked by another 1976 patent issued in 1980 to Cylink, a Stanford University spinoff. As SSL became the dominant technology in the area of secure websites, the Internet Engineering Task Force (IETF) managed to persuade RSA Security (the MIT spinoff) to yield some intellectual property to the public standard in the late 1990s. Then in 2001, Leon Stambler sued RSA Security and Verisign over his 1993 patents, which claimed to cover SSL public key encryption. In 2005, RSA Security and Verisign were found not to have infringed the Stambler patents.[17] Several other disputes of this kind ended in these patents being invalidated, but others led to settlements with undisclosed royalty payments. This history illustrates the complexity both of the technology and of the disputes in the case of a valuable standard.

Because many of the past cases ended in some kind of settlement with undisclosed terms, it is difficult to form a precise picture of the licensing royalties involved. It is, however, noteworthy that most of the cases concerned internet patents rather than "pure" business method patents. Following Lanjouw and Schankerman (2001), this suggests that internet patents are the high-value and enforceable patents in this area. The more frivolous business method patents (such as 6,257,248, for cutting hair with scissors in both hands, or the previously mentioned 6,368,227, for a method of swinging on a swing) are probably unenforceable.

B. *Business Method Patenting Outside the United States*

According to the TRIPS agreement of the World Trade Organization (WTO), neither business methods nor software is specifically excludable subject matter for patentability (Diallo 2003). With respect to software, national treatment varies, but in most countries at least some types of software (especially those with a "technical effect" or where they are embodied in hardware) are now patentable.[18] At the present time, business methods are patentable (with some restrictions) in the United States, Canada, Australia, Japan, Singapore, and possibly Korea, but not in Europe including the United Kingdom. For example, the UK Patent Office introduced special treatment for business method applications in November 2004 because of

[16] This author was one of many who was incredulous when this patent, which solves the Y2K two-digit year problem by redefining the base year, issued. Like some others, she had software (in this case, TSP) on the market using this method a good fifteen years before patent 5,806,063 was applied for. The Patent Commissioner ordered a reexamination of this patent in 1999, and a final rejection of all claims was issued on June 10, 2005. After appeal, the rejection was finally affirmed by the PTO Board of Appeals on March 16, 2009 (!). Among other things, this case illustrates the time and resources that can be consumed even by a dubious patent in this area.

[17] Stambler v. RSA Sec., Inc., 123 Fed. Appx. 982 (Fed. Cir. 2005).

[18] See Spindler (2003) for a useful discussion of the current state of play in Europe and European Commission (2002) for the draft European directive on software patent policy.

the increasing number that had little or no chance of being granted (Managing Intellectual Property 2004). In so doing, the director of the Patent Office cited applications from Fujitsu for optimizing the scheduling of airline crews and a system for managing a debt-recovery process as being inherently unpatentable. In general, practitioners view UK practice with respect to software as more restrictive than that at the EPO (Managing Intellectual Property 2007).

Several researchers have looked at various types of business method patents applied for or granted at the EPO. Wagner (2008) examined 1901 EPO applications that had granted U.S. equivalents in class 705, finding that these patents had more claims and a longer pendency than other patents and were mostly taken out by large U.S. and Japanese electronic and computer firms. About 70% were granted (fewer for U.S. applicants), and of those granted, 16% were opposed, a relatively high rate. The most interesting finding was the very active opposition (44% of granted patents) in a single technology area – franking devices – dominated by one American (Pitney-Bowes) and three European firms. The fact that Pitney-Bowes, by far the largest patent holder, was the opposed and the other three firms were the opposers in most cases suggests that these competitors (Societe Secap, Neopost Ltd, and Francotyp-Postalia) feared being locked out of technologies they were already using without having patented them.

Hall, Thoma, and Torrisi (2009) studied financial method patents at the EPO, using a variety of definitions to identify them. They found that the majority are held by large established firms in nonfinancial sectors, as Lerner (2001) found for the United States and Wagner for Europe. Decisions on these patent applications take longer and they are more likely to be rejected, suggesting uncertainty over subject matter eligibility and their value to the applicant. As Wagner found for the subset of these patents with U.S. equivalents, they are more likely to be opposed once issued, which is consistent with the fact that their other value indicators such as citations are also higher than for patents as a whole.

It would be interesting to ask whether the difference in treatment of business method and financial patents at the PTO and the EPO has made any difference for business method and internet innovation in United States and Europe. Unfortunately, this particular research has not yet been undertaken, probably because it is still too early for there to be much evidence and also because there are confounding influences that make the comparison difficult. Thus I turn to the empirical evidence on the effects of having a patent system on innovation in general in the next section of this chapter.

II. DOES THE PATENT SYSTEM INCREASE INNOVATIVE ACTIVITY?

Although almost the holy grail of innovation policy research, this question has proved exceedingly difficult to answer because of the absence of real experiments. As I suggested in the Introduction, economic theory does not supply an unambiguous answer to the question, so that it is essential to rely on empirical observations where a patent system has been introduced, eliminated, or changed in major ways. In this part, I first review the theoretical results briefly and then turn to the empirical evidence on innovation and the patent system.

A. *Theoretical Results*

The first result from theory is the well-known argument that granting a patent on an innovation will incentivize the inventor – raising welfare – and create a temporary monopoly with its attendant deadweight loss. This rather stark result is mitigated somewhat by two observations. First, inventors are often motivated by a variety of factors, not all of which are financial. Second, innovators are often creative in securing returns to their inventions even in the absence of a patent by bringing the innovation to the market speedily and by secrecy. Based on these observations, we might expect the patent system to be an important incentive system when (1) considerable funds are needed to develop an invention, as in the case of pharmaceuticals or complex modern information technology, and (2) it is difficult to keep the innovation secret or imitation is easy.

More recently, a number of theorists beginning with Scotchmer (1991, 1996) and Green and Scotchmer (1995) have stressed the negative effects of patenting in industries with cumulative or sequential technology where each innovation builds on the last, as well as the impossibility of getting the incentives right unless there is enough information to enable contracts to be written before the first invention. Incentives to develop follow-on innovation in these industries are reduced by the need to pay licensing fees to the earlier inventors. In principle, for industries with very complex technologies, the problem of contracting for many small pieces of technology may be so severe that transactions costs discourage invention altogether (Heller and Eisenberg 1998; Grindley and Teece 1997).

For my purposes here, the work of Bessen and Maskin (2006) and Hunt (2001a) is probably the most directly appropriate. Bessen and Maskin used a model of sequential innovation where each invention builds on the preceding to show that patent protection does not encourage innovation as much as in the static nonsequential setting, and it may even discourage it. Hunt modeled sequential innovation along with a variable standard of patentability (nonobviousness) and asked how a patent system is likely to affect innovation in this case. He assumes an environment where the profitability of inventions is continuously eroded by the introduction of new, competing technologies and where the strength of the nonobviousness requirement for obtaining a patent determines the proportion of new discoveries that do not affect the profits earned by older proprietary discoveries. He then analyzed the consequences of lowering the nonobviousness requirement, showing that there are two competing effects: a static effect in which research and development (R&D) incentives are increased because more inventions are patentable and a dynamic effect in which incentives are decreased because the profit from any given invention is lower since it will be replaced more quickly.

Two conclusions are drawn from this analysis: (1) There exists a unique standard of nonobviousness that maximizes the rate of innovation in a given industry, and (2) contrary to the conventional wisdom, reductions in the nonobviousness requirement are more likely to encourage innovation in industries that innovate slowly than in industries that innovate rapidly. The implication is that in rapidly innovating industries where each new product builds on others, welfare is more likely to be enhanced by having a high hurdle for obtaining a patent. O'Donoghue (1998) uses a slightly different model of sequential innovation and draws a similar conclusion – that increasing the standard of patentability can increase R&D as firms go after larger innovations, even though the overall cost of obtaining a patent has risen.

As a general rule, the theoretical work discussed here has abstracted from the frictions introduced by uncertain patent validity, transaction costs such as those needed to negotiate licenses, and the costs of litigation for infringement and validity that arise either because of bargaining breakdown or real uncertainty about the patentability. Yet there is considerable anecdotal (Federal Trade Commission 2003) and some empirical evidence (e.g., Lerner 1995) that these frictions can be an important component of the cost of a patent system, and hence more patents or lower quality patents may be a drag on innovation because they increase transactions costs without increasing innovation incentives. In a recent article, Farrell and Shapiro (2008) consider the problem of uncertain validity and show that, when downstream firms compete with themselves or with the upstream firm that holds the patent, social welfare is improved by determining the validity of the patent before licensing. As they conclude, weak patents can be surprisingly strong so that it is worth eliminating them early in the process.

The main conclusion from theoretical work in this area is that whether patents are a socially useful way to encourage innovation turns on the characteristics of the innovation process and the complexity of the products that "read on" the patents. For this reason, I now turn to a review of the empirical evidence on the question.

B. *Empirical Evidence*

Most researchers who have investigated the question of innovation and the patent system empirically have looked at historical eras when there were changes to the system and examined the consequences for subsequent innovative activity. Recently there have been a pair of studies that use mainly nineteenth-century data (when there was substantial variation across countries in patent systems). One uses invention data from World Fairs and Expositions, and the other uses patenting itself as the innovation measure.

Moser (2005) found that inventors in countries without a patent system do not innovate more than inventors in countries with patent systems. However, when inventors in countries without patent systems do innovate, they tend to do so in areas that are more easily protected with trade secrecy. Lerner (2002) found that, when a country strengthens its patent system, inventors from other countries patent more in that country. However, in his study, inventors from the country itself did not appear to invent more – they neither patented more in their own country nor in Great Britain (which was chosen as a reference country, because it was a very important market in the nineteenth century and one with a well-functioning patent system that was widely used).

Results using data from the twentieth century are harder to find, but survey evidence exists. The first study was probably that by Mansfield (1986), who surveyed 100 U.S. manufacturing firms in the early 1980s, finding that patents were important for innovation only in pharmaceuticals and chemicals, although firms in all sectors reported that they patented more than half of their patentable inventions. This basic result has held up to the present day.

The Carnegie-Mellon and Yale surveys (Cohen, Nelson, and Walsh 2000 and Levin et al. 1987) demonstrate fairly clearly that patents are NOT among the important means to appropriate returns to innovation, except perhaps in the pharmaceutical industry. Similar results have been obtained by other researchers for Europe and Japan. Arundel (2001) reported the results of the PACE survey of large European firms, accounting for more than 75% of the patenting in Europe. In both the United States and Europe, firms rated superior sales and service, lead time, and secrecy as far more important than patents in securing the returns to innovation. They usually reported patents to be important primarily for blocking and defensive purposes.

Using a somewhat more complex economic model and the same survey evidence, Arora, Ceccagnoli, and Cohen (2003) found that the patent premium, which they describe as the difference in payoffs to patented and unpatented inventions net of patent application costs, is not positive on average except for the medical instruments sector. Nevertheless, selecting on those inventions that actually are patented, the premium is generally positive and provides an incentive for R&D that is considerable in the health-related industries and still positive in other sectors.

The most positive results are those obtained using time series cross-section data at the country level. Unfortunately such studies are rarely free of the criticism that the relationship between innovative activity and patenting at the country level is largely simultaneously determined and not causal. In a 1997 paper using aggregate data across sixty countries for the 1960–90 period, Park and Ginarte (1997) found that the strength of the IP system (an index based on coverage, especially whether pharmaceuticals are covered; membership in international agreements; lack of compulsory licensing and working requirements; strength of enforcement; and duration) is positively associated with R&D investment in the thirty countries with the highest median incomes (that is, G-7 and other developed countries, mostly in Europe). In the other countries, the relationship is positive but not significant. Unfortunately their estimates are cross-sectional and not corrected for the simultaneity (reverse causality) between doing R&D and having a patent system, which may explain why they are so different from those of Moser and Lerner. Similar results were reported by Kanwar and Evenson (2003), who also did not control for simultaneity.

Using a database of twenty-six countries whose pharmaceutical patenting laws changed between 1978 and 2002 and applying propensity score matching techniques, Qian (2007) provides a more nuanced view. There was no evidence that the change itself had an impact on innovative activity, measured as cite-weighted patents, R&D, or pharmaceutical exports. However, countries with higher levels of education, development, and economic freedom did experience an increase in innovation. That is, there was an interaction effect, but this effect diminished at the highest levels of patent protection, suggesting that an intermediate level was optimal.

Sakakibara and Branstetter (2001) studied the effects of expanding patent scope in Japan in 1988. According to the Japanese firms and patent attorneys whom they interviewed, a statutory change that allowed multiple claims per patent (as has always been true in the United States) had the effect of increasing patent scope in Japan. They found that this change to the patent system had a very small positive effect on R&D activity in Japanese firms.

Hall and Ziedonis (2001) looked at a single industry (semiconductors) that doubled its patenting-R&D rate after the creation of the CAFC and other changes to patent legislation in 1982. Interview evidence suggested that the increase was due to the fact that inventions in this industry use technology that is covered by hundreds of patents held by a number of firms and that firms increasingly feared litigation and preliminary injunctions if they failed to have cross-licensing agreements in place. Negotiating such agreements was greatly facilitated by having a large patent portfolio of one's own, so several firms – large and small – were engaged in defensive drives to increase their patenting rate. These efforts had little to do with encouraging innovation and in fact looked like a tax on innovative activity. The result also highlights the fact that the one-product/one-patent model of innovation is very far from the reality in many industries.

Hall and Ziedonis (2001) also noted another effect of stronger patents in the semiconductor industry: They appear to have facilitated the entry of pure "design" firms, those that produce semiconductor designs but do no manufacturing. This result was supported both by interview evidence (executives reported that patents were important for securing venture capital financing where there were few other assets) and by the fact that the share of design firms in the industry increased from approximately 0% in 1982 (before the strengthening of the system) to 30% in 1995.

Several conclusions emerge from this survey of empirical work on the effects of the patent system on innovation. Although introducing or strengthening a patent system (lengthening the patent term, broadening subject matter coverage, and so forth) usually results in an increase in patenting, it is not clear that these changes result in an increase in innovative activity at all times and in all places. If there is an increase in innovation due to patents, it is most likely to be centered in the pharmaceutical, biotechnology, and medical instrument sectors, and possibly also specialty chemicals. Patents in many of these areas are relatively easy to define, because they are based on molecular formulas, and therefore they are also relatively easy to enforce. Thus empirical research supports those who argue that a unitary patent system is far from optimal for supporting innovation.

The most interesting and not immediately obvious conclusion is that the existence and strength of the patent system have a tendency to affect the organization of industry, by allowing trade in knowledge and facilitating the vertical disintegration of knowledge-based industries and the entry of new firms that possess only intangible assets. It is very clear that this disruptive feature of the patent system has been important with respect to business method and internet patents. In many (but by no means all) cases, the first step taken by an inventor/entrepreneur with an idea for an internet-based business model is to attempt to acquire a patent on it, and certainly one of the first questions asked by the venture capitalist approached for financing is whether the startup owns patents on its technology.[19]

C. *Implications for Business Method Innovation*

What does the body of literature just surveyed have to say about the implications of allowing business method patents on innovation in business methods and finance? The only conclusion that is certain is that doing so will cause an increase in the patenting of business methods, one we have already experienced. And along with this increase in patenting, especially one that introduces patents of less certain quality, will come an increase in litigation, raising the costs of the system as a whole. It is noteworthy that Lerner (2006b) found that the probability of a lawsuit involving a financial patent held by a small entity is above unity, which suggests both that these patents are relatively valuable and that the primary role they play is the collecting of royalties from other firms.[20] Overall, he found that the lawsuit rate for financial patents awarded between 1976 and 2003 was about 30%, to be compared with the relatively low overall rate of 1–2% reported by Lanjouw and Schankerman (2001). As Farrell and Shapiro (2008) have shown, even weak patents whose validity is uncertain can be surprisingly effective in litigation.

Unfortunately, although we can be confident that the use of patents will increase when they are allowed, it is much more difficult to make predictions about the effects of this subject matter expansion on innovation. We know that patents are not considered essential for capturing the returns to innovation in many industries, and there seems no reason to think that financial patents are any different. Casual

[19] See Mann and Sager (2007) for more detail on the use of patents by venture-backed software startups, which is by no means universal, and varies considerably within the software sector. Also see Merges (2003) on the possible implication of financial patents.

[20] More precisely, Lerner found that firms with less than 200 employees in the year a patent was awarded experienced 1.153 lawsuits per patent, adjusted for the grant and suit lags.

observation suggests that business method patents are not being used to provide innovation incentives as much as they are being used to extract rents ex post, but this evidence could be misleading. We do not know whether there would have been as much entry into internet businesses or new financial offerings in the absence of the patent system or even whether such entry is a good or a bad thing (recent difficulties among innovative financial firms suggest the latter possibility).

A recent study by Duffy and Squires (2008) discusses the tradeoff between secrecy and patenting for financial innovations in sophisticated trading mechanisms, valuation metrics, or innovative financial products, suggesting that as transparency becomes more important to regulators, the desirability of patenting may increase. However, at the present time, such inventions are not generally protectable outside the United States, so patenting is less attractive because it enables easy imitation of an intangible product that can be produced anywhere in the world. Duffy and Squires then looked at 100 patents issued in class 705/35 (Finance – banking, investment, or credit) during 2008 and concluded that only a handful were for such sophisticated new financial products, suggesting either that these products are not yet being patented or that they are still stuck in the PTO.[21] Kumar and Turnbull (2008) provide a model of the decision to patent in the case of new financial products, suggesting that it depends a great deal on the extent to which there is a need to develop a market for the new product, which would involve revealing the idea to potential imitators.

In a slightly different technology area, one possible evolution of practice in the banking and financial services industry can be hypothesized, however. This industry depends heavily on secure communication and transactions exchange among banks and brokerage houses, and such communications depend on standards; that is, they depend on different institutions communicating information to each other in exactly the same way. The industry carries out millions of such transactions daily and requires a very high level of accuracy, which implies a need for highly stable common standards. If components of new transactions' standards or particular ways of doing things are patented by many different institutions, it is possible that a situation could develop like that in the semiconductor/computer industry, where it is necessary to have a portfolio of patents for cross-licensing purposes. This in turn may raise the cost of doing business and make it harder for new firms to enter without access to the requisite intellectual property.

I close this discussion with the observation by Merges (2003) about the potential consequences of the introduction of patenting into the financial sector, which has not been welcomed by the established large players in that sector. According to Merges, two other U.S. industries (railroads in the nineteenth century and commercial software in the twentieth) greeted the arrival of patents on a large scale in their

[21] Note that because this type of patent is unlikely to be applied for outside the United States and therefore will not be published at eighteen months after application, the current seven-year pendency means that a number of applications could be pending and not yet observed.

sectors with alarm and then learned to live with them, with no obvious decline in innovative activity or even profitability. As he puts it, "Perhaps patents overall simply do not affect the 'big variables' of economic life – industry structure, the basic pace of innovation, etc. – in such an industry to any great extent" (Merges 2003, p. 21).

III. PATENT QUALITY[22]

Many critics of the wave of business method patents in the first couple of years following the *State Street* decision have pointed to their low quality rather than their existence as the real policy problem (see Barton 2000, Dreyfuss 2001, and other references in Table 7.4). But what is meant by patent quality? The statutory definition of a patentable invention is that it be novel, nonobvious, and have utility.[23] Both the economic and legal view suggest that high-quality patents are those that describe an invention that is truly "new," rather than an invention that is already in widespread use but not yet patented.[24]

In addition to the three statutory requirements, a fourth criterion for granting a patent on an invention is that the patent application must disclose sufficient details about the invention. These disclosures in the published patent can facilitate knowledge spillovers to others who might use or improve on the invention. Another criterion for a "high-quality patent" therefore is that it enable those "skilled in the art" to comprehend the invention well enough to use the patent document for implementation of the described invention.

From a social welfare perspective, an important characteristic of a high-quality patent is that there be relatively little uncertainty over the breadth of its claims (i.e., over what specific features of a technical advance are claimed under the terms of the patent, as well as whether these claims are likely to be upheld in legal proceedings following the issue of the patent). Uncertainty about the validity of a patent has several potential costs: It may cause the patent holder to underinvest in the technology, it could reduce investment by potential competitors in competing technical advances, and it may lead to costly litigation after both the holder and potential competitors have sunk sizable investments. A recent book by Bessen and Meurer (2008) argues very clearly that lack of clear notice renders the patent right very unlike an ordinary real property right.

A. *Consequences of Low Patent Quality*

Although some scholars, notably Lemley (2001), have argued that the costs of having higher quality patents may exceed the benefit, recent experience suggests that there

22 Parts of this section are drawn from Hall et al. (2003).

23 See Lunney (2001) for an argument that the nonobviousness test has been weakened since the creation of the Federal Circuit Court of Appeals in 1982.

24 Presumably, if the invention has already been reduced to practice by others, the potential gain from incentivizing an inventor is zero, so we are left only with the deadweight loss from monopoly.

TABLE 7.4. *Recent recommendations on patent policy*

Author(s)*	Date	Type	Recommendation(s)
Dreyfuss	2001	business method	Prior-art search weak and generates low-quality patents; costs of business method patents greatly exceed benefits and they should be statutorily excluded
Merges	1999	business method	Business method patent flood and issuing low-quality patents; calls for opposition system
Meurer	2002	business method	PTO and the courts should use the subject matter and nonobviousness standards for patentability to limit grants of business method patents. Favors reversal of *State Street* and restoration of the business method exception. Short of reversal, argues for a narrow reading of *State Street* and rigorous application of the nonobviousness standard.
Lunney	2001	business method	Federal Circuit has gone too far in loosening nonobviousness test, requiring written documentation. Should limit e-commerce patents to those that are very creative (i.e., raise patentability standards)
AIPLA	2000	business method	Recommends that business methods with useful, concrete, or tangible results, including internet- and software-implemented business methods, receive the same treatment as other technologies. Where implemented in software, business method patent applications should be examined as software-related applications are examined today for compliance with 35 U.S.C. §§§ 101, 102, and 103
Thomas	1999	business method	Restrict patentable advances to the repeatable production or transformation of material objects and exclude subject matter founded on the aesthetic, social observation, or personal skill. Consistent with TRIPS, the industrial application requirement would restore a sense of patentable subject matter that matches our sensibilities.
Wegner	2001	business method	Favors opposition system modeled on Europe and Japan and also designated trial courts for patent cases
Bakels and Hugen-holtz	2002	software	(1) Stronger inventive step test; (2) exclude business method patents "as such"; and (3) create a European Patent Observatory to monitor system performance
Cohen and Lemley	2001	software	(1) Limited right to reverse engineer patented programs, in order to duplicate unprotected elements; and (2) courts should enforce doctrine of equivalents narrowly for software

(*continued*)

TABLE 7.4 *(continued)*

Author(s)	Date	Type	Recommendation(s)
Somaya	2001	software	Software components should be reused, as in Lemley and O'Brien
Lemley and O'Brien	1997	software	Software patents will encourage the reuse of software components, because trade secrecy will no longer be necessary.
Dam	1995	software	Software patents sound, although badly administered by PTO; sui generis protection for software not desirable
Samuelson	1995	Software	Recommends limited protection for software interfaces (sui generis)
Warren-Boulton, Baseman, and Woroch	1995	Software	(1) Copyright should not extend to de facto standards; (2) software interfaces should not be copyrighted, because of market power extension; and (3) allow reverse engineering for interoperability
Kasdan	1994	software	Lack of computer science personnel among PTO examiners means prior-art search incomplete (e.g. Knuth's book ignored); software patents undesirable
Kingston	2001	general	Lower cost of patent disputes in complex technologies via (1) compulsory expert arbitration with legal aid and (2) shared-risk compulsory licensing
Levin and Levin	2002	general	Introducing a patent opposition process would yield substantial welfare gains
Lemley	2001	general	Do not try to improve patent quality by increasing exam time because PTO is "rationally ignorant," given cost of higher quality patents
Quillen	2001	general	(1) Raise standards for patentability; (2) reduce resulting uncertainty and delay in validity determination; (3) reduce excessive damages in patent infringement litigation; and (4) return appellate jurisdiction to regional courts so alternative views can be heard on the same issue
Barton	2000 2001	general	(1) Raise standards for patentability by using a real nonobviousness test; (2) clarify research exemption; (3) ease legal attack on invalid patents (strengthen reexam, remove presumption of validity)
Janis	1997	general	Institute an inter partes reexam system modeled on trademark reexam and similar to European opposition system

* Complete citations are given in the References section.

are also some unintended consequences in the form of complicating property rights and feedback effects. In this part we review the arguments for increasing patent quality.

"Low-quality patents" can create considerable uncertainty among inventors or would-be commercializers of inventions and slow either the pace of innovation or investment in the commercialization of new technologies. Lerner (1995) has shown that fear of litigation may cause smaller entrant firms to avoid areas where incumbents hold large numbers of patents. Such entry avoidance may be rational and even welfare enhancing if the incumbents' patents are known for certain to be valid, but low-quality patents held by incumbents may also deter entry into a technological area if the costs of invalidating the patents are too high. In these circumstances, technological alternatives may not be commercialized and consumer welfare suffers. Also, as Farrell and Shapiro (2008) argue, low-quality patents can harm consumer welfare if used to restrain downstream competition.

The lack of relatively rapid processes for resolving patent validity and ensuring higher patent quality also may slow the pace of invention in fields characterized by "cumulative invention" (i.e., those in which one inventor's efforts rely on previous technical advances or advances in complementary technologies). If these previous technical advances are covered by patents of dubious validity or excessive breadth, the costs to inventors of pursuing the inventions that rely on them may be so high as to discourage such cumulative invention. Alternatively, large numbers of low-quality patents may dramatically increase the level of "fragmentation" of property rights covering prior-generation or complementary technologies, raising the transaction costs for inventors of obtaining access (e.g., through licenses) to these technologies (Shapiro 2001). Finally, the issue of a large number of low-quality patents will increase uncertainty among inventors concerning the level of protection enjoyed by these related inventions, which in turn will make it more costly and difficult for inventors to build on these related inventions in their own technical advances.

The issuance of low-quality patents also is likely to spur significant increases in patent applications, further straining the already overburdened examination processes of the PTO. A kind of vicious circle may result, in which cursory examinations of patent applications result in the issue of low-quality patents, which triggers a rapid growth in applications, further taxing the limited resources of the PTO, further limiting the examination of individual applications, and further degrading the quality of patents.

Decisions in the early 2000s by the CAFC, the specialized appeals court for patent cases, concerning the validity of "important" patents (those deemed sufficiently valuable by the patent holder or competitor to litigate and appeal) create still another reason for serious consideration of a nonjudicial process for post-issue validity challenges. For example, in 2002 it ruled that the PTO had incorrectly rejected two applications for "obviousness," arguing that if an examiner rejects an application using "general knowledge," that knowledge "must be articulated and placed on the record."[25] At the time, according to Deputy Commissioner Esther Kepplinger, this meant "we can't reject something just because it's stupid."[26] It is possible that decisions such as this one have significantly weakened the level of scrutiny provided by the already costly and overcrowded patent litigation system.

The PTO has responded both to critics of the quality of patents being issued and the increasing flood of patent applications in several ways. First, it introduced a second pair of eyes for the examination of business method patents in March 2000 and later extended this practice to other new technology areas. Second, in 2007, together with the Peer-to-Patent Project at the New York University Law School, it begin a pilot program that allows third parties to submit prior art for selected patent applications in the computing and business method areas that are in the system but not yet examined. It is clear that these initiatives have had some effect, both on the decline in the number of 705 patents issuing and in the initial patent allowance rate, which has fallen from 70% in 2001 to 45% in 2008 (Crouch 2009).

Finally, then-Commissioner Dudas proposed a series of rules changes in 2008 that were designed to reduce the PTO workload by discouraging continuation applications, requests for continued examinations, and applications with large numbers of claims. After litigation by inventors opposed to these changes, the CAFC allowed at least some to stand (Foley & Lardner LLP 2009).

IV. SURVEY OF POLICY RECOMMENDATIONS

In an effort to find a consensus, this part collects and organizes the many policy recommendations with respect to business method, internet, and software patents that have been made by other scholars. Table 7.4 summarizes the recommendations of a number of legal and economic scholars. Several points emerge from this table and from a reading of the papers referenced.

First, there is a remarkable amount of agreement, if not a consensus, that the average quality of patents being issued during the 1990s was too low, especially in the software and business method areas. There is also some agreement on the reasons: an overburdened PTO, lack of expertise in the relevant areas, lack of prior-art databases, and the weakening of the nonobviousness test, partly through court decisions.

Recommendations center on correcting these problems in software and business methods, although many of the suggestions would apply more broadly. Many authors suggest that standards of patentability and nonobviousness should be increased across

[25] This decision presumably made it more difficult to reject such patents as US 6368227, the patent on a swinging method that uses a technique known by children for years but not placed "on the record." Note that this particular patent has been subject to a reexamination request of the U.S. Patent Commissioner because of the publicity it received. The problem with patents like this is not necessarily that they are enforceable in the courts, but that they clog the system and raise its total cost.

[26] As quoted in the *Los Angeles Times*, February 7, 2003.

all technologies, but especially in software and business methods (Barton 2000, 2001, Kasdan 1994, Bakels and Hugenholtz 2002, Lunney 2001, Quillen 2001, Dreyfuss 2001, Meurer 2002). This recommendation appears to have been followed to some extent by the PTO after about 2001 and was reinforced by the Supreme Court decision in *KSR* v. *Teleflex*.[27]

In contrast, recommendations with respect to subject matter extensions to software and business methods vary considerably, ranging all the way from the AIPLA position that business methods receive the same treatment as other technologies to Thomas's (1999) recommendation that subject matter be restricted to "the repeatable production or transformation of material objects." Nevertheless, a number of legal scholars, including Dreyfuss, Meurer, and Bakels and Hugenholtz, have called for reinstatement of the business method exception. Again, to a limited extent this has happened with the *Bilski* decision.

With respect to software more broadly, Lemley and O'Brien (1997) and Somaya (2001) have argued that patenting of software may have a beneficial effect if it leads to the reuse rather than the reinvention of software components as a result of patent publication, instead of the use of secrecy to protect them. However, Lemley and Cohen (Cohen and Lemley 2001), Warren-Boulton, Baseman, and Woroch (1995), and Samuelson (1995) have recommended both narrow construction of patents for software and limited rights to reverse engineer in order to ensure interoperability and transparent interfaces.

Finally, several authors have endorsed the idea that a greatly strengthened inter partes post-grant reexamination system modeled on the European opposition system would encourage competitors and other third parties to bring forth prior art, especially in new subject matter areas where the PTO has inadequate searching facilities (Janis 1997, Levin and Levin 2003, Graham et al. 2003, Hall et al. 2003, Wegner 2001). The primary argument for such a system is that it would lead to invalidity determinations being made earlier and at less cost than under the current system, which relies primarily on infringement suits accompanied by countersuits for patent validity. A second argument is that, by housing validity determination within the PTO, useful feedback on the performance and accuracy of examination can be generated relatively quickly and communicated at somewhat lower cost than if it is generated by the courts. I refer the reader to Graham et al. (2003) for further information on the comparative operation of the ex parte U.S. reexamination system and the inter partes European opposition system.

CONCLUSIONS

Broad evidence that the patent system encourages innovation always and everywhere is hard to come by. The patent system does encourage publication rather

[27] KSR v. Teleflex, 550 U.S. 398 (2007).

than secrecy; it is probably good at providing incentives for innovations with high development costs that are fairly easily imitated and for which a patent can be clearly defined (e.g., pharmaceuticals). When innovations are incremental and when many different innovations must be combined to make a useful product, it is less obvious that the benefits of the patent system outweigh the costs. Business and financial methods are more likely to fall into the second class than the first.

It is useful to think about recommendations for policy toward business methods patents in two very distinct ways. First, there is widespread agreement among legal scholars that the nonobviousness test has not been applied carefully enough in the case of internet and business method patents and that the lack of prior-art databases has led to the issuance of many invalid patents in software and business methods. Second, some scholars go further and argue that business methods per se should be excluded from patentability, Judge Rich not withstanding. Given the number of such patents now outstanding, this outcome is unlikely.

With respect to the former critique, a number of scholars have advanced the use of a strengthened post-grant reexamination system to encourage third parties to bring prior art to the attention of the PTO. Although the PTO strengthened the examination process with respect to these patents (USPTO 1999), some believe that this proposal still has some merit, especially if it could be used to weed out patents in these areas that were issued prior to the administrative changes at the PTO. In the meantime, legal decisions and the PTO's own actions seem to have mitigated the problems that arose following the *State Street* decision.

Excluding business and financial methods per se from patentability, although perhaps desirable, is not feasible given the difficulty of defining what they are. Even at the EPO, where there is a general exclusion, such patents do exist whenever the invention solves a particular technical problem. The language in the recent *Bilski* decision in the United States seems to move in that direction, excluding those patents with overbroad and vague claims that many perceive to be the main drag on the innovative system.

REFERENCES

Allison, J. R. and E. H. Tiller (2003). "Statistical Analysis of Internet Business Method Patents," in W. M. Cohen (ed.), *Intellectual Property in the Knowledge-Based Economy*. Washington, DC: National Academies Press.

Arora, A., M. Ceccagnoli, and W. Cohen (2003). *R&D and the Patent Premium*. Cambridge, MA: NBER Working Paper No. W9431.

Arundel, A. (2001). "Patents in the Knowledge-Based Economy," *Beleidstudies Technology Economie* 37: 67–88.

Bakels, R. and P. B. Hugenholtz (2002). *The Patentability of Computer Programs*. Amsterdam: IViR.

Barton, J. H. (2001). "Non-Obviousness." Stanford University Law School (August), manuscript.

———. (2000). "Reforming the Patent System," *Science* 287: 1933–34.

Bessen, J. E. and R. M. Hunt (2004). *An Empirical Look at Software Patents*. Philadelphia, PA: Federal Reserve Bank of Philadelphia Working Paper No. 03–17/R.

Bessen, J. E. and E. Maskin (2006). *Sequential Innovation, Patents, and Imitation*. Princeton, NJ: Institute for Advanced Study, School of Social Science.

Bessen, J. E. and M. J. Meurer (2008). *Patent Failure: How Judges, Bureaucrats, and Lawyers Put Innovators at Risk*. Princeton, NJ: Princeton University Press.

Blind, K., J. Edler, and R. Nack (2001). *Micro- and Macro-economic Implications of the Patentability of Software Innovations. Intellectual Property Rights in Information Technologies between Innovation and Competition*. Karlsruhe/Munich: Fraunhofer Institute and Max Planck Institute.

Cockburn, I. (2001). "Issues in Business Method Patents." Boston, MA: Boston University and NBER, manuscript.

Cohen, J. E. and M. A. Lemley (2001). "Patent Scope and Innovation in the Software Industry," *California Law Review* 89(1): 1–57.

Cohen, W. M., R. R. Nelson, and J. P. Walsh (2000). *Protecting Their Intellectual Assets: Appropriability Conditions and Why Firms Patent or Not?* Cambridge, MA: NBER Working Paper No. 7552

Crouch, D. (2009). Patently-O Blog. http://www.patentlyo.com.

Dam, K. W. (1995). "Some Economic Considerations in the Intellectual Property Protection of Software," *Journal of Legal Studies* 24: 321–77.

Davis, L. (2002b). "Is Appropriability a 'Problem' for Innovations in Digital Information Goods?" in G. Eliasson and C. Wihlborg (eds.), *The Law, Economics and Technology of the Internet*, unknown publisher.

———. (2002a). "Patents and the Internet," in G. Eliasson and C. Wihlborg (eds.), *The Law, Economics and Technology of the Internet*, unknown publisher.

Diallo, B. (2003). "Historical Perspectives on IP Protection for Software in Selected Countries Worldwide," *World Patent Information* 25: 19–25.

Dreyfuss, R. C. (2001). "Examining *State Street Bank*: Developments in Business Method Patenting," *Computer und Recht International* 2001(1): 1–9.

———. (2000). "State Street or Easy Street: Is Patenting Business Methods Good for Business?" in *Intellectual Property Law*, Vol. 6, Ch. 14. London: Juris Publishing Company.

Duffy, J. F. and J. A. Squires (2008). "Disclosure and Financial Patents: Revealing the Invisible Hand." Paper presented at the Bank of Finland-CEPR Conference, Helsinki, October 2008.

European Commission. (2002). "Proposal for a Directive of the European Parliament and of the Council on the Patentability of Computer-implemented Inventions," Brussels: European Commission.

Farrell, J. and C. Shapiro (2008). "How Strong Are Weak Patents?" *American Economic Review* 98 (4): 1347–69.

Federal Trade Commission (2003). *To Promote Innovation: The Proper Balance of Patent and Competition Law Policy*. Washington, DC: U.S. Government Printing Office.

Foley & Lardner LLP (2009). "Did the Patent Office Win? Tafas v. Doll Opens the Door to Substantial Changes in the USPTO's Practice, but Finds that Limits on Continuation Applications Exceed USPTO Authority," *Legal News Alert*, March 2009. http://www.foley.com/publications/pub_detail.aspx?pubid=5859, accessed March 12, 2011.

Graham, S. J. H., B. H. Hall, D. Harhoff, and D. C. Mowery (2003). "Post-Issue Patent Quality Control: A Comparative Study of US Patent Re-Examinations and European Patent Oppositions," in W. M. Cohen and S. A. Merrill (eds.), *The Patent System in the Knowledge-Based Economy*. Washington, DC: National Academies Press, pp. 74–119.

Graham, S. J. H. and D. C. Mowery (2003). "Intellectual Property Protection in the U.S. Software Industry," in W. M. Cohen and S. A. Merrill (eds.), *The Patent System in the Knowledge-Based Economy*. Washington, DC: National Academies Press.

Green, J. and S. Scotchmer. (1995). "On the Division of Profit in Sequential Innovation," *RAND Journal of Economics* 26: 20–33.

Grindley, P.C and Teece, D.J. (1997). "Managing Intellectual Capital: Licensing and Cross-Licensing in Semiconductors and Electronics," *California Management Review* 39: 1–34.

Hall, B. H. (2007). "Innovation in Non-Bank Payment Systems." Paper presented at the Kansas City Federal Reserve Conference, Santa Fe, NM, May 2007.

Hall, B. H. (2003). *Business Method Patents, Innovation, and Policy*. Cambridge, MA: NBER Working Paper w9717.

Hall, B. H., S. J. H. Graham, D. Harhoff, and D. C. Mowery (2003). "Prospects for Improving U.S. Patent Quality via Post-grant Opposition," *Innovation Policy and the Economy* 4: 115–43.

Hall, B. H., and M. MacGarvie (2006). *The Private Value of Software Patents*. Cambridge, MA: NBER Working Paper w12195.

Hall, B. H., G. Thoma, and S. Torrisi (2009). "Financial Patenting in Europe," *European Management Review*, 6: 45–63.

Hall, B. H., and R. H. Ziedonis (2001). "The Patent Paradox Revisited: An Empirical Study of Patenting in the U.S. Semiconductor Industry, 1979–1995," *RAND Journal of Economics* 32:101–28.

Hart, P., P. Holmes, and J. Reid (1999). *The Economic Impact of Patentability of Computer Programs*. London: Intellectual Property Institute.

Heller, M. A. and R. S. Eisenberg (1998). "Can Patents Deter Innovation? The Anticommons in Biomedical Research," *Science* 280: 698–701.

Hunt, R. M. (2008). *Business Method Patents and U.S. Financial Services*. Research Department Working Paper No. 07–21. Philadelphia: Federal Reserve Bank of Philadelphia.

______. (2001a). Patentability, Industry Structure, and Innovation. Working Paper No. 01–13. Philadelphia: Federal Reserve Bank of Philadelphia Research Dept.

______. (2001b). "You Can Patent That? Are Patents on Computer Programs and Business Methods Good for the New Economy?" *Philadelphia Federal Reserve Bank Business Review* 2001(Q1): 5–15.

Janis, M. D. (1997). "Rethinking Reexamination: Toward a Viable Administrative Revocation System for U.S. Patent Law," *Harvard Journal of Law and Technology* 11 (1): 1–122.

Kanwar, S. and R. Evenson (2003). "Does Intellectual Property Protection Spur Technical Change?" *Oxford Economic Papers* 55: 235–64.

Kasdan, J. (1999). Obviousness and New Technologies. Working Paper No. 146. New York: Columbia University Center for Law and Economics Studies.

______. (1994). Fascinatin' Algorithm: Patent Protection for Computer Programs. Working Paper No. 94. New York: Columbia University Center for Law and Economics Studies.

Kingston, W. (2001). "Innovation Needs Patents Reform," *Research Policy* 30 (3): 403–23.

Kumar, P and S. M. Turnbull (2008). "Optimal Patenting and Licensing of Financial Innovations," *Management Science* 54 (12): 2012–23.

Lanjouw, J. O. and M. Schankerman (2001). "Characteristics of Patent Litigation: A Window on Competition," *RAND Journal of Economics* 32 (1): 129–51.

Lemley, M. A. (2001). "Rational Ignorance at the Patent Office," *Northwestern University Law Review* 95 (4): 1495–1532.

Lemley, M. A. and D. W. O'Brien (1997). "Encouraging Software Reuse," *Stanford Law Review* 49(2): 255–304.

Lerner, J. (2006a). "The New New Financial Thing: The Origins of Financial Innovations," *Journal of Financial Economics* 79 (2): 223–55.

———. (2006b). "Trolls on State Street? The Litigation of Financial Patents, 1976–2005." Boston, MA: Harvard Business School, manuscript.

———. (2002). "Patent Protection and Innovation over 150 Years," *American Economic Review* 92 (2): 221–25.

———. (2001). Where Does State Street Lead? Harvard Business School Working Paper No. 01–005.

———. (1995). "Patenting in the Shadow of Competitors," *Journal of Law and Economics* 38(2): 463–96.

Levin, R. C., A. K. Klevorick, R. R. Nelson, and S. G. Winter (1987). "Appropriating the Returns to Industrial R&D," *Brookings Papers on Economic Activity*: 783–820.

Levin, R. C. and J. Levin. (2003). "Benefits and Costs of an Opposition Process," in W. M. Cohen and S. A. Merrill (eds.), *The Patent System in the Knowledge-Based Economy*. Washington, DC: National Academies Press, pp. 120–44.

Lunney, G. S., Jr. (2001). "e-Obviousness," *Michigan Telecommunications Technology Law Review* 7: 363–422.

Managing Intellectual Property (2007). "A Sliver of Hope for UK Software Patents." *Weekly News*, June 1. http://www.managingip.com/Article/1377101/A-sliver-of-hope-for-UK-software-patents.html.

Managing Intellectual Property (2004). "UK Acts over Business Method Applications." *Weekly News*, November 28. http://www.managingip.com/Article/1258644/Latest-News-Magazine/UK-acts-over-business-method-applications.html.

Mann, R. J. and T. W. Sager (2007). "Patents, Venture Capital, and Software Startups," *Research Policy* 36: 193–208.

Mansfield, E. (1986). "Patents and Innovation: An Empirical Study," *Management Science* 32: 173–81.

Mazzoleni, R. and R. R. Nelson (1998). "Economic Theories About the Benefits and Costs of Patents," *Journal of Economic Issues* 32(4): 1031–52.

Merges, R. P. (2003). The Uninvited Guest: Patents on Wall Street. Berkeley, CA: University of California at Berkeley Public Law Research Paper No. 126.

———. 1999. "As Many As Six Impossible Patents Before Breakfast: Property Rights for Business Concepts and Patent System Reform," *Berkeley Technology Law Journal* 14 (2): 577–616.

Meurer, M. J. (2002). "Business Method Patents and Patent Floods," *Washington University Journal of Law and Policy* 8: 309–40.

Moser, P. (2005). "How Do Patent Laws Influence Innovation? Evidence from Nineteenth-Century World's Fairs," *American Economic Review* 95 (4): 1214–36.

O'Donoghue, T. (1998). "A Patentability Requirement for Sequential Innovation," *RAND Journal of Economics* 29 (4): 654–79.

Park, W. G. and J. C. Ginarte (1997). "Intellectual Property Rights and Economic Growth," *Contemporary Economic Policy* XV (July): 51–61.

Qian, Y. (2007). "Do Additional National Patent Laws Stimulate Domestic Innovation in a Global Patenting Environment?" *Review of Economics and Statistics* 89 (3): 436–53.

Quillen, C. D., Jr. 2001. "The U.S. Patent System: Is it Broke? And Who Can Fix it, if It Is? Presentation to the Association of General Counsel.

Sakakibara, M., and L. Branstetter (2001). "Do Stronger Patents Induce More Innovation? Evidence from the 1988 Japanese Patent law Reforms," *RAND Journal of Economics* 32: 77–100.

Samuelson, P. (1995). "An Entirely New Legal Regime Is Needed," *The Computer Lawyer* 12 (2): 11–17.
Scotchmer, S. (1996). "Protecting Early Innovators: Should Second Generation Products be Patentable?," *RAND Journal of Economics* 27: 322–31.
______. (1991). "Standing on the Shoulders of Giants: Cumulative Research and the Patent Law," *Journal of Economic Perspectives* 5: 29–41.
Shapiro, C. (2001). "Navigating the Patent Thicket: Cross Licenses, Patent Pools, and Standard-Setting," *Innovation Policy and the Economy* 1: 119–50.
Somaya, D. (2001). *Incentives, Organizational Choices and Transactional Challenges in Software Production*. College Park, MD: University of Maryland.
Spindler, G. (2003). "The European Legal Framework for Software Patents." Paper presented at the EPIP conference on New Challenges to the Patent System, EPO, Munich, Germany, April 24/25, 2003.
State Street Bank and Trust Co., Inc. v. Signature Financial Group, Inc., 149 F.3d 1368 (Fed. Cir. 1998).
Takalo, T. and M. Komulainen. (2008). "Empirical Study of European patent applications in class G06Q 40/00B Exchange." Helsinki, manuscript.
Thomas, J. R. (1999). "The Patenting of the Liberal Professions," *Boston College Law Review*. 40: 1139–90.
USPTO (1999). *White Paper on Automated Financial or Management Data Processing Methods (Business Methods)*. http://www.uspto.gov/web/menu/busmethp/index2.htm.
Wagner, S. (2008). "Business Method Patents in Europe and their Strategic Use – Evidence from Franking Device Manufacturers," *Economics of Innovation and New Technology* 17 (3–4): 173–94.
Warren-Boulton, F. R., K. C. Baseman, and G. A. Woroch. (1995). "Copyright Protection of Software Can Make Economic Sense," *The Computer Lawyer* 12 (2): 18–28.
Wegner, H. C. (2001). "Invalidity Defenses to e-patent Infringement: A Comparative View of the Differing Ways to Achieve Patent Justice in the United States," Paper presented at the SOFTIC 2001 Symposium, Tokyo, Japan.

8

The Litigation of Financial Innovations

*Josh Lerner**

INTRODUCTION

The impact of financial innovation is widely accepted. For instance, the economic importance of new products and services in the financial arena has been heralded by Miller [1986] and Merton [1992], questioned by Van Horne [1985], and empirically documented by Tufano [1989]. However, the empirics of financial innovation have attracted remarkably little academic attention, as highlighted in a review article by Frame and White [2004].

In the past decade, there has been a profound change in the conditions under which financial innovations are pursued. The *State Street Bank* case in the late 1990s opened the door to the widespread patenting of financial inventions. (The history of financial patenting is summarized in the next section.) Because patents fundamentally alter the way in which innovations can be used – for instance, they make the type of rapid diffusion documented by Tufano [1989] less feasible – assessing the impact of patenting is critical to understanding the future of financial innovation. We know almost nothing about the way in which these financial patents, having been granted, are utilized by firms.

This chapter seeks to understand the litigation of financial patents. Litigation is crucial to delineating the boundaries of patent awards. Moreover, because patent litigation typically entails several millions of dollars of expenditures for each party in a suit (AIPLA [2005]), the lawsuits in this sample represent a significant expenditure of resources.

* Harvard University and National Bureau of Economic Research. Chris Allen, Sarah Eriksen, Chris Johnson, Erika McCaffrey, Jacek Rycko, Sarah Woolverton, and especially Lori Santikian provided excellent research assistance. Harvard Business School and the Toulouse Network on Information Technology provided financial support. I thank Peter Tufano for permission to use some of our joint work in Part I. I thank Bronwyn Hall, Bob Hunt, Vivian Maese, Sam Peltzman, Rufus Pollock, Mark Schankerman, Enrique Schroth, two anonymous referees, and seminar participants at Columbia, Harvard, the NBER, the Securities Industry Association, and Toulouse for helpful conversations. All errors are my own.

After framing the chapter through a discussion of the economics literature on suit and settlement, I empirically examine the litigation of all financial patents awarded between January 1976 and August 2003 through the end of 2005. I find that financial patents are being litigated at a rate twenty-seven to thirty-nine times greater than that of patents as a whole. The rate is more than an order of magnitude higher than even the most extensively litigated major category of patents (drugs and health). It is also far greater than that in the early years of another emerging industry where the extent and breadth of patent protection were initially ambiguous: biotechnology.

The bulk of this chapter seeks to understand the litigation of financial patents in greater depth. I show the following:

- The financial patents being litigated are disproportionately those issued to individuals. Inasmuch as those granted to corporations are being adjudicated, it is overwhelmingly those issued to smaller, private entities. This seems inconsistent with suggestions that larger firms will be able to detect infringements more accurately or will have more resources to pursue infringers.
- Litigated patents appear to be more important than other financial patents: They have more claims and disproportionately cite and are cited by other patents. This result appears consistent with standard economic models of suit and settlement.
- Litigation does not appear to have increased for patents awarded after the *State Street Bank* decision, despite the likely increase in uncertainty about these awards. If these years also saw an increase in the awarding of lower quality patents, the lack of a temporal pattern may be consistent with theory.
- The defendants in these cases are dominated by larger firms. Differences in the cost of litigation may explain the greater propensity of well-off firms to be the target of lawsuits, and individuals and smaller firms to be plaintiffs.

The chapter is structured as follows. Part I summarizes the history of financial patenting. Part II briefly reviews the relevant literature on the economics of litigation. Part III describes the construction of the dataset. Part IV analyzes which patents are litigated. Part V examines which firms are defendants in lawsuits. The final section explores the implications.

I. THE PATENTING OF FINANCIAL INNOVATIONS[1]

There has long been ambiguity about the patentability of financial innovations in the United States. American law did not explicitly forbid such patents, as many nations in the French and German legal traditions did. But after the 1908 court decision

[1] This section is based in part on Lerner [2002] and Lerner and Tufano [2003], as well as a number of practitioner interviewers.

that established the "business methods exception,"[2] many judges and lawyers presumed that financial and other business methods were not patentable subject matter. Although the U.S. Patent and Trademark Office (PTO) has issued patents on financial and other business methods for several decades – Merrill Lynch's 1982 patent (U.S. Patent no. 4,346,442) on the Cash Management Account was a high-profile pioneering award – many observers questioned their validity. Consequently, patent holders were reluctant to incur the time and expense to litigate their awards.

As a result, financial innovators took different approaches to managing their key intellectual assets than did other industries. Key innovations by one investment bank were rapidly copied by their competitors, with imitative products usually appearing after the innovator had an opportunity to market only a single issue of the new security (Tufano [1989]). Firms boasted that they could use the information in required securities filings to "reverse engineer" virtually any discovery. Whole prospectuses were copied virtually verbatim. Defecting employees frequently carried knowledge with them from one employer to the next, and vendors would transfer insights developed during projects with financial institutions to their competitors. Although firms tried to protect their insights (e.g., trading strategies) through the use of trade secrets, these protections were frequently modest at best. Firms also used branding, in the form of service-marked products, to differentiate their offerings from one another.

Attitudes toward business method patents changed with the July 1998 appellate decision in *State Street Bank and Trust* v. *Signature Financial Group*.[3] This case originated with a software program used to determine the value of mutual funds, on which Signature had obtained a patent (U.S. Patent no. 5,193,056) in 1993. State Street Bank sued to have the patent invalidated on the grounds that it covered a business method and was hence not patentable. Although State Street Bank's argument prevailed in the district court, the Court of Appeals for the Federal Circuit (CAFC), the centralized appellate court for patent cases, reversed the finding. In its decision, the court explicitly rejected the notion of a "business method exception."[4] The Supreme Court declined to hear State Street Bank's appeal of the appellate decision in January 1999. In the numerous articles in the trade press that followed the two decisions, the case was interpreted as unambiguously establishing the patentability of business methods. A rapid expansion in the number of finance patents issued soon followed.[5]

The decision appears to have led to a substantial increase in the filing and granting of business method patents, including financial patents. In interviews with a number of financial institutions, Peter Tufano and I found firms undertaking a variety of

[2] Hotel Security Checking Co. v. Lorraine Co., 160 F. 467 (2d Cir. 1908).

[3] 927 F. Supp. 502, 38 USPQ2d 1530 (D. Mass. 1996); 149 F.3d 1368 (Fed. Cir. 1998).

[4] On the day when Signature won its suit, State Street's stock fell 2.3%, or $277 million.

[5] There is no definitive definition of a financial patent. It can be defined as encompassing awards on products and processes relating to banking, insurance, investing, payment systems, securities issuance, and trading. In the Appendix I present a definition using the PTO's patent classification scheme.

responses. In some instances, the firms engaged in strictly defensive patenting that protected innovations to ensure that others did not patent them later and gathered patents with careful consideration of a possible counterattack should any rival accuse them of patent infringement. In other instances, financial institutions saw patents as having a broader use by, for instance, allowing them to establish a strategic position in the municipal bond market, where the widespread distribution of prospectuses had traditionally made it difficult to protect innovations (see, for instance, U.S. Patents no. 7,246,094 and 7,376,607). By far the most aggressive responses were from individual inventors and patent-holding companies, which have accounted for a disproportionate share of the awards (Lerner [2002]) and have aggressively sought in many cases to monetize these awards through demands for royalties and litigation.

But this growth of patenting has not been without controversy. One of the major concerns expressed about the expansion of awards in this area has been about their quality. Many accounts have focused on particularly problematic patents, such as U.S. Patent no. 5,884,286, a 1999 award to a graduate of Georgia Tech's MBA program that covered the valuation of infinitely lived call and put options, despite the fact that the academic literature on the pricing of these instruments dates back to 1965. These concerns are at least partially supported by Lerner [2002], who shows that, although academic research is highly relevant to many financial patents, these works are far less often cited in patents than in other academically related areas, such as biotechnology.

The status of finance patents was again thrown into uncertainty by the CAFC's ruling in the *In re Bilski* case in October 2008.[6] In a 9–3 decision, the court upheld a ruling made by the Board of Patent Appeals and Interferences that denied a patent for a method of hedging in commodities trading developed by Bernard Bilski and Rand Warsaw. While disallowing this patent, the court made clear that business methods will still be patentable. In particular, it indicated that it would disallow patents where every step of the claimed process may be performed entirely in the human mind, rather than needing to rely on a machine: "of course, a claimed process wherein all of the process steps may be performed entirely in the human mind is obviously not tied to any machine and does not transform any article into a different state or thing. As a result, it would not be patent-eligible." Press commentaries after the decision highlighted the resulting uncertainty surrounding the patentability of business methods and the status of existing awards, especially given the Supreme Court's decision to review the case.

II. MODELING AND ANALYZING SUIT AND SETTLEMENT

Since the pioneering work of Priest and Klein [1984], economists have understood that the decision to litigate rather than settle disputes is a function of the expected

[6] 543 F. 3d 943 (Fed. Cir. 2008) (en banc).

payoffs. To summarize a well-developed literature (see the survey by Cooter and Rubinfeld [1989]), conditional on a legal harm being done, four considerations can be seen as increasing the probability of a trial being held:

1. the likelihood that the offense is detected by the potential plaintiff
2. the size of the stakes under dispute
3. the uncertainty about the outcome of the controversy between the two parties
4. the cost of settlement relative to that of trial

These hypotheses can be tested in the context of financial patent litigation:

- The extent to which infringements are identified may be a function of the characteristics of the patentees. It is likely that larger, more established firms will have better information about the state of the market and the activities of their rivals, as well as more resources for defending their intellectual property, so they might be more likely to initiate litigation.[7] Among the ways we can characterize an entity are whether the patent holder is a corporation, whether it is publicly traded, its size, and its sales.
- Although we cannot directly measure the value of patents, several indirect measures can be employed. The literature (e.g., Harhoff et al. [1999, 2003]; Jaffe and Trajtenberg [2002]; Lanjouw, Pakes, and Putnam [1998]) has suggested that patent value can be captured through the number of claims made in the issued patent, the number of citations in other patents that the patent subsequently received (an indication that subsequent inventions have built on this discovery), and the number of citations made by the patent (which has been interpreted as reflecting the care with which the patent drafters have searched the prior patents). Theory suggests that these more valuable patents will be more frequently litigated.
- The extent of uncertainty surrounding financial patents increased substantially after the *State Street* decision. Prior to this period, there was a general consensus that financial innovations were unlikely to be patentable. After *State Street*, questions about the future of business method patent awards, the scope of these grants, and the size of the monetary damages associated with the infringement of financial patents have proliferated. However, it should also be noted that the acceleration in the number of filings after the decision (documented in Lerner [2002]) suggests that more marginal discoveries may have been patented post–*State Street*. These less important discoveries may be less frequently litigated for the reasons delineated in the previous bullet.

7 Typically, patent litigation is initiated by the patent holders themselves. Although potential infringers can sue for "declaratory judgment" that they do not infringe a patent, these actions are only permitted when the alleged infringer has already been threatened with litigation. Other parties are not allowed to sue to have a patent declared invalid.

- Assessing the relative costs of settlement rather than trial is challenging. An overall time trend may be difficult to discern. For instance, lawyers have been increasingly willing to work for plaintiffs on a contingency basis in patent cases, which reduces the cost of litigation sharply. Danzon [1983] shows how such contingency arrangements can lead to a greater willingness of plaintiffs to file suit in some cases, but not others.

One complication is introduced by the fact that most theoretical depictions are of the decision to proceed to trial once a suit has been filed. Here, the empirical analysis focuses on the initial decision to file litigation. In part, this focus is due to necessity: It is the exceptional patent case that proceeds to the end of a trial.[8] It can thus be argued that the decision to initiate litigation is the critical one in this setting. More importantly, basic models of suit and settlement (e.g., Cooter and Rubinfeld, [1989, section II.C]) suggest that factors affecting the decision to settle a dispute prior to trial should also drive the decision to settle prior to the inception of litigation. The same considerations – the probabilities of success, the extent of uncertainty, and the rewards if successful – should largely shape the decision to file a lawsuit and to proceed to trial.[9]

It should be noted, however, that models of nuisance litigation suggest that the decision to file a suit may be different in some instances from the decision to proceed to trial. In particular, a plaintiff may be willing to file a suit that would have a negative expected value were it to go to trial if certain conditions are met, such as if the defendant has greater costs in litigating disputes or if the defendant's costs are more "front-end loaded" (see, for instance, Bebchuk [1988], Cooter and Rubinfeld [1989], and Rosenberg and Shavell [1985]). In these instances, a plaintiff may rationally initiate a losing suit.

Earlier literature (e.g., Lerner [1995]) has suggested that firms, particularly large firms, as opposed to individuals, should have more litigation experience and consequently lower litigation costs due to "learning curve" effects. This might lead us to conclude that nuisance litigation against large firms should be rare. Recent developments, however, raise questions about this interpretation. For instance, the reliance on injunctions, both prior to (preliminary injunctions) and after (injunctive relief) a finding of patent infringement, means that the cost of an adverse judgment to a larger firm – where a shutdown and the associated reputational damage may affect a wide variety of product lines – may be greater than to a small firm or to an individual with a single product (or no product at all). If this suggestion holds, we may see disproportionate numbers of lawsuits directed against large firms by individuals.

8 For instance, in Lanjouw and Lerner's [2001] sample, a verdict was rendered in only 11% of the patent suits.

9 A similar assumption has been made in other empirical research on litigation, such as Browne and Puelz [1999] and Lanjouw and Schankerman [2003].

Recent works, specifically on the licensing and litigation of patents, have reinforced these conclusions and given us fresh insights into these patterns. The earlier literature on profitable sham litigation is related to insights from the model of "weak" (i.e., highly uncertain) patents developed by Farrell and Shapiro [2008]. The authors show that questionable patents can command surprisingly high royalties in certain settings. When weak patents are licensed to downstream firms that are not rivals, low royalties are the rule, but when these awards are licensed to downstream firms that are rivals (to each other or to the patent holder), the share of revenues going to the patent holder can be quite substantial. Although in Farrell and Shapiro's model the parties settle prior to the filing of litigation, it is plausible in many instances that parties use preemptive suits as part of the bargaining process.

Henkel and Reitzig [2007] present a model that corroborates these speculations about the types of entities that seek to profit from the licensing and litigation of low-value patents. In particular, they argue that firms can exploit institutional "loopholes" in the patent system. For instance, by patenting a trivial technology that has been overlooked by others, but that imposes high switching costs not to infringe, they can create a threat of injunction, which then drives the alleged infringers to settle. Similarly, it may be possible to exploit the limitations of the way in which the courts calculate damages. The model suggests that the entities that may face retaliatory action are typically those without operations of their own.

III. CONSTRUCTING THE DATASET

This part summarizes how I constructed the dataset used in this analysis. More details are in the Appendix.

Patent awards. I identified awards using the online database of the PTO, which summarizes all patents awarded since January 1976. Because I wanted to be able to assess the quality of issued patents (which relies on being able to identify how frequently the awards are cited in subsequent documents), I only included patents in the sample awarded through August 2003 (which gives me three years to observe citations). In total, there are 2944 awards in the sample.

Litigation. I employed the Derwent LIT/ALERT patent litigation database to determine if, and how often, each patent in the sample has been litigated through the end of 2005. I did not observe cases where litigation was threatened but no lawsuit was filed. The ideal way to address this concern would have been through a Heckman-style regression. But in the classic Heckman analysis, there typically are strong priors about what considerations lead to nonresponses (e.g., that young children or a wealthy spouse may deter a woman's labor force participation). It was much more difficult to identify observable variables in this dataset that could plausibly explain settlement prior to the filing of a lawsuit.

Characteristics of patentees. Using public databases, I characterized the features of the parties to whom the patents were assigned in the year of the award.

Features of the patents. I compiled the number of forward and backward citations through July 2006 in order to have as full depiction of the patents as possible. I also identified those forward and backward citations that are self-citations. The interpretation of self-citations is ambiguous: Although the number of self-citations may indicate awards that are more valuable to the patentees, earlier work suggests that large firms disproportionately cite themselves. Finally, I computed two alternative measures of patent quality: generality and originality (see Hall, Jaffe, and Trajtenberg [2002]).

Potential defendants. In the final analysis in Part V, I examine which firms are sued for infringement. To identify potential infringers, I collected annual data on all firms in the "Finance, Insurance and Real Estate" industry category (except for Standard Industrial Classification class 65, which contains real estate operators) listed in Compustat in every year between 1990 and 2002.

IV. ANALYSIS OF THE LITIGATION OF PATENTS

A. *Summary Statistics*

Table 8.1 provides an overview of the firms and patents included in the sample. Among the key patterns in Panel A are the disproportionate citation levels relative to the typical U.S. award;[10] the dominance of financial patenting by U.S. firms, which account for 74% of the awards (in recent years, approximately one-half of all patent awards have gone to non-U.S. entities); and the very skewed distribution of litigation.

The second panel indicates a few characteristics of the lawsuits themselves. Most involve a single financial patent, but several encompass multiple awards. More interestingly, the role of third parties here is much greater than elsewhere. Only 46% of the disputes involve an inventor or an original assignee as a plaintiff or a defendant. In other cases, third parties are conducting the litigation instead. This share of third parties is much greater than seen elsewhere. For instance, Lanjouw and Schankerman [2001, table 1] found that in 68.5% of their cases, the assignee is either a plaintiff or defendant. (They did not examine cases where the inventor but not the assignee was a litigator, which would increase the share at least modestly.)

Analysis of patent reassignments using PTO's Patent Assignment database[11] reinforces the finding that parties other than the inventor or the original assignee

[10] Jaffe and Trajtenberg [2002, p. 439] find that the typical twelve-year-old patent had received just fewer than seven citations, or one-quarter the level seen here. The predicted number of citations is slightly lower if one computes a weighted average based on the actual ages of the awards in the financial patents sample.

[11] Available at http://assignments.uspto.gov/assignments/?db=pat. The PTO Patent Assignment data include information on many types of patent ownership transfers, including assignee name changes and security interests associated with loans, I restricted the definition of "reassignments" to transactions after the patent issuance that involve the transfer of patent ownership away from the original assignee or inventor.

TABLE 8.1. *Characteristics of patents and lawsuits*

Panel A: Patent awards	Mean	Std. dev.	Min.	Max.
Year patent issued	1994.7	7.3	1976	2003
Application year	1992.1	7.1	1969	2002
Claims made	20.9	20.9	1	375
Citations made	13.3	17.6	0	243
Citations made per claim	1.2	3.1	0	121.5
Citations received through July 2006	24.0	33.2	0	407
Citations received through July 2006 per claim	2.3	6.0	0	129
Self-citations made	0.6	2.1	0	60
Self-citations received through July 2006	0.4	1.0	0	15
Generality	0.44	0.25	0.07	1
Originality	0.53	0.27	0.06	1
Sales of assignee in issue year (billions of 2003$s)	24.9	37.8	0	467
Employment of assignee in issue year (000s)	86.0	113.3	0.01	891
Assignee is a U.S.-based individual	16.0%			
Assignee is a non-U.S.-based individual	2.3%			
Assignee is a U.S.-based public corporation	32.5%			
Assignee is a non-U.S.-based public corporation	16.2%			
Assignee is a U.S.-based private firm	24.9%			
Assignee is a non-U.S.-based private firm	7.7%			
Nationality of assignee (if non-U.S.):				
Japanese	57.6%			
British	8.5%			
French	6.5%			
German	6.3%			
Lawsuits involving patent through end of 2005	0.08	0.59	0	15
Docket entries in lawsuits involving patent through end of 2005	8.4	60.1	0	955
Panel B: Lawsuits				
Number of financial patents in suit	1.32	1	1	7
Plaintiff is listed as patent inventor?	5.9%			
Plaintiff is listed as original assignee?	32.6%			
Defendant is listed as patent inventor?	1.1%			
Defendant is listed as original assignee?	6.4%			
Neither plaintiff nor defendant is inventor or original assignee?	54.0%			

Notes: The sample consists of 2,942 financial patents issued between January 1976 and August 2003. The table presents the key features of the patents and if the 246 lawsuits involving these patents through the end of 2005.

(third parties) play a significant role in litigation. First, the incidence of reassignments of litigated patents is twice that of nonlitigated patents. Twenty-three percent of the nonlitigated patents were reassigned from their original assignees at some time between their issue date and January 2009, compared to 47.7% of the litigated patents. These rates are significantly different in a chi-squared test at the 0.1% level of significance. Second, looking more specifically at the litigated patents, only 46% of the disputes involved a patent whose owner at the time of the suit was the inventor or original assignee and was a plaintiff or defendant. In 34% of the cases, a reassignee was both the owner at that point and a party in the suit. In 18% of the cases, inventors or original assignees continued to own the patents at the time of the filing, but were not parties in litigation. Finally, the small set of remaining cases involved instances where the patent was reassigned, but the new assignee was not a party in the dispute. Presumably in the latter two cases, the patent owner worked out an arrangement with one of the litigating parties, but did not file a formal ownership transfer with the PTO.

I also undertook some additional exploration of the features of the litigated patents. There was little obvious differentiation between the litigated patents and the financial patents more generally. For instance, a χ^2-test of the primary patent classes of the litigated and nonlitigated patents was unable to reject the null hypothesis of no difference with an associated *p*-value of 0.91. Nor were there any significant differences between the technology classes of litigated and nonlitigated patents when I specifically considered awards to individuals and small entities.

The diversity of the litigated patents can be illustrated by the following summary descriptions of three of the most litigated financial patents:

1. The most litigated patent is an award to an individual inventor, Lawrence B. Lockwood, which is being litigated through the patent holding company Pangea Intellectual Properties. The patent – no. 6,289,319 – covers an automated "financial transaction processing system" and is cast in broad terms sufficient to cover all e-commerce transactions, as well as those employing automated teller machines. Pangea has been targeting small firms in its litigation in a successful effort to obtain settlements of hundreds of thousands of dollars, each from firms that are reluctant to bear the cost of litigation.[12]
2. Meridian Enterprises' U.S. Patent no. 5,025,372 covers a method of administering an incentive award program through the use of credit cards. It successfully sued a larger competitor in the sales incentive market, Carlson Marketing Group (part of the group that owns the Radisson Hotel chain). After a jury handed down a verdict overwhelmingly favorable to Meridian with substantial

[12] See, for instance, the discussion in http://www.infoworld.com/articles/hn/xml/02/05/15/020515hnpangea.html (accessed October 10, 2006).

TABLE 8.2. *Most frequently represented firms*

Innovators	Patentees	Plaintiffs	Defendants
Merrill Lynch	Hitachi	Pangea Intellectual Properties, LLC	American Express
Citigroup	International Business Machines	Divine Technology Ventures	Citigroup
American Express	NCR	Source, Inc.	Chicago Board of Trade
Citicorp	Citigroup	Meridian Enterprises Corp.	New York Mercantile Exchange
McGraw-Hill	Fujitsu	Travelers Express Co.	JP Morgan Chase

Notes: The table summarizes the firms most frequently represented in the tabulations of financial innovators between 1990 and 2002, financial patentees between 1976 and 2003, and litigators of financial patents between 1975 and 2005. The tabulations of plaintiffs and defendants exclude cases where an alleged infringer sued for declaratory relief; they also exclude the compilation of defendants and actions against frequent patent plaintiffs.
The source of the first column is Lerner [2006].

monetary damages, it successfully licensed the patent to Bank of America, CapitalOne, and many other major credit card providers.[13]

3. Patent no. 6,088,685, which covers the creation of a tradable security out of one or more mutual funds, was assigned to a startup firm, Mopex, by its founders. In a series of lawsuits with major exchanges, the patent holder claimed that a wide variety of exchange-traded funds, such as the popular iShares, infringed this award. Ultimately, prior art was discovered in the form of a regulatory filing by Morgan Stanley that led to the dismissal of Mopex's primary lawsuit.

The nature of the litigating patentees, suggested in these vignettes, is highlighted in Table 8.2, which presents the most frequently represented firms in several categories, which prove to be dramatically different:

- The first column presents the most frequently represented financial innovators, as reported in Lerner [2006]. This compilation is based on stories in the *Wall Street Journal* on financial innovation between 1990 and 2002.[14] It is dominated by financial institutions and includes a major publisher.

[13] See the discussion in http://www.managingip.com/Article/1255476/Finance-companies-rush-to-patent-business-methods.html (accessed January 16, 2009).

[14] Mergers and acquisitions introduced complications to the tabulations. Citicorp appears in the first column because it was an active innovator until its acquisition by the Travelers Group in 1998. Subsequent innovations by this institution were attributed to Citigroup, its corporate parent in 2003 (which is credited with innovations developed by the new combined entity and the old Travelers Group). Lerner [2006] provides a more detailed description of the procedure used.

TABLE 8.3. *Distribution of adjusted and unadjusted lawsuits, by year*

Patent award year	No. of patents	Unadjusted lawsuits/ 1,000 patents	Rate, adjusted using all patents	Rate, adjusted using finance patents
1976–1979	110	45.5	285.9	285.9
1980–1984	258	19.4	62.4	62.4
1985–1989	443	101.6	235.4	266.4
1990–1994	294	210.9	411.9	607.1
1995–1999	762	86.6	299.2	491.4
2000–2003	1,075	58.6	337.1	506.6
All patents	2,942	83.6	293.5	429.3

Notes: The sample consists of 2,942 financial patents issued between January 1976 and August 2003. The table presents for each time period the number of financial patents issued and the adjusted and unadjusted rate of lawsuits involving these patents. See text for discussion of the adjustment processes.

- The second column presents the most frequent financial patentees between January 1976 and August 2003. This list is dominated by information technology companies. These firms began filing for patents on innovations that were developed in the course of projects for financial service firms soon after the *State Street* decision (or even before).
- The most frequent plaintiffs[15] in financial patent litigation between 1976 and 2005 are reported in column 3. This list is dominated by patent-holding companies that have no lines of business other than licensing and litigating patent awards.
- The most frequent defendants in financial patent litigation between 1976 and 2005 are reported in the fourth column. In contrast to the plaintiffs, the compilation of the most frequently represented defendants is dominated by major investment banks, trading exchanges, and other established financial institutions.

B. *The Overall Level of Litigation*

I then examined the propensity for these patents to be litigated. The change in patent awards and suits over time is shown in Table 8.3. The litigation data in column 2, however, have two limitations. First, not all cases are reported to the PTO. Lanjouw

[15] In some cases, entities file for "declaratory relief," or for a ruling that a patent they are being threatened with litigation about is invalid. These cases appear relatively rarely in the sample. Before making this and the subsequent tabulation in the fourth column of Table 8.2, I eliminated cases where the defendant is an assignee or an inventor of a patent in contention, but the plaintiff is not. I also eliminated from the list of defendants parties that appear twice or more as plaintiffs, because these cases are also likely to be suits for declaratory relief. In the third and fourth columns, when two firms are involved in the same number of suits, I ranked them based on the number of patents over which they have litigated.

and Schankerman [2003] address this issue by comparing the number of cases reported to the PTO with the number of case filings identified as patent related by the Federal Judicial Center. This administrative office compiles a comprehensive database of all litigation. It does not, however, indicate which patents were involved in individual cases, so cannot be used as the basis for the analysis here. From this information, Lanjouw and Schankerman were able to compute an adjustment factor (reported in Appendix I of their 2003 paper), which scales up the number of reported cases to reflect nonreporting.

The second limitation has to do with the fact that all patents are not litigated immediately after issue. Rather, a considerable number of cases involve patents that are a few years old (the probability of litigation drops considerably for older patents). Because many of the patents in the sample are quite young (having been awarded as recently as mid-2003), this truncation bias may be significant. I reported two adjustments to the number of lawsuits. First, based on the actual distribution of litigation over time of all patents awarded between 1982 and 1986, Lanjouw and Schankerman [2003, Appendix I] report adjustment factors (i.e., factors that allow one to compute the total expected amount of litigation over a patent's lifetime based on the extent of such activity in the initial years after the award).[16] Second, I looked at the propensity to litigate financial patents specifically. Using the number of lawsuits in each year after each patent award in the sample as the dependent variable, I estimated the propensity of patents in different age groups, technology classes, and grant dates to be litigated. I then used these coefficients to predict the amount of litigation over the patent's lifespan. Because the litigation of financial patents tends to be more concentrated in the later years after the award, this approach generated larger estimates than the first approach.

Columns 3 and 4 present the adjusted amount of litigation. Once these corrections are made, there is no clear time trend in the amount of litigation; the upward adjustments are greatest for the oldest patents (due to the severe nonreporting biases in early years) and for the most recent ones (because of their greater truncation). Comparing the litigation rates in the third column to the similarly adjusted data of Lanjouw and Schankerman [2001, Table 1], the overall rate of litigation is twenty-seven times greater than in their overall sample of awards; using the fourth, it is thirty-nine times greater.

This rate of patent litigation is far greater than that in other fields. The technology group with the highest litigation rate in the Lanjouw-Schankerman sample, "drugs

[16] There are two subtle differences between my procedure and Lanjouw and Schankerman's. First, the earlier authors assumed that there was only one patent per lawsuit due to the limitations in the early Derwent data noted earlier, whereas I researched the cases to determine missing patents. Because there are on average 1.3 patents per case in my sample, my reported litigation rate will be slightly higher. Second, approximately 20% of the entries in the Derwent database are duplicate records, referring to different actions in the same suit. I deleted these entries (which apparently was not done by Lanjouw and Schankerman). Thus, collectively these two adjustments should have a very modest effect on the comparisons.

TABLE 8.4. *Adjusted lawsuits by firm type*

Firm type in award year	Adjusted lawsuits/ 1,000 patents — Using all patents	Adjusted lawsuits/ 1,000 patents — Using finance patents
By Assignee Status		
Publicly Traded Firm	114.5	175.4
Privately Held Firm	396.6	579.1
Individual	591.7	846.5
p-value, test of no difference	0.000	0.000
By Nation of Assignee		
United States	382.8	560.9
Japan	29.9	34.8
Other	61.0	95.8
p-value, test of no difference	0.000	0.000
By Employees in Award Year		
0–200	1153.0	1581.9
201–1,000	313.1	488.0
1,001–50,000	80.3	115.7
50,001–200,000	47.1	70.8
>200,000	0.0	0.0
p-value, test of no difference	0.000	0.000
By Revenues in Award Year (millions of 2003$s)		
0–10	790.9	1238.0
10.1–100	681.5	1096.9
100.1–1,000	74.7	119.9
1,000.1–10,000	84.5	113.9
10,000.1–50,000	45.1	72.8
>50,000	0.0	0.0
p-value, test of no difference	0.000	0.000

Notes: The sample consists of 2,942 financial patents issued between January 1976 and August 2003. The table presents for various subclasses of assignees the adjusted rate of lawsuits involving these patents. See text for discussion of the adjustment processes.

and health," has a litigation rate that is less than 7% that seen in financial patents. Nor do other emerging technologies – where uncertainty is presumably greater – appear to have rates approaching those of financial patents. For instance, in Lerner [1995] I examined the litigation of the first 2048 biotechnology awards and found that the rate of litigation was less than one-fifth the rate seen here.

C. *The Distribution of Litigation*

Table 8.4 considers the litigation rate for patents with different classes of owners. Patents assigned to individuals and U.S. entities are far more likely to be litigated than

TABLE 8.5. *Comparison of means for litigated and nonlitigated patents*

	Domestic		Foreign	
	Litigated	Not litigated	Litigated	Not litigated
Claims	31.00	22.73***	24.83	14.40*
Forward citations/year	4.04	2.40***	4.07	1.40***
Backward citations	19.39	14.78**	9.83	8.24
Forward cites/year/claim	0.28	0.20*	0.21	0.16
Backward cites/claim	1.77	1.18*	0.61	0.96

Notes: The sample consists of 2,942 financial patents issued between January 1976 and August 2003. The table presents characteristics of the patents assigned to domestic and foreign assignees.
*, **, and *** denote significance at the 10%, 5%, and 1% significance level.

those held by public corporations, and the litigation rate of firms of different sizes differs dramatically, with smaller firms disproportionately owning litigated patents.

I compare the characteristics of the patents themselves in Table 8.5. Here, I examine domestic and foreign patentees separately, because their citation practices may differ. In particular, foreign patent applicants tend not to cite the relevant U.S. patents, but rather their foreign counterparts. These citations thus do not show up in standard citation counts and indeed, it is extremely labor intensive to extract and reconcile these cites with those of U.S. patentees. Thus, the number of citations by foreign patentees (and perhaps of foreign patents, if citations tend to be localized) may be depressed. Given that financial patenting, so far, has been dominated by U.S. entities, however, the impact of this bias should be minor.

Table 8.5 shows contrasts between patents that are and are not litigated. Like litigated patents, overall, litigated financial patents have more forward citations and claims. The difference in the number of forward citations, however, is much smaller and no longer statistically significant at the 5% confidence level when I compute citations per claim. Thus, although litigated financial awards may be more expansive in their claims, they are not disproportionately cited once the number of claims is controlled for. However, litigated patents do cite more prior art.[17]

[17] In the earlier discussion, I argued that forward citations are a proxy for importance, which drives litigation. There might be another relationship between citations and innovation, however: Patents that are litigated might be cited more frequently not because they are more important, but rather because the publicity generated by the lawsuit calls attention to the award. This might lead to false inferences. In an unreported table, I tested for the presence of a publicity effect. In particular, for all litigated patents, I looked at the mean number of citations obtained in the years before and after the patent was litigated. Part of the difference in the number of citations between litigated and nonlitigated patents appears to be driven by a "publicity effect." In the three years after the dispute, the litigated patents garnered 5.2 more forward citations relative to the baseline before the inception of litigation. (By the fourth year, the citation rate returned to the baseline.) For the mean patent in the sample, which is twelve years old, this translates into a little under one-half of a citation per year. This accounts for roughly 23% of the difference in annual forward citation rates for litigated and nonlitigated financial patents (4.0 and 2.1).

TABLE 8.6. *Regression estimates of number of lawsuits*

	Dependent variable: Was patent litigated?	Dependent variable: Number of lawsuits involving patent				
	Probit	Poisson	Negative binomial			
	(1)	(2)	(3)	(4)	(5)	(6)
Logarithm of number of claims in patent	0.55	1.06	1.13	0.98	0.81	0.85
	[0.07]***	[0.10]***	[0.18]***	[0.18]***	[0.18]***	[0.18]***
Log of forward citations per claim	0.35	0.67	0.96	0.84	0.7	0.78
	[0.08]***	[0.12]***	[0.25]***	[0.24]***	[0.24]***	[0.24]***
Log of backward citations per claim	0.55	0.89	1.05	0.92	0.7	0.71
	[0.11]***	[0.15]***	[0.30]***	[0.29]***	[0.28]**	[0.29]**
Was assignee a public corporation?				−1.09	−0.02	0.09
				[0.27]***	[0.36]	[0.44]
Was assignee an individual?				0.43	0.34	0.28
				[0.28]	[0.28]	[0.28]
Was assignee based in the United States?				1.31	1.39	1.25
				[0.39]***	[0.40]***	[0.39]***
Log of employment in year of issue (000s)					−0.57	
					[0.12]***	
Log of sales in year of issue (millions of 2003$s)						−0.25
						[0.07]***
Year of issue dummy variables	Y	Y	Y	Y	Y	Y
Zero or missing data dummy variables	Y	Y	Y	Y	Y	Y
Controls for self-citation rate	Y	Y	Y	Y	Y	Y
p-value, χ^2-test	0.00	0.00	0.00	0.00	0.00	0.00
Pseudo R2	0.10	0.13	0.07	0.11	0.12	0.13
Observations	2757	2941	2941	2941	2941	2941

Notes: The sample consists of 2,942 financial patents issued between January 1976 and August 2003. The dependent variable in the first regression is a dummy variable indicating whether the patent was ever litigated; in the remaining regressions, it is the count of lawsuits involving the patent. The first regression employs a probit specification, the second is a Poisson estimation, and the rest use negative binomial specifications.

Coefficients are reported in the top line; robust standard errors in brackets below.

*,**, and *** denote significance at the 10%, 5%, and 1% significance level.

I then turn in Table 8.6 to a regression analysis to explain the prevalence of litigation. The unit of observation is each patent award in the sample. I employed two dependent variables in the reported regressions. The first is an indicator, denoted as one where the patent was litigated before the end of 2005 and as zero otherwise. This is reported in the first column, which features a probit analysis. The second variable (reported in the remaining columns) is the count of lawsuits in which the patent was involved. In these cases, I estimated Poisson and negative binomial specifications. (I did not adjust the dependent variable here for truncation or reporting biases, but instead used dummy variables for each patent award year.)

The regressions paint a consistent story.[18] More important patents – those with more claims and with more forward and backward citations – are more likely to be litigated, as are those of smaller U.S. entities. Table 8.7 explores the magnitude of the coefficients. The first column reports the predicted dependent variable at the means of the continuous variables and with the binary variables coded as zero. In the rows, I show the change in predicted dependent variable as one independent variable at a time is changed. For instance, regression 4 shows that, for patents awarded to public corporations, the predicted litigation rate falls by two-thirds. A one standard deviation increase in employment in the fifth regression reduces the expected amount of litigation by 70%. I discuss the implications of these results in Part V.

Another natural question is whether there is a time trend in the pattern of litigation. On the one hand, the uncertainty around patent value is likely to have increased markedly after the *State Street* decision. On the other hand, the increase in financial patent filings after this decision may mean that more marginal discoveries were being patented post-decision. Figure 8.1 shows the coefficient on each annual dummy variable in the first negative binomial regression in Table 8.6 (the third regression). Not only are there no consistent patterns over time but also the year dummies are collectively and individually insignificant in this and other regressions.

D. *Robustness Checks*

I conducted a variety of robustness checks to examine whether the results are sensitive to the specification used. The first addressed the concern that there are systematic patterns in the patents applied for over time. I repeated in unreported regressions the specifications presented in Table 8.6 while also using dummy variables for the application (as well as the award) year. The key results were little changed.

Another possibility is that the specification is problematic because it fails to account for the large number of zero observations in the sample. One way to address this problem is to estimate a zero-inflated negative binomial specification, in which the first stage estimates the probability that the patent is litigated at all and the second focuses on the number of suits filed conditionally on whether or not litigation took place. The key results were qualitatively unchanged.

18 The sample size is smaller in the first regression. Some observations were dropped from the probit regression because a zero or one outcome is perfectly predicted.

TABLE 8.7. *Estimated litigation probabilities*

	At means	+1 Standard deviation in log claims	+2 Standard deviations in log claims	+1 Standard deviation in log forward citations per claim	+2 Standard deviations in log forward citations per claim	+1 Standard deviation in log backward citations per claim	+2 Standard deviations in log backward citations per claim
Probability of litigation (regression #1 in Table 8.6)	3.22%	8.45%	18.37%	5.57%	9.08%	5.71%	9.49%
Count of lawsuits (#3)	0.024	0.064	0.170	0.049	0.099	0.040	0.067
Count of lawsuits (#4)	0.014	0.033	0.076	0.026	0.048	0.022	0.035
Count of lawsuits (#5)	0.005	0.010	0.021	0.009	0.014	0.007	0.010
	At means	**Patent holder is a public corporation**	**Patent holder is an individual**	**Patent holder is from the United States**	**+1 Standard deviation in log employment**	**+2 Standard deviations in log employment**	
Probability of litigation (regression #1 in Table 8.6)	3.22%	–	–	–	–	–	
Count of lawsuits (#3)	0.024	–	–	–	–	–	
Count of lawsuits (#4)	0.014	0.005	0.021	0.052	–	–	
Count of lawsuits (#5)	0.005	0.005	0.007	0.020	0.002	0.000	

Notes: The sample consists of 2,942 financial patents issued between January 1976 and August 2003. The dependent variable in the regression in the first row is a dummy variable indicating whether the patent was ever litigated; in the remaining regressions, it is the count of lawsuits involving the patent. The regression in the first row employs a probit specification, and the rest use negative binomial specifications. The first column presents the predicted dependent variable at the means of the continuous variables and with the binary variables coded as zero; the other columns show the change in the predicted dependent variable as one variable at a time is shifted.

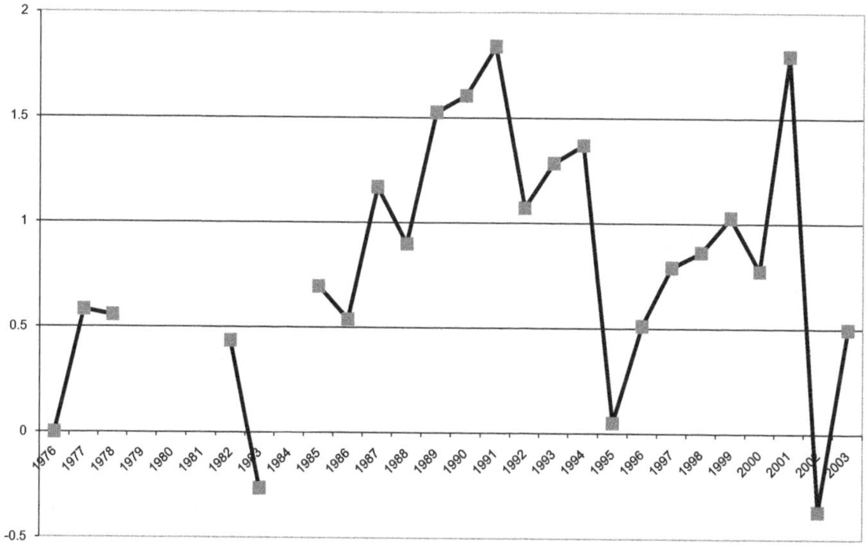

FIGURE 8.1. Annual Dummy Variables from Regression 3 in Table 6. The table presents the coefficients from the 3rd regression in Table 6. The coefficient for 1976 is normalized to zero. No financial patents awarded in 1979 through 1981 and 1984 were litigated.

Another concern is that lawsuits may vary in intensity. In some cases, suits may be dropped or settled soon after being filed; in others, litigation may progress for years. To measure the intensity of the effort expended by the parties in the litigation, I totaled the number of docket filings in each case using the records of the PACER system[19] and used the cumulative number of docket entries in the lawsuits associated with each patent as the dependent variable. Table 8.8 reports the regressions corresponding to the negative binomial analyses in columns 3 through 6 of Table 8.6. The primary results that appeared in the earlier regressions continue to go through as before.

I also undertook the following robustness checks in unreported regressions: using the adjusted counts of lawsuits, as in Tables 8.3 and 8.4, rather than the actual counts as the dependent variable in the regressions; employing alternative measures of patent importance, such as originality and generality (Hall, Jaffe, and Trajtenberg [2002]), in lieu of the citation counts; introducing additional financial data available about publicly traded firms; adding fixed and random effects for the patentees; and dividing the patentees by those above and below the median employment (or sales). The earlier results continued to hold. One exception was that the relationship

[19] In approximately 5% of the cases, I was unable to obtain the index of the docket file, either through PACER or an examination of the physical docket. In these instances, I assumed that the case had zero docket entries. I also repeated the analysis, assuming that these missing cases have the mean number of docket entries and found that the results are essentially unchanged.

TABLE 8.8. *Regression estimates for litigation intensity*

	Dependent variable: Number of filings in lawsuits involving patent			
	Tobit			
	(1)	(2)	(3)	(4)
Logarithm of number of claims in patent	253.61 [37.23]***	217.64 [36.74]***	196.73 [36.11]***	200.24 [36.17]***
Log of forward citations per claim	132.28 [41.20]***	116.13 [40.90]***	98.6 [40.80]**	108.18 [40.74]***
Log of backward citations per claim	284.91 [52.24]***	252.23 [51.07]***	231.94 [51.11]***	228.62 [50.85]***
Was assignee a public corporation?		−225.99 [49.88]***	−35.12 [69.37]	14.71 [75.58]
Was assignee an individual?		−29.67 [50.89]	−44.86 [52.85]	−56.75 [51.19]
Was assignee based in the United States?		246.57 [76.88]***	243.37 [78.42]***	234.98 [76.19]***
Log of employment in year of issue (000s)			−89.99 [22.20]***	
Log of sales in year of issue (millions of 2003$s)				−41.59 [12.54]***
Year of issue dummy variables	Y	Y	Y	Y
Zero or missing data dummy variables	Y	Y	Y	Y
Controls for self-citation rate	Y	Y	Y	Y
p-value, χ^2-test	0.00	0.00	0.00	0.00
Pseudo-R2	0.05	0.07	0.08	0.08
Observations	2941	2941	2941	2941

Notes: The sample consists of 2,942 financial patents issued between January 1976 and August 2003. The dependent variable is the count of filings in all lawsuits involving the patent. All regressions employ Tobit specifications.
Coefficients are reported in the top line; standard errors in brackets below.
*,**, and *** denote significance at the 10%, 5%, and 1% significance level.

between firm size and the probability of litigation was only statistically significant among the smaller firms.

PART V. ANALYSIS OF DEFENDANTS

The analysis in Part IV focused on which patents are litigated. I now examine which firms are especially likely to be named as defendants in these actions. Because it is difficult to observe the entire pool of potential defendants, I focus on publicly traded firms, which I can identify and characterize.

TABLE 8.9. *Regression estimates of financial patent litigation defendants*

	Dependent Variable: Number of Lawsuits Involving Firm		
	Negative binomial		
	Entire sample (1)	U.S.-based firms only (2)	1999 and after observations only (3)
Log years firm has been publicly traded	0.18	0.43	0.30
	[0.25]	[0.28]	[0.26]
Log of firm's assets	0.46	0.36	0.44
	[0.14]***	[0.13]***	[0.14]***
Profit margin	−0.13	0.04	−0.07
	[0.39]	[0.55]	[0.41]
Leverage	−1.62	−1.67	−2.04
	[1.14]	[1.35]	[1.09]*
Innovations by firm	0.52	0.38	0.20
	[0.40]	[0.34]	[0.27]
Academic connectedness	−0.76	−1.39	−0.61
	[1.02]	[2.80]	[0.46]
Other innovations in ZIP code	−0.27	−0.17	0.01
	[0.24]	[0.23]	[0.21]
Industry controls	Y	Y	Y
Nationality of patentee dummy variables	Y	N	Y
p-value, χ^2-test	0.000	0.000	0.000
Observations	15,937	15,034	5,472

Notes: The sample consists of 15,397 annual observations of financial firms and financial innovators (see text) in Compustat between 1990 and 2002. The dependent variable is the count of filings in all patent lawsuits with the firm as a defendant in the year of the observation. All regressions employ negative binomial specifications.

Coefficients are reported in the top line; robust standard errors in brackets below.

*,**, and *** denote significance at the 10%, 5%, and 1% significance level.

Theoretical work on the propensity to file litigation suggests that the costs of litigation should matter. But, as discussed in Part II, the predicted effects are not obvious: Larger firms should have lower litigation costs due to "learning curve" effects, but are also more vulnerable to damage to other product lines and their reputation from an adverse judgment. I used several proxies for firms' potential litigation costs, including experience (the logarithm of its age as a public entity),[20] financial scale

[20] I computed the age and other measures using the Compustat GVKEY identifier associated with the firm at the time of the innovation. I mapped in the count of innovations using the appropriate identifier. These assignments are not always apparent, but can be determined by reviewing the corporation's history using the Hoover's directory, Lexis-Nexis, the SDC Mergers and Acquisitions database, and online sources.

(the logarithm of assets), financial condition (pre-tax operating income over sales), leverage (the ratio of the book value of long-term debt to the book value of long-term debt and preferred stock plus the market value of common stock), headquarters location, and the extent of innovation (measured by the number of innovations associated with that firm reported in the *Wall Street Journal*, the extent of the firm's interconnections to academia, and the financial innovations occurring in the firm's zip code, all computed in the year of the observation). I confined the analysis to all firms with a primary assignment to Standard Industrial Classification (SIC) codes 60–69 or those that developed a financial innovation that was reported in the *Wall Street Journal* during these years. (See Lerner [2006] for the identification of these innovations; the results are robust to just using financial firms.)

The analysis, reported in Table 8.9, suggests that the strongest determinant of a firm being a defendant in financial patent litigation is its scale. The measures of innovation are consistently insignificant, and the dummies for the firm headquarters are inconsistent in sign. One interpretation of these patterns – as well as the earlier finding that patents owned by individuals and smaller firms are much more likely to be litigated – harkens back to the discussion of the costs of litigation in Part II. If large firms find litigation substantially more costly than do other parties – presumably due to the risk of damage to their reputation or to other lines of business from a possible injunction – they may disproportionately be the subject of nuisance litigation, in which entities with lower litigation costs rationally target them with dubious claims, confident that the defendants will find it in their interest to settle the cases.

CONCLUSIONS

This chapter examines the litigation of financial patents and finds that they are being litigated two to three dozen times more frequently than patents as a whole. The awards being litigated are disproportionately those awarded to individuals and to smaller, private entities. Patents with more claims and more citations are also more frequently litigated. Additionally, larger firms are disproportionately targeted in litigation.

I argue that many of the patterns here are consistent with theoretical models of suit and settlement. In particular, the selection of more important patents for litigation follows directly from theoretical suggestions that high-stakes disputes should lead more frequently to litigation. If we accept the suggestion that larger firms have significantly greater costs of litigation, the patterns regarding the initiation of lawsuits and the targets in those suits would be consistent with theories of nuisance litigation.

In particular, the patterns are consistent with recent models of the strategic exploitation of weak patents, such as those by Farrell and Shapiro [2008] and Henkel and Reitzig [2007]. These authors suggest that the exploitation of these awards – frequently by small entities and free standing entrepreneurs – can have socially detrimental effects beyond the deadweight losses associated with the licensing payments. These effects range from distortions in the incentives to innovate to spending on socially unproductive litigation.

Why is there such an extraordinary high level of litigation of financial patents, even when compared to other emerging technology classes? The theoretical literature would lead us to attribute this phenomenon to the substantial uncertainty about the extent of patent protection, the intensity of the product market competition, the differences in the litigation costs between the various parties, and the high potential rewards associated with these patents. Although we can hypothesize several explanations, the definitive explanation for the intensity of litigation remains elusive.

This chapter suggests a number of unanswered questions. Foremost among these are the consequences of these patterns of litigation for innovation in financial services. Several of the authors cited earlier suggest that the litigation of weak patents may distort innovation, but much remains to be understood about the potential distortions. For instance, has the high level of intellectual property litigation deterred or encouraged the introduction of new products and services in this area? How have firms' innovative choices been affected by this new intellectual property regime? Finally, how has this affected social welfare? Understanding the consequences of these shifts is important, given the economic impact of financial innovation.

REFERENCES

American Intellectual Property Law Association [AIPLA], 2005, *2005 Report of the Economic Survey*, Washington, DC, AIPLA.

Bebchuk, Lucian A., 1988, Suing solely to extract a settlement offer, *Journal of Legal Studies* 17, 437–450.

Browne, Mark J., and Robert Puelz, 1999, The effect of legal rules on the value of economic and non-economic damages and the decision to file, *Journal of Risk and Uncertainty* 18, 189–213.

Cooter, Robert D., and Daniel L. Rubinfeld, 1989, Economic analysis of legal disputes and their resolution, *Journal of Economic Literature* 27, 1067–1097.

Danzon, Patricia M., 1983, Contingent fees for personal injury litigation, *Bell Journal of Economics* 14, 213–224.

Farrell, Joseph, and Carl Shapiro, 2008, How strong are weak patents?, *American Economic Review*, 98, 1347–1369.

Frame, W. Scott, and Lawrence J. White, 2004, Empirical studies of financial innovation: Mostly talk and not much action? *Journal of Economic Literature* 42, 116–144.

Hall, Bronwyn H., Adam B. Jaffe, and Manuel Trajtenberg, 2002, The NBER patent citations data file: Lessons, insights and methodological tools, in Adam B. Jaffe and Manuel Trajtenberg, *Patents, Citations, and Innovations: A Window on the Knowledge Economy*, Cambridge, MIT Press.

Harhoff, Dietmar, Francis Narin, F. M. Scherer, and Katrin Vopel, 1999, Citation frequency and the value of patented inventions, *Review of Economics and Statistics*, 81, 511–515.

Harhoff, Dietmar, F. M. Scherer, and Katrin Vopel, 2003, Citations, family size, opposition, and the value of patent rights, *Research Policy*, 32, 1343–1364.

Henkel, Joachim, and Markus G. Reitzig, 2007, Patent sharks and the sustainability of value destruction strategies, Unpublished working paper, available at http://ssrn.com/abstract=985602.

Jaffe, Adam B., and Manuel Trajtenberg, 2002, *Patents, Citations, and Innovations: A Window on the Knowledge Economy*, Cambridge, MIT Press.

Lanjouw, Jean O., and Josh Lerner, 2001, Tilting the table? The use of preliminary injunctions, *Journal of Law and Economics*, 44, 573–603.

Lanjouw, Jean O., Ariel Pakes, and Jonathan Putnam, 1998, How to count patents and value intellectual property: Uses of patent renewal and application data, *Journal of Industrial Economics* 46, 405–433.

Lanjouw, Jean O., and Mark Schankerman, 2001, Characteristics of patent litigation: A window on competition, *RAND Journal of Economics* 32,129–151.

Lanjouw, Jean O., and Mark Schankerman, 2003, An empirical analysis of the enforcement of patent rights in the United States, in Wesley Cohen and Steven Merrill, eds., *Patents in the Knowledge-Based Economy*, Washington, DC, National Academy Press, pp. 145–179.

Lerner, Josh, 1995, Patenting in the shadow of competitors, *Journal of Law and Economics* 38, 563–595.

Lerner, Josh, 2002, Where does *State Street* lead? A first look at finance patents, 1971–2000, *Journal of Finance* 57, 901–930.

Lerner, Josh, 2006, The new new financial thing: The origins of financial innovations, *Journal of Financial Economics* 79, 233–255.

Lerner, Josh, and Peter Tufano, 2003, Patently valuable assets: What are the consequences of the knowledge revolution in financial services?, Unpublished working paper, Harvard University.

Merton, Robert C., 1992, Financial innovation and economic performance, *Journal of Applied Corporate Finance* 4 (Winter), 12–22.

Miller, Merton H., 1986, Financial innovation: The last twenty years and the next, *Journal of Financial and Quantitative Analysis* 21, 459–471.

Priest, George L., and Benjamin Klein, 1984, The selection of disputes for litigation, *Journal of Legal Studies* 13, 1–55.

Rosenberg, David, and Stephen Shavell, 1985, A model in which suits are brought for their nuisance value, *International Review of Law and Economics* 5, 3–13.

Tufano, Peter, 1989, Financial innovation and first-mover advantages, *Journal of Financial Economics* 25, 213–240.

Van Horne, James C., 1985, Of financial innovation and excesses, *Journal of Finance* 40, 621–631.

SAMPLE CONSTRUCTION

Patents: Following the procedure in Lerner [2006], I identified all patents assigned to relevant U.S. Patent Classification subclasses. Patents are classified at the time they issue to one or more classifications. There are more than one hundred thousand such classes. The PTO takes such classifications very seriously, because they ensure that examiners will be able to identify the relevant earlier awards when they engage in subsequent patent searches. I used all patents with a primary assignment to the following subclasses of class 705, "Data Processing: Financial, Business Practice, Management, or Cost/Price Determination":

- 705/4: Insurance (e.g., computer-implemented systems or methods for writing insurance policies, processing insurance claims, etc.)
- 705/35: Finance (e.g., banking, investment, or credit)
- 705/36: Portfolio selection, planning, or analysis
- 705/37: Trading, matching, or bidding
- 705/38: Credit (risk) processing or loan processing (e.g., mortgages)
- 705/39–705/45, which focus on bank back office operations (e.g., ATM networks, remote banking, and electronic funds transfer)

Although class 705 has traditionally been the primary class in which finance patents were classified, there has been a tendency for applicants in recent years to seek to get their financial applications classified in class 902 instead. The reason for this is a program initiated in 2000 by the PTO, in response to the controversy surrounding many internet-related patents (which typically had also been classified in class 705). Since this date, the PTO has undertaken a "second review" of patent applications in class 705 before making grants. Savvy applicants have sought to avoid the delay and expense associated by this review by seeking a primary assignment in another class. Reflecting this behavior, I also included patents assigned to class 902: Electronic funds transfer.

Litigation: The Derwent database is built using reports to the PTO from the district courts where the patent litigation is initiated. Although filing of these reports is mandatory, as Lanjouw and Schankerman document [2001, 2003], in a considerable number of instances (about 35% in recent years and more earlier), no such report is made. (To address this deficiency, I adjusted the computed patent litigation rates, as discussed in detail in Part IV.B.) The data on litigation were downloaded in May 2006. There appears, however, to be substantial reporting lags: I found no suits from 2006 and only one after August 2005.[1] From the database, I gathered information

[1] I assumed that the database contains all records involving patent litigation filed through the end of 2005. Thus, the estimates of the amount of litigation – and the disparities from other areas of patent litigation – are slightly understated.

on the key dates, parties, and location of each case, as well as the patents that were involved.[2] Because the lists of litigating parties provided by Derwent are incomplete (it only assigned one patent to each lawsuit prior to 1990, even if there were multiple ones at issue), I obtained the docket filings for the earlier cases and augmented their records. I counted the number of lawsuits involving each patent, regarding each case as one suit even if multiple defendants were named.

Patentees: I defined publicly traded entities as those for which financial and related information for the year prior to the award was available from Compustat, WorldScope, or filings with the U.S. Securities and Exchange Commission. I classified as private firms all other cases where there is a nongovernmental, nonacademic assignee other than the inventor.[3] For private entities, I employed a variety of sources, including the *Moody's* manuals, the *Corporate Technology Directory*, national directories of firms (particularly of Japan), and directories of various segments of the financial services industry. In these cases, I simply sought to obtain information on the revenues and employment of the firm, as well as the nation in which its headquarters is based. If I was unable to identify the relevant information in the year of award, I used information from the previous year or, if this information was not available, the year after the award. In many cases, however, I was unable to locate the sales and revenue information: Many of the assignees were small patent-holding companies that keep extremely low profiles. I was, however, able to characterize the location of all assignees: If information on firm location was not available from the above databases, I used the location of the assignee as identified in the issued patent. If there was no assignee, I used the location of the inventor.

Potential defendants: Information on financial health and headquarters location was taken from Compustat. I counted innovations by a given firm by totaling the stories about innovative financial products or services introduced by that firm in the *Wall Street Journal* in a given year. I characterized the potential for knowledge spillovers by totaling the number of innovations by firms headquartered in the same zip code in the same year. I characterized the extent to which each firm is close to the academic frontier by using the firm's representation on the editorial boards of four leading academic-practitioner journals, normalized by the firm's assets. I calculated each firm's editorial board seats at the beginning of each year. I counted a firm that is a sponsor of a journal as having the equivalent of two editorial board seats. Lerner [2006] provides more details on these measures.

[2] Because the considerable majority of patent cases ultimately settle, and these settlements are highly diverse and rarely disclosed to the public, it is impossible to characterize the outcomes of these cases in a systematic manner.

[3] Because it is difficult to determine whether non-U.S. foreign firms are publicly traded, some public firms may be misclassified as private. Given that corporate financial patentees are dominated by U.S. and large Japanese firms, this problem should be limited.

9

Patent Search and Cumulative Innovation

*Michael J. Meurer**

Cumulative innovation, the process of one innovator building on the efforts of earlier innovators is common and important. Economists who study innovation readily accept this assertion (as do I), even though it is hard to evaluate empirically. Because of the work of Suzanne Scotchmer and others, economists also recognize that cumulative innovation poses a serious challenge to those who try to design an optimal patent system. When one innovation builds on another, the patent system can be used to divide profits between two distinct innovators. But under normal conditions it cannot be designed to make both innovators full claimants on the flow of value created by their respective innovations.

Several articles have taken up the challenge of uncovering policy concerns that should help determine the division of profit beyond early and late innovators. Green and Scotchmer (1995) note that, when different firms contribute innovations to a sequence, total patent-based profits will need to be higher than the profits required to induce a single firm to invest in the same sequence of innovations. Scotchmer and Green (1990) observe that a weak nonobviousness standard encourages disclosure that has social value because it speeds further development and reduces redundant innovation. O'Donoghue, Scotchmer, and Thisse (1998) argue for broad and short patents in a quality ladder model because broad patents reduce duplicative investment. In contrast, Denicolò (2000) observes that a weak nonobviousness standard and narrow breadth reduce possibly wasteful racing to achieve a first-generation innovation.

* Abraham and Lillian Benton Scholar and Professor of Law at Boston University School of Law. Thanks to Ben Depoorter, Ted Sichelman, and participants at the GMU/Microsoft Conference, Washington University Conference on the Economics of Law and Innovation, and BU Conference on Property Law and IP for helpful comments. Support from the Ewing Marion Kauffman Foundation is gratefully acknowledged.

Curiously, the lessons from these articles best apply to what is usually classified as discrete rather than cumulative technology. Drug discovery is a discrete technology in the sense that there are few inventions and few patents per product. The standard models of cumulative innovation apply well to problems such as how to divide patent profits between the inventor of a new drug and follow-on innovators who find a new use or new formulation of the drug.

The models, however, do not work very well for cumulative technologies like the information and communications technologies (ICT). Three simplifying assumptions in these models are more problematic for richly cumulative technologies than they are for discrete technologies. First, the division of patent profits is often crucial in the pharmaceutical industry, but often not very important in ICT, because the total patent profits are small; see Cohen, Nelson, and Walsh (2000); Bessen and Meurer (2008). Second, the models assume that there is value in the disclosure contained in the early patent and that the early invention is essential to later innovation. In ICT, independent invention and inadvertent patent infringement are common (Bessen and Meurer 2008). Third, the models emphasize ex ante licensing as an option for coordinating early- and late-stage innovation. But such coordination is impossible if the potential contracting parties cannot identify one another. Cockburn and Henderson (2003) find that most firms do not engage in product clearance patent searches before they introduce a new product. Conversely, pharmaceutical firms are religious about doing patent searches at several different decision points in the innovation process.

My goal in this chapter is to modify a standard model of cumulative innovation to better account for some of the factors that cause patents (especially outside pharmaceutical technology) to perform badly as property. Bessen and Meurer (2008) show that patents fail as property in the sense that they deliver small net rewards to innovators (even negative rewards), because they fail to communicate information about patent-based property boundaries to strangers. To lawyers this is known as failure of the notice function of property.

PART I. CUMULATIVE INNOVATION, HOLDUP, AND EX ANTE PATENT LICENSING

In this chapter, I combine a model of cumulative innovation and patent licensing that follows Green and Scotchmer (1995) with a search model. The model has two players: a patent owner and an innovator. They hold symmetric information. In the first stage, the innovator conducts a search for a patented technology to incorporate into its innovation. The goal of the search is to find and license a patent that might be asserted against the innovator, and to reduce development costs by building on the patented technology held by the patent owner. The search is costly because the patent system does not provide perfect notice.

If the search is fruitful and reveals a relevant patent (I assume there is at most one), then the innovator has a chance to negotiate a license before sinking its development cost. Regardless of whether an ex ante license is negotiated, the innovator then decides whether to develop the innovation. Lacking an ex ante license, the innovator is vulnerable to a patent lawsuit, and it may be forced to negotiate an ex post license following development.

If the search does not reveal a relevant patent, then the innovator can do nothing or develop the innovation. I assume the development cost is (weakly) greater after a failed search. Development exposes the innovator to a possible patent lawsuit, and it might negotiate an ex post license with the patent owner.

In this part, I analyze the subgame that follows a search that uncovers a relevant patent. The next part analyzes the subgame that follows a fruitless search, and the entire game including search. Let V measure the value of the innovation. The cost of development is c, where $c \leq V$. Thus, the social planner always prefers development. If the firms go to trial, they each bear the litigation cost L. The probability of victory by the innovator is α; thus, the patent owner is sure to win at trial if $\alpha = 0$. If the patent owner wins at trial, the remedy is an injunction; the innovator cannot profit from the innovation, which includes the patented technology, unless it gets permission from the patent owner. I will assume that the innovator can design around the patent and deploy an alternative innovation with value X, where $X \in [0, V]$. I assume that the design-around alternative is not available to the innovator until after the patent claims are interpreted at trial and that the innovator can determine the boundaries of the patent claims. The value X is net of additional development costs.

Licensing does not occur if the patent owner lacks a credible threat of going to trial. The patent owner's expected profit is

$$\frac{1-\alpha}{2}(V-x)-L. \qquad (1)$$

This profit expression arises because the patent owner bears its own litigation cost L regardless of the trial outcome; the patent owner wins with probability $1-\alpha$; and following a win, the patent owner negotiates a post-trial license and equally splits the surplus achieved when the innovator deploys the original technology instead of inventing around the patent. If expression (1) is less than zero, then there is no license, the patent owner earns zero, and the innovator earns $V-c$. I will call this outcome *acquiescence*.

My assumption of symmetric information means that a trial will not occur in equilibrium. Instead, it provides the threat point for ex post licensing (that is, a license after development, but before trial). If the expression in (1) is non-negative, then the threat point for the patent owner is given by (1), and the threat point for the innovator is: $\frac{1-\alpha}{2}(V+x)+\alpha V-c-L$. The firms will negotiate a license to avoid the litigation costs. Assuming an equal split of the surplus, then the *ex post*

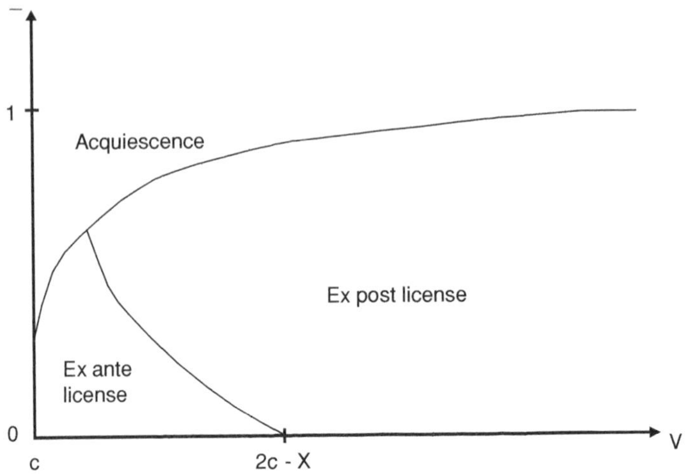

FIGURE 9.1. Licensing subgame outcomes after a relevant patent is identified by the innovator's search, assuming $2L + X \leq c$.

license outcome gives the patent owner an expected profit of: $\frac{1-\alpha}{2}(V - x)$, and the innovator gets an expected profit of

$$\frac{1-\alpha}{2}(V + x) + \alpha V - c. \tag{2}$$

Green and Scotchmer observe that the innovator is subject to holdup and may find that development is not profitable without an ex ante license. In particular, if expression (2) is less than zero, then the innovator will not develop the technology unless the patent owner agrees to bear some of the development cost.

The equilibrium outcome is ex ante licensing when the patent owner has a credible threat to sue and the innovator has a credible threat to forego development. In other words, ex ante licensing requires that expression (1) is non-negative and expression (2) is negative. The threat points for the negotiation of an ex ante license are zero for both firms. The surplus is $V - c$, which is divided equally so that each firm gets $(V - c)/2$ from an ex ante license.

Figure 9.1 displays the set of (V, α) parameter values that correspond to different outcomes of the licensing subgame that occur after a relevant patent is identified by the innovator's search. The figure is drawn on the assumption that $2L + X \leq c$. A relatively high development cost makes the region of ex ante licensing larger. If $2c \leq 2L + X$, then ex ante licensing is not an equilibrium outcome. The intermediate case is similar to the case displayed in Figure 9.1, except for values of V sufficiently close to c, where the patent owner does not have a credible threat to sue even if victory is certain; in other words, even if $\alpha = 0$.

Remark 1. As noted by Green and Scotchmer, ex ante licensing has social value because it ensures development of the innovation when its value exceeds development cost. Social value is realized only in the region of Figure 9.1 labeled *ex ante licensing*. There is no social (or private) value to ex ante licensing for sufficiently large values of α, L, V, or X, because either the patent owner lacks a credible threat of a lawsuit to induce licensing or the innovator lacks a credible threat of foregoing development.

Remark 2. Ex ante licensing and the threat of holdup also have implications for the division of profits. For certain parameter values, the patent owner makes more money if its patent is made weaker. This counterintuitive result arises because when the innovator has a credible threat to forego development, it shifts part of the development cost to the patent owner through the terms of the ex ante license. A small increase in α or X that changes expression (2) from negative to positive can shift the equilibrium outcome from ex ante licensing to ex post licensing and raise the profit of the patent owner, because the innovator loses its credible threat to forego development.

PART II. SEARCH, DEVELOPMENT, AND PATENT LICENSING

If the innovator conducts a fruitless search and decides to develop the innovation anyway, then it faces a potential dispute with the patent owner. For now, I will assume that the patent owner is sure to observe the innovation. I will also assume that the innovator knows the strength of the patent – that is, the values of α and X – before investing in development. Then the parties will negotiate an ex post license unless the patent owner lacks a credible threat of going to trial. If expression (1) is negative, then the patent owner acquiesces. If expression (1) is non-negative, then the parties agree to an ex post license yielding the same profits as those given in Part I.

Before I can analyze the development decision I need to specify the remaining features of the model. Rather than assuming that the patent owner's technology is essential to the innovation, I assume that it reduces the development cost. Let $C \geq c$ be the development cost when the innovator has not located the relevant patented technology. The innovator commits to an investment of s on search. It knows that there is at most one patented technology available that is relevant to the innovation it is contemplating. The probability that the relevant patented technology exists is given by p. Conditional on the existence of a relevant patent the search technology finds it with probability $f(s)$. Thus, $pf(s)$ is the probability of finding a patent, $p[1 - f(s)]$ is the probability of finding nothing even though a relevant patent exists, and $1 - p$ is the probability that there is no relevant patent. Assume that $f(0) = 0$, $f' > 0 > f''$, and $f(s) < 1$ for all s.

Given this search technology I can now evaluate the profitability of a decision to develop the innovation after a fruitless search. If there is no relevant patent, then the innovator will capture $V - C$ from development. If there is a relevant patent that the innovator did not find and the patent owner has a credible threat to sue, then the profit from an ex post license is $\frac{1-\alpha}{2}(V+x)+\alpha V - C$. Weighing these profits by the updated probabilities gives an expected profit of

$$\frac{1-p}{1-pf}V + \frac{p(1-f)}{1-pf}\left[\frac{1-\alpha}{2}(V+x)+\alpha V\right] - C. \tag{3}$$

If this expression is non-negative, then the innovator will develop the technology despite not finding a relevant patent. If the expression is negative, then the innovator will not develop the technology after a fruitless search. Alternatively, if the relevant patent is weak and the patent owner does not have a credible threat, then the profit is simply

$$V - C. \tag{4}$$

Three considerations drive the equilibrium investment in search. First, a successful search reduces development cost by $C - c$, and thus search increases with development cost savings. Second, search grows more attractive as the probability that there is a relevant patent grows. The relationship between equilibrium search and the holdup problem is more complex. As noted in Part I, an ex ante license can overcome a holdup problem and assure development. This problem arises when $V \geq c$, but expression (2) is negative. Of course, an ex ante license is only possible if the innovator finds the relevant patent and its owner. Furthermore, a thorough but failed search can give an innovator confidence to develop a technology when $V \geq C$. An intensive search that does not turn up a relevant patent reduces the ex post probability that there is a relevant patent and that holdup will occur. In other words, expression (3) grows with search intensity, and increasing search can shift the value of the expression from negative to positive.

Proposition 1. Either the equilibrium search intensity, s^*, solves $pGf'(s) = 1$, where G is the private gain to the innovator from successful search, or the equilibrium search intensity $s^* = \bar{s}$, where expression (3) equals zero at $\bar{s}$.

Proof. When the innovator chooses s it knows which of the three licensing outcomes from Part I will prevail. Let us first consider the *acquiescence* outcome. If $V \geq C$, then the innovator will develop regardless of the search outcome, and the expected profit from search is: $V - pf(s)c - (1-p)f(s)C - s$. The private gain from search is simply the development cost savings $G = C - c$, and the first-order condition follows. If $V < C$, so that condition (4) is negative, then the innovator will only develop after successful search, and the expected profit from search is $V - pf(s)c - s$. The private gain from search is the development surplus, $G = V - c$, and the first-order condition follows.

Next, suppose that the parameter values are such that the *ex post licensing* outcome prevails after the innovator has identified the relevant patent owner. The expected profit function may have a kink because expression (3) can be negative for some values of s and positive for others. It is easy to show that expression (3) is increasing in s. It is possible that (3) is positive for all values of s, it possible that it is negative for all values of s, and it is possible that it is negative for $0 \leq s < \bar{s}$ and positive for $\bar{s} < s$. The expected profit from search when (3) is negative is $pf(s)[\alpha V + (1-\alpha)\frac{V+X}{2} - c] - s$ The expected profit from search when (3) is non-negative is $p[\alpha V + (1-\alpha)\frac{V+X}{2}] - pf(s)c - p[1 - f(s)]C + (1-p)(V - C) - s$. Notice that these profits are equal when expression (3) is zero.

When (3) is always positive or always negative, then the first-order condition in Proposition 1 applies with an appropriate definition of G that I will give soon. When (3) is negative for small values of s and positive for large values, then the first-order condition is satisfied at s^*, and it may also be satisfied at another local minimum. The first-order condition must be satisfied at s^* because the slope of the expected profit function at $s = \bar{s}$ is smaller approaching from the left than approaching from the right. Intuitively, the profit function may have two humps, but it must have at least one. The private gain from search if (3) is negative for all s, or when $0 \leq s^* < \bar{s}$, is $G = \alpha V + (1-\alpha)\frac{V+X}{2} - c$. And the private gain from search if (3) is positive for all s, or when $\bar{s} < s^*$, is $G = C - c$.

Finally, suppose the parameter values are such that the *ex ante licensing* outcome prevails after the innovator has identified the relevant patent owner. The same three possibilities regarding expression (3) that applied with an ex post licensing outcome also apply with an ex ante licensing outcome. The situations differ because the slope of the expected profit function at $s = \bar{s}$ is smaller approaching from the right than approaching from the left – the opposite from the analysis of the ex post licensing outcome. This means that it is possible when $s^* = \bar{s}$ that the slope of the profit function is positive when approaching from the left and negative when approaching from the right, so that the first-order condition is not satisfied at the optimum. Putting that case to the side, the first-order condition in Proposition 1 will hold with the appropriate definition of G.

The expected profit from search when (3) is negative is $pf(s)\frac{V-c}{2} - s$. In this case the private gain from search is $G = \frac{V-c}{2}$. The expected profit from search when (3) is non-negative is $pf(s)\frac{V-c}{2} + p[1 - f(s)][\alpha V + (1-\alpha)\frac{V+X}{2} - C] + (1-p)(V - C) - s$. In this case the private gain from search is $G = \frac{V-c}{2} - [\alpha V + (1-\alpha)\frac{V+X}{2} - C]$.

To gain a better understanding of the equilibrium, let us consider a special case. If the patented technology is unnecessary to the innovator, so that $C = c$, then there is no search given an acquiescence outcome. The patent owner does not have a credible threat to sue; thus, the only reason to search for the patent is to gain a development cost benefit. Next, notice that expression (3) is greater than or equal to expression (2) when the development costs are equal. Hence, if the ex post licensing outcome prevails given a fruitful search, development will occur following a fruitless search. This in turn means that the private gain from search $G = C - c = 0$, and there will be no search.

In contrast, positive equilibrium search may occur given the ex ante licensing outcome, even when $C = c$. If the innovator foregoes development following a fruitless search (expression (3) is negative given an optimal search), then search is profitable because ex ante licensing overcomes the holdup problem. If the innovator develops despite a fruitless search, search is still profitable because when search is successful, the patent owner will share some of its rents with the innovator in the ex ante license.

PART III. COMPARISON OF PRIVATE AND SOCIAL INCENTIVES TO SEARCH

The U.S. government has a variety of policy instruments that it could use to reduce the cost of performing a patent search. It could require publication of all U.S. patent applications. It could prohibit or limit claim language changes in continuing applications. It could limit the number of patents in force by raising fees or standards of patentability. It could reward innovators that conduct product clearance searches, or at least it could reduce the penalties imposed on searchers through the operation of the willfulness doctrine (and possibly the inequitable conduct doctrine).

Before we attempt to formulate policy reforms that encourage search, we should ask whether current search levels are too low. Or perhaps the easier question is: How do private incentives to search compare to social incentives? If the social planner were in charge of the search choice, but not the litigation, licensing, or development decisions, then the objective function when development always occurs would be

$$pf(s)(V-c) + p[1-f(s)](V-C) + (1-p)(V-C) - s, \tag{5}$$

and otherwise:

$$pf(s)(V-c) - s. \tag{6}$$

Proposition 2. If a fruitful search yields an acquiescence outcome or an ex post licensing outcome in which expression (3) is non-negative, then the private and social incentives to search are the same. If the expression (3) is negative and a fruitful search yields an ex ante or ex post licensing outcome, then the innovator performs too little a search compared to the socially preferred amount. If a fruitful search yields an ex ante licensing outcome in which expression (3) is non-negative, then the innovator performs too much search compared to the socially preferred amount.

Proof. Looking back to the proof of Proposition 1 we see the private gains to search are $G = C - c$, when innovation occurs regardless of the search outcome and when the acquiescence or ex post licensing outcome prevails. This matches the social gain that is derived from (5). In words, the social planner derives a benefit from search when it reduces development cost. Because the entire benefit of reduced development cost is captured by the innovator, the social and private incentives are aligned.

In the acquiescence outcome in which the innovator does not invest in development given a fruitless search, the private gain $G = V - c$. This matches the social gain that is derived from (6).

In the cases in which a fruitless search leads to no development and either ex ante or ex post licensing prevails, then there is too little search. Once again the social gain is $V - c$, but the private gain in the ex ante licensing case is only $G = \frac{V-c}{2}$, and in the ex post licensing case the private gain is $G = \alpha V + (1-\alpha)\frac{V+X}{2} - c$. The private gains are smaller in both cases (recall that $X \leq V$). Private search is too low because the innovator does not appropriate the full value of the innovation.

In the remaining case there is too much search. The innovator develops the innovation regardless of the search outcome. The innovator seeks both the benefit of reduced development cost and the enhanced bargaining power associated with an ex ante license. The social planner cares about the former but not the latter. The social gain from search is $C - c$, and the private gain is $G = \frac{V-c}{2} - [\alpha V + (1-\alpha)\frac{V+X}{2} - C]$. The fact that expression (2) is negative is sufficient to prove that the private gain is larger.

Proposition 2 is especially interesting when evaluated in the context of a stylized comparison between pharmaceutical and ICT innovation. If patent notice and patent protection are both strong for pharmaceutical technology, we might associate the problem of oversearching with that technology. In terms of the model, if search is cheap and the equilibrium value of f is high, then expression (3) is more likely to be positive. If patent protection is strong and X is small compared to V, then (2) is more likely to be negative. If the opposite assumptions are appropriate for ICT, then we are more likely to see too little search.

CONCLUSION

Cumulative innovation is the norm in many areas of technology, but both existing patent law and economic models focus on discrete innovation. New models, such as those proposed in this chapter, may guide policy makers in developing more nuanced approaches to these areas, particularly for information and communication technologies, where patents routinely fail to provide the notice function of property. These improved approaches should encourage search and reduce coordination costs, ultimately resulting in more ex ante licensing and less litigation.

REFERENCES

Bessen, J. and Meurer, M. J., *Patent Failure: How Judges, Bureaucrats, and Lawyers Put Innovators at Risk*. Princeton: Princeton University Press, 2008.

Cockburn, I. and Henderson, R., "The IPO Survey on Strategic Management of Intellectual Property." *Intellectual Property Owners Association*. Washington, DC, November 2003.

Cohen, W., Nelson, R. R., and Walsh, J. P 2000. "Protecting Their Intellectual Assets: Appropriability Conditions and Why U.S. Manufacturing Firms Patent (or Not)." *NBER Working Paper* No. 7752.

Denicolò, V. 2000. "Two Stage Patent Races and Patent Policy." *RAND Journal of Economics* 31, 488–501.

Green, J. and Scotchmer, S. 1995. "On the Division of Profit in Sequential Innovation." *RAND Journal of Economics* 26:20–33.

O'Donoghue, T., Scotchmer, S. and Thisse, J.-F. 1998, "Patent Breadth, Patent Life and the Pace of Technological Progress." *Journal of Economics and Management Strategy* 1–32.

Scotchmer, S. and Green, J. 1990. "Novelty and Disclosure in Patent Law." *RAND Journal of Economics* 21:131–146.

10

The Vonage Trilogy

A Case Study in "Patent Bullying"

*Ted R. Sichelman**

This chapter presents an in-depth case study of a series of infringement suits filed by "patent bullies." Unlike the oft-discussed "patent trolls" – which typically sell no products or services and perform no R&D – patent bullies are large, established operating companies that threaten or institute costly patent infringement actions of dubious merit against smaller companies, usually in order to suppress competition or garner licensing fees. In an ideal world of high-quality patents and optimal patent licensing and litigation, infringement suits by aggressive incumbents would have a cleansing, almost Darwinian effect. Yet, defects and distortions in patent examination, licensing, and litigation – the very problems that are raised constantly in the context of patent trolls – generally apply with equal and often greater force to patent bullies. Nonetheless, patent bullies have scarcely been discussed in the academic literature or popular press, especially in recent years.

Specifically, this chapter examines three patent infringement suits filed by incumbent telecommunications carriers – Sprint, Verizon, and AT&T – against Vonage, then an early-stage company providing consumer telephone services over the internet. Based on a detailed analysis of the patents-at-issue, prior art, court documents, and news accounts, it shows that the incumbents were able to exploit defects in the patent system in order to prevent Vonage's disruptive technologies from competing

* Professor, University of San Diego School of Law. This chapter is an annotated version of an article in 90 Notre Dame L. Rev. (2014). I thank Colleen Chien, William Gallagher, Stuart Graham, David Jones, Mark Lemley, David McGowan, Lisa Ramsey, Pam Samuelson, David Schwartz, and participants at the University of San Diego School of Law IP Speakers' Series, Law & Society Annual Meeting at the Sturm College of Law – University of Denver, Patents and Entrepreneurship in Business and Information Technologies Conference at George Washington University Law School, Conference on Innovation and Communication Law at Louisville Law School, and the IP Scholars Conference at Cardozo Law School for helpful suggestions and comments, as well as Dylan Aste, Jennifer Barlock, Alan Chang, Ryan Rafferty, and Dan Taskalos for their invaluable research assistance. This research was funded in part by a grant from the Ewing Marion Kauffman Foundation, which I thank for its support. The contents are solely my responsibility.

with their outmoded products and services. Because startups like Vonage typically lack the resources to vigorously defend against even weak patent suits, patent bullying can result in severe anticompetitive effects. Indeed, the suits filed against Vonage wound up costing it more than $200 million in settlement payments. The incumbents achieved their intended result – drastically reducing Vonage's stock price, severely weakening its position in the market, and placing it at the brink of insolvency.

The chapter concludes with reflections on the Vonage trilogy, particularly the potential for abuse that patent bullies can wreak on smaller companies. This case study demonstrates that further theoretical and empirical study is warranted to assess the full extent of the patent bullying problem.

I. INTRODUCTION: THE OVERLOOKED PROBLEM OF PATENT BULLYING

In the last ten years or so, academics, the media, the Federal Trade Commission, and even the Supreme Court have been fixated on so-called patent trolls – loosely, entities and individuals that generate the bulk of their revenue from patent litigation and licensing, but do not make and sell products that embody their patents and that, typically, perform little to no research and development (R&D) relating to their patents.[1] Yet, the exact problem that trolls present to the patent system has remained somewhat elusive.[2]

Many focus their attention on the nonpracticing nature of trolls, exhorting that patent holders that do not sell commercial products embodying their patents are

[1] Some might characterize individual inventors or small companies that had once performed R&D, but no longer do, as patent trolls. In general, there is a substantial debate over how to define the term "troll," but all definitions appear to require that a troll not make and sell products (at least in substantial numbers) that embody the patents it owns. *See generally* Christopher Anthony Cotropia, Jay P. Kesan & David L. Schwartz, Unpacking Patent Assertion Entities (PAEs) (working paper, 2014), *available at* http://ssrn.com/abstract=2346381; Colleen V. Chien, *Of Trolls, Davids, Goliaths, and Kings: Narratives and Evidence in the Litigation of High-Tech Patents*, 87 N.C. L. Rev. 1571, 1579 (2009). Focusing on the nonpracticing nature of trolls, many commentators have begun using "nonpracticing entity" (NPE) as a less disparaging substitute. For the reasons I present later, I think the term "troll" is justified, but only for those NPEs that *abuse* the patent system by exploiting *weak* patents. In this regard, the current shift in terminology may do more injustice to those NPEs that assert strong patents – which I generally view as welfare enhancing – than retaining the use of the "troll" term.

[2] Following the dissemination of this chapter online, Mark Lemley and Douglas Melamed offered a trenchant critique of the common rhetoric of patent trolls. *See* Mark A. Lemley & A. Douglas Melamed, *Missing the Forest for the Trolls*, 113 Colum. L. Rev. 2117, 2129–45 (2013) (contending that, in many respects, practicing entities potentially generate more social costs than trolls) (citing an earlier version of this chapter). However, in contrast to this chapter, Lemley and Melamed do not focus their efforts on describing how large practicing entities abuse the patent system by "bullying" smaller practicing entities, instead grounding their analysis in a comparison of the activities of practicing entities to those of non-practicing entities. *See id.*

behaving contrary to the goals of the patent system.[3] However, this view is clearly wrong, at least as a descriptive matter, because the Supreme Court has firmly held that "it is the privilege of any owner of property [including patents] to use or not use it, without question of motive."[4] Indeed, the most widely accepted explanation of the patent system – the "reward theory" – posits that patents are designed to spur invention and its disclosure in patents to the public, but generally are unnecessary to promote the *commercialization* of inventions.[5] Instead, reward theorists believe that once inventions are created and disclosed, the market will efficiently yield commercial embodiments of those inventions. Although there is a strong normative argument that the patent system should actively promote commercialization – and I am squarely in favor of this view – American patent law has long shied away from this approach.[6] Thus, under current law, trolls not commercializing their inventions can scarcely justify the views of those aligned against them.[7]

3 *See, e.g.*, Amy L. Landers, *Let the Games Begin: Incentives to Innovation in the New Economy of Intellectual Property Law*, 46 SANTA CLARA L. REV. 307, 332–35 (2006); Sannu K. Shrestha, Note, *Trolls or Market-Makers? An Empirical Analysis of Nonpracticing Entities*, 110 COLUM. L. REV. 114 (2010). *But see* Damien Geradin et al., Elves or Trolls? The Role of Non-Practicing Patent Owners in the Innovation Economy (TILEC Discussion Paper No. 2008–018, May 2008), *available at* http://papers.ssrn.com/sol3/papers.cfm?abstract_id=1136086 (proposing a business-model-neutral policy for analyzing patent licensors).

4 Continental Paper Bag Co. v. Eastern Paper Bag Co., 210 U.S. 405, 429 (1908); *see also* eBay Inc. v. MercExchange, L.L.C., 547 U.S. 388, 393-94 (2006) ("The [district] court's categorical rule is also in tension with *Continental Paper Bag Co. v. Eastern Paper Bag Co.*, which rejected the contention that a court of equity has no jurisdiction to grant injunctive relief to a patent holder who has unreasonably declined to use the patent.") (citations omitted). Although lower courts have latched onto Justice Kennedy's concurrence in *eBay* to deny injunctive relief to a nonpracticing patentee, *see, e.g.*, Commonwealth Sci. and Indus. Research Org. v. Buffalo Tech. Inc., 492 F.Supp.2d 600, 607–08 (E.D. Tex. 2007), *rev'd on other grounds by*, 542 F.3d 1363 (Fed. Cir. 2008), such a patentee is just as entitled to a suitable legal remedy as a practicing entity, *see* Ted Sichelman, *Purging Patent Law of "Private Law" Remedies*, 92 TEXAS L. REV. 516, 551-552 (2014) [hereinafter Sichelman, *Purging Private Law*]. Moreover, although post–*eBay* denials of injunctions to nonpracticing entities may be effectuating more of a commercialization-oriented view of patent law: On a theoretical level, Justice Kennedy's pronouncement is analytically flawed because he implicitly assumes without basis that nonpracticing entities enjoy "undue leverage in negotiations" involving complex technologies whereas practicing entities do not. *eBay*, 547 U.S. at 396–97. Whether a patentee is practicing or not, an injunction may suboptimally diminish the social incentives to commercialize because the patentee can often gain more leverage in negotiations than attributable to the social value of the patent. *See* Sichelman, *Purging Patent Law*. One might argue that nonpracticing entities tend to gain greater "undue" leverage than practicing entities – for example, because they are repeat players and relatively risk neutral – but these fine distinctions played no role in Justice Kennedy's conclusory assertions. *eBay*, 547 U.S. at 396–97.

5 *See* Ted Sichelman, *Commercializing Patents*, 62 STAN. L. REV. 341, 358–62 (2010).

6 *See id.*

7 Some defendants make a more nuanced argument regarding trolls' lack of commercial activity – namely, that trolls thwart accused infringers' efforts to defend against infringement lawsuits by eliminating defendants' ability to assert infringement counterclaims so as to spur settlement. *See* Wendy H. Schacht & John R. Thomas, C.R.S. REPORT FOR CONGRESS, PATENT REFORM: INNOVATION ISSUES 9 (2005) ("Because patent speculators do not otherwise participate in the marketplace, however, they are immune to such counterclaims."), *available at* http://patentlaw.typepad.com/patent/RL32996.pdf.

Another oft-touted criticism of trolls is that they perform little to no R&D on their patents. Yet, this view seems as odd as the commercialization concern. Patents have always been tradable, either through outright sale or licensing, and nobody would argue that only the original inventor should be able to sue for infringement. Although trolls themselves might not perform R&D, the inventors listed on the patents presumably did, so saying that "trolls thwart the patent system because they undertake no R&D" is not much different from saying GE thwarts the patent system, because only its engineers – who assign their patents to their employer, GE – perform research. Rather, from the perspective of contemporary economics, there is little difference between a vertically integrated entity like GE and an effective joint venture between independent inventors and a troll assignee – indeed, the joint ventures are often more efficient means of producing inventions.[8]

In sum, the two key features of trolls as they are commonly defined – namely, that they do not commercialize their patents and perform little to no R&D – are red herrings when it comes to the problems they create for the patent system, at least on the widely accepted reward theory of patent law.[9] Rather, the major concern over trolls seems to stem from their single-minded goal of earning revenue from patent litigation and licensing. This quest for patent-induced profits appears to channel many trolls into aggressively exploiting defects in patent examination, licensing, and litigation in ways that other patent holders often do not. Indeed, on this view, the term "troll" should be limited only to – and is well deserved for – those nonpracticing entities that *abuse* the patent system. However, to be certain, *any patent holder can – and many do – take advantage of these systemic defects.*

There are at least four serious defects in the patent system. First, although the empirical research is limited, it appears the U.S. Patent & Trademark Office (PTO) issues many patent claims that are arguably anticipated or obvious in view of prior technology; overly broad given the scope of the patent disclosure; vague, ambiguous, and generally difficult to interpret; and introduced and amended long after the original patent disclosure is filed.[10] Despite the seemingly endless number of "bad" patents, there is a "presumption of validity" that patents are properly granted, which makes invalidating them in litigation quite costly – usually a million dollars or more. Second, patentees and potential infringers face unusually high transaction costs in

But the only *policy* reasons in favor of promoting these kinds of counterclaims would be to lower the social costs of defending against "bad" patents or the costs arising from other systemic defects, neither of which is endemic to patent trolls. *See infra* notes 10–13 and accompanying text.

8 *See* Henry William Chesbrough, Open Innovation: The New Imperative for Creating and Profiting from Technology (2003).

9 As noted earlier, if one views the patent system as important to promoting commercialization, then trolls' failure to make and sell products embodying their patents is certainly a serious problem. *See supra* text accompany notes 5–6. But only a minority of scholars and judges hold such a view. *See* Sichelman, *supra* note 5, at 358–62, 393; Michael Abramowicz & John Duffy, *Intellectual Property for Market Experimentation*, 83 N.Y.U. L. Rev. 337, 401–02 (2008).

10 *See* Sichelman, *supra* note 5, at 356–57, 383–84.

licensing negotiations and litigation, which are fueled in large part by uncertainty and instability in many patent law doctrines. The distorting effects of these costs are especially problematic in technological fields for which patent search and analysis are difficult.[11] Third, patent holders can delay assertions of infringement until a relevant market is well developed and the costs of switching to a non-infringing technology are exorbitant.[12] Fourth, asymmetric resources, stakes, and levels of risk aversion between repeat players – such as trolls and large patent holders versus one-time players, such as startup companies – can result in highly skewed litigation outcomes.[13]

Although trolls appear to be especially adept at exploiting these defects, they are not the only group doing so. Another important class of patent holders – namely, large practicing entities that often hold many patents – appear to be exploiting the same sorts of defects, and potentially at much greater rates. Just like the trolls, these "patent bullies" take full advantage of weak, uncertain, and vague patents; the high costs of litigation; the ability to delay lawsuits; and their massive resources in order to engage in highly anticompetitive behavior, often against market entrants and startups. Specifically, patent bullies assert their patents against entrants to prevent innovative, disruptive technologies from competing with the bullies' outmoded products.[14] Additionally, bullies desiring to enter a new market wield their patents against startups that are already well positioned in the market. Specifically, a patent bully can file an infringement suit to compel a license from a startup to its innovative technology – which, in turn, the bully uses to trounce the startup by leveraging preestablished production capacity, marketing channels, and general goodwill, as well as by engaging in effective predatory pricing by tying the innovative product to the sale of preexisting products. These effects are often compounded by keiretsu-style, cross-licensing agreements among industry incumbents, which provide a veritable zone of freedom to the incumbents, but a wall of impenetrability to entrants.[15]

The remainder of this chapter provides an in-depth description and analysis of the patent bullying problem by engaging in a case study of a trilogy of suits filed by incumbent telecommunications carriers against Vonage, an early-stage company that provides consumer telephone services over the internet. By evaluating the decisions of Vonage's and Sprint's counsel in the context of the patents-in-suit,

[11] *See id.*

[12] *See* Sichelman, *Purging Patent Law, supra* note 3.

[13] *See* Stuart J. H. Graham & Ted Sichelman, *Why Do Start-ups Patent?*, 23 Berkeley Tech. L.J. 1063, 1086 (2008).

[14] *See infra* Part II.

[15] *See* F. Scott Kieff, *Coordination, Property, and Intellectual Property: An Unconventional Approach to Anticompetitive Effects and Downstream Access*, 56 Emory L.J. 327, 413 (2006) ("[F]ollowing the FTC recommendations may lead to a system under which large players could regularly trade large numbers of weak patents with each other while at the same time frustrating market entry."); F. Scott Kieff, *A Keiretsu Approach to Patents*, Intell. Asset Mgmt., Feb./Mar. 2001, at 51 (discussing the mechanism behind the "keiretsu" effect of cross-licensing networks).

accused technology, prior art, and hired experts, this chapter offers an atypical, "law in action" approach for assessing the defects of the present patent system.[16] Such a mode of inquiry is radically different from not only the doctrinally oriented analyses that generally ignore the effects of counsel on case outcomes and judicial opinions but also the high-level empirical analyses that tend to abstract away from the day-to-day decisions of parties, lawyers, and judges.

More concretely, this chapter examines how Sprint, Verizon, and AT&T filed suits to prevent Vonage from continuing to gain market share from the carriers with its disruptive internet-based, consumer telephony services. Although it appears that all or nearly all of the patents in suit were very likely not infringed, invalid, or unenforceable, Vonage lacked the resources and experience to vigorously and skillfully defend against these suits. As a result, it paid more than $200 million in settlement payments to the carriers. Ultimately, Vonage's seemingly unwarranted settlement payments placed it at the brink of insolvency – drastically reducing its stock price and severely weakening its position in the market. Perhaps more importantly, the outcome of the Vonage trilogy – which was widely publicized in the mainstream media – has provided a strong signal to incumbents that patent litigation, even when the underlying case is weak, can be an effective tool to quash competition.

Despite the serious nature of patent bullying, scant attention has been paid to it in the popular press and academic literature, especially in recent years.[17] Arguably, the paucity of discussion of patent bullying stems in large part from the ability of certain practicing entities to effectively divert attention away from their own exploitative behavior by placing the blame on so-called nonpracticing entities (NPEs) and patent assertion entities (PAEs), often taken to be synonymous with "patent trolls." Although I do not contend that abusive behavior by trolls should be condoned, it should be viewed in the light of rampant abusive behavior by nonpracticing *and practicing* entities alike. The Vonage case study presented herein indicates that as "patent bullies," practicing entities can engage in similar levels of abuse as the nonpracticing trolls.

II. THE GENESIS, SUCCESS, AND BULLYING OF VONAGE

This part begins by recounting the genesis of Vonage in 2000 and its rapid growth over the next five years. Next, it describes the suits filed against Vonage by Sprint,

[16] I only provide a brief account of the AT&T suit because I represented Vonage in that case. *See infra* note 54. Additionally, because of space considerations and the lack of electronic access to most of the documents in the Verizon case, I analyze that suit in less detail.

[17] Notable exceptions to this trend include Jean O. Lanjouw & Joshua Lerner, *Tilting the Table? The Use of Preliminary Injunctions*, 44 J.L. & Econ. 573, 575 (2001); Michael J. Meurer, *Controlling Opportunistic and Anticompetitive Intellectual Property Litigation*, 44 B.C. L. Rev. 509 (2003); Gwendolyn G. Ball & Jay P. Kesan, Transaction Costs and Trolls: Strategic Behavior by Individual Inventors, Small Firms, and Entrepreneurs in Patent Litigation (working paper, Feb. 6, 2009), *available at* http://ssrn.com/abstrat=1337166; Graham & Sichelman, *supra* note 13; Chien, *supra* note 1.

Verizon, and AT&T, including an in-depth analysis of the patents and technologies at issue in the Sprint case. In so doing, I conclude that Vonage failed to raise (or waived) potentially determinative defenses in the Sprint case, which it settled for roughly $80 million. Last, I examine several suits filed against Vonage by ostensible "trolls," as well as a suit Vonage acquired that was directed against the incumbent carriers. In general, I conclude that the patent system was not effective for Vonage as a plaintiff – and more importantly – afforded ample opportunity for patent bullying by industry incumbents, with results far worse than those inflicted on Vonage by the trolls.

As a preliminary matter, the reader might wonder whether a legal academic is suitably positioned to play "Monday-morning quarterback" in evaluating the decisions of lawyers in cases involving highly complex technologies and spanning several years and hundreds of pleadings. Normally, the answer to this question would be an indubitable "no." However, in this situation, I believe the answer is a qualified "yes." Specifically, before practicing as a patent litigator, I founded and ran a software communications company that sold Voice over IP (VoIP) systems that included technology similar to that used by Vonage. In this regard, I was heavily involved in the design, development, and installation of my company's VoIP-related products.

Additionally, I represented Vonage in its action against AT&T – albeit briefly, because the case settled shortly after filing – and also represented Skype, the largest provider of VoIP services in the world, in two unrelated patent infringement actions. As part of my professional and legal work, I have become quite familiar with the types of VoIP technology employed by Vonage, including prior art relevant to the patents-in-suit in the Vonage trilogy. Although I have not read every pleading in detail in the Sprint case – nor do I even have access to all of them, because many were filed under seal – in drafting this chapter, I spent numerous hours reading the patents-in-suit, pleadings, and orders, as well as searching for and reviewing potential prior art. Although I can legitimately convince only those intimately familiar with the facts of case of the correctness of my conclusions, hopefully the analysis presented herein will inform any reader of the weakness of Sprint's suit and the critical omissions Vonage made in defense.[18]

A. *Traditional Telephony and the Birth of Vonage*

Up until the mid-1990s, voice-based telephone communications comprised a combination of traditional "circuit switched" (effectively analog) networks – often known collectively as the "public switched telephone network" (PSTN) – and private

[18] As I mentioned earlier, this chapter only briefly examines the *Verizon* and *AT & T* cases because of space limitations, the lack of readily available court documents, and my representation of Vonage in the AT & T case.

"packet-based" (effectively digital) networks, which were typically used to carry long-distance traffic between local "relay" points connected to the PSTN. With the rise of the internet, a number of companies endeavored to carry voice traffic over that effectively public, packet-based network. Early providers, such as the Israeli company, Vocaltec, required that all users be on the internet to place and receive calls. Yet, in early 1996, Vocaltec demonstrated an innovative Internet Protocol (IP)-PSTN gateway that bridged the PSTN and IP worlds. This sort of gateway allowed callers on a standard telephone network to call someone on the internet and vice versa. Soon after Vocaltec released its gateway, other manufacturers, such as Cisco Systems, offered similar gateways. With a large variety of cost-affordable and reliable gateways available, a number of internet telephony companies were founded to offer consumers standard telephone services that used the internet to substantially reduce the costs of carrying long distance calls

The fastest growing of these companies in the early 2000s was Vonage Holdings Company (Vonage). Founded in 2000, by 2005, Vonage had more than 1.2 million subscribers, a number that was growing at more than 300% per year.[19] The driver behind Vonage's phenomenal growth and revenue was its ability to offer "unlimited" local and long-distance calling on any ordinary telephone for about $40 per month.[20] Although Vonage's calls are carried over the internet, a user simply plugged an adapter into an ordinary phone and connected it to a router – and with some minimal installation – started placing calls in a manner essentially indistinguishable from a traditional phone service.[21] Thus, Vonage was not simply an add-on, but an entire replacement for the services offered by the incumbent carriers.[22] Not only were carriers losing many subscribers and substantial revenue to Vonage in the mid-2000s, they were implicitly funding Vonage's low-cost service because they built and maintained most of the underlying network for the internet in the United States. Although subscribers paid carriers for their use of the internet, because landline data plans in the United States typically provided (and still provide) for *unlimited* data transmission and downloads, the carriers were effectively subsidizing Vonage's discounts. Moreover, by providing its services over the "preexisting" internet, Vonage was able to avoid being classified as a traditional telephone service, which allowed it to escape burdensome regulation and taxes.[23] As such, the incumbent carriers were

[19] Vonage Timeline, http://www.vonage.com/corporate/about_timeline.php (last visited Feb. 17, 2011); Yahoo! Finance, Profile for Vonage Holdings Corporation, http://finance.yahoo.com/q/pr?s=VG (last visited Feb. 16, 2014).

[20] *See* Ted Hearn, *An Advantage for Vonage? VoIP Rival Rides Cable Pipe*, MULTICHANNEL NEWS (Jan. 6, 2003), http://goliath.ecnext.com/coms2/gi_0198–97572/An-advantage-for-Vonage-VoIP.html (last visited Feb. 7, 2011).

[21] *See* Lev Grossman, *On the Internet, Talk Is Cheap*, TIME, Apr. 15, 2002, at 77.

[22] *See* Chris Williams, *Vonage: Patent Smackdown Won't Bring Shutters Down*, REGISTER, Feb. 26, 2007, http://www.theregister.co.uk/2007/02/26/vonage_defends_-against_verizon.

[23] Jonathan E. Nuechterlein, *Eighth Circuit Upholds FCC Order Preempting State Regulation of VoIP*, Apr. 18, 2007, http://www.wilmerhale.com/publications/whPubsDetail.aspx?publication=3657.

presumably highly motivated to find any way to prevent Vonage from expanding its subscriber base.

B. *The Vonage Trilogy*

1. Sprint v. Vonage

In October 2005, Sprint filed an infringement suit on seven patents against Vonage in the District of Kansas.[24] In terms of relative resources – and using 2006 as a benchmark (2005 data are not available for Vonage because it was a private company then) – Sprint had 600 patents, $41 billion in revenue, $2.4 billion in net profits, 50,000 employees, and 50 million customers, whereas Vonage had no issued patents, $600 million in revenue, $338 million in net losses, 1,500 employees, and 2.2 million customers. Notably, Vonage's lack of a patent portfolio (by definition) precluded it from the preferred tactic of "defending" against suit by asserting its patents back against Sprint. Indeed, as recounted in more detail later, Vonage settled the case after purchasing a set of patents that Sprint was accused of infringing in another case.

The seven patents-in-suit all disclosed technological systems and methods to route voice traffic on a traditional telephone network – the "public switched telephone network" (PSTN) – to and from a digital packet-based network that uses an "asynchronous transfer mode" (ATM), non-internet protocol. Like so-called patent trolls, Sprint admitted in its interrogatories that it never practiced the patents, though there was some evidence that Cisco Systems, Inc. ("Cisco") was a licensee of the patents-in-suit and that Cisco sold products that could be used in practicing the patents.[25] One critical fact in the case was that Vonage purchased most of its communications equipment from Cisco, which led to potential defenses I explore later.

Because the specifications of the patents-in-suit disclosed carrying voice traffic over an ATM-based network, as opposed to the internet, claim construction revolved around whether Sprint's patents could cover an IP network. In this regard – like savvy trolls – Sprint filed an original patent application, which it abandoned, and then filed a series of "continuation" applications, including those that resulted in the seven patents-in-suit. By using continuations, Sprint was able to rely on the filing date of its original application for new claims that purported to cover non- ATM networks. Indeed, Sprint's earliest issued patent's claims are limited to ATM networks, whereas its later patents removed this limitation, presumably in an attempt to reach IP networks such as those used by Vonage. Importantly, because

[24] Complaint, Sprint Communications Co. LP v. Vonage Holdings Corp., 2005 WL 3776507 (D. Kan. Oct. 4, 2005) (No. 05–2433-JWL).

[25] *See* Vonage's Memorandum in Support of Vonage Holdings Corp. and Vonage America, Inc.'s Motion Seeking Leave to Amend Their Respective Answers, Affirmative Defenses and Counterclaims Pursuant to Fed. R. Civ. P. 15, Sprint Communications Co. LP v. Vonage Holdings Corp., Case No. 05–2433 (Mar. 30, 2007).

Sprint's later patent applications were entitled to rely on the 1994 filing date of the original application, all of the developments in the field of internet telephony between then and the late 1990s (the actual filing date of the patents-in-suit) were excluded from the set of potential prior art that could be used to invalidate the patents.

Although Vonage was able to win a key claim construction battle that limited the *literal* scope of many of the asserted claims to ATM networks, as I recount later, it apparently failed to mount arguments that would have probably given it a winning defense of non-infringement of three of the seven patents under the "doctrine of equivalents." In addition to Vonage's failure to limit the patents to ATM networks – despite the seemingly wide array of prior art available to it and strong evidence showing the inventor of the patents never considered his invention to apply to IP networks[26] – it did not move for many defenses of invalidity on summary judgment, including anticipation and obviousness, and was unsuccessful in showing invalidity at trial. Finally, Vonage waived the potentially decisive defenses of "implied license" and "exhaustion" by waiting to assert them until the last day of discovery. Taken together, these omissions arguably turned Sprint's seemingly "weak" case into an effectively "strong" one.

Part of Vonage's failure to mount these defenses presumably stemmed from the inexperience of its experts, who – as I explain later – appeared relatively unfamiliar with the technology-at-issue. Of course, ultimately it is counsel who is responsible for selecting experts, gathering evidence, and mounting a case. Yet, according to the court and all other indicators, Vonage's counsel was quite experienced in patent litigation matters. Thus, one might surmise that Vonage's omissions and waivers – some of them quite serious – resulted more from a lack of time and resources, rather than skill, arguably brought on by a constrained litigation budget. With these caveats, I now turn to the details of the case.

A. BATTLE OF THE EXPERTS (OR NOT). Perhaps the first – and, surely, one of the most important – strategic gaffes by Vonage's counsel was hiring a non-infringement expert who was arguably unqualified and an invalidity expert with very little relevant knowledge in the field. For its non-infringement expert, Vonage hired Joel M. Halpern, a consultant in the field of networking. Although Halpern had extensive experience in the area of ATM and IP networks,[27] as Sprint recognized in a motion to exclude his expert opinions, his expertise only encompassed data networking, but not

[26] *See* Vonage's Memorandum in Opposition to Sprint's Motion for Partial Summary Judgment at 6–7, Sprint Communications Co. LP v. Vonage Holdings Corp., 2007 WL 2813950 (D. Kan. June 11, 2007) (citing a PowerPoint slide of the inventor stating the invention's purpose was to "describe a new switched ATM/circuit network architecture").

[27] Joe Halpern-Biography, Network Computing, http://www.networkcomputing.com/713/713f2HALPERN.html (last visited Aug. 17, 2013) (noting that Halpern is one of two key designers of Public Network-to-Node Interface (PNNI), the protocol for routing ATM-switched virtual circuits).

traditional telephony, including the PSTN.[28] Because the patents and technology at-issue all involved transferring calls between the PSTN and packet networks (such as ATM and IP networks), Vonage's non-infringement expert only had knowledge on half of the equation. Although Sprint's motion to exclude Halpern was not granted, Vonage arguably suffered from his lack of expertise. As discussed later, it appears Vonage failed to introduce important non-infringement arguments at summary judgment and presented a poor case of non-infringement at trial.

Vonage's invalidity expert, Frank R. Koperda, had some experience in interfacing traditional telephony platforms with digital networks, but it was in the mid-1980s, more than ten years before the critical date of the patents-in-suit.[29] The rest of Koperda's experience – like Halpern's – was mainly in data networking, and his small amount of experience in VoIP did not involve connections between the PSTN and IP networks.[30] Indeed, as with Halpern, Sprint eventually moved to disqualify Koperda as a qualified expert. Although the court denied the motion, it is somewhat telling that Sprint decided to file such a motion at all.

B. MISSED PRIOR ART AND KEY DEFENSES. More specifically, Vonage was unable to mount a substantial invalidity defense of anticipation or obviousness. Although I have not exhaustively searched for or analyzed the prior art relevant to the patents-in-suit, industry observers indicated that Sprint's patents were likely invalid, and the failure of Vonage to lodge substantial prior art likely seems to be a significant oversight.[31] Despite the ostensive gaps in Vonage's prior art disclosures, because Sprint's patents only disclosed communications technologies in an ATM environment, but the claims in the patents-in-issue were drafted to cover any type of network – including an IP environment – it should at least have been apparent to Vonage's counsel that lack of written description would be a critical defense. In this regard, recall that the enablement requirement demands that the specification "describe how to make and use the invention," whereas the written description requirement mandates that the specification "show that the inventor actually invented the invention claimed."[32]

Although Vonage's counsel apparently recognized the importance of a non-enablement defense – and although Vonage's expert's invalidity report is sealed – other documents show that Vonage's counsel apparently overlooked the lack of

[28] Sprint's Brief in Support of its Motion to Exclude the Opinions of Vonage's Expert Joel M. Halpern, Sprint Communications Co. LP v. Vonage Holdings Corp., 2007 WL 2821679 (D. Kan. May 15, 2007).

[29] Frank R. Koperda-Resume, NextGen Datacom, http://www.nextgendc.com/resume_skill.htm (last visited Feb. 11, 2014).

[30] *See id.*

[31] *See, e.g.*, Mike Masnick, *AT&T Joins the Party of Jealous Telcos: Sues Vonage for Patent Infringement*, TECHDIRT, Oct. 22, 2007, http://www.techdirt.com/articles/20071019/184443.shtml.

[32] Ariad Pharmaceuticals, Inc. v. Eli Lilly & Co., 598 F.3d 1336, 1345, 1351 (Fed. Cir. 2010); *see also In re* Gosteli, 872 F.2d 1008, 1012 (Fed. Cir. 1989) (stating that for written description, the critical question is whether "the description clearly allow persons of ordinary skill in the art to recognize that he or she invented what is claimed").

written description as a separate defense at summary judgment.[33] In particular, in a response brief to Sprint's motion to exclude the testimony of Vonage's expert, Vonage's counsel merely discussed enablement, but not written description. Additionally, Vonage's opposition brief to Sprint's motion for partial summary judgment appeared to confuse the indefiniteness and written description doctrines.[34] In the very likely event that Vonage did not lodge a separate defense of written description at summary judgment, this failure appears to be a critical oversight, because the inventor of the patents-in-suit "regarded his invention as being directed to an ATM system rather than including the Internet as a component."[35] Such a statement seems the essence of a lack of "possession" of the "claimed subject matter."[36] In other words, it appears the specification did not "describe[e] the claimed invention with all of its limitations using such descriptive means as words, structures, figures, diagrams, and formulas that fully set forth the claimed invention."[37] Although "[t]he subject matter of the claim need not be described literally (i.e., using the same terms or *in haec verba*)," the patents would have needed to disclose sufficient material to "clearly allow persons of ordinary skill in the art to recognize" that the specification related to any type of network, including IP networks.[38] Because the patents' disclosure described "the invention" as relating solely relating to *ATM* networks – which was apparently supported by statements from the inventor and other Sprint engineers – and portions of the patents were construed to cover *non-ATM* networks, it is unlikely that Sprint satisfied the written description requirement.[39]

33 Although the court remarked that "Vonage contends that the asserted patents are invalid pursuant to 35 U.S.C. § 112 for failure to comply with the written description, enablement, and definiteness requirements," the court only addressed indefiniteness in its summary judgment order, indicating that Vonage did not raise a separate written description defense. Sprint Communications Co. L.P. v. Vonage Holdings Corp., 500 F. Supp.2d 1290, 1328–32 (D. Kan. 2007).

34 Vonage's Memorandum in Opposition to Sprint's Motion for Partial Summary Judgment, Sprint Communications Co. LP v. Vonage Holdings Corp., 2007 WL 2813950 (D. Kan. June 11, 2007). Specifically, Sprint argued that the fact that "[e]very document authored by Mr. Christie states that his invention was directed to an ATM system for voice communication" supports a rejection under § 112 ¶ 2 (indefiniteness), rather than the much stronger argument for failure to meet ¶ 1 (written description/enablement). *Id.*

35 *Sprint*, 500 F. Supp.2d at 1332 ("Vonage directs the court to evidence which it contends shows that Mr. Christie regarded his invention as being directed to an ATM system rather than including the Internet as a component. This evidence consists of documents authored by Mr. Christie as well as the deposition testimony of a Sprint employee and one of Sprint's patent attorneys.").

36 Ralston Purina Co. v. Far-Mar-Co, Inc., 772 F.2d 1570, 1575 (Fed. Cir. 1985).

37 MPEP 2163.02 (citing Lockwood v. American Airlines, Inc., 107 F.3d 1565, 1572, 41 USPQ2d 1961, 1966 (Fed. Cir. 1997)).

38 *Gosteli*, 872 F.2d at 1012.

39 Moreover, as I describe further herein, although there is some basis to believe that the specification disclosed a "structure" relating to IP networks, even if this basis were sufficient to support claims over IP networks, it would preclude any theory of infringement under the doctrine of equivalents under the "dedication" rule. Thus, even if Sprint failed on a written description defense, the same arguments would have very likely knocked out three patents that the court found were not literally infringed. *See infra* notes 57–58 and accompanying text.

Vonage's apparent failure to mount a solid written description defense was not its only critical omission. In particular, according to the district court, "Vonage built its VoIP telephony system with the technical advice of, and using components purchased from, Cisco."[40] Importantly, Sprint and Cisco had executed an "Alliance Agreement" that provided for the "joint development and ownership of products and intellectual property relating to the asserted patents."[41] In the agreement, "Sprint agreed to license to Cisco patents," including the patents-in-suit, and "covenanted not to sue Cisco customers for infringement of any [licensed] patent."[42] Based on the Sprint-Cisco agreement, Vonage arguably had viable implied license and exhaustion defenses, even before the Supreme Court's opinion in *LG* v. *Quanta*.[43] Yet, inexplicably – although Vonage's counsel had received the Sprint-Cisco agreement two months before the close of discovery – Vonage's counsel waited until the last day of discovery to move to amend its answer to include these defenses.[44] As a result, the magistrate judge rejected Vonage's motion to amend its answer, which the district court subsequently upheld.[45]

C. A MEAGER SUMMARY JUDGMENT MOTION (AND MORE MISSED DEFENSES). Vonage's tactical daftness continued at the summary judgment stage. The court began by stating that "it was struck by many . . . deficiencies in Vonage's brief."[46] It noted that a substantial portion of Vonage's brief failed to comply with local rules governing motions for summary judgment, because they were "largely cluttered with improper attorney argument and commentary as well as legal conclusions, none of which are 'facts that would be admissible in evidence.'"[47] Indeed, the court lambasted Vonage for its poorly drafted brief, stating,

> It contains mostly argument, attorney commentary, and conclusory statements regarding the patents and technology at issue, with only cursory citations to the record. Vonage's purported "factual" description of the Sprint patents in Section II is actually attorney argument that roughly paraphrases the patent disclosures to support Vonage's contentions in this case and, notably, selectively omits those portions of the patents which do not. . . . Additionally, it is even more troubling because it contains paragraphs, some of which are lengthy, which purport to describe Vonage's technologically complex system with nothing more than a single cursory citation to the record at the end of each paragraph. This makes it virtually impossible for the court to determine what, if any, portions of the record Vonage is relying on to

40 *Sprint*, 500 F. Supp.2d at 1334.
41 *Id.*
42 *Id.*
43 Quanta Computer, Inc. v. LG Electronics, Inc., 553 U.S. 617 (2008).
44 *Sprint*, 500 F. Supp.2d at 1347.
45 *See id.* at 1348–49.
46 *Id.* at 1303.
47 *Id.* at 1304.

> support each of the statements which allegedly describes its system. . . . Vonage has no legitimate excuse for its decision to ignore these rules, as Vonage is represented by sophisticated counsel and competent local counsel who should be familiar with the court's rules governing summary judgment practice. . . . Accordingly, the court will grant Sprint's motion to the extent that it will largely disregard the arguments set forth in Sections II, III, and IV of Vonage's brief.[48]

With the court predisposed to Sprint's arguments – not to mention the court's decision to "largely disregard" most of Vonage's arguments for procedural reasons – it decided in favor of Sprint on summary judgment for all but its weakest arguments.

First, the court incorporated Sprint's hyperbole regarding the importance of the patents-in-suit, stating that the invention in the patents "was significant in that it had the potential to render obsolete major components with the PSTN [public switched telephone network], breaking the grip that a handful of switch manufacturers held on service providers like Sprint."[49] In reality, the invention appeared to be well known in the art (see the later discussion), and the court failed to note that Sprint never even practiced the putatively "significant" patents-in-suit.[50]

Second, on claim construction issues, the court pointed out repeatedly that Vonage improperly read limitations from the specification into the claim language.[51] Nonetheless, Vonage was successful in its effort to limit the scope of the term "interworking device," which the court interpreted as limited to "an ATM internetworking multiplexer." In particular, citing the Federal Circuit's decision in *Honeywell International* v. *ITT Industries*,[52] the court narrowed the plain meaning of the term, because it found that the common specification of the patents-in-suit described "the invention" as providing "virtual connections 'through an *ATM* internetworking multiplexer.'"[53]

Vonage's win on the term "interworking device" set the stage for it to knock out three of seven asserted patents on non-infringement, because its network operates across IP – not ATM – networks. Clearly, with such an interpretation, there could be no literal infringement of these three patents, and the court was quick to recognize as much.[54] Yet, the court found that material disputes of fact remained on the doctrine of equivalents. As an initial matter, Vonage missed an opportunity to eliminate the doctrine of equivalents as a theory of infringement. In particular, under the Supreme

[48] *Id.* at 1304–05.
[49] *Id.* at 1301.
[50] *See id.*
[51] *See id.* at 1311–12. After the summary judgment order issued, in a pretrial order, the court construed a number of additional terms and addressed several other arguments. Memorandum and Order, Sprint Communications Co. LP v. Vonage Holdings Corp. (D. Kan. Sept. 19, 2007) (No. 05-2433-JWL). I briefly address this order herein in the description of the trial phase. *See infra* Part II.B.1.d.
[52] 452 F.3d 1312 (Fed. Cir. 2006)
[53] *See Sprint*, 500 F. Supp.2d at 1310–1311 (emphasis added).
[54] *See id.* at 1316–1318.

Court's decision in *Festo*, amendments made during patent prosecution typically preclude reliance on the doctrine of equivalents. However, because Vonage raised this argument only in its summary judgment reply brief, the court found that it was waived and disregarded it.[55]

With the doctrine of equivalents in play, the court found that "Sprint had raised a genuine issue of material fact" of whether Vonage's technology satisfied the standard "function-way-result" test typically used to determine whether an accused product is "equivalent" to the asserted patent claims.[56] Although one could debate whether the court should have held that a reasonable juror could find that the "way" Vonage's gateways worked was substantially the same as that in Sprint's claims, the court noticeably failed to consider whether Sprint effectively disclosed, but failed to claim, "IP interworking devices" in the specifications of the patents-in-suit. This was potentially a critical oversight, because it is black-letter law that "when a patent drafter discloses but declines to claim subject matter . . . this action dedicates that unclaimed subject matter to the public."[57] Although the applicable patents-in-suit did not expressly disclose IP interworking devices, they did disclose the use of the internet "IP" protocol several times.[58] Moreover, although the advent of full-blown IP gateways was a few years away, IP "interworking devices" were well known in the prior art at the time of the priority date of the patents-in-suit. For example, I located a patent assigned to Motorola filed in 1993 that discloses a telephone that includes an "interworking function" that connects it between a traditional PSTN telephone network and a data network.[59] The Motorola patent further discloses connecting the telephone to a TCP/IP network.[60] Although these facts are not decisive, Vonage could have likely made a strong argument that one of skill in the art would have read Sprint's patents-at-issue to have disclosed, but not claimed, IP interworking devices.[61] Because the claim term was construed as covering only "ATM interworking devices," it seems very likely that Vonage did not present such an argument or

55 Assuming Sprint had amended the claims in the patents-in-suit in response to prior art, because IP interworking devices were clearly foreseeable at the time of the amendment, it seems very likely that *Festo* would have precluded the doctrine of equivalents. *See* Festo Corp. v. Shoketsu Kinzoku Kogyo Kabushiki Co., Ltd., 535 U.S. 722, 738 (2002).

56 *See Sprint*, 500 F. Supp.2d at 1316–18 (citing Aquatex Indus., Inc. v. Techniche Solutions, 419 F.3d 1374, 1382 (Fed. Cir. 2005)).

57 Johnson & Johnston Associates Inc. v. R.E. Service Co., Inc., 285 F.3d 1046, 1054 (Fed. Cir. 2002) (en banc).

58 *See* U.S. Pat. No. 6,665,294 (filed Aug. 5, 2002) ("the '294 patent"), at 4:20–23, 6:20–25, 10:16–21, 11:19–28, 15:27–31.

59 *See* U.S. Pat. No. 5,426,643 (filed Nov. 1, 1993), at 3:12–19.

60 *See id.* at 1:25–44.

61 *See* PSC Computer Products, Inc. v. Foxconn Intern., Inc., 355 F.3d 1353, 1360 (Fed. Cir. 2004) ("We thus hold that if one of ordinary skill in the art can understand the unclaimed disclosed teaching upon reading the written description, the alternative matter disclosed has been dedicated to the public.").

evidence on summary judgment,[62] but that had it done so,[63] it might have prevented Sprint from relying on the doctrine of equivalents.[64]

As mentioned earlier, it appears Vonage failed to raise a written description defense on summary judgment. Yet, Vonage likely had a strong defense of lack of written description, because the sole inventor of the patents-in-suit had apparently admitted that he viewed his invention as only applying to ATM, not IP, networks. Although this defense is ultimately a question of fact,[65] presumably, the underlying facts were not genuinely disputed. As such, it seems Vonage made a tactical mistake not arguing for summary judgment of invalidity of all asserted patents on this ground. At the very least, evidence of the lack of written description would likely have more favorably colored the judge's findings on non-infringement, particularly the doctrine of equivalents. Of course, the publicly available pleadings indicate that Vonage's counsel did not even recognize written description as a defense separate from non-enablement and indefiniteness, and this potential oversight may explain Vonage's failure to lodge it at summary judgment, not to mention sufficiently developing the facts to do so.

Vonage also failed to raise any anticipation or obviousness defenses at summary judgment. Despite the seemingly wide array of available prior art, Vonage was unable to find anything suitable to support a summary judgment motion. This omission is particularly notable, because just a few months earlier, the Supreme Court had issued its landmark opinion in *KSR* v. *Teleflex*,[66] providing a firm basis for judges to invalidate patents at the summary judgment stage on grounds of obviousness. If Vonage had further developed what appeared to be a relatively meager collection of prior art, it arguably would have been able to file a strong motion for invalidity due to obviousness. Presumably, part of its failure to do so stemmed from its experts' lack of familiarity with the technology of the patents-in-suit.

Vonage's ostensible fumbling at summary judgment is evidenced further by Sprint's success in excluding a number of Vonage's proffered defenses. In particular, the court granted Sprint's motion on Vonage's asserted defense of claim

[62] Vonage filed its motion for summary judgment and supporting brief under seal. *See* Defendants Vonage Holdings Corp. and Vonage America, Inc.'s Motion for Summary Judgment, Sprint Communications Co. LP v. Vonage Holdings Corp. (D. Kan. May 15, 2007) (No. 05–2433-JWL). However, given the apparent strength of the "unclaimed matter" argument – and the notable absence of any discussion of the issue in the court's summary judgment order – it is very likely that Vonage did not present it to the court.

[63] Vonage's apparent inability to assert strong arguments on the doctrine of equivalents was also apparent in the court's opinion for another patent-in-suit, in which it stated, "[Vonage's] argument is so cursory and undeveloped that the court cannot even begin to find that Vonage is entitled to judgment as a matter of law based on this theory." *Sprint*, 500 F. Supp.2d at 1324.

[64] Sprint also waived other potentially decisive non-infringement defenses. *See, e.g., Sprint*, 500 F. Supp.2d at 1326 ("Once again, the court will not consider this argument because it was not raised for the first time until Vonage's reply.").

[65] *See* Falko-Gunter Falkner v. Inglis, 448 F.3d 1357, 1363 (Fed. Cir. 2006).

[66] KSR International Co. v. Teleflex Inc., 550 U.S. 398, 401-02, 419-20 (2006).

indefiniteness. Indefiniteness is difficult to show, because it requires that the claims be "insolubly ambiguous,"[67] and for this very reason, it is not usually successful as a defense.[68] Not only was the claim language well outside this narrow standard, but the district court also found that Vonage's expert "report provided no opinion or analysis on this defense."[69] Next, the court easily rejected Vonage's laches, estoppel, acquiescence, misuse, unclean hands, and patentable subject matter defenses, mainly because Vonage introduced no facts that could support them, but also because the court prevented it from relying on the Sprint-Cisco licensing agreement. In this regard, the court pointed out Vonage's confusion between a laches defense, which relates to when suit is filed, and a prosecution laches defense, which relates to the amount of time a patentee spends prosecuting its patent.[70]

Additionally, the court chastised Vonage once again for its failure to meet imposed deadlines:

> The court might be willing to put the parties to this inconvenience if Vonage had offered a legitimate justification for its belated reliance on the prosecution histories as the basis for its laches defense. Significantly, however, Vonage has not done so. In this respect, it is important to note that Vonage's approach to this issue is not unique. Rather, it is entirely typical of the manner in which Vonage has approached the entire pretrial phase of this case. Vonage has repeatedly raised arguments in a belated fashion and has engaged in tactics which the court believes are designed to delay the trial of this case. Its overall approach leads the court to believe that either (1) Vonage has not adequately prepared this case for trial, or (2) Vonage is attempting to benefit from "hide-the-ball" tactics. The court discounts the likelihood that Vonage is unprepared, as Vonage is represented by counsel who are undoubtedly well versed in patent litigation as well as the disclosure and supplementation requirements of the Federal Rules of Civil Procedure. Thus, the court can only conclude that Vonage's belated assertion of this patent prosecution defense theory must have been a strategic litigation decision.[71]

As some consolation, the court did leave intact Vonage's marking defense, because although Sprint did not practice the patents, its licensee Cisco possibly did.[72] Of course, because Vonage could not introduce evidence of the Sprint-Cisco licensing agreement, its win here was essentially moot. And although Vonage's non-infringement expert was perhaps a poor hire – and apparently did not even meet the requirements of one of skill in the art that he set out in *his own* expert

[67] Amgen v. Hoechst Marion Roussel, 314 F.3d 1313, 1342 (Fed. Cir. 2003).
[68] University of Houston Law Center, Decisions for 2005–2009, http://www.patstats.org/2005–2009_composite.htm (last visited Feb. 12, 2014) (showing that at the district court level, accused infringers raised the defense in only 78 decided cases over a five-year period and prevailed only 38% of the time).
[69] *Sprint*, 500 F. Supp.2d at 1331.
[70] *See id.* at 1329–30.
[71] *Id.* at 1338–39.
[72] *See id.* at 1334.

report[73] – the court, perhaps taking pity on Vonage at this point in the opinion, decided nonetheless that he passed *Daubert* muster.[74]

In sum, Vonage failed to raise or waived not just one, but several seemingly strong defenses at summary judgment. Its behavior was so notable that the court rebuked Vonage for its "cursory citations," selective omissions, "decision to ignore the[] rules," "belated" arguments, and "hide-the-ball tactics." Sprint, in contrast, won on the most of the issues it raised, eliminating a large number of potential defenses from the case. With such a one-sided result, the parties headed into trial with the odds strongly favoring Sprint.

D. VONAGE'S TRIAL LOSS AND ULTIMATE SETTLEMENT. At trial, Vonage was in a precarious situation. In addition to losing key arguments at summary judgment, Vonage lost potentially decisive issues in an important pretrial order construing further claim terms and rejecting its prosecution history estoppel arguments.[75] Ultimately, the jury found infringement of all fourteen claims at issue in six different patents and held none of the claims were invalid.[76] It awarded \$69.5 million in damages for past infringement at a 5% reasonable royalty rate, which applied to future sales.[77] Sprint then moved to modify the judgment to include an injunction against future infringement. Before the court ruled, the parties settled for an estimated \$80 million.[78] Presumably, part of the settlement was driven by a set of patents that Vonage purchased from Digital Packet Licensing, which had a pending infringement suit against Sprint, as well as AT&T and Nortel Networks.[79] Before

73 *See* Sprint's Brief in Support of its Motion to Exclude the Opinions of Vonage's Expert Joel M. Halpern, Sprint Communications Co. LP v. Vonage Holdings Corp., 2007 WL 2821679 (May 15, 2007). Specifically, Halpern stated in one of his expert reports,

> A person of ordinary skill in the art at the time of the effective filing dates of the Sprint Patents would have had a bachelors degree in electrical engineering, computer engineering or computer science, and at least three years experience in the telecommunications industry. The person would also have some familiarity with narrowband and broadband networks, telecommunications signaling requirements and the Public Switched Telephone Network ("PSTN").

Halpern did not appear to have familiarity with signaling requirements for the PSTN. *See id.*

74 *Sprint*, 500 F. Supp. 2d at 1342–45 (citing Daubert v. Merrell Dow Pharmaceuticals, Inc., 509 U.S. 579, 589–93 (1993) (instructing district courts to perform a "gatekeeping" function by restricting expert testimony to that by witnesses qualified by "knowledge, skill, experience, training, or education").

75 Memorandum and Order, Sprint Communications Co. LP v. Vonage Holdings Corp. (D. Kan. Sept. 19, 2007) (No. 05–2433-JWL).

76 Verdict, Sprint Communications Co. LP v. Vonage Holdings Corp. (D. Kan. Sept. 25, 2007) (No. 05–2433-JWL).

77 *Id.*

78 See Nathan Eddy, Vonage, AT&T Agree on Patent Lawsuit Settlement, CHANNEL WEB, Dec. 26, 2007, http://www.crn.com/networking/205203144.

79 Vonage Acquires Three Key VoIP Patents from Digital Packet Licensing Inc., *Asterisk VoIP News, July 18, 2006, http://www.asteriskvoipnews.com/vonage/vonage_acquires_three_key_voip_patents_from_digital_packet_licensing_inc.html (last visited May 11, 2011).

settlement, there were reports that Sprint might purchase Vonage as part of settling the case, but no deal was consummated.[80]

2. Verizon v. Vonage

The Verizon suit was similar in many ways to the Sprint suit.[81] After Vonage had taken away hundreds of thousands of Verizon subscribers, Verizon sued Vonage for patent infringement in June 2006 in the so-called rocket docket of the Eastern District of Virginia.[82] The seven patents-at-issue covered gateway interfaces between packet-switched networks, such as the internet, and circuit-switched networks, like the PSTN;[83] billing and fraud detection;[84] call forwarding and voicemail;[85] and the use of wifi cordless handsets on a VoIP network.[86]

In the midst of discovery and pretrial disputes, the parties briefed claim construction issues.[87] Overall, the district court construed the disputed claim terms broadly.[88] A few days later the court denied both parties summary judgment.[89] Unfortunately, a copy of the order is neither available from the federal courts' PACER database nor Westlaw or Lexis. However, based on a review of the docket in the case, Vonage apparently filed only a summary judgment motion of non-infringement, but not invalidity.[90] In this regard, Vonage hired the same invalidity expert as in the Sprint case, Frank Koperda, who as I recounted earlier had some experience in interfacing traditional telephony platforms with digital networks, but not since the

80 Eric Savitz, Vonage up on Inexplicable Rumors Sprint May Buy It, SEEKING ALPHA, http://seekingalpha.com/article/32645-vonage-up-on-inexplicable-rumors-sprint-may-buy-it (last visited May 11, 2013).

81 However, because of the fewer available electronic documents in the *Verizon* case as well as space considerations, I recount this case in much less detail than the *Sprint* case.

82 Complaint for Injunctive and Other Relief, Verizon Services Corp. et al. v. Vonage Holdings Corp. et al., 2006 WL 1682996 (E.D. Va. June 12, 2006).

83 U.S. Pat. Nos. 6,104,711 (filed Mar. 6, 1997); 6,282,574 (filed Feb. 24, 2000); 6,128,304 (filed Oct. 23, 1998).

84 U.S. Pat. Nos. 6,430,275 (filed Jul. 28, 1999); 6,137,869 (filed Sep. 16, 1997).

85 U.S. Pat. No. 6,298,062 (filed Oct. 23, 1998).

86 U.S. Pat. No. 6,359,880 (filed Jul. 30, 1999).

87 Docket, Verizon Services Corp. et al. v. Vonage Holdings Corp. et al., Case No. 1:06-cv-00682 (E.D. Va. June 12, 2006).

88 Verizon Services Corp. v. Vonage Holdings Corp., 2007 WL 528749 (E.D. Va. 2007). For instance, the court construed "maintaining by said unitary logical object of a record of the . . . progress" as "[m]aintaining by a single logical database, which includes related call processing logic and supporting infrastructure, a record of call status (e.g., setup, in progress, termination) that can be used for billing, usage tracking, and other purposes." *Id.* at *3. Because "unitary logical object" was interpreted as a "single logical database," presumably a distributed database with multiple sub-databases connected "logically" into one database would meet the limitation. As the remainder of the limitation concerns standard functions in telecommunications systems, any VoIP system designed to support end-user subscribers would have likely met the court's interpretation of this claim element.

89 Docket, Verizon Services Corp. et al. v. Vonage Holdings Corp. et al., Case No. 1:06-cv-00682 (E.D. Va. June 12, 2006).

90 *Id.*

mid-1980s.[91] Like the Sprint case, presumably Koperda's lack of recent experience weakened Vonage's invalidity case.

After a several-week trial, the jury found that Vonage infringed three of Verizon's patents. Overall, it awarded $58 million in reasonably royalties for past infringement and a 5.5% royalty rate on future sales.[92] Subsequently, the court granted an injunction against future infringement,[93] which the Federal Circuit subsequently stayed pending appeal.[94] On appeal, the Federal Circuit upheld claim constructions on two of the three patents, affirming the findings of infringement and validity, and reversed and remanded on one of the patents.[95] With the injunction in place from the two infringed patents, Vonage decided to settle the case for between $80 and $120 million.[96]

3. AT&T v. Vonage

After Vonage had settled the suits filed by Sprint and Verizon, totaling more than $160 million,[97] less than one month later, AT&T launched a suit against it in another rocket docket, the Western District of Wisconsin.[98] Like the Sprint patents, AT&T's patent disclosed telephony across an ATM network, but contained claims not expressly limited to any type of network.[99] (Because I represented Vonage in this matter, I have chosen to refrain from a detailed analysis of infringement, invalidity, and enforceability.) Although at least some industry observers believed that Vonage had a strong defense of non-infringement and invalidity,[100] it quickly settled the case for about $40 million.[101] Presumably, Vonage had become skeptical by that point of its ability to convince judges and juries that the patents asserted against it were invalid or unenforceable or that its technology was sufficiently different from traditional packet networks, such as ATM networks, so as not to infringe. Assuming as much, Vonage's decision to settle was certainly understandable.

[91] Frank R. Koperda-Resume, NextGen Datacom, http://www.nextgendc.com/resume_skill.htm. (last visited Feb. 11, 2014).

[92] Verdict Form, Verizon Services Corp. v. Vonage Holdings Corp., 2007 WL 1751100 (E.D. Va. 2007).

[93] Docket, Verizon Services Corp. et al. v. Vonage Holdings Corp. et al., Case No. 1:06-cv-00682 (E.D. Va. June 12, 2006).

[94] Verizon Services Corp. v. Vonage Holdings Corp., 228 Fed. Appx. 986 (Fed. Cir. 2007).

[95] Verizon Services Corp. v. Vonage Holdings Corp., 503 F.3d 1295 (Fed. Cir. 2007).

[96] Anne Broache, *Vonage, Verizon Settle Patent Spat for up to $120 Million*, CNET NEWS, Oct. 25, 2007, http://news.cnet.com/8301–10784-3–9804709–7.html. If Vonage were such a competitive threat to Verizon, one might wonder why Verizon did not leave its injunction in place, thereby shutting down Vonage entirely. In this regard, Vonage had stated that it could implement a non-infringing design-around to avoid infringing Verizon's patents. *See id.* Presumably, Verizon decided that a settlement was preferable to the risk that Vonage could switch to a non-infringing alternative.

[97] *See* Eddy, *supra* note 78.

[98] AT&T Corp. v. Vonage Holdings Corp.,Case No. 07-CV-858 (W.D. Wis. Oct. 19, 2007).

[99] *See* U.S. Pat. No. 6,487,200 (issued Nov. 6, 2002).

[100] *See* Masnick, *supra* note 31.

[101] *See* Eddy, *supra* note 97.

C. *The Aftermath of the Trilogy and Subsequent Cases*

Following the settlements of roughly $200 million,[102] which was about one-quarter of Vonage's annual revenue at the time,[103] Vonage's marketing expenditures decreased and its subscriber growth slowed substantially.[104] Indeed, Vonage was almost delisted from the New York Stock Exchange,[105] and some observers predicted bankruptcy.[106] From the time of Vonage's IPO (about seven months after the Sprint suit was filed) through the AT&T settlement, its stock price declined from $17 per share to about $2 per share.[107] Although other factors certainly accounted for the decline, the trilogy of lawsuits arguably played a major role, particularly given the substantial declines in Vonage's stock price following unfavorable rulings in the case.

The highly damaging effects imposed on Vonage by the patent bully carriers stand in contrast to the relative minor effects of a series of suits filed against Vonage before and afterward by a variety of nonpracticing entities (NPEs). Overall, Vonage was involved in three different NPE suits around the time of the trilogy, which all settled.[108] However, unlike the suits filed by the incumbent carriers, none of the NPEs extracted a large toll from Vonage.[109] So, at least for Vonage, the "bullies" inflicted much more damage than the "trolls."

[102] *See id.*

[103] *See* Yahoo! Finance, Income Statement for Vonage Holdings Corporation, http://finance.yahoo.com/q/is?s=VG&annual (last visited Feb. 1, 2014) (Dec. 31, 2007 data).

[104] David Shabelman, *Some Hope for Vonage*, THEDEAL.COM, Nov. 9, 2007, *available at* Lexis-Nexis, News-All file; *see also* Seth Wallis-Jones, *Growth Slows Bbut Vonage Trims Losses on Path to Profits*, GLOBAL INSIGHT, Feb. 14, 2008.

[105] *See* João-Pierre S. Ruth, *Vonage Faces Hangup from Stock Exchange*, NJBIZ, Feb. 16, 2009, *available at* 2009 WLNR 3234320.

[106] *See* Shabelman, *supra* note 104.

[107] *See* Yahoo! Finance Vonage Holdings Corporation, http://finance.yahoo.com/echarts?s=VG+Interactive#chart3:symbol=vg;range=my;charttype=line;crosshair=on;ohlcvalues=0;logscale=off;source=undefined (last visited May 12, 2013).

[108] Rates Technology Inc. v. Vonage America, Inc. et al., Case No. 2:05-cv-04727-DRH-ARL (E.D.N.Y.) (filed October 6, 2005); Klausner Technologies, Inc. v. Vonage Holdings Corp. et al., Case No. 2:06-cv-00275-LED-JDL (E.D. Tex.) (filed July 11, 2006); Web Telephony, LLC. v. Bell Atlantic Communications, Inc.(dba Verizon Long Distance) et al., Case No. 2:07-cv-00085-DF-CE (filed Mar. 14, 2007).

[109] *See* Vonage Holding Co., 10-Q/A, Q3–2007, *available at* http://yahoo.brand.edgar-online.com/EFX_dll/EDGARpro.dll?FetchFilingHtmlSection1?SectionID=5804337–35029–110848&SessionID=mN3HHSCKotpm047 (noting that neither the Rates Technology nor the Klausner Technologies settlements were "material" transactions); Vonage Holding Co., 10-K, May 27, 2010 ("As part of the settlement, we agreed to pay eight quarterly payments totaling $800,000 over the next two years between April 2009 and December 2010. Under the transaction, we expensed $339,000 of the patent settlement costs during the year ended March 31, 2009 that were related to benefits received by us in and during the periods prior to fiscal year 2009. We recorded the remaining license fee of $432,000 as other long term assets as of March 31, 2009 and we are amortizing this amount to cost of service revenues in the Consolidated Statements of Operations over the remaining life of the primary patent, which expires in September 2017.").

Furthermore, Vonage did not fare so well in the infringement suits it purchased to fend off Sprint. In those suits, Digital Packet Licensing, LLC – the original plaintiff – had sued Sprint, AT&T, Nortel, MCI, and others.[110] After Vonage acquired the patents, Nortel shrewdly asserted a number of patents of its own against Vonage.[111] Ultimately, the cases settled with Vonage and Nortel licensing their patents to each other for no fee,[112] and Vonage appeared to collect little to nothing from the other defendants.[113] Of course, Vonage likely spent millions in litigation fees on the cases.

III. CONCLUSION: REFLECTIONS ON THE TRILOGY AND THE NEED FOR FURTHER STUDY

As I have recounted, Vonage – a startup company providing a highly competitive, low-cost telephone service that drew millions of subscribers away from the incumbent carriers – did not fare well in the U.S. patent system. Most importantly, Vonage paid out roughly $200 million in settlement amounts, plus millions in attorneys' fees, placing it at the brink of insolvency. Although Vonage ultimately escaped the "death penalty," its value decreased precipitously, and the suits very likely caused permanent damage to the health of the company.

One might quip that if Vonage lost its Sprint and Verizon cases, then the payout was deserved. However, as I described earlier, much of Vonage's woes in the Sprint case appeared to stem from tactical errors. Presumably, those errors were driven in large part by Vonage's limited litigation budget and experience in patent suits, especially compared with Sprint's very large budget and extensive litigation experience. These sorts of differentials among litigants highlight a problem in the patent bullying context not present in the patent troll context – namely, that patent bullies not only can force settlements in weak cases but also can win at judgment in weak cases. The ability of patent bullies to achieve such results, of course, compounds the distortions already present in patent litigation and licensing. Indeed, the so-called trolls – which were much smaller than Sprint and Verizon – did not achieve as favorable results against Vonage. Nor do trolls use litigation to acquire competitors at bargain basement prices – which Sprint had apparently considered. Furthermore, when Vonage attempted to cash out on its patents against Nortel Networks, it was smacked right back and ultimately settled for nothing.

110 Vonage Holdings Corporation v. MCI, Inc. et al., Case No. 2:05-cv-00451-LED (E.D.Tex.) (filed Sept. 20, 2005).

111 Nortel's Answer and Counterclaims, Vonage Holdings Corp. v. Nortel Networks Inc. et al., Case No. 1:07-cv-00507-GMS (D. Del.) (filed Aug. 17, 2007).

112 *See Vonage and Nortel Settle Patent Dispute*, Reuters, Dec. 31, 2007, http://www.reuters.com/article/2007/12/31/us-vonage-patentdispute-idUSWNAS541520071231.

113 I could find no reports of the settlement amounts with these defendants, but presumably if the amounts had been large, they would have been reported in Vonage's public filings.

Generalizing from the Vonage trilogy, a few important problems for the patent system as a whole emerge. First, like the trolls, patent bullies can take advantage of high litigation costs and the complexity of patent litigation to gain leverage in suit against smaller defendants. Importantly, this leverage can stem from bullies' increased odds of winning otherwise "weak" suits. And, unlike in the troll context, patent bullies will ordinarily be entitled to injunctions. Coupled with the high risk aversion of many small defendants, these advantages can place extreme pressure on defendants to settle or else result in inaccurate judgments, leading to substantial economically distorting effects. Second, unlike in the troll context, settlements and judgments with bullies do not only result in money changing hands. Rather, bullies often desire to acquire a smaller competitor's technology, either through a coerced license or a forced purchase of the competitor's entire company. Arguably, these results can wreak even more damage on the competitive environment than suits by trolls.

Of course, Vonage's story is just one, and it may not be illustrative of suits by large practicing entities against smaller competitors. One fact is certain, however – the prevalence of large company–small company suits is not low. In a study by Gwendolyn Ball and Jay Kesan of nearly all U.S. patent infringement actions filed in 2000 and 2002, roughly 25% of the cases were filed by a plaintiff that was substantially larger than the defendant.[114] Nonetheless, in order to assess whether these suits present a serious public policy problem, a comprehensive determination and analysis of the outcomes and effects of such suits are needed. As such, only further work can decidedly answer whether these suits truly present a systemic "patent bully" problem. In the meantime – much like the "patent troll" problem – we are left mainly with anecdote to fashion policy.

[114] *See* Ball & Kesan, *supra* note 17.

11

University Software Ownership and Litigation

A First Examination

*Arti K. Rai, John R. Allison, and Bhaven N. Sampat**

INTRODUCTION

Software patents and university-owned patents represent two of the most controversial intellectual property developments of the past few decades. Various scholars have quarreled with the alleged vagueness and undue breadth of software patent claims.[1] Some have also suggested that, given the poor quality of prior-art documentation and patent examiner training in the area of software, many issued software patents

* Arti K. Rai is the Elvin R. Latty Professor at Duke University School of Law; John R. Allison is the Spence Centennial Professor of Business Administration at the McCombs School of Business, University of Texas, Austin; and Bhaven N. Sampat is Assistant Professor at Mailman School of Public Health, Columbia University. The authors gratefully acknowledge the support of the National Human Genome Research Institute, the U.S. Department of Energy, and the Ewing Marion Kauffman Foundation. Earlier versions of this chapter were presented at the University of Arizona Law School, University of North Carolina School of Law, the University of California, Berkeley (Boalt) School of Law, Columbia University School of Law, and the Washington University in St. Louis School of Law. We thank the participants in those symposia for their comments. We also thank Gerald Barnett, Jim Bessen, Richard Brandon, Robert Cook-Deegan, Rick Friedman, Bob Hunt, David Kappos, Ronald Mann, Robin Rasor, Mark Schankerman, and Manny Schecter for their comments. Thanks are also due to Matt Block, Nina Knierim, Erik Smith, and Cameron Westin for excellent research assistance. Finally, Colin Crossman provided invaluable help with the interviews. A different version of this chapter was previously published in the *North Carolina Law Review*. See Arti K. Rai et al., *University Software Ownership and Litigation: A First Examination*, 87 N.C. L. Rev. 1519 (2008–09).

1 *See, e.g.*, James Bessen & Michael Meurer, Patent Failure: How Judges, Bureaucrats, and Lawyers Put Innovation at Risk 187–214 (2008); Dan Burk & Mark Lemley, *Policy Levers in Patent Law*, 89 Va. L. Rev. 1575, 1623 (2003) (arguing that the Court of Appeals for the Federal Circuit, which hears all appeals in patent cases, has an exaggerated sense of the skill of the ordinary computer scientist and is therefore likely to allow broad patents); Arti K. Rai, *Engaging Facts and Policy, A Multi-Institutional Approach to Patent System Reform*, 103 Colum. L. Rev. 1035, 1053–54 (2003) (arguing that because pure software patents are not limited to a particular physical machine or process, they may be problematic in terms of breadth). *But see* Robert P. Merges, *Software and Patent Scope: A Report from the Middle Innings*, 85 Tex. L. Rev. 1627, 1649–52 (2007) (arguing that some recent Federal Circuit cases have interpreted disclosure requirements for software patents more rigorously).

are likely to be obvious.[2] More generally, there is significant debate over the extent to which software patents are likely to foster (or hinder) innovation.[3] Because software products are often "complex" and may infringe many patents, some incumbent providers of information technology (IT) products support limiting patentability.[4]

In contrast with software patents, university-owned patents have existed for more than a few decades. The number of university-held patents has increased substantially, however, since the 1980 passage of the Bayh-Dole Act.[5] Although the legal question was sometimes murky before 1980, Bayh-Dole made it unequivocally clear that universities can patent federally funded research.[6]

[2] *See generally* Glynn Lunney, *E-Obviousness*, 7 MICH. TELECOMM. & TECH. L. REV. 363 (2001) (making this argument and further arguing that the Federal Circuit tends to affirm lower court determinations that a patent is nonobvious while reversing determinations that a patent is obvious and thus does not meet a prerequisite of patentability).

[3] *Compare* James Bessen & Robert Hunt, *An Empirical Look at Software Patents*, 16 J. ECON. & MGMT. STRATEGY 157, 173–74, 180–85 (2007) (arguing that software patents are substitutes for research and development), *with* Ronald Mann, *Do Patents Facilitate Financing in the Software Industry*, 83 TEX. L. REV. 961, 999–1003 (2005) (arguing that software patents may help certain types of small software firms attract financing). Similarly, a study by Noel and Schankerman that is in tension with the findings of Bessen and Hunt examines software firms only. *See* Michael Noel & Mark Schankerman, *Strategic Patenting and Software Innovation* 12 (London Sch. of Econ. & Pol. Sci., Ctr. for Econ. Policy Research, Paper No. EI43, June 2006), *available at* http://papers.ssrn.com/sol3/papers.cfm?abstract_id=1158320. These papers can be reconciled to the extent that Mann's argument in favor of patents is largely limited to small software firms, wherea Bessen and Hunt focus on software patents held by large firms both within and outside the software industry. For discussion of another empirical study on software patents, see *infra* note 144 and accompanying text.

[4] These firms have supported legislative and judicial efforts to make patents easier to challenge and injunctive relief, particularly by nonmanufacturing entities, more difficult to secure. *See generally* eBay Inc. v. MercExchange, L.L.C., 547 U.S. 388 (2006) (clarifying that injunctive relief is not necessarily automatic on a finding of infringement); Patent Reform Act of 2007, S. 1145, 110th Cong. § 321 (2007) (proposing a robust system of post-grant opposition proceedings). In contrast, although products in the biopharmaceutical industry may require many patented inputs for their creation, the products *themselves* are likely to be covered by only a few patents. Thus, one common strategy for avoiding patent thickets is secret infringement. *See* John Walsh et al., *Working Through the Patent Problem*, 299 SCIENCE 1021, 1021 (2003).

[5] Bayh-Dole Act of 1980, Pub. L. No. 96–517, 94 Stat. 3017 (codified at 35 U.S.C. §§ 200–210 (2006)). *See* NAT'L SCI. BD., NAT'L SCI. FOUND., SCIENCE & ENGINEERING INDICATORS 2006, at 50–51 (2006), *available at* http://www.nsf.gov/statistics/seind06/pdf/ volume1.pdf (noting that numbers of patents issued to academic institutions quadrupled from approximately 800 in 1988 to more than 3200 in 2003).

[6] Although not all university research is federally funded, the federal share represented 64% of university research and development in fiscal year 2004. *See* RONDA BRITT, NAT'L SCI. FOUND., ACADEMIC RESEARCH AND DEVELOPMENT EXPENDITURES: FISCAL YEAR 2004, at 8 (2006), *available at* http://www.nsf.gov/statistics/nsf06323/pdf/tab1.pdf. In electrical engineering and computer science (EE/CS), the federal percentage of university R&D in fiscal year 2004 was even higher: 73% and 68%, respectively. *Id.* In contrast, industry accounts for only about 5% of university R&D (including EE/CS R&D). *Id.* These percentages have been fairly consistent over the last 20 years. *Id.* For example, from 1996 to 1998, the years probably most relevant to patents issued in 2002, the federal funding percentage for EE/CS was 70%, 68%, and 67% in each respective year. *Id.* The overall federal funding percentage during those years was about 60%. *Id.*

Assertive university patenting has attracted attention in both scholarly and popular literature.[7] Additionally, because universities and sometimes even their exclusive licensees are nonmanufacturing patentees, the intense debate over whether such patentees employ "holdup" strategies deleterious to innovation when they assert patents against successful commercializers directly implicates universities.[8] That said, almost all analyses of university patenting have focused on patenting within the life sciences.[9] This focus is perhaps not surprising, because the major economic argument put forward in the legislative history of the Bayh-Dole Act – that patents on publicly funded invention promote commercialization of such invention[10] – would appear to apply most clearly to areas of the life sciences, such as drug development. Conventional wisdom suggests that, without the quasi-monopoly protection of a patent on the small molecule chemical, few firms would be interested in taking a potentially promising drug candidate through the expensive clinical trial and approval process.[11]

We report these statistics to buttress our supposition that most software-related research done by universities is federally (or at least publicly) funded and thus subject to the types of economic analysis usually employed in thinking about publicly funded research. Unfortunately, although Bayh-Dole requires universities to report federal funding when they file for patents, many do not. *See* University of California, The Bayh-Dole Act: A Guide to the Law and Implementing Regulations, http://www .ucop.edu/ ott/faculty/bayh.html (last visited Apr. 21, 2009). Thus, we cannot rely on such reports to determine the funding source of research that led to specific software patents.

7 In a popular account, Jennifer Washburn suggests that universities are being corrupted by their interest in commercial activities, including patenting. *See generally* JENNIFER WASHBURN, UNIVERSITY, INC.: THE CORPORATE CORRUPTION OF AMERICAN HIGHER EDUCATION (2005) (discussing universities and their interest in commercial activities). For a comprehensive analysis of available data on the impact of Bayh-Dole, see generally DAVID C. MOWERY ET AL., IVORY TOWER AND INDUSTRIAL INNOVATION (2004).

8 *See generally* Mark Lemley, *Are Universities Patent Trolls?*, 18 FORDHAM INTELL. PROP. MEDIA & ENT. L.J. 611 (2008) (providing a nonempirical analysis of whether universities should be considered patent "trolls"). The most celebrated recent example of a lucrative holdup strategy was that pursued by a patent holding company, NTP, against Research in Motion (RIM), the maker of the BlackBerry. In that case, RIM settled for $612.5 million in order to avoid the imminent threat of court-ordered injunctive relief, even though the PTO had called into question the validity of several of the asserted patents. *See* Yuki Noguchi, *BlackBerry Patent Dispute Is Settled*, Wash. Post, Mar. 4, 2006, at A1. For discussion of holdup litigation by universities, see *infra* Part IV.B.

9 *See, e.g.*, Pierre Azoulay, Ryan Michigan & Bhaven N. Sampat, *The Anatomy of Medical School Patenting*, 357 NEW. ENG. J. MED. 2049, 2049–56 (2007); Pierre Azoulay, Waverly Ding & Toby E. Stuart, *The Determinants of Faculty Patenting Behavior: Demographics or Opportunities?*, 63 J. ECON. BEHAV. & ORG. 599, 599 (2007); Fiona Murray & Scott Stern, *Do Formal Intellectual Property Rights Hinder the Free Flow of Scientific Knowledge: An Empirical Test of the Anti-Commons Hypothesis*, 63 J. ECON. BEHAV. & ORG. 648, 648 (2007).

10 Although the text of Bayh-Dole does not suggest a particular licensing model, the legislative history of the bill that eventually became the Bayh-Dole Act, as well as that of similar bills that were being discussed at the time, indicates a focus on exclusive licenses. House Report 96–1307 notes the importance of exclusive licensing for attracting capital necessary for development. H.R. Rep. No. 96–1307, pt. 1, at 3, 5 (1980). Senate Report 96–480 asserts that, because nonexclusive licenses were generally viewed dismissively in the business community "as no patent protection at all," nonexclusive licensing by the government had not been successful in producing development. S. Rep. No. 96–480, at 28 (1979).

11 The empirical evidence also indicates that patents are more important for recouping R&D investment in the pharmaceutical industry than in other manufacturing industries. *See* Wesley Cohen,

In the case of publicly funded software, by contrast, the need for a patent and exclusive license to promote further development is less apparent.[12] Although development costs are not uniformly low, they are likely to be low relative to those in the biopharmaceutical industry.[13] Indeed, in certain cases of open source software development, firms derive revenue not from property rights over the software product itself, but from a strategy that monetizes the value of support services and complementary hardware.[14] Thus, if universities are in fact making strong proprietary claims on software, scholars should be concerned. The social welfare argument for such claims is more tenuous than in the life sciences.

Despite IT sector complaints about university behavior,[15] as well as prominent lawsuits involving software patents,[16] the subject of university software ownership and litigation has not been studied systematically. Indeed, this chapter represents the first systematic study of which we are aware.[17] We rely in part on a unique, hand-curated database of university software patents.[18] This quantitative analysis is supplemented by interviews conducted with technology transfer officers at those universities that

Richard R. Nelson & John P. Walsh, *Protecting Their Intellectual Assets: Appropriability Conditions and Why U.S. Manufacturing Firms Patent (or Not)* 2 (Nat'l Bureau of Econ. Research, Working Paper No. 7552, Feb. 2000), *available at* http://www.nber.org/papers/w7552.pdf (discussing the recouping of R&D costs in the context of the pharmaceutical industry and other manufacturing industries).

[12] Even in the life sciences, the availability of patents on improvements, as well as the presence of absorptive capacity in commercial firms, may diminish the need for exclusive licensing on certain inventions, such as research tools. MOWERY ET AL., *supra* note 9, at 158 (discussing the manner in which Columbia's DNA co-transformation technology was developed commercially without the need for exclusive licensing).

[13] *See* Joseph A. DiMasi et al., *The Price of Innovation: New Estimates of Drug Development Costs*, 22 J. HEALTH ECON. 151, 166 (2003) (giving an estimate of $802 million for new chemical molecules developed entirely in the private sector). This estimate, which includes an opportunity cost of capital of about $400 million, would presumably be somewhat lower where some of the relevant work had already been done in a federally funded institution. *See id.*

[14] *See generally* Andrea Bonaccorsi & Cristina Rossi, *Why Open Source Software Can Succeed*, 32 RES. POL'Y 1243 (2003) (discussing examples ranging from software publishers such as Red Hat to hardware manufacturers such as IBM).

[15] *See, e.g., Hearing on "Bayh-Dole – The Next 25 Years" Before the H. Comm. on Science and Technology*, 110th Cong. 46–56 (2007) (statement of Wayne Johnson, Vice-President, University Relations Worldwide, Hewlett-Packard); Steve Lohr, *IBM and Universities Plan Collaboration*, N.Y. Times, Dec. 14, 2006, at C11 (noting a statement by an IBM vice president that "[u]niversities have made life increasingly difficult to do research . . . because of all the contractual issues around intellectual property").

[16] *See, e.g.*, Eolas Techs. Inc. v. Microsoft Corp., 399 F.3d 1325 (Fed. Cir. 2005).

[17] Ajay Agrawal and Rebecca Henderson touch on a related subject in their examination of the patenting practices of the MIT EE/CS faculty. Ajay Agrawal & Rebecca Henderson, *Putting Patents in Context: Exploring Knowledge Transfer from MIT*, 48 MGMT. SCI. 44, 44 (2002). Based on their research, they conclude that patenting is a "minority activity" for most faculty members in the EE/CS department (and the mechanical engineering department). *Id.*

[18] Our quantitative analysis focuses on patents primarily because there is no comprehensive data on the extent to which copyright is asserted by universities. Copyright attaches as soon as the software is created. Because there is no need to register copyrights, it is difficult to know the total volume of university software protected by copyright.

own large numbers of software patents, as well as academic scientists and other officials prominent in the open source movement.

The combination of our quantitative and qualitative inquiry yields a number of important results. First, software patents represent a significant and growing percentage of university patent holdings.[19] Second, university software patenting practices tend to mimic their nonsoftware patenting practices. The data suggest that those universities that have a higher patent propensity in general are also more likely to obtain software patents.[20] Similarly, our interviews show that some universities view software as similar to other, more physical inventions.[21] The difficulty with this view is that software is likely to follow a different commercialization path than other inventions. Thus, it is perhaps not surprising that we see a fair number of litigated cases involving software patents and that almost all of these appear to represent situations where the university or its exclusive licensee is asserting the patent against an entity that has successfully commercialized software independent of the patent.[22] Notably, in the majority of these cases, the university's argument has lost on grounds of either patent invalidity or non-infringement.[23]

The main rationale for supporting patenting would, therefore, appear to be the promotion of startup businesses, presumably on the theory that startups, and market-based activities more generally, are likely to be more innovative than activities in large, vertically integrated incumbent firms.[24] However, whether patents are necessary for startup promotion is not as clear in the software area as it is, for example, in the biotechnology industry. Moreover, in contrast with biotechnology, where copyright is not available, universities can use software copyright to achieve revenue-generation goals.[25]

It may be that university software patenting is a transient phenomenon. As we discuss later,[26] some technology transfer officers argue that they no longer view the patenting of software as a particularly good mechanism for technology transfer.[27] In addition, the 2006 Supreme Court decision in *eBay Inc.* v. *MercExchange, L.L.C.*,[28] allowing district courts discretion to award damages even after finding validity and infringement, could make software patenting and litigation less attractive to universities in the future.

This chapter proceeds as follows. Part I discusses the history of software patenting and how it influenced our methodology for compiling a database of university

19 *See infra* Part II.A.
20 *See infra* Part II.B.
21 *See infra* Part III.
22 *See* discussion *infra* Part IV.B.
23 *Id.*
24 *Id.*
25 *See* discussion *infra* Part V.B.
26 *See infra* Part V.C.
27 *Id.*
28 547 U.S. 388 (2006).

software patents. Next, Part II presents our quantitative results; specifically, we identify trends in and determinants of university software patenting. Part III integrates these quantitative results with results from our interviews. Part IV then discusses the "holdup" features present in much university litigation over software patents. More generally, it provides a policy analysis of why universities' apparent *one-size-fits-all* approach to patenting is problematic. Finally, Part V discusses the path forward, with a focus on whether we are likely to see more of this unitary approach (and concomitant litigation) in the future.

I. SOFTWARE PATENTING: HISTORY AND METHODS OF IDENTIFYING

To identify university patents, we began by using the U.S. Patent and Trademark Office's (PTO) Cassis database to identify all patents issued in 1982, 1987, 1992, 1997, and 2002 that were assigned to institutions classified as Research or Doctoral Universities in the Carnegie Commission of Higher Education's 1972 or 1994 reports. We chose these particular years because they span a series of shifts in the legal regime surrounding software produced at universities.[29] Not only did university patenting increase significantly after the 1980 passage of the Bayh-Dole Act,[30] but patent jurisprudence in the area of software also evolved considerably. Because this evolution is closely related to the manner in which we define the term "software patent," we describe it in some detail next.

A. *The History of Software Patents*

In the 1970s, the dominant intellectual property regime for software was copyright, not patent.[31] A 1972 Supreme Court case, *Gottschalk* v. *Benson*,[32] appeared to reject software (in that case, a computerized method for converting decimal numbers to binary numbers) as patentable subject matter on the grounds that patent law did not

29 A methodology that sampled one year of filing would have tracked more precisely the impact of particular software cases on filing behavior. However, because we did not aim to measure the precise impact of specific cases, sampling by year of issue was sufficient for purposes of getting a general sense of trends. In theory, sampling by year of issuance could be an issue for our regression analyses, which require that we assess patenting against (inter alia) R&D expenditures. However, when we did sample by year of filing (for filing years 1998–2002), our regression results were roughly similar.

30 *See supra* note 7 and accompanying text.

31 *See generally* Peter S. Menell, *An Analysis of the Scope of Copyright Protection for Application Programs*, 41 STAN. L. REV. 1045 (1989) (analyzing various means of legal protection for computer technologies, including copyright and patent law, and their scope of protection). To be sure, some software patents may have been issued in disguised form in the 1970s. *See* E-mail from Richard Brandon, Assistant Gen. Counsel, Univ. of Mich. Office of Tech. Transfer, to Arti K. Rai, Professor of Law, Duke Univ. Sch. of Law (Nov. 21, 2006 17:19 EST) (on file with the *North Carolina Law Review*). This fact is not relevant for our purposes.

32 409 U.S. 63 (1972).

encompass abstract scientific or mathematical principles.[33] Further, several years later, in the 1980 amendments to the Copyright Act of 1976, Congress expressly endorsed copyright as an appropriate protection regime for software.[34]

The intellectual property terrain shifted in the 1980s. In the 1981 decision *Diamond v. Diehr*,[35] the Supreme Court gave its first clear indication that certain types of software-implemented inventions were patentable. *Diehr* narrowed *Gottschalk* by upholding as patentable subject matter a rubber-curing process that used software to calculate cure time. According to the *Diehr* Court, the physical transformation of the rubber "into a different state or thing" took the invention being claimed out of the realm of abstraction.[36]

Through the 1980s, the Court of Appeals for the Federal Circuit generally followed a test somewhat similar to that enunciated in *Diehr*. Under this test, if an invention's claims involved nothing more than an algorithm, then the invention could not be patented.[37] However, if the claims involved a mathematical algorithm that was "applied to, or limited by, physical elements or process steps," such claims would constitute patentable subject matter.[38] The overall message to patent attorneys was that software could be patented, but it had to be claimed as something else. Assuming an approximate examination pendency of two years during the relevant period,[39] patents issued in our sample years of 1987 and 1992 should reflect patenting of software as "something else."

Moreover, as the patent option was becoming more attractive, copyright was becoming much less so. In the early 1990s, a series of appellate court decisions made it clear that copyright covered primarily the literal source code of the program.[40]

Greater changes lay in store. In the 1994 case of *In re Alappat*,[41] the Federal Circuit effectively eliminated any limitation on patenting software by concluding

33 Although *Gottschalk* is generally considered a subject matter case, the Court may also have been concerned with breadth – the patent in question was not restricted to any particular implementation of the algorithm. *Gottschalk*, 409 U.S. at 65–72. In general, as noted earlier, pure software patents of the type at issue in *Gottschalk* may be broader than patents covering software restricted to a particular physical process or machine. *See* Rai, *supra* note 1, at 1104–05.

34 Act of Dec. 12, 1980, Pub. L. No. 96–517, § 10, 94 Stat. 3105, 3028 (codified as amended at 17 U.S.C. §§ 101, 117 (2006)).

35 450 U.S. 175 (1981).

36 *Id.* at 175. In fact, the *Diehr* Court argued that it had long viewed "[t]ransformation and reduction of an article 'to a different state or thing' [as] *the* clue to the patentability of a process claim that does not include particular machines." *Id.* at 184 (emphasis added) (citations omitted).

37 *See* Arrhythmia Research Tech., Inc. v. Corazonix Corp., 958 F.2d 1053, 1058 (Fed. Cir. 1992).

38 *Id.*

39 The PTO calculates that average pendency was about two years over the period from 1988 to 2000. *See* John L. King, *Patent Examination Procedures and Patent Quality*, *in* PATENTS IN THE KNOWLEDGE-BASED ECONOMY 54, 63 (Wesley M. Cohen & Stephen A. Merrill eds., 2003) (citing data from Annual Reports of the PTO).

40 *See, e.g.*, Lotus Dev. Corp. v. Borland Int'l, Inc., 49 F.3d 807, 817 (1st Cir. 1995), *aff'd*, 516 U.S. 233 (1996); Computer Ass'n Int'l v. Altai, Inc., 982 F.2d 693, 702 (2d Cir. 1992).

41 33 F.3d 1526, 1545 (Fed. Cir. 1994). The *Alappat* decision was anticipated to some extent by cases like *In re Iwahashi*, 888 F.2d 1370, 1375 (Fed. Cir. 1989) (holding that just because an apparatus is operated as an algorithm does not make it nonstatutory).

that subject matter criteria could be met by claiming software as a new machine – a "special purpose" computer – when it was executed.[42] Presumably all software could produce such a special-purpose computer and hence be patentable. Again, assuming a two-year examination pendency, patents issued in 1997 should begin to incorporate any effects that decisions such as *Alappat* had on filing incentives. Also, in 1996, the PTO issued software guidelines that broadly allowed software as patentable subject matter whether the software was claimed as a machine or a process.[43] Two years later, the Federal Circuit's decision in *State Street* v. *Signature Financial Group*[44] similarly rejected any special subject matter test for software, finding that it (like all inventions) is patentable if it produces a "useful" result.[45] After *State Street,* there was no need for even the fig leaf of a physical machine or process. Thus, patents issued in 2002 should incorporate any impact of the PTO guidelines and the *State Street* decision on filing incentives.[46]

B. *Identifying University Software Patents*

Given this history, it is perhaps not surprising that identifying "software" patents is very difficult. Even now, there is no universally accepted definition of what a software patent is. To our knowledge, there have been only a few significant efforts to identify a large dataset of software patents.[47] An initial paper by Stuart Graham and David Mowery,[48] which does not attempt to define the term "software patent," relies on certain International Patent Classifications (IPCs)[49] as limited to patents in those classes owned by large software firms.[50] A more recent paper by Graham and Mowery uses particular U.S. patent classes, once again limited to patents in

[42] *Alappat,* 33 F.3d at 1545.

[43] *See* Examination Guidelines for Computer-Related Inventions, 61 Fed. Reg. 7,478, 7,478 (Feb. 28, 1996) (outlining how PTO examiners should scrutinize computer-related inventions).

[44] 149 F.3d 1368 (Fed. Cir. 1998).

[45] *Id.* at 1375 (arguing that the question of whether a claim encompasses patentable subject matter should focus on "practical utility").

[46] In contrast with *State Street,* the Supreme Court 2010 decision in *Bilski v. Kappos* states that patents can issue on "abstract" claims. However, as discussed further, whether this decision will have an impact on software claims is unclear.

[47] We exclude from our discussion a paper by Iain Cockburn and Meghan MacGarvie that focuses on patents held by firms in twenty-seven specific software markets. *See* Iain M. Cockburn & Megan J. MacGarvie, *Entry, Exit and Patenting in the Software Industry* 12 (Nat'l Bureau of Econ. Research, Working Paper No. 12563, Oct. 2006), *available at* http://www.nber.org/papers/w12563 (finding that firms are less likely to enter software markets in which there are more software patents but that, all else equal, firms that have software patents are more likely to enter these markets).

[48] Stuart J. H. Graham & David C. Mowery, *Intellectual Property Protection in the U.S. Software Industry, in* Patents in the Knowledge-Based Economy 219, 231 (Wesley M. Cohen & Stephen A. Merrill eds., 2003).

[49] Graham and Mowery use IPC classes G06F (subclasses 3, 5, 7, 9, 11, 12, 13, and 15), G06K (subclasses 9 and 15), and H04L (subclass 9). *Id.*

[50] *See id.* at 232 n.37 (noting that analysis focuses on patents assigned to large, publicly traded software firms).

those classes owned by large software firms.[51] The Graham and Mowery approach is not likely to be significantly overinclusive so long as it is limited to patents owned by packaged software firms. However, their approach may be quite underinclusive, missing software patents assigned to other firms as well as software patents in other patent classes.[52]

Another significant effort to identify a large set of software patents, by James Bessen and Bob Hunt,[53] defines "software patent" to include patents on inventions in which the data-processing algorithms are carried out by code either stored on a magnetic storage medium or embedded in chips ("firmware").[54] Rejecting the use of patent

[51] Stuart J. H. Graham & David C. Mowery, *Software Patents: Good News or Bad News?, in* INTELLECTUAL PROPERTY RIGHTS IN FRONTIER INDUSTRIES: SOFTWARE AND BIOTECHNOLOGY 45, 56–57 (Robert Hahn ed., 2005). The U.S. patent classes are 345, 358, 382, 704, 707, 709, 710, 711, 713, 714, 715, and 717. Similarly, Bronwyn Hall and Meghan MacGarvie rely on PTO classes. They do not, however, limit their use of these classes to packaged software firms. *See* Bronwyn H. Hall & Meghan MacGarvie, *The Private Value of Software Patents* 16–19 (Nat'l Bureau of Econ. Research, Working Paper No. 12,195, May 2006), *available at* http://www.nber.org/papers/w12195 (discussing datasets that are not confined to packaged software firms).

[52] To get a sense of false positives and false negatives, we assessed how the two Graham and Mowery approaches classified the 2,942 university patents issued in 2002. As shown in the Appendix Tables 11.A1 and 11.A2, very few of the patents classified by us as nonsoftware were classified as software by either the GM-IPC approach or the GM-PTO approach. However, the GM-IPC approach did not classify as software 86% of the patents we classified as software. Similarly, the GM-PTO approach did not classify as software 82% of the patents we classified as software. An analysis conducted by Bronwyn Hall and Meghan MacGarvie compared Graham-Mowery with earlier datasets manually compiled by Allison and determined that an approach that uses patent classifications misses about 50% of software patents. *See* Hall & MacGarvie, *supra* note 53, at 17 (finding mixed effects of changes in legal doctrine on the market value and stock returns of software firms).

Of course, as the analysis by Hall and MacGarvie suggests, *see* Table 11.A2 Appendix *infra*, even significant percentages of Type I and Type II errors do not necessarily have a systematic impact on regression results. In our case, however, because the number of patents in our dataset was tractable, and we needed to do manual work to determine departmental origin in any event, *see infra* Part II.C, we preferred a more precise approach.

[53] *See* Bessen & Hunt, *supra* note 3.

[54] As Bessen and Hunt note, one of the current authors, John Allison, earlier employed a definition of software patent that excluded firmware, including only inventions in which the code implementing the data-processing algorithms are stored on a magnetic storage medium. *See* John R. Allison & Mark Lemley, *Who's Patenting What? An Empirical Exploration of Patent Prosecution*, 53 VAND. L. REV. 2099, 2110 (2000). Allison also employed this definition in later articles. *See* John Allison & Mark Lemley, *The Growing Complexity of the Patent System*, 82 B.U. L. REV. 77 (2002) (discussing patent trends over the last thirty years); John Allison & Emerson Tiller, *The Business Method Patent Myth*, 18 BERKELEY TECH. L.J. 987 (2003) (arguing that business method patents should not receive special treatment by the PTO). The reasons for using this definition were a combination of initial doubt and compromise with a co-author, followed by a need for consistency. Each of these articles made use of the same dataset of 1000 randomly selected patents issued between mid-1996 and mid-1998. After a great deal more experience gained from closely reading thousands of computer-related patents, Allison became convinced that the definition should include firmware. When he used the same set of 1000 randomly selected patents in a subsequent article, he studied each patent again and reclassified them using a definition that included firmware. *See generally* John R. Allison et al., *Valuable Patents*, 92 GEO. L.J. 435 (2004) (discussing characteristics of litigated patents). Allison has used this more inclusive definition in studying the approximately 20,000 patents issued during 1998–2002 to almost

classifications,[55] Bessen and Hunt study a random sample of patents and classify them according to their definition. Using characteristics of patents Bessen and Hunt find to fit their definition, they then develop a keyword search algorithm to identify software patents.[56]

Although the Bessen and Hunt definition of software patent is reasonable, there are pitfalls associated with using automated keyword searches to identify such patents. From one of the co-author's (John Allison's) study of thousands of computer-related patents, it is clear that the use of language in the titles, abstracts, written descriptions, and claims of patents, even in those dealing with the same area of technology, can be highly idiosyncratic among different patent owners. In general, a common criticism of patents in the IT industries is that the industries lack a standardized vocabulary for claims.[57] Moreover, software is a critical part of inventions in so many fields that reliance on particular search terms could produce a dataset that has both false positives and false negatives.[58]

Instead of relying on prior approaches, we formulated a definition of "software patent" based on the extensive experience one of us (Allison) has had in reading

1000 firms appearing in the Software 500 list in those years. This list ranks firms according to their gross revenues in software and services and includes many firms that are primarily manufacturers in addition to firms that produce only software. *See* John R. Allison et al., *Software Patents, Incumbents, and Entry*, 85 TEX. L. REV. 1579, 1594–95 (2007) (detailing methodology). *See generally* John R. Allison & Ronald J. Mann, *The Disputed Quality of Software Patents*, 85 WASH. U. L. REV. 297 (2007) (analyzing firm-held patents and their characteristics).

55 *See* Bessen & Hunt, *supra* note 3, at 163–64 (discussing methodology for identifying software patents). The Bessen and Hunt definition of a software patent appears to include patents on inventions that "use" software as part of the invention, but excludes those that "use" off-the-shelf software:

> Our concept of software patent involves a logic algorithm for processing data that is implemented via stored instructions; that is, the logic is not "hardwired." These instructions could reside on a disk or other storage medium, or they could be stored in "firmware" – that is, a read-only memory – as is typical of embedded software. But we want to exclude inventions that do not use software as part of the invention. For example, some patents reference off-the-shelf software used to determine key parameters of the invention; such uses do not make the patent a software patent.

Id. at 163.

56 The keyword search algorithm initially identifies a set of patents that use the words "software," "computer," or "program" in the claims or specification. *Id.* at 185. Patents within the set that contain the word "semiconductor," "chip," "circuit," "circuitry," or "bus" are then excluded, as well as patents that contain the word "antigen," "antigenic," or "chromatography." *Id.*

57 *See, e.g.*, BESSEN & MEURER, *supra* note 1.

58 *See generally* Bessen & Hunt, *supra* note 3 (identifying substantial degrees of over- and underinclusiveness in the dataset generated by their keyword search). Table 11.A3 in the Appendix uses university patents issued in 2002 to compare the Bessen and Hunt (BH) approach with our own approach. The two approaches yield an approximately comparable number of total patents (396 patents using our approach versus 415 using the BH approach). However, 51% of the patents our approach identifies as software are not identified as such by the BH algorithm. Moreover, we classify as nonsoftware 53% of the patents that BH classify as software. Similarly, one recent study that used software experts to read a sample of the BH patents asserts that more than 50% represented Type II errors. *See* Anne Layne-Farrar, *Defining Software Patents: A Research Field Guide* 1–21 (AEI-Brookings Joint Ctr., Working Paper No. 05–14, Aug. 2005), *available at* http://aei-brookings.org/admin/authorpdfs/redirect-safely.php?fname=../pdffiles/phpAW.pdf.

software patents. Our definition of software patent is "a patent in which at least one claim element consists of data processing – the actual manipulation of data – regardless of whether the code carrying out that data processing is on a magnetic storage medium or embedded in a chip." Not only is it possible to apply this definition consistently but it also captures the realities of claim drafting. In Allison's experience, patent claims often include the prior art, with only one or two elements covering the purportedly novel and nonobvious advance. For example, a claim may read as though it covers a generic router, printer, magnetic resonance imaging machine, or other hardware, when in fact the only purported novelty is in one element consisting of a function carried out by algorithms. This drafting practice may be partly a consequence of the fact that, before *Alappat* and the 1996 PTO guidelines, software had to be claimed not as a new algorithm per se but instead as a new machine that allegedly did something different because of the new algorithm.[59] More fundamentally, a claim covers the entire invention, and in a case such as this, the entire invention is not just the new algorithm in isolation; rather, it is a piece of hardware that allegedly does something different because of the new algorithm.

In a large set of patents, it is a practical impossibility to include only those patents in which the software element (as contrasted with other elements of the invention) is novel and nonobvious. To restrict ourselves to patents in which the software element was novel and nonobvious, we would need to employ a person having ordinary skill in the art to conduct a very thorough study of the relevant prior art. Even then, the question would be plagued by doubt because issues of novelty and nonobviousness are typically difficult to resolve even after a full evidentiary exploration in court. But the fact that, under our definition, the data processing must be identified in a claim element does suggest that software is sufficiently important to novelty and nonobviousness for the patent claim drafter to include it as a limitation of the claim (thereby narrowing the claim). In other words, it would be foolhardy for a patent attorney to include such an element unless it was a critical part of the invention.

Our approach does have limits. One problem is that it involves the slow and laborious process of reading patents. Although the decision on many patents is clear, there will always be a substantial percentage that must be studied with great care.[60] Moreover, a degree of subjective judgment is occasionally required. However, at least in the case of a relatively small dataset, we believe that increased accuracy more than compensates for time intensity and that the absence of algorithmic criteria is readily replicable by automated methods. We do not claim that our dataset of university-owned software patents is perfect, but we do contend that our error rate is very small – certainly smaller than in any dataset acquired by means of patent classifications or keyword searches.

59 *See supra* notes 43–45 and accompanying text.

60 However, if one is studying a large population of patents from the computer-related industries, the percentage that must be carefully scrutinized is far higher than if one is studying a population of patents across a broad array of fields (as in this chapter).

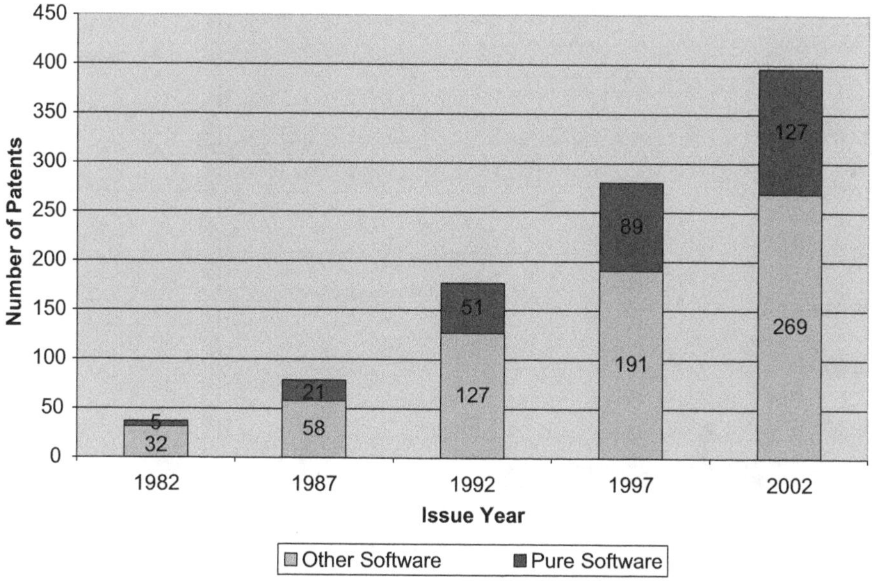

FIGURE 11.1. University software patents, by type and year.

In addition to identifying which patents of the more than 7600 university-owned patents in our sample are software patents, we also identified a subset that may be called "pure software patents." These are patents in which the claims consist only of data processing – that is, the entire invention consists of algorithms.[61] This task required thorough study of each of the patents that had already been identified as a software patent. Although the process of identifying "pure" software patents was accomplished with a high degree of accuracy, there was a small number of patents about which reasonable minds could differ. Thus, for this second stage, we also do not profess to have achieved perfection, but we do maintain that our error rate is very low.

II. UNIVERSITY SOFTWARE PATENTING: TRENDS, DETERMINANTS, AND DEPARTMENTAL ORIGIN

A. *Trends*

Figure 11.1 shows that university software patenting increased more than tenfold over the 1982–2002 period, from 37 patents in 1982 to 396 patents in 2002. Over this period, the "pure software" proportion of university software patents also increased

[61] These sorts of patents could presumably issue with any frequency only after the Federal Circuit's 1994 *Alappat* decision. However, as discussed further, *see infra* Part V.A, even these pure software claims typically involve the use of a computer and, in some cases, a trivial nondata-processing element such as a generic input, output, or storage element. Thus, they may survive even after *In re Bilski*.

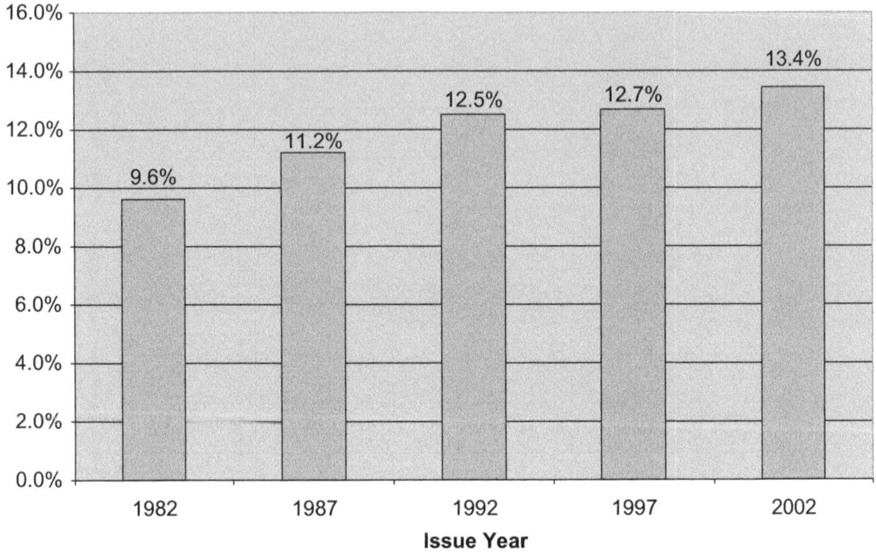

FIGURE 11.2. University software patents as a share of all university patents.

dramatically, from 13% to 32% of all university software patents. The latter change is hardly surprising. Whereas the patentability of pure software was unclear in the 1980s, its status became much more secure in the 1990s.[62] Over these two decades, university software patenting also grew at a faster rate than university patenting overall. As a consequence, the software share of university patents rose from 9 percent in 1982 to 13 percent in 2002, as seen in Figure 11.2.

Table 11.1 lists the fifteen universities that received the most software patents in 2002.[63] Together, these institutions accounted for 60% of all university software patents issued in 2002. The top five institutions alone – the Massachusetts Institute of Technology (MIT), the University of California, Stanford University (Stanford), the California Institute of Technology (Caltech), and the University of Texas – accounted for more than a third (34.2%) of all university software patents. The top five patentees also represented the top five university patentees overall in 2002. However, moving further down the list of the top fifteen, we see that a number of the top software patentees are not among the top university patentees overall. The University of Washington (sixth in software patenting/fifteenth in overall patenting), the Georgia Institute of Technology ("Georgia Tech") (eighth/twentieth), Carnegie Mellon (ninth/fifty-first), the University of Rochester (twelfth/fiftieth), and the

[62] *See supra* notes 42–45 and accompanying text.

[63] To be sure, the 2002 data may be somewhat unusual in that it reflects patent filings that occurred during the "dot-com" bubble of the late 1990s. However, with a few exceptions, these universities also received the largest number of software patents over the course of the sampling.

TABLE 11.1. *University software patenting, overall patenting, and pure software patenting in 2002*

University	Rank in patenting (issue year 2002)		
	Software	Overall	Pure software
Massachusetts Institute of Technology	1	2	1
University of California	2	1	2
Stanford University	3	4	4
California Institute of Technology	4	3	23
University of Texas	5	5	41
University of Washington	6	15	6
University of Wisconsin	7	7	8
Georgia Institute of Technology	8	20	3
Carnegie Mellon University	9	51	13
Johns Hopkins University	10	6	11
State University of New York	11	8	20
University of Rochester	12	50	14
University of Pennsylvania	13	13	42
University of Illinois	14	28	5
Columbia University	15	14	10

University of Illinois (fourteenth/twenty-eighth) particularly stand out as institutions substantially more prominent in software patenting than in overall patenting.

With respect to the patenting of "pure" software, Table 11.1 shows that the top three patenting institutions overall also ranked among the top recipients of pure software patents (first, second, and fourth). In contrast, although Caltech and the University of Texas ranked high in overall software patenting (fourth and fifth, respectively), they ranked relatively low in the patenting of pure software (twenty-third and forty-first, respectively). The University of Washington, Georgia Tech, Carnegie Mellon, the University of Rochester, and the University of Illinois – mentioned earlier as standing out in software patenting relative to overall patenting – also stand out with respect to numbers of pure software patents (sixth, third, thirteenth, fourteenth, and eleventh, respectively).

As these examples suggest, several factors may affect university software patenting. First, the amount of software-related R&D and thus the output of software may matter. Second, the size of the overall research enterprise may matter, because software can be developed in many parts of the university. Third, an individual university's nonsoftware-related propensity to patent (i.e., the share of nonsoftware research outputs it patents either because its researchers are prone to file invention disclosure statements and push for patents on those disclosures or because technology transfer officers are prone to seek patents on disclosures, may also affect software patenting.[64]

[64] In our quantitative discussion, we cannot distinguish between motivations of university technology transfer offices and motivations of university scientists. In any event, these motivations may be related.

Although there are undoubtedly other factors that affect software patenting – for example, how software ownership in particular is viewed in the technology licensing office or among faculty[65] – these factors are difficult to measure quantitatively. We examine some of these factors in our qualitative analyses.

B. *Patent Production Functions*

To examine the relationship of software R&D, overall R&D, and nonsoftware patent propensity to university-level software patenting, we collected data on R&D funds as well as nonsoftware patenting for all of the 202 Carnegie research universities in our sample. The unit of analysis for the "patent production functions" we estimate is a university in a given issue year. For each institution, we created variables measuring the number of software patents and number of other patents issued in 1982, 1987, 1992, 1997, and 2002. We used the National Science Foundation's WebCaspar database[66] to collect R&D data for these universities for the 1977–2002 time period.[67] Specifically, we collected data on computer science R&D and overall R&D and used this information to construct variables measuring the sum of computer science and other R&D over the previous five years. The main empirical analyses relate a university's software patenting to its nonsoftware patenting in a given issue year and to its computer science R&D and other R&D over the five years prior. We decided to use a five-year time frame because it is difficult to estimate precisely when the research that led to a particular invention disclosure (let alone an issued patent) was conducted. By using a relatively long time frame, we aimed to get a sense of the research commitment of the university, both inside and outside the software arena, around the time an invention disclosure was likely to have been submitted.[68]

To facilitate interpretation, we took natural logarithms of the independent variables.[69] Because the dependent variables are integer valued, we estimated

For example, Azoulay et al., *supra* note 11, at 600, 615–19, find that, in a study of 3862 life sciences researchers, the overall "patent stock" of the university where the researcher is employed has an effect on the number of patents held by the life sciences researcher.

65 In the life sciences context, for example, one study that examined patenting activity for 3862 researchers found that having co-authors who patent has a positive effect on patenting behavior. *Id.* at 615.

66 This database is available at WebCASPAR: Integrated Science and Engineering Resources Data System, http://caspar.nsf.gov (follow "Info" hyperlink for "NSF Survey of R&D Expenditures at Universities and Colleges") (last visited Apr. 21, 2009).

67 This database uses information from NSF's *Survey of R&D Expenditures at Universities and Colleges*, a survey conducted annually by NSF's Division of Science Resource Statistics. For more on this data source, see *id.* (follow "Info" hyperlink for "NSF Survey of R&D Expenditures at Universities and Colleges").

68 For purposes of our regression analyses, the strong persistence in university-level R&D funding and composition over time is very helpful. As one indicator of this persistence, computer science R&D funding at a point in time has a correlation of 0.965 with its sum over the previous five years, and other R&D funding has a correlation of 0.996 with its sum over the previous five years.

69 Following convention, we use natural logs of one plus the variable.

TABLE 11.2. *Negative binomial models, determinants of 1982 software patenting*

	Model 1 (1)	Model 2 (2)	Model 3 (3)	Model 4 (4)
ln Lagged CS Funds	.218*	.167	.770**	.748**
	(.128)	(.124)	(.336)	(.358)
ln Lagged Other Funds	.612**	−.043	1.435**	.709
	(.270)	(.193)	(.635)	(.774)
ln Other Patents		1.326***		.742
		(.272)		(.501)
Const.	−10.317***	−4.045**	−27.910***	−19.811**
	(2.824)	(1.798)	(8.697)	(10.044)
Obs.	202	202	202	202

Notes: Robust standard errors in parentheses. ***$p < .001$; **$p < .01$; *$p < .05$.

negative binomial regressions relating software patents and pure software patents to research expenditures.[70] Tables 11.2 through 11.6 show the main results from these simple cross-sectional regressions for 1982 to 2002, respectively. The dependent variable in Models 1 and 2 is the number of software patents issued to a university in a given year. In Models 3 and 4, the dependent variable is the number of pure software patents.

In negative binomial models, coefficients on log-transformed variables can be interpreted as elasticities. Model 1 for the 1982 sample (Table 11.2) shows that both computer science R&D and other R&D are related to software patenting. After introducing the nonsoftware patenting variable, neither of the R&D variables is significant, but the number of nonsoftware patents is – with a 1% increase in other patenting associated with a 1.3% increase in software patenting. Both software and nonsoftware R&D are related to the number of pure software patents (Model 3), but the latter is no longer statistically significant after introducing the nonsoftware patenting variable. Thus, the only clear implication of the 1982 cohort is the strong correlation of nonsoftware patenting with overall software patents.

Tables 11.3 and 11.4 show that, in 1987 and 1992, once nonsoftware patents are taken into account, neither computer science nor other R&D has a consistently strong association with either overall software patenting or pure software patenting. Nonsoftware patenting is, however, strongly related to software patenting and pure software patenting, after controlling for R&D. Depending on the specific model and gear, elasticities range from 0.797 to 1.035.

[70] We could not reject the hypothesis of overdispersion and thus chose negative binomial models over Poisson models. However, we obtained qualitatively similar results from Poisson models with standard errors adjusted to account for overdispersion and from log-log models estimated via ordinary least squares. These results are available from the authors on request.

TABLE 11.3. *Negative binomial models, determinants of 1987 software patenting*

	Model 1 (1)	Model 2 (2)	Model 3 (3)	Model 4 (4)
ln Lagged CS Funds	.343***	.314***	.289	.210
	(.122)	(.092)	(.194)	(.162)
ln Lagged Other Funds	1.013***	.291	.864**	.094
	(.236)	(.198)	(.351)	(.319)
ln Other Patents		.797***		1.035***
		(.163)		(.303)
Const.	−16.411***	−8.430***	−15.243***	−6.796**
	(2.592)	(2.117)	(3.792)	(3.261)
Obs.	202	202	202	202

Notes: Robust standard errors in parentheses. $^{***}p < .001$; $^{**}p < .01$; $^{*}p < .05$.

Further, Tables 11.5 and 11.6 show that, after the mid-1990s – the post–*Alappat*[71] era – universities that had larger stocks of computer science R&D also tended to do more software patenting and pure software patenting. This conclusion is consistent with the descriptive data for issue year 2002 in Table 11.1. In each of the models, however, after controlling for computer science R&D and other R&D, nonsoftware patenting was significantly related to both software patenting and pure software patenting, with elasticities ranging from 0.78 to 0.91 depending on the specific model and year.

The finding that nonsoftware patenting (conditional on overall and computer science R&D) has a qualitatively and statistically significant relationship with software patenting suggests that universities with a higher nonsoftware patenting propensity also tend to patent more software.

This correlation between nonsoftware and software patenting propensity could be driven by several factors. One potentially omitted variable from these analyses is university success in getting patent applications issued. If some universities are systematically better at securing patents, this could drive the observed correlation even if the propensity to file patent applications on software is unrelated to the propensity to file applications on other inventions. We explored this question for the 2002 cohort for the subset of 130 universities where Association of University Technology Managers (AUTM) data on "application success" were available.[72] As

[71] *In re* Alappat, 33 F.3d 1526 (Fed. Cir. 1994).

[72] More specifically, data on the number of patent applications filed by the university were available. Combining this data with PTO data on issued patents based on 2002 applications (as of December 2007) allowed us to measure the university's "application success." Because the application success variable captures university patent prosecution ability based on applications filed in 2002 (and issued over the next five years) rather than in the years prior to the issuance of the 2002 patents, the application success measure is potentially a noisy one. However, we suspect that university success in obtaining patents is relatively invariant over time.

TABLE 11.4. *Negative binomial models, determinants of 1992 software patenting*

	Model 1 (1)	Model 2 (2)	Model 3 (3)	Model 4 (4)
ln Lagged CS Funds	.143*	.082	.122	.071
	(.077)	(.073)	(.110)	(.107)
ln Lagged Other Funds	1.083***	.348*	.968***	.264
	(.192)	(.206)	(.287)	(.323)
ln Other Patents		1.027***		.955***
		(.199)		(.318)
Const.	−15.295***	−7.610***	−14.735***	−7.392**
	(2.213)	(2.221)	(3.357)	(3.446)
Obs.	202	202	202	202

Notes: Robust standard errors in parentheses. $^{***}p < .001$; $^{**}p < .01$; $^{*}p < .05$.

TABLE 11.5. *Negative binomial models, determinants of 1997 software patenting*

	Model 1 (1)	Model 2 (2)	Model 3 (3)	Model 4 (4)
ln Lagged CS Funds	.245***	.172**	.348***	.275**
	(.076)	(.072)	(.134)	(.131)
ln Lagged Other Funds	.986***	.308	1.005***	.271
	(.160)	(.196)	(.252)	(.320)
ln Other Patents		.832***		.813***
		(.185)		(.282)
Const.	−14.941***	−7.394***	−17.358***	−9.023**
	(1.878)	(2.179)	(2.975)	(3.587)
Obs.	202	202	202	202

Notes: Robust standard errors in parentheses. $^{***}p < .001$; $^{**}p < .01$; $^{*}p < .05$.

TABLE 11.6. *Negative binomial models, determinants of 2002 software patenting*

	Model 1 (1)	Model 2 (2)	Model 3 (3)	Model 4 (4)
ln Lagged CS Funds	.110**	.097**	.588***	.523***
	(.049)	(.045)	(.121)	(.110)
ln Lagged Other Funds	.839***	.073	.223	−.395**
	(.118)	(.141)	(.161)	(.163)
ln Other Patents		.910***		.781***
		(.141)		(.167)
Const.	−11.577***	−3.613**	−9.017***	−2.182
	(1.406)	(1.510)	(1.615)	(1.576)
Obs.	202	202	202	202

Notes: Robust standard errors in parentheses. $^{***}p < .001$; $^{**}p < .01$; $^{*}p < .05$.

TABLE 11.7. *Negative binomial models, determinants of 2002 software patenting, AUTM universities*

	Model 1 (1)	Model 2 (2)	Model 3 (3)	Model 4 (4)
ln Lagged CS Funds	.100**	.537***	.091	.583***
	(.046)	(.111)	(.057)	(.120)
ln Lagged Other Funds	−.040	−.524**	.428**	−.008
	(.169)	(.235)	(.202)	(.254)
ln Other Patents	.807***	.717***		
	(.160)	(.219)		
Application Success Rate	−.207	.068		
	(.360)	(.426)		
ln TTO FTEs			.503**	.407*
			(.208)	(.247)
Const.	−1.663	−.317	−6.420***	−6.356**
	(1.914)	(2.530)	(2.468)	(3.046)
Obs.	130	130	101	101

Notes: Robust standard errors in parentheses. $^{***}p < .001$; $^{**}p < .01$; $^{*}p < .05$.

Models 1 and 2 in Table 11.7 show, for all software patents and pure software patents, respectively, application success is not significantly related to software patenting.

Another possible explanation for the correlation between nonsoftware and software patenting propensity could be scale economies: The marginal costs of obtaining a software patent (or any additional patent) may be lower for universities that have larger technology transfer operations. To test this possibility, we used data on the size of technology transfer offices. Reports from the AUTM contain data on the number of licensing officers employed by each university in 2002, though only for a subset (102) of universities in our sample.[73] Models 3 and 4 in Table 11.7 show that, after controlling for nonsoftware and software R&D, this variable is significantly related to both pure and software patenting, consistent with the scale economies hypothesis.

Finally, we estimated a panel version of these regressions for the entire period with university and year fixed effects. This model identifies the estimated changes in R&D and other patenting using within-university variation over time. Thus, any time-invariant university factors (including "fixed" university technology transfer abilities) would not affect estimates from this model.

Table 11.8 shows the results. Notably, the year dummies are positive and their magnitude increases over time, reflecting the overall growth in university patenting over the 1982–2002 period. Model 1 shows that the main factor affecting overall software patenting is change in nonsoftware patenting, with a 1% increase in

73 Association of University Technology Managers, FY 2002 AUTM Licensing Survey (on file with author).

TABLE 11.8. *Negative binomial models, determinants of software patenting, panel model*

	Model 1 (1)	Model 2 (2)
Log Lagged CS Funds	.039	.107
	(.047)	(.096)
Log Lagged Other Funds	−.387	−.118
	(.289)	(.628)
Log Other Patents	.457***	.054
	(.093)	(.167)
Year Dummy 1987	.688***	1.363**
	(.244)	(.583)
Year Dummy 1992	1.381***	2.193***
	(.324)	(.754)
Year Dummy 1997	1.767***	2.708***
	(.400)	(.897)
Year Dummy 2002	2.090***	3.045***
	(.472)	(1.040)
Const.	−17.388	−15.120
	(5379.716)	(418.959)
Obs.	1010	1010

Notes: All models include university fixed effects. The left-out year category is 1982. Robust standard errors in parentheses. $^{***}p < .001$; $^{**}p < .01$; $^{*}p < .05$.

nonsoftware patenting implying a 0.46% increase in software patenting. The corresponding finding for pure software patenting is neither qualitatively nor statistically significant. Additionally, none of the R&D measures are statistically significant for either software or pure software. This last set of results should be interpreted with caution, however. Because the panels are short and there is limited within-university variation, it is difficult to draw strong inferences.

Taken together, we read these results as consistent with the impressions from our interviews (discussed later) that university software patenting practices are related to their nonsoftware patenting practices. An ideal test of this hypothesis would control for the number of disclosed software inventions for which patents would indeed facilitate technology transfer. If we had such a measure, and found that nonsoftware patent propensity nonetheless affected the volume of software patenting, this would provide strong support for the argument that university software patenting is less about "technology transfer" and more about "business as usual." Unfortunately, such a measure is unlikely to be obtained.[74]

74 Another limitation of our data is that we must rely on R&D generally (and computer science R&D in particular) as an imperfect proxy for the volume of software output at a university.

TABLE 11.9. *Departmental origin of inventors on software patents issued to the top fifteen recipients of software patents in issue year 2002*

Department	N	Percent	Cumulative percent
EE/CS	47	9.67	9.67
Electrical Engineering	47	9.67	19.34
Computer Science	42	8.64	27.98
Neuroscience	23	4.73	32.72
Robotics Institute	23	4.73	37.45
Medical Physics	20	4.12	41.56
Radiology	19	3.91	45.47
Lawrence Livermore	15	3.09	48.56
Chemistry	13	2.67	51.23
Mechanical Engineering	12	2.47	53.70

Note: Counts and percentages calculated at the patent-inventor level.

C. *Departmental Origin*

To explore the sources of software patenting in greater detail, we also identified the departmental origin of the inventors in the top fifteen academic software patentees in 2002. As noted earlier, these institutions accounted for 60% of 2002's overall academic software patenting.[75]

These 241 patents had 544 distinct inventors. Based on web searches, we were able to locate the primary departmental affiliation for 73.5% (400) of these inventors. Seen another way, these 241 patents included 661 unique inventor-patent dyads. For example, if an inventor was included on three patents, she generated three inventor-patent dyads. For 26.5% of these dyads, we could not identify the inventor's department.

Table 11.9 shows the top ten departments for dyads where the department is known. Slightly fewer than 30% of the inventors are from electrical engineering, computer science, and joint EE/CS departments. Moreover, consistent with arguments that software is produced across the university, a number of biomedical departments are also represented, including Neuroscience, Radiology, and Medical Physics. To the extent that software is being treated just like other inventions for purposes of patenting, this may be in part because a significant proportion of it emerges from biomedical departments where patenting is the norm. In this regard, it bears emphasis that, of the 970 software patents in our overall sampling, 333 (more than one-third) represented software with biomedical applications.

Table 11.10 shows the analogous table for pure software patents. Perhaps not surprisingly, more than half of the patent-inventor dyads on pure software patents emanate from electrical engineering, computer science, or joint EE/CS departments. Other

75 *See supra* Part II.A.

TABLE 11.10. *Departmental origin of inventors for pure software patents issued to the top fifteen recipients of software patents in issue year 2002*

Department	N	Percent	Cumulative percent
Computer Science	33	23.57	23.57
EE/CS	29	20.71	44.29
Electrical Engineering	12	8.57	52.86
Lincoln Laboratory	6	4.29	57.14
Aeronautics and Astronautics	5	3.57	60.71
Robotics Institute	5	3.57	64.29
Agricultural and Biological Engineering	3	2.14	66.43
Chemistry and Biochemistry	3	2.14	68.57
Mathematics	3	2.14	70.71
Biostatistics and Medical Informatics	2	1.43	72.14

Note: Counts and percentages calculated at the patent-inventor level.

departments are less prominent in the production of pure software patents than in the production of other software patents.

III. UNIVERSITY OWNERSHIP POLICIES

Our quantitative results demonstrate that, on the whole, for software patent applications filed in the 1980s and 1990s, universities appeared to take a one-size-fits all approach to technology. Those universities that tended to file a lot of nonsoftware patents also filed a lot of software patents (both ordinary software and pure software). The regression results underscore what can be seen through a casual review of the descriptive statistics in Table 11.4: the top five software patentees in 2002 – MIT, University of California, Stanford, Caltech, and the University of Texas – were also the top five overall patentees. Notably, none of these five was in the top five in computer science R&D spending for the years 1996–98.

Yet, a qualitative review of our descriptive data also indicates some anomalies in this general pattern. For example, of the top five software patentees in 2002, two – Caltech and the University of Texas – did *not* have significant numbers of pure software patents.[76] Moreover, five universities – the University of Washington, Georgia Tech, Carnegie Mellon University, the University of Rochester, and the University of Illinois – ranked substantially higher in software/pure software patenting than in overall patenting.

To get a more fine-grained sense of factors that might be influencing individual universities, we investigated technology transfer policies at the fifteen universities that received the most software patents in 2002. In addition to reviewing publicly available materials, we conducted interviews with two groups of relevant parties: (1) technology

[76] Caltech and the University of Texas ranked twenty-third and forty-first, respectively.

transfer managers responsible for software at the universities[77] and (2) academics and graduate students prominent in software development. The latter group was selected through snowball sampling. Interviews were conducted by telephone, lasted approximately 45 minutes to one hour, and were semi-structured. On occasion, follow-up discussions were necessary and were conducted either via e-mail or by telephone. A list of questions asked in each interview is shown in the Appendix.[78]

Several of the interviews confirmed the results of our quantitative analysis – that technology transfer officers treat software like other inventions. Lita Nelsen, director of the MIT technology transfer office, noted that, when discussing pure software, "if there are no strong feelings on the part of the authors to open source their work, we will look at it *like any other invention*."[79]

Our qualitative investigation also suggested reasons for the relatively low numbers of pure software patents at the University of Texas and Caltech. At the University of Texas, complaints from computer science faculty resulted in the explicit adoption of a policy allowing faculty freedom to share their work as they wanted.[80] Such freedom includes express permission to use the GNU General Public License (GPL), a "viral" open source license that requires software source code to be open but also requires those who redistribute the software to make any modifications they have made to the source code available.[81] This policy was adopted in the 1990s and therefore would have affected the number of pure software patents that issued in 2002.[82]

The explanation for Caltech's small number of pure software patents is less transparent. Because we were unable to speak with the technology licensing office,[83] our knowledge of the Caltech situation is based on reports from scientists who worked

77 We were able to obtain interviews with officials at all technology transfer offices except Caltech and Columbia University.

78 All interviews were recorded; transcripts of recordings (with portions where interviewees wished to remain anonymous deleted) are available on request from the authors.

79 E-mail from Lita Nelsen, Director, MIT Tech. Licensing Office, to Colin Crossman, Faculty Fellow, Duke Law Sch. (July 27, 2005, 13:45 EST) (on file with the North Carolina Law Review). According to Nelsen, software tends to be worth patenting when the primary value is in the algorithm and when it is likely to give "a substantial return." *Id.*; *see also* Telephone Interview with Gerald Barnett, Dir., Univ. of Wash., Software & Copyright Ventures (Oct. 2, 2003) (emphasis added) (noting that universities that have a long history of patenting tend to see software, including pure software, through the lens they use for other invention).

80 Telephone Interview with Georgia Harper, Attorney, Intellectual Prop. Section, Univ. of Tex. Office of Gen. Counsel (Feb. 26, 2004).

81 For information about the GPL license, see GNU General Public License, Free Software Foundation, Inc. (3d version, June 29, 2007), http://www.gnu.org/licenses/ gpl.html.

82 *See* Telephone Interview with Georgia Harper, *supra* note 82. Various University of Texas websites document the university's continuing support of open source under GPL or similar licenses where the faculty inventor and a software consultant determine that such distribution is in the best interest of the university and the public. *See, e.g.*, Administrative Policy Regarding Disclosure, Distribution and Licensing Software, University of Texas (Dec. 15, 2004), http://www.utsystem.edu/ogc/intellectualproperty/ swadmpol.htm.

83 The Caltech technology transfer staff refused requests for an interview.

there. According to one prominent open source software developer at Caltech, most software developed there is for internal, in-house use and is probably not even reported to the technology transfer office.[84] For software that is reported, the faculty researcher decides how the software should be exploited.[85] The technology transfer office is not only familiar with open source but also is apparently eager to use the viral GPL license; the viral GPL allows for the future possibility of "forking," with one fork continuing to be available without charge via the GPL and the other fork converted into a nonviral license for which corporate clients might be willing to pay.[86]

In contrast, the positions of two of the other top five software patentees – MIT and the University of California – are (or at least have been) less explicitly favorable to open source.[87] According to MIT's director of technology transfer, MIT allows researchers to use the open source approach and even manages their licenses, but this position is not part of an official policy.[88] The University of California system appears to have a highly complex set of positions on open source licensing. Although some campuses, such as Berkeley and San Diego, are familiar with the open source model, other campuses are less so.[89] Complexity is compounded by the fact that various important campuses, including Berkeley, have been actively fine-tuning their policies.[90] As of early 2002, officials from the Berkeley office were quoted as criticizing the decision made by Berkeley a decade earlier, in 1992, to release as open source the Unix operating system and TCP/IP networking protocol.[91] At about the same time, Berkeley computational biologist Steven Brenner encountered difficulties in releasing his lab's software under an open source license.[92]

As for the five schools that rank substantially higher in software/pure software patenting than in other patenting – the University of Washington, Georgia Tech, Carnegie Mellon, the University of Rochester, and the University of Illinois – the first three of these schools have unique characteristics that may explain their high levels of pure software patenting. At the University of Washington, a separate technology

84 Telephone Interview with C. Titus Brown, Graduate Student, Cal. Inst. of Tech., Dept. of Biology (Aug. 17, 2005).

85 *Id.*

86 *See id.*

87 Where Stanford University fits in the picture is not clear. Stanford did not adopt an explicit policy in favor of open source until 2004. It adopted this policy in response to a number of requests received from professors. *See* Telephone Interview with Katherine Ku, Dir., Stanford Office of Tech. Licensing (Sept. 6, 2005). However, Stanford has long had a policy allowing professors to put their inventions into the public domain if they so desire.

88 Telephone Interview with Lita Nelsen, Dir., Mass. Inst. of Tech. Licensing Office (Aug. 8, 2005).

89 Telephone Interview with William Decker, Assoc. Dir., Univ. of Cal. at San Diego Tech. Transfer Office (Aug. 28, 2003).

90 *See infra* notes 180–83 and accompanying text.

91 *See* Jeffrey Benner, *Public Money, Private Code*, SALON, Jan. 4, 2002, http://www.salon.com/tech/feature/2002/01/04/university_open_source/index.html.

92 Telephone Interview with Steven Brenner, Assoc. Professor, Univ. of Cal. at Berkeley Dept. of Plant & Microbial Biology (Mar. 8, 2004).

licensing office, now called the Digital Ventures Office, is responsible for managing pure software (and digital products more generally).[93] By 2005, the office employed seven full-time professionals as well as two to four part-time students.[94] As for Georgia Tech, its level of computer science R&D funding relative to other funding is quite high – it ranks fifth in computer science funding and only thirty-second in other funding. Finally, Carnegie Mellon ranks second in computer science funding and eighty-seventh in other funding. Carnegie Mellon is also home to the Software Engineering Institute (SEI), a research consortium founded by software firms.[95] Patents from SEI are assigned to Carnegie Mellon, and the software firms in the consortium receive an automatic, royalty-free license.[96]

IV. UNIVERSITY SOFTWARE OWNERSHIP: A POLICY ANALYSIS

A. *General Considerations*

Our results indicate that universities have become active patentees of software, including pure software. They have clearly availed themselves of the opportunities afforded by the Bayh-Dole Act and the Federal Circuit decisions in the 1990s. Moreover, at least for our sample – which, because of prosecution lag time, terminates with patents filed around 2000 – behavior with respect to total software patents and pure software patents is strongly affected by nonsoftware patent propensity. Although there are anomalies in the overall pattern – largely explicable through policies at particular universities that either strongly favor open source or favor a particular focus on software[97] – the correlation is clear.

From a private point of view, this correlation may make sense, especially if the reason for the effect is, as some of our data suggest, economies of scale at the technology transfer office.[98] To the extent such scale economies exist, they are likely to lower the private marginal cost of patent acquisition.[99] From a social point of view, however, patenting based on scale economies is quite problematic. Ideally, we would want decisions about whether to patent publicly funded academic research to be based not only on the private marginal costs of patent acquisition but also on

93 Digital Ventures Home Page, http://depts.washington.edu/ventures/ (last visited Apr. 29, 2007).

94 Telephone Interviews with Charles Williams, Dir., Univ. of Wash. Digital Ventures (Apr. 21, 2004 & Sept. 1, 2005).

95 *See* Carnegie Mellon University, Software Engineering Institute, http://www.sei. cmu.edu/ (last visited Apr. 21, 2009).

96 Telephone Interview with Carl P. Mahler II, Dir. of Intellectual Prop., Ctr. for Tech. Transfer & Entm't (Sept. 2, 2005).

97 *See supra* Part III.

98 *See* David C. Mowery & Bhaven N. Sampat, *Patenting and Licensing University Inventions: Lessons from the History of the Research Corporation*, 10 INDUS. & CORP. CHANGE 317, 322–24 (2001).

99 *See id.* at 325.

whether a patent is needed to facilitate commercialization in a specific case, which is likely to vary across inventions and fields.

Stated differently, a lack of differentiation between software and other research could be problematic. As the data on the varying importance of patents as incentives in different industries suggest,[100] and as case study research on the disparate development trajectories of university technologies specifically emphasizes,[101] the optimal mode of university–industry technology transfer is likely to vary by industry and invention.[102] More specifically, as indicated earlier, the theory espoused in the legislative history of Bayh-Dole – that patents and exclusive licenses are necessary to create incentives for firms to develop and commercialize "embryonic" university inventions[103] – does not apply neatly in the software context, where development costs are often low relative to other types of inventions.[104]

Another major argument often advanced in favor of patents is that the prospect of licensing royalties induces university researchers to work with industry licensees and thereby transfer tacit knowledge necessary for commercialization.[105] Although this argument could in theory be compatible with exclusive or nonexclusive licenses, the assumption tends to be that an academic researcher would have sufficient time for only one exclusive licensee. However, in comparison to the life sciences, software (particularly pure software) is an area of invention where knowledge is likely to be relatively codified. Object-oriented programming is based on principles of modular design, and one of the reasons that open source methods of software production have been successful is that the development task can be broken up into modular

[100] *See* Cohen et al., *supra* note 13, at 5–30 (examining the diverse methods used by R&D labs to protect profits made from their inventions, as well as the diverse motives to patent across different industries).

[101] *See generally* Jeannette Colyvas et al., *How Do University Inventions Get into Practice*, 48 MGMT. SCI. 61 (2002) (discussing eleven case studies from Columbia University and Stanford University).

[102] In addition to differential incentive effects, university patents and licenses have different informational effects across different industries. Of particular relevance to our study, the comprehensive Carnegie Mellon survey, conducted on a broad range of large and small firms in the early 1990s, indicates that outside of the pharmaceutical and biotechnology industries, industrial R&D managers rate patents and licenses very low relative to other sources of information on public research (e.g., publications, conferences, informal interaction with university researchers, and consulting). *See* Cohen et al., *supra* note 13, at 4–5 (surveying various sizes of firms and their R&D managers). Even within the pharmaceutical industry, patents and licenses were less important than research publications and conferences. *Id.*

[103] *See supra* note 12 and accompanying text.

[104] To be sure, such costs may be higher in situations where the software is not pure software. However, even in those cases, to the extent that the novel or nonobvious element is likely software, development costs are probably still low relative to the biopharmaceutical industry.

[105] The evidence generally cited for this argument is survey data presented in Richard Jensen & Marie Thursby, *Proofs and Prototypes for Sale: The Licensing of University Inventions*, 91 AM. ECON. REV. 240, 240 (2001). The Jensen and Thursby survey of sixty-two technology transfer offices (TTOs) found that TTO managers thought that inventor involvement was often important in the commercialization of inventions. *Id.* at 255.

pieces that are then reassembled.[106] So, the need for the transfer of tacit knowledge may not be as pervasive as it is in the life sciences.

Indeed, in some well-known cases, it appears that the university patent allowed the university and/or its exclusive licensee to extract rents from other firms without aiding in technology transfer. For example, in the prominent case of *Eolas Technologies, Inc.* v. *Microsoft Corp.*,[107] Microsoft's commercialization does not appear to have been aided by the activities of the University of California/Eolas.[108] Even worse, in *Eolas*, the university patent was arguably being used to "hold up" the commercializer – that is, to use the threat of injunctive relief to extract rents significantly larger than the inventive contribution made by the patentee (and thus also significantly larger than any licensing fee the university inventor could have charged ex ante).[109]

B. *The Problem of Holdup Litigation*

To study the litigation question more systematically, we conducted two related empirical inquiries.[110] First, we used four different search methods to collect case studies involving university software litigation.[111] Second, by running the patents in our database against the Derwent LitAlert database of patent cases filed, we

[106] *See* Yochai Benkler, *Coase's Penguin, or, Linux and* The Nature of the Firm, 112 YALE L.J., 369, 383–88 (2002).

[107] 399 F.3d 1325 (Fed. Cir. 2005).

[108] According to a University of California website on the *Eolas* case, Microsoft and other firms were approached about licensing the technology in 1994 but declined to do so. University of California, Questions and Answers About UC/Eolas Patent Infringement Suit Against Microsoft, http://www.ucop.edu/news/archives/2003/aug11art1qanda.htm (last visited Apr. 21, 2009).

[109] The legal and economic literature on holdup through property rights assertion (both within and outside the patent context) is voluminous. *See, e.g.*, Arti K. Rai, *Regulating Scientific Research: Intellectual Property Rights and the Norms of Science*, 94 NW. U. L. REV. 77, 127–28 (1999) (summarizing literature). For a recent contribution, see Mark Lemley & Carl Shapiro, *Patent Holdup and Royalty Stacking*, 85 TEX. L. REV. 1991, 2008–10 (2007).

[110] To our knowledge, empirical work on university patent litigation has not been technology specific. The empirical work to date indicates that, across all technologies, university patents are litigated at about the same rate as other patents, that such litigation has tripled in the period from 1985–2000, and that litigation tends to consume time and resources that might otherwise be spent in marketing technology and establishing licenses. *See* Scott Shane & Deepak Somaya, *The Effects of Patent Litigation on University Licensing Efforts*, 63 J. ECON. & BEHAV. ORG. 739, 740–41 (2007).

[111] Specifically, we gleaned our cases from four sources: (1) searches of the U.S. Patent Quarterly (USPQ) database for cases where a university was a party to the litigation, (2) searches of the Derwent LitAlert database for cases where a university was a litigation party, (3) searches of general news databases for discussions of university-related patent litigation, and (4) running the patent numbers for all university software patents in our database against the LitAlert database. All inquiries were conducted through September 2006. When we found cases of interest, we used PACER docket records to supplement our inquiry. In general, our discussion of cases is unlikely to be biased based on underinclusiveness. The USPQ database is underinclusive to the extent that it contains information only about cases from which a written order has emerged. Although the LitAlert database is supposed to include all cases involving a patent, it actually includes a little more than half of such cases. *See* Deepak Somaya, *Strategic Determinants of Decisions Not to Settle Patent Litigation*, 24 STRATEGIC MGMT. J. 17, 21–22

determined whether the software patents in our sample were litigated at rates higher (or lower) than the nonsoftware patents in our sample.[112]

With respect to the latter inquiry, there was no statistically significant difference in rates of litigation between the software and nonsoftware patents in our sample.[113] However, we did generate a number of case studies in which university software patents appeared to have been used in a manner that hindered, rather than promoted, commercialization. Research Corporation Technologies (RCT), a firm that is the assignee of patents from the University of Rochester, has actively pursued litigation on a group of six patents covering the so-called Blue Noise Mask printing technology.[114] This technology, which was developed at the University of Rochester and assigned to RCT under a technology evaluation and commercialization agreement dating back to 1953, allows for high-quality "half-tone" printing.[115] It is used by firms ranging from Hewlett-Packard to Microsoft.[116] The firm's website emphasizes the patent suits it has brought against Hewlett-Packard, Epson, and Microsoft and "invites current and potential users of this landmark technology to contact [RCT] about licenses under RCT's patent rights."[117] The lawsuits against Hewlett-Packard and Epson were settled in 1999 and 2001, respectively.[118] At the time of writing, the litigation against Microsoft is ongoing.[119]

In 2003 MIT and its exclusive licensee, Akamai, were involved in lawsuits against two firms, Speedera Networks Inc. and C&W Wireless Internet Services, that allegedly infringed the MIT/Akamai patent on software for decreasing congestion and delay in accessing Web pages on the internet.[120] The Akamai technology, which was launched in 1999 at the height of the "dot-com" boom, was similar to technologies developed by other firms before Akamai.[121] The district court granted a permanent injunction on finding that the patent was valid and had been infringed.[122] On appeal, however, the Court of Appeals for the Federal Circuit determined that

(2008). However, there is no reason to believe the underinclusiveness is biased in favor of, or against, software patent litigation.

112 This patent search includes all cases filed before September 2006. As noted earlier, although this database is underinclusive, there is no reason to believe its underinclusiveness is biased in favor of or against software patent litigation. These results are available on request.

113 In part, this may be because the total numbers (five software cases and forty-six nonsoftware cases filed with respect to the patents in our sample) were small.

114 *See* Research Corporation Technologies, Licensing: Blue Noise Mask, http://www.rctech.com/licensing/lic-blue-noise-mask.php (last visited Apr. 21, 2009).

115 *See id.*

116 *See id.*

117 *See id.*

118 *See id.*

119 Research Corp. Techs. v. Microsoft Corp., No. CV-01–658-TUC-MLR, 2006 U.S. Dist. LEXIS 66875 (D. Ariz. June 13, 2006), *vacated*, 536 F.3d 1246, 1247 (Fed. Cir. 2008).

120 *See* Akamai Techs., Inc. v. C&W Internet Servs., 344 F.3d 1186, 1188–89 (Fed. Cir. 2003).

121 *Id.* at 1193 (quoting *Akamai* brief noting this point).

122 *Id.* at 1188.

the broadest claims of the patent were invalid, because the C&W software actually predated them.[123]

In other cases, university patents have been asserted for large damage awards (usually for the statutory maximum of six years of past infringement) immediately before they were about to expire. For example, MIT and an exclusive licensee, Electronics for Imaging, have sued ninety-two firms, including Microsoft and IBM, alleging infringement of a patent covering image-editing software.[124] This lawsuit was filed in December 2001, six months before the patent was set to expire.[125] The technology in question is a color imaging method that can be applied to any system that produces color pictures.[126] Similarly, in March and May 2005, a few months before the relevant patent was due to expire, the University of Texas filed three lawsuits against forty-two electronics manufacturers alleging infringement on a software patent that allows text messaging through a standard telephone keypad.[127] In some cases, the patent in question was not due to expire immediately, but was nonetheless relatively old. In 2002, for example, Cornell sued Hewlett-Packard over a 1989 patent obtained by a Cornell professor for a technique that accelerates a computer's processing speed.[128] Similarly, a 2001 suit by MIT against Lockheed-Martin involved a 1989 patent on systems for analyzing acoustic waveforms.[129]

In all of these cases, commercialization by firms other than the university licensee was going forward, and patent rights/exclusive licenses did not appear to have been necessary to facilitate "technology transfer."[130] Moreover, there is no evidence in these cases that the other firms' development efforts were "free-riding" on licensees' investments.[131] In fact, in at least three of these cases, the patent had not (apparently) been licensed at all.[132] Contrary to the spirit of Bayh-Dole, these patents

[123] *Id.* at 1194–95. Even the narrower claims were found valid only because the Federal Circuit required C&W to establish that there be a "suggestion or motivation to combine" prior-art references. *Id.* at 1196. This "suggestion" test has been controversial, and the rigid application of it was rejected by the Supreme Court in *KSR* v. *Teleflex*, 550 U.S. 398, 418 (2007).

[124] Mass. Inst. of Tech. v. Abacus Software, 462 F.3d 1344, 1349 (Fed. Cir. 2006).

[125] *Id.*

[126] In April 2002, MIT and EFI expanded their complaint to include 214 defendants. In the course of litigation, plaintiffs settled with some defendants and dismissed their claims against others, so that only four remained: Corel, Microsoft, Roxio, and MGI Software. *Id.* at 1344. As discussed further, the Federal Circuit overturned a district court claim construction that favored the defendants in this case. *See infra* note 142 and accompanying text.

[127] Bd. of Regents v. Benq Am. Corp., 533 F.3d 1362, 1365 (Fed. Cir. 2008).

[128] *See* Cornell Univ. v. Hewlett-Packard Co., 313 F. Supp. 2d 114, 120 (N.D.N.Y. 2004).

[129] Mass. Inst. of Tech. v. Lockheed Martin Global Telecomms., Inc., 251 F. Supp. 2d 1006, 1007 (D. Mass. 2003) (granting defendant's motion for summary judgment on non-infringement).

[130] *See supra* notes 116–31 and accompanying text.

[131] *Id.*

[132] *See, e.g., Benq America Corp.*, 533 F.3d at 1365 (listing only the University of Texas as a plaintiff); *Cornell Univ.*, 313 F. Supp. 2d at 118 (naming only Cornell University and its research foundation as plaintiffs); *Lockheed Martin*, 251 F. Supp. 2d at 1007 (naming only MIT as a plaintiff).

simply allowed universities to extract rents and perhaps even hold up development efforts.[133]

Attempts to extract rents from firms that have commercialized successfully may be a particular concern where the case is ultimately very weak. Thus, it is notable that in a number of litigated cases, the university's argument was unequivocally rejected.[134] For example, in 2005 the University of Texas lost a case involving patents on positron emission technology (PET), a medical imaging technology that uses gamma rays to detect cancer, heart disease, brain disorders, and other health conditions.[135] The University of Texas claimed that CTI Molecular Imaging Inc., a leading provider of PET equipment, infringed two of its patents.[136] In that case, both the district court and the Federal Circuit held that the defendant did not infringe.[137] Similarly, in a suit brought by the University of California and its exclusive licensee over patented software for eliminating edge artifacts when compressing digital images, both the district court and the Federal Circuit found in 2005 that the patent in question was neither invalid nor infringed.[138] In 2003, a lawsuit by the University of Illinois against Fujitsu on software patents relating to plasma display panels resulted in a summary judgment determination that the relevant patent claims were invalid.[139] In contrast, our search found only one case in which a university's assertions regarding its patented software were largely vindicated by the court system, either in a final district court decision that was not appealed or in an appellate court decision.[140]

Even if patenting and exclusive licensing of software do not facilitate commercialization per se, one might argue that exclusive licenses to university patents are useful for software startups and that promoting such startups is a socially valuable goal.[141] But, even assuming that the "generating startups" argument has merit, the force with which it applies to software is not clear. Whereas most small biotechnology firms that receive venture financing have patents, the available empirical evidence indicates that most software startups that receive venture financing, particularly in the first round, do not have patents.[142] Moreover, although there is some evidence

[133] *See supra* note 12 and accompanying text.

[134] In the cases discussed earlier, by contrast, the university patentee lost on many of its arguments but won on some others.

[135] Bd. of Regents v. CTI Molecular Imaging, Inc., 164 F. App'x 982, 982 (Fed. Cir. 2005) (per curiam) (unpublished); *see CTI Molecular Imaging, Inc. Announces Dismissal of Lawsuit*, BIOSPACE, Feb. 28, 2005, http://www.biospace.com/news_story.aspx?News EntityId=19216020.

[136] *See CTI Molecular Imaging, Inc.*, 164 F. App'x at 982.

[137] *See id.*

[138] LizardTech. Inc. v. Earth Res. Mapping Inc., 424 F.3d 1336, 1337 (Fed. Cir. 2005).

[139] Competitive Techs. v. Fujitsu Ltd., 286 F. Supp. 2d 1161, 1209 (N.D. Cal. 2003).

[140] Mass. Inst. of Tech. v. Abacus Software, 462 F.3d 1344, 1347 (Fed. Cir. 2006).

[141] *See, e.g.*, Ashish Arora & Robert P. Merges, *Specialized Supply Firms, Property Rights, and Firm Boundaries*, 13 INDUS. & CORP. CHANGE 451, 451 (2004). Although Arora and Merges do not specifically discuss university-generated research, the logic of their argument presumably applies to such research.

[142] *See* Ronald J. Mann & Thomas W. Sager, *Patents, Venture Capital, and Software Start-ups*, 36 RES. POL'Y 193, 197 (2007). One limitation of the Mann and Sager data, however, is that it includes only the

that small software firms with patents tend to fare better than firms without such patents,[143] the evidence also indicates that the disparity is much less significant than that between biotechnology firms with and without patents.[144] At a minimum, the "generating startups" argument for patenting software is less compelling than it is for biotechnology. In any event, in many of the cases we found, the university was suing on its own behalf; it did not appear to have found a licensee.[145]

Of course, litigated cases are not likely to be representative of all university software patents. There are certainly cases of successful commercialization where the firm in question did have an exclusive license to a university patent. The company Google, which was the exclusive licensee of a patent assigned to Stanford,[146] is a prominent example, as is RSA Security, the exclusive licensee of various data-encryption patents assigned to MIT.[147] Moreover, as noted earlier, university software patents do not appear to be litigated at rates significantly different from those of university patents in other fields.[148] Thus, we cannot state unequivocally that the incidence of holdup in the software patent context is higher than that for university patents in other fields.

Nonetheless, there is reason to believe that holdup is more likely in software than in other fields, mainly because patents and exclusive licenses are less likely to be important for commercialization in this field than in others. To put the point another way, the ratio of false positives (patenting and giving an exclusive license when it is not necessary for commercialization) to false negatives (failing to patent and giving an exclusive license when it is necessary for commercialization) is likely to be higher in software than in the life sciences. In this regard, it bears mention that some of the most successful cases of software commercialization have not involved patents and exclusive licenses. For example, a number of unpatented Stanford programs have been widely adopted by the industry: Both MINOS, a linear and nonlinear optimization program, and Genscan, a gene structure prediction program, have been used (via a copyright license) by dozens of different commercial firms.[149]

patents that software firms hold in their own names. *Id.* It does not include patents to which firms may have exclusive licenses. *Id.* Another, perhaps more important, limitation is that the Mann and Sager study firms received venture financing during the 1997–99 "bubble" years, before the 2001 market crash. *Id.* at 195.

143 *See id.* at 194–204; *see also* Cockburn & MacGarvie, *supra* note 49, at 33–34 (finding that in software markets where patenting is intense, entry for firms with patents is easier than entry for firms without patents).

144 Mann & Sager, *supra* note 142, at 194–204.

145 *See, e.g.*, Cornell Univ. v. Hewlett-Packard Co., 313 F. Supp. 2d 114, 118 (N.D.N.Y. 2004); Mass. Inst. of Tech. v. Lockheed Martin Global Telecomms., Inc., 251 F. Supp. 2d 1006, 1007 (D. Mass. 2003).

146 Exclusive Patent License Agreement Dated July 2, 2001 Between Google and Stanford, http://www.techagreements.com/agreement-preview.aspx?num=66564 (last visited Apr. 21, 2009).

147 *See* RSA Security Inc. Company History, http://www.fundinguniverse.com/ company-histories/RSA-Security-Inc-Company-History.html (last visited Apr. 21, 2009). Whether patents and exclusive licenses were particularly important to commercial success in these cases is unclear, however.

148 *See supra* note 115 and accompanying text.

149 *See* Katherine Ku, *Software Licensing: Stanford's Approach*, Computing Res. News, Jan. 2002, at 3, 8.

V. THE WAY FORWARD

As the Stanford example suggests, models of successful software commercialization absent patents are possible. More generally, the future of university software ownership may not be one in which universities are using patents as holdup opportunities.

A. *The Impact of* eBay *v.* MercExchange *and* In re Bilski

As an initial matter, the holdup threat that patentees can wield may have been mitigated by the Supreme Court's decision in *eBay Inc.* v. *MercExchange, L.L.C.*[150] In that case, the Court made it clear that permanent injunctive relief is not automatic on a finding of patent infringement.[151] Rather, the plaintiff must prove each element of the traditional four-factor test for permanent injunctive relief: (1) that it has suffered irreparable harm; (2) that remedies available at law, such as monetary damages, are inadequate to compensate for that harm; (3) that the balance of hardship between the patentee and infringer argues in favor of a remedy in equity; and (4) that the public interest would not be disserved by a permanent injunction.[152] Although the Supreme Court opinion explicitly addresses only permanent injunctive relief,[153] lower courts have interpreted this ruling as raising the burden faced by plaintiffs in requests for preliminary injunctive relief.[154] The application to preliminary injunctive relief is important because, as illustrated by the famous $612.5 million settlement that RIM, the maker of the BlackBerry device, paid on patents that had been seriously questioned by the PTO,[155] even the threat of a preliminary injunction – before validity and infringement have been proven – can be used to extract large settlements.

Lower court cases interpreting *eBay*, particularly in the context of permanent injunctive relief, have tended to emphasize that irreparable harm should be presumed, and injunctive relief is thereby available, where the patentee and the infringer are direct competitors; in that case, infringement is likely to cause the patentee to lose market share and profits.[156] In an instructive opinion, the *eBay* district court noted on remand that irreparable harm may also be found where a patentee is seeking

[150] 547 U.S. 388 (2006).

[151] *Id.* at 391–93.

[152] *Id.*

[153] *Id.* at 394.

[154] *See* The Fire of Genius, Injunction (Dec. 31, 2007), http://www.thefireofgenius. com/injunctions/ (noting that, as of December 31, 2007, twelve cases had cited *eBay* in denying requests for preliminary injunction).

[155] *See supra* note 10 and accompanying text.

[156] For cases emphasizing direct competition when discussing irreparable harm, see generally Smith & Nephew, Inc., v. Synthes, 466 F. Supp. 2d 978, 983 (W.D. Tenn. 2006), *appeal dismissed*, 269 F. App'x 972 (Fed. Cir. 2008); Tivo Inc. v. Echostar Commc'ns Corp., 664 F. Supp. 2d. 664, 669 (E.D. Tex. 2006), *aff'd in part, rev'd in part, and remanded by* 516 F.3d 1290 (Fed. Cir. 2008); z4 Techs. v. Microsoft Corp., 434 F. Supp. 2d 437, 440 (E.D. Tex. 2006), *aff'd*, 507 F.3d. 1340 (Fed. Cir. 2007); Visto Corp. v. Seven Networks Inc., No. 2:03-CV-333-TJW, 2006 WL 3741891, at *4 (E.D. Tex. Dec.

to develop its patent in partnership with others (the classic Bayh-Dole rationale).[157] In contrast, where the patentee secures revenues by approaching firms that have already developed, so as "to maximize the value of a license," monetary damages should be sufficient to compensate for infringement.[158] Thus, at least in those situations where the university patent is being asserted without a partner licensee that practices the patent in competition with infringers, one might suppose that the university's post–*eBay* bargaining leverage would be reduced.

The question of how universities should be treated for purposes of injunctive relief was the subject of a recent Federal Circuit appeal, *Commonwealth Scientific and Industrial Research Organisation* v. *Buffalo Technology Inc.*[159] Although the patentee in that case, Commonwealth Scientific and Industrial Research Organisation (CSIRO), is an Australian research institute, not a U.S. university, it generates and licenses technology in precisely the same manner as do U.S. universities.[160] Moreover, the patent in question was a software patent that covers wireless LAN technology, specifically a number of 802.11 standards.[161] In *CSIRO I* and related cases, CSIRO asserted its patent against not only Buffalo Technology but also Toshiba, SMC, 3Com, and Microsoft.[162] The district court decision granting injunctive relief to CSIRO emphasized the *eBay* Court's reluctance to categorically rule out injunctive relief for universities.[163] The court then went further, ordering injunctive relief on the theory that a failure to grant such relief would create irreparable harm by

19, 2006); Paice LLC v. Toyota Motor Corp., No. 2:04-CV-211-DF, 2006 WL 2385139, at *4 (E.D. Tex. Aug. 16, 2006), *aff'd in part, rev'd in part, and remanded by* 504 F.3d. 1293 (Fed. Cir. 2007).

157 MercExchange, L.L.C. v. eBay, Inc., 500 F. Supp. 2d 556, 572 (E.D.Va. 2007), *appeal dismissed*, 273 F. App'x 856 (Fed. Cir. 2008) & 273 F. App'x 857 (Fed. Cir. 2008). In this regard, the district court's opinion was in accord with the Supreme Court's refusal to categorically exclude universities from the possibility of injunctive relief. *See* eBay Inc. v. MercExchange, L.L.C., 547 U.S. 388, 393 (2006) ("[S]ome patent holders, such as university researchers or self-made inventors, might reasonably prefer to license their patents, rather than undertake efforts to secure the financing necessary to bring their works to market themselves. Such patent holders may be able to satisfy the traditional four-factor test, and we see no basis for categorically denying them the opportunity to do so.")

158 *MercExchange, L.L.C. v. eBay, Inc.*, 500 F. Supp. 2d at 572.

159 542 F.3d 1363 (Fed. Cir. 2008), *reh'g denied*, No. 2007–1449, 2008 U.S. App. LEXIS 25268 (Fed. Cir. 2008) (*CSIRO I*).

160 Commonwealth Scientific & Indus. Research Org. v. Buffalo Tech., Inc. (*CSIRO II*), 492 F. Supp. 2d 600, 604 (E.D. Tex. 2007), *remanded*, No. 2007–1449, slip op. at 36 (Fed. Cir. Sept. 19, 2008), *available at* http://www.cafc.uscourts.gov/opinions/07–1449.pdf.

161 *CSIRO I*, 542 F.3d at 1367.

162 Dell, Intel, and Marvell are plaintiffs in declaratory judgment actions against CSIRO. Microsoft Corp. v. Commonwealth Scientific & Indus. Research Org., 572 F. Supp. 2d 786, 792 (E.D. Tex. 2008) (describing the suits filed against Toshiba, SMC, 3com, and Microsoft). Dell, Intel, and Marvell are plaintiffs in declaratory judgment actions against CSIRO. *See* Microsoft Corp. v. Commonwealth Scientific & Indus. Research Org., Nos. 6:06 CV 549, 6:06 CV 550, 2007 WL 4376104, at *1 (E.D. Tex. Dec. 13, 2007) (describing the declaratory judgment actions brought by Dell, Intel, and Marvell against CSIRO).

163 *CSIRO II*, 492 F. Supp. 2d at 603–04 (E.D. Tex. 2007), *remanded*, No. 2007–1449, slip op. at 36 (Fed. Cir. Sept. 19, 2008), *available at* http://www.cafc.uscourts.gov/opinions/07–1449.pdf.

making it difficult for CSIRO to license its patents and thus support its research enterprise.[164] Therefore, the extent to which university patentees could continue to exercise the threat of holdup would appear to have turned on the Federal Circuit's resolution of *CSIRO I*. However, the Federal Circuit remanded the case on invalidity grounds without ruling on the issue of injunctive relief.[165]

As noted earlier, the Supreme Court recently decided the much anticipated case of *Bilski v. Kappos*. In *Bilski*, the Court held that process claims are invalid to the extent they cover material that is "abstract." Because the *Bilski* decision largely leaves open the question of how abstraction should be defined, its impact on university software patents is difficult to gauge fully. To the extent that *Bilski* has an impact, however, that impact is likely to be limited to pure software patents. Moreover, if the recitation of a computer is deemed to take a process out of the realm of the abstract, virtually all of the pure software patents in our study should pass muster.

B. *Revenue Generation Without Holdup*

Contrary to the district court's theory in *CSIRO II*, university interests in revenue generation can be achieved without the innovation-chilling threat of holdup. Specifically, the alternative of ex ante nonexclusive licensing at reasonable rates (which CSIRO allegedly *did not* attempt to do despite a promise to the Institute of Electrical and Electronics Engineers [IEEE] to license on "reasonable and nondiscriminatory" terms[166]) could be a mechanism for satisfying university interests while minimizing potential harms.[167] Although nonexclusive licenses are something of a tax on commercialization, a small royalty rate is unlikely to deter most commercialization.

Sound practical reasons may, however, counsel against nonexclusive licensing of *patents*. Although, as noted earlier, economies of scale may reduce prosecution costs for large technology transfer offices,[168] the prosecution of patents still requires some investment of money and staff time. Whereas exclusive licensees typically pay patent application costs, nonexclusive licensees generally do not.[169] Notably, however, software (particularly pure software) differs from virtually every other university

[164] *CSIRO II*, 492 F. Supp. 2d at 604.

[165] *See* Commonwealth Scientific & Indus. Research Org. v. Buffalo Tech., Inc., No. 2007–1449, slip op. at 36 (Fed. Cir. Sept. 19, 2008), *available at* http://www.cafc.uscourts. gov/opinions/07–1449.pdf.

[166] Brief of Accton Technology Corp. (Taiwan) et al. as Amici Curiae in Support of Appellants Buffalo Technology (USA), Inc. and Buffalo, Inc. and Reversal of Injunction Order at 6–7, Commonwealth Scientific & Indus. Research Org. v. Buffalo Tech., Inc., No. 2007–1449 (Fed. Cir. Sept. 19, 2008), *available at* http://www.mmblaw.com/media/news/ media.326.pdf (using RAND as an abbreviation for reasonable and nondiscriminatory).

[167] *See, e.g.*, Ku, *supra* note 151, at 8 (indicating that Stanford uses nonexclusive licenses to make software available for "modest fees").

[168] *See supra* note 100 and accompanying text.

[169] Statement from Joel B. Kirschbaum, Ph.D., UCSF Office of Technology Management, Non-exclusive Patent Licenses – Who Benefits? (on file with the North Carolina Law Review).

invention in that patents do not have to serve as the foundation of a nonexclusive licensing scheme. Copyright, which attaches without cost on creation of the software, will do the job.[170] For this reason, at least some technology transfer offices state that they are beginning to refrain from seeking patents.[171] At the University of Washington, for example, the Digital Ventures office says that it uses patenting only if there is a real need to improve the technology (presumably via an exclusive license).[172] Digital Ventures has also convinced startups to "go without a patent."[173] For example, MINOS, which is available via a nonexclusive copyright license, is one of Stanford's largest money generators.[174]

Because copyright has been interpreted by the courts to cover little more than source code,[175] it generally does not, by itself, confer a great deal of power. For this reason, commentators concerned about the negative effects of strong proprietary rights have typically focused on patents. Even so, firms appear to be willing to license software because they do not want to bear the costs of independent creation.

Even nonexclusive copyright licensing with relatively low fees, however, can be problematic for nonprofit researchers. Thus, universities that want to balance the goal of academic access with revenue generation, such as the University of Washington, are assessing which licenses and royalty structures are appropriate for which situations.[176] The technology transfer offices at the University of Washington, the University of California at Berkeley, and Stanford University have all embraced the idea of dual licenses that give relatively inexpensive access to the nonprofit sector, but allow for revenue generation from the commercial sector.[177] Indeed, Stanford's lucrative MINOS business software program is available via a dual copyright license – the commercial use costs more than ten times as much as the academic use.[178]

C. *Evolving Policies at "Pro-Patent" Institutions?*

Our research has also generated some evidence of evolving policies at institutions that have historically sought large numbers of software patents. In 2004, the University of

[170] *See* Ku, *supra* note 151, at 8.

[171] *See* Frequently Asked Questions, Office of Intellectual Property and Industry Research Alliances, University of California, Berkley, http://ipira.berkeley.edu/page.php? nav=75 (last visited Apr. 21, 2009).

[172] E-mail from Charles Williams, Director, Tech. Transfer, Univ. of Or., to Arti K. Rai, Prof., Duke Univ. Sch. of Law (Sept. 2, 2005 01:19 EST) (on file with the North Carolina Law Review).

[173] *Id.*

[174] Telephone Interview with Katherine Ku, *supra* note 89.

[175] *See supra* note 42 and accompanying text.

[176] *See Meet Charles Williams*, Ingenuity, Summer 2004, at 1, 2, *available at* http://depts.washington.edu/techtran/aboutus/Newsletter/Summer04.pdf.

[177] *See, e.g.*, Frequently Asked Questions, *supra* note 175.

[178] *See* Stanford Business Software Inc., Minos 5.5, http://www.sbsi-sol-optimize.com/asp/sol_product_minos.htm (last visited Apr. 21, 2009).

California at Berkeley announced a policy that appeared to give a relatively strong endorsement to the open source model. In this new policy, the Berkeley Technology Transfer Office states that it will work with researchers who want to release their code under an open source model.[179] Although it is not clear whether researchers have the final say in cases of conflict, the new policy appears encouraging toward open source. Berkeley has also developed, and encourages researchers to use, an "academic" license, under which source code is made available free of charge to academic institutions and nonprofits, while being made available for a fee to commercial users.[180] In general, the new Berkeley policy appears to encourage the possibility of releasing software under different types of licenses for different purposes.

Moreover, although the University of Washington, Georgia Tech, and Carnegie Mellon have a significant software patent presence, this level of patenting may not represent a continuing pattern. Current technology transfer officials assert that they promote other models of software ownership. In fiscal year 2005, the University of Washington's Digital Ventures office generated 90% of its revenue from copyright licensing.[181] The Digital Ventures website features a large variety of unpatented software that can be secured for commercial use through an online license with a standard rate.[182] Like Berkeley, the University of Washington also encourages "forking" in its licenses – licenses in which software (and underlying source code) is made available free of charge for certain uses and available for a fee for other uses.[183] Officials at Georgia Tech's technology licensing office note that they oversee dozens of open source-type software licenses each year and that, given the short technology life cycle in the software industry, algorithm patents are often not very valuable.[184] Finally, at Carnegie Mellon, the current technology transfer team states that it almost never patents unless another entity is willing to pay for such patenting.[185]

Furthermore, information technology can substantially facilitate the task of low-transaction cost, nonexclusive licensing. Universities such as Stanford already make software like MINOS available through simple web-based interfaces.[186] Several dozen universities are currently participating in the Kauffman Foundation's web-based I-Bridge project, which aims to reduce the transaction costs associated with

[179] Frequently Asked Questions, *supra* note 175 (discussing open source options available on Berkeley's software disclosure form).
[180] *See id.*
[181] E-mail from Charles Williams, *supra* note 176.
[182] University of Washington, Digital Ventures: Express Licensing Program, http://depts.washington.edu/ventures/UW_Technology/Express_Licenses/ (last visited Apr. 21, 2009).
[183] *Id.*
[184] Telephone Interview with Kevin Wozniak, Interim Dir. of Tech. Licensing, Ga. Tech. Research Corp. (Sept. 1, 2005).
[185] Telephone Interview with Carl P. Mahler II, *supra* note 98.
[186] *See* Minos 5.5, *supra* note 182.

licensing: Many of the projects available on the I-Bridge site represent software.[187] Additionally, some large technology firms have decided to sponsor software projects at universities under an explicit "open collaboration" model.[188] In 2005, four technology firms (IBM, Hewlett-Packard, Intel, and Cisco) announced a set of "Open Collaborative Research" principles under which certain types of sponsored research in software would be made freely available.[189] IBM is now embarking on specific software projects at seven universities under the rubric of these principles.[190]

D. *The Role of Open Source*

The related question of using copyright to promote open source within the university is an interesting one. As we have noted, some universities have long embraced open source, and these universities tend to have smaller numbers of pure software patents.[191] But even among technology transfer officials sympathetic to the goals of open source, some mention difficulties that open source may create in the university setting.[192] For example, faculty may prefer open source as a method of distribution, not because of ideological commitment but because open-source–related consulting revenues, unlike licensing royalties, do not have to be shared with the university.[193] Indeed, at least one prominent technology transfer officer (who preferred to remain anonymous) believes that some faculty make software open source for the purpose of attracting widespread interest, but have every intention of asserting proprietary rights over the source code at some later point.[194] Additionally, software is often developed by groups, and technology transfer officers sometimes find themselves in the middle of disputes among group members about the best open source mechanism to use (or, indeed, whether open source should be used at all).[195] Technology transfer officers are also wary that particular types of open source licenses will conflict with

[187] Ibridge, http://www.ibridgenetwork.org/ (search "Search Innovations" for "software") (last visited Apr. 21, 2009) (listing participating organizations).

[188] *See* Lohr, *supra* note 17.

[189] *Id.*

[190] *Id.* These universities are Berkeley, Carnegie Mellon, Georgia Tech, the University of Illinois, Rensselaer, Stanford, and the University of Texas, Austin.

[191] *See supra* notes 82–88 and accompanying text.

[192] *See supra* notes 81–88 and accompanying text.

[193] E-mail from Patrick Jones, Director, Office of Tech. Transfer, Univ. of Ariz., to Arti K. Rai, Prof., Duke Univ. Sch. of Law (Apr. 3, 2004) (on file with the North Carolina Law Review).

[194] This technology transfer officer did not specify precisely how a faculty member would assert proprietary rights. In the context of a viral license, one mechanism for doing so would be to "fork" the license. One prong of the license would remain viral, while the other, made available to paying customers, would not be viral in character. The software producer MySQL has adopted this strategy. *See* MySQL, Commercial License for OEMS, ISVs, and VARs (Oct. 9, 2008), http://www.mysql.com/about/legal/licensing/oem/.

[195] Telephone Interview with Lita L. Nelsen, *supra* note 90; Telephone Interviews with Charles Williams, *supra* note 96.

obligations to sponsors, including the federal government under Bayh-Dole.[196] Thus, to the extent funding agencies are interested in an open source approach because they think such an approach is likely to produce better software, they need to be aware of possible institutional impediments.

One final point bears emphasis. Because our quantitative data extend only to the late 1990s, we cannot say that university software holdings have continued to grow. Indeed, as noted, technology transfer officers from universities with significant software patent holdings, such as the University of Washington and Carnegie Mellon, state that they are now quite receptive to nonpatent-based modes of technology transfer.[197] Whether university patenting and licensing practices are currently different from practices in the late 1990s would be a valuable subject for further research. Even if filing practices have changed, however, the existing stock of software patents may represent a lucrative source of revenues when asserted against firms that have commercialized successfully. The extent to which such holdup strategies are successful may depend on how the *CSIRO* line of cases are resolved.

CONCLUSION

In this chapter, we have presented the first systematic investigation of university software ownership and litigation. We found that software patents represent a significant and growing percentage of university patent holdings. Moreover, our qualitative results and research from a complementary econometric analysis suggest that universities have followed a one-size-fits-all approach: Those with higher patent propensities in other fields also tend to patent more software. From a policy standpoint, this finding suggests a problem. Software – and particularly pure software – is likely to follow a different commercialization path than invention in other fields. Therefore, patenting and exclusive licensing of software may yield a higher proportion of situations where the exclusive licensee uses a patent to hold up an entity that has successfully commercialized without the need for an exclusive license. Moreover, even if the goal is not promoting commercialization per se, but promoting startups, exclusive patent licenses are not necessarily critical to that goal.

To be sure, university practices with respect to software are not uniform. For example, universities that have policies friendly to open source are less likely to patent pure software. Moreover, universities may in the future move away from patenting and exclusive licensing of software. However, the lingering impact of a substantial

[196] In theory, under Bayh-Dole, if the university and researcher choose not to patent, the government has the option of patenting. Bayh-Dole Act of 1980, Pub. L. No. 96–517, 94 Stat. 3015 (codified as amended at 35 U.S.C. §§ 200–11 (2006)). Whether a decision to release software under an open source license represents an unwarranted interference with the government's option remains an open question, at least in theory. In practice, however, we are unaware of any situation where a decision to release software under an open source license has interfered with an agency's desire to patent.

[197] *See supra* notes 185–89 and accompanying text.

university portfolio of patents , some of which has been licensed exclusively, may continue to be felt in socially unproductive litigation.

APPENDIX

Questions for Technology Transfer Officers

1) Is there an official university policy regarding ownership and dissemination of software and software-based inventions? If yes, what is it?
2) Are there more informal guidelines or norms that govern ownership and dissemination of software or software-based inventions? If yes, what are they?
3) How does the technology transfer office decide whether it should seek a patent on software or software-based inventions?
4) What is the university's policy, if any, toward open source software?
5) Are there any trends or changes in university policy toward ownership of software or software-based inventions that are worthy of note?
6) Have you had any conflicts with faculty members regarding how software or software-based inventions should be owned or disseminated? In cases of conflict, who makes the determination?

Questions for Academics/Graduate Students

1) Are you aware of an official university policy regarding ownership and dissemination of software and software-based inventions? If yes, what is it?
2) Are you aware of informal guidelines or norms that govern ownership and dissemination of software or software-based inventions? If yes, what are they?

TABLE 11.A1. *Comparison of bessen-hunt keyword-based classification of software patents with our classification*

Bessen-hunt classification	Our classification: Non SW	SW	Total
Non SW	2,325	202	2,527
	92.01	7.99	100
	91.32	51.01	85.89
SW	221	194	415
	53.25	46.75	100
	8.68	48.99	14.11
Total	2,546	396	2,942
	86.54	13.46	100
	100	100	100

TABLE 11.A2. *Comparison of graham-mowery IPC-based classification of software patents with our classification*

Graham-mowery IPC classification	Our classification		
	Non SW	SW	Total
Non SW	2,544	341	2,885
	88.18	11.82	100
	99.92	86.11	98.06
SW	2	55	57
	3.51	96.49	100
	0.08	13.89	1.94
Total	2,546	396	2,942
	86.54	13.46	100
	100	100	100

3) Do you know how the technology transfer office decides whether it should seek a patent on software or software-based inventions?
4) Are you aware of any university policy toward open source software? If yes, what is it?
5) Are there any trends or changes in university policy toward ownership of software that are worthy of note?
6) Have you had any conflicts with the technology transfer office regarding how software or software-based inventions should be owned or disseminated? In cases of conflict, who makes the determination?
7) Do you produce or use open source software?
8) Do you generally disclose software or software-based inventions to the technology transfer office?

TABLE 11.A3. *Comparison of graham-mowery USPC-based classification of software patents with our classification*

Graham-mowery USPC classification	Our classification		
	Non SW	SW	Total
Non SW	2,541	328	2,869
	88.57	11.43	100
	99.80	82.83	97.52
SW	5	68	73
	6.85	93.15	100
	0.20	17.17	2.48
Total	2,546	396	2,942
	86.54	13.46	100
	100	100	100

12

The Individual Inventor Motif in the Age of the Patent Troll†

*Christopher A. Cotropia**

INTRODUCTION

The garage inventor is as American as apple pie.[1] We enjoy stories of independent inventors, working against all odds to provide society with amazing technological

† Editors' Note: This chapter was written prior to the passage of the Leahy-Smith America Invents Act, Pub. L. No. 112-29, 125 Stat. 284 (2011). However, the provisions of the America Invents Act are mostly a subset of previous patent reform bills, and many of the themes discussed in this chapter are directly applicable to the legislative history of the Act.

* Professor of Law, Intellectual Property Institute, University of Richmond Law School. Thanks to Kevin Collins, Jim Gibson, Jack Preis, Arti Rai, Josh Sarnoff, and the participants at the Patents and Entrepreneurship in Business and Information Technologies symposium hosted at George Washington University Law School for their comments and suggestions on an earlier draft. Special thanks to the Ewing Marion Kauffman Foundation, the Microsoft Corporation, and the George Washington University Law School Intellectual Property Center for the research grant that supported the writing of this chapter. A version of this chapter was originally published in the *Yale Journal of Law and Technology*. *See* Christopher A. Cotropia, *The Individual Inventor Motif in the Age of the Patent Troll*, 12 YALE J.L. & TECH. 52 (2009).

[1] *See* Mark D. Janis, *Patent Abolitionism*, 17 BERKELEY TECH. L.J. 899, 910 (2002); Michael J. Meurer, *Inventors, Entrepreneurs, and Intellectual Property Law*, 45 HOUS. L. REV. 1201, 1202–03 (2008).

An important point of clarification needs to be made up front concerning this chapter's use of the term "individual inventor." Although this term clearly includes individuals, who invent by themselves, the term has also been used in the literature to include small businesses and entrepreneurs. *See* Meurer, *id.*, at 1201–04 (using the terms such as "small innovative firms," "small business," "small entities," "entrepreneurs," and "inventors" interchangeably when discussing how patent law handles this class of inventors); Janis, *supra* note 1, at 920 (discussing both "independent inventors" and "small business" when exploring the "heroic inventor motif"). Even the PTO lumps these individuals together when defining "small entity." *See* 37 C.F.R. § 1.27 (2009) (including a "person, small business concern, or nonprofit organization" in the definition).

This chapter follows the same custom and includes all of these inventors when using the term "individual inventors." However, these classes of inventors have their differences, and these differences could come out in both the usage of distinct motifs (individual inventor versus small business inventor motif) and substantive impact. Such fidelity is not explored in this chapter, mainly it lumps these different inventors together, like those commentators and the PTO before, both in rhetoric and substantive analysis. I thank the editors at the *Yale Journal of Law and Technology*, particularly Molly Boyle, for raising this point.

breakthroughs. The stories are so entertaining that popular movies are made about such individuals – such as *Flash of Genius*, telling the story of Robert Kerns, the inventor of the intermittent windshield wiper system.[2] Intel has even launched an ad campaign championing the individual inventor, portraying individuals such as Alay Bhatt, the inventor of the Universal Serial Bus (USB), as modern-day rock stars.[3]

The individual inventor story generally goes as follows: A lone individual toils in her limited free time – evenings after work and perhaps the weekend – to come up with an amazing breakthrough that turns out to be incredibly beneficial to society.[4] This entrepreneur is unconstrained by both the bureaucracy of a large corporate structure and the traditional thinking in a given technological field. The drive and ingenuity of these small inventors are the life-blood of American innovation. Hard-working, creative individuals like Thomas Edison, Steve Jobs, and Bill Gates are the ones who bring about true innovations.

This "individual inventor motif" – that small inventors play a crucial role in creating revolutionary inventions and, in turn, spurring the American economy – is, for the most part, widely accepted.[5] It is perhaps strongest in those technologies where independent invention is most likely – such as the information technologies and business methods. These are technological areas where resources do not act as a high barrier to invention, and thus small inventors can easily participate.[6] The patent system has traditionally taken the individual inventor motif to heart and seen patents as a vehicle both to fuel individual inventors and protect them from large corporations.[7]

There is another, newer narrative that Americans are becoming more and more aware of – the story of the "patent troll."[8] The narrative is as follows: Patent trolls are patent holders who, while not commercializing the patented invention themselves, seek royalties from other companies who have.[9] They hold up such companies, asserting their patent rights at the right time to maximize the royalties they can get. For patent trolls, patenting is about profit, not invention.

[2] *See* FLASH OF GENIUS (2008), available at http://www.imdb.com/title/tt1054588 (last visited Mar. 21, 2011).

[3] *See* An "Intel Start" TV Ad – Sponsors of Tomorrow, http://www.youtube.com/watch?v=jqLPHrCQr2I (last visited Nov. 11, 2009). **Video has been removed by user.**

[4] *See* Meurer, *supra* note 1, at 1202–03 ("Received wisdom holds that small business plays an especially important role in the American economy in terms of job creation, and that entrepreneurs are disproportionately responsible for revolutionary innovations.").

[5] *Id.*; *see also* Janis, *supra* note 1, at 910–11.

[6] *See* John R. Allison, et al., *Software Patents, Incumbents, and Entry*, 85 TEX. L. REV. 1579, 1580–81 (2007).

[7] *See, e.g.*, J. Douglas Hawkins, *Importance and Access of International Patent Protection for the Independent Inventor*, 3 U. BALT. INTELL. PROP. L.J. 145, 148 (1995) ("Independent inventors accounted for about half of all patent filings in the United States around fifty years ago.").

[8] *See, e.g.*, Laurie J. Flynn, *Chip Maker Wins Battle, but Faces Bigger War*, N.Y. TIMES, Sept. 29, 2008, at C8 ("Patent troll is a derogatory term used to describe companies or individuals who make their money suing companies for patent infringement.").

[9] John M. Golden, *"Patent Trolls" and Patent Remedies*, 85 TEX. L. REV. 2111, 2112 (2007).

If a defendant is sued by one of these patent trolls, the alleged infringers do not have the usual retaliatory mechanism – the ability to assert their own patents in return – because the patent troll does not sell any products or offer any services that could infringe. The lack of production by the patent troll also means that society receives no benefit from the patent, just the tax of the patent troll.[10] Such "trolling" is common in the same fields that most individual inventors operate in – information technologies and business methods. These technological areas are more susceptible to holdup because many of the products are multicomponent, allowing a patent covering even the smallest part of the product to hold up the whole technology.[11] When the product is particularly valuable, even a patent on a small component can facilitate the extraction of a large rent.

The intersection of these two popular narratives – that of the individual inventor and that of the patent troll – is the focus of this chapter. Patent trolls are the targets of the current patent reform movement.[12] One of the difficulties that has plagued the push for change, however, is a definitional one: What exactly is a patent troll?[13]

This is where the individual inventor – the person who is supposed to be promoted by the patent system – comes in. The individual inventor could easily fit within some definitions of a patent troll – both are individuals who are nonproducing and monetize their patents by seeking royalty arrangements with larger companies. The biggest difference is that traditional thinking vilifies one and reveres the other.

This chapter examines this intersection to gain a better understanding of the place of the individual inventor motif in patent law. The individual inventor has been championed even before there was U.S. patent law. But how has the hunt for the patent troll affected the individual inventor motif? This chapter answers that question by looking at both the rhetorical use of the motif and the impact of substantive changes on individual inventors in all three branches of government – Congress, the U.S. Patent and Trademark Office (PTO), and the courts (particularly the Supreme

[10] *See* Mark A. Lemley & Doug Lichtman, *Rethinking Patent Law's Presumption of Validity*, 60 Stan. L. Rev. 45, 48 (2007) ("Sadly, a large and growing number of 'patent trolls' today play this exact strategy, using patents on obvious inventions quite literally to tax legitimate business activity."); Daniel J. McFeely, *An Argument for Restricting the Patent Rights of Those Who Misuse the U.S. Patent System to Earn Money Through Litigation*, 40 Ariz. St. L.J. 289, 290–91 (2008) (discussing how the patent troll "causes harm to society").

[11] Mark A. Lemley & Carl Shapiro, *Patent Hold-up and Royalty Stacking*, 85 Tex. L. Rev. 1991, 2008–09 (2007).

[12] *See* Paul J. Heald, *Optimal Remedies for Patent Infringement: A Transactional Model*, 45 Hous. L. Rev. 1165, 1199 (2008) ("To conclude, one thrust of current patent reform efforts focuses on remedies, with the most frequent object of discussion being the 'patent troll,' the nonexploiting owner of a patent whose business model is based on extracting licensing fees from unintentional infringers.").

[13] Ronald J. Mann, *Do Patents Facilitate Financing in the Software Industry?*, 83 Tex. L. Rev. 961, 1023–24 (noting that it "is difficult to discern any principled distinction between the desire of the inventor to appropriate the value of his invention and the desire of operating firms to appropriate the value of their inventions.").

Court).[14] What this chapter finds is that the individual inventor motif is incredibly resilient, at least rhetorically, remaining essentially unscathed by the introduction of the patent troll into the discourse.[15] This inquiry also unveils additional, beneficial information about the motif. For example, the motif's positive rhetoric is completely divorced from the mostly negative substantive impacts of patent law changes on individual inventors. While the rhetoric lives on, almost every recent patent law change has been to the detriment of small inventors.[16] Variations in the motif's usage also tell a great deal about the various governmental institutions' roles in the patent system – with the PTO catering the most to individual inventors and the courts being the most insulated from and apathetic toward such interests.[17]

This chapter proceeds in three parts. Part I describes the individual inventor motif and looks at the use and treatment of the motif in the patent system prior to the advent of the patent troll. Part II then examines the impact of the introduction of the patent troll on the motif's rhetorical usage and the substantive impact of patent law changes on the individual inventor. Finally, Part III explores the implications of the chapter's findings, both for the motif itself and for understanding the roles of various institutions in the patent system. Furthermore, pushes for patent reform at all three institutions have been constant over the past several years. Those who engage the patent system for reform can also learn about the motif's effectiveness from this chapter's findings.[18] The additional insight into how the different institutions operate within the patent system can help such activists further, shedding light on which arguments play better in different venues.

I. THE INDIVIDUAL INVENTOR AND THE U.S. PATENT SYSTEM

A. *The Individual Inventor Motif Defined*

Americans see the individual inventor as crucial to the production of new inventions and innovations. This view of the individual inventor, what I call "the individual inventor motif," is infused throughout much of the history of the U.S. patent system.[19] The motif's use supports the conclusion that one of the main goals of the patent system should be to assist and, in some ways, protect the individual inventor.[20]

14 *See infra* Part II.B.

15 *See infra* Part III.A.

16 *See infra* Part III.B.

17 *See infra* Part III.C.

18 *See, e.g.*, Amy Kapczynski, *The Access to Knowledge Mobilization and the New Politics of Intellectual Property*, 117 YALE L.J. 804, 838 (2008) ("The process that has led to this reform effort has also turned up significant rifts in the coalition of IP industries.").

19 The motif's origins trace back well before creation of the U.S. patent system. Janis, *supra* note 1, at 908–10 (discussing the British patent system's invocation of the individual inventor motif).

20 *Id.* at 910–12. Meurer points out that it is far from clear that patents actually help individual inventors, particularly the slightly larger small company, in obtaining patents. Meurer, *supra* note 1, at 1230–35.

The patent laws do very little to prompt this view.[21] The U.S. Constitution does identify "Inventors" – the individual creator, not corporations – as the target of the patent incentive.[22] And many of the founding fathers, the same individuals who played a significant role in shaping the U.S. patent system, were solo inventors themselves.[23] Yet, rather than resulting from any legislation, statute, or even the Constitution, invocations of the individual inventor motif in patent discourse are the product of the collective belief in the narrative itself: that small inventors are crucial to technological innovation and that the patent system should support their activities.

B. *Historic Usage of the Motif*

All three governmental branches have employed the individual inventor motif and have often made it part of their analysis of the patent system. Mark Janis noted in his discussion of what he calls the "heroic inventor motif"[24] that "[c]ommentaries and legislative studies on U.S. patent law reform in the mid-twentieth century periodically acknowledged the interests of independent inventors."[25] The PTO has also played to the motif, mainly through its separate fee structure and tailored resources for individual inventors.[26] The courts, though not as much as the legislative and administrative actors, have also given credence to the individual inventor narrative.[27]

Janis cataloged usage of the individual inventor motif in patent law in the late 1990s and early 2000s. All three branches paid homage to the individual inventor, albeit in varying degrees.

1. Legislative

In Congress, the main reform effort during the period Janis studied was the legislation that eventually passed as the American Inventor's Protection Act of 1999.[28] Key

[21] *Id.* at 1203–04 ("Only a few IP law doctrines target small firms for specific benefits. . . . ").

[22] U.S. CONST. art. I, § 8 ("To promote the Progress of Science and useful Arts, by securing for limited Times to Authors and Inventors the exclusive Right to their respective Writings and Discoveries"). The patent statutes also award patents to the named inventor, not corporations. 35 U.S.C. § 116 (2009).

[23] *See* Dana Rohrabacher & Paul Crilly, *The Case for a Strong Patent System*, 8 HARV. J.L. & TECH. 263, 270 (1995) (noting that many of nation's founding fathers were technologists).

[24] Although Janis uses the term "heroic inventor motif" versus this chapter's usage of "individual inventor motif," there is not much substantive difference between what he and I are discussing. Janis focuses more on what the individual inventor does – create a major invention – whereas I am focusing on a larger class of individuals: all individual inventors, regardless of the significance of their discovery.

[25] Janis, *supra* note 1, at 916.

[26] Janis also notes "[a]nother example comes from mid-1960's symposium commentary from PTO officials in honor of the 175th anniversary of the U.S. Patent System. A symposium article published in the *Journal of the Patent Office Society* offered a poetic ode to the 'Godly Inventor,' commencing, 'A spark ignites your restless mind, a fearless soul, it starts to grind. . . . '" *Id.* at 911–12.

[27] *Id.* at 912 ("The heroic inventor motif also manifests itself in judicial opinions.").

[28] *Id.* at 919–20.

provisions in the bill dealt with the publication of the patent application prior to issuance.[29] The proposed legislation changed the long-standing practice that kept applications secret until the patent was allowed and issued.

As originally proposed the legislation would publish all applications eighteen months after filing.[30] Janis noted that this publication requirement met strong resistance from the individual inventors' lobby, which argued that early publication would essentially lead to theft of the small inventor's ideas by large corporations.[31] As William P. Parker, president of the Vermont Inventors Association, put it, "[t]he idea-thieves can make money from the idea before the patent even issues and when they are challenged, are in a better position financially to defend themselves than the legitimate owner."[32]

Congress responded by amending the proposed legislation to allow patent applicants to opt out of the eighteen-month publication if the applicant was willing not to file for patents in foreign jurisdictions (which required such prepublication).[33] This amendment allowed individual inventors – who most likely would not be filing for foreign patents given the high cost and low benefit of such filing to individuals – to avoid the danger of theft from early publication. Congress also changed the name of the legislation to the American Inventor's Protection Act, explicitly paying homage to the individual inventor.[34] The legislation also included provisions to help protect small inventors from the invention-promotion business.[35] The final legislation did, however, contain provisions that individual inventors opposed,[36] but the changes made in response to their lobbying and the final naming of the act evidenced Congress's willingness to assist the individual inventor.

2. Administrative

The motif was also alive and well at the PTO in the late 1990s and early 2000s. Its website contained a special set of resources for small inventors. As Janis noted, the PTO's "Independent Inventor Resources"[37] section started with the following text: "To paraphrase our Declaration of Independence, America is the land of the free,

29 *Id.*

30 *Id.*

31 *Id.*

32 *Id.* (quoting *The Omnibus Patent Act of 1997: Hearings on S. 507 and H.R. 400 (S. Hrg. 105–95) Before Comm. on the Judiciary*, 105th Cong. 49 (1997)).

33 35 U.S.C. § 122(b), 154(b).

34 Janis, *supra* note 1, at 920.

35 35 U.S.C. § 297; Janis, *supra* note 1, at 921.

36 Janis, *supra* note 1, at 919–21; Phyllis Schlafly, *Don't Fall for "Phony Patent Reform,"* Inventors Voice, August 1, 1999, http://www.inventionconvention.com/inventorsvoice/urgentalerts/080199schlafly.html (last visited Apr. 4, 2011) ("This bill is called the American Inventors Protection Act, but should be called the Inventors Elimination Act. The independent inventors would be squeezed out and their inventions stolen from them, all for the benefit of the foreigners and the giant corporations.").

37 Janis, *supra* note 1, at 911–12.

home of the brave, and haven for the independent inventor. Nowhere else in the world does a government exist that supports its independent inventors to the extent that we do. The independent inventor is America's natural resource."[38] As it has historically, the PTO also maintained a separate fee schedule for small inventors, allowing those who qualified for small entity status to pay essentially half the usual amount for most patent application filing fees.[39]

3. Judicial

Some judges, although not as much as Congress and the PTO, have also shown some concern for individual inventors during the time period studied by Janis. For example, Judge Linn of the U.S. Court of Appeals for the Federal Circuit dissented from the court's en banc ruling on prosecution history estoppel, arguing, in part, that the majority's rigid rule "wrongfully set[] in place a regime that increases the cost and complexity of patent prosecution to the detriment of individual inventors" and "discounts the intrinsic worth in treating more fairly the individual inventor whose patent right is under administrative scrutiny."[40] Janis also identified other times when Federal Circuit judges, during this time period, discussed a particular patent rule's impact on small inventors.[41] Notably, however, the individual inventor motif never really played a deciding role in a majority decision during the time period Janis studied. Although individual judges have discussed individual inventors, the courts, in majority opinions, have not.

II. "PATENT TROLLS" AND THE INDIVIDUAL INVENTOR MOTIF

Given the persistence of the motif's presence in patent law, Janis's conclusion in 2002 that "[o]ne cannot help but expect that patent law reform debates will continue to revert periodically to narratives about the heroic inventor" seemed, at the time, incontrovertible.[42] However, recently a new "favorite villain" of the patent system has arrived – the "'patent troll' . . . one of a class of patent owners who do not provide end products or services themselves, but who do demand royalties as a price for authorizing the work of others."[43] This description arguably includes the individual inventor, perhaps jeopardizing the individual inventor's role in the patent reform debate. The question, explored later, is whether the advent of the patent troll has affected the individual inventor motif in the patent system – both the rhetorical use of the motif and the substantive impact on individual inventors.

38 *Id.* (quoting the website as it appeared on Dec. 20, 2001).

39 Muerer, *supra* note 1, at 1203–04.

40 Festo Corp. v. Shoketsu Kinzoku Kogyo Kabushiki Co., 234 F.3d 558, 620 (Fed. Cir. 2000) (en banc) (Linn, J., concurring in part and dissenting in part).

41 *See* Janis, *supra* note 1, at 913–14 (citing examples in the on-sale bar, public use bars, and remedies areas).

42 *Id.* at 922.

43 Golden, *supra* note 9, at 2112.

A. *Patent Trolls and the Current Patent Reform Movement*

A major concern of current patent reformists is patent holdup.[44] A patentee has a patent on a given product, or more likely on a single component of a given product, and uses that patent to hold up the product and its producer after the producer has made a significant investment getting the product to market.[45] This holdup situation is particularly problematic when the patent holder is a nonproducer.[46] That is, the patentee does not manufacture the patented invention herself. This exacerbates the situation because society does not gain anything from the patentee herself because the product does not go to market, and the alleged infringer has little recourse, because the common counterstrategy of threatening the patent holder with patent infringement is often useless.[47]

1. The Patent Troll

The patentees who are nonproducing and engage in holdup behavior have been labeled "patent trolls."[48] Patent troll activity is generally frowned on because the trolls act only as "tollkeepers" on the road of innovation.[49] Patent trolls tax innovation by extracting licensing revenue without giving back anything in return.[50] Instead, "[b]y acquiring [patent] claims and threatening or pursuing litigation, the patent trolls seek and often receive economic settlements from genuine innovators and producers that greatly exceed the true economic value of the patents in question."[51] The holdup is "harmful rent-seeking," extracting more value than what the patent is worth.[52]

Modern patent reform efforts have been directed toward solving the patent troll/holdup problem. Two of the initial reports that sparked the modern patent reform movement – the Federal Trade Commission's 2003 report on innovation and competition and the National Research Council's 2004 study of the patent system – both identified holdup as a significant problem of the U.S. patent

44 Lemley & Shapiro, *supra* note 11, at 2008–09.

45 *Id.*

46 *Id.*

47 There is, however, some societal value even in a patent being used by a patent troll – value in the information disclosed in the patent itself, for example. *See* Jeanne C. Fromer, *Patent Disclosure*, 94 Iowa L. Rev. 539, 547–550 (2009).

48 *See, e.g.*, Jeremiah Chan & Matthew Fawcett, *Footsteps of the Patent Troll*, 10 Intell. Prop. L. Bull. 1, 5 (2005); Robert P. Merges, *Introductory Note to Brief of Amicus Curiae in* eBay v. MercExchange, 21 Berkeley Tech. L.J. 997, 997 (2006).

49 Robert P. Merges & Richard R. Nelson, *On the Complex Economics of Patent Scope*, 90 Colum. L. Rev. 839, 907 (using the term "tollkeeper[]" to identify a patentee that does not assist the real-world development of the invention but simply takes license revenue for that development).

50 *See* Brief of Amicus Curiae Yahoo! Inc. in Support of Petitioner, eBay Inc. v. MercExchange, L.L.C., 547 U.S. 388 (2006) (No. 05–130), at 2–3.

51 *Id.* at 6–7.

52 Michael J. Meurer, *Controlling Opportunistic and Anti-Competitive Intellectual Property Litigation*, 44 B.C. L. Rev. 509, 509 (2003); *see also* Lemley & Shapiro, *supra* note 11.

system.[53] Recent books on the problems with the patent system also identify holdup and the patent troll as critical components of the current patent problems.[54]

2. Definitional Problems

The hunt is on, but it faces a significant hurdle recognized by many: Who exactly is being hunted? Some view a patent troll as anyone having certain inherent characteristics – never practicing the patented invention and seeking only to license it.[55] Others go further with the definition, looking for more specific actions, such as asserting patents against practicing entities when a holdup situation is highly possible in order to maximize royalties.[56]

It has become difficult to pick a definition that is not over- or underinclusive. For example, as Mark Lemley points out, under an overly broad definition, most universities can be viewed as patent trolls.[57] Universities rarely, if ever, actually commercialize the patented technology they invent.[58] Instead, universities seek to transfer their inventions to others and, in the process, may assert patents in the hope of seeking royalties.[59] Such actions could be defined as the work of a patent troll, but university-originated inventions, purposively spurred in part by the patent system, are seen by most as beneficial, not problematic.[60]

Just like universities, individual inventors can also arguably fall under the umbrella of patent trolls.[61] Garage inventors do not have the means to commercialize. Their main goal from the beginning, most likely, is to sell their patented technology to a larger company who has the capability to bring it to market. In the process, they may have to assert their patent to obtain such a royalty. These characteristics and actions are part of the individual inventor's narrative, but now they are also part of

53 *See* Fed. Trade Comm'n, To Promote Innovation: The Proper Balance of Competition and Patent Law and Policy (2003), http://www.ftc.gov/os/2003/10/innovationrpt.pdf; Nat'l Research Council, A Patent System for the 21st Century (Stephen A. Merrill et al. eds., 2004).

54 *See, e.g.*, James Bessen & Michael J. Meurer, Patent Failure: How Judges, Bureaucrats, and Lawyers Put Innovators at Risk 160 (2008) (noting that "'troll-like' behavior is certainly a problem"); Dan L. Burk & Mark A. Lemley, The Patent Crisis and How Courts Can Solve It 28–30 (2009).

55 Brenda Sandburg, *Trolling for Dollars*, Law.com, July 30, 2001, http://www.law.com/jsp/PubArticle.jsp?id=900005370205 (describing the term as defined by its creator, Peter Detkin, then assistant general counsel for Intel Corporation).

56 Mark Lemley, *Are Universities Patent Trolls?*, 18 Fordham Intell. Prop. Media & Ent. L.J. 611, 630 (2008) ("Instead of singling out bad actors, we should focus on the bad acts and the laws that make them possible. We will solve the troll problem not by hunting down and eliminating trolls, but by hunting down and eliminating the many legal rules that facilitate the capture by patent owners of a disproportionate share of an irreversible investment.").

57 *Id.* at 629.

58 *Id.*

59 *Id.*

60 *Id.* at 629–30.

61 *See, e.g.*, Andrew Beckerman-Rodau, *The Supreme Court Engages in Judicial Activism in Interpreting the Patent Law in* eBay, Inc. v. MercExchange, L.L.C., 10 Tul. J. Tech. & Intell. Prop. 165, 173 (2007) ("[S]o-called patent trolls are often independent inventors or small startups.").

that of the patent troll.[62] According to one definition, a patent troll is "one of a class of patent owners who do not provide end products or services themselves, but who do demand royalties as a price for authorizing the work of others."[63] The same could be said of the individual inventor.

As Ronald Mann puts it, "any effort to design a suitable definition of the term 'troll' is likely to lend credence to the view that the status as a troll is in the eye of the beholder."[64] Some individual inventors will introduce real holdup problems, and thus are legitimately patent trolls. However, a significant number will certainly not.[65]

B. *The Patent Troll's Impact on the Individual Inventor Motif*

Given the focus on eradicating the patent troll and the individual inventor's similarities to a patent troll, the individual inventor motif may be in real trouble in modern patent discourse. Has the individual inventor universally become the villainous patent troll or has the motif remained unscathed (or is it sitting somewhere in between)?

This section attempts to measure the current status of the individual inventor motif in patent law in two ways. First, it examines the usage of individual inventor rhetoric by all three governmental branches to see if the motif is invoked as strongly as it was before the current emphasis on the patent troll.[66] Second, it examines major patent law changes by the three branches to see if these changes – most seeking to remedy the harms of patent trolls – negatively affect individual inventors. Examining both the rhetorical use and the substantive impact of the motif since the rise of the patent troll should clarify the current status of the individual inventor, at least in the eyes of major government actors.

1. Legislative View

The major modern patent reform bill has been before Congress in one form or another since 2005.[67] Although the specifics of the legislation proposed over the

[62] *See supra* Part II.A.

[63] Golden, *supra* note 9, at 2112.

[64] Mann, *supra* note 13, at 1023–24 (noting that "[i]t is difficult to discern any principled distinction between the desire of the inventor to appropriate the value of his invention and the desire of operating firms to appropriate the value of their inventions").

[65] *See* Marc Morgan, *Stop Looking Under the Bridge for Imaginary Creatures: A Comment Examining Who Really Deserves the Title Patent Troll*, 17 FED. CIR. B.J. 165, 177 (2008) ("[I]ndividual inventors should not be considered patent trolls. Though they do not produce their innovations, individual inventors are crucial to America's technological growth and account for 18% or more of the patent filers in the USPTO.").

[66] The study performed by this chapter can be contrasted to Janis's work. Janis's work covers a perfect, contrasting time frame – right before the reform movement that focuses on patent trolls and the major patent system reports. *See* Janis, *supra* note 1, at 913–22.

[67] Patent Reform Act of 2005, H.R. 2795, 109th Cong.

next four years varied, a majority of the amendments – from damages reform to post-grant opposition mechanisms – were meant to remedy the holdup/patent troll problem. None of the proposed legislation passed, with the 2009 version failing to be passed by either the House or Senate.[68] The Patent Reform Act of 2007 – H.R. 1908 – came the closest to becoming law – passing in the House, but failing in the Senate.[69] Thus, the discourse surrounding the proposed patent reform bills – particularly H.R. 1908 – and their substance provide insight as to Congress's current view of the individual inventor in the age of the patent troll.

A. RHETORIC. In general, the discussions surrounding pending patent reform legislation include a very positive individual inventor narrative. No one in Congress during this period questioned the need to support individual inventors or look out for their special concerns.[70] Discussions of patent trolls and holdups were kept distinct and separate from mentions of the small inventor.[71]

In fact, small inventors were affirmatively made a part of the legislative process. Almost every committee meeting on patent reform included a panelist who was herself, or represented, an individual or small inventor.[72] The House Committee on Small Business even had a full committee hearing on the impact of patent reform on small businesses.[73]

The floor debate concerning the 2007 House version of the patent reform legislation – H.R. 1908 – provides a very interesting perspective on Congress's rhetorical use of the individual inventor motif. The legislation before the House contained many provisions that were seen as hostile to small inventors.[74] H.R. 1908 would switch

68 *See* Patent Reform Act of 2009, S. 515, 111th Cong. (2009).

69 Patent Reform Act of 2007, H.R. 1908, 110th Cong., 153 Cong. Rec. H 10270, 10307.

70 *See* 153 Cong. Rec. H at 10301 (statement of Rep. Jackson-Lee) ("[W]e must always be mindful of the importance of ensuring that small companies have the same opportunities to innovate and have their inventions patented and that the laws will continue to protect their valuable intellectual property.").

71 *See Patent Trolls: Fact or Fiction?: Hearing Before the H. Subcomm. on Courts, the Internet, and Intellectual Property of the H. Comm. of the Judiciary*, 109th Cong. 4 (2006) (statement of Congressman Bass) ("Dean Kamen really works and represents what is the heart of America's economics and industrial future. He is truly an inventor, and he owns and runs one of the Nation's few really successful modern development labs.").

72 *See, e.g.*, *Patent Reform in the 111th Congress: Legislation and Recent Court Decision: Hearing Before the S. Judiciary Comm.*, 111th Cong. (2009), *available at* http://judiciary.senate.gov/hearings/hearing.cfm?id=3701 (last visited Apr. 4, 2011) (including testimony from Taraneh Maghame, vice president of a small company); *Patent Trolls*, *supra* note 72 (including the testimony of Dean Kamen, individual inventor).

73 *The Importance of Patent Reform to Small Businesses: Before H. Comm. on Small Business*, 110th Cong. (2007).

74 See, e.g., Adam J. Sedia, *Legislative Update: Storming the Last Bastion: The Patent Reform Act of 2007 and its Assault on the Superior First-to-Invent Rule*, 18 DEPAUL J. ART, TECH. & INTELL. PROP. L. 79, 79 (2007) ("The bill, currently on the Senate's legislative calendar and likely to come up for vote soon, faces heavy opposition from several interest groups, particularly small inventors and the biotechnology industry.").

the U.S. patent system from first–to-invent to first-to-file and provided for automatic publication of all patent applications at eighteen months.[75] H.R. 1908 also modified the damages provisions and established a post-grant review system.[76] Some saw these provisions as providing large companies an unfair advantage in defending against allegations of patent infringement by individual inventors.[77]

Almost everyone who spoke out against the legislation, in particular against the provisions just identified, invoked the individual inventor motif to explain the reason the legislation was harmful. For example, Reprehensive Gohmert argued as follows:

> [The legislation must be sponsored by] huge defendants who wanted to drag small entrepreneurs into dilatory situations so that their invention or component could be usurped without proper compensation, even though it might mean the bankruptcy of the inventor and the destruction of the opportunity for the little guys with the inventive vision and spirit, which actually spurred some of the greatest developments and wealth we know and have in this country.[78]

One House member, Representative Rohrabacher even went so far as to call the legislation the "Steal American Technologies Act."[79]

Those supporting the legislation did not question the need to protect the individual inventor.[80] Some said that the legislation as proposed would actually help small inventors.[81] They also promised that changes to the legislation were made or were going to be made to address the individual inventors' concerns.[82] A few supporters went a step further, framing the discussion as one of balancing – a tradeoff between

75 Patent Reform Act of 2007, H.R. 1908, 110th Cong. §§ 3, 9(a) (2007).

76 *Id.* § 6.

77 *See, e.g.*, Darren Cahr et al., *Of Pacs and Trolls: How the Patent Wars May Be Coming to a Hospital Near You*, 19 HEALTH LAW. 15, 16 n.9 (2006) ("Although large corporations argue in favor of changes that reduce the risks of patent litigation, small inventors criticize proposals that disadvantage individuals trying to enforce their patent rights while these same corporations often have significant intellectual property licensing arms.").

78 153 Cong. Rec. H 10,270, 10,278 (statement of Rep. Gohmert, Member, Crime Subcomm. of the Judiciary Comm.) ("[I]t is big companies who do not want others to have the opportunities that they did.").

79 *Id.* at 10,273–74 (statement of Rep. Rohrabacher) (noting that the legislation "would be a disaster for individual inventors").

80 *See id.* at 10,276 (statement of Rep. Lofgren) (recognizing the interests of "small inventors"); *id.* at 10,301 (statement of Rep. Jackson-Lee) ("On the other hand, Mr. Chairman, we must always be mindful of the importance of ensuring that small companies have the same opportunities to innovate and have their inventions patented and that the laws will continue to protect their valuable intellectual property.").

81 *See id.* at 10,282 (statement of Rep. Wexler) ("This bill will nurture and protect inventors, thereby promoting future Alexander Graham Bells and tomorrow's Microsofts.").

82 *See id.* at 10,279 (statement of Rep. Jackson-Lee) ("I am delighted that even though there are questions about, for example, the first-to-file over the first-to-invent, this committee saw fit to add my amendment which means that there will be periodic review so Congress will be instructed on whether or not this works on behalf of all inventors big and small.").

eradicating patent trolls and aiding the small inventor.[83] But such comments were incredibly sparse and came in a far second to pro-individual inventor commentary from those who supported the legislation.

B. SUBSTANCE. In sharp contrast to the unanimity of the rhetoric, the pending legislation, particularly the H.R. 1908 version of patent reform legislation, would negatively affect individual inventors. Most of the legislation's provisions – particularly damage reforms and the post-grant review provisions – were provisions that assisted companies to defend against allegations of infringement, particularly allegations by patent trolls.[84] Although such provisions helped those who were defendants in patent suits, they generally hurt those who would be asserting patents, especially plaintiffs with fewer resources and less sophistication, including small inventors. In addition, given the unlikelihood that they will manufacture or sell products or services, small inventors benefit more from patent strength than they do from laws that make patent defense easier. In addition to its pro-defendant provisions, the legislation also included the aforementioned shifts to first-to-file and automatic publication. Both moves were made to harmonize U.S. patent law with most foreign patent systems, but these provisions were also generally seen as harmful to individual inventors.[85]

The legislation was, however, eventually defeated. The 2009 version, which included similar, albeit not as many, anti-individual inventor provisions, has still not passed at the time of this writing.[86] And the provisions that were contained in H.R. 1908 as approved by the House and in more recent versions of the legislation include compromises to soften its impact on small inventors.[87] Some of these provisions are changes that were made during the House floor debate of H.R. 1908.[88] Accordingly, the substantive impact of the patent troll on the individual inventor

[83] *See id.* at 10,276 (statement of Rep. Lofgren) ("I represent Silicon Valley, which has a diversity of high tech. Biotech, large companies, small companies, universities, small inventors, pharmaceutical companies, we have got them all, including small inventors working out of a garage. A balanced approach to innovation is essential to all of these entities."); *id.* at 10,277 (statement of Rep. Johnson) ("In order to continue to stimulate growth and reward inventors in these various sectors, we in Congress are charged with finding the right balances between protecting inventions and stimulating innovation."); *id.* at 10,280 (statement of Rep. Jackson-Lee) ("Thus, it is very important that we take care not to harm this incubator of tomorrow's technological breakthroughs. The bill before us strikes the proper balance.").

[84] *See supra* note 76.

[85] *See supra* note 74; *but see* Karen Simon, *The Patent Reform Act's Proposed First-to-File Standard: Needed Reform or Constitutional Blunder?*, 6 J. MARSHALL REV. INTELL. PROP. L. 129, 138 n.77 (2006) (noting that the current first-to-invent regime in the United States is "costly" to small inventors because it prompts "large inventors to challenge the patents of small inventors more frequently" by filing interferences).

[86] *See* Patent Reform Act of 2009, S. 515, 111th Cong. (2009).

[87] *See* 153 Cong. Rec. H. 10,270, 10297 (statement of Rep. Issa) (offering a floor amendment to the early publication portion of H.R. 1908); *see also* Patent Reform Act of 2009, S. 515, 111th Cong. § 7 (2009) (removing the automatic publication requirement).

[88] *See* 153 Cong. Rec. at 10,297.

is currently nil, and the compromises and defeats may evidence the work of the individual inventor motif as continuing to protect small inventors in the patent system.[89]

2. Administrative View

The PTO's own literature, particularly on its website, provides insight into its view of individual inventors. Its response to comments on two rule packages also provides indication that the motif is alive and well at the PTO. This part examines both the rhetoric used by the PTO regarding individual inventors and the substantive impact of its rulemaking.

A. RHETORIC. The PTO has continued to describe the individual inventor in a positive light. Its website has an entire section devoted to resources for independent inventors.[90]

The PTO has also espoused positive rhetoric concerning individual inventors in its response to comments on one of the two rule packages issued in 2007. In the first rule package, the USPTO issued rules concerning the continuation of patent application filings and claim limitations rules that were set to go into effect on November 1, 2007.[91] The rules essentially limited the number of times a patent applicant could file for continuations of patent prosecution for a single application.[92] It also limited the number of claims per application.[93]

A significant number of the comments received by the PTO asserted that the rules would have a particularly harmful impact on small inventors or, as the PTO identifies them, small entities.[94] The PTO confronted these comments head on. It did not dispute the underlying premise that small inventors' concerns were worth addressing, but instead answered whether the rules would have a negative impact

[89] *See, e.g.*, John R. Allison et. al., *Valuable Patents*, 92 GEO. L.J. 435, 468 (2004) (discussing the success of the small inventors lobby). Another explanation, explored more in Part III.B of the chapter, is that the changes were made to protect the pharmaceutical industry, not the small inventor.

[90] *See* http://www.uspto.gov/inventors/independent/index.jsp (last visited Apr. 4, 2011).

[91] *See* Changes to Practice for Continued Examination Filings, Patent Applications Containing Patentably Indistinct Claims, and Examination of Claims in Patent Applications, 72 Fed. Reg. 46,716, 46,716 (Aug. 21, 2007) (to be codified at 37 C.F.R. pt. 1). Because of litigation over the validity of the rules, the effective date, if they ever become effective, is still uncertain. *See* Tafas v. Doll, 559 F.3d 1345, 1364–65 (Fed. Cir. 2009) (finding the claim limitation rules valid and the continuation rules invalid because they conflicted with 35 U.S.C. § 120, and remanding the case to the district court).

[92] *See* Changes to Practice for Continued Examination Filings, 72 Fed. Reg. 46,716 (Rule 78, pertaining to continuations, and Rule 114, pertaining to requests for continued examination).

[93] *See id.* (Rule 75, limiting the total number of claims per application to no more than five independent claims and twenty-five total claims, and Rule 265, describing the examination support document needed to be submitted to go beyond these limitations).

[94] *See id.* at 46,743–44, 46,745, 46,754, 46,758, 46,759–60, 46,763, 46,765–66, 46,783, 46,788, 46,793, 46,798, 46,801, 46,811, 46,824, 46,828 (containing comments concerned with the proposed rules' impact on small entities. A small entity, as defined by the PTO, includes a "person, small business concern, or nonprofit organization." 37 C.F.R. § 1.27.

on individual inventors and whether such concerns needed addressing.[95] The PTO also articulated the overall purpose of the rules as inventor-neutral.[96] It stated that the rules were meant to reduce examination backlog and improve the quality of examination across the board, not to address the patent holdup problem or, more specifically, the patent troll problem.[97]

B. SUBSTANCE. The PTO continues to adjust filing fees based on the filing entity's size.[98] Small entities still have their fees essentially cut in half as compared to other applicants.[99] The rationale is that higher fees uniquely bar individual inventors' access to the patent system because of their lack of resources.[100] The adjustment of filing fees is meant to equalize access to the patent system between large and small inventors. In addition to these fee adjustments, the PTO also made changes to the two rule packages described earlier to address substantive concerns of individual inventors.

One of the main substantive concerns with the continuation rule package was that limiting the continuations available would harm small inventors. This is because such inventors are both more likely to file continuations and have fewer resources to effectively obtain adequate patent rights when continuations are limited.[101] Individual inventors need patents earlier in the development process to secure investment. Thus, they need to separate earlier allowed claims and then continue prosecution on still-rejected claims. In addition, small inventors often cannot spend as much up front and thus need continuations to spread out their application costs.[102] The package also addressed the argument that small entities make up the majority of continuation filings.[103]

The PTO responded to these comments, as well as those from other types of inventors, by relaxing the limitation on continuations.[104] As compared to the initially

95 *See* Changes to Practice for Continued Examination Filings, 72 Fed. Reg. at 46,743–44, 46,745, 46,754, 46,758, 46,759–60, 46,763, 46,765–66, 46,783, 46,788, 46,793, 46,798, 46,801, 46,811, 46,824, 46,828.

96 *See, e.g., id.* at 46,760 ("The changes being adopted in this final rule [Rule 78] do not disproportionately impact small entities.").

97 *See* Tafas v. Doll, 559 F.3d 1345, 1350 (Fed. Cir. 2009); Changes to Practice for Continued Examination Filings, 72 Fed. Reg. 46,716.

98 *See* 37 C.F.R. § 1.16(a)(1) (2008) (setting forth the filing fee for both a regular applicant and a small entity).

99 *Id.*

100 *See* Mike R. Turner, Note, *The Future of the Corroboration Requirement in Patent Law: Why a Clear, Strict Standard Benefits All*, 2008 U. ILL. L. REV. 1319, 1344 ("[T]he government has been careful to avoid shutting the door to the patent office on small entities.").

101 Changes to Practice for Continued Examination Filings, 72 Fed. Reg. at 46,759, 46,765–66.

102 *Id.* (reporting comments asserting that "the rule changes could stifle the building of patent portfolios for small companies and cause a reduction of capital investment in these companies and in new technologies").

103 *Id.*

104 *Id.* at 46,759 ("The Office has made modifications to these proposed changes such that this final rule will permit an applicant to file two continuation applications or continuation-in-part applications, plus a single request for continued examination in an application family, without any justification.").

proposed rules, instead of one continuation, an applicant could now file two as a matter of right. To obtain further time, an applicant could in addition file a request for continued examination. Furthermore, as the PTO pointed out, small inventors can file even more than two continuations, as long as they meet the justification criteria.[105]

The PTO also conducted a study to examine the substantive impact of the continuation limitations on small inventors. It found that 2.9% of applications filed by small inventors included enough continuations to require special justification under the new rules.[106] This was in comparison to a slightly lower rate, 2.7%, for all patent applications.[107]

There was also concern about the continuation rules' requirement that divisional applications be filed during the pendency of the initial application.[108] This would prevent small inventors from spreading out their prosecution costs over the sequential filing of divisional applications, particularly as aspects of the invention became commercially viable. The PTO responded by amending the rules to allow for sequential filing of divisionals.[109]

Finally, there was an argument that the limitation on the number of claims available under the continuation rules would harm small inventors.[110] Individual inventors may need more claims than the average inventor to provide adequate protection for their inventions and cannot pay the financial and procedural price of meeting the special requirement under the rules to get more claims.[111]

The PTO responded by changing the proposed rules to allow for more claims to be filed than originally proposed.[112] It also studied the filings of small entities and found that 24.4% of the cases would exceed the amended limitation on claims, as compared to a 23.7% rate for all applicants.[113] The difference in impact on applicants as a general population and on individual inventors did not appear to be large. Finally, small entities could file an examination support document (ESD) to obtain claims beyond those initially allowed.[114] The PTO amended the rules to make this requirement less burdensome on small entities, with § 1.256(f) removing the most onerous part of the ESD – the requirement to apply prior art to the proposed claims

[105] *Id.* at 46,745 (noting that if an applicant wishes to pursue more than two continuation applications, he must file a petition "showing that the amendment, argument, or evidence sought to be entered could not have been submitted during the prosecution of the prior-filed application.").

[106] *Id.* at 46,760.

[107] *Id.*

[108] *Id.* at 46,745.

[109] *Id.* ("In response to those concerns and suggestions, § 1.78(d)(ii) as adopted in this final rule does not require that a divisional application be filed during the pendency of the initial application.").

[110] *Id.* at 46,765–66.

[111] *Id.*

[112] *Id.* at 46,788.

[113] *Id.*

[114] *Id.* at 46,788.

and to articulate why the claims are allowable over that art – exclusively for small entities.[115]

There were also substantive concerns regarding the second, more recent rule package that contained procedural changes to filing appeals to the Board of Patent Appeals and Interferences (BPAI).[116] There was discussion about whether the rules added an additional filing cost, which would significantly affect small inventors.[117] This debate arose not so much in response to comments, but from the PTO's discussion in response to the requirements of the Regulatory Flexibility Act.[118] After making some assumptions about the number of individual inventor applicants who would incur a fee for exceeding page limits, the PTO concluded that the impact would be small and that further change was unnecessary.[119]

3. Judicial View

Although the Federal Circuit is usually the first judicial body that comes to mind when discussing patent law,[120] there has been a significant amount of patent law activity at the Supreme Court during the patent troll era. Seven opinions on significant patent law areas were issued from 2006–08,[121] and in almost every single one, amicus briefs were filed asserting that individual inventor's interests were at stake. Accordingly, the following analysis focuses on the Supreme Court and looks at both

[115] *Id.* at 46,798, 46,743–44 (noting that this inclusion was also in response to the Regulatory Flexibility Act). *See also id.* at 46,798.

("A number of comments argued that the search and analysis necessary to prepare an examination support document would add significant cost to the preparation of an application, that the cost would be significantly more than the $2,500 predicted by the Office, and that this would significantly disadvantage independent inventors and small businesses.")

[116] *See* Rules of Practice Before the Board of Patent Appeals and Interferences in Ex Parte Appeals, 73 Fed. Reg. 32,938 (June 10, 2008) (to be codified at 34 C.F.R. pt. 41).

[117] *Id.* at 32,972.

[118] *Id.* at 32,969. Section 603 of the Regulatory Flexibility Act requires administrative agencies to analyze the costs of regulations to small businesses and consider alternatives to reduce the impact on such small businesses. 5 U.S.C. § 603 (2006).

[119] *Id.*

("When [the assumption of the number of applicants going over the page limit] is compared to the 5,977 small entities that filed a notice of appeal with the Office in FY 2007 (21,653 notices of appeal were filed by large entities in the same period), it demonstrates that the petition fee has the potential to affect only 2.8% of the small entities filing an appeal. An effect on 2.8% of the small entities filing an appeal is not a disproportionate impact on small entities, nor is the actual number of 166 impacted small entities a substantial number.").

[120] *See* John M. Golden, *The Supreme Court as "Prime Percolator": A Prescription for Appellate Review of Questions of Patent Law*, 56 UCLA L. Rev. 657 (2009); Mark D. Janis, *Patent Law in the Age of the Invisible Supreme Court*, 2001 U. Ill. L. Rev. 387.

[121] *See* Quanta Computer, Inc. v. LG Elecs., Inc., 128 S. Ct. 2109 (2008); KSR Int'l Co. v. Teleflex Inc., 550 U.S. 398 (2007); Microsoft Corp. v. AT&T Corp., 550 U.S. 437 (2007); MedImmune, Inc. v. Genentech, Inc., 549 U.S. 118 (2007); Lab. Corp. of Am. Holdings v. Metabolite Labs., Inc., 548 U.S. 926 (2006); eBay Inc. v. MercExchange, L.L.C., 547 U.S. 388 (2006); Ill. Tool Works Inc. v. Independent Ink, Inc., 547 U.S. 28 (2006).

the rhetoric in and substantive effect of these decisions concerning the individual inventor.[122]

A. RHETORIC. In only one patent case out of the eight that the Supreme Court has issued since 2003 has the Court explicitly mentioned the individual inventor. In *eBay, Inc.* v. *MercExchange, L.L.C*, the Supreme Court held that the general four-factor test for determining whether a permanent injunction should issue must be used in patent cases.[123] Under the facts of the case, there was a question as to whether nonpracticing entities could obtain permanent injunctions.[124]

In the Court's decision, the majority rejected the categorical rule that all patentees who are both willing to license and are not commercially practicing their patents should not be awarded injunctions. The Court identified "university researchers" and "self-made inventors" as those who "may be able to satisfy the traditional four-factor test."[125] The Court essentially stated that the "self-made inventor[]" – the individual inventor – could still obtain an injunction after the *eBay* decision.

One of the concurrences also focused on the type of patent holder seeking an injunction. That concurrence, authored by Justice Kennedy and joined by Justices Stevens, Souter, and Breyer,[126] indicated that district courts should take note of "the nature of the patent being enforced and the economic function of the patent holder," and in *eBay*, the function of the patent holder was "quite unlike earlier cases," presumably because it involved a business method patent and, arguably, a patentee who was only trying to license the patent, not commercialize it.[127] The concurrence identified the existence of industries where firms use patents mainly to obtain licensing fees. Injunctions in these instances "can be employed as a bargaining tool to charge exorbitant fees to companies that seek to buy licenses to practice the patent."[128] In this context, the concurrence discussed the patent holdup problem, noting that "[w]hen the patented invention is but a small component of the product the companies seek to produce and the threat of an injunction is employed simply for undue leverage in negotiations, legal damages may well be

[122] Interestingly, there was little mention of the individual inventor by the Federal Circuit over the five years preceding the writing of this chapter. A search was done on the CTAF database on Westlaw – ("small inventor" "small inventors" "small entity" "individual inventor" "individual inventors" "individual inventor" "individual inventors" "entrepreneur" "entrepreneurs" "small entities" "small business" "small businesses" "garage inventor" "garage inventors" "start-up" "self-made inventor") & da(last 5 years) & patent! – and only one case included a discussion related to the individual inventor motif, in *Voda v. Cordis Corp.*, 536 F.3d 1311, 1329 (Fed. Cir. 2008), where the Federal Circuit dismissed Voda's argument that the denial of a permanent injunction to Voda conflicted with the provision permitting "self-made inventor[s]" to obtain injunctions in the Supreme Court's *eBay* holding.

[123] 547 U.S. 388 (2006).

[124] *Id.* at 393.

[125] *Id.*

[126] *Id.* at 396–97 (Kennedy, J., concurring).

[127] *Id.*

[128] *Id.* at 396.

sufficient to compensate for the infringement and an injunction may not serve the public interest."[129] Justice Kennedy's concurrence focused on patentees that exhibit patent-troll-like characteristics, concluding that injunctions should not be available to such individuals.

The majority took a neutral view of the individual inventor – telling district courts not to immediately conclude that a small inventor does not deserve an injunction.[130] The majority did not, however, go so far as to require that all individual inventors receive an injunction – like large firms, they have to satisfy the four-factor test. However, the concurrence authored by Justice Kennedy muddled this message by focusing on the patent troll. The concurrence encouraged district courts to watch out for patent holdup situations caused by patent holders just looking to monetize their patents. These cases, involving nonpracticing entities using patents solely for monetary purposes, signify the rise of the patent troll problem, not seen in the "earlier cases."[131] In the concurrence's view, the focus is on removing the unfair advantages injunctions give to some nonpracticing entities who seek to license – a category of patentee that is commonly comprised of individual inventors.

B. SUBSTANCE. When comparing the majority decision in *eBay* to Justice Kennedy's concurrence, the Court's rhetorical use of the individual inventor motif is inconclusive at best. The substantive story, however, is a bit clearer. Almost all of the Court's recent patent decisions have reached holdings that are detrimental to individual inventors, mainly because all the decisions essentially weaken patent rights, and it is the patent right – not the shielding from accusations of patent infringement – that benefits individual inventors the most.[132]

For example, although the majority in *eBay* expressly indicated that "self-made inventors" should not have been uniquely harmed by the Court's decision, this rhetoric has not stopped lower courts from denying injunctions to individual inventors. In fact, that language has been cited and then dismissed in a majority of cases denying injunctions to small inventors.[133] This is because the four-factor test for an injunction places small inventors at a disadvantage, particularly when read in light of Justice Kennedy's concurrence. As John Golden summarizes it,

> Despite the unanimous Court's warning against "certain expansive principles suggesting that injunctive relief could not issue in a broad swath of cases," district courts have responded in apparent lockstep to Justice Kennedy's concerns about trolls. Since the Supreme Court issued its opinion in *eBay*, district courts appear to have consistently denied permanent injunctions in cases where an infringer has

[129] *Id.* at 396–97.

[130] *Id.*

[131] *Id.* at 396.

[132] *But see* BESSEN & MEURER, *supra* note 55, at 173–77 (concluding that patents are not as valuable to individual inventors as other methods of appropriating value from their innovation).

[133] *See, e.g., Voda v. Cordis Corp.*, 536 F.3d 1311, 1329 (Fed. Cir. 2008).

contested the patent holder's request for such relief and the infringer and patent holder were not competitors.[134]

Golden continues in his analysis by noting that "[s]ystematically curtailing injunctive relief for such patent holders may inflict injury on patent trolls, but it may also victimize those classes of inventors whom patent law should be most careful to protect."[135] The class he is referencing includes individual inventors.

Many other patent decisions by the Court seem to come out against positions advocated for by individual inventors. For example, in *Microsoft Corp.* v. *AT&T Corp.*, the Court held that 35 U.S.C. § 271(f), while making the combination of a patented invention outside the United States actionable infringement in some cases, does not cover the sending of software from the United States to a foreign manufacturer who uses the software to make a U.S. patented invention abroad.[136] The argument by small companies and universities was that holding such activity not to be infringement created a loophole that corporations such as Microsoft could exploit.[137] Companies with foreign ties would be able to send their manufacturing abroad to avoid infringement, thereby avoiding liability for stealing a less powerful entity's invention.[138]

The Supreme Court's decision in *MedImmune, Inc.* v. *Genentech, Inc.* disadvantages individual inventors because it makes it easier for potential infringers – those that individual inventors will enforce their patents against – to avoid contractual obligations and to forum shop.[139] In *MedImmune*, the Supreme Court concluded that a licensee can challenge the licensed patent's validity without terminating or breaching the underlying license.[140] This holding also lowered the bar as to what creates an "actual controversy" for the purposes of sparking a valid declaratory judgment action, essentially enabling alleged infringers to control forum selection in patent suits by allowing them to file declaratory judgment actions even before breaching the license.[141] Such a result, as some amici argued to the Supreme Court, "erode[s] the sanctity of contracts and interfere[s] with vital policies favoring amicable resolution of commercial matters" that are so crucial for patentees who depend on royalty streams to monetize their patents.[142] It also puts small inventors, who would

[134] Golden, *supra* note 9, at 2113–14 ("Thus, the district courts' post-eBay practice may be in some tension with the Supreme Court's warning against the 'categorical denial of injunctive relief' to broad classes of patent holders.").

[135] *Id.* at 2160.

[136] 550 U.S. 437 (2007).

[137] *See* Brief of Amicus Curiae Wisconsin Alumni Research Foundation et al., *Microsoft*, 550 U.S. 437 (No. 05–1056), at 5–6.

[138] *Id.*

[139] 549 U.S. 118 (2007).

[140] *Id.* at 119–23.

[141] *SanDisk Corp. v. STMicroelectronics, Inc.*, 480 F.3d 1372, 1377–79 (Fed. Cir. 2007).

[142] *See* Brief of Amici Curiae The Trustees of Columbia University in the City of New York et al., *MedImmune*, 549 U.S. 118 (No. 05–608), at 2.

normally be looking for licenses as opposed to overtly seeking out litigation, at a disadvantage to large corporations that can take advantage of the forum advantages that filing early declaratory judgment actions present.[143]

Individual inventors are also disadvantaged by the Court's decision in *KSR International Co. v. Teleflex Inc.* because the case's change to the nonobviousness requirement makes patentability determinations unpredictable.[144] The *KSR* decision rejected a "rigid" test for nonobviousness and replaced it with a "flexible" and "functional" approach.[145] Some argued that such a shift would render most significant individual inventors' inventions obvious.[146] "While large business may be only slightly impacted" by the hindsight the Court's test introduces, "small business concerns and struggling innovators [would be] certain to face an instant and devastating diminishment of corporate value."[147] Others asserted that a flexible nonobviousness requirement would make it more difficult for individual inventors to secure financing for their research and development because "potential investors cannot evaluate the likelihood that the venture's pending patent applications will be approved or that its issued patents will be enforced."[148]

In *Quanta Computer, Inc. v. LG Electronics, Inc.*, the Court's holding is detrimental to individual inventors because it limits their ability to license their patents effectively.[149] The Court in *Quanta* determined that a license with a computer components manufacturer exhausted patent rights against purchasers of such components who used them to make, without an expressed license, a patented system and perform a patented method.[150] Multiple amici argued that tiered licensing, which the decision in *Quanta* makes more difficult, is a crucial vehicle by which small inventors recoup their costs of inventing.[151] Small inventors also rely on others

143 Even before *MedImmune*, courts were concerned about the advantages an alleged infringer might have if the requirements for filing declaratory judgment actions were relaxed in patent cases. *See, e.g.*, Fresenius USA, Inc. v. Transonic Sys., Inc., 207 F. Supp. 2d 1009, 1012–13 (N.D. Cal. 2001) ("Exercising jurisdiction over declaratory-relief actions under [expanded] circumstances would create a strong disincentive for patentees to communicate with potential infringers before filing suit, for fear of being sued first and thus forced to litigate in the defendant's forum of choice.").

144 550 U.S. 398 (2007).

145 *Id.*

146 Brief of Harold W. Milton, Jr. as Amicus Curiae in Support of Respondent, KSR Int'l Co. v. Teleflex Inc., 550 U.S. 398 (2007) (No. 04–1350), at 2 (stating that the inventions of inventors such as the Wright brothers and Thomas Edison might be rendered obvious in hindsight).

147 Brief of the United Inventors Association as Amicus Curiae in Support of the Respondents, *KSR*, 550 U.S. 398 (No. 04–1350), at 2.

148 Brief of Altitude Capital Partners et al. as Amici Curiae in Support of Respondents, *KSR*, 550 U.S. 398 (No. 04–1350), at 4 ("Similarly, a firm like Altitude Capital Partners will be less inclined to back an independent inventor, or will do so only on much less favorable terms that diminish incentives to innovate, if Altitude cannot predict with reasonable confidence whether the inventor's patents will be upheld in court.").

149 128 S. Ct. 2109 (2008).

150 *Id.*

151 *See* Brief for Wi-LAN Inc. as Amicus Curiae Supporting Respondent, *Quanta*, 128 S. Ct. 2109 (No. 06–937), at 19–22; Brief of Amici Curiae Interdigital Communications, LLC and Tessera, Inc. in

TABLE 12.1. *Patent troll era handling of individual inventors*

	Rhetoric	Substance
Legislative	Positive	Mixed
Administrative	Positive	Positive
Judicial	Nonexistent[152]	Negative

to manufacture and distribute their product because they do not have the in-house capabilities or resources to do so.[153]

III. IMPLICATIONS

The rhetoric regarding individual inventors has remained extremely positive in both Congress and the PTO during this period of legislative and administrative reform. Both of these bodies also at least proposed substantive changes that took individual inventors' interests into account, even if they were not overtly pro-individual-inventor proposals. The PTO changed its proposed rules to take the concerns of individual inventors into consideration, even creating a special exception for small entities in its claim limitation rules. Although Congress never passed any significant patent legislation during the period studied, it did seriously consider changes that would be harmful to small inventors. The proposed legislation, however, was modified, to take into account at least some of the small inventors' interests. The judiciary essentially did not take any notice of individual inventors' concerns – either on a rhetorical or a substantive level. The Supreme Court's recent decisions did, however, reduce the value of patents, particularly for individual inventors. Table 12.1 summarizes these results, and this section examines their implications.

A. *Resilience of the Motif's Rhetoric*

When the rhetoric observed by Janis shortly before the modern patent reform efforts and the focus on the patent troll is compared to the rhetoric examined in Part II.B, one can see that not much has changed at all. Congress still engages heavily in the

Support of Respondent, *Quanta*, 128 S. Ct. 2109 (No. 06–937), at 12; Brief of Amberwave Systems Corp. as Amicus Curiae in Support of Respondent, *Quanta*, 128 S. Ct. 2109 (No. 06–937), at 10.

152 The Court in *eBay Inc. v. MercExchange, L.L.C.* does mention "self-made inventors." 547 U.S. 388, 393 (2006). Justice Kennedy's concurrence focuses on patent trolls, but not necessarily individual inventors. *eBay*, 547 U.S. at 396 (Kennedy, J., concurring). However, the majority's discussion is still neutral and mentions individual inventors sparingly – it does not establish a pro-individual-inventor view of injunctions. And Justice Kennedy never discusses the size of the patent trolls he is focused on, so whether he is considering the individual inventor in his analysis is unclear.

153 Brief for Wi-LAN Inc., *supra* note 151, at 19.

individual inventor rhetoric,[154] the PTO is still the strongest ally of the individual inventor,[155] and litigants continue to invoke the rhetoric in litigation, while the courts, maybe even less so now, do not seem to engage the motif at all.[156]

Other than perhaps the slight dropoff in engagement by the courts, the individual inventor motif remains rhetorically intact – at least as much as it was before the advent of the patent troll. Those primarily engaged in the usage of rhetoric – mainly Congress and the PTO – are able to keep the small inventor and the patent troll separate.[157] The definitional concerns that the patent troll hunt presents for the individual inventor motif are not justified: The garage inventor is still a narrative that policy makers find worth telling.

B. *Lack of Substance Behind the Motif*

It has been suggested before that, although the motif is strong, there is very little doctrine specifically designed to benefit the individual inventor:[158] Other than a few patent rules, there are no positive laws protecting individual inventors.[159] The Congress attempts to stay, at best, neutral and simply avoid passing laws that disadvantage individual inventors.[160] Arguably, the Supreme Court tried to do the same in *eBay*, albeit perhaps unsuccessfully.[161] Although the rhetoric is still employed, there is just no substance standing behind it. Other than the PTO's reduction of some of the application filing burden on small inventors, there is little else that the patent system does to assist such individuals or address their concerns specifically.

In fact, most of the patent law changes either proposed or actually made, mainly in the courts, have come out against individual inventors' interests. The provisions being discussed in Congress at the time of this writing focus on providing defendants with recourse to combat infringement actions and are thus opposed by small inventor interest groups.[162] The same, anti-individual-inventor effect can be found in Supreme Court decisions, with each recent patent decision making it more difficult to successfully enforce patent rights.[163] Thus, although the rhetoric remains strong, its emptiness is self-evident. The troll hunt may have not damaged the individual inventor's image, but it certainly has created substantive changes that cut against small inventors.

The House debate of H.R. 1908 epitomizes the emptiness of the individual inventor motif. Opponents of the bill focused solely on the bill's impact on the small

[154] *See supra* Part II.B.1.a.
[155] *See supra* Part II.B.2.a.
[156] *See supra* Part II.B.3.a.
[157] *See supra* Parts II.B.1.a, II.B.2.a.
[158] *See* Meurer, *supra* note 1, at 1202–03.
[159] *Id.*
[160] *See supra* Part II.B.1.b (describing Congress's recent patent lawmaking efforts).
[161] Golden, *supra* note 9, at 2113–14.
[162] *See* Patent Reform Act of 2009, S. 515, 111th Cong. (2009).
[163] *See supra* Part II.B.3.b (cataloging these decisions).

inventor.[164] Proponents, unwilling to verbally attack the individual inventor, played along rhetorically, despite the fact that the law they were supporting made substantive changes that were potentially adverse.[165] What makes this exchange even more interesting is that the real substance of the debate was probably not big business versus the little inventor, but the information technology industry versus pharmaceutical companies.[166] And yet the opposition to the bill – mostly by big pharma – did not harp on the legislation's impact on the pharmaceutical industry, but on the individual inventors. It is highly unlikely that the small inventor was the main concern of opponents, but at least externally that is how it appeared.[167] Pharmaceutical companies have an interest in stronger patent laws, and because their interests aligned with those of individual inventors, who also commonly benefit from stronger patent laws, pharma found a friend.[168] The motif was an empty vessel that could dress up the concerns of another, perhaps less sympathetic interest group.[169] Presumably, if the interests of another powerful industry lined up with those of individual inventors, that industry would utilize the rhetoric of individual inventors for the same reason.

An examination of the recent discourse involving individual inventors shows that it truly is only a rhetorical motif and not much more, particularly outside the PTO. The motif invokes a very powerful narrative – a story that almost all Americans understand[170] – but one that does not drive dramatic substantive change, particularly substantive change in favor of individual inventors.[171] Instead, the motif is coopted – particularly in Congress – by those parties whose interests are best furthered by policies that strengthen patent rights.

C. *Roles of the Different Institutions in Patent Law*

How different institutions have handled individual inventors' interests, particularly in the age of the patent troll, illustrates a great deal about their role in patent law.

[164] *See, e.g., supra* notes 79–84.

[165] *See, e.g., supra* note 86.

[166] *See* Meurer, *supra* note 1, at 1214 ("Recent discussions of patent reform emphasize the disparate interests of the pharmaceutical and biotechnology industries on one side, and the information and communication technology industries on the other. Some of the discussion also notes tension between small inventors and big information and communications technology firms.").

[167] *Id.*

[168] *See* Jay P. Kesan & Andres A. Gallo, *The Political Economy of the Patent System*, 87 N.C. L. Rev. 1341, 1353 (2009) ("Other sectors, for example, biotechnology and pharmaceutical companies, which depend heavily on patents to support their R&D projects and sustain their market positions, will prefer a strong patent system to foster market value for their innovations.").

[169] *See* Janis, *supra* note 1, at 911 ("One might expect patent reformers to be drawn to the strategy of reconceptualizing the reform debate by attempting to couple technical reform measures with the romantic imagery of the lone inventor struggling against a recalcitrant bureaucracy.").

[170] *Id.* ("[T]he heroic inventor motif, with its overtones of Jeffersonian self-reliance and Yankee ingenuity, may simply mesh uniquely well with the American perception of its own identity.").

[171] *See supra* Part II.B.

The PTO has been the most receptive to the rhetorical use of the individual inventor motif and actually has substantively acted on it, modifying proposed rules to give individual inventors specific exemptions.[172] Such action makes sense from an institutional perspective for several reasons. First, the PTO engages patentees almost exclusively on the patent acquisition side of the equation. It focuses on when individuals should and should not obtain patent rights.[173] This turns out to be the side of the patent system that individual inventors engage most. It is also the side the motif focuses on – the ability of individual inventors to create ground-breaking inventions. The motif should have the most impact on the front-end of patent law, and thus on the PTO. Second, the USPTO's receptiveness to the motif also exemplifies the customer service nature of the agency.[174] Finally, there are larger pro-small business attitudes at play when considering the administrative agency. For example, the Regulatory Flexibility Act is focused solely on helping small businesses interact with regulatory agencies such as the PTO.[175] Many of the PTO's responses to individual inventors' comments on the recently proposed rules were regarding, in part, its duty under the Act.

This individual-inventor-friendly environment at the PTO sits in sharp contrast to the judiciary's ambivalence to individual inventors' concerns. Every time individual inventors came up in the briefs, except arguably in *eBay*, the Supreme Court ignored them in its ultimate decision.[176] This makes sense from an institutional perspective, given that the law that governed each of those cases made no special exceptions for small inventors. In fact, nothing within the Patent Act treats such inventors differently.[177] Given that overt direction, or lack thereof, by Congress, courts address only those concerns identified by legislators, as they arguably should. The Supreme Court's handling of the motif evidences restraint, a lack of judicial activism, for want of a better term.[178] The judiciary's failure to consider the motif is the way it is supposed to work – with the courts immune to rhetoric and popular opinion, particularly popular opinion that is not expressed in any specific statutory provision.[179] This explanation for the general absence of the motif seems especially

[172] *See supra* Part II.B.2.

[173] *See* Stuart Minor Benjamin & Arti K. Rai, *Who's Afraid of the APA? What the Patent System Can Learn from Administrative Law*, 95 Geo. L. J. 269, 276–77 (2007) ("Instead of asking whether a given patent is necessary to promote innovation, the patent statute directs the PTO to determine whether the patent application meets validity standards that have scientific and technical underpinnings.").

[174] *See* Rochelle Dreyfuss, *Pathological Patenting: The PTO as Cause or Cure*, 104 Mich. L. Rev. 1559, 1567 (2006) (reviewing Adam B. Jaffe & Josh Lerner, Innovation and Its Discontents: How Our Broken Patent System Is Endangering Innovation and Progress, and What To Do About It (2004)) ("[T]he PTO's profit orientation disposes it to grant its customer/clients' patents. Nor are these patents invalidated when they get to court.").

[175] *See* 5 U.S.C. §§ 601–612 (2006).

[176] *See supra* Part II.B.3.b.

[177] *See* Meurer, *supra* note 1, at 1202–03.

[178] Giacomo A. M. Ponzetto & Patricio A. Fernandez, *Case Law Versus Statute Law: An Evolutionary Comparison*, 37 J. Legal Stud. 379, 393–94 (2008) (setting forth a definition of judicial activism).

[179] *Id.*

likely given the Court's language in *eBay*. The case discusses the application of equitable remedies, an area in which courts are least constrained by statute. And *eBay* is the only case in which the individual inventors' interests made their way into the opinion.[180]

The motif's lack of influence on the judiciary is also a product of the fact that, whereas the PTO is on the front end, courts are, for all intents and purposes, on the back end of the patent system. They see the patented invention in the context of a lawsuit in which an allegedly infringing defendant has produced her own product or service.[181] This context is also the one where the impact of patent trolls is most noticed, because in those cases, the plaintiffs have produced nothing.[182] Sometimes it is also the context in which the individual inventor is not the only innovator, particularly because most cases involve a defendant that did not copy the invention, giving them some moral ground.[183] That is, the defendant is likely to have gone through the complete invention and development process herself and simply come in second, behind the first to invent.[184] The motif is, therefore, at its weakest at the enforcement stage and perhaps most susceptible to being ignored.

Finally, Congress's handling of the individual inventor motif makes sense. Congress sits in the middle of these issues – with individual inventors needing to be protected on the front end and patent trolls thwarted on the back end. Congress also is more likely to engage in rhetoric, particularly rhetoric its constituents understand and support.[185] And rhetoric that, in the end, turns out to be empty.

CONCLUSION

These findings have tremendous import for the individual inventor motif and the patent system in general. The individual inventor motif has been around for a long time and has continuously been invoked in patent discourse. At least in its modern form, the motif has maintained its rhetorical strength in spite of the current negative focus on patent trolls. The prevalence of individual patent holders whose sole focus is to license their patents, not commercialize the underlying technology – the so-called patent trolls – has not discouraged usage of the classic American story of the individual inventor.

There are very few substantive changes, however, that match the more extensive usage of strong, pro-individual-inventor rhetoric. Individual inventors fare better before the actor in the patent system that sees them the most – the PTO. But even at the PTO, there are not a large number of regulations being adopted that specifically

180 35 U.S.C. § 283 (2006) (indicating that district courts "may grant injunctions"); eBay v. MercExchange, 547 U.S. 388, 389 (2006).
181 35 U.S.C. § 281 (2006) (giving a patentee a remedy of a "civil action for infringement of his patent").
182 *See supra* Part II.A.1.
183 Christopher A. Cotropia & Mark A. Lemley, *Copying in Patent Law*, 87 N. C. L. Rev. 1421 (2009).
184 *Id.*
185 *See* Janis, *supra* note 1, at 911.

benefit the individual inventor. Thus, those who engage the patent system for reform should take this chapter's findings to heart, to better understand in which institutions the motif has more power and greater potential to prompt true change. This study also provides a broader picture as to how the various institutions are operating in the patent system to the benefit or detriment of small, independent inventors, additional information that reformists can use going forward.

13

Anything Under the Sun Made by Humans

Patent Law Doctrines as Endogenous Institutions for Commercializing Innovation

*James E. Daily and F. Scott Kieff**

INTRODUCTION

This chapter was presented at the 2012 Randolph W. Thrower Symposium, which is part of the endowed lecture series sponsored by Mr. Thrower's family and hosted by the *Emory Law Journal* and Emory University School of Law. The subject of the 2012 symposium was *Innovation for the Modern Era: Law, Policy, and Practice in a Changing World*. This chapter was part of the panel titled *The Role of Institutions in Fostering and Disseminating Technological Innovation* and offers a comparative, institutional analysis of different approaches to one of today's hot topics in modern patent law – the issue of patentable subject matter[1] – to elucidate how different approaches to institutional design in patent law can have different impacts on the markets for commercializing innovation.

This chapter proceeds as follows: Part I introduces a précis on institutions and their application to intellectual property. Part II highlights some links that can be found between, on the one hand, a patent system's overall goals and the types of

* James E. Daily is a research technologist with the Washington University in St. Louis School of Law's Center for Empirical Research in the Law. F. Scott Kieff worked on this book while serving as Fred C. Stevenson Research Professor, George Washington University Law School, and Ray & Louise Knowles Senior Fellow, Stanford University Hoover Institution on War, Revolution, and Peace, before taking up his government post as a Commissioner at the U.S. International Trade Commission (USITC). He took a leave of absence from George Washington University Law School and resigned from Stanford University Hoover Institution to take up his government post. The views expressed in this chapter are those of the chapter authors and do not necessarily reflect those of the other chapter authors or co-editors. Nor are the views expressed in this book properly attributable to the USITC. A version of this chapter was published in the *Emory Law Review*.

1 *See, e.g.*, Andrew Pollack, *Justices Send Back Gene Case*, N.Y. Times, Mar. 27, 2012, at B1 (describing case about whether technologies relating to genes associated with breast and ovarian cancer are eligible subject matter for patenting); Eduardo Porter, *Tech Suits Endanger Innovation*, N.Y. Times, May 30, 2012, at B1 (describing case about whether technologies relating to computer software are eligible subject matter for patenting).

dispute resolution it conducts, and on the other hand, the different relationships these features set up between the government and market actors. Part III lays out as a benchmark the "anything under the sun made by man" approach to patentable subject matter that was featured in the 1952 Patent Act, championed by the Supreme Court in the 1980s, and followed by Congress through most of the second half of the twentieth century,[2] as well as a contrasting, more subjective approach the Court deployed in its most recent cases. This chapter concludes by elucidating some reasons why, to the extent society wants to increase the overall rate of invention commercialization and overall competition as reflected in diversity in firm size among participants in the markets for commercializing innovation, society should consider largely returning to the prior approach to the law of patentable subject matter, updating only its gender-biased language.

I. A PRÉCIS ON INSTITUTIONS

In the social sciences, the term *institutions* refers to constraints that are human-imposed – laws, rules, norms, and their enforcement characteristics – and the field known as New Institutional Social Sciences, including the narrower field known as New Institutional Economics, studies the nature and degree of the impact that institutions can have on overall economic and social performance.[3] Institutions are usually considered to be largely endogenous to a given democratic society – meaning that they are seen as internally generated rather than imposed from outside – because generally at least some subset of the people in that society decide which institutions are implemented.[4]

2 *See* Diamond v. Diehr, 450 U.S. 175, 182 (1981); Diamond v. Chakrabarty, 447 U.S. 303, 309 (1980); S. Rep. No. 82–1979, at 5 (1952); H.R. Rep. No. 82–1923, at 6 (1952). The historical and revision notes for 35 U.S.C. § 101 state that the 1952 Act expanded the definition of process to include a "new use of a known process, machine, manufacture, composition of matter, or material," 35 U.S.C. § 101 hist. n. (2006), which is highly relevant to many technologies such as software, which is fundamentally about finding new uses for existing machines (i.e., computers). *See also* Act of Sept. 30, 1996, Pub. L. No. 104–208, 110 Stat. 3009 (1996) (codified as amended at 35 U.S.C. § 287(c)) (statute providing a safe harbor for certain medical methods but declining to exclude them from patentability); American Inventors Protection Act of 1999, Pub. L. No. 106–113, 113 Stat, 1501 (1999) (codified as amended at 35 U.S.C. § 273) (statute providing a prior user defense for business method patents but declining to exclude them from patentability).

3 For a general discussion of these terms in relation to intellectual property, see F. Scott Kieff, *Coordination, Property, and Intellectual Property: An Unconventional Approach to Anticompetitive Effects and Downstream Access*, 56 Emory L.J. 327, 338–40 (2006); and Henry E. Smith, *Institutions and Indirectness in Intellectual Property*, 157 U. Pa. L. Rev. 2083, 2083–2101 (2009).

4 *See* Stanley L. Engerman & Kenneth L. Sokoloff, *Debating the Role of Institutions in Political and Economic Development: Theory, History, and Findings*, 11 Ann. Rev. Pol. Sci. 119, 124–25 (2008) (discussing the definition of institutions and their endogenous and exogenous origins). In contrast, sometimes laws are imposed largely by outside forces, such as when a society is controlled by a foreign power. For more on endogenous institutions, see *id.*

This chapter outlines a comparative institutional analysis among various doctrines in patent law to show how they can have different impacts on the way inventions are commercialized. It recognizes that one size rarely fits all because different societies have different goals that they intend to further within the systems of institutions they implement, that no one approach to furthering any particular set of goals is perfect, and that it may make sense to eliminate patent systems in their entirety. In so doing, this chapter builds on a prior body of work about the positive role that property rights in patents can play in commercializing innovation to show how recent shifts in approaches to the particular laws about what types of subject matter are eligible for patent protection can be expected to have different effects on the commercialization of inventions than prior approaches.[5]

The particular institution that is the focus of this chapter is the area of patent law known as the "patentable subject matter requirement," which is distinct from the other, more widely known legal requirements for a valid patent, such as novelty, nonobviousness (known outside the United States as "inventive step"), and adequate disclosure.[6] The patentable subject matter requirement is an additional requirement that is designed to entirely exclude from patent eligibility particular fields of inventive activity, even if they satisfy those other requirements for patentability.[7] Common targets of the patentable subject matter requirement include those inventions relating to life, such as biotechnology;[8] those relating to computers, such as software;[9] those relating to business, such as financial techniques;[10] and those relating to fun, such as sports moves.[11] This area of the law has again become a hot spot, and the Supreme Court recently decided two high-profile cases in it: *Bilski*, involving finance and software, and *Mayo*, involving biotechnology.[12]

5 *See* Stephen H. Haber et al., *On the Importance to Economic Success of Property Rights in Finance and Innovation*, 26 Wash. U. J.L. & Pol'y 215 (2008) (surveying recent developments surrounding property rights and their economic impact).

6 *See* 35 U.S.C. §§ 102, 103, 112 (setting forth the substantive requirements in patent law for novelty, nonobviousness, and disclosure). For more on all of these requirements see F. Scott Kieff, Pauline Newman, Herbert F. Schwartz & Henry E. Smith, Principles of Patent Law, 154–688 (5th ed. 2011) (chapters three, four, and five, discussing disclosure, novelty, and nonobviousness).

7 Rebecca S. Eisenberg, *Wisdom of the Ages or Dead-Hand Control? Patentable Subject Matter for Diagnostic Methods After* In re Bilski, 3 Case W. Res. J. L. Tech. & Internet 1 n.2 (2012).

8 *Id.*

9 James Bessen, *A Generation of Software Patents* (Boston Univ. Sch. of Law Working Paper No. 11–31, 2011), *available at* http://papers.ssrn.com/sol3/papers.cfm?abstract_id=1868979.

10 John F. Duffy, *Why Business Method Patents?*, 63 Stan. L. Rev. 1247 (2011).

11 F. Scott Kieff et al., *It's Your Turn, but It's My Move: Intellectual Property Protection for Sports "Moves,"* 25 Santa Clara Computer & High Tech. L.J. 765 (2009).

12 Bilski v. Kappos, 130 S. Ct. 3218 (2010) (regarding patent on methods for hedging against the risk of price changes in the commodities market); Mayo Collaborative Servs. v. Prometheus Labs., Inc., 132 S. Ct. 1289 (2012) (regarding a patent on methods for adjusting the dosage of a drug in response to metabolite levels in a patient's blood). The Court has also vacated and remanded other important subject matter cases to the Federal Circuit to be considered in light of *Mayo*. *E.g.*, Ass'n for Molecular Pathology v. Myriad Genetics, Inc., 132 S. Ct. 1794 (2012) (regarding patent on BRCA 1&2 breast

II. BASIC GOALS FOR A PATENT SYSTEM AND BROAD INSTITUTIONAL DESIGN

Although a searching study of patent theory is beyond the scope of this chapter, this part offers a brief outline of some basic goals and broad institutional features of the patent system to set the stage for the more focused comparative institutional analysis on the topic of patentable subject matter. The discussion in this part is designed to highlight the types of links that can be found between, on the one hand, a patent system's goals and the types of dispute resolution it conducts, and on the other hand, the different relationships these links set up between the government and market actors.

Although patents often are seen as tools that societies use to encourage inventors to invent, significant and politically diverse voices among those studying and implementing the U.S. patent system have instead focused on the role of strong and predictable rules for patent procurement and enforcement in facilitating competition and the commercialization of inventions.[13] Economic history has taught that a defining feature of the early U.S. patent system that was central to its economic success was the way in which it used a property rights approach to facilitate private ordering.[14] Analysis of legal history reveals that the principal draftsman of the statute that implemented the patent system that operated in the United States from 1952 through the end of the twentieth century was explicit in focusing on the role of the system in facilitating coordination among many diverse market participants in order to commercialize innovation, rather than on getting inventions made.[15] As Abraham Lincoln described it, the patent system "added the fuel of interest to the fire of genius, in the discovery *and production* of new and useful things."[16] As shown

cancer markers in cancer screening); WildTangent, Inc. v. Ultramercial, LLC, 132 S. Ct. 2431 (2012) (patent on methods of distributing copyrighted products over the internet in exchange for viewing an advertisement).

13 B. Zorina Khan & Kenneth L. Sokoloff, *History Lessons: The Early Development of Intellectual Property Institutions in the United States*, 15 J. ECON. PERSP., Summer 2001, at 235.

14 *See, e.g.*, Naomi R. Lamoreaux & Kenneth L. Sokoloff, *Intermediaries in the U.S. Market for Technology, 1870–1920*, *in* FINANCE, INTERMEDIARIES, AND ECONOMIC DEVELOPMENT 209, 210–11 (Stanley L. Engerman et al., eds., 2003); Khan & Sokoloff, *supra* note 13, at 235.

15 *See* Giles S. Rich, *The Relation Between Patent Practices and the Anti-Monopoly Laws*, 24 J. PAT. OFF. SOC'Y 159, 177–80 (1942) (five-part series of articles written by principal drafter of the 1952 Patent Act), reprinted as Giles S. Rich, *The Relation Between Patent Practices and the Anti-Monopoly Laws*, 14 FED. CIR. B.J. 5, 21, 37, 67, & 87, at 34 (2004). Leading progressive jurists immediately recognized the power of the 1952 Act in strengthening patents, having championed strong patents as tools for helping smaller market entrants compete against larger, established firms. *See* Reiner v. I. Leon Co., 285 F.2d 501, 503 (2d Cir. 1960) ("There can be no doubt that the Act of 1952 meant to change the slow but steady drift of judicial decision that had been hostile to patents. . . . "); Picard v. United Aircraft Corp., 128 F.2d 632, 643 (2d Cir. 1942) (Frank, J., concurring) (discussing the role of predictable rules for patent enforcement in helping a smaller "David" compete with a larger "Goliath").

16 Abraham Lincoln, Second Lecture on Discoveries and Inventions (Feb. 11, 1859), *in* 3 THE COLLECTED WORKS OF ABRAHAM LINCOLN 356, 363 (Roy P. Basler ed., 1953) (emphasis added).

through an analysis of legal history, this approach to strong patents has enjoyed support across the U.S. political spectrum.[17]

Although focusing on getting inventions made has much appeal, the difference between the goals of inventing and commercializing reveals some key institutional features of the patent system. Consider that the goal of getting inventions made generally involves the use of targeted incentives that can be provided by a host of alternatives to patents, such as tax credits, prizes, grants, rewards, and the like.[18] Providing these targeted incentives requires an immense amount of information about who exactly should be targeted and how large the incentive should be, and those operating under the regime have stronger incentives to seek their own rewards than to discipline the giver to be more frugal in giving rewards to others.[19] Not only is amassing all of that information hard for the government to do but it is also likely that large, established market actors will be better able than smaller market entrants to wield the powerful political influence needed to get the government to act on that information.

One feature that patents have in contrast with other such rewards is that patent applicants themselves bring to the government much of the information needed to grant and enforce the patent. They do this through the process of submitting and prosecuting their patent applications. In addition, competitors of the patentee and the patentee's business associates, who are putative patent infringers, bring to the attention of the government the rest of the relevant information needed to evaluate the patent when the patent is asserted against them, in court or during Patent and Trademark Office (PTO) reexamination.[20]

To be sure, the incentive to invent is well supported by a host of factors that are likely to exist in the absence of a patent system, including invention's famous mother, necessity, as well as innate curiosity and the funding of basic research, each of which

[17] *See, e.g.*, Pauline Newman, *The Federal Circuit in Perspective*, 54 Am. U. L. Rev. 821, 822–23 (2005) (reviewing history of the 1982 statute designed to strengthen the U.S. patent system, included as a major domestic policy initiative of the Carter Administration before being signed into law by the Reagan Administration); *see also* Federal Courts Improvement Act of 1982, Pub. L. No. 97–164, 96 Stat. 25 (1982) (codified as amended at 28 U.S.C. § 171) (creating the U.S. Court of Federal Claims); Indus. Advisory Subcomm. on Patent and Info. Policy, Report on Patent Policy, *in* Advisory Committee on Industrial Innovation: Final Report 147, 155 (1979).

[18] *See, e.g.*, Michael Kremer, *Patent Buy Outs: A Mechanism for Encouraging Innovation* 113 Q.J. Econ. 1137 (1998) (suggesting the government buy out patents after conducting an auction to determine an appropriate buy-out price to better address these same fields and others); Steven Shavell & Tanguy van Ypersele, *Rewards Versus Intellectual Property Rights* 44 J.L. & Econ. 525 (2001) (suggesting government-sponsored cash rewards as partial or full replacements for patents and a means to better address fields where the disparity between average cost and marginal cost is typically large, citing as an example modern biotechnology and computer software, which are both focal points in today's debates about patentable subject matter).

[19] For a general critique of rewards-focused approaches to patents, see F. Scott Kieff, *Property Rights and Property Rules for Commercializing Inventions*, 85 Minn. L. Rev. 697, 705–17 (2001). *See also* Daniel F. Spulber, *Should Business Method Inventions Be Patentable?*, 3 J. Legal Analysis 265, 298–304 (2011).

[20] Kieff, *supra* note 19, at 712.

is to be celebrated. The point here is to highlight some important benefits that come from having the patent system focus on getting inventions commercialized, rather than on only getting inventions made.

Getting an invention commercialized requires coordination of a large number of complementary users of an invention, including venture capitalists, managers, marketers, laborers, and often the owners of other inventions. But getting these diverse actors coordinated is not that difficult when inventions can be patented and those patents can be enforced under systems having relatively low administrative costs and less reliance on flexible discretion over subjective factors. When an inventor has a patent backed up by credible enforcement in court, then that patent can act like a beacon in a dark room to draw to itself all of those interested in that technology and can start conversations among them.[21] As long as the patent is predictably enforced, this beacon effect is followed by a bargain effect, because those parties know that only those who strike deals with each other involving the patent can avoid being excluded by the patent in court.[22] Through the enforcement of that patent right and those contract rights, the government is able to help patentees and their contracting parties appropriate the returns to any of their rival inputs to developing and commercializing innovation – labor, lab space, capital, etc. – without the government itself having to trace the relative contributions of each participant.[23] This decentralized, ad hoc coordination occurs spontaneously, without the government needing to amass any of the specified information it would need to directly target each of the parties.[24] Instead, each party brings its own expertise and other assets to the negotiating table and knows – without necessarily having to reveal it to other parties or the government – enough about its own level of interest and capability to decide whether to strike a deal or not.

Just as the difference between the societal goals of inventing and commercializing reveals a significant difference in degree with respect to the relationship the government needs to have with market actors to implement a patent system, the difference between using court adjudication and administrative agency examination to assess patents reveals a significant difference in the nature of that same relationship. As explored in more detail in prior work, although court litigation is more expensive and time consuming, it is also less open to political influence, and its link between issues of patent validity and infringement provide important, self-disciplining effects on both patentees and alleged infringers.[25] As a result, present trends toward an

[21] F. Scott Kieff, *On Coordinating Transactions in Intellectual Property: A Response to Smith's* Delineating Entitlements in Information, 117 Yale L.J. Pocket Part 101, 102 (2007); *see also* Henry E. Smith, *Intellectual Property as Property: Delineating Entitlements in Information*, 116 Yale L.J. 1742, 1751–52 (2007).

[22] *See* Kieff, *supra* note 21, at 102.

[23] *See* Smith, *supra* note 21, at 1745.

[24] *Id.* at 1763–65.

[25] *See* F. Scott Kieff, *The Case for Preferring Patent-Validity Litigation over Second-Window Review and Gold-Plated Patents: When One Size Doesn't Fit All, How Could Two Do the Trick?*, 157 U. Pa. L.

increased reliance on administrative agency proceedings instead of court litigation may be expected to make it harder for new firms to enter and compete in markets; that is because larger firms are much more likely to bring political influence to bear in agency determinations, in which they are less subject to that self-disciplining effect.[26]

The discussion thus far has offered a thumbnail sketch of two basic choices a society can make about the patent system as an institution: overall goals and types of dispute resolution or enforcement. The particular choices a society makes on both of these basic fronts can tilt the system to favor those large, established market actors that will be better able to wield political influence than smaller market entrants. The discussions that follow show how a similar anticompetitive effect can be caused by certain approaches to the more legally technical doctrine known as *patentable subject matter*.

III. ALTERNATIVE APPROACHES TO THE PATENTABLE SUBJECT MATTER DOCTRINE

Written against a background in which disputes were known to have arisen about what types of subject matter would even be eligible for patent protection, and in which several types of subject matter had temporarily been ruled out of bounds, the 1952 Patent Act explicitly ruled everything in.[27] In its first provisions (§§ 100 and 101) of the chapter setting forth the substantive requirements for obtaining a patent, the statute provides that "[w]hoever invents or discovers any new and useful process, machine, manufacture, or composition of matter, or any new and useful improvement thereof, may obtain a patent therefor, subject to the conditions and requirements of this title."[28] It further defines the term *invention* to mean "invention or discovery," and the term *process* to mean "process, art, or method, [including] a new use of a known process, machine, manufacture, composition of matter, or material."[29] The linguistic work these statutory clauses were set up to accomplish is simple: breadth. That is why the lists are exemplary, not restrictive; the restrictions on obtaining a patent come through the requirements listed elsewhere in the statute. For example, even the mention in this statutory text of the word *new* has not been read to provide any separate novelty requirement beyond the novelty and

REV. 1937, 1949–50 (2009) [hereinafter Kieff, *The Case for Preferring*]; F. Scott Kieff, *The Case for Registering Patents and the Law and Economics of Present Patent-Obtaining Rules*, 45 B.C. L. REV. 55, 118–22 (2003) [hereinafter Kieff, *The Case for Registering*].

[26] Kieff, *The Case for Preferring*, *supra* note 25, at 1949.

[27] *Id.* at 106; *see also In re* Bilski, 545 F.3d 943, 985–90 (Fed. Cir. 2008) (en banc) (Newman, J., dissenting), *aff'd*, 130 S. Ct. 3218 (2010); Michael Risch, *America's First Patents*, 64 FLA. L. REV. 1279, 1286–94 (2012). *But see* Joshua D. Sarnoff, *Patent-Eligible Inventions After* Bilski: *History and Theory*, 63 HASTINGS L.J. 53 (2011).

[28] 35 U.S.C. § 101 (2006).

[29] 35 U.S.C. § 100(a)-(b).

nonobviousness requirements that are more famously associated with other statutory provisions.[30]

Despite the plain textual meaning and evident historical context of the 1952 Patent Act, the courts eventually reintroduced the set of subjective limitations on patentable subject matter. The leadoff case in the Supreme Court was the 1972 *Gottschalk* v. *Benson* decision, in which the Court read in to the patentable subject matter requirement some vague notions of the other substantive patentability requirements that are more generally known: novelty, nonobviousness, and disclosure.[31] It was followed a few years later by the 1978 *Parker* v. *Flook* decision.[32] In *Flook*, the Court was more explicit in reading the novelty, nonobviousness, and disclosure requirements into the patentable subject matter inquiry.[33]

The double-dipping approach to the patentable subject matter test the Court used in *Benson* and *Flook* can be problematic because it has often become a highly subjective inquiry that largely turns on a court's own reasoning to determine whether "the patent claims add *enough* . . . to qualify as patent-eligible processes that *apply* natural laws."[34] This problem would be exacerbated if, as some advocate, courts were encouraged (or even required) to make determinations on the issue of patentable subject matter a question appropriate for summary, policy-based, discretionary determination at the early phases of a patent litigation, long before a factual record is developed.[35] Because courts, like other government organizations, are also subject

30 *See* P.J. Federico, *Commentary on the New Patent Act, in Title 35, United States Code Annotated 1 (West 1954), reprinted in* 75 J. PAT. & TRADEMARK OFF. SOC'Y 161, 178 (1993) ("The general part of the Committee Report states that section 102 'may be said to describe the statutory novelty required for patentability, and includes, in effect, an amplification and definition of 'new' in section 101.'"); *see also In re* Bergy, 596 F.2d 952, 960 (1979) ("Notwithstanding the words 'new and useful' in § 101, the invention is not examined under that statute for novelty because that is not the statutory scheme of things or the long-established administrative practice."), *vacated*, 444 U.S. 1028 (1980).

31 Gottschalk v. Benson, 409 U.S. 63 (1972). For example, the Court's analysis in *Benson* begins by citing to older cases on the radio, telegraph, and the telephone (*MacKay Radio & Telegraph Co.* v. *Radio Corp.*, 306 U.S. 86, 94 (1939), *O'Reilly* v. *Morse*, 15 U.S. (1 How.) 62 (1854), and *The Telephone Cases*, 126 U.S. 1 (1888)) as though they stand for the proposition that a claim may be so abstract and sweeping as to cover both the "known and unknown." *See Benson*, 409 U.S. at 67–69. But this line of reasoning essentially imports into the patentable subject matter analysis concerns that are addressed by the other substantive patent law requirements of novelty, nonobviousness, and disclosure. Furthermore, as Adam Mossoff has shown, such fears about the preclusive effects of these historical patents are far overblown. *See* Adam Mossoff, *The Rise and Fall of the First American Patent Thicket: The Sewing Machine War of the 1850s*, 53 ARIZ. L. REV. 165, 203–05 (2011).

32 *See, e.g.*, Parker v. Flook, 437 U.S. 584, 600 (1978) (Stewart, J., dissenting) ("The Court today . . . strikes what seems to me an equally damaging blow at basic principles of patent law by importing into its inquiry under 35 U.S.C. § 101 [regarding patentable subject matter] the criteria of novelty and inventiveness [which is also known as nonobviousness].")

33 *See id.* at 586, 594 (majority opinion) (requiring an "inventive application" or "inventive concept" and discussing the application's failure to adequately define the input variables of the claimed formula).

34 Mayo, 132 S.Ct. at 1297 (emphasis in original).

35 *See* MySpace, Inc. v. GraphOn Corp., 672 F.3d 1250, 1264 (Fed. Cir. 2012) (Mayer, J., dissenting) ("The issue of whether a claimed method meets the subject matter eligibility requirements contained in 35

to political influence, this type of subjective standard leaves them favoring those large, established companies better able to muster the expensive government communications and outreach efforts needed to bring cases to the Supreme Court.[36] It has long been recognized in the patent community that the *Benson* decision was the direct result of exactly that type of influence,[37] and the several published opinions by the en banc Federal Circuit in the later *Alappat*[38] decision make the record explicit while disagreeing with each other over the possible nullifying impact of a similar politically influenced process.[39] As Judge Rich explained when endeavoring to ascertain the cause and effect of *Benson* in *In re Johnston*,

> I find it more significant to contemplate the identities of the troops lined up for battle in *Benson* and observe which side obtained the victory. On the one side was the Government, against patenting programs or software, supported by the collective forces of major hardware (*i.e.*, computer) manufacturers and their representative associations who, for economic reasons, did not want patents granted *on programs* for their machines. On the other side was Benson et al. and their assignee and assorted lawyers and legal groups who were in favor of patent protection for programs or software. The anti-patenting forces won the victory. . . . [40]

To be sure, the image to keep in mind is not that courts and other government organizations – nor the officials within them – are receiving inappropriate payoffs or other forms of influence. To the contrary, it makes sound sense for government organizations and officials to seek out and receive information about how their actions can best affect society, and interested members of society are exercising a vital First Amendment constitutional right to make their voices heard by their government.

U.S.C. § 101 is an 'antecedent question' that must be addressed before this court can consider whether particular claims are invalid as obvious or anticipated."); Smartgene, Inc. v. Advanced Biological Labs., SA, 852 F.Supp.2d 42, 51 (D.D.C. 2012) ("[A] 35 U.S.C. § 101 subject matter patentability inquiry *is* the threshold analysis for determining patent validity.") (holding that the patent claims were not directed to patentable subject matter).

36 *See* John F. Duffy, *The Federal Circuit in the Shadow of the Solicitor General*, 78 GEO. WASH. L. REV. 518 (2010) (showing how lobbying efforts before the Solicitor General's Office can influence outcomes in Supreme Court patent cases).

37 *See, e.g., infra* notes 40–41.

38 *In re* Alappat, 33 F.3d 1526 (Fed. Cir. 1994) (en banc), *abrogated by In re* Bilski, 545 F.3d 943 (Fed Cir. 2008).

39 *See* F. Scott Kieff, *Welcome to Patent Purgatory*, DEFINING IDEAS (June 9, 2011), http://www.hoover.org/research/welcome-patent-purgatory: "The elimination of effective patent protection for computer software through the Supreme Court's 1972 *Benson* decision was the direct result of intensive influence wielded by Nicholas Katzenbach, who became general counsel of IBM in 1969, over the U.S. Department of Justice, which he formerly ran as Attorney General during the Kennedy/Johnson Administration. And a similar influence was applied, albeit ultimately unsuccessfully, during the first Bush administration, in the lead up to the 1994 appellate court *Alappat* decision. The Patent Office Commissioner had made the decision to reconstitute the office's internal Board of Appeals to hold a rehearing before a specially packed Board designed to reject the patent on a type of software."

40 *In re* Johnston, 502 F.2d 765, 774 (C.C.P.A. 1974) (Rich, J., dissenting), *rev'd*, Dann v. Johnston, 425 U.S. 219 (1976).

The reason for concern is that the result has been reliance on an additional subjective standard that is duplicative of more objective standards embodied in the other substantive patentability requirements that are more generally known, namely novelty, nonobviousness, and disclosure. The addition of this easily influenced test for patentability is what further tilts the playing field in favor of those large, established companies better able to muster the expensive government communications and outreach efforts, which have given their voices an outsized effect compared to the voices of smaller, market-challenging competitors.

Although the *Benson* and *Flook* approach established a beachhead in the debates about patentable subject matter, the broader view embodied in the 1952 Patent Act successfully pushed back almost immediately. In the 1980 and 1981 decisions in *Diamond* v. *Chakrabarty* and *Diamond* v. *Diehr*, the Court rejected efforts to exclude from patentable subject matter inventions relating to biotechnology and software, respectively.[41] In both of these cases, the Court pointed out that "Congress intended statutory subject matter to 'include anything under the sun that is made by man.'"[42]

There are good reasons to think that it was this return to the broad view of patentable subject matter that played a crucial role in the relative success of the U.S. markets for both biotechnology and software.[43] After the 1980 *Chakrabarty* decision, the U.S. biotechnology sector enjoyed far more certainty about eligibility for patent protection than the same sectors in Europe and Japan, and only in the United States was there remarkable growth in the number of small and medium-sized biotechnology companies and a drastic increase in the number of new drugs and new medical devices brought to market.[44] Contrary to the expectations of some commentators, widespread patenting in biotechnology did not lead to a patent thicket or anticommons, nor did it result in significant restrictions on research.[45]

41 *See* Diamond v. Diehr, 450 U.S. 175 (1981); Diamond v. Chakrabarty, 447 U.S. 303 (1980).

42 Chakrabarty, 447 U.S. at 309 (quoting S. Rep. No. 82–1979, at 5 (1952); H.R. Rep. No. 82–1923, at 6 (1952)); *accord* Diehr, 450 U.S. at 182 (quoting S. Rep. No. 82–1979, at 5 (1952); H.R. Rep. No. 82–1923, at 6 (1952)).

43 *See* Classen Immunotherapies, Inc. v. Biogen Idec, 659 F.3d 1057, 1075 (Fed. Cir. 2011) (Rader, J., concurring) (discussing how "with some considerable blame on its eligibility doctrines, Europe lost innovation investment to the United States"); Ass'n for Molecular Pathology v. Myriad Genetics, Inc., 653 F.3d 1329, 1368 (Fed. Cir. 2011), *vacated* 132 S. Ct. 1794 (2012), *remanded to* 689 F.3d 1303 (Fed. Cir. 2012) (Moore, J., concurring) ("This outpouring of scientific creativity, spurred by the patent system, reflects a substantial investment of time and money by the biotechnology industry to obtain property rights related to DNA sequences.").

44 *See* Heather Hamme Ramirez, *Defending the Privatization of Research Tools: An Examination of the "Tragedy of the Anticommons" in Biotechnology Research and Development*, 53 Emory L.J. 359, 359 (2004) ("Since 1992, the number of biotech patents granted has increased substantially, and the industry has more than tripled in size. New biotech drug and vaccine approvals rose from two in 1982 to thirty-five in 2002."); *see also* Kieff, *supra* note 3, at 411–12.

45 *See* Richard A. Epstein & Bruce N. Kuhlik, *Is There a Biomedical Anticommons?*, CATO Rev. Bus. & Gov't Reg., Summer 2004, at 54; Kieff, *supra* note 3, at 391–96; Kieff, *supra* note 21, at 106–09; Mossoff, *supra* note 31, at 168–70; Timothy Caulfield et al., *Evidence and Anecdotes: An Analysis of Human*

Similarly, although there was no reliable protection for software patents after *Benson* and *Flook* essentially until after the 1994 *Alappat* decision,[46] that later period in which software patents enjoyed meaningful protection is when Google arrived with a portfolio of strong patents and trade secrets and soon grew to become Microsoft's largest competitive threat.[47]

Despite the success of the broad approach to patentable subject matter in biotechnology and software, the Supreme Court has recently returned to the narrow approach of *Benson* and *Flook*. In the 2010 *Bilski* v. *Kappos* decision and the 2012 *Mayo* v. *Prometheus* decision, the Court again imported into the patentable subject matter inquiry a vague and substantively duplicative version of the novelty, nonobviousness, and disclosure requirements.[48] Taken together, *Bilski* and *Mayo* create what some have called an "I know it when I see it" test for patent eligibility.[49]

Gene Patenting Controversies, 24 NATURE BIOTECHNOLOGY 1091, 1092 (2006);. Biotechnology research has also not been impeded by aggressive enforcement against researchers. *See* Ass'n for Molecular Pathology v. Myriad Genetics, Inc., 689 F.3d 1303, 1331 (Fed. Cir. 2012) ("[P]atents are rarely enforced against scientific research, even during their terms."). The recent *Myriad* and *Mayo* cases involved commercial competitors rather than scientists engaged in basic research, and in *Myriad* the patent challengers had to provoke a dispute via a declaratory judgment action. See Ass'n for Molecular Pathology v. Myriad Genetics, Inc., 653 F.3d 1329, 1345, 1348 (Fed. Cir. 2011); Mayo, 132 S. Ct. at 1296.

46 *In re* Alappat, 33 F.3d 1526 (Fed. Cir. 1994) (en banc), *abrogated by In re* Bilski, 545 F.3d 943 (Fed Cir. 2008).

47 According to its own patent information database, Google is the original assignee of more than 730 U.S. patents. *See Advanced Patent Search*, GOOGLE, http://www.google.com/advanced_patent_search (last visited Feb. 9, 2013) (The number of patents was determined by searching the database for issued patents where Google is the original assignee). U.S. Patent 6,285,999, the patent on PageRank – the foundational algorithm for Google's search technology – is owned by Stanford University and exclusively licensed to Google. *See* Richard Brandt, *Starting Up: How Google Got Its Groove*, STANFORD MAG., Nov.–Dec. 2004), *available at* http://alumni.stanford.edu/get/page/magazine/article/?article_id=35436; U.S. Patent No. 6,285,999 (filed Jan. 9, 1998). In 2012 Google obtained 17,000 patents as part of its acquisition of Motorola Mobility. Steve Lohr, *On Google, F.T.C. Set Rules of War over Patents*, N.Y. TIMES, Jan. 5, 2013, at B1. Although Google recently committed to antitrust authorities to limit its own ability to enforce those newly acquired patents to the extent they are subject to enforceable commitments to be licensed on fair, reasonable, and nondiscriminatory (FRAND) terms, that new commitment does not appear to reach all of the newly acquired patents or any of the patents within Google's treasure trove of original patents on search. In the Matter of Motorola Mobility LLC, No. 1210120 at 4, 7 (F.T.C. Jan. 3, 2013), *available at* http://www.ftc.gov/os/caselist/1210120/130103googlemotorolado.pdf. Furthermore, such a high-profile case imposing limits on enforceability of FRAND-related patents may set a precedent that plays out to the advantage of Google and other large companies when defending against patent infringement allegations.

48 *See* Mayo Collaborative Servs. v. Prometheus Labs., Inc., 132 S. Ct. 1289, 1302 (2012) (stating that broad claims foreclose future invention and tie up future use of laws of nature); *Id.* at 1297 (stating claims must "add *enough* to their statements of the correlations to allow the processes they describe to qualify as patent-eligible processes that *apply* natural laws"); Bilski v. Kappos, 130 S. Ct. 3218, 3218, 3229 (2010) (discussing the need to set a higher bar for patentable subject matter because some business method patents are vague and of "suspect validity"); *Id.* at 3231 (holding the claimed invention patent ineligible because its claims are overbroad and rely on a "long prevalent" economic practice and "well-known . . . techniques").

49 Kevin Emerson Collins, Bilski *and the Ambiguity of "An Unpatentable Abstract Idea,"* 15 LEWIS & CLARK L. REV. 37, 39 (2011).

If these new precedents play out that way, then the test for patentable subject matter may have again become subject to the influence of larger, more-established industrial parties due to their ability to better communicate with agencies such as the PTO and the courts, including the Supreme Court.

CONCLUSION

There are several possible consequences of the Court's return to a narrow view of patentable subject matter. For example, the restriction on the patentability of financial and business methods may constrain the commercialization of new technologies and lead to a loss of the economic efficiency provided by new business methods.[50]

A more immediate consequence appears to have been a decline in the value of biotechnology companies.[51] This may suggest that a similar effect will be seen for companies that rely on business method and software patents. This decline in value may be exacerbated by a decrease in venture capital funding.[52] Given that venture capital funding is correlated with patenting,[53] this may result in an overall decrease in investment in new technologies and their commercialization.

Weaker patents also tend to give more power to large, established companies at the expense of smaller companies, startups, and individual inventors.[54] Combined with an overall trend toward consolidation in these industries,[55] weaker patents may have significant anticompetitive effects.[56] A potential consequence may be lower rates of commercializing innovation and higher prices as larger companies no longer feel as much pressure from an already reduced number of new market entrants. Returning to a broad view of patentable subject matter may significantly mitigate such risks.

[50] Spulber, *supra* note 19, at 287–88.

[51] *See, e.g.*, Brent Kendall et al., *Top Court Decision Alarms Biotech*, WALL ST. J., Mar. 21, 2012, at A1 (reporting a 5.2% drop in the value of Myriad Genetics stock out of concern that its patents could be invalidated in the wake of *Mayo*).

[52] Jonathan D. Rockoff & Pui-Wing Tam, *Biotech Funding Gets Harder to Find*, WALL ST. J., Mar. 19, 2012, at B1.

[53] Stuart J.H. Graham et al., *High Technology Entrepreneurs and the Patent System: Results of the 2008 Berkeley Patent Survey*, 24 BERKELEY TECH. L.J. 1255, 1281 (2009).

[54] *See* Picard v. United Aircraft Corp., 128 F.2d 632, 643 (2d Cir. 1942) (Frank, J., concurring); Kieff, *supra* note 3, at 411; Kieff, *supra* note 21, at 105.

[55] *See, e.g.*, Cyrus Sanati, *A Different Kind of Drug Deal*, N.Y. TIMES DEALBOOK (April 17, 2009, 7:10 AM), http://dealbook.nytimes.com/2009/04/17/a-different-kind-of-drug-deal/ (reporting on the rapid consolidation in the pharmaceutical industry).

[56] *See, e.g.*, Richard A. Epstein, et al., *The FTC, IP, and SSOs: Government Hold-Up Replacing Private Coordination*, 8 J. COMPETITION L. & ECON., 1, 2 (exploring example of administrative agency applying subjective tests for various patent-related issues in a way that ends up substituting a small likelihood of a small holdup effect caused by property rights in patents with a large likelihood of a large holdup effect caused by the government in coordination with large market participants to the disadvantage of market entrants).

Index